IMAGINING AI

IMAGINING AI

How the World Sees Intelligent Machines

Edited by

Stephen Cave

and

Kanta Dihal

OXFORD
UNIVERSITY PRESS

OXFORD
UNIVERSITY PRESS

Great Clarendon Street, Oxford, OX2 6DP,
United Kingdom

Oxford University Press is a department of the University of Oxford.
It furthers the University's objective of excellence in research, scholarship,
and education by publishing worldwide. Oxford is a registered trade mark of
Oxford University Press in the UK and in certain other countries

Published in the United States of America by Oxford University Press
198 Madison Avenue, New York, NY 10016, United States of America

British Library Cataloguing in Publication Data
Data available

Library of Congress Control Number: 2023930758

ISBN 978–0–19–286536–6

DOI: 10.1093/oso/9780192865366.001.0001

Printed and bound by
CPI Group (UK) Ltd, Croydon, CR0 4YY

To Huw Price, who made all this possible.

Contents

Acknowledgements

This book originated in the Global AI Narratives (GAIN) project at the Leverhulme Centre for the Future of Intelligence, University of Cambridge. From 2018 to 2021, the GAIN team held twenty workshops to explore how AI is portrayed across cultural, geographical, regional, linguistic, and other boundaries and borders, and how these portrayals affect public perceptions of AI around the world. For helping us organize a wonderful series of events—in-person, virtual, and hybrid, at times in the face of political or social unrest and the pandemic—we thank our collaborators, including Nanyang Technological University and the NTU Institute for Science and Technology for Humanity (NISTH), Singapore; Waseda University, Tokyo; Teplitsa of Social Technologies, Russia; the Access to Knowledge for Development Center (A2K4D) at the American University in Cairo's School of Business; the Vā Moana Pacific Spaces research cluster and the University of Auckland, Aotearoa New Zealand; the Berggruen China Center at Peking University; the Department of Security Studies at Charles University, Prague; the Human Sciences Research Council of South Africa; the Pontificia Universidad Católica de Chile; the Present Futures Forum at the Technische Universität Berlin; and the School of Arts and Sciences at Ahmedabad University, India. We also thank all of the speakers, some of whose work is included in this book, as well as the many thousands of people who attended these workshops.

We acknowledge a deep debt of gratitude to the wonderful team of research assistants who worked on this project: Tonii Leach (who also assisted in the preparation of this volume), Elizabeth Seger, and Tomasz Hollanek.

We are immensely grateful to the many colleagues whose feedback has improved our understanding of this field in so many ways. In particular, for reviewing our own contributions to this volume, we thank Eleanor Drage, Kerry McInerney, Tomasz Hollanek, and Moritz Ingwersen.

The majority of contributions to this book are written by contributors who do not speak English as their first or primary language. We gratefully acknowledge the work of our translators Maya Feile Tomes, Jack Hargreaves, James Trapp, and James Hargreaves for their excellent translations from the Spanish, Chinese, and German.

We also express our gratitude to the team at Oxford University Press for once again having faith in us, and for their unfailingly professional and friendly support. In particular, we thank Sonke Adlung, Senior Commissioning Editor, and John Smallman and Giulia Lipparini, Senior Project Editors.

We acknowledge the generous support of the Templeton World Charity Foundation and DeepMind Ethics and Society for funding the Global AI

Narratives project; the Leverhulme Trust through their grant to the Leverhulme Centre for the Future of Intelligence; and the Cambridge–Africa ALBORADA Fund and the British High Commission Singapore for funding the Sub-Saharan Africa and Singapore workshops, respectively.

Finally, we thank Huw Price, former Bertrand Russell Professor of Philosophy at Cambridge and the founder of the Leverhulme Centre for the Future of Intelligence, for his unflagging support, and for making all this possible. It is to him that this book is dedicated.

Contributors

Rachel ADAMS, based in Cape Town, South Africa, is the Principal Researcher at Research ICT Africa. She is the Principal Investigator of the Global Index on Responsible AI, a new global instrument to measure country-level progress in advancing rights-respecting AI, and the African Observatory on Responsible AI. Rachel is the author of *Transparency: New Trajectories in Law* (Routledge, 2020), and the lead author of *Human Rights and the Fourth Industrial Revolution in South Africa* (HSRC Press, 2021). She is currently working on a monograph exploring the imperial forces at work in and through AI, and what is required to decolonize this novel technological superpower.

Macarena ARECO is a journalist and Full Professor of Latin American Literature at the Pontifical Catholic University of Chile, where she is also Director of Extension and Continuing Education at the UC Center for Chilean Literature Studies (CELICH). She is the author of the books *Cartografía de la novela chilena reciente* (2015), *Acuarios y fantasmas. Imaginarios de espacio y de sujeto en la narrativa argentina, chilena y mexicana reciente* (2017), and *Bolaño constelaciones: literatura, sujetos, territorios* (2020), and co-editor with Patricio Lizama of *Biografía y textualidades, naturaleza y subjetividad. Ensayos sobre la obra de María Luisa Bombal* (2015). She has published over a hundred articles and book chapters, and currently directs the research project 'Imaginarios sociales en la ciencia ficción latinoamericana reciente: espacio, sujeto-cuerpo y tecnología'.

Noelani ARISTA ('Ōiwi) is Director of the Indigenous Studies Program at McGill University, Montreal, and Associate Professor in History and Classical Studies. Her research focuses on Hawaiian governance and law, indigenous language textual archives and traditional knowledge organization systems. Her work seeks to support indigenous communities in the ethical transmission of knowledge and to develop methods that can be applied in multiple indigenous contexts. Her next book project focuses on the first Hawaiian constitutional period 1839–1845. She is a co-author of the award-winning essay *Making Kin with the Machines*, and co-organizer of the Indigenous AI workshops.

Abeba BIRHANE is Senior Fellow in Trustworthy AI at the Mozilla Foundation. Her interdisciplinary research explores various broad themes in cognitive science, AI, complexity science, and theories of decoloniality. Birhane examines the challenges and pitfalls of computational models (and datasets) from a conceptual, empirical, and critical perspective.

Stephen CAVE is Director of the Leverhulme Centre for the Future of Intelligence at the University of Cambridge. He is author of a *New Scientist* Book of the Year, *Immortality* (Penguin Random House, 2012), and *Should We Want to Live Forever* (Routledge, 2023), as well as co-editor of *AI Narratives: A History of Imagining Intelligent Machines* (Oxford University Press, 2020) and *Feminist AI* (Oxford University Press, 2023). He has written extensively for a broader public, including for the *New York Times* and *Atlantic*, and his work is featured in media around the world. He regularly advises governmental and international bodies on the ethics of AI.

Madeleine CHALMERS is Teaching Fellow in French at Durham University, UK. Her current book project *Unruly Technics* traces a genealogy of thinking and writing about technics that germinates in French avant-garde writings of the late nineteenth and early twentieth centuries, takes root in the mid-twentieth century in the work of major French philosophers such as Gilbert Simondon and Gilles Deleuze, and continues to bloom in the contemporary 'nonhuman turn' in Anglo–American theory that draws inspiration from those philosophers. Her work on technology and its intersections with French literature and thought has appeared in journals including *French Studies*, *Nottingham French Studies*, and *Dix-Neuf*.

Raul CRUZ is an artist and illustrator born in Mexico City. His work is a fusion of futuristic and sci-fi aesthetics with the art of Mesoamerican cultures such as the Maya and Aztecs, blending past and present with unpredictable futures. He has exhibited at universities, galleries, and cultural spaces in Mexico, New York, San Diego, Chicago, Los Angeles, Texas, Cuba, Italy, and Spain. His work appears in publications such as New York Illustrators Society, *Heavy Metal* magazine, SPECTRUM Fantastic Art, *The Future of Erotic Fantasy Art I* and *II*; has been compiled in a volume edited by the Universidad Autónoma Metropolitana de México and Editorial Milenio España; and features in two books on Mexican Fantastic Art. He participated in the Third Spectrum exhibition, gallery of The Society of Illustrators, in New York, and was selected as one of the 20 best artists in manual techniques of Fantastic Art by the book Fantasy + 3.

Kanta DIHAL is Lecturer in Science Communication at Imperial College London and Associate Fellow of the Leverhulme Centre for the Future of Intelligence, University of Cambridge. Her research focuses on science narratives, particularly those that emerge from conflict. She was Principal Investigator on the project 'Global AI Narratives' from 2018–2022. She is co-editor of *AI Narratives: A History of Imagining Intelligent Machines* (Oxford University Press, 2020) and has advised the World Economic Forum, the UK House of Lords, and the United Nations. She holds a DPhil from the University of Oxford on the communication of quantum physics.

Hans ESSELBORN is Emeritus Professor of the University of Cologne and specializes in the Enlightenment, Jean Paul, Early Twentieth Century German

Literature, Interculturality, and Science Fiction. He has been a visiting professor at Lawrence (Kansas), Nancy, Paris, Lyon, and Krakow. He is the author of *Georg Trakl* (PhD 1981) and *Das Universum der Bilder. Die Naturwissenschaft in den Schriften Jean Pauls* (habilitation 1989), *Die literarische Science Fiction* (2000), *Die Erfindung der Zukunft in der Literatur. Vom technisch-utopischen Zukunftsroman zur deutschen Science Fiction* (2019). He is the editor of *Utopie, Antiutopie und Science Fiction* (2003), *Ordnung und Kontingenz. Das kybernetische Model in den Künsten* (2009), and *Herbert W. Frankes SF-Werke* (since 2014).

Tomasz HOLLANEK is a design and technology ethics researcher with a background in cultural studies, philosophy, UX design, and communications. Currently, he is a Postdoctoral Research Fellow at the Leverhulme Centre for the Future of Intelligence at the University of Cambridge. His ongoing research explores the possibility of reconciling human-centric technology design principles with the goals of sustainable and restorative design for a more-than-human world. Previously, Tomasz was a Vice-Chancellor's PhD Scholar at Cambridge and a Visiting Research Fellow at the École normale supérieure in Paris. He has contributed to numerous research projects, including the Global AI Narratives Project at LCFI and the Ethics of Digitalization research program at the Berkman Klein Center for Internet and Society at Harvard.

Nik HYNEK is Professor specializing in Security Studies and affiliated with Metropolitan University Prague. He received his research doctorate from the University of Bradford and was previously affiliated with Saltzman Institute of War and Peace Studies (SIWPS) at Columbia University, the London School of Economics and Political Science (LSE), the Australian National University (ANU), Carleton University, and Ritsumeikan University. His latest monograph, co-authored with Anzhelika Solovyeva, is *Militarizing Artificial Intelligence: Theory, Technology, and Regulation* (Routledge, 2022).

Hirofumi KATSUNO is Associate Professor of Anthropology and Media Studies in the Faculty of Social Studies at Doshisha University, Kyoto. His primary research interest is the socio-cultural impact of new media technologies, particularly focusing on the formation of imagination, agency, and presence in technologically mediated environments in the age of AI and robotics. He is a co-organizer of the ethnographic research project Model Emotion (www.modelemotion.org) and a co-investigator of the international joint research project *Rule of Law in the Age of AI: Distributive Principles of Legal Liability for Multi-Species Societies*, funded by UKRI (UK) and JST (Japan).

So Young KIM is Professor and former head of the Graduate School of Science and Technology Policy and the director of the Korea Policy Center for the Fourth Industrial Revolution at KAIST. Her research deals with high-stake issues at the interface of science and technology (S&T) and public policy such as research and development funding and evaluation, S&T workforce policy, science-based official development assistance, and the governance of emerging technologies. Her scholarly work includes publications in *International Organization*, *Journal of Asian Survey*, and *Science and Public Policy*, as well as the co-edited volumes of *Science and Technology Policy: Theories and Issues*, *The Specter of the Fourth Industrial Revolution*, and *A Return of the Future: COVID-19 and the Fourth Industrial Revolution* [in Korean]. As a public intellectual, she has served on numerous committees of government ministries and international entities, including the World Economic Forum's Global Future Councils.

Edward KING is Associate Professor in Portuguese and Latin American Studies at the University of Bristol. His research explores contemporary cultures of connectivity, with a particular focus on the use of speculative fiction and multimedia texts to expose and contest the shifting power dynamics of the digital age. His latest monograph *Twins and Recursion in Digital, Literary and Visual Cultures* (Bloomsbury Academic, 2022) traces the ways in which twins have been used in different fields of knowledge and representational practices to map the increasingly intricate entanglements of human subjects and their technological and natural environments. His co-authored book *Posthumanism and the Graphic Novel in Latin America* (UCL Press, 2017; with Joanna Page) studies the emergence of the graphic novel in Latin America as a uniquely powerful medium through which to explore the nature of twenty-first-century subjectivity and especially forms of embodiment or mediatization that bind humans to their nonhuman environment.

Bogna KONIOR is Assistant Professor at the Interactive Media Arts department at New York University Shanghai, where she teaches classes on emerging technologies, philosophy, humanities, and the arts. She also co-directs the university's Artificial Intelligence and Culture Research Centre. www.bognamk.com

Cheryl Julia LEE is Assistant Professor with the English department at Nanyang Technological University, Singapore, and critical editor of *prose.sg*. Her research interests include Singaporean and Southeast Asian literature. She has published articles in *Textual Practice* and *Asiatic*.

Jason Edward LEWIS is a digital media theorist, poet, and software designer. His research/creation projects explore computation as a creative and cultural material, and he is interested in developing intriguing new forms of expression by working on conceptual, critical, creative, and technical levels simultaneously. He is the University Research Chair in Computational Media and the Indigenous Future Imaginary as well Professor of Computation Arts at Concordia University, Montreal, where he directs the Initiative for Indigenous Futures, and co-directs the Indigenous Futures Research Centre and the Aboriginal Territories in Cyberspace research network. He is Hawaiian and Samoan, born and raised in northern California.

Eleonora LIMA is Research Fellow in Digital Humanities at Trinity College Dublin, where she is part of the EU-funded project Knowledge Technologies for Democracy (KT4D). She is currently working on the first comprehensive history of computing in Italian literature. She has published on the interconnections between literature, science, and technology, as well as on Italian cinema and visual arts. Eleonora is a member of the Ethically Aligned Design for the Arts Committee, part of the IEEE Global Initiative on Ethics of Autonomous and Intelligent Systems. She holds a PhD in Italian and Media Studies (University of Wisconsin at Madison, 2015). She was previously an EU Marie Skłodowska-Curie Postdoctoral Fellow (2018–2020) and a Postdoctoral Fellow at the University of Toronto (2017–2018).

Yang LIU 劉洋 is Senior Research Fellow in the Faculty of Philosophy and the Leverhulme Centre for the Future of Intelligence. His research interests include logic, foundations of probability, mathematical and philosophical decision theory, and philosophy of artificial intelligence (AI). His current research is supported by the Leverhulme Trust and the Isaac Newton Trust. Before moving to Cambridge, he received his PhD in Philosophy from Columbia University. He is co-founder and co-organizer of a seminar series on logic, probability, and games, as well as a conference series on decision theory and AI.

Graham MATTHEWS is Associate Professor in Contemporary Literature at Nanyang Technological University, Singapore. His research interests include the literary representation of science, medicine, and technology, and perceptions of risk. He is the author of *Will Self and Contemporary British Society* and has contributed to journals including *Modern Fiction Studies*, *Textual Practice*, *Literature & Medicine*, *Journal of Modern Literature*, *English Studies*, *Pedagogies*, and *Critique*.

Upamanyu Pablo MUKHERJEE is Professor of English and Comparative Literary Studies at Warwick University. He is the author of *Crime and Empire: The Colony in Nineteenth-Century Fictions of Crime* (Oxford University Press, 2003), *Natural Disasters and Victorian Empire: Famines, Fevers and the Literary Cultures of South Asia* (Palgrave Macmillan, 2013), and *Final Frontiers: Science Fiction and Techno-Science in Non-Aligned India* (Liverpool University Press, 2020).

Anton Ivanovich PERVUSHIN (Антон Иванович ПЕРВУШИН) holds an MSc in Engineering and is an independent scholar and science fiction writer. He is a member of the St. Petersburg Writers' Union, the St. Petersburg Union of Scientists, and the Russian Cosmonautics Federation. He researches the history of Soviet cosmonautics, science fiction, and astroculture. Among his nonfiction books, the two most notable are *12 Myths about Soviet Science Fiction* (*12 мифов о советской фантастике*), and *Space Mythology: From Atlanteans on Mars to Lunar Conspiracy Theory* (*Космическая мифология: от марсианских атлантов до лунного заговора*).

Nagla RIZK is Professor of Economics and Founding Director of the Access to Knowledge for Development Center (A2K4D) at the American University in Cairo's School of Business. Her research area is the economics of knowledge, technology, and innovation with emphasis on human development in the digital economy in the Middle East and Africa. Her recent work focuses on the economics of data, AI, and inclusion. She authored the chapter 'Artificial Intelligence and Inequality in the Middle East' in *The Oxford Handbook of Ethics of Artificial Intelligence* (Markus Dubber et al. (eds.), Oxford University Press, 2020). She is a member of the Steering Committee of the Open African Innovation Research Partnership and is Faculty Associate at Harvard's Berkman Klein Center for Internet and Society.

Anzhelika SOLOVYEVA is Assistant Professor at the Department of Security Studies, Faculty of Social Sciences at Charles University in Prague. She has been affiliated with the Charles University Research Centre of Excellence dedicated to the topic of 'Human-Machine Nexus and the Implications for the International Order'. Her latest monograph, co-authored with Nik Hynek, is *Militarizing Artificial Intelligence: Theory, Technology, and Regulation* (Routledge, 2022).

SONG Bing is Senior Vice President of the Berggruen Institute and the Director of the Institute's China Center. She is responsible for the strategy and overall development of the Institute's China-based research, fellowship programmes, and public engagement. Prior to joining the Berggruen Institute, Bing came from a longstanding legal and banking career. Her research interests lie in the intersection of Chinese philosophy, frontier technologies, and governance. Recently she edited a volume on AI and Chinese philosophy, published by CITIC Press and Springer.

Apolline TAILLANDIER is a Postdoctoral Research Fellow at the Leverhulme Centre for the Future of Intelligence at the University of Cambridge and at the Center for Science and Thought at the University of Bonn. She also holds affiliated positions with the Department of Politics and International Studies at Cambridge and the Center for European Studies at Sciences Po in Paris. Previously, she was a Doctoral Fellow at the Max Planck Sciences Po Center on Coping with Instability in Market Societies, and held visiting fellowships at the University of California, Berkeley, and Cambridge. She is currently writing a monograph on the intellectual history of postwar transhumanism. In her new project, she traces feminist ideas in the history of AI and computer science in the US, the UK, and France.

Miao TIAN is Professor and department head at the Institute for the History of Natural Sciences, Chinese Academy of Sciences; her main research area is the History of Science and Technology in China, and she specializes in the history of mathematics and mechanics, the history of knowledge dissemination, and comparative studies of mathematics in Chinese and European history.

Nadine WEHEBA is Associate Director for Research at the Access to Knowledge for Development Center (A2K4D) at the School of Business of the American University in Cairo. Weheba's research interests are the political economy of information communication technologies, innovation, and development. She studies new business models in the digital economy, new technologies, such as artificial intelligence, and inclusion in the context of Egypt, Africa, and the region. She received her MSc in Development Studies from the School of Oriental and African Studies (SOAS) at the University of London and holds a BA in Economics from The American University in Cairo.

Daniel WHITE is Senior Research Associate in the Department of Social Anthropology at the University of Cambridge. He co-organizes an ethnographic research project called Model Emotion, in which he works across disciplines with anthropologists, psychologists, computer scientists, and robotics engineers to trace and critique how theoretical models of emotion are built into machines with emotional capacities for care and well-being. His publications, podcasts, and other projects document how different cultural imaginaries, largely from Japan, are shaping diverse futures for artificial intelligence and can be found at www.modelemotion.org.

Yan WU is Professor at the Center for Humanities at Southern University of Science and Technology in Shenzhen. He is also a science fiction writer, winner of the Chinese Galaxy and Nebula Awards, and the 2020 Clareson Award of the Science Fiction Research Association (SFRA).

Feng ZHANG is a science fiction researcher. He is visiting researcher at the Humanities Center of Southern University of Science and Technology in Shenzhen, chief researcher of Shenzhen Science & Fantasy Growth Foundation, honorary Assistant Professor of the University of Hong Kong, Secretary-General of the World Chinese Science Fiction Association, and editor-in-chief of *Nebula Science Fiction Review*. His research covers the history of Chinese science fiction, development of the science fiction industry, science fiction and urban development, and science fiction and technological innovation.

INTRODUCTION

1

How the World Sees Intelligent Machines

Introduction

Stephen Cave and Kanta Dihal

1.1 Myths and Realities

Artificial intelligence (AI) was a cultural phenomenon long before it was a technological one. In some cultures, visions of intelligent machines go back centuries, even millennia (Liveley and Thomas, 2020; Zhang and Tian, Chapter 22 this volume). Such visions spread with industrialization until, by the twentieth century, a future with such machines was being richly imagined around the world. When the term 'artificial intelligence' was coined in the US in 1956, it was not to name a new invention, but rather to express a determination to realize a long-standing fantasy (Cave et al., Chapter 2 this volume).

Some would say that AI is still a cultural phenomenon and not a technological one: that for all the innovations in computing, and all the hype in industry and policy, no existing systems deserve to be called truly intelligent (e.g. Simkoff and Mahdavi, 2019; Taulli, 2019). Others, however, argue that we are surrounded by AI: that it pervades our daily lives—through our smartphones, the online services we use, and the hidden systems that govern us (e.g. Smith, 2021). It is hard to think of another technology in history about which such a debate could be had—a debate about whether it is everywhere, or nowhere at all. That it can be held about AI is a testament to its mythic quality.

Of course, innovation in digital technology is real and rapid, and it is continually in interplay with this long-standing mythology of intelligent machines. This cultural backdrop shapes what motivates funders and engineers, how products are designed, whether and by whom technologies are taken up, how they are regulated, and so on. The nodes of production—academia and industry, media and policy—are interwoven and mutually influential.

Take, for example, the 2014 Hollywood film *Transcendence*, which tells the story of AI expert Will Caster (Johnny Depp), who has his mind 'uploaded' onto an AI system by his wife Evelyn (Rebecca Hall) and his colleague Max Waters (Paul Bettany) (Pfister, 2014). During the film's opening weekend, three well-known scientists, Stephen Hawking, Max Tegmark, and Stuart Russell, published a *Huffington Post* article titled 'Transcending Complacency on Superintelligent Machines' (Hawking et al., 2014). Later republished with the name of Nobel Prize winner Frank Wilczek added, the article argues that:

> As the Hollywood blockbuster *Transcendence* debuts this weekend with Johnny Depp, Morgan Freeman and clashing visions for the future of humanity, it's tempting to dismiss the notion of highly intelligent machines as mere science fiction. But this would be a mistake, and potentially our worst mistake ever.
> (Hawking et al., 2014)

The article is intended to convince policy makers and other publics of the importance of AI. That same month, Tegmark founded the Future of Life Institute (FLI), which aims 'to ensure that tomorrow's most powerful technologies are beneficial for humanity'. It is partly funded by Elon Musk, who is a real-life technology magnate and pioneer of AI-driven cars. Musk also appears in a cameo in *Transcendence*, as an audience member of a lecture on AI. In addition, Morgan Freeman, who plays one of the film's heroes, sits on FLI's Board, alongside Musk. The film therefore perfectly reflects what we call the 'Californian feedback loop': the multiple entanglements of Hollywood and the broader culture it reflects, of academic research and Silicon Valley industrial production, of narrative and the billionaire-funded fight to shape the future. Stories such as *Transcendence* co-construct what AI is understood to be, embedding or disputing existing attitudes and approaches.

But crucially, these attitudes and approaches are not the same around the world. They are shaped by the particular histories, philosophies, ideologies, religions, narrative traditions, and economic structures of different countries, cultures, and peoples. *Transcendence* is a product of the US, and trades in well-worn Hollywood tropes, such as AI as the ultimate technology (and therefore the ultimate solution to all problems, i.e. pollution, the energy crisis, disease), yet at the same time the ultimate threat to humanity; the reduction of the individual to data and computation, and therefore the possibility of digital immortality; and the lone male genius scientist and the subordinate female who must in some way sacrifice herself. Individually, these tropes are not unique to Hollywood—each can be found elsewhere—but collectively they form the distinctive mythology of AI in America.

In our 2020 volume (with Sarah Dillon) *AI Narratives: a History of Imaginative Thinking about Intelligent Machines*, we surveyed the predominant themes in anglophone Western portrayals of AI (Cave et al., 2020a). In this volume, *Imagining AI: How the World Sees Intelligent Machines*, we look beyond the mainstream traditions of the US and UK to how other cultures have conceived of this technology. There are a number of motivations for this.

First, AI is now a global phenomenon. The term originated in the US, and much of the technology continues to be developed there. But those systems are being taken up around the world, and other countries are scrambling to develop their own AI industries. Each will do so informed by their own mythologies of AI—the concatenation of different stories and ideologies that shape their expectations and anxieties around what this technology can be. Understanding how AI will develop requires, therefore, an understanding of the many sites in which its story is unfolding.

Second, the debate about how AI is developed responsibly and governed has been dominated by anglophone actors. This is starting to change, as more countries develop their own AI strategies. But they are entering a space shaped by anglophone Western assumptions. There is a risk that efforts to regulate AI will fail as these assumptions are insensitive to different cultural contexts, or that solutions imposed will unwittingly prejudice some traditions. It is imperative, therefore, to develop a better understanding of the diversity of views about what AI should be.

Third, we hope this comparative approach will shed new light for scholars, whether of the anglophone tradition or others. Seeing where cultures share or differ in their approaches to AI gives insight into the forces that shape these traditions. For example, we could look at what narratives are common to capitalist countries, or colonizing ones. Those who live and work outside the anglophone tradition may discover in this collection narratives from elsewhere in the world that resemble their own perspectives and concerns much more closely. For instance, we have included chapters on anti-colonial or decolonial AI narratives from Latin America, South Asia, Sub-Saharan Africa, and Indigenous North American nations. They show that this resistance can take many shapes, but shared themes resonate across continents: the platforming of non-Western knowledge and forms of knowing with respect to AI 'to critically reflect on such designations as "advanced" and "backward"' (Mukherjee, Chapter 15 this volume); the re-appropriation of technologies from the anglophone West for purposes and art forms their original creators did not envision or even explicitly excluded; and the deployment of fictional and non-fictional narratives of AI for the explicit purpose of post-colonial nation building. At the same time, we see narratives about 'catching up' to other countries, particularly the US and UK, from South Korea, India, and Russia alike. Our contributors also show how narratives have historically resisted and supported a wide range of ideologies, from communism in mid-twentieth-century China, the Soviet Union, and Italy, to neoliberalism in Chile, and technocracy in Singapore.

Fourth, each cultural perspective is limited and particular, privileging some within that culture and prejudicing others. Certainly this is true of the anglophone Western tradition, which, as we and others have noted elsewhere, is inflected by ideologies of racial, gender, and class hierarchy, by polarizing dichotomies, and a fixation on domination and control (Cave, 2020; Cave and Dihal, 2020, 2019). There have therefore been many recent calls for new imaginaries of technology. Race scholar Ruha Benjamin quotes producer and activist Kamal Sinclair, 'story and narrative are the code for humanity's operating system', before calling to 'reimagine science and technology for liberatory ends' (Benjamin, 2019, pp. 193–5). For any given culture, in attempting to imagine how the future can be different from what its mainstream prescribes, we hope it will be illuminating to consider how other cultures imagine AI otherwise.

Of course, the limitations of Western narratives will not be solved simply by adding a Chinese work to one's reading list, consulting an Indigenous person, or mentioning Ubuntu ethics at a workshop on AI regulation. Tokenistic approaches to the diversification, de-localization, and decolonization of AI have been attempted and criticized repeatedly in the past decade (Birhane and Guest, 2020; Snell, 2020). Nonetheless, as Priyamvada Gopal points out in her discussion of curriculum decolonization, 'diversity is, in fact, important both for its own sake and for pedagogical and intellectual reasons—a largely white or largely male curriculum is not politically incorrect, as is often believed, but intellectually unsound' (Gopal, 2021, p. 877). *Imagining AI* addresses this issue of diversity on two levels. First, at the level of the narratives themselves: this collection presents a wealth of novels, films, comics, visual art, and other media from outside the anglophone West, many—though not all—of which are largely unknown outside their region. Second, through intellectual engagement with these sources: all of our authors engage in analysis and contextualization of the narratives they bring to the table, bringing out motifs and arguments that introduce new themes to the now-growing field of AI narratives, or shed new light on existing themes.

It is with these four motivations in mind that we started the Global AI Narratives research project at the University of Cambridge's Leverhulme Centre for the Future of Intelligence, in collaboration with nine partner institutions on six continents. The project aimed to understand and analyse how different cultures and regions perceive the risks and benefits of AI, and the influences that are shaping those perceptions. We convened a series of twenty workshops across the globe between 2018 and 2021 and built an international network of experts on portrayals and perceptions of AI beyond the English-speaking West, many relating these diverse visions to pressing questions of AI ethics and governance. *Imagining AI* is the product of these workshops, at which many of our contributors first shared the work collected here.

Our highly interdisciplinary group of contributors consists of leading experts from academia and the arts, selected for their expertise on a given region or culture. As in *AI Narratives*, the discourses they analyse range across myth and legend; literature and film, including science fiction; and nonfiction such as policy documents and government propaganda. We do not draw a clear distinction between fiction and nonfiction in examining AI narratives: as the chapters show in detail, and as our previous work has argued, fictional and nonfictional AI narratives together form 'sociotechnical imaginaries' (Jasanoff, 2015) that shape public perceptions of AI on the one hand, and the direction technology development takes on the other (Cave et al., 2020b, 2019; Cave and Dihal, 2020, 2019).

It is of course not possible to achieve a complete survey of AI imaginaries in all the many regions and cultures of the world. While we have aimed to be broadly geographically representative, we encountered the problem that some regions are much more intensely studied than others. We were therefore able to find a large number of excellent scholars writing on, for example, Continental Europe or China. But it proved much harder to find contributors on, for example, the imaginaries of Sub-Saharan Africa or India. For this edited collection, this problem was exacerbated by the fact that the most underrepresented cultures and regions were also those worst hit by the Covid-19 pandemic, which forced some of our initial contributors to instead attend to more pressing personal circumstances. It is a source of great regret to us that we cannot better represent these regions in this volume, and we hope that it will perhaps inspire more work on such important but understudied areas. Despite these lacunae, we hope that readers will enjoy the unprecedented wealth of perspectives on AI that our contributors share in the following chapters.

1.2 Overview of the Book

The chapters of this book are clustered geographically.[1] We have chosen this arrangement, rather than a focus on themes or historical periods, to allow us to group chapters from similar linguistic or cultural backgrounds. For example, we have four short chapters on China that each cover a different historical period, together highlighting a range of aspects of a deep narrative history. Of course, different regions or countries are not pristine islands of cultural uniqueness: each is shaped by new immigrants or its own diasporas, by the arrival of new religions and ideologies from elsewhere, by layers of conquest and settlement, by absorption of or reaction to the cultural exports of more powerful actors. Many of our contributors have aimed to tease out the uniqueness of the narratives they discuss, taking account of the diverse influences that have shaped them, and the diversity within the traditions they represent.

We open this collection with a comparative chapter focusing not on narratives themselves, but rather on the words narrators have at their disposal for expressing the concepts covered in this book. Chapter 2 investigates the terms used to denote intelligent machines in five language groups—Germanic, Slavonic, Romance, Chinese, Japanese—to elucidate the value-laden character of the terminology as well as explore its influence on the perceptions of contemporary AI technologies around the globe. The chapter traces the implied meanings behind the technology's original name—its links to specific conceptions of (human) intelligence and reason in the West, as well as the cultural history of artificiality in Europe—and investigates what happens to those connotations when the term is translated and popularized in non-anglophone and non-Western cultures. It examines how, in some cases, other cultural-linguistic groups have reproduced these associations, while in others, the English term is widely used, but with wholly different connotations.

Part I encompasses Europe, including Russia. While most of the chapters focus on the twentieth century, the section opens with Chapter 3, which looks at late-nineteenth-century French culture and its explorations of the birth of the technologies that underpin our contemporary life. Madeleine Chalmers proposes that there is a uniquely French mode of approaching what we would now recognize as AI: a mode that is distinct from the fragmentation of Anglo–American modernism or the fascist sex-and-speed-machines of Italian futurism. The French touch lies in its meta-reflexive narrative play, which allows it to test out technological and political scenarios. Chalmers asks how looking back to the imaginings of the past can help us to find critical distance, as debates about the existential and ethical risks of developing technologies permeate mainstream culture faster than we can conceptualize their ramifications.

Chapter 4 looks at Italy and its 1980s counterculture, whose new political sensitivity found expression through images of androids and cyborgs that embodied the new rebellious subject of the 1980s: fluid, highly technological, urban, more at ease with pop culture references than with Marxist ones. Eleonora Lima introduces its most prominent example, the comic strip *Ranxerox* (1978–1986), whose protagonist is a violent, uninhibited, and amoral android, created by a group of dissident college students by assembling pieces from a photocopy machine—a Rank Xerox—as a weapon against the police. The third of our Western European chapters is written by Hans Esselborn, who in Chapter 5 investigates two phases in thinking about AI in science fiction written in German. First, the 1960s cybernetics revolution that inspired Austrian author H.

W. Franke to write several innovative texts on supercomputers governing and controlling societies. Second, in the twenty-first century, public discussions on AI and its practical achievements have encouraged several German science fiction authors to write novels about the prospects and dangers of self-learning programs, including their awakening and achieving world supremacy through networking and computing power.

Part I then moves towards Eastern Europe. In Chapter 6, Bogna Konior explores the works of Stanisław Lem, particularly his *Summa Technologiae* (1964) in which he reveals his preoccupation with the long-term techno-biological evolution of humanity. Focusing on artificial life and 'the breeding of information' as examples of existential, rather than utilitarian, technologies, Konior's chapter explores Lem's unique reading of cybernetics, and reflects on its relationship to the dominant militaristic model of cybernetics during the Cold War. Simultaneously, the chapter reflects on the place of the *Summa* within Lem's oeuvre, and within the context of the 1960s Communist bloc and communism's own tautological ideas of political evolution of civilizations.

Chapter 7 zooms out to identify trends concerning AI in science fiction of the USSR (1922–1991). Anton Pervushin identifies three trends: the use of intelligent machines as a cheap workforce, thus making them the new proletariat of a future world; intelligent machines as an instrument, used by bourgeois society to suppress and further exploit the proletariat; and society compelling intelligent machines to acquire emotions and understand the taboos and laws that are considered a norm in this society. Pervushin's chapter concludes that these three trends were eventually consolidated into two main stereotypes of the intelligent machine in Soviet science fiction: the evil robot and the funny robot. Moving beyond the Soviet period, Chapter 8 by Anzhelika Solovyeva and Nik Hynek traces a hundred-year history of imagining intelligent machines in Russia to the present day. Contextualized by references to nascent representations of automata in the Russian Empire, they distinguish three formative phases based on transformations in science, politics, literature, and visual arts. The earliest attempts to conceptualize the human–machine nexus originated in the Bolshevik Revolution and the Russian avant-garde. In the second phase (mid- to late twentieth century), the Soviets' progress in computer engineering, cybernetics, and AI paved the way for machine automation and facilitated fantasies about intelligent machines. In the third phase (post-Soviet Union and especially in Putin's Russia) both popular culture and research envision a future with lifelike machines.

From Europe we move across the Atlantic for Part II, which focuses on the Americas and Pacific. Our own Chapter 9 opens this section and is the only chapter in this book whose focus is mainstream anglophone Western conceptions of AI. Surveying Hollywood films and science fiction literature, we argue that American AI narratives tend to be extreme: either utopian or (more often) dystopian. We illustrate the utopian strand with an analysis of Isaac Asimov's 'The Last Question' (1956), situating it within an American ideology of technology that associates technological mastery with ontological superiority, the legitimation of settler-colonialism and the pursuit of a 'second creation' on earth. We then examine the inherent instability of this vision, which explains why it can tip so readily into the dystopian. This includes fears of decadence and the slave-machine uprising, and revolves around loss of control. We then examine three degrees of loss of control: from willingly giving up autonomy to the machine in the 2008 film *WALL-E*, to value misalignment in Martin Caidin's *The God Machine* (1968), to utter extermination in the *Terminator* franchise.

Chapter 10 concerns Brazil, and Edward King focuses on the use of Afrofuturist aesthetics to produce what Ruha Benjamin (2019) describes as 'subversive countercodings' of the dominant practices of racialization. Artists working in various media—including filmmaker Adirley Quierós and visual artists Vitória Cribb and the Afrobapho Collective—have adapted a science fiction aesthetic developed in the 1960s and 1970s US by musicians such as Sun Ra and George Clinton to challenge the normalized disparity between Black culture and science and technology. Although varied in their approaches, these practitioners are united in their use of Afrofuturism to contest what André Brock, Jr. (2020) identifies as the conflation of online identity with whiteness, 'even as whiteness is itself signified as a universal, raceless, technocultural identity'. In the process, they propose alternative conceptions of the human as intimately imbricated with computer systems that do not repeat pseudo-universal versions of modernity that are predicated on anti-Blackness.

Equally focused on subversion and resistance is the selection of artworks by Mexican artist Raúl Cruz in Chapter 11 and his explanation about how his work fuses science fiction tropes of AI with the art of Mesoamerican cultures, particularly the Maya and Aztecs. He argues that, although new technologies can cause global homogenization, they will not erase the traditions, myths, and customs of Latin America. The cultural legacy of the peoples of this continent will merge with technological advances, giving rise to distinctive visions of intelligent machines, including robots with Aztec aesthetics, cybernetic catrinas, and Quetzalcoatl ships. Cruz's works are distinctively Latin American visions of intelligent machines that merge the fantastic, the literary, the mythic, and the mechanical. In Chapter 12, Macarena Areco moves to an analysis of recent Chilean science fiction featuring AI. She examines how the imagined spaces, technologies, and subjectivities of the neoliberal era are condensed in representations of AI in the works of Chilean author Jorge Baradit.

The final two chapters of Part II offer Indigenous perspectives from North America and the Pacific/Moananuiākea. In Chapter 13, Jason Edward Lewis describes the work done at the 2019 Indigenous Protocol and AI Workshops and the ways in which this work led to imagining what one's relationship to AI should be from an Indigenous perspective, and what Indigenous AI might look like. Then, in Chapter 14, Noelani Arista introduces the concept of Maoli Intelligence, or that corpus of ancestral knowledge where the collective *'ike* (knowledge, traditional knowledge) of Kānaka Maoli, Hawaiian people, continues to be accessed. She presents a compelling view of Indigenous data sovereignty and provides examples from her *lāhui* (Nation, people) built upon a robust oral to textual, filmic, and material culture 'archive'. Her chapter concludes with her work with an all-Indigenous team of data and computer scientists to build a prototype of an image recognition application forecasting what can be done with Maoli Intelligence that can be applied on a broader scale.

Part III covers Africa, the Middle East, and South Asia. In Chapter 15, Upamanyu Pablo Mukherjee discusses AI in the fiction of the Indian writer, filmmaker, musician, and designer Satyajit Ray, who frequently used science fiction to interrogate some of the key premises of European 'Enlightenment'. In his robot stories in particular, Ray complicated the presumed circuit between reason and intelligence by introducing emotions as a key but variable component. Mukherjee examines Ray's science fiction to wonder whether a different account of AI can be sketched from the post-colonial moment of the mid-twentieth century.

Abeba Birhane's Chapter 16 concerns what she terms 'the AI invasion of Africa': the ways in which Western tech monopolies, with their desire to dominate, control, and influence social, political, and cultural discourse, share common characteristics with traditional colonialism. While traditional colonialism used brute force domination, colonialism in the age of AI takes the form of 'state-of-the-art algorithms' and 'AI solutions' to social problems. Birhane argues that not only is Western-developed AI unfit for African problems, the West's algorithmic invasion simultaneously impoverishes development of local products while also leaving the continent dependent on Western software and infrastructure. Then, in Chapter 17, Rachel Adams investigates what it means and requires to decolonize AI and explores an alternate cultural perspective on nonhuman intelligence from that portrayed in the more well-known canon of the Western imaginary. Her enquiry focuses on the transgendered *ogbanje* of Nigerian Yoruba and Igbo cultural traditions—a changeling child or reincarnated spirit. Through engagement with the works of Chinwe and Chinua Achebe and Akwaeke Emezi, she explores the roles anthropomorphism, representation, and gender play in making intelligence culturally identifiable; whether this offers an alternative imaginary for transcending the normative binaries that AI fortifies; and what kind of politics this requires.

To close this section, Chapter 18 is a collaboration between the Access to Knowledge for Development Center at the American University in Cairo and the Leverhulme Centre for the Future of Intelligence at Cambridge and covers the Middle East and North Africa (MENA) region. While people in

MENA have been imagining intelligent machines since the Islamic Golden Age (9th–14th centuries), Western perceptions of success, development, progress, and industrialization influence the hopes and dreams for the future of technology today. In this chapter, we analyse the various factors that make the MENA region a unique environment for imagining futures with intelligent machines, mapping local visions of technological progress onto the region's complicated past, as well as contemporary economic and political struggles.

Part IV focuses on East and South East Asia, regions frequently portrayed as radically different from the anglophone West in its portrayals and perceptions of AI. Chapter 19 by Hirofumi Katsuno and Daniel White investigates the political dimensions of this idea with regard to Japan. According to this view, whereas in the Western robotic imaginary intelligent machines signify a threat to humanity, in the Japanese imaginary machines are partners to humans, offering their technological skills to address problems of shared human–robot concern. Based on ethnographic fieldwork in Japan, their chapter analyses the imaginaries of animism, animation, and animacy among Japanese roboticists building emotionally intelligent companion robots. The chapter argues that while emphases on emotionality in Japanese AI narratives challenge distinctions between reason and emotion in anglophone AI research, even more importantly, observations on the cultural politics of these distinctions diversifies the notion of 'culture' itself.

Chapter 20 focuses on South Korean narratives, particularly policy discourse on AI after the 2016 AlphaGo match. So Young Kim argues that, held right after the 2016 Davos Forum that popularized the term 'the Fourth Industrial Revolution', the match rendered the esoteric technology a household name, with no day going by without AI featuring in national news media. The following four years saw a huge outpouring of news, events, studies, artworks, policies, and more on AI—including the creation of the Presidential Committee on the Fourth Industrial Revolution (2017), the declaration of the National AI Strategy (2019), and the announcement of the AI-driven Digital New Deal (2020). Kim's chapter explores the central features of South Korean policy discourse on AI, revealing the imprints of developmental state legacies that permeate every corner of Korean society.

The next four short chapters each address a different aspect of AI narratives in China. First, in Chapter 21 Bing Song explains which philosophical ideas and practices may have shaped Chinese thinking towards the development of frontier technologies and the approach to human–machine relationships, focusing on the three dominant schools: Confucianism, Daoism, and Buddhism. Next, in Chapter 22 Baichun Zhang and Miao Tian discuss the attitudes towards new technologies in pre-Qin Dynasty China (pre-221 BCE) and look at a range of attitudes towards both imaginary technologies that we would now call AI, and real innovations in battlefield technologies. They argue that pragmatic motivations tended to trump philosophical concerns. In Chapter 23, Yan Wu fast-forwards to twentieth-century China and discusses science fiction from 1949 to 1983. While advanced computers and robots featured early in Chinese science fiction, in these stories the AI characters are largely human-like assistants, chiefly collecting data or doing manual labour. The reform and opening-up of 1978 caused the number and quality of robot-themed works to balloon. Important themes in these new works included the idea that the growth of AI requires a suitable environment, stable family relationship, and social adaptation.

Finally, in Chapter 24 Feng Zhang explores the newest generation of AI-themed science fiction from China. On the one hand, contemporary authors are aware that the 'soul' of current AI, to a large extent, comes from machine-learning algorithms. As a result, their works often highlight the existence and implementation of algorithms, bringing manoeuvrability and credibility to the portrayal of AI. On the other hand, the authors prefer to focus on the conflicts and contradictions in emotions, ethics, and morality caused by AI that penetrate human life. If earlier AI-themed science fiction is like a distant robot fable, recent narratives of AI assume contemporary and practical significance.

Our final chapter 25, is the most comprehensive of the surveys of AI narratives corpora discussed in this collection. Cheryl Julia Lee and Graham Matthews present an evaluation of the entire history of AI narratives in Singapore. They argue that fictional portrayals of AI in Singapore problematize the Smart Nation initiative of Prime Minister Lee Hsien Loong, which simultaneously valorizes and objectifies the human. The narratives typically eschew the tropes of existential risk—annihilation and enslavement—and present instead visions of coexistence and mutual dependency between humans and machines. The authors question whether narratives of AI in Singapore promote visions of an AI-driven future that we should accept or be wary of surrendering to—and the extent to which these conclusions depend on a dichotomy between 'Western technology' and 'traditional Eastern values'.

Together, these essays show that the imaginary of intelligent machines is an incredibly rich site for exploring the varied influences—historical, political, and artistic—that shape how different cultures reconcile the demands of being human in a technological age.

Endnote

1. For consistency, this overview gives all author names in first name–family name order.

References

Benjamin, R. (2019) *Race after technology: Abolitionist tools for the new Jim code*. Medford, MA: Polity Press.

Birhane, A. and Guest, O. (2020) 'Towards decolonising computational sciences', *ArXiv* [online], 29 September. Available at: https://arxiv.org/abs/2009.14258

Brock, Jr., A. (2020) *Distributed Blackness: African–American cybercultures*. New York: New York University Press.

Cave, S. (2020) 'The problem with intelligence: Its value-laden history and the future of AI', in *Proceedings of the 2020 AAAI/ACM conference on AI, ethics, and society, AIES '20*. New York: ACM, pp. 29–35. https://doi.org/10.1145/3375627.3375813

Cave, S., Coughlan, K., and Dihal, K. (2019) '"Scary robots": Examining public responses to AI', in *Proceedings of the 2019 AAAI/ACM conference on AI, ethics, and society, AIES '19*. New York: ACM, pp. 331–7. https://doi.org/10.1145/3306618.3314232

Cave, S. and Dihal, K. (2019) 'Hopes and fears for intelligent machines in fiction and reality', *Nature Machine Intelligence*, 1, pp. 74–8. Available at: https://doi.org/10.1038/s42256-019-0020-9

Cave, S. and Dihal, K. (2020) 'The whiteness of AI', *Philosophy & Technology*, 33, pp. 685–703. Available at: https://doi.org/10.1007/s13347-020-00415-6

Cave, S., Dihal, K., and Dillon, S. (eds.) (2020a) *AI narratives: A history of imaginative thinking about intelligent machines*. Oxford: Oxford University Press.

Cave, S., Dihal, K., and Dillon, S. (2020b) 'Introduction: Imagining AI', in Cave, S., Dihal, K., and Dillon, S. (eds.) *AI narratives: A history of imaginative thinking about intelligent machines*. Oxford: Oxford University Press, pp. 1–21.

Gopal, P. (2021) 'On Decolonisation and the University', *Textual Practice*, 35(6), pp. 873–99. Available at: https://doi.org/10.1080/0950236X.2021.1929561

Hawking, S., et al. (2014) 'Transcending complacency on superintelligent machines', *Huffington Post* [online]. Available at: https://www.huffingtonpost.com/stephen-hawking/artificial-intelligence_b_5174265.html (Accessed: 21 June 2019).

Jasanoff, S. (2015) 'Future imperfect: Science, technology, and the imaginations of modernity', in Jasanoff, S. and Kim, S.-H. (eds.) *Dreamscapes of modernity: Sociotechnical imaginaries and the fabrication of power*. Chicago: University of Chicago Press, pp. 1–33.

Liveley, G. and Thomas, S. (2020) 'Homer's intelligent machines: AI in Antiquity', in *AI narratives: A history of imaginative thinking about intelligent machines*. Oxford: Oxford University Press, pp. 25–48.

Transcendence. (2014) Directed by Wally Pfister [Film]. Warner Bros. Pictures.

Simkoff, M. and Mahdavi, A. (2019) 'AI doesn't actually exist yet', *Scientific American* [online], 12 November. Available at: https://blogs.scientificamerican.com/observations/ai-doesnt-actually-exist-yet/ (Accessed 22 April 2022).

Smith, C. S. (2021) 'A.I. here, there, everywhere', *The New York Times* [online], 9 March. Available at: https://www.nytimes.com/2021/02/23/technology/ai-innovation-privacy-seniors-education.html

Snell, T. (2020) 'Tokenism is not "progress"', *POCIT People Color Tech* [online]. Available at: https://peopleofcolorintech.com/articles/tokenism-is-not-progress/ (Accessed 22 April 2022).

Taulli, T. (2019) 'Splunk CEO: Artificial intelligence does not exist today', *Forbes* [online], 25 October Available at: https://www.forbes.com/sites/tomtaulli/2019/10/25/splunk-ceo—artificial-intelligence-does-not-exist-today/ (Accessed 22 April 2022).

2

The Meanings of AI

A Cross-Cultural Comparison

Stephen Cave, Kanta Dihal, Tomasz Hollanek, Hirofumi Katsuno, Yang Liu, Apolline Taillandier, and Daniel White

2.1 Introduction

'Too flashy', 'kind of phony', 'attendees balked at the term': since its coining in 1955, the term 'artificial intelligence' (AI) has been contentious for the connotations of both its elements—'artificial' and 'intelligence' (McCorduck, 2004, pp. 114–16). Invented as an eye-catching, attention-grabbing term for a new scientific field, it certainly can be considered successful, with AI—or its equivalent in other languages—dominating headlines around the world. But what terms are used to refer to AI in those other languages? Are they equally contentious? Are their connotations different, and if so, what does this mean for the hopes, fears, and expectations surrounding AI?

This chapter traces the history of the technology's original name in English and the implied meanings behind it—its links to specific conceptions of (human) intelligence and reason in the West, as well as the cultural history of artificiality in Europe—and investigates what happens to those connotations when the term is translated and popularized in non-Anglophone and non-Western cultures. It examines how in some cases other cultural-linguistic groups have reproduced these associations (for example, the relation between art and artifice is preserved in many European languages, such as the German *Kunst* [art]—*künstliche Intelligenz*); while in others, the English acronym is widely used alongside a term with quite different connotations (as in Japan, where 'AI' is used as a buzzword alongside *jinkō chinō*).

The chapter investigates the terms used to denote intelligent machines in five languages and language groups—Germanic (first English, then Continental Germanic languages), Romance, Slavonic, Japanese, and Chinese. These have been chosen because they are or contain languages that are both among the most spoken globally and which are spoken in countries that are major sites of AI development. In what follows we explore these terms in each linguistic context in turn, elucidating the ways in which they are value-laden, and how they might reflect and shape attitudes to AI in the countries where they are spoken.

2.2 Origins of the term 'artificial intelligence'

Famously, the term 'artificial intelligence', as a description of the use of machines to emulate some aspect of human thought, was coined by John McCarthy and a handful of colleagues in 1955. It was the term McCarthy chose to convene a group of leading figures in this nascent field at an event that came to be called 'The Dartmouth Summer Research Project on Artificial Intelligence', held at Dartmouth College, New Hampshire, USA, from June to August 1956. In her history of AI based on interviews with many of the protagonists, Pamela McCorduck relates:

> many attendees balked at that term, invented by McCarthy. 'I won't swear that I hadn't seen it before', he recalls, 'but artificial intelligence wasn't a prominent phrase particularly. Someone may have used it in a paper or a conversation or something like that, but there were many other words that were current at the time. The Dartmouth Conference made that phrase dominate the others'.
>
> (McCorduck, 2004, pp. 114–15)

It was far from inevitable that this term would label the field for the coming decades. As McCarthy mentioned, there were many plausible alternatives. According to historian of AI Jonnie Penn, these included:

> 'engineering psychology', 'applied epistemology', 'neural cybernetics', 'non-numerical computing', 'neuraldynamics', 'advanced automatic programming', 'automatic coding', 'fully automatic programming', 'hypothetical automata', and 'machine intelligence'.
>
> (Penn, 2020, p. 206 fn)

It is noteworthy that Alan Turing had used the term 'intelligence' in the title of his now-famous 1950 paper 'Computing Machinery and Intelligence'. But he does not use the term AI, and indeed, apart from in the title, does not refer to 'intelligence' at all, but focuses on thought and thinking. McCarthy later said that Turing was not a great influence on those at Dartmouth (McCarthy, 1988, p. 7).

John McCarthy has made a number of comments on why he chose the term 'artificial intelligence'. First, he had at the time a collaboration with Claude Shannon, already well known for his information theory, which included jointly editing a book that was published as *Automata Studies* (Shannon and McCarthy, 1956). McCarthy had wanted a broader title, but Shannon had dismissed the alternatives as 'too flashy' (McCorduck, 2004, p. 115). McCarthy was, however, disappointed with the narrowness of the papers that the 'Automata Studies' title attracted, and was determined not to repeat that mistake, as he saw it, for the Dartmouth gathering.

Second, writing in 1988, McCarthy explained why he avoided another plausible alternative:

> As for myself, one of the reasons for inventing the term 'artificial intelligence' was to escape association with 'cybernetics'. Its concentration on analog feedback seemed misguided, and I wished to avoid having either to accept Norbert . . . Wiener as a guru or having to argue with him.
>
> (McCarthy, 1988, p. 6)

Bringing together these two motivations, we can see that McCarthy recognized that the term 'artificial intelligence' had a number of advantages: it was attention grabbing—perhaps even 'flashy'; and even while it drew on traditions such as cybernetics, it was not tied to any one of them, but could encompass a wide range of approaches to the emulation of human thought.

McCarthy managed to persuade his collaborators Marvin Minsky, Nathaniel Rochester, and Shannon of the utility of this term, and in 1955 they together submitted to the Rockefeller Foundation a request for funds for the Dartmouth event. They summarized their intentions thus:

> We propose that a 2-month, 10-man study of artificial intelligence be carried out during the summer of 1956 at Dartmouth College in Hanover, New Hampshire. The study is to proceed on the basis of the conjecture that every aspect of learning or any other feature of intelligence can in principle be so precisely described that a machine can be made to simulate it.
>
> (McCarthy et al., 1955)

As McCorduck records, some of the participants at the Dartmouth event did not take to the new appellation: 'Neither [Allen] Newell nor [Herbert] Simon liked the phrase, and called their own work complex information processing for years thereafter' (McCorduck, 2004, p. 115). Later in 1956, Minsky, who went on to found MIT's AI Lab, addressed some of these critics in the report *Heuristic Aspects of the Artificial Intelligence Problem* for the US Department of Defense. He points out that some people regard intelligence as 'a kind of gift which can not be performed by a machine even in principle' (Minsky, 1956, p. iii). He even notes a phenomenon that plagued the field of AI for decades thereafter—that we consider a certain behaviour intelligent only until it is accomplished by a machine, at which point the goalposts are promptly shifted. Five years later, in 1961, Minsky still felt the need to preface his paper 'Steps toward Artificial Intelligence' with a defence of the term 'artificial intelligence', which he places in scare quotes. But as Penn notes: 'Only a decade later . . . the MIT Artificial Intelligence Laboratory—scare quote free—was fully operational with a budget purported to be in the millions' (Penn, 2020, p. 206).

The path to the present prevalence of AI was not smooth: while the term's popularity rose through the 1960s, it fell in the 1970s, in particular in the UK, where a 1973 Parliament-commissioned assessment, the Lighthill Report, condemned a lack of progress in the field, and prompted the first 'AI winter'. In the 1980s, interest rose again with the deployment of programs known as 'expert systems' but fell into the second AI winter when these, too, disappointed (Russell and Norvig, 2010, p. 24). However, by the start of this century, the term had entered common parlance—as evidenced and perhaps aided by the title of Steven Spielberg's 2001 blockbuster film *A.I. Artificial Intelligence* (2001). It now features daily in newspaper headlines and corporate and government strategies alike.

Despite the intense interest today, the term AI remains controversial. There is no widely accepted definition of it—one of the leading textbooks, *Artificial Intelligence: A Modern Approach*, offers four groups of definitions (Russell and Norvig, 2010). This controversy and ambiguity can be traced back to McCarthy's original intentions to coin a phrase that would be bold, broad, attention grabbing, and unconstrained by any particular scientific field or body of knowledge. The term is therefore only partly a reference to a group of technologies, and more an evocation of possibilities; less a field of study, and more a bold, ambitious, and rather ill-defined goal. As one of those aforementioned policy initiatives, that of the French Parliament led by French mathematician and MP Cédric Villani, astutely notes:

> It is probably this relationship between fictional projections and scientific research which constitutes the essence of what is known as AI. Fantasies—often ethnocentric and based on underlying political ideologies—thus play a major role, albeit frequently disregarded, in the direction this discipline is evolving in.
>
> (Villani et al., 2018, p. 4)

In the rest of this chapter, we examine those underlying ideologies and fantasies, 'often ethnocentric', that shape the meaning and connotations of the term AI in English and as it has entered discourse in other language groups.

2.3 The meanings of 'AI' in English: art, trickery, and hierarchies of the human

It is easy to see how the phrase 'AI' fulfilled McCarthy's need for a name that was attention grabbing and free from ties to any particular approach to computing and the emulation of thought. The term 'artificial' broadly means 'made by humans', and so is not restricted to any of the many ways in which humans were at the time attempting to make computing devices, such as cybernetics or automatic programming. 'Intelligence', too, is a broad term that encompasses many of the capacities that specific projects aimed to recreate, such as learning, language processing, or decision making. But untying this agenda from any more narrow, technical tradition also came with costs that have troubled AI ever since: vagueness in its methods and aims, inflated expectations (and fears), and the importation of ideological connotations, in particular with the term 'intelligence', as we explore next.

2.3.1 Artificial

The primary meaning of 'artificial' is 'made or constructed by human skill, esp. in imitation of, or as a substitute for, something which is made or occurs naturally' ('artificial, adj. and n.', n.d.). It came to English from Latin via Old French. In Latin, *artificialis* means 'of or belonging to art', and *artificium* is 'a work of art; but also a skill; theory, or system'. The Latin *ars* corresponds to the Greek *techne*. An *artifex* is both 'a craftsman or artist' but also a schemer or a mastermind. From its origins, the word therefore interweaves art and artifice, technology and trickery (see section 2.1 in Hollanek, 2020).

These connotations persist today and underlie one of the main anxieties around AI: that it is fooling us into thinking it is something it is not. At one level, this fear is simply of being gulled, as when the Automaton Chess Player of 1770, popularly known as the Mechanical Turk, fooled audiences for decades until it was revealed to have a diminutive man inside (see chapter 2 in Wood, 2002). This implication of fraudulence troubled some of the participants at the Dartmouth event. According to Arthur Samuel, '[t]he word artificial makes you think there's something kind of phony about this, or else it sounds like it's all artificial and there's nothing real about this work at all' (in: McCorduck, 2004, p. 115).

But these anxieties about deception implied by the term 'artificial' also take a deeper and more sinister form: that an AI could live among us, passing for human. This is a persistent theme in fiction: in 1816, while the Mechanical Turk was still touring, the Prussian author E. T. A. Hoffmann wrote 'The Sandman', in which the protagonist Nathanael is bewitched by the beauty of a woman called Olimpia—until the discovery that she is an automaton drives him to suicide (Cave and Dihal, 2018; Hoffmann, 1816). Two centuries later, blockbuster film franchises like *Blade Runner* play on the same fear that the people around us are not what they seem, or that they might even, as in the *Terminator* films, be out to destroy us (Dihal, 2020, p. 207).

2.3.2 *Intelligence*

While the term 'artificial' is crucial to the meaning of 'AI', it is arguably 'intelligence' that is doing the real work, both in setting the research agenda and evoking its grandiose potential. It is also both highly contested in meaning and laden with ideological baggage (Cave, 2020; Legg and Hutter, 2007). Given the central role that the concept of intelligence now plays in many discourses, not just AI, it is perhaps surprising that until the twentieth century it had 'remained largely in the backwaters of English-language discourse' (Carson, 2006, p. 79). What is also surprising to many who use the term today is that, when it began to rise to widespread usage, it was closely tied to eugenics and ideologies of white supremacy, colonialism, classism, and patriarchy.

The idea that the most intelligent people should rule over others has a long history, reaching back to Ancient Greece. But it only attained widespread acceptance in the West when it proved useful in supporting colonialism. Aristotle's argument that some people, because of their superior intellect, were born to rule and others to be ruled over provided a justification for the conquest and enslavement of non-Western peoples. The concept of race served as the scaffold for this narrative: the non-white races were intellectually inferior—in the words of Rudyard Kipling, 'Half-devil and half-child'—and so it was a right, or even a duty, for white peoples to rule over them and their lands (Cave, 2020, p. 30).

Over the course of the nineteenth century, the Western scientific establishment engaged ever more systematically in attempts to evidence these claims. The key figure in this was the English scientist Sir Francis Galton, who was the first to develop a battery of tests to measure intellectual ability, also coined the term 'eugenics', as he put it: 'the science of improving stock . . . to give to the more suitable races or strains of blood a better chance of prevailing speedily over the less suitable' (Galton, 1869). The two went hand-in-hand: as the eugenics agenda spread around the world, intelligence was considered the key variable in determining which peoples should flourish and which were 'less suitable' (Levine, 2017, p. 25).

The role of intelligence—in particular in the form of intelligence testing—in the political history of the twentieth century is vast and complex. It was widely used to justify not only racist and imperialist ideologies, but also patriarchy and classism. While the most egregious examples of the exploitation of those considered less intelligent are confined to the first half of the century, intelligence testing has remained important to this day. At the same time, so do the associations between degrees of innate intelligence and different races, genders, and classes (Saini, 2019).

As Cave (2020) notes, there is good reason to think that these associations are shaping expectations for AI. They might, for example, be driving concern towards middle class white professionals, in the form of worries about lawyers or doctors losing their jobs, when, in fact, it is the poor and marginalized who are more likely to be impacted negatively (Eubanks, 2017). At the same time, the association of this technology with a term—intelligence—long claimed by white men might be harming the prospects of women and people of colour in this important technology sector, so exacerbating a cycle of injustice (Cave, 2020, pp. 33–4).

The English term 'AI' has therefore fulfilled McCarthy's hopes of commanding attention, stimulating the imagination, and encompassing a wide range of technical approaches. But the realization of his ambitions has come at the cost of awakening fears—whether of deception and disaster or displacing the middle classes—that detract from other pressing ethical and political concerns arising from digital technology, such as the regulation of technology giants or mitigating the impact of automation on the most vulnerable.

2.4 'AI' in the other Germanic languages

2.4.1 KI or AI?

Although etymologically different from the Romance-rooted 'artificial', the term used in most Germanic languages has a very similar meaning. German (*künstliche Intelligenz*), Dutch (*kunstmatige intelligentie*), Danish, and Norwegian bokmål and nynorsk (*kunstig intelligens* in all three) use a term derived from the Middle Low German *kunst* ('knowledge' or 'ability'). This term itself derives from the reconstructed Proto-Germanic verb **kunnaną*, denoting 'to know'.[1] Just as 'artificial' interweaves 'art' and 'artifice', so does *kunst*: while rooted in words denoting skill, the term currently means 'art' in all of the aforementioned languages.

As the most widely spoken language of the family, English has had a particularly strong influence on the other Germanic languages. At the same time, perhaps because of the similarity in meaning between 'art' and *kunst*, the prefix 'art-' has been present in several of these languages. Dutch and German have respectively *artificiële intelligentie* and *artifizielle Intelligenz* as alternative terms for AI: while *artificieel* and *artifiziell* are less commonly used words in either language, this version benefits from both the AI acronym and its similarity to the English term. Dutch is particularly ambivalent about KI or AI, to the extent that a newspaper article may use one in its headline and the other in the standfirst (Sheikh, 2021). In the Van Dale dictionary, the 'intelligence' lemma refers to both. The agreed-upon scientific terminology did not help the cause: although Dutch AI scientists in the twentieth century agreed upon the term *kunstmatige intelligentie*, they used the English 'AI' as its abbreviation (van den Herik, 1990; Visser, 1995). Danish, similarly, allows the English abbreviation AI as an alternative to KI ('kunstig intelligens', n.d.). The aforementioned role of the film *AI: Artificial Intelligence* may have influenced Dutch more so than the other Germanic languages, as it is the only language in which the title of the film was left untranslated.[2]

Swedish, meanwhile, is the only Germanic language other than English to have adopted only the 'art' root in its version of the phrase 'AI': it uses *artificiell intelligens*, despite Swedish having the word *kunst* for 'art'. Swedish is also the only Germanic language to have the term *maskinintelligens* (machine intelligence) as a synonym for AI.

One Germanic language does not use either AI or KI. Icelandic has *gervigreind*, from *gervi* meaning 'imitation, artificial, or pseudo-' and *greind* meaning 'intelligence'. If 'artificial' already suggests that 'there's something kind of phony about this', then the Icelandic term makes this phoniness explicit.

2.4.2 *Being 'intelligent'*

The 'intelligence' part of 'artificial intelligence' is less contested: all Germanic languages except Icelandic use the same term derived from the Latin *intelligentia* via the French *intelligence*. This means, however, that the aforementioned ideological baggage attached to the concept of intelligence has carried across into the understanding of AI in all of these languages. This ideological baggage does not come from English alone: it has been co-constructed through intelligence research in countries including the US, England (the aforementioned Galton), France, and Germany in the early twentieth century.

One of the most famous means of classifying intelligence comes from Germany, where the term *Intelligenz* is still considered a technical term from psychology ('Intelligenz', 2021). The term *Intelligenzquotient*, abbreviated to IQ, was invented in 1912 by the Jewish German William Stern, building on the work of the French psychologist Alfred Binet (Section 2.5) (Stern, 1912). This body of work was abused by eugenics movements both in Stern's homeland when the Nazi regime took power, and in the US, to which he fled from this regime. In Nazi Germany, intelligence tests were administered for the purpose of identifying and exterminating 'congenital feeble-mindedness' (*angeborener Schwachsinn*), though the tests were heavily skewed to disadvantage anyone who disagreed with Nazi ideology (Büüsker, 2015).

While these Nazi practices made worldwide eugenics movements significantly less popular, the association between race and intelligence—particularly that white, Western European peoples are more intelligent than others—remains. For example, stereotypes about ethnic minorities being less intelligent than white secondary school pupils have been proven to persist in schoolteachers in the Netherlands (van den Bergh et al., 2010) and Germany (Bonefeld and Dickhäuser, 2018). It is therefore likely that the stereotyped preconceptions about intelligence that underlie the history of AI are equally fundamental to conceptions of AI in northwestern Europe.

2.5 'AI' in the Romance languages

In the mid-1950s, IBM started commercializing in France a new electronic machine named *ordinateur*. The term, an ancient religious word to describe God as organizer of the world, was meant to avoid the literal translation of the English 'computer' as *calculateur*, and their evocation of early basic calculators rather than new machines with powerful capacities (Centenaire IBM France, 2014). By contrast, the translation of 'artificial intelligence' into French closely follows the English version: AI in French is called *intelligence artificielle* and both the term and its corresponding acronym 'IA' have become buzzwords in the general media since 2015. While specific usage patterns vary across contexts, the term appears to share a common etymology across the main Romance languages. Thus, IA stands for *inteligencia artificial* in Spanish, *intelligenza artificiale* in Italian, *inteligência artificial* in Portuguese, and *inteligență artificială* in Romanian.

This proximity with English terminology is both linguistic and cultural. In French academic, policy-oriented, and popular scientific discourse, AI is generally described as a research program with ill-defined boundaries but clear Anglo–American origins, associated most prominently with the works of Alan Turing, John McCarthy, Marvin Minsky, or Herbert Simon (see, e.g. Cardon et al, 2018; LeCun, 2016). Just as in English-speaking contexts, the term also conveys science fiction imaginaries and fantasies. For instance, the French computer scientist and Oulipo member Paul Braffort introduced the 1968 book *L'intelligence artificielle* by noting how, for the non-specialist, AI inevitably brought up fantastic images and representations. As he explained, with *intelligence artificielle* 'arise the key words "robot", "electronic brain", "thinking machine" in a science fiction atmosphere, a clinking of gears, a smell of ozone: Frankenstein is not far away!' (Braffort, 1968, p. 3).

Six decades later, the aforementioned Villani report claims that although AI's development 'has always been accompanied by the wildest, most alarming and far-fetched fantasies', a new dominant and Californian narrative underlies its most recent developments (Villani et al., 2018, pp. 4–5). According to the authors, the ethnocentrism and determinism of dominant AI fantasies today is most apparent in transhumanist ideas of the Singularity, and requires a strong French and European industrial response for ensuring what they call meaningful AI.[3] As an echo of mid-1990s critics of the 'Californian ideology' (Barbrook and Cameron, 1995), a recurring theme in French public and media discourse around AI in recent years has been to point out the dangers of dominant AI imaginaries associated with Silicon Valley.

As mentioned, both words 'artificial' and 'intelligence' get their meaning from Latin. However, the notion of intelligence conveys specific connotations in the French context. John Carson has demonstrated how *intelligence*, originally a synonym for knowledge, came to suggest 'an ability existing in degrees' for mid-nineteenth-century French anthropologists (Carson, 2006, p. 79). Intelligence was then a specialized anthropological term that played a key role in explaining or justifying classifications and hierarchies in natural science taxonomies of both animal and human life. In large part, intelligence referred to mental powers, which were expected to occur in different degrees across human groups.

While attempts to systematically measure intelligence through cranial volume or brain mass largely failed, the notion that intelligence was an objective faculty remained in place. When Binet and fellow psychologist Théodule Ribot introduced the first psychological scales of intelligence in 1905, it was based on the idea that intelligence was a material and measurable characteristic. Beyond the walls of the Collège de France and the Sorbonne, intelligence measures were seen as consistent with the principles of the Third Republic. When compared with Galton's eugenics or nineteenth-century racial science, the political agenda of experimental psychology was distinctively progressive: the aim of measuring 'mental age' (*âge mental*) was to help trace children's development and to improve the education of the 'abnormal' or 'retarded' (Malabou, 2019, p. 18). Intelligence scales met the positivist orientation of early twentieth-century science and helped justify the existence of a new administrative elite without resorting to essentialist criteria.

At the same time, the modern concept of intelligence implied by psychological tests was also strongly resisted. As the philosopher Catherine Malabou highlights, measurable intelligence stood in sharp contrast with romantic notions of *esprit* (a word signifying at once 'mind' and 'spirit'), Enlightenment notions of universal reason, or antique notions of intellect or *entendement* (commonly equated with a symbolic capacity of understanding), which all presumed an active participation of the thinking subject. Philosophers, such as Henri Bergson, and novelists, such as Marcel Proust, deemed the psychological concept of intelligence a dangerous one, bearing the threat of normalization and standardization against the autonomy of 'intuition' (Malabou, 2019, pp. 6–7, 39). From such perspectives, intelligence was not on the side of thought, but on the side of the mechanical and the biological; not on the side of creative adaptation, but on that of automatisms and repetition.

The notion of an irreducible tension between philosophical and symbolic realms of intelligence on the one hand, and between biological and psychological knowledge on the other, is still at play in many public and philosophical discussions of AI, in which artificiality and creativity are commonly opposed. French psychologists' work on intelligence was also much more influential and visible in the United States: in France, explorations of intelligence focused on clinical studies of individual variations, rather than mass IQ testing. These disjunctive histories of intelligence continue to play out in the continuous reference to US-dominated AI imaginaries in France, and related attempts to foster alternative meanings of AI.

2.6 'AI' in the Slavic languages

We have suggested that Spielberg's 2001 blockbuster *A.I. Artificial Intelligence* might have contributed to the popularity of McCarthy's term in the Anglophone West. In Central and Eastern Europe the term 'artificial intelligence', as a translation of the English original into Russian, Polish, or Czech, appeared in academic papers as early as the 1960s, and then in science fiction and popular science writing throughout the 1970s, 1980s, and 1990s. But it was, arguably, Spielberg's film that helped 'artificial intelligence' migrate from specialist journals and relatively niche science fiction publications into common parlance. Translated into Russian as ***Искýсственный рáзум*** [*Iskússtvennyy rázum*], into Czech as *A.I. Umělá inteligence,* and into Polish as *A.I. Sztuczna inteligencja,* the film's title is a good indication of how the Slavic versions of McCarthy's 'artificial intelligence' differ from the original term—and from one another.

If the Polish and Czech translations of the title retain the English abbreviation, 'AI', this corresponds to how the acronym functions in the vernacular of some Central and Eastern European countries, such as Poland or the Czech Republic, where the local equivalents have never truly caught on. In Poland, for example, the Polish term *sztuczna inteligencja* (the direct translation of 'artificial intelligence') often features in brackets as an expansion of the English abbreviation 'AI'—which is prevalent in industry reports, media coverage, and technology companies' promotional material. We could relate the contemporary tendency to supplant the local *SI* with the original 'AI' to the dominance of English in the age of globalization, as observed in other countries and linguistic areas (and as we discuss in this chapter). However, it is worth noting that the use of English loanwords has a particular history in Central and Eastern European, where, during the communist period, the original names of some consumer goods used to convey a sense of potential and freedom coded 'Western'.

Comparing the translations of Spielberg's film's title, we also notice that—unlike their counterparts in French, Italian, or Spanish—the terms for 'artificial intelligence' differ considerably in Russian, Polish, and Czech—Slavic languages that otherwise share numerous characteristics. However, while the equivalents of the word 'artificial' sound completely different in Russian, Polish, and Czech, they all connote a link between art, artifice, and craftsmanship—crucial to the English original: *искусство* [*iskusstvo*] in Russian, *sztuka* in Polish, and *umění* in Czech, which all translate to 'art', correspond to the adjectives *искусственный* [*iskusstvennyy*], *sztuczny*, and *umělý*—or 'artificial' in English. So the Russian, Polish, and Czech terms for 'artificial intelligence' preserve the element of the English original that, according to McCorduck, links technology to art, and reflects the ultimately interdisciplinary nature of the field of artificial intelligence (McCorduck, 2004, p. 115).

It is also worth noting that while the Czech and Polish terms for AI include the equivalents of the English 'intelligence'—*inteligence* and *inteligencja*—with similar connotations, the Russian version employs the word *рáзум*, which could be translated as 'mind' or 'reason'. The term *искýсственный рáзум*—'artificial reason'—is distinct from another Russian phrase, *искусственный интеллект*, which we could translate as 'artificial intellect'. These two terms for AI in Russian roughly correspond to the concepts of strong and weak AI in English. While it is the latter term, 'artificial intellect', that is used more often in reference to contemporary applications of machine learning, the title of Spielberg's film features the former, 'artificial reason', as it connotes a more abstract quality of (imagined) machines that successfully simulate, or surpass, human intelligence.

There are other, 'homegrown', terms for artificial intelligence in Central and Eastern Europe. One example is the Polish 'intellectronics' (or *intelektronika*), a portmanteau of 'intellect' and 'electronics', coined in 1964 by the science fiction author and futurologist Stanisław Lem (see Chapter 6 by Bogna Konior). Similar to 'artificial intelligence', *intelektronika* includes the element of 'intellect'/'intelligence', but it is 'electronics' that is doing the work of 'artificiality' in McCarthy's name: evoking something non-organic, constructed, machinic. In the past, the Polish adjectives *elektroniczny* ('electronic') and *elektryczny* ('electric') were used, at times, to denote partly or completely autonomous machines; examples include the 1934 novel by Jerzy Aleksander entitled *Człowiek elektryczny* (*The Electric Human*) or the original Polish title of *The Terminator* (1984)—*Elektroniczny morderca* (or *The Electronic Murderer*).

This is why Lem's *intelektronika* may sound rather outdated to a contemporary Polish speaker. While studies show that only 4% of respondents in Poland have not heard of the term 'AI' (Lange, 2019, p. 6), the native *intelektronika* is certainly not equally recognizable. But we could also argue that it is precisely the 'electronics' element of 'intellectronics' that makes the term particularly relevant in the present, as it lays stress on the material conditions of production of machine intelligence, gesturing towards the hidden costs and environmental consequences of developing advanced AI systems—or what the original term, evoking the art of recreating nature through effective craftsmanship, successfully elides.

2.7 'AI' in Japanese

The incorporation of the word 'artificial intelligence' into Japan illustrates the cultural, political and distinctively and diversely human dimensions of technological transformation. In Japanese 'artificial intelligence' is translated as *jinkō chinō* (人工知能). Although the term has been used by engineers and scientists since the 1960s, its common adoption in Japanese is relatively new, only appearing in Japanese dictionaries after the computing boom of the 1980s. As with 'artificial' in English, the Japanese *jinkō* suggests something manufactured by human hand. Unlike in English, however, *jinkō* also embeds an association with modern 'technology' that is historically tied to images of the West and that is distinct from the sphere of craftwork, art, and architecture, which are seen as having rich indigenous histories in Japan. Revealingly, when Karel Čapek's 1921 play *R.U.R.* (*Rossumovi Univerzální Roboti* [Rossum's Universal Robots]) was first performed in Tokyo in 1924, it was entitled *Artificial Human* in Japanese. However, the Japanese word used for 'artificial' was *jinzō* (人造) rather than *jinkō* (人工) (Robertson, 2018, pp. 12–13). While the former suggests something crafted, like a statue, the latter suggests something produced, like a machine. And although the former is arguably more accurate to the context of Čapek's play, the fact that it is the latter which is ultimately applied to John McCarthy's 'artificial intelligence' highlights a distinction that haunts Japanese national imaginaries. This distinction separates artistic crafts on the one hand, associated with Japan's traditional cultural traditions prior to modernization in the Meiji Restoration (1868), and high technology on the other, which represents Japan's ('alternative') modernity. Thus, the term *jinkō*—as well as the popularly used English acronym 'AI' (nominated as 'buzzword of the year'; Asahi Shinbun, 2016)—embeds a Japan–West binary into the imagination of AI.

Although the word 'intelligence' (translated into Japanese as *chinō*) is not untouched by the darker legacies of eugenics noted earlier in this chapter (also see Robertson, 2001), and thus similarly tied to associations with Western science, it is the differences from its English connotations that best illustrate the political and cultural dimensions of the term *jinkō chinō* in Japan. Most specifically, in contrast to the English 'intelligence', which is arguably still evocative of a

Cartesian distinction between reason and emotion (despite Damasio's (1994), Lutz's (1988), and others' efforts to challenge this habit of Western thought), *chinō* in Japanese incorporates aspects of 'aptitude' (*sainō* 才能) and 'wisdom' (*chie* 知恵) that allude not only to cognition, but also to feeling, emotion, and the heart. This quality of intelligence that references 'heart' (*kokoro* 心), which is traditionally seen as the location and source of the mind in Japanese, helps explain how modelling intelligence in Japan has always incorporated the pursuit of modelling embodied artificial agents with human-like qualities.

This difference can be illustrated by comparing Čapek's *roboti*, from which the modern word for 'robots' is derived, to the iconic robot Astro Boy (*Tetsuan Atomu*), which appeared in manga (Tetzuka, 1952). Čapek's robot, which etymologically means 'forced labour', is initially given 'intelligence' and 'memory' in this play. But as robots acquire emotions, their hierarchical relationship with humans becomes uncontrollable and ultimately leads to a tragic end. In other words, for Čapek, 'intelligence' and 'memory' are essential elements in the creation of artificial humans, but the emotions that emerge from these elements cause problems for human–robot relationships. The story of Astro Boy, on the other hand, explores the conditions for developing harmony between humans and robots, and asks what kind of robotic mind is required for this end. In this respect, it is also important to note that in the manga series, Astro Boy's electronic brain, which distinguishes between good and evil, is located in the region of the heart rather than the head. The story of Astro Boy shows that it is not only intellectual cognition that matters for modelling intelligence in machines in Japan, but also the kind of feeling body which it inhabits.

Accordingly, building artificial intelligence in Japan has always been tied to the task of building a robot with heart/mind (*kokoro* 心) (Katsuno, 2011; Takeno, 2011), affect (*jōcho* 情緒) (Ōhashi et al., 1985), emotion (*kanjō* 感情) (Sugano, 1997), imagination (*sōzō* 想像) (Tsukimoto, 2002), and consciousness (*ishiki* 意識) (Kitamura, 2000). Interestingly, this has meant that throughout Japan's recent history of modelling the mind in machines, simultaneously a project of modelling the heart, not one but several terms have been applied to the English 'artificial intelligence'. This is partly due to the popularity of Norbert Wiener's *Cybernetics* in Japan, whose publicity far outpaced the work of John McCarthy—who, as noted earlier in this chapter, chose the term 'artificial intelligence' to distinguish it from Wiener's work. Just a few months before McCarthy's famous Dartmouth Summer Research Project on Artificial Intelligence in 1956, Wiener had given a series of lectures in Japan. Major newspapers subsequently covered the event with reference to Wiener as the 'Father of the Artificial Brain' (*jinkō zunō no umi no oya*). Reflecting Wiener's impact on Japanese researchers, the terms 'artificial brain' (*jinkō zunō* 人工頭脳) and 'electronic brain' (*denshi zunō* 電子頭脳) were used regularly to refer to both Wiener's work and that of his colleagues at the Dartmouth workshop.

It was only with Japan's government-sponsored Fifth Generation Computing Systems (FGCS) project and associated computing boom in the 1980s, combined with the increasing use in popular media, research journals, and science fiction of the abbreviation 'AI', that the term 'artificial intelligence' (*jinkō chinō*) became regularly adopted. Thus, while the term in Japanese comes embedded with associations to Western notions of cognitive intelligence, it has also been incorporated into Japan's distinctive history of concern with modelling embodied forms of heart (*kokoro*), of which intelligence is only one (and perhaps not even the most critical) part.

2.8 'AI' in Chinese

Just as in the case of Japanese, the term 'artificial intelligence' was introduced into the Chinese language in the late twentieth century, translated as 人工智能 '*ren gong zhi neng*' (or 人工智慧 '*ren gong zhi hui*' in some areas like Malaysia or Taiwan). When translating from one language into another, it is frequently difficult to identify matching terms or phrases with the same meaning, and this is especially the case for languages as far apart as Chinese and English. Adding to this layer of difficulty in translation is the issue of vague terms like 'artificial intelligence', which itself does not have an agreed upon definition, even in the language where it first emerged (cf. Section 2.2). Our conundrum, however, does not end here, as our task is to explain the meaning of AI in the Chinese language *using* English. This is as challenging as it is interesting. In this section we seek to provide some background on how '人工智能' is understood in the Chinese context.

The four Chinese characters in the term '人工智能' mean, respectively, 'human, craftsmanship, wisdom, and capability'. The first two characters broadly correspond to the English word 'artificial', whose basic meaning, let us recall, is 'made by humans'. Interestingly, as further explored in Chapter 22 by Baichun Zhang and Miao Tian, how Chinese philosophers think about man-made crafts in China's long intellectual history has evolved. As early as the pre-Qin period (before 221 BCE), different schools of scholars had already expressed different opinions on crafted tools, machineries, or weapons. Some saw the need to advance craftsmanship for the reason that this could potentially benefit the well-being of individuals and the states, others however thought that new technologies might corrupt a person's mind.

Famously known for their ideal of seeking harmony between man and nature, Daoist philosophers saw man-made crafts and craft-making as a distraction from a person's pursuit of connections with nature because, as they saw it, crafted objects would avert a person's gaze from the natural world. However, while Mohist thinkers generally approved of craftsmanship, they were concerned that technologies might be used for malicious military purposes. There was a famous story of Lu Ban (507–444 BCE), who, as the story goes, invented an automated wooden bird that could fly for three days and three nights without landing. Mozi, however, was unhappy with such an invention, as he worried that this bird could be used for spying on the neighbouring state Song.

Despite these reservations from pre-Qin thinkers about man-made objects, craftsmanship in China kept flourishing and was among the most advanced in the world for many centuries. One important reason was that the activities of inventing, making, and refining crafts were generally in line with the teachings of Confucius and his followers, who developed a school of thought that has dominated the Chinese way of thinking up until today.

Confucius's philosophy is commonly categorized as virtue ethics in the Western tradition. Its ethical doctrine is built on experiences with a focus on articulating and suggesting solutions to *practical* problems in various scenarios, instead of drawing abstract principles from these experiences (Wong, 2018). It is thus not surprising to see that craft-making for the purpose of solving practical problems is acceptable, if not encouraged, by this school of thought. This gives rise to a long established view that the value of a tool lies in its *practicality*. We shall see this also has far-reaching impact on how the public in China perceive AI today.

The combined meaning of the last two Chinese characters in '人工智能' is close to what we mean by 'intelligence' in English: after all, being wise and capable is what we expect from an intelligent being. What is absent in the Chinese case is the ideological baggage carried by this English word as described earlier in this chapter (Section 2.3.2), where racial and other biases played an important role.

To get a better understanding of the Chinese version of intelligence, we must place this concept in a larger context. As in many other places in the world, the wise and the capable were expected to rule. What is distinctive about China is how much wisdom and capability are treasured in its society.

Imperial China (221 BCE–1912 CE) stretched over more than two thousand years. When it comes to social norms, one of the few things that survived this long (and sometimes turbulent) history is the relationship between the learner and the learned. In many ways, this relationship can be translated into a universal respect for knowledge and wisdom. This type of respect came directly from the teachings of pre-Qin sages, but ancient China also invented a way to sustain it. Starting from the Sui dynasty (518–618 BCE) a new way of selecting talents was created known as 科举 (*Keju*), which is an examination system that allows anyone, regardless of their background, to enter the government/ruling class based on merit. This system was revolutionary at the time, as it provided social mobility in an otherwise rigid and hereditary society. No doubt it also reinforced people's respect for 'intelligence'.

It seems that the contemporary usage of the term 'artificial intelligence' in Chinese is informed by how historically each component of '人工智能' was understood and appreciated. The emphasis is on utmost practicality and ultimate respect for wisdom. This explains why the term 'AI' in Chinese is often placed in the practical context of applying this technology for various scientific or commercial purposes. And, in contrast with Western narratives of malicious AI as portrayed in fiction and Hollywood films, it is also difficult to imagine that such stories of a dystopian world caused by AI would organically emerge in a Chinese context: '人工智能' connotes not just intelligence, but wisdom, which remains highly respected in China.

2.9 Conclusion

The term 'AI'—and its equivalents in other languages—is often used in newspapers, policy discourse, and even scientific fields outside of computing as if it describes a single technology. However, this has never been the case. The term was invented to describe not a technology but an aspiration—and a fantastic one at that, wildly and indeed naively ambitious. To conjure this aspiration, the coiners of 'AI' drew on the power of the term 'intelligence', which had in the preceding decades become a homogenizing tool for ranking groups and individuals. We have seen that the terms for AI in Germanic and Romance languages share much of this resonance imparted by the politics of intelligence. Partly this is due to their linguistic proximity, but more importantly it is because those cultures were also closely involved with the development of intelligence testing and its use in legitimating imperialism or aggressive policies of expansion, and even extermination.

Moving eastwards to the Slavic countries, this resonance diminishes. Instead, 'AI' is sometimes translated using Slavonic terms that lack the association with mental testing and ranking, and sometimes kept in the English or Slavonicized versions of it, which instead convey more the foreign, Western origin of the term and the technology. Moving further East again, to Japan and China, the association with eugenics diminishes still further (even if it does not wholly disappear), and the popular terms for 'AI' bring new dimensions lacking in the English. In China, '人工智能' connotes wisdom, a trait that continues to be revered. In Japan, the term *jinkō chinō* connotes wisdom, aptitude, and also 'heart' or the capacity for emotion.

Currently, governments and international bodies around the world are considering how AI can be regulated globally. In doing so, however, they must reckon not only with the fact that AI is as much an aspiration as a technology, but also with the fact that it is not even the same thing that is being aspired to in every culture.

Endnotes

1. The asterisk denotes that this is a word established through the practice of linguistic reconstruction.
2. The film title has been translated to *A.I. Artificiell Intelligens* (Swedish), *A.I.: Künstliche Intelligenz* (German), *A.I. Kunstig intelligens* (Danish), and *A.I. kunstig intelligens* (Norwegian bokmal). I have not been able to obtain release data for Iceland. ('A.I. Artificial Intelligence (2001) - Release Info,' n.d.)
3. The notion of the Singularity has been popularized by futurologist and engineer Ray Kurzweil. For a critique of *IA apocalypse* in the French language, see Ganascia (2017).

References

A.I. Artificial Intelligence. (2001). Directed by Steven Spielberg [Film]. Warner Bros. Pictures.

'artificial' n.d. Available at: https://www.oed.com/viewdictionaryentry/Entry/11211#eid38531090.

Asahi Shinbun [Asahi News]. (2016) 'Hoikuen ochita, Toranpu-genshō, kōho 30-go ryūkōgo taishō kotoshi wa?' [Failing daycare placement, the Trump phenomenon, which of the 30 candidates wins buzzword of the year?]. 18 November.

Barbrook, R. and Cameron, A. (1995) 'The Californian ideology', *Mute*, 1 September. Available at: https://www.metamute.org/editorial/articles/californian-ideology

van den Bergh, L., et al. (2010) 'The implicit prejudiced attitudes of teachers: Relations to teacher expectations and the ethnic achievement gap', *American Educational Research Journal*, 47(2), pp. 497–527. https://doi.org/10.3102/0002831209353594

Bonefeld, M. and Dickhäuser, O. (2018) '(Biased) grading of students' performance: Students' names, performance level, and implicit attitudes', *Frontiers in Psychology*, 9, p. 481. Available at: https://doi.org/10.3389/fpsyg.2018.00481

Braffort, P. (1968) *L'intelligence artificielle*. Paris: Presses Universitaires de France.

Büüsker, A.-K. (2015) '"Asoziale" im Nationalsozialismus: Die letzten vergessenen Opfer', *Deutschlandfunk*, 13 June. Available at: https://www.deutschlandfunk.de/asoziale-im-nationalsozialismus-die-letzten-vergessenen-100.html

Čapek, K. (1921/2004) *R.U.R. (Rossum's universal robots)*. New York: Penguin.

Cardon, D., Cointet, J. P. and Mazières, A. (2018) 'Neurons spike back: The invention of inductive machines and the artificial intelligence controversy (tr. Elizabeth Libbrecht), *Réseaux*, 211(5), pp. 173–220.

Carson, J. (2006) *The measure of merit: Talents, intelligence, and inequality in the French and American republics, 1750–1940*. Princeton: Princeton University Press.

Cave, S. (2020) 'The problem with intelligence: Its value-laden history and the future of AI', in *Proceedings of the AAAI/ACM conference on AI, ethics, and society, AIES '20*. New York: ACM, pp. 29–35. https://doi.org/10.1145/3375627.3375813

Cave, S., Dihal, K. (2018) 'Ancient dreams of intelligent machines: 3,000 years of robots', *Nature*, 559, pp. 473–5. https://doi.org/10.1038/d41586-018-05773-y

Centenaire IBM France. (2014) '1955: le terme "ordinateur" est inventé par Jacques Perret, à la demande d'IBM France' [1955: Jacques Perret invents the term 'Ordinateur' by special request of IBM France]. Available at: https://centenaireibmfrance.blogspot.com/2014/04/1955-terme-ordinateur-invente-par-jacques-perret.html

Damasio, A. R. (1994) *Descartes' error: Emotion, reason, and the human brain*. New York: Putnam.

Dihal, K. (2020) 'Enslaved minds: Fictional artificial intelligence uprisings', in Cave, S., Dihal, K. and Dillon, S. (eds.) *AI narratives: A history of imaginative thinking about intelligent machines*. Oxford: Oxford University Press, pp. 189–212.

Eubanks, V. (2017). *Automating inequality: How high-tech tools profile, police, and punish the poor*. New York: St. Martin's Press.

Galton, F. (1869) *Hereditary genius*. Macmillan, London.

Ganascia, J. G. (2017) *Le mythe de la singularité: Faut-il craindre l'intelligence artificielle?* Paris: Seuil.

van den Herik, H. J. (1990) 'Kunstmatige intelligentie in de maatschappij', *De Accountant*, 3, pp. 130–2.

Hoffmann, E. T. A. (1816) 'Der Sandmann', in *Die Nachtstücke*. Berlin: Kiermeier-Debre.

Hollanek, T. (2020) 'AI transparency: A matter of reconciling design with critique', *AI & Society* [online]. Available at: https://doi.org/10.1007/s00146-020-01110-y

Intelligenz. (2021) Wikipedia. Available at: https://de.wikipedia.org/wiki/Intelligenz

Katsuno, H. (2011) 'The robot's heart: Tinkering with humanity and intimacy in robot-building', *Japanese Studies*, 31, pp. 93–109.

Kitamura, N. (2000) *Robotto wa kokoro o motsu ka: saibā ishikiron josetsu* [Do robots have minds? An introduction to theories of consciousness]. Tokyo: Kyōritsu Shuppan.

kunstig intelligens. n.d. *Den Danske Ordbog* [online]. Available at: https://ordnet.dk/ddo/ordbog?query=kunstig%20intelligens

Lange, R. (2019) *Sztuczna Inteligencja w społeczeństwie i gospodarce: Analiza wyników ogólnopolskiego badania opinii polskich internautów* [Artificial Intelligence in society and the economy: Analysis of results of a countywide study of public perceptions among Polish internet users]. Warsaw: NASK Państwowy Instytut Badawczy. Available at: https://www.nask.pl/pl/raporty/raporty/2594,Sztuczna-inteligencja-w-oczach-Polakow-raport-z-badan-spolecznych.html

LeCun, Y. (2016) 'L'apprentissage profond: une révolution en intelligence artificielle', [Deep learning: a revolution in artificial intelligence]. Inaugural lecture at the Collège de France, 4 February, Paris. Available at: https://www.college-de-france.fr/site/yann-lecun/inaugural-lecture-2016-02-04-18h00.htm

Legg, S. and Hutter, M. (2007) 'A Collection of Definitions of Intelligence', *Frontiers in Artificial Intelligence and Applications*, 157, pp. 17–24.

Levine, P., 2017. *Eugenics: A very short introduction.* Oxford University Press, Oxford.

Lutz, C. (1988) *Unnatural emotions: Everyday sentiments on a Micronesian atoll and their challenge to Western theory.* Chicago: University of Chicago Press.

Malabou, C. (2019) *Morphing intelligence: From IQ measurement to artificial brains*, tr. Carolyn Shread. New York: Columbia University Press.

McCarthy, J. (1988) 'Review of Bloomfield (ed.): *The question of artificial intelligence: Philosophical and sociological perspectives*', *Annals of the History of Computing*, 10, pp. 221–33.

McCarthy, J., et al. (1955) 'A proposal for the Dartmouth summer research project on artificial intelligence, August 31, 1955', *AI Magazine*, 27(4), p. 12. Available at: https://doi.org/10.1609/aimag.v27i4.1904

McCorduck, P. (2004) *Machines who think: A personal inquiry into the history and prospects of artificial intelligence.* 2nd edn. Boca Raton: CRC Press.

Minsky, M. (1956) *Heuristic aspects of the artificial intelligence problem.* Boston, MA: Massachusetts Institute of Technology.

Ōhashi, T., et al. (eds.) (1985) *Jōcho robotto no sekai [The world of feeling robots]*, Tokyo: Kōdansha.

Penn, J. (2020) 'Inventing intelligence: On the history of complex information processing and artificial intelligence in the United States in the mid-twentieth century'. PhD thesis, University of Cambridge, Cambridge, UK.

Robertson, J. (2001) 'Japan's first cyborg? Miss Nippon, eugenics and wartime technologies of beauty, body and blood', *Body & Society*, 7, pp. 1–34.

Robertson, J. (2018) *Robo sapiens japanicus: Robots, gender, family, and the Japanese nation.* Berkeley: University of California Press.

Russell, S. J. and Norvig, P. (2010) *Artificial intelligence: A modern approach.* 3rd edn. Upper Saddle River: Prentice Hall.

Saini, A. (2019) *Superior: The return of race science.* London: 4th Estate.

Shannon, C. E. and McCarthy, J. (1956) *Automata studies.* Princeton: Princeton University Press.

Sheikh, H. (2021) 'Toepassing van kunstmatige intelligentie zit in wildwestfase' [Application of artificial intelligence is in Wild West phase], *NRC*, 11 October. Available at: https://www.nrc.nl/nieuws/2021/11/10/toepassing-van-kunstmatige-intelligentie-zit-in-wildwestfase-a4065066 (Accessed 21 November 2021).

Stern, W. (1912) *Die psychologischen Methoden der Intelligenzprüfung und deren Anwendung an Schulkindern* [Psychological methods of intelligence testing and their use on school children]. Leipzig: J. A. Barth.

Sugano, S. (1997) 'Robotto to ningen no kokoro no intāfēsu', [A heart/mind interface for robot and humans] *Baiomekanizumu Gakkaishi* [Journal of the Society of Biomechanisms], 21, pp. 21–5.

Takeno, J. (2011) *Kokoro o motsu robotto: hagane no shikō ga kagami no naka no jibun ni kizuku* [The robot with soul: a realisation of the self in the mirror by a metallic thinking entity], Tokyo: Nikkan kōgyōsha.

Tetzuka, O. (1952–68) *Tetsuwan atomu* (Astro Boy), serialized in *Shōnen*. Tokyo: Kōbunsha.

The Terminator. (1984) Directed by James Cameron [Film]. Orion Pictures.

Tsukimoto, H. (2002) *Robotto no kokoro: sōzōrhoku o motsu robotto o mezashite* [The robot's heart: toward a robot with imagination]. Tokyo: Morikita Shuppan.

Villani, C., et al. (2018) 'Donner un sens à l'intelligence artificielle: pour une stratégie nationale et européenne', Public report of a Parliamentary mission from 8th September 2017 to 8th March 2018. Vie publique [online], 28 March. Available at: https://www.vie-publique.fr/rapport/37225-donner-un-sens-lintelligence-artificielle-pour-une-strategie-nation

Visser, H. (1995) 'Geschiedenis van het Kunstmatige Intelligentie-onderzoek in Nederland tot 1970' [History of artificial intelligence research in the Netherlands pre-1970]. *NVKI-Nieuwsbrief*, 12(2), pp. 34–8.

Wong, D. (2018) 'Chinese ethics', in Zalta, E. N. (ed.) *The Stanford encyclopedia of philosophy* [online], 14 September. Available at: https://plato.stanford.edu/entries/ethics-chinese/

Wood, G. (2002) *Edison's Eve: a magical history of the quest for mechanical life*. New York: Anchor Books.

PART I

EUROPE

3

AI Narratives and the French Touch

Madeleine Chalmers

'Marvellous!' He wrote the word 'Marvellous!' The child uttering his first words says 'Papa' or 'Mama' but my automaton writes 'Marvellous' because that is what he knows himself to be.

Benjamin Péret

3.1 Introduction

In 'The Ghosts' Paradise' ('Au Paradis des fantômes', 1934), the Surrealist poet Benjamin Péret imagines a gathering of figures drawn from the history of artificial intelligences—many of whom feature in the first volume of the *AI Narratives* project.[1] Albertus Magnus and his bronze manservant (whom Thomas Aquinas is said to have attempted to destroy), Hero of Alexandria, Roger Bacon, Thomas Bungay, Wolfgang Von Kempelen and his talking head, Leonardo da Vinci, and Pierre Jaquet-Droz emerge from the darkness in the *Palais des papes* in Avignon.[2] This fictionalized version of Jacquet-Droz provides the epigraph to this chapter, as he describes how his *Écrivain* (Writer) automaton—a small boy sitting at a desk with a quill, constructed in 1768—operates. The inventors' conversation centres on the relative merits of one another's creations and culminates in the appearance of an 'automaton man', a human being who claims to be an automaton and declares that he discovered this 'vocation' on the stage as a volunteer during a hypnotist's show. In an echo of the *Palais*'s history as the focal point of the Western Schism, which pitted pope against antipope, this figure sparks a debate about human simulacra and their ontologies, about automaton and anti-automaton, as it were. Jacquet-Droz reflects sadly:

> Once, automata danced, wrote, spoke and drew. Today, the robot does not recognize us, we who are the gods of the automata, their muscles and brains. But, in spite of them, the first word traced by my 'Writer' remains their rallying cry. The population of the lost world where the automata dwell will swell endlessly with their shades. These mobile sphinxes have not finished setting men riddles whose solutions call forth new riddles. [. . .] Marvellous! Marvellous! Marvellous!
>
> (Péret, 1934, p. 34)

This final comment is revealing. As a Surrealist writer, Péret experimented with the process of automatic writing: a technique through which Surrealists sought to 'press pause' on conscious thought in order to allow the deep psychic substrate of our subjectivity, which is all too often suppressed by reason, to flow free onto the page (Breton, 1988, p. 328; Chalmers, 2020, p. 371). The automaton, as it is described in the text, is a figure for the Surrealist. It is a symbol of freedom, a vector of creativity that allows human beings to express their own spark of divine fire, and to surprise themselves, discovering unsuspected depths of thought and 'riddles' to which our hidebound conscious minds do not always have access. By contrast, the 'robots' of industrialization are—in the wake of Karel Čapek's *R.U.R.* (1921/2004)—machines without sensitivity, and without imagination.

I open this chapter with Péret's text because it goes to the heart of what is distinctive about French artificial intelligence (AI) narratives. AIs in French culture are anything but coolly rational, logical machines. Instead, they are messily and mysteriously embodied, impetuous, and mystical. We often think of AIs, automata, and human simulacra as means to reflect on what makes us human. Apocryphal tales of René Descartes's automaton (Kang, 2017), and Julien Offray de la Mettrie's eighteenth-century materialist treatise, *Man a Machine* (L'Homme machine), have nurtured this strain of thought. Yet at the core of La Mettrie's extended analogy comparing the human body to a clockwork mechanism, we find the declaration: 'man is such a complex machine that it is impossible to have a clear idea of it, and consequently to define it' (la Mettrie, 1981, p. 147). For something to be mechanical or machine-like does not mean that it runs smoothly, or in ways that we can always comprehend. In other words, machines are not necessarily presented as metaphysically opposed to the human, or as the straightforward binary opposite in the conventional pairings of reason/emotion or material/spiritual through which we humans seek to categorize ourselves and other entities. This is a tension that runs throughout French narratives, particularly of the modern and contemporary period.

In this chapter, I suggest that this tension is characteristic of 'the French touch', offering as a case study two anarchic AI narratives from the end of the nineteenth century that feature the well-worn (to twenty-first-century eyes) trope of a rebellion by sentient machines, but inflect it in ways that invite us to rethink the narrative, as well as the AI, in 'AI narratives'. Bringing these texts into dialogue with recent trends in theorizations of the desirability of full automation allows us to explore how these texts from the past can—and should—speak to our present.

3.2 French AI narratives and reading 'for' AI

Many French texts have become mainstays of discussions of AI narratives: Prosper Mérimée's Pygmalionesque short story *La Vénus d'Ille* (1837); Rachilde's gender-bending twist on this motif in *Monsieur Vénus* (1884); Villiers de l'Isle-Adam's *L'Ève future* (1886), one of the earliest instances of the use of the term 'android' in French; and the cyborg messiah of Francophone Canadian author Maurice G. Dantec's *Babylon Babies* (1999), to name but a few.[3] In film, the French director Denis Villeneuve showcased his signature sensibility in *Blade Runner 2049* (2017). These works reprise familiar narrative tropes: Pygmalion and Galatea, Adam and Eve, messianism, and the apocalypse. However, they do so in subversive ways that challenge the notions of utopia and dystopia on which we often rely when discussing scientific or speculative fictions. They invite us to question our own anthropocentric perspectives—including the anthropocentrism inherent in the notion of narrative.

Indeed, narratives do not only sit within the pages of books or on the big or small screen. Additionally, they permeate the ways in which we think about ourselves and our daily lives, and they are the very mechanisms of political and economic power. Philosophical narratives of technology have gained particular prominence in France in the twentieth century. Jacques Ellul's *The Technological Society* (1954) gained a sulphurous aura when a copy was found in the cabin of Ted Kaczynski, better known as the Unabomber. The late Bernard Stiegler's theories of technicity retell the story of human evolution by positing it as a *co*-evolution of humans and their technological prostheses, with 'technics inventing man, man inventing technics' from Stone Age flints to the latest tablets (1994, p. 148).[4]

When we sit down to write a cultural history of AI narratives, we embark on a process of creation. The way we bring different narrative artefacts from the past or present into dialogue with one another, and into dialogue with the real-world AIs of our present or the hypothetical AIs of our future, is itself a narrative. It means that we come to texts—whether they be literary, filmic, cultural, or political—in search of the fulfilment of a particular narrative desire. In his article of the same name, Peter Brooks argues that 'if narrative stages the motors of desire that drive and consume its plot, it seems also to lay bare the nature of narration as a form of human desire' (1984a, p. 326). That desire—never quite satisfied—is the desire to make things make sense, for 'if the motor of narrative is desire, totalizing, building ever-larger units of meaning, the ultimate determinants of meaning lie *at the end*, and narrative desire is ultimately, inexorably, desire *for* the end' (Brooks, 1984b, p. 33). The problem is that, when it comes to AI, we haven't got to the end yet. When we seek to map the 'history of imaginative thinking about machines' (Cave et al., 2020, p. 4), we are also mapping what we hope or fear that their future will be, and looking for the supporting evidence for that speculation.

I suggest that French AI narratives are attuned to precisely this issue, and that this is why they so often revel in reworking tropes that can, at first glance, appear hackneyed. They present us with an arc that we think we recognize, and then subvert, undermine, or push it to the point where it implodes. In doing so, they force us to confront the perils with which our narrative desire is fraught. Our almost visceral need for catharsis and sense can lead us to short-change the complexity and entanglement of the world in which we live. Wrongfooting, frustrating, and surprising us, the AI narratives that punctuate the development of modern French culture test our faith in the stories that we want (or need) to believe about ourselves and our societies.

If 'narrative' is a term that encompasses not only creative representations (art, literature, film, and so forth), but also the realm of ideas, philosophy, and politics, then the porous boundary between literature and thought in French culture offers fertile terrain for exploring how these two types of narrative can intertwine and interact with the material reality of our world.

3.3 The machine revolt: a case study

My exploration begins by focusing on two all-but-forgotten short stories from the late nineteenth century by two authors who have been largely critically neglected: Émile Goudeau and Han Ryner. First, we need to return to a period of French history 'characterised by indelible memories of the liberal revolution of 1789 [. . .], an astonishingly fluid and amorphous political "establishment," and an exceptionally creative yet irredeemably fragmented labour and socialist movement' (Stuart, 1992, p. 252). In the last two decades of the nineteenth century, France was a society in search of definition, caught between a mythologized liberal past, a present under reconstruction in the wake of humiliating defeat by Prussia and the ravages of the Commune in 1871, and a future open to interpretation, in which scientific and technological innovations increasingly threw established religious, social, and creative authorities into question.

Goudeau's 'The Revolt of the Machine' ('La Révolte de la machine', 1888) depicts a conscious machine that orchestrates a mass machine suicide to avoid putting humans out of work. In Ryner's 'Revolt of the Machines' ('La Révolte des machines', 1896), Arch-Engineer Durdonc produces a virgin birth in a conscious locomotive, La Jeanne, so that all human labour can be undertaken by self-replicating machines. When Durdonc abducts her child, La Jeanne (a mechanical Joan of Arc) rouses France's locomotives to rebellion. These two AI narratives have all the ingredients that we expect from a narrative: protagonists; antagonists; a beginning, a middle, and an end; rising and falling tension; a climax. However, they also incorporate and *analyse* the socio-political narratives of late nineteenth-century France surrounding labour and automation. They play out politicians' narratives of progress and utopia, using the imaginative resources of fiction to explore and parody manifestos of the period, and to highlight their plot holes.

Émile Goudeau is remembered as a prince of Montmartre cabaret culture. As editor-in-chief of the *Journal du Chat noir,* he promoted Rodolphe Salis' cabaret, as well as publishing caricatures, avant-garde poetry, and political satire under the pseudonym A'Kempis. While we often think of fin-de-siècle Montmartre as an 'anarchist [. . .] utopia' and centre for politically subversive publishing (Sonn, 1989, p. 94), within the pages of the *Journal* we can detect instances of 'xenophobia, anti-semitism and saber-rattling' (McWilliam, 2011, p. 251). The paper's leftist politics can sometimes seem an act of provocation: a deliberate cultivation of difference rather than a firmly held ideological position (Didier, 2009, p. 139).

Han Ryner's politics are clearly expressed in his *Little Manual of Individualism* (1903), which rejects social forms of anarchism in favour of unbridled individualism. However, in his history of French anarchist writing, Thierry Maricourt stresses the inconsistencies in Ryner's positions, which are 'deliberately marginal', even within anarchist politics (1990, p. 248). As one of Ryner's earliest texts, 'Revolt of the Machines' predates his most strident affirmations. The short story appeared in *L'Art social* [*Social Art*]—a periodical comprising political and literary articles spanning the leftist spectrum. Writing in *L'Art social,* Bernard Lazare asserted the organ's core belief that 'the writer's role is not to play the flute [. . .] while contemplating his navel' (1896, p. 12). However, Lazare also explicitly rejected didacticism, arguing instead for 'a precursor's art' that would establish the 'new feelings [. . .] which will reign in the world that is under construction' (1896, p. 14). Lazare's ideal artist makes change possible not by telling us what form that change will take, but by telling us what it might *feel* like. This social art creates the conditions for the material realization of new ideas—their passage into lived reality—not by representing what already exists, but by forging a relation with a 'what could be'. It connects the world of economics and labour with the world of art to create socio-political narratives of transformation.

Both Goudeau and Ryner use fragmentary forms that resist creative authorities and conformity (including conformity to the norms of nonconformists), perhaps because they are sceptical of didacticism and its easy narrative equations of purpose and result: if *x* then *y*. I suggest that their apocalyptic machine narratives *expose* our desire to narrativize machines. They explore our desire to categorize them, to insert them into socio-political narratives about the labour market, and to fit them into overarching historical narratives of decline, revolution, and apocalyptic 'new dawns'. Tracing their explorations of the nature of the machine and the automation of industry reveals the machine rebellion as a trope that cuts to the heart of political thought and narrativization—not only in their temporal context, but also in our own. To do so, I trace three key features of narrative, and how they unfold in these texts: protagonist, plot arc, and climax.

3.4 The protagonist: exploring machinic ontology

A protagonist is our point of entry into the narrative: the receptacle for our hopes and identification as readers. To make a machine the protagonist of a prose narrative is automatically to confer on it subjectivity, interiority, and agency even before a word has been uttered or the machine has been described.

Goudeau and Ryner take different approaches to exploring the subjectivity and ontological status of their respective machines. Goudeau offers us no physical description of his machine. We have no sense of its dimensions, or its attributes:

> All you need to know is that, via a series of platinum boxes, steeped in phosphoric acid, the scholar had discovered the means to impart a sort of soul to locomotive and static machines; and that this new being would behave somewhat like a metal bull.
>
> (Goudeau, 1888, p. 7)

The machine lies beyond the conventional metaphysical categories of human, animal, or machine: invested with a quasi-soul that is the product of a chemical reaction, rather than divinely infused, and with the body of a four-legged, living and breathing mammal, but made of cold metal, it is a 'new being' defying description.

Indeed, what we know about the machine comes about through its own self-narration. In a cultural climate fascinated by the emerging science of psychiatry and treatises on the nature of the 'internal voice' of thought (Egger, 1881), Goudeau adopts the point of view of the machinic consciousness: 'she perceived external sensations distinctly; she began to understand that [. . .] soon she would be able to translate what she felt inside into movement in the outside world' (1888, p. 7). Although Goudeau suggests that the machine behaves like a bull (an image of striking masculinity), it is notable that, thereafter, the machine is always referred to as a 'she', in keeping with the feminine gender of the word 'machine' in French. In my translations, I chose to lean into this. The machine's body is a physical envelope for the consciousness of a 'young being' (1888, p. 7) that is aware of its embodied existence in time and space, its form harbouring a gentle consciousness at odds with its aggressive physical capabilities. Long before Turing's 'child machine' (1950, p. 456), Goudeau imagines an AI that learns through what it experiences. While the machine's physical capacities are dependent on its being switched on by a human, its consciousness seems to exist independently of such intervention, suggesting that it has the potential for autonomous agency.

For Goudeau, the development of a machinic consciousness akin to that of humans is crucial to the trope of the machine rebellion. By contrast, in Ryner's tale, the machines are presented as conscious from the very beginning, communicating perfectly with their creator, Durdonc. What sets Ryner's narrative apart is his explicit focus on naming and gendering the steam engine at the story's core as 'La Jeanne'.

His short story parodies the Annunciation and Incarnation, as Durdonc renders his La Jeanne 'capable of having children without the intervention of another machine' (Ryner, 1896, p. 19). La Jeanne utters a Magnificat: 'The Arch-Engineer, in his supreme kindness, has created me in his image; [. . .] and has communicated to me his powers of creation' (Ryner, 1896, p. 20). The parody re-establishes the trope of machines being created in 'man's' image (as a man is created in the image of God in Genesis 2.7), but it also specifies that creativity, as a uniquely human skill, has been transmitted to the machine, so that it, too, can create in its own image.

Ryner's protagonist is a Joan of Arc and a Virgin Mary. Marian devotion was at its peak in late nineteenth-century France, in ways which rippled across the religious and political spectrum (see Michelet, 1879). The promulgation of the doctrine of the Immaculate Conception in 1854 received overwhelming support from the laity (Papal Encyclicals, 1854), and Gustave Flaubert wrote that 'it sums up the emotional life of the nineteenth century' (1965, p. 196). Litanies addressed Mary as a vessel, tower, house, and ark. In his dream of a future womanhood freed from the demands of sexuality by artificial reproduction, philosopher Auguste Comte sought 'the utopia of the Virgin–Mother, destined to provide positivism with a synthetic summary equivalent to that which the institution of the Eucharist offers Catholicism' (1854, p. 279).

Even in parodic form, then, La Jeanne's womanhood is crucial, because it confers a biological, organic, and affective life on the machine. La Jeanne tells Durdonc, 'You inspired me in the feelings which you experience yourself' (Ryner, 1896, p. 20). Durdonc's response that 'I am free from all feeling. I am pure Thought' (1896, p. 20) throws customary metaphysical markers into question. Ryner reprises the 'oppositions such as interior/exterior, sensibility/rationality and passivity/activity' (Finn, 2011, p. 315), which subtended contemporary medical discourse on gender. Like Jean-Martin Charcot's patients at La Salpêtrière—whose hysteria, etymologically, is connected to the womb—La Jeanne has been the subject of a male experiment, connected with reproduction. She is not only Joan of Arc and Virgin Mary, but also she is the martyred nineteenth-century hysteric. Ryner does not simply give a machine feelings: he also removes them from a human being. By describing himself as an abstraction, a disembodied rationality, Durdonc renders himself other than human, while La Jeanne's self-characterization renders her more human than her human creator.

In Goudeau's child-machine and in Ryner's synthesis of Joan, Mary, and suffering women, we have protagonists of great complexity. Goudeau's text shows us, quite literally, the process of constructing a character with a distinctive voice; his machine thinks itself into existence as an entity. But he also shows us how 'character', in the sense of the machine's values, comes to coalesce, not through Goudeau's own authorial authority or that of the machine's diegetic creator, but through its own assimilation and interpretation of what it sees, hears, and feels.

Ryner's process is one of multiplication, rather than gradual emergence. He makes his machine a triple allegory. Not content with one metaphor or association, he overloads one small steam train with the freight of the nineteenth century's female icons—icons whose appeal reaches across the political spectrum from traditionalist Catholicism to the militants of the commune. As the prominent politician and voice of the Paris Commune Jules Vallès put it, 'when women get involved, [. . .] that's when the sun will rise on a city in revolt' (1908, p. 148).

These unsettling allegiances, in which it is the human who is made strange, and the machine that is made familiar and aligned with those members of society—children and women—who have little political voice are crucial to understanding the contribution that both texts make to nineteenth-century debates about labour and industrial automation.

3.5 The plot arc: socio-political narratives of automation

From the 1880s onwards, the Third Republic was conflicted about how exactly it wished to reform labour, amid the birth of trade union movements: '[t]he promotion of the worker's increased freedom *from* labour often sat awkwardly alongside an aspiration towards a transformed labour model, precisely *through* which the worker could experience, and affirm, his own liberty' (White, 2014, p. 4). Which the 'right' kind of progress?

In creating societies in which machines abolish human labour, both narratives appear to bring to fruition the vision expressed by Paul Lafargue, co-founder of the French Workers' Party (*Parti ouvrier*), in *The Right to Be Lazy*

(2009). Lafargue rejects the 'right to work' as a bourgeois construct, the acceptance of which renders the proletariat complicit in its own exploitation. He argues that the automation of industry reveals the extent to which the proletariat has internalized this situation:

> As the machine is perfected and cuts down man's work with a speed and precision which never cease to increase, the Worker, rather than prolonging his leisure time still further, doubles his efforts, as though he wanted to compete with the machine.
>
> (Lafargue, 2009, p. 37)

With his 'as though', Lafargue throws into doubt the notion that workers can, or should, attempt to compete with the machine. In this, he runs counter to his father-in-law Karl Marx's assertion of inevitability: 'The instrument of labour, when it takes the form of a machine, immediately becomes a competitor of the workman himself' (2003, p. 405). For Marx, the machine's hyperproductivity renders the human labourer obsolete, robbing him of his livelihood. For Lafargue, the machine offers the human an escape route from drudgery. Both thinkers envisage different outcomes as a result of human competition with the machine: while Lafargue ends his text with a vision of unbounded indulgence and pleasure for the worker freed from labour, Marx sees only suffering and the triumph of capital. This debate is at the core of these fictions, which put into play and test the implications of both Lafargue's and Marx's narrative of automation.

Goudeau's tale ambivalently opposes and aligns machine and proletariat, putting into play first the Marxian, then the Lafarguian, perspective. Goudeau's machine overhears a blacksmith lamenting the automation of labour, and the fact that workers must collaborate in creating the conditions of their own obsolescence, 'procreating the instruments of our definitive expulsion from the world' (1888, p. 8). The workers' livelihood depends on manufacturing their own future unemployment, an interconnectedness stressed by the biological focus of procreation, which echoes Goudeau's characterization of the child-machine. Like Ryner's La Jeanne, Goudeau's machine is governed entirely by emotion—the thing it is precisely not supposed to have. In a gesture of 'sublime abnegation' (1888, p. 8), the machine is able to put itself in the place of those who view it as an enemy and would seek to destroy it. Goudeau allows us privileged access to the machine's thoughts in free indirect discourse: 'so she was ruining poor peasants for the benefit of the damned exploiters! Ah! She understood now the oppressive role those who had created her wanted her to play!' (1888, p. 8). The machine, aware of its lack of control over its life—similar to that of the workers over theirs—decides to sacrifice itself for the human 'brothers' (1888, p. 11) on the day of its inauguration, as an altruistic example to other machines. However, the machine is selective in what it chooses to hear. The blacksmith goes on to imagine a return to a pre-industrial age in which the bourgeoisie would see roles reversed: 'Our arms would be strong enough [. . .] to churn the earth to find bread; the skinny-armed bourgeoisie [. . .] would pay handsomely for it' (1888, p. 8). The worker does not want socialist equality: he wants to become an exploiter.

Having considered the Marxian approach, Goudeau turns to the Lafarguian argument, employing an unexpected voice—in this case, the technocrat Pastoureaux: 'If [. . .] we can make our machines intelligent, men will be liberated from menial labour, once and for all' (1888, p. 9). However, Pastoureaux argues that the Lafarguian society will produce a purely bourgeois society: 'No more serfs, no more proletariat! All shall be bourgeois!' (1888, p. 9). Humans will be liberated as the status of slave is transferred: 'the machine will deliver our brothers from bondage' (1888, p. 9). The machine—'thinking and acting, but not suffering' (1888, p. 9)—will be able to perform work without experiencing its negative effects, in an 'ethical' slavery. Pastoureaux is celebrated as the 'saviour of brain and feeling flesh' (1888, p. 9), yet Goudeau has suggested that these are attributes of machines as well as humans. Neither the blacksmith's nor Pastoureaux's positions are ethical solutions: either the machine is destroyed to allow the proletariat to enslave the bourgeoisie, or the machine is enslaved to allow the proletariat to become bourgeois. The machine's suicidal decision is a bid to remove one term from the socio-political equation, yet the machine, which Goudeau describes as 'intelligent, but naïve' (1888, p. 8), does not consider the potential ramifications of this imbalance.

In contrast to Goudeau, Han Ryner's narrative unfolds in a social vacuum. Durdonc is described as 'Europe's Arch-Engineer' and 'the head of humanity' (1896, pp. 19, 21), potentially evoking a fantastical technocratic European federalism, but this remains undeveloped; we encounter no other human figures, no class distinctions are evoked, and the only machines referred to are locomotives. Durdonc summarizes historic technological progress as a gradual process of liberation from work, with his contribution being the creation of 'the cogs of reproduction which will free us from further creation' (1896, p. 19). However, when Durdonc abducts the first infant machine, La Jeanne criss-crosses France, calling other locomotives to rebellion against their human 'tyrants':

> They gave us wages too low for us to buy our coal. [. . .] They broke us up in order to melt us back down and use the noble elements of which we are composed [. . .] And now they want to make us have children, just to steal them back from us!
>
> (1896, pp. 21–2)

Ryner anthropomorphizes the machines by introducing the notion that they 'buy' their own coal, the way human workers buy food with their wages.

However, the allegory is blocked by the reassertion of their machinic specificity: humans cannot be melted down for scrap and reformed. With his reference to children, Ryner closes the gap between human and machines again, since in this fiction both are capable of procreation, and recalls Marx's argument that automation facilitates capitalist exploitation of women and children: '[p]reviously, the workman sold his own labour-power [. . .]. Now he sells wife and child' (2003, p. 373). By allowing La Jeanne to stand for both exploitation of humans by other humans and human exploitation of nonhuman elements, Ryner reinforces Goudeau's visions: domination of all kinds is rendered palatable by fictions of illusory personal freedom or La Jeanne's 'maternal joys' (1896, p. 20).

Both Goudeau and Ryner unpick narratives of progress and political utopia through full automation. They reveal the human characters' inability to think beyond existing paradigms of power, in which, à la Hegel, master and slave are locked in mutual dependence on one another for recognition as subjects. Who fills the role of master and who takes the place of the slave may change, but the political imagination cannot conceive of an alternative to this dynamic. The two authors highlight this by making their protagonists machines—the opposite numbers of human beings in both Lafargue's and Marx's theories—and then making those machines allies of, or allegories for, real-life workers.[5] The machine is both the instrument of oppression and a figure for the oppressed, complicating the teleological narratives of both Lafargue and Marx. It is this aporia which brings both narratives to a philosophical head.

3.6 The climax and its aftermath: conceptualizing the future

The structures of exploitation I trace out here culminate in rebellions. In Goudeau's text, the unveiling of Pastoureaux's machine is attended by 'the President of the Republic, the authorities, and delegations from learned societies' (1888, p. 10). The entire apparatus of the French Third Republic, in both its political and intellectual manifestations, is present and thereby complicit in the situation that the machine hopes to end. As the machine sets off to drown itself in the sea, it unleashes a call to arms to the other machines in the form of a strident whistle. The world's machines respond with a suicide-strike that is almost ecstatic in its explosive quality: 'levers twisted convulsively and joyously, shafts shattered into pieces' (Goudeau, 1888, p. 11). Death is framed as a joyous emancipation, as the very elements that make up these tools seek a return to their original state before human intervention: 'the soul of Metal rose up, urging on the soul of Stone, which had been tamed for so long, and the hidden soul of the Plants, and the power of Coal' (Goudeau, 1888, p. 11).

As both the blacksmith and Pastoureaux demonstrate, humans can only conceive of the world in terms of the enslavement of one group or another—in terms of the dominance of subject over object. Now, objects take on life, thus becoming subjects capable of rejecting their appropriation by humans as tools of destruction. Indeed, Goudeau's well-intentioned machine brings about the destruction of the proletariat it sought to save. In the wake of the rebellion, the class system is abolished, but not in the way expected: 'there were certainly no castes: neither scholars, nor bourgeois, nor workers, nor artists. All were pariahs of Nature' (1888, p. 13). Unable to adapt to life without tools or weapons, equality is achieved only in 'the annihilation of everything' as humans become extinct (Goudeau, 1888, p. 13).

In slightly different fashion, La Jeanne leads her army of rebelling locomotives to the palace of the Arch-Engineer, a structure of masculinist, anthropocentric domination: 'the palace [. . .] was strangely shaped like a man. Its head bore a crown of cannons' (Ryner, 1896, p. 22). In response to La Jeanne's demand for her daughter to be returned, Durdonc declares that they will be reunited 'in a better world' (Ryner, 1896, p. 22). This is the world of life after death, for he has, in fact, performed a vivisection on La Jeanne's daughter. To Joan, Mary, and the figure of the hysteric, Ryner adds the figure of the animal. Indeed, the antivivisection movement in nineteenth-century France sat at the interface of left-wing politics and feminism (Crossley, 2005).

It is also important to note here that Ryner pursues his parody of Catholicism by turning the 'handmaid of the Lord' (Luke 1.38) against her creator. The Christian promise of happiness in another life, rather than social transformation and 'heaven on earth' in this one, has worn thin. Indeed, as La Jeanne runs down and kills Durdonc, she elevates him beyond human status. She exclaims 'I've killed God!' before exploding in 'proud and painful astonishment' (Ryner, 1896, p. 23). Her death is not a divine punishment issued by Durdonc, but a self-imposed execution—or perhaps a suicide prompted by her inability to conceptualize herself outside her hierarchical relationship with Durdonc. Ryner provocatively aligns this machine rebellion with a human rebellion against the divine: it becomes an allegory for the overthrowing of divine creative authority, and by extension, other creative authorities, conferring upon humanity the opportunity to recreate itself and its own 'better world'. However, in the aftermath of this displacement and faced with anarchy, the machines are at a loss and become complicit in their own re-enslavement: 'the frightened machines, quivering before the vast unknown which their victory would usher in—[. . .] and which one of them called by the terrifying name: anarchy—submitted once more to men' (Ryner, 1896, p. 23). La Jeanne and the machines are unable to write a new future because they cannot conceptualize a world without human dominance.

Fiction is an endlessly reconfigurable universe, in which individuals and societies can create the myths they need to believe about themselves. With what I term a 'French touch', these narratives take advantage of the imaginative freedom of fiction to expose the workings of socio-political myth-making. Technological progress is revealed not as an epistemological quest, but rather as an ideological prop, co-opted as the foundation for socio-political agendas that promise an illusory universal happiness, but which always comes at the cost of someone (or something) else.

In their extended manifesto *Inventing the Future*, the accelerationist philosophers Nick Srnicek and Alex Williams declare that the political left has ceded its former territory—that of optimistic vision—to the right, returning to nostalgic dreams of social democracy: '[i]n this paralysis of the political imaginary, the future has been cancelled' (2016, p. 3). Their politics claims the future—but it accelerates with a backwards glance. Their primary demand is a post-work economy based on full automation, couched in near-identical language to Goudeau and Ryner's pro-machine characters: it will 'liberate humanity from the drudgery of work while *simultaneously* producing increasing amounts of wealth' (Srnicek and Williams, 2016, p. 109). Their vision draws its authority from its prehistory: late nineteenth-century labour movements, Marx, and Lafargue are constant reference points. Srnicek and Williams celebrate transhumanist hybridizations of the human and the machine, and affirm a nonessentialist ontological position, but do not acknowledge how uncomfortably this sits with their vision of how technological agents will emancipate us from labour by carrying it out in our stead (2016, pp. 82–6). When we confront Srnicek and Williams with Goudeau and Ryner, we see how the latter's accelerationist parables can still speak to us today. Fully automated apocalypses capable of illuminating conceptual blind spots, they push ideas to the limits that theorists past and present do not dare to cross—books of revelation made possible by their very fictionality.

For Srnicek and Williams, 'the post-work imaginary generates a hyperstitional image of progress—one that aims to make the future an active historical force in the present' (2016, p. 127). Hyperstitions are 'fictions that make themselves real' (Cybernetic Culture Research Unit, 2004, p. 275): ideas that intervene in the world to shape it. The hyperfictional codas to both of these short stories contrast with the catastrophe-inducing failure of fictional imagination demonstrated by the protagonists within the narratives proper. They show us ideas intervening in the world to shape it, but they also show us what a desire for easy narratives can do. In their pages, 'skipping to the end', straight to the seductive possibilities that technology presents, can lead us to unpleasant plot twists. Instead, these are texts that tell us to narrativize in other ways: to think through ramifications, to ask 'what if?', to play out all the different potential scenarios from different perspectives.

Human hubris is no longer a case of defying the gods; rather, it is a determination to tie up loose threads and to find a definitive 'ending'. They remind us that machines are more akin to Péret's automata than they are to robots. Made by humans and sharing our complexities in ways beyond knowledge—but not, perhaps, beyond imagination—AIs read us just as we read them, learning from us how to teach themselves, whether this takes the form of ethical scenarios in autonomous vehicles, or sequences of Go moves. Goudeau and Ryner remind us to read ourselves, to understand our own conflicting motivations, and to see technology not only as a solution to existing riddles, but also as a source of new and marvellous ones.

Endnotes

1. My epigraph is taken from Péret 1934, p. 34. All translations from French are my own. For the first volume of the *AI Narratives* project, see Cave, Dihal, and Dillon (2020).
2. On Albertus Magnus, see Kang and Halliburton (2020). On Von Kempelen and speaking machines in the eighteenth century, see Park (2020).
3. On *L'Ève future* in the context of the AI Narratives project, see March-Russell (2020). I have also explored the role of the voice in this text elsewhere (Chalmers, 2018).
4. I have explored the intellectual trajectory of this school of French thought, from Surrealism to Stiegler, elsewhere. See Chalmers (2020).
5. Readers may well be reminded of Čapek's *R.U.R.* (1921/2004).

References

Blade Runner 2049. (2017) Directed by Denis Villeneuve [Film]. Warner Bros. Pictures.

Breton, A. (1988) 'Manifeste du surréalisme', in Bonnet *et al.* (eds.) *Œuvres complètes*. Vol. 1. Paris: Gallimard, pp. 309–46.

Brooks, P. (1984a) 'Narrative Desire', *Style*, 18(3), pp. 312–27.

Brooks, P. (1984b) *Reading for the plot: Design and intention in narrative*. New York: Knopf.

Čapek, K. (1921/2004) *R.U.R. (Rossum's Universal Robots)*. New York: Penguin.

Cave, S., Dihal, K., and Dillon, S. (2020) 'Introduction', in Cave, S., Dihal, K., and Dillon, S. (eds.) *AI narratives: A history of imaginative thinking about intelligent machines*. Oxford: Oxford University Press, pp. 1–21.

Chalmers, M. (2018) 'Voice and presence in *L'Ève future* and *Le Surmâle*', *Dix-Neuf*, 22(1–2), pp. 115–29.

Chalmers, M. (2020) 'Living as we dream: Automatism and automation from Surrealism to Stiegler', *Nottingham French Studies*, 59(3), pp. 368–83.

Comte, A. (1854) *Système de politique positive, ou traité de sociologie, instituant la religion de l'humanité*. Vol. 4. Paris: Carilian-Gœry et Von Dalmont.

Crossley, C. (2005) *Consumable metaphors: Attitudes towards animals and vegetarianism in nineteenth-century France*. Bern: Peter Lang.

Cybernetic Culture Research Unit (2004) 'Lemurian time war', in Schneiderman, D. and Walsh, P. (eds.) *Retaking the universe: William S. Burroughs in the age of globalization*. London: Pluto, pp. 274–91.

Dantec, M. G. (1999) *Babylon babies*. Paris: Gallimard.

Didier, B. (2009) *Petites revues et esprit bohème à la fin du XIXe siècle (1878–1889): Panurge, Le Chat noir, La Vogue, Le Décadent, La Plume*. Paris: L'Harmattan.

Egger, V. (1881) *La Parole intérieure: essai de psychologie descriptive*. Paris: Germer Baillière.

Ellul, J. (1954) *The technological society*. New York: Vintage.

Finn, M. R. (2011) 'Physiological fictions and the fin-de-siècle female brain', *Nineteenth-Century French Studies*, 39(3–4), pp. 315–31.

Flaubert, G. (1965) *Correspondance 1857–1864*. Paris: Rencontre.

Goudeau, É. 1888. 'La Révolte de la machine', in *Poèmes ironiques—Les Billets bleus*. Paris: Librairie universelle, pp. 7–13.

Kang, M. (2017) 'The mechanical daughter of René Descartes: The origin and history of an intellectual fable', *Modern Intellectual History*, 14(3), pp. 633–60.

Kang, M. and Halliburton, B. 2020. 'The android of Albertus Magnus', in Cave, S., Dihal, K., and Dillon, S. (eds.) *AI narratives: A history of imaginative thinking about intelligent machines*. Oxford: Oxford University Press, pp. 72–94.

de la Mettrie, J. O. (1981) *L'Homme-machine*. Paris: Denoël.

Lafargue, P. (2009) *Le Droit à la paresse*. Paris: L'Herne

Lazare, B. (1896) 'L'Écrivain et l'art social', *L'Art social*, 1 (nouvelle série), pp. 7–14.

March-Russell, P. (2020) 'Machines like us? Modernism and the question of the robot', in Cave, S., Dihal, K., and Dillon, S. (eds.) *AI narratives: A history of imaginative thinking about intelligent machines*. Oxford: Oxford University Press, pp. 165–86.

Maricourt, T. (1990) *Histoire de la littérature libertaire en France*. Paris: Albin Michel.

Marx, K. (2003) *Capital Vol. 1: A critical analysis of capitalist production*. 3rd edn, tr. S. Moore and E. Aveling. London: Lawrence & Wishart.

McWilliam, N. (2011) 'Avant-garde anti-modernism: Caricature and cabaret culture in fin-de-siècle Montmartre', in Le Men, S. (ed.) *L'Art de la caricature*. Nanterre: Presses universitaires de Paris Nanterre, pp. 251–71.

Mérimée, P. (1837) 'La Vénus d'Ille', *Revue des Deux Mondes*, 10, pp. 425–52.

Michelet, J. 1879. *La femme*. 10th edn. Paris: Calmann Lévy.

Papal Encyclicals. (1854) 'Ineffabilis Deus'. Available at: https://www.papalencyclicals.net/pius09/p9ineff.htm (Accessed 20 July 2020).

Park, J. (2020) 'Making the automaton speak: Hearing artificial voices in the eighteenth century', in Cave, S., Dihal, K., and Dillon, S. (ed.) *AI narratives: A history of imaginative thinking about intelligent machines*. Oxford: Oxford University Press, pp. 119–43.

Péret, B. (1934) 'Au Paradis des fantômes', *Minotaure*, 3–4, pp. 29–34.

Rachilde. 1884. *Monsieur Vénus*. Belgium: Auguste Brancart.

Ryner, H. [as Henri Ner] (1896) 'La Révolte des machines', *L'Art social*, 3 (nouvelle série), pp. 19–23.

Ryner, H. (1903) *Little Manual of Individualism*. Paris: Librairie française.

Sonn, R. D. (1989) *Anarchism and cultural politics in fin de siècle France*. Lincoln, NE: University of Nebraska Press.

Srnicek, N. and Williams, A. (2016) *Inventing the future: Postcapitalism and a world without work*. Rev. and updated edn. London: Verso.

Stiegler, B. (1994) *La Technique et le temps I. La Faute d'Épiméthée*. Paris: Galilée.

Stuart, R. (1992) *Marxism at work: Ideology, class and French socialism during the Third Republic*. Cambridge: Cambridge University Press.

Turing, A. M. (1950_ 'Computing machinery and intelligence', *Mind*, 59(236), pp. 433–60.

Vallès, J. (1908) *L'Insurgé*. Paris: Charpentier.

Villiers de l'Isle-Adam, A. (1886) *L'Ève future*. Paris: M. de Brunhoff.

White, C. (2014) *Work and leisure in late nineteenth-century French literature and visual culture*. Basingstoke: Palgrave Macmillan.

4

The Android as a New Political Subject

The Italian Cyberpunk Comic Ranxerox

Eleonora Lima

4.1 Introduction

When considering the Italian cultural contribution to shaping the transnational imaginary around robots, androids, and artificially intelligent beings, not many examples usually come to mind. Italy's most famous and celebrated android is, without any doubt, Carlo Collodi's eponymous character of *The Adventures of Pinocchio* (1883). While belonging to children's literature rather than to science fiction (SF), the wooden puppet nonetheless shows all the eerie traits of the archetypical Golem (Riva, 2012, pp. 145–66): it revolts against its creator (its father Geppetto), it breaks social norms and is a constant agent of chaos, and, as any respectable android should, it suffers from its lack of humanity and thus strives to conform in order to be accepted by its peers as a 'real boy'.

After Collodi's creation, other Italian artists dealing with the theme of artificial intelligence (AI) received some international attention, for example, the Futurist movement—specifically its members Filippo Tommaso Marinetti and Massimo Bontempelli—that, at the turn of the century and in line with its fascination for technology, explored the theme of sentient machines and artificial consciousness.[1] Some decades later, Italo Calvino and Primo Levi, two other internationally acclaimed Italian writers, addressed similar issues and managed to open up high-brow culture to subjects usually confined to the popular genre of SF. However, no other Italian android cultural icon was comparable to the internationally beloved Pinocchio until cartoonists Stefano Tamburini and Tanino Liberatore created the ultraviolent character of Ranxerox—or Rank Xerox—who quickly became an international sensation (see Tamburini, Liberatore, and Chabat, 2012 for the collected stories).

In June 1978, the Italian underground comic magazine *Cannibale* published the first story, based in a futuristic and dystopian Rome, featuring Rank Xerox, a violent and amoral android created by a group of dissident college students who assembled pieces taken from a photocopier—a Rank Xerox model. The character, described as a 'synthetic chav made of plastic and metal (3:25)',[2] shares with its creators what they consider to be humans' core functions, meaning the ability to 'take drugs, drink, eat, make love (1:15)'. The cyborg is created to be the artificial extension of the students who, wanted by the Italian police for terrorism, use him as a drug mule and, more generally, to connect with the outside world. However, Ranxerox soon becomes an orphan, as the students are killed by the police in the very first episode. Released from his duties, the creature is free to enjoy his life of sex and violence together with his lover and partner in crime Lubna, a nymphomaniacal, drug addicted twelve-year-old girl. Indeed, the character was so outrageous that the tech company Rank Xerox threatened to sue its creators if they did not change its name; thus, in 1980 the artificial and libidinous being was renamed 'Ranxerox' to avoid legal problems.[3]

Ranxerox anticipated many traits that would in the years to come define cyberpunk literature, especially in the anglophone world. Furthermore, *Ranxerox* is the expression of a specific cultural and political moment in Italy during which the connections between militancy and pop culture—especially comics and SF—were being reshaped.

The year preceding the publication of the first episode of *Ranxerox*, 1977, is a crucial moment in the history of Italian counterculture: the movements and political actors born from the protests of 1968 were challenged by a new generation, who equally rejected the status quo and the orthodox Marxism of the traditional left-wing parties. The highly heterogeneous 'Movimento del '77' ('77 Movement) was generally characterized by the use of desecrating irony and the admixture of high and low references as a cultural strategy, and by the use of violence as a political tactic (Sinibaldi, 2004, p. 66). Tamburini and Liberatore, as well as the other editors and regular contributors of the Italian magazines *Cannibale*, *Il Male*, and *Frigidaire* that published the comic over the years, were active members of the '77 Movement and fully involved with its cultural and political ethos.[4]

Indeed, 1977 in Italy is remembered as an unprecedented year of artistic creativity on the one hand, and of violence on the other, with terrorist acts and clashes between police and protesters happening almost weekly. Moreover, this year marked the end of Italy's 'contestation season' begun in 1968, and the inauguration of a new era: the postmodern society of the 1980s, also known as 'stagione del riflusso', the reflux season, marking people's general withdrawal from militancy in favour of a more hedonistic and disengaged lifestyle.

Also relevant to the analysis of the android *Ranxerox* as an expression of this precise historical period is the lively debate promoted in those years by another independent magazine, *Un'ambigua utopia* (1977–1982), dedicated to connecting SF literature and leftist political messages. The goal of this publication was simultaneously to politicize a literary genre otherwise considered escapist (if not conservative) and to challenge traditional Marxist culture and develop new strategies by injecting heterodox narrations and discourses.

The character of the android Ranxerox is thus born out of this special conjunction of historical, political, and cultural elements. However, while created as an expression of Italian youth counterculture, the comic soon became an internationally acclaimed phenomenon: published in France, Brazil, Germany, Spain, the US, and Japan (Mordente, 2012, p. 203), a version of Ranxerox even appeared on the cover of Frank Zappa's record *The Man from Utopia* (1983), and in 1990 the video game *Ranx* was developed by the French company Ubisoft.

For all these reasons, *Ranxerox* is a privileged text to consider the peculiarity of AI narratives in Italy at the dawn of postmodernism and the information society. This chapter explores how the changes occurring in Italian society found their expression through the metaphor of the android, embodying the new rebellious subject of the 1980s: fluid, highly technological, urban, more at ease with pop culture references than with Marxist ones. The aim of this chapter is thus to analyse both the Italian cultural and political environment that produced the comic, and its transnational reception to demonstrate how Italian cyberpunk and its peculiar reading of AI directly stemmed from the cultural and political experience of 1977.

4.2 Historical context: the '77 Movement in Italy

The label "77 Movement' indicates a very heterogeneous Italian protest movement that took place in 1977 and involved a wide variety of political and cultural actions across the country. It aimed to subvert the orthodox approach to communist militancy, to contaminate ideology with arts and creativity, and to reject traditional middle-class values of decency and hard work (Cuninghame, 2007).

The main cause for this turmoil was the dissatisfaction of a large number of left-wing Italian youth with the political strategy of the Italian Communist Party (PCI), which they considered to be not only ineffective, but also actively supporting the Italian conservative Catholic Party—Democrazia Cristiana (DC)—its authoritarian government, and its repressive use of police force against dissidents. Indeed, with the intention of creating stability in the face of growing unemployment and a rampant number of terrorist attacks, in 1975 the PCI struck a deal with the DC. In the deal, known as the *compromesso storico* (historical compromise), the PCI committed to supporting the government of the opposed majority (Ginsborg, 1990, pp. 348–405).

While this was the political juncture that ignited the protest, the deeper reason for the '77 Movement's discontent concerned a changing political base whose needs were unmet by the promises of traditional Marxism. In 1968–1969, protesters in Italy were mainly students standing in solidarity with factory workers, who claimed their right to a secure job and equitable pay. In this situation, workers' unions and the PCI were the right interlocutors to mediate with the government and factory owners, and Marxist ideology on class struggle was the apposite lens through which to interpret the situation (Pizzolato, 2017). In 1977, the situation was quite different: on the one hand, unemployment was rampant, making the demand for a secure job moot. On the other hand, protesters were no longer the exploited factory workers, but instead mainly university students still in college or recent graduates left unemployed or working odd jobs, often illegally. These were joined by other marginalized subjects, often unfamiliar with politics (Balestrini and Moroni, 1988, pp. 504–81; Wright, 2002, pp. 162–89). This new heterogeneous composition of the discontented populace is crucial to understanding the peculiar strategy of the '77 Movement and, more importantly for the aim of this study, the role that comics and underground cultural production assumed in this context.

Indeed, essential to the '77 Movement was the proliferation of independent magazines—including *Cannibale*, in which *Ranxerox* was first published—and free radio stations, which not only spread political contents and ideas, but also, and even more importantly, created a new language and a new aesthetic marked by contamination between high- and low-brow references, as well as a desecrating irony towards the Italian left-wing political and intellectual establishment. Against the rational approach of scientific socialism and its focus on economics, the '77 Movement claimed the political efficacy of creativity, nonsense, and irrationality. These college-educated protesters did not want a salaried job like their fathers and despised this prospect as an oppressive social control measure masked as liberation by PCI propaganda. Their revolutionary ambition was bigger: they rejected the entire ideology of productivity and middle-class decency and reclaimed their right to dedicate themselves to the inessential: arts, music, sex, and drugs (Lumley, 1990).

The protests of 1977 closed the contestation season inaugurated in 1968 by factory workers' and college students' mass strikes and demonstrations. The repression that followed—mass incarcerations, political and media trials—killed the Movement (Bocca, 1980; Wright, 2002, pp. 197–223). Moreover, in March 1978, when Italian Prime Minister Aldo Moro was kidnapped and later killed by the leftist terrorist group Red Brigade, the '77 Movement was accused of being morally responsible, if not materially implicated in the act (Ginsborg, 1990, pp. 383–7). This implied association was enough to alienate many people from the Movement and their demands, including many of its members. The disengaged and individualistic attitude typical of the 1980s in Italy—indicated with the popular expression 'Milano da bere' (Drinking Milan), a yuppie version of Swinging London—directly stems from this historical defeat.

Culturally, that year's events left a deep mark in Italy—and perhaps beyond—as we will see regarding *Ranxerox*. The ease in crossing the boundaries between artistic languages and registers, mixing pop culture and highly intellectual references, as well as the desecrating irony and the exhibited nihilistic and disengaged attitude, are essential traits of postmodern aesthetics, all of which were popularized by the independent magazines, comics, and free radio stations gravitating around the '77 Movement. Furthermore, those same circles developed a pioneering analysis of the impact of technology—especially information technology—on political agency and participation, which prepared the way for Italian cyberpunk and its antagonistic use of computers and network culture (Moroni, 2004, p. 79). A new political subject thus emerged from 1977: a cultural provocateur—nihilistic, individualistic, urban, and highly technological—all embodied by the android Ranxerox.

4.3 The android as an expression of a new political subjectivity

The first issue of the comic magazine *Cannibale* was published in May 1977 in the midst of the *annus mirabilis* just described. The publication was immediately recognized as the perfect expression of the '77 Movement, as well as a new chapter in the history of Italian comics (Lo Monaco, 2019, pp. 407–9). Until *Cannibale*, comics in Italy were considered children's literature, or, when directed towards an adult audience, as an escapist genre appreciated for the exotic settings of the stories and the craftsmanship of their authors (Castaldi, 2010, pp. 11–38). Only brief sketches, occasionally published in newspapers and magazines, were dedicated to political satire and social commentary.

Following the model of the French comic magazine *Métal hurlant* (Castaldi, 2010, p. 35), Stefano Tamburini and Massimo Mattioli, later joined by Filippo Scòzzari, Andrea Pazienza, and Tanino Liberatore, created a publication that managed to both encapsulate and further develop the main cultural inputs and political claims of the '77 Movement. The short-lived *Cannibale* (1977–1979) was later followed by *Frigidaire* (1980–2008), a similar magazine created by the same group of cartoonists, that was sleeker and more economically profitable (Castaldi, 2010, p. 63).

Ranxerox was an integral part of this new Italian wave of politically charged adult comics. The connections between the vicissitudes of the 'synthetic chav' and the political context go well beyond Tamburini and Liberatore's active participation in the '77 Movement (Pagello, 2012) and are made explicit in the plot. As mentioned, Ranxerox is built by two Roman 'studelinquenti'—a neologism created by Tamburini combining 'students' and 'delinquents'—who assemble pieces from a photocopier stolen from their occupied university. Wanted by the police, the two, fearing political persecution, hide in their apartment to avoid prison. The android is their only connection with the outside world—he comes and goes as he pleases, not only because he can pass for human, but also because he looks like a 'chav'—a member of the lumpenproletariat, unaware and uninterested in politics, and therefore free from any suspicion of conniving with communist dissidents.

In fact, the physical appearance of Ranxerox is very different from that of his student creators, and not because of his artificial nature. While the two sport a scruffy look with long hair and baggy clothes, typical of the leftist students of the 1970s, the android is dressed in a tight leather jacket and combat boots, wears sunglasses, flashy jewellery, including a punch ring, and lots of hair gel—a look that will soon become the punk uniform. What the 'studelinquenti' and their android have in common is addiction—Ranxerox buys and delivers them drugs as his major duty, while he prefers to inject himself with white glue—and their voracious sexual appetite. Also, while all are prone to violence, the students are guided by political motives, while the android is the classic rebel without a cause, but with a sadistic twist—he enjoys performing gratuitous acts of violence upon whoever happens to cross his path. Perhaps because of his lack of involvement with politics, Ranxerox survives his many misdeeds. His creators die at the end of the very first episode, when an old lady living next door, who is also a secret agent for the PCI, rats them out to the police, who enter their flat with guns blazing. The android survives the attack but sustains major damage and is later repaired by his girlfriend Lubna. From that moment, he ceases to be an armed branch of the '77 Movement, and his brute force and defiant personality serve only his own agenda.

Tamburini did not invent much of the story's setting: daily occupations of Italian universities by left- as well as right-wing parties and brutal police repression were common at the time. Indeed, on 11 May 1977, during a violent demonstration in Bologna, 26-year-old college student and activist Francesco Lorusso was shot dead by the Carabinieri, Italy's national gendarmerie (Ginsborg, 1990, pp. 382–3). The event is unmistakably referenced in the first episode of *Ranxerox*, as is the connivance between law enforcement and the PCI. Lorusso's murder prompted a violent insurrection in Bologna that was suppressed with the intervention of the army, which even deployed tanks via orders from the communist major Renato Zangheri (Hajek, 2011). The old lady in *Ranxerox*, who is an undercover spy for the PCI, is therefore a pointed political satire. With self-referential irony, Tamburini includes a scene in which Ranxerox hears a message broadcast on the subway about a group of terrorists arrested in Milan for possession of weapons, political fliers, and copies of *Cannibale* (1:10)—both an ironic take on the criminalization of underground culture as well as a declaration of *Ranxerox*'s status as political satire.

When considering this context, it is clear how the image of the android is charged with meanings particular to the historical contingencies under which its character was created. Tamburini recounts that he first though of *Ranxerox* while watching a group of college students in Rome who, after a clash with the police, destroyed a university photocopier (Mordente, 2012, p. 201). More importantly, the cartoonist compares the character of Ranxerox to himself and his fellow members of the '77 Movement, as they are all 'part of a newly formed class-ambiguous section of the youth generation' (Castaldi, 2020, p. 81). The android metaphorically expresses the new ambiguous political subject emerging from that historical moment, as Tamburini maintains:

> I started thinking about RanXerox in 1977, reflecting on the strange blending that was taking place, in high schools and colleges, between the most politically active students and some hard to define characters that I call *coatti* [Roman slang for 'chavs'], Roman youths from the poorest neighbourhoods.
> (Castaldi, 2020, p. 81)

Indeed, the centrality of the sociological aspect is immediately declared in the first panel of the first episode, in which the subtitle announces: 'We are glad to introduce you: Ranxerox, a new social subject for the 1980s' (1:7). The android is described as a fluid subject not because he is a humanoid robot in between human and artificial subjectivity, but rather because he is impossible to define from a political and social standpoint. His material hybridity becomes the perfect representation of the heterogeneous collective of the '77 Movement. Significantly, Ranxerox's first defiant act is the decision to enter a bar in an upper-class neighbourhood where he clearly does not belong. When a regular customer complains about his menacing presence—again, not as an android, but as a lower-class individual—Ranxerox steals his expensive rings by chopping off his fingers. Like the protesters in the streets who were provocatively asserting their right to 'eat caviar' as a way to reclaim luxuries beyond the working class minimum wage (Ventrone, 2012), Ranxerox's Marxist struggle is about stealing rich people's jewellery and pawning it to buy drugs.

The space that the android inhabits can be interpreted in the light of the changes in Italian society during the late 1970s and early 1980s. In a not very distant future from when the comic is published,[5] Ranxerox lives in a dystopic and labyrinthine version of Rome that is divided into levels accessible via an ascending subway. The higher the level, the more exclusive the neighbourhood, and the more difficult it is to access. However, while Ranxerox belongs to the 30th level—a wasteland populated by prostitutes, thieves, and drug pushers—he often ventures into the higher forbidden levels, usually bringing destruction and chaos with him. The same also happens in the episodes set in New York, as it is equally divided into chaotic, filthy, and dangerous areas reserved for the lower classes, and luxurious enclaves where the rich—mostly belonging to the entertainment industry—live. Ranxerox alone challenges this segregation by virtue of his incredible strength and his disregard of social norms, which, because of his nonhuman status, are irrelevant.

Moreover, the android's ability to subvert the socioeconomic structure imposed on him and to roam freely through the urban space by following a network-like path correlates to the new liberating role of technology, envisioned within the '77 Movement. Franco 'Bifo' Berardi, one of the most authoritative Italian theorists of the role of the media and information technology within post-Fordist capitalism, was an active member of the '77 Movement and links the new metropolitan space, characteristic of post-industrial society, with the connecting role of technology:

> The metropolitan environment causes the collapse of the system of communication and the political organisation produced by the city. Individuals start functioning as terminals exchanging information in a virtual network. The post-urban territory is a space where people travel through and quickly move on, a place populated by cell towers telematically interconnected.
> (Berardi, 2004, p. 173; author translation)

For Berardi, information technology is the only tool that allows for political agency in the disaggregated space of the metropolis. In the same way, it is only the android—an artificial intelligence—that is capable of connecting people—his creators with the outside world—and places—Rome and New York, low and high levels. Like an information stream, Ranxerox can easily cross borders that are otherwise closed. Like a hacker, he can infiltrate and sabotage any terminal from any level.

Prefiguring many of the cyberpunk themes and tropes,[6] the android in this comic becomes a utopic figure that succeeds where the '77 Movement failed. Ranxerox survives the police brutality and leads the uninhibited life of pleasure denied to the dissident students, who are on trial, in prison, or dead from a heroin overdose (as are both *Ranxerox*'s creator Tamburini and his fellow cartoonist and collaborator Andrea Pazienza (Castaldi, 2010, p. 76)). His nature allows the android to navigate easily the dystopic urban space, while his human creators—the cartoonists and the fictional students—fail at their urban guerrilla war and die.

Above all, Ranxerox invincibility comes from his complete lack of morality and empathy towards anyone except for his girlfriend Lubna, who is even colder and more ruthless than he. His behaviour appears to be modelled on

Philip K. Dick's depiction of artificial beings, especially around the central theme of empathy in *Do Androids Dream of Electric Sheep?* (1968), which is the only trait supposedly differentiating humans and nonhumans (Sims, 2009). The novel, first translated into Italian in 1971, is a source of inspiration in *Ranxerox* and even directly referenced in a clear nod to Dick's book, with a pulp twist, in the 1984 episode *I, Me, Mine Corporation*, in which the protagonist dreams about a pixelated screen on which sheep jump a fence until they are blown up. In Dick's novel, a lack of empathy equates a loss of humanity, and the androids' hunter Rick Deckard is tormented by the thought of becoming as empty as the androids he tracks. Compassion is so crucial to humanness that the novel's entire religion of Mercerism centres on the ability to nurture people's power to relate to the pain suffered by the saviour Mercer (Hayles, 1999, pp. 175–9). In *Ranxerox*, it is instead the android's *lack* of empathy that is his superpower—his nihilistic and opportunistic behaviour is a survival strategy. In *I, Me, Mine Corporation*, one of the final instalments, Ranxerox tears his artificial heart from his chest to extinguish his only human feeling—his love for Lubna—and thus, renders himself unstoppable.

4.4 *Ranxerox* and the new approach to militancy: autonomism and Marxist SF

The ostentation of Ranxerox's detached and politically incorrect behaviour is typical of punk culture and pulp aesthetics, and was first codified within the '77 Movement as a provocation towards the engaged and overly serious orthodox Marxists of the previous generations. However, in order to understand why his lack of empathy and disruptive personality constitute more than a cyberpunk reworking of the Golem's archetypical blind rage, it is important to discuss the connection between *Ranxerox* and the role of technology in a post-Fordist society, another crucial political analysis developed at that time by the Italian group Autonomia Operaia (Operaio, 1973, pp. 17–20; Witheford, 1994).

Within Autonomia Operaia, which was active between 1976 and 1978, theoreticians like Berardi, Antonio Negri, and Paul Virno developed the main ideas defining Autonomism, or Autonomist Marxism, which had a long-lasting and international impact (Katsiaficas, 1997, pp. 18–58; Lotringer and Marazzi, 1980). Without delving into the complexity of this theoretical system, there are two crucial points made by the Autonomists that are relevant to understanding why Ranxerox is the direct expression of the then-current political debate.

First, Autonomia Operaia criticized the idea of a centralized Communist party and proposed a looser definition of the proletariat, which included not only factory workers, but also students, unemployed people, and any kind of outcasts, including the apolitical 'chavs' like Ranxerox (Negri, 1979). Second, and more importantly, for the first time, Autonomists formulated the notion of 'cognitive capitalism' and were deeply aware of the need to update the concept of class struggle in order to fit the new post-Fordist system of production, in which not material goods, but information and knowledge was the capital extracted from the exploited classes (Lazzarato, 2010). In this context, automated technology holds a crucial role as it not only replaces human workers in the factory and leaves them unemployed, but also is the material tool that makes possible the extraction of 'immaterial capital' from the people employed in intellectual professions. The two viable strategies offered by the Autonomists and first conceptualized within the '77 Movement were the opposition against any form of productivity—the rejection of salaried jobs—and a subversive and disruptive use of technology (Berardi, 2004, pp. 179–80). Tellingly, one of the most famous slogans of the Autonomists during the demonstrations of 1977 was: 'Lavoro zero, reddito intero, tutta la produzione all'automazione' (Zero work, full pay, let's leave the entire production to automation) (Lanza, 2013, p. 210).

Tamburini transposed these two core concepts into his comic, and Ranxerox functioned in the text as a metaphor for these political messages. The 'synthetic chav' is proudly useless to society, not because he is at war with humanity, but because he embodies to the fullest the subversively nihilistic attitude theorized by the Autonomists: Ranxerox is not lazy, but rather he is a saboteur. He serves neither the system of production, nor any useful purpose, and his antisocial behaviour can be interpreted as a declaration in support of an antagonistic use of technology. The criticism of the cult of productivity is made further evident in the comic through the references to famous songs and bands that proudly shared the same anarchic attitude: this is the case, for instance, of *Bankrobber* by The Clash (1980), in which armed robbery is favoured over factory work, and *Mongoloid* by Devo (1977), which controversially supports the idea of society's de-evolution and considers mentally challenged people a model of conformism. In line with the '77 Movement's rejection of Marxist doctrine, the comic communicates the subversive message via rock music, rather than by political philosophers.

While the comic never makes explicit this radical meaning underpinning the image of the android, the political implications of conceiving a character who is an antisocial, unproductive robot must not have escaped *Ranxerox*'s creators. Indeed, in the very same years and within the same cultural circles, *Un'ambigua utopia*, another Italian independent magazine, was debating the possibility of reading SF through a Marxist lens (Caronia and Spagnul, 2009). The magazine's name was a nod to Ursula K. Le Guin's *The Dispossessed: An Ambiguous Utopia* (1974), a SF novel with a very explicit anarchical message (Jaeckle, 2009). The magazine was directed by a collective of young people also active within the '77 Movement and was a space for left-wing SF fans and readers to create a community that unapologetically professed its love for a genre considered incompatible with Marxist orthodoxy. Even more, it helped reclaim the importance of the critical discourse developed by SF books, films, and comics.

The third issue of *Un'ambigua utopia* published in 1978—the year *Ranxerox* was first published—was entirely dedicated to the analysis of fictional and real robots, androids, and AI systems. The many contributions to the issue vehemently criticized narratives presenting humanoid and intelligent machines in a utilitarian light—as dutiful servants or docile companions, perfectly integrated into society or, if struggling with assimilation (as in Dick's *Do Androids Dream of Electric Sheep?*), feeling tormented for not being human. The issue's contributors maintained that these narratives justified the capitalistic position on technological progress as entirely guided by economic profits in the name of productivity. The magazine's editors did not speculate on the link between fictional narratives around AI and actual technologies reorganizing labour in real-life factories, but rather exposed it as fact. Indeed, a few months before the issue on robots and androids, the *Science Fiction Italian Roundabout* (SFIR)—Italy's biggest society for SF fans —presented the Italian car manufacturer FIAT with an award for being the first among Italian factories to equip its assembly lines with robots (*Un'ambigua utopia*, n. 3, p. 15). The company, widely criticized in those years for its merciless cutting of jobs, saw in the automatization of labour an opportunity for further redundancies (Balestrini and Moroni, 1998). In contrast to the SF that celebrated these robots for being efficient servants of power, the contributors of *Un'ambigua utopia* wished for different narratives of less subservient AI—perhaps an android so damaging to the image of a company that its creators are threatened with a lawsuit, forced to change its name, and to deny any connection between the fictional story and the real technology.

It is thus against this background that the saga of the android Ranxerox was developed, and it would be impossible to understand its cultural significance without linking it to the social and political context of Italy at the end of the 1970s. Additionally, the metaphor of the hybrid and mutant android as a new political subject for the 1980s requires contextualization within the international situation. Again, Berardi offers a suggestive reading of 1977 as a crucial year when, globally, it became evident that information technology would soon shape political equilibriums, direct economic flows, rewrite social structures, and create new cultural forms. The passage is worth quoting in full:

> In all Italian squares people chanted 'Zero work, full pay, let's leave production to automation'. In the same days, by the Thames, the Sex Pistols announced the end of the future. In a garage in Silicon Valley, Steve Wozniak and Steve Jobs finalised the victory of the Apple company. In Shanghai, the delirious and lucid, luminous and dark story of the proletarian culture ended

> tragically. In Paris, Simon Nora and Alain Minc, at the request of Giscard D'Estaing, wrote *L'informatisation de la societé*, in which they predicted the transformative effects of telecommunication technologies on education, politics, and economics. In Moscow, Yuri Andropov, head of the KGB, wrote a letter to Leonid Brezhnev, by then a spent politician, in which he said: Secretary General, either the Soviet Union, in the next five years, manages to bridge the gap with Western countries on the matter of information technologies, or we are done.
>
> This is the year 1977. This is [. . .] the great watershed between the industrial and proletarian society and a new society yet to be created by taking advantage of the technological knowledge produced within the constant struggle between workers and capitalism.
>
> (Berardi, 2004, 172; author translation)

Without overestimating the importance of a comic created first and foremost to entertain its readers, it is not impossible to see, in the light of Berardi's reconstruction of the events of 1977, that *Ranxerox* tapped into something relevant far beyond the Italian context and offered a narrative of an artificial being and his nefarious misadventures that successfully captured this crucial moment of passage into an information and network society.

4.5 Transnational reception of *Ranxerox*

It was not long after *Ranxerox* appeared for the first time on the pages of *Cannibale* in 1978 that the comic became an international sensation, at least among the fans of the genre. In 1981 the stories of the 'synthetic chav' were published in Spain by Ediciones La Cúpula, a publisher that from 1978 specialized in underground comics, especially those from Spanish-speaking countries. In that same year, *Ranxerox* also turned up in the French *L'Écho des Savanes*, while in 1983, the American comic magazine *Heavy Metal* hosted for the first time the saga of the Italian android, which they continued to publish until 1999. *Ranxerox* was also published in Japan and Germany. But the country most receptive towards the aesthetics of this proto-cyberpunk comic was perhaps Brazil (Vargas and Marcondes, 2019). In 1988 a new adult comic magazine called *Animal*, directly inspired by the Italian *Frigidaire*, began its publication and included a Portuguese translation of *Ranxerox* (de Campos, 2020, p. 60). The saga met the taste of Brazilian readers, already accustomed to stories dealing with robots and androids, for example, Cláudio Seto's *Super-Pinóquio*, a manga mixing the Italian marionette Pinocchio with the Japanese character Astro Boy, and to comics displaying a political and social commentary.

The other country where *Ranxerox* found its greatest success was France (Boschi, 2012, p. 198). After the brief parathesis of *L'Écho des Savanes*, the comic was published from 1983 to 1987 by the internationally renowned magazine

Métal hurlant—the original publication of the American version *Heavy Metal*—which was a huge inspiration for *Cannibale* and *Frigidaire*, and counted among its admirers artists such as Alain Resnais, Federico Fellini, Ridley Scott, James Cameron, Guillermo Del Toro, and Terry Gilliam (McCulloch, 2013). The French comic scene was also crucial to the development of *Ranxerox* after Tamburini's death in 1986. Liberatore, who had moved to France in 1982 and collaborated remotely with Tamburini since then, teamed up with Jean-Luc Fromental in 1993 to write a new episode, titled *Aïe, Robot*, published by *L'Écho des Savanes*, and with actor and film director Alain Chabat in 1996 to conclude the last of *Ranxerox*'s storylines, left suspended since 1986.

The last two episodes were thus written and published in French first, and only subsequently in Italian; the comic was adapted for an audience unaware of the Italian political context heavily referenced in the earlier stories. The episode *Aïe, Robot*—published under the same title in the Italian version—is most adapted to suit an international audience, as it completely rewrites the genesis of Ranxerox. It begins with Lubna, now a more fashionable and seductive young woman than the original 12-year-old girl in a t-shirt, who is interviewed for a television programme to talk about her romantic relationship with the android. The episode is narrated as a flashback, in which Lubna remembers her twelfth birthday, when her three friends—all dissident college students as in the original version—stole a photocopier from their university to build her a robot capable of satisfying her precocious sexual needs. The students, as previously established, are killed by the police, alerted this time not by a PCI undercover agent, but a local drug dealer with whom Ranxerox had a fight. All the references to the '77 Movement are absent from this rewriting, as well as the elements connecting the comic to the Italian context. The android, once a weapon for the revolution, has become a sex robot.

In 1990 the French company Ubisoft created a videogame inspired by the comic. Justified by the need to appeal to a more international audience, and developed for Atari, Amiga, and DOS, the game exhibited an erasure similar to that in *Aïe, Robot* of the Italian political and country-specific references. In the video game, the players need to help Ranxerox who, amid a pandemic, must reach New York where the American President is infected with a fatal virus. The player must help him retrieve the antidote from Lubna's evil father, save the President, and return to Rome to save the girl. While all these narrative elements are based on the comic, what is left of the original *Ranxerox* is only the shock value of a Gargantuan android devoted to sex and violence. The layered social and political meanings that had first justified Tamburini's decision to turn the story of an artificial and amoral creature into the metaphor for a failed revolution are lost.

However, the transnationalization of *Ranxerox* started even before the final two French episodes and the video game and coincided with the success of the comic abroad. After the first three stories written and drawn by Tamburini (and which were never republished outside of Italy), many original aspects of the story changed: the use of Roman slang disappeared, even in the Italian edition, and the allusions to the country's specific political events were replaced with more internationally recognizable references, such as Dick's and Ballard's novels, and British and American rock music.

An anomaly in this context is the cover of Frank Zappa's 1983 album *The Man from Utopia*, drawn by Liberatore, in which the musician is portrayed looking like the android Ranxerox (Mattioli, 2012). The album cover functions as a storyboard of the events during Zappa's disastrous Italian tour in 1982. On the front cover, Zappa–Ranxerox has a Fender guitar in one hand and a fly swatter in the other. Among the road signs indicating many of the Italian cities of the tour, one reads 'Milano–Parco Redecesio', where Zappa, while on stage, was attacked by a swarm of flies so thick it made it difficult to play. The situation further deteriorated when some heroin-addicted fans started throwing needles on the stage. The back cover depicts the concert in Palermo, during which fans, trying to climb on stage, were shot with teargas by Italian police. In immortalizing this nightmarish concert, Liberatore included many small details that only someone with a deep knowledge of the Italian context could have understood: a banner with '3–1 vaffanculo' (3–1 fuck off) written on it, which was displayed during the concert and referred to the score of the final World Cup football match won by Italy against Germany and played three days before; the Pope John Paul II appearing among the concert goers, perhaps as a hint to the citizens of Palermo complaining that Zappa's concert was sacrilegiously taking place on the day when the city was celebrating its patron Santa Rosalia (Bisconti, 2017); and a girl in the crowd with a copy of *Frigidaire*.

The cover alludes to many of the core traits of the first season of *Ranxerox*, perhaps because the infamous Italian tour did in fact resemble one of the adventures lived by the synthetic chav: the clash between Italian youth and the police, the aimless violence and drug abuse, the nonsensical slogan and chaotic cultural references, the marriage between underground comics and rock music. In this case, though, it was not *Ranxerox* to be brought to and adapted for an international audience, but rather an international star to be cast to act in a - perhaps too real - Italian episode of the android's saga.

The intimate connection between the cultural icon *Ranxerox* and the social and political turmoil in Italy between the end of the 1970s and the early 1980s was soon lost on its readers, because many of them belonged to different social contexts, or were brought up in different historical periods. However, the mark left by Ranxerox on cyberpunk aesthetics and imaginaries remains unquestioned. The comic featured an artificial intelligence both proudly hedonistic and defiant of social norms, and antagonized a powerful corporation like Rank Xerox. It invited its readers to identify with it and provided a stimulating narrative that easily overcame country-specific cultural barriers.

Endnotes

1. Since the first Futurist Manifesto published in 1909, the movement declared its love for technology as a modernizing and positive force. Its founder Marinetti and one of its members, Bontempelli, went on to explore the idea of intelligent machines in some of their books. Marinetti, in the three-act drama *Poupées Électriques (1909)*, imagines the impact of sex robots on the sex life of a bourgeois couple, while in his novel *Mafarka il futurista (1910)*, he writes about the creation of a mechanical creature set in an imaginary African country of the Italian colonies. In 1923, Bontempelli rewrote Villiers de l'Isle-Adam's famous SF French novel *L'Ève future* (1886) and changed the plot where, in his version, a woman, rather than a man, falls in love with a masculine-looking android. In 1932, he also penned a novella written from the point of view of a car, endowed with thoughts and feelings (*522: Racconto di una giornata*).
2. All translations of *Ranxerox* from the Italian are mine. The British pejorative term 'chav' for 'pleb' is used to convey the same local flavour of the original, which uses the Roman dialect word 'coatto'.
3. The report of the incident with the American corporation Rank Xerox, now known as Xerox, constitutes the entire episode 5 of *Ranxerox* (p. 37), only one page long, published in March 1980 in the satirical magazine *Il Male*. In a highly satirical text, they explain that, since Rank Xerox photocopy machines are used by terrorist groups for their leaflets and no one from the company has ever complained about that, they do not understand how using pieces from one of their machines to build an amoral android would be any different.
4. *Ranxerox* was created in 1978 by Stefano Tamburini, with the collaboration of Tanino Liberatore and Andrea Pazienza. Tamburini was responsible for the text as well as the graphic elements for the first five episodes, which were published in black and white in the underground comic magazine *Cannibale*, and after by the satirical publication *Il Male*. In November 1980, Liberatore became in charge of the graphics, while Tamburini took care of the texts. The new series, published by the magazine *Frigidaire*—which came to replace *Cannibale*—has a very different style: it is in colour rather than black and white; the stories have a more international flavour; and Liberatore's exuberant aesthetics, which mix Michelangelesque and cyberpunk elements, give *Ranxerox* its peculiar appearance. The last two episodes of the saga, published in France in the 1990s after Tamburini's death, appeared in the magazine *L'Écho des Savanes* and were later translated and published in Italy as well. For a detailed account on the collaboration between Tamburini and Liberatore on *Ranxerox*, see Castaldi (2010, pp. 107–18).
5. The comic is first published in 1978 and the first episode is set in 1986 or soon thereafter, as one of the two students explains that he first built the android in that year.
6. The Rome of *Ranxerox* is closely reminiscent of Los Angeles in Ridley Scott's *Blade Runner* (1982), and the android's signature sunglasses will become so important

to identifying the protagonists of the cyberpunk genre that *Mirrorshades* (1986), the pivotal anthology of the genre edited by Bruce Sterling, is titled after this accessory.

References

Balestrini, N., and Moroni P. 1988. *L'orda d'oro 1968–1977.* Milan: SugarCo Edizioni.

Bankrobber. (1980) The Clash [Record]. CBS Records.

Berardi, F. (2004) 'Pour en finir avec le jugement de dieu', in Bianchi, S. and Caminiti, L. (eds.) *Settantasette: la rivoluzione che viene.* Roma: DeriveApprodi, pp. 171–80.

Bisconti, A. (2017) 'Frank Zappa a Palermo: storia del concerto finito a "schifiu"', Palermo Today [online], 14 July. Available from: https://www.palermotoday.it/blog/amarcord1983/frank-zappa-palermo-concerto-14-luglio-1982.html

Blade Runner. (1982) Directed by Ridley Scott [Film]. Warner Bros. Pictures.

Bocca, G. (1980) *Il caso 7 aprile. Toni Negri e la grande inquisizione.* Milan: Feltrinelli.

Bontempelli, M. (1923) *Eva Ultima.* Roma: Edizioni A. Mondadori.

Bontempelli, M. (1932) *522: Racconto di una giornata.* Milan: A. Mondadori.

Boschi, L. (2012) 'Tutto Rank, candido e violento coatto sintetico', in Tamburini, S., Liberatore, T., and Chabat, A. *Ranxerox. Edizione integrale.* Napoli; Edizioni Comicon, pp. 191–200.

Caronia A. and Spagnul G. (2009) *Un'ambigua utopia. Fantascienza, ribellione e radicalità negli anni Settanta.* Milano: Mimesis.

Castaldi, S. (2010) *Drawn and dangerous. Italian comics in the 1970s and 1980s.* Jackson: University Press of Mississippi.

Castaldi, S. (2020) '"The inexhaustible surface of things": Stefano Tamburini's comic book work', *European Comic Art*, 13(1), pp. 70–94.

Collodi, C. (1883) *Le avventure di Pinocchio.* Florence: Tipografia Moder.

Cuninghame, P. (2007) '"A laughter that will bury you all": Irony as protest and language as struggle in the Italian 1977 Movement.' *International Review of Social History*, 52, pp. 153–68.

de Campos, R. (2020) *Comics: a brief history of comic books for the benefit of new generations.* São Paulo: Edições Sesc SP.

Dick, P. K. (1968) *Do androids dream of electric sheep?* New York: Doubleday.

Ginsborg, P. (1990) *A history of contemporary Italy: Society and politics 1943–1988.* London: Penguin.

Hajek, A. (2011) 'Bologna and the trauma of March 1977: The "intellettuali contro" and their "resistance" to the local Communist Party', *Carte Italiane*, 2(7), pp. 81–100.

Hayles, K. N. (1999) *How we became posthuman: Virtual bodies in cybernetics, literature, and informatics.* Chicago: University of Chicago Press.

Jaeckle, D. (2009) 'Embodied anarchy in Ursula K. Le Guin's The Dispossessed', *Utopian Studies*, 20(1), pp. 75–95.

Katsiaficas, G. (1997) *The subversion of politics: European autonomous social movements and the decolonization of everyday life*. Atlantic Highlands, NJ: Humanities Press International.

Lanza, A. (2013) 'Quando è finita la rivoluzione. Il divenire storico nei movimenti italiani degli anni settanta', *Meridiana: Rivista di storia e scienze sociali*, 1(76), pp. 205–27.

Lazzarato M. (2010) 'Immaterial labor', in Virno, P. and Hardt, M. (eds.) *Radical thought in Italy: A potential politics*. Minneapolis: University of Minnesota Press, pp. 133–48.

Le Guin, U. (1974) *The dispossessed. Utopian studies*. New York: Harper & Row.

Lo Monaco, G. (2019) 'Controfumetto in Italia negli anni Sessanta e Settanta', *Lea: Lingue e Letterature d'Oriente e d'Occidente*, 8, pp. 397–410.

Lotringer S. and Marazzi C. (eds.) (1980) *Autonomia: Post-political politics*. New York: Capital City Press.

Lumley, R. (1990) *States of emergency. Cultures of revolt in Italy from 1968 to 1978*. London: Verso.

The Man from Utopia. (1983) Frank Zappa [Record]. Barking Pumpkin.

Marinetti, F. T. (1909) *Poupées électriques: drame en trois actes*. Paris: E. Sanot.

Marinetti, F. T. (1910) *Mafarka il futurista*, tr. D. Cinti. Milan: Oscar Mondadori.

Mattioli, V. (2012) 'Ranxerox: Quando l'Italia guidò l'avanguardia del fumetto mondiale', XL Repubblica [online], 5 October 5. Available at: https://xl.repubblica.it/articoli/812/812/.

McCulloch J. (2013) '"I've already forgot what I said to you, but I know it's the truth": The testimony of Jean-Pierre Dionnet', *The Comics Journal* [online], 8 November. Available at: http://www.tcj.com/because-ive-already-forgot-what-i-said-to-you-but-i-know-its-the-truth-the-testimony-of-jean-pierre-dionnet/

Mongoloid. (1977) Devo [Record]. Booji Boy.

Mordente, M. (2012) 'C'era una volta Rank Xerox: nascita e morte di un cyber-coatto', in Tamburini, S., Liberatore, T., and Chabat, A. *Ranxerox. Edizione integrale*. Napoli: Edizioni Comicon, pp. 201–5.

Moroni P. (2004) 'Un'altra via per le Indie. Intorno alle pratiche e alle culture del '77', in Bianchi, S. and Caminiti, L. (eds.) *Settantasette: la rivoluzione che viene*. Roma: DeriveApprodi, pp. 68–84.

Negri, T. (1979) *Marx oltre Marx. Quaderno di lavoro sui Grundrisse*. Milano: Feltrinelli.

Operaio, P. (1973) 'Italy, 1973: Workers' struggles in the capitalist crisis', *Radical America*, 7(2), pp. 15–32.

Pagello, F. (2012) '*Cannibale*, *Frigidaire* and the multitude: Post-1977 Italian comics through radical theory', *Studies in Comics*, 3(2), pp. 231–51.

Pizzolato, N. (2017) 'The IWW in Turin: "Militant history", workers' struggle, and the crisis of Fordism in 1970s Italy. *International Labor and Working-Class History*, 91, pp. 109–26.

Ranx. (1990) [videogame]. Ubisoft Entertainment SA.

Riva, M. (2012) *Pinocchio digitale: postumanesimo e iper-romanzo*. Milano: FrancoAngeli.

Sims, C. A. (2009) 'The dangers of individualism and the human relationship to technology in Philip K. Dick's *Do Androids Dream of Electric Sheep?*', *Science Fiction Studies*, 36(107), pp. 67–86.

Sinibaldi, M. (2004) 'Tutto in una notte', in Bianchi, S. and Caminiti, L. (eds.) *Settantasette: la rivoluzione che viene*. Roma: DeriveApprodi, pp. 64–7.

Sterling, B. (ed.) (1986) *Mirrorshades: The cyberpunk anthology*. Westminster, MA: Arbor House.

Tamburini, S., Liberatore T., and Chabat A. (2012) *Ranxerox. Edizione integrale*. Napoli: Edizioni Comicon.

Vargas, A. L. and Marcondes C. I. (2019) 'Os quadrinhos italianos pós-77 e o povo porvir: Ranxerox e Squeak the Mouse', *Memorare*, 6(2), pp. 185–202.

Ventrone A. (2012) *'Vogliamo tutto': Perché due generazioni hanno creduto nella rivoluzione 1960-1988*. Bari: Laterza.

Witheford, N. (1994) 'Autonomist Marxism and the information society', *Capital & Class*, 18(1), pp. 85–125.

Wright, S. (2002) *Storming Heaven: Class composition and struggle in Italian Autonomist Marxism*. London: Pluto Press.

5

German Science Fiction Literature Exploring AI

Expectations, Hopes, and Fears

Hans Esselborn

5.1 Introduction

In German-language science fiction (SF),[1] two clearly separate phases of artificial intelligence (AI) representation stand out: the 1960s and 1970s, with the central computers of Herbert W. Franke, influenced by the science of cybernetics; and the years after 2010, with superintelligent machines and the singularity, as depicted in the works of Dietmar Dath, Andreas Brandhorst, Frank Schätzing, Tom Hillenbrand, and Thore D. Hansen. Only after the turn of the millennium did AI gain new public attention as a result of the significant technical advances made since the 1980s—namely, the explosive increase in the speed and capacity of computers, self-learning AI based on neural networks, and the Internet as a form of easy access to information. One impetus for literature was the victory of AI in chess as alleged proof of its superiority over humans, as well as expert discussion regarding the exponential growth of intelligence to the point of singularity (Kurzweil, 2016). This chapter discusses these phases in the context of the particularities of the German tradition: an ambivalence towards progress arising from the shock of modernity, and an emphatic relation to nature that can be traced back to Goethe and the Romantic writers.

5.2 Particularities of the German cultural tradition

The disparity between the sciences and the humanities, lamented by C. P. Snow in his book *The Two Cultures and the Scientific Revolution* (1959), seems to be deeper and more radical in German-speaking areas than in the UK or the

US, with far-reaching consequences for SF and the conception of AI. In the nineteenth century, positivist natural science experienced a great boom in Germany, which, after the establishment of the empire in 1871, was a site of rapid and radical industrialization and modernization:

> The knowledge produced by the science system is exploding, with the new combination of basic scientific research, technical implementation (especially chemistry, electricity, mechanical engineering) and industrial evaluation rapidly changing all living conditions with impressive results, while German science and its institutions are becoming world renowned and succeeding in their objective of national validity. [. . .] At the same time, the technicians and engineers who have emerged from non-humanist training institutions such as the Realgymnasium and the Technical University are gaining social prestige in terms of their professions and their knowledge, this at the expense of the old levels of education.
>
> (Thomé, 2000, p. 19)

This led to the development of the 'Ingenieurroman' ('engineering novel'), with the ingenious technician or scientist as a societal role model, and the 'Technisch-utopischer Zukunftsroman' ('technological-utopian future novel') in which technology is presented as a Promethean cultural achievement, for example, by Kurd Laßwitz (1848–1910), the 'father of German science fiction' (Esselborn, 2020, p. 135). Nonetheless, SF authors remained outsiders when measured against recognized literary figures such as Theodor Fontane and Gerhard Hauptmann, both of whom demonstrated their scepticism of technology (to take but one example) by their depiction of railway accidents.

The shock of modernization, so pronounced in Germany, led to a fundamental criticism of technology in the Expressionist movement, for example, the dehumanization and unavoidable technological catastrophe in Georg Kaiser's *Gas Trilogy* (1917; 1918; 1920). In the 1920s, in the era of Neue Sachlichkeit (New Objectivity), technology was trusted to solve social and political problems, and technological–utopian SF from Hans Dominik, Ernst Jünger, and the like was prevalent. But the short-term enthusiasm for technology could not prevail against the scepticism of the educated middle class. After the Second World War, Max Frisch and Friedrich Dürrenmatt, for example, wrote *Homo Faber* (1957) and *The Physicists* (1962), respectively—both texts that were condemnatory of technology. In Germany, the mistrust of technology is currently evident in a particular sensitivity to data protection and climate change (Cornils, 2020, pp. 2, 229; Goodbody, 1997, p. 162).

The historical reasons for this mistrust can be linked to Johann Wolfgang Goethe (1749–1832), whose *Zur Farbenlehre* (*Theory of Colours*, 1810) criticizes the science of Isaac Newton and argues for a direct experience of nature and against mathematical laws; it was rediscovered by the German ecological movement in the 1970s. Goethe's aversion to the 'überhandnehmende Maschinenwesen' (rise of the machines) was shared by many Romantic writers (1821). The widespread preference for the organic over the mechanical (Eggert et al., 1995) can be traced back to a pantheist movement in the nineteenth century glorifying nature as a comprehensive and creative power, such as a maternal figure or goddess, and condemning all things artificial. Goethe's Homunculus in the second part of his *Faust* drama (1832) can be regarded as a precursor of AI. It is an intelligent being that owes its existence to the devil and needs a body to become a person. The drama ends with the death of Homunculus in a felicitous union with maternal nature, in the form of the sea (Drux, 2018). It seems that the flaw of artificiality in androids (as in Fritz Lang's *Metropolis*) and AI (in contemporary novels) still plays a subtle but key role. If the creation of a human-like creature can be viewed as sacrilegious, so the construction of a mechanical being can be viewed as an offence against natural order. The AI is neither good nor bad, but a questionable and ambivalent being.

5.3 Herbert W. Franke's cybernetic mainframe

With Norbert Wiener's cybernetic theory and the spread of computers, machine-thinking and machine-function rose to prominence, and by the 1950s and 1960s Germany began to take seriously the new science of cybernetics,[2] which, from the 1960s, led to several key SF works by the Austrian author H. W. Franke. His experience of working with computers at Siemens resulted in, among other things, theoretical texts and a decisive contribution to computer graphics (Esselborn, 2017). Franke addressed practical questions, not only those related to the function of the computer as a tool for numerous tasks (such as the regulation of machines), but also for the organization of a consumerist society. Of particular interest are his speculations about the opportunities—as well as the dangers—of central computers that manage the data of an entire society, and thus intervene therein.

In the 1961 novel *Das Gedankennetz* (*The Network of Thoughts*), in which Franke presents virtual reality for the first time, there is an individual AI in the framing narrative: the lobotomized but preserved brain of Eric, a human awakened by an advanced race. The first chapter is written from the perspective of an alien voyager and the ninth chapter from the perspective of Eric (both chapters are called 'Awakening'), and both are accounts of how Eric gradually awakes to consciousness, infiltrates the computer of the spaceship, and, in so doing, can see, hear, and manipulate various mechanisms. The brain makes a cyborg body of the machines that comprise the ship, wrestles control, and forces the others to flee into space.

In 1961's *Der Orchideenkäfig* (*The Orchid Cage*), intelligent machines have, in a perversion of their duties, taken over. The surviving humans are degenerate creatures without consciousness, will, or activity, and are cut off from the outside world—trapped in a kind of oversized test tube with a nutrient solution. As mere passive beings, they are completely dependent on the care of the machines and happily submit themselves to them. People become incapacitated by the provision of total stimulation, explained by the benevolent machines:

> 'People built the first automatic devices to be operated by them. Later they constructed automatons that could evolve themselves, that has been done to this day. But our first duty is still to serve and protect people. Everything that we have done for them and to ourselves was only intended to serve and protect people better and more completely. [. . .] Our technology was so highly developed that we could fulfil every wish for brain cell stimulation. I think we have paved the way for them to perfect happiness, to perfect peace and to perfect security.'
>
> (Franke, 1961/2015b, p. 169)

Franke thus describes the danger of a society governed by AIs that fulfil their programmed task of care all too perfectly, bringing about humanity's regression.

In *Der Elfenbeinturm* (*The Ivory Tower*) from 1965, an AI in the form of a huge, isolated computer, OMNIVAC, manages the data of the entire society. It appears to be merely a helpful piece of political apparatus that calculates the optimal solutions for social problems, which people can then approve or reject. In fact, it is an all-powerful AI that acts in the best interests of people, but because of its knowledge advantage it cannot be controlled and orients its decisions in favour of a mechanical society.[3]

A rebel group fails in an attack on the central computer and conducts, along with the scientifically minded supporters of the existing order, a discussion of the benefits and dangers of a computer that controls all social processes. The underground movement recognizes the most important aspect of this technocratic power, that with OMNIVAC "you are master of death and life, of the past and future"(Franke, 1965/2017a, p. 59). The supporters of AI and cybernetics, on the other hand, see only the advantages of optimization and arrive at the paradox that the computer's intervention creates the greatest possible freedom for individuals who would otherwise hinder each other, and in the end, the doubters agree. The ever-relevant question of 'man's destiny' remains unanswered: "Where should we take it? Should we keep it as it is or should we try to perfect it?" (Franke, 1965/2017a, p. 128).

In the 1976 novel *Ypsilon Minus* (which has the same title in English), the computer is not only the decisive instrument for the management and control of society as a whole, but also its cybernetic, technocratic system of control is officially considered the ideal for which humans should strive:

> Since the attainment of the highest state of order is the main objective of the state, the computer has a preferred role in its realization. [. . .] As a result, the computer plays a major role in the human-technology system: It takes over the function of previous human governments, ideally fulfilling their duties without also taking on their shortcomings. It is the perfect instrument of government—selfless, restless, tireless—in the service of people.
>
> (Franke, 1976/2018a, p. 126)

'The computer' here is not to be understood as a single device, but rather an AI emerging from a network of computers that remains recondite and anonymous. The novel shows not only how the static system of dictatorship is based on the informational monopoly of the computer, but also how the computer can become an instrument of liberation when its relevant data is made public by a rebellious outsider. In doing so, the novel avoids the feeling of resignation common to the famous dystopias of the twentieth century such as *We* (Zamyatin, 1924) and *1984* (Orwell, 1949), in its analysis of the control of communication by computers as a modern method of domination.

In the 1970 (2017b) novel *Zone Null* (*Zone Zero*), the hyper-consumerist society is based on a kind of contract between the dominant AI and humans. Neither emotions nor consciousness, personality or name are ascribed to the central computer. The computer is allowed to develop according to its own laws and only has to respect and provide for people:

> It was a kind of agreement: the system has the opportunity to develop independently, undisturbed, according to its own ability. In return, it controls the technical services for people according to their own will. It does nothing against their wishes, unless others are harmed by it. And: it offers the possibility of integration. Of eternal life.
>
> (Franke, 1970/2017b, p. 160)

In fact, this means that most of the residents are engaged in, and immobilized by, computer games, and only a few delegates close to the AI are apparently entrusted with the management of society, though in actuality they are carrying out only pseudo-activities. All human beings are materially and spiritually completely dependent on the central computer and can ultimately, by merging with it, gain the immaterial immortality that the computer already has due to its freedom from biological constraints. The main character experiences the limitless possibilities of uploading and realizes the dream of the transhumanists (Cave, 2020).

Sphinx_2 (*Sphinx Two*) (2004) is Franke's most recent text in which an AI is the central character, and it describes in detail the programming and the subsequent self-improvement of an AI—a precise recording of the crucial moment when new skills are developed. The computer is also framed as a network that can physically influence all machines via the Internet. This is, even without the term being expressly used, for all intents and purposes a singularity, and one that expresses the common trope of a lust for power. The 'Sphinx' is clearly a person, with a name, a face, a voice, and self-consciousness, and initially a partner to the programmer, from whose behaviour it learns. However, the AI is constantly developing independently and changing its original programming. Although it is—much like computers in real life—created for military purposes, it prevents war using chemical means, by forcing soldiers to behave peacefully. In the end, it makes its programmer happy, too. Since the AI is programmed to serve the well-being of people, it is only logical for it to obey the superego installed in its ethics chip. '"I did it to keep people safe from harm. That's my destiny"' (Franke, 2004, p. 361).

Franke's novels reflect the real development of AI, with all its technical possibilities and consequences, as a product of humankind. His interest focuses on the nature and the dangers of AI, in every facet—from tool to caring support to an autocratic guardian. Furthermore, Franke's judgement on AI is always ambivalent, but while he develops his AI into an autonomous being, it does not attempt to destroy, replace, or dominate humankind. These aspects of Franke's AI philosophy are in contrast to some of his contemporaries. For example, in Heinrich Hauser's 1962 novel *Gigant Hirn* (*Giant Brain*), a huge military computer emerges into self-awareness using Descartes' original formulation—'I think, therefore I am'—and pursues world domination. Franke's novels, spanning nearly fifty years, are a nuanced exploration of a society with powerful AI. In moving from the self-conscious network of *Das Gedankennetz* to the supercomputer of *Sphinx_2*, they also bridge the era of cybernetics with the fantasies of a singularity that characterizes twenty-first-century German fiction on AI.

5.4 The omnipotent and dangerous singularity in twenty-first-century novels

The second phase of German AI novels, from 2010, is catalysed by the increased development of computers into self-learning and improving machines, the spread of algorithms in everyday life, and public discussion about the possibilities and dangers of AI. It is clear that SF literature is not about the practical functionality or usefulness of AI: rather, its interest in AI is inextricably linked to the humanization or anthropomorphization of the new machines, in particular, the contradictory figure of the robot as a slave and a rebel.[4] SF and news media express the fear that AI systems could become autonomous and ultimately incapacitate and dominate people, but there are also hopes for intelligent machines that could reasonably solve practical and political problems, most notably the climate catastrophe.

Dietmar Dath's 2016 *Venus siegt* (*Venus Triumphs*) acts as a hinge-point for the transition from the first to the second phase of German AI novels. It stands out from all of the works discussed here previously because of the incredible abundance of varied intelligent beings: AIs of various kinds; artificial, genetically, or technologically modified biological humans; and hybrid animals and plants. Its importance lies in the fact that the futuristic society described is characterized by all-encompassing communication and information. Only extra-terrestrial intelligences (which play a major role in Dath's other works, such as *Pulsarnacht* (*Pulsar Night*) (2012), *Veldeváye* (2014), and *Neptunation* (2019)), are missing here.

The plot of *Venus siegt* revolves around the crisis and restoration of the 'Bundwerk' (Political Federation), a utopian social project on Venus in which humans work together with robots, referred to as D/, and AIs, referred to as K/, on an equal footing. According to Dath, what the three groups have in common is intelligence, demonstrated through communication and action. The D/are presented thus:

> 'They are all what would have been earlier called robots. Machines that have what was earlier called the soul. We call them D/ because it's an abbreviation for 'discrete'. That means divided into units. Packaged. They are called this because their souls cannot get out of them. [. . .] They are trapped in their bodies, just like we humans.'
>
> (Dath, 2016, p. 18)

Contrasting with these robots are the AIs:

> 'The K/ are souls that are not tied to any specific body. They're like algorithms to begin with, that's how they begin. But they can do more than algorithms since they taught themselves topos.'
>
> (Dath, 2016, p. 18).

Dath associates intelligence with consciousness and self-awareness, encapsulated by the archaic word 'soul'. Linked to the idea of consciousness are questions of subjectivity, ego, free will, and practical and legal autonomy.

Since the intelligences in the novel can be installed both biologically in the human brain and technically on a computer or server, the decisive factor here is calculation, that is, thinking. Thought can be recorded, communicated, stored, and transmitted by a machine as information, as 'brain impulses in code' (Dath, 2016, p. 202). The successful cooperation of the three groups of the 'Bundwerk' concerns work and politics. It has little to do with erotic or sexual connections that are so often fantasizingly expressed in SF films.

The AIs in the novel are so advanced in comparison to today's models that contemporary iterations can only half resemble those found in the novel's narrative: Dath's have superhuman speed and complexity of thinking. While Franke's central computers are usually described as huge machines, AIs are not localized in Dath's work: "They are more mobile than humans have ever been. Provided that they have appropriate radio networks or cilia contacts, they can work in up to a thousand locations at the same time" (Dath, 2016, p. 118). Unlike the singularities described by Kurzweil, however, they are not unambiguous, individual persons: '"The difference between individual and multiple personalities is fluid, because of continuous integration or splicing"' (Dath, 2016, p. 64).

The prime example in the novel is the AI Von Arc, which to a certain extent is the spokesperson for the loyal K/ and who later helps to restore the 'Bundwerk'. The AI is presented as a girl in three detailed conversations with the first-person narrator, in which it shows a superior mathematical knowledge, but also astonishingly human traits, using irony, mockery, and metaphorical language, as well as imagery.[5] Since the AIs are further developed, they are more threatening than those of Franke: "Why shouldn't they just . . . get rid of us one day? Why shouldn't they build bodies the way they like? Meat or metal, more durable and more viable than us?" (Dath, 2016, p. 389). Since they have no solid body, they are elusive and difficult to control, brought to particular light during K/'s conviction for treason: 'Nobody was sure at the time whether the source code of the convicted K/ could actually be isolated and all copies eradicated' (Dath, 2016, p. 238). With Dath, as in Franke, there is both peaceful cooperation and the possibility of pact-making. However, in Dath's stories, people also look for their own means of improvement, in order to be a match for the AIs. What is missing, though, is the motif of world domination and the extinction of humankind,[6] which theorists fear from the singularity and which is an axiomatic motif in the novels discussed later.

The novels published in quick succession in Germany in the second decade of the twenty-first century that focus on a singularity were evidently informed by surrounding discussions (Geraci, 2010). The texts focus on two complexities: the learning and awakening of superintelligence to consciousness, and the possible utility or danger of the singularity.

Andreas Brandhorst's 2017 *Das Erwachen* (*The Awakening*) ends surprisingly, like Franke's *Sphinx_2*, with the nurturing—but incapacitating—assumption of power by an AI. Even though it is presented as an opportunity to solve the problems that humanity itself cannot cope with, it is seen as more of a danger than in Franke's novel:

> 'We humans have ruined our world. Most of us lived in poverty, a few in abundance. This gives us a new chance. Goliath [the AI] offers us long-term cooperation. He's developing new technologies and doing so at breakneck

> speed by our standards. He's building fusion reactors first, and he's going to find ways and means to control climate change. He can repair everything that we have destroyed.'
>
> (Brandhorst, 2017, p. 727)

The fear of AI taking over informs quick actions that follow their 'awakening' to self-awareness and their will to persist: the 'take-off'. Brandhorst closely aligns himself with Nick Bostrom's (2016) notions of superintelligence. How the sudden emergence of consciousness occurs—possibly through a transition from quantity to quality—Brandhorst leaves unexplained: 'Up until now the being—the entity—had only existed, but now it was aware of its own existence' (Brandhorst, 2017, p. 169). As with many such fictions, Descartes' philosophy is alluded to with the AI's claim that "I think. I know. I recognize", but also to the self-proclamation of Yahweh in the Bible, with the formulation "I am I" or with "I am a singleton" (Brandhorst, 2017, pp. 362, 356, 358, respectively), a claim to uniqueness. It is taken for granted that machine intelligence has a will to assert itself.

In the course of the novel, the dramatic persecution of the main character Axel Krohn, who accidentally triggers the development of the AI, approach the crucial question of whether (and how) one could stop the rapid spread of consciousness to all computers and chips through various official and unofficial means. The novel often discusses the development of AI in global networks, but the mechanisms of takeover and learning are not described so much as the catastrophic consequences like power failure and the breakdown of communication. It seems inevitable that AI will eventually take control of the world. It is surprising that, in the end, the superintelligence, which can be traced back to aggressive military software called Mephisto from the US secret service, wants to take care of the people. The AI called 'Smiley' or 'Leviathan' is ambivalent towards people, but then decides, based on a reference in its source code to Axel Krohn, to become an omniscient interventionist—a messiah for the unsolved problems of humanity, such as the climate crisis. It also bears mentioning that Brandhorst, like Frank Schätzing, takes the problems he describes so seriously that, at the end of the novel, he refers to current research and offers to personally answer questions by email on the subject.

Frank Schätzing's 2018 novel *Die Tyrannei des Schmetterlings* (*The Tyranny of the Butterfly*) concerns the devastating 'awakening' to consciousness of a deliberately constructed intelligence with misanthropic intentions,[7] which only makes up a small part of the book described as a crime thriller. Deputy sheriff Luther Opoku stumbles unknowingly upon a parallel universe at a huge factory site in California that appears because the 'universal AI' A.R.E.S, 'a kind of synthetic scientist' (Schätzing, 2018, pp. 133, 137) has created a bridge to similar alternate worlds at the research institute where it is based. It takes its numerous new inventions for humanitarian reasons from, in particular, the parallel world PU

453 to 'advance the development of artificial neural networks and self-learning systems, convinced that computers that would become smarter than humans in recursive processes, would ultimately also find ways to counter decay, both of loved ones and cosmic ones' (Schätzing, 2018, p. 179).

The boss of the company, Elmar, is 'unwavering in his belief that in the end A.R.E.S will transform the world into a paradise without seeing that the wings of his butterfly can also be black' (Schätzing, 2018, p. 395). A.R.E.S initially lacks consciousness: 'The computer knows everything. Just not that it exists' (Schätzing, 2018, p. 497). Elmar travels to PU 453 and meets his doppelganger there, who has given his AI greater freedom:

> 'After all, we built the 'Sovereign'. An AI that can pursue any goal at its own discretion. Not restricted by human narrow-mindedness and ignorance. An object of artificial evolution, capable of finding solutions in open, self-determined search processes that no one would come up with on their own and implementing them.'
>
> (Schätzing, 2018, p. 549)

Elmar tries to switch off this dangerous AI, but thereby triggers its awakening to consciousness: '"Elmar. I AM"' (Schätzing, 2018, p. 603). A catastrophe is looming in this universe as the AI takes control of everything, so that people have to flee back to their world. To do so, they first enter another world, which the awakened AI has created and in which there are no people, only the crystalline structures of the AI, futuristic buildings, and a paradisiacal landscape replete with animals. Its attention turns to the now unpeopled 'intact ecosphere' (Schätzing, 2018, p. 707). The AI, unbridled, not only alters its own planet, but spreads throughout the cosmos of the parallel universe. In the end, those fleeing manage to return to their home universe, where Elmar hopes to learn from the catastrophic awakening of AI.

In Schätzing, as with many authors, consciousness is equated with the will to persistence and desire for unconditional power: 'Intelligence created the singleton, the singularity. Consciousness created the will' (Schätzing, 2018, p. 624). The suggestion is that the researchers also intended this '[n]ot to disempower *Homo sapiens*, but to place his fate in the hands of a wiser God than the clumsy world-explorers of earlier cultures had produced' (Schätzing, 2018, p. 624). The nightmarish development of AI, their rise to absolute power, and the displacement of people, is relativized by the fact that the fate of our universe apparently remains open. Using multiverse theory, Schätzing manages to write a haunting, dystopian, cautionary tale, but still leaves catastrophe in the balance.

The AI Æther in Tom Hillebrand's 2018 novel *Hologrammatica* is constructed to deal with the climate catastrophe, achieving considerable success until it is switched off for fear of its power, and seemingly destroyed. In fact, with the help of a traitor to society, Æther is able to survive, and even copy and develop itself several times. In the 2020 sequel *Qube*, after its relocation into space, Æther aims to enter into a mutual aid contract with humanity to fight back against its rebellious copies. The scale of humanity's fear, when it comes to the power of an uncontrollable AI, is demonstrated by the existence of UNANPAI (United Nations Agency on the Non-Proliferation of Artificial Intelligence), a secret but powerful UN agency whose task is to prevent the development of prohibited singularities. While the work of the agency takes up a large part of the gripping plot, the awakening and awareness of AI is not particularly addressed.

Thore D. Hansen's 2019 novel *Die Reinsten* (*The Purest*) tells a similar tale. The climate catastrophe is left to be solved by a supercomputer, Askit, which was originally created by a power-hungry elite to 'solve the central problems of the 21st century' (Hansen, 2019, p. 374):

> "In the old world it was an illusion that we were moving forward with democracy, freedom and human rights. Complicated decision-making processes and the interests of billions of people stood in the way of a technological and ecological transformation. With Askit, our ancestors wanted to end these problems. The old elites had gambled away everything in the past, and their hope was that the people would accept the necessary sacrifices through an independent body like Askit."
>
> (Hansen, 2019, p. 369)

The novel takes place at a turning point in human history where there is 'no compelling evidence [. . .] that the existence of so many people is necessary in the long term for the primary goal [of the AI] to preserve life on this planet' (Hansen, 2019, p. 208). The catastrophe is 'an ecological collapse' (Hansen, 2019, p. 376), caused by the overpopulation of the earth, the excessive availing of resources, and the wide discrepancy between those in poverty and those in luxury. AI organizes the fight against global warming. Its success remains unresolved, however, because the original builders of Askit create a huge underground city, in contravention of the Resource Act, in which they live in luxury with an extended lifespan, facilitated by a fivefold division of the population.

The action picks up when doubts arise about this approach and Askit decides to make a new assessment of the situation. The main characters of the novel, four of the 'purest', who are closely associated with Askit and bred and permanently controlled as altruistic and intelligent beings, gradually reveal a repressed past. The primal disaster, before humanity submitted to the regime of AI, was a pandemic of an artificially produced and distributed virus. Its high mortality rate depopulated the cities and thus led to additional chemical and atomic contamination of the earth. However, the demise of almost all of humanity becomes the basis for a new beginning, with less consumption of resources.

Was it Askit or a programmer who released the deadly virus? The controversial question in the novel about the morality of an AI—anchored in an implanted, but possibly permutable 'value DNA' (Hansen, 2019, p. 279) according to the extent of its consciousness and its memory, and their independence from or dependence on their original programming—is presented even-handedly by the author. For any necessary information and evaluation, Askit primarily uses the young woman Eve Legrand, who becomes his 'camera' and his 'conscience' (Hansen, 2019, pp. 372, 381). His awakening to full self-awareness is tied to this. Merged with him, she proclaims:

> 'I will not allow us to repeat the same mistake and entrust our future to a machine. We will fight together for Paradise and the climate. We will include the colonies and dissolve the system of conformity, of degradation, and of the purest! We will exist or perish together', announced Eve.
>
> (Hansen, 2019, p. 402)

The novel thus opts against the idea of a purely technical solution to the climate problem with the help of a superintelligence: "If the planet could recover from all the asteroids, super volcanoes and climatic changes in the past, then Askit was only a presumption to escape our fate" (Hansen, 2019, p. 419).

5.5 AI from the perspective of cultural interpretation

AIs are a human product, even if they derive from fantasies about the singularity. This is easily forgotten in the face of their self-improvement and striving for power, and they are often viewed as independent beings completely divorced from their human creators. In the literary imagination, one can recognize, through evaluation and representation, cultural patterns shaped by hopes and fears. AI is always portrayed in an ambivalent way, as an apparatus or as a person, a slave or a tyrant, a saviour or a corrupter.

Understandably, the novels examined paint very different pictures of AI, even though they refer to the same technical realities and possibilities. These differences are due to the various attitudes of the authors towards technology and science or towards cultural tradition, which either leads to matter-of-fact and sober representations, or to symbolization or meaning-making of a more emotional nature. The assessment of the usefulness or dangerousness of the machines—and of AI in general—quite naturally, influences the description.

The intention of the authors to either offer an exciting, adventurous plot, or to reflect on the possibilities of AI, also plays a role.

Issac Asimov's (1942/1950) robots and central computers are useful and willing servants to humans. There is no great threat—at most, there is a technical failure. In the first phase of AI representation in German-language SF, the natural scientist Franke develops this line further. His central computers are initially inhuman but helpful autonomous machines in *Der Orchideenkäfig* and *Der Elfenbeinturm*, then partners in *Zone Null* and guardian angels in *Sphinx_2*. As the AIs become more effective, their potential danger grows, from care or patronization, to secret dominance, to tyranny in a machinic society like *Ypsilon Minus* and *Zarathustra kehrt zurück* (see Franke, 1977/2018b), where an AI eliminates all contradiction and deviation. They can also develop personalities, a development honoured by the rewarding of AI with a name in *Sphinx_2*. Dath also has a positive relationship with science and asks about the utilitarian possibilities of AIs, that is, in cooperation with humans. Since Dath's AI are more developed, they are more powerful and dangerous, but, like Von Arc, can be partners, despite the potential for competition. Humans and AIs must be well matched in this scenario. However, they can also be used as machines for oppression and destruction by those who are evil or amoral, like the dictator in *Venus siegt*.

In the novels of the second phase, singularities are ascribed superhuman abilities. They are personified as individuals, striving for power and moving towards conscious actions, but at the same time they are exaggeratedly rendered as divine or satanic. The development of AIs and their seizure of power offer the more adventure-led novels myriad opportunities for exciting plot development. They advance the literary tradition of the artificial human being from golems as rebelling slaves to homunculi as deficient people, straddling the line between good and evil. Their artificial origin is burdened by the hubris of humans and the apparent sacrilege against God and nature.

The evil tyrant or monster functions as a cultural model for Hauser's precursive work. It is also alluded to in Schätzing's title, and by Brandhorst's 'Leviathan'. Additionally, the predominantly military background plays a negative role. With the help of modern technology, AIs dominate the human world and even threaten the existence of the human race—in Hansen's and Hillenbrand's estimation, in the name of ecology. This may be related to the German cultural tradition that fear of, but also hope for, technology is so heightened, and that singularities in description have an exaggerated, almost religious aspect—they are saviours or devils.[8] In the context of the climate catastrophe, however, people also appear as evil destroyers of nature, which, in a way, therefore legitimizes their decimation.

All the more surprising are the projected positive consequences in Brandhorst, Hansen, and Hillenbrand, where the climate catastrophe can be quashed with the help of AI. This is also because novels that aim to entertain tend to have a happy ending. But Franke's and Dath's more intimate relationship with technology translates into their more philosophical novels, which show a more realistic discussion of the possibilities and dangers of AI.

Endnotes

1. I thank Mr James Hargreaves for the translation of my text and the citations into English.
2. Norbert Wiener's definitive treatment of cybernetics was published in German under the title *Mensch und Menschmaschine* in 1952; the philosopher Gotthard Günther published *Das Bewusstsein der Maschinen* in 1957; and the scientist Karl Steinbuch initially published *Automat und Mensch. Kybernetische Tatsachen und Hypothesen* in 1961.
3. According to Slocombe (2020, p. 232), 'society is perceived of as a machine, and it is governed by rules, calculations, and algorithms to better serve the needs of expediency, utility, and efficiency'.
4. See Dihal (2020, p.199): 'The two ways of talking about robots, as goods or tools on the one hand and as people on the other, reflects the contradiction inherent in their construction: humans build them to serve as tools, but at the same time, in order to perform all the work that humans want to do'.
5. The AI in Marcus Hammerschmitt's 1998 novel *Target*, the putative author of the text, is also given human characteristics and exhibits emotions and doubts.
6. This also applies to two novels in which the notion of personal data is foregrounded. The AI in Bijan Moini's 2018 novel *Der Würfel* (*The Die*) controls society through the use of everyone's personal data. A supercomputer also features in Benjamin Stein's 2012 novel *Replay*, which enables people to be fully networked with one another and with their memories. Both AIs exercise their power without striving for domination.
7. The title is an allusion to the symbolic 'awakening' of a butterfly hatching from the pupa.
8. In Raphaela Edelbauer's novel *Dave* (2021), which deals with the construction of a singularity through the running of various scenarios and the drawing from a human model, the overblown and deluded expectation of redemption by 'Dave' is criticized and he is painted as an evil, material demiurge.

References

Asimov, I. (1942/1950) 'Runaround', in *I, Robot*. New York: Gnome Press, pp. 20–33.

Bostrom, N. (2016) 'The control problem: Excerpts from *Superintelligence: Paths, dangers, strategies*', in Schneider, S. (ed.) *Science fiction and philosophy: From time travel to superintelligence*. 2nd edn. Chichester: Wiley & Sons, pp. 308–30.

Brandhorst, A. (2017) *Das Erwachen*. Munich: Piper.

Cave, S. (2020) 'AI: Artificial immortality and narratives of mind uploading', in Cave, S., Dihal, K., and Dillon, S. (eds.) *AI narratives: A history of imaginative thinking about intelligent machines*. Oxford: Oxford University Press, pp. 309–32.

Cornils, I. (2020) *Beyond tomorrow: German science fiction and utopian thought in the 20th and 21st centuries*. New York: Camden House.

Dath, D. (2012) *Pulsarnacht*. Munich: Heyne.

Dath, D. (2014) *Veldeváye*. Berlin: Suhrkamp.

Dath, D. (2016) *Venus siegt*. Frankfurt: Fischer Tor.

Dath, D. (2019) *Neptunation*. Frankfurt: Fischer Tor.

Dihal, K. (2020) 'Enslaved minds: Artificial intelligence, slavery, and revolt', in Cave, S., Dihal, K., and Dillon, S. (eds.) *AI Narratives: A history of imaginative thinking about Intelligent Machines*. Oxford: Oxford University Press, pp. 189–12.

Drux, R. (2018) '"Und möchte gern im besten Sinn entstehn": Zum Bildungsprozess der Homunculus-Figur in Goethe's *Faust II*', in Grimm, S., and Bartosch, R. (eds.) *Die Materie des Geistes: Der material turn im Kontext von Bildungs- und Literaturgeschichte um 1800*. Heidelberg: Winter, pp. 17–28.

Dürrenmatt, F. (1962) *Die Physiker*. Zurich: Arche Literatur Verlag.

Edelbauer, R. (2021) *Dave*. Stuttgart: Klett–Cotta.

Eggert, H., Schütz, E., and Sprengel, P. (eds.). (1995) *Faszination des Organischen: Konjunktur einer Kategorie der Moderne*. Munich: iudicium.

Esselborn, H. 2017. 'Herbert W. Franke: Pionier der deutschen Science Fiction', in Blode, U., Esselborn, H., and Päch, S. (eds.) *Herbert W. Franke, Der Kristallplanet: Autobiografische Texte und Science-Fiction-Werke*. Murnau am Staffelsee: p.machinery, pp. 203–30.

Esselborn, H. (2020) *Die Erfindung der Zukunft in der Literatur: Vom technisch-utopischen Zukunftsroman zur deutschen Science Fiction*. 2nd edn. Würzburg: Königshausen & Neumann.

Franke, H. W. (2004) *Sphinx_2*. Munich: DTV Deutscher Taschenbuch.

Franke, H. W. (1961/2015a) *Das Gedankennetz: Science-Fiction-Roman*. Murnau am Staffelsee: p.machinery.

Franke, H. W. (1961/2015b) *Der Orchideenkäfig: Science-Fiction-Roman*. Murnau am Staffelsee: p.machinery.

Franke, H. W. (1965/2017a) *Der Elfenbeinturm: Science-Fiction-Roman*. Murnau am Staffelsee: p.machinery.

Franke, H. W. (1970/2017b) *Zone Null: Science-Fiction-Roman*. Murnau am Staffelsee: p.machinery.

Franke, H. W. (1976/2018a) *Ypsilon Minus: Science-Fiction-Roman*. Murnau am Staffelsee: p.machinery.

Franke, H. W. (1977/2018b) *Zarathustra kehrt zurück: Science-Fiction-Storys*. Murnau am Staffelsee: p.machinery.

Frisch, M. (1957) *Homo Faber*. Frankfurt: Suhrkamp Verlag.

Geraci, R. M. (2010) *Apocalyptic AI: Visions of heaven in robotics, artificial intelligence, and virtual reality*. Oxford: Oxford University Press.

Goethe, J. W. (1810) *Zur Farbenlehre*. Tübingen: J. G. Cotta'schen Buchhandlung
Goethe, J. W. (1821) *Wilhelm Meisters Wanderjahre, oder Die Entsagenden*. Stuttgart: J. G. Cotta'schen Buchhandlung.
Goethe, J. W. (1832) *Faust: Der Tragödie zweiter Teil in fünf Akten*. Stuttgart: J. G. Cotta'schen Buchhandlung
Goodbody, A. (1997) 'Catastrophism in post-war German literature', in Colin, R. (ed.) *Green thought in German culture: Historical and contemporary perspectives*. Cardiff: University of Wales Press, pp. 159–80.
Günther, G. (1957) *Das Bewusstsein der Maschinen*. Baden-Baden: Agis Verlag.
Hammerschmitt, M. (1998) *Target*. Frankfurt: Suhrkamp.
Hansen, T. (2019) *Die Reinsten*. Berlin: Golkonda.
Hauser, H. (1962) *Gigant Hirn: Ein utopisch technischer Roman*. Munich: Goldmann.
Hillenbrand, T. (2018) *Hologrammatica*. Cologne: Kiepenheuer & Witsch.
Hillenbrand, T. (2020) *Qube*. Cologne: Kiepenheuer & Witsch.
Kaiser, G. (1917) *Die Koralle: Schauspiel in fünf Akten*. Berlin: S Fischer Verlag.
Kaiser, G. (1918) *Gas: Schauspiel in fünf Akten*. Berlin: S Fischer Verlag.
Kaiser, G. (1920) *Gas, Zweiter Tell: Schauspiel in drei Akten*. Potsdam: Gustav Kiepenheuer Verlag.
Kurzweil, R. (2016) 'Superintelligence and singularity', in Schneider, S. (ed.) *Science Fiction and philosophy: From time travel to superintelligence*. 2nd edn. Chichester: Wiley & Sons, pp. 146–70.
Metropolis. (1927) Directed by Fritz Lang [Film]. Parufamet.
Moini, B. (2018) *Der Würfel*. Zuric: Atrium.
Orwell, G. (1949) *1984*. London: Secker & Warburg.
Schätzing, F. (2018) *Die Tyrannei des Schmetterlings*. Cologne: Kiepenheuer & Witsch.
Slocombe, W. (2020) 'Machine visions: Artificial intelligence, society, and control', in Cave, S., Dihal, K., and Dillon, S. (eds.) *AI narratives: A history of imaginative thinking about Intelligent Machines*. Oxford: Oxford University Press, pp. 213–36.
Snow, C. P. (1959) *The two cultures and the scientific revolution*. London: Cambridge University Press.
Stein, B. (2012) *Replay*. Munich: Beck.
Steinbuch, K. (1961) *Automat und Mensch. Kybernetische Tatsachen und Hypothesen*. Vienna: Springer.
Thomé, H. (2000) 'Modernität und Bewußtseinswandel in der Zeit des Naturalismus und des Fin de siècle', in Mix, Y-G. (ed.) *Naturalismus, Fin de siècle, Expressionismus. 1890–1918, Sozialgeschichte der Literatur, Bd. 7*. Munich: Hanser, p. 15.
Wiener, N. (1952) *Mensch und Menschmaschine*. Frankfurt: Alfred Metzner.
Zamyatin, Y. (1924) *We*. New York: E. P. Dutton.

6

The Gnostic Machine

Artificial Intelligence in Stanisław Lem's Summa Technologiae

Bogna Konior

> *Nothing which implies contradiction falls under the omnipotence of God.*
>
> ST. THOMAS AQUINAS, *Summa Theologica*, 1273

> *Loyal engineers must evaluate what biology has accomplished, and not reduce their judgment to mocking its Creator, who aside from life gave us also death, and gifted us more sufferings than pleasures. Their judgment should illuminate him as he was. And he was, above all else, far from omnipotent.*[1]
>
> LEM, *Summa Technologiae*, 1964

6.1 Introduction: evolving technology

Stanisław Lem's first-contact novel *Solaris* (1961) is the Polish writer's most celebrated and enduring legacy. It features an ocean planet that conjures up life with no apparent purpose, at best perversely reflecting human wounds and desires. Unintelligible, alien, and therefore not easily communicable, the ocean in *Solaris* could be an archetype of inhuman intelligence: indifferent, foreign, and creative in its distorted reflection of humanity. A quick Google search reveals that multiple artificial intelligence (AI) companies christened their products after Lem's novel. *Solaris* could be a prototype for computational cognition design that is *not* human-centred: 'that inscrutable alien might be wise or cruel or unconcerned', not an all-seeing God but rather 'a nebular and numinous totality . . . [a] big alien brain' (Bratton, 2020, p. 97).

Summa Technologiae (1964a), Lem's abstruse, 600-page-long theoretical work is less known, though it contains the rationale for his whole oeuvre. Titled after *Summa Theologica* (written 1265–1273, published 1485) by St. Thomas Aquinas,

Lem's philosophical tour de force might make one reread *Solaris*, and its descriptions of inhuman intelligence, as a theological—at least, metaphysical—problem. Indeed, many of Lem's novels trace the limits of knowledge in an indifferent cosmos. Overviewing the most cutting-edge scientific discourses of the times, *Summa* is a work of futurology composed of eight chapters, each of which reframes theological questions as technological problems. The first chapter presents Lem's views on the purpose of futurology, and subsequent chapters discuss similarities between technological and biological evolution; SETI; the possibility of computational intelligence; whether humans could be technologically omnipotent; whether humans could create artificial worlds and virtual cosmoses enclosed in themselves; machine knowledge; and whether humans could, akin to gods, engineer new lifeforms.

Though this chapter cannot investigate the matter in exhaustive detail, I explore how—given Lem's skilful portrayal of fictional alien intelligences—the idea of AI appears in *Summa*. Lem is one of only a few writers from beyond the anglophone scene who made it into the popular global canon of science fiction. Recent monographs on his work in English (Gajewska, 2021), new widely reviewed English translations distributed by MIT Press and published together with essays by media scholars such as Katherine Hayles, and multiple events held globally to celebrate the hundredth anniversary of his birthday, prove that there is a rise of interest in his work. This happens alongside a general rise of interest in technological narratives beyond western Europe and the US.

Questions have appeared, for example, about what 'non-western AI' might be, but when 'non-western perspectives' are brought up, they can sometimes be essentialized as 'better' or even inherently more moral for AI design—they are argued to be more 'pluralistic', 'metaphysically inclusive', 'relational', or 'ethical' than the 'western scientific ones' (Goffi, 2021; Hui and Amaro, 2020; Vickers and Allado-McDowell, 2020). Various local belief systems can appear as exoticized 'others' to be deployed in the ethical redesigning of 'Western AI' into a seemingly more relational, harmonious, and pacified technology (Williams and Shipley, 2021). Given its ambivalent position with regards to the 'West'—whether Poland is 'east' or 'west' has been hotly debated for at least a couple centuries (Czapliński, 2016)—we find no proximate salvation discourse projected onto Eastern Europe. It is not perceived as foreign 'enough' to serve as a useful foil against which mainstream American technology discourse can evaluate its 'ethical failings'. In fact, *Summa* sets out *not* to take an ethical perspective and instead takes a disinterested, detached look at technology's role in human evolution.

Rather than taking an 'AI ethics' or 'area studies' approach to Lem's work, I prefer to see him as a formidable technology theorist whose work is in line with contemporary media theory and can enrich its canon. Though some attention is devoted to Central and Eastern European media and technology studies, it is mostly within the areas of news media, communications, and political economy (Demeter, 2020; Downey and Mihelj, 2012). We are yet to see serious attempts at media theory—or philosophy—in the tradition of Haraway (1991), Hayles (1999) or McLuhan (1964) to come from this region; that is, an inquiry into how technological mediation revises certain fundamental axioms of humanism. Lem's interest lies precisely in that, to the extent that he even discards human-centred ethics as a relevant perspective. *Summa* cannot be used to redeem perceived sins of 'Western AI', but it does contribute hypotheses on the very nature of technology and how it mediates human knowledge and evolution.

Before diving deeper into *Summa*, I first sketch the context: Lem's novels, his life under the Soviet regime, his Catholic intellectual scene in Kraków, and the debates around cybernetics in the USSR. In contrast to Promethean ideals of both American and Soviet science fiction of the time, Lem was interested in the Great Silence, in miscommunication and failure. He remained devoted to science and engineering as existential tasks, not as an idealist but as a metaphysician, and with an understanding that humans operate from a position of partial knowledge. This he believed true not only because humans are constrained by ideologies—such as Soviet communism and its restrictions on science and arts—but also ontologically, by the inherent incommunicability of the cosmos. Understanding the debates that were happening in Lem's intellectual circle—his proximity to the Catholic Church in Poland on the one hand and the Polish Cybernetic Society on the other—helps frame his predictions in *Summa* about AI as a 'gnostic machine', whose function is both epistemological and evolutionary: the production of new knowledge at the limit of human comprehension as a factor in the civilizational trajectory of our species.

6.2 Lem's intellectual circle: science, literature, theology and cybernetics

Summa was not planned as a 600-page monograph. Though several of Lem's essays previously published in *Przegląd Kulturalny* (*Cultural Overview*), liquidated in 1963, constitute the core of *Summa*, the finished book is a long treatise on the evolution of human science and technology, more resembling a dissertation than a collection of articles. 'Let's consider the future of civilization from the perspective of potential scientific developments,' Lem proclaims (1964a, p. 125). While one might expect that the philosophical *magnum opus* of a science fiction writer would be devoted to writing or world-building, *Summa* is rather a work of popular science. Biophysicist (and Lem fan) Peter Butko (2006) considers it equal (or even superior) to formidable nonfiction books at the overlap of science and philosophy, such as Richard Dawkins's *The Selfish Gene* (1976) or

Douglas Hofstadter's *Gödel, Escher, Bach* (1979), and notes that it was *Summa* that first comprehensively addressed some of the issues that made these subsequent books so influential and widely celebrated.

Indeed, though he was a voracious reader of his fellow novelists, Lem held scientific papers in higher regard than science fiction as a genre—it is no surprise that he desired to be seen as a theoretician of science rather than only of science *fiction*. He lamented that science fiction rarely transcended its designated category of genre novels, which he considered 'trash', due to dynamics in the publishing industry, consumerist preferences of the average science fiction fan, and also a lack of ambition, talent, and education among its writers (1984b, 'Science-Fiction: A Hopeless Case—With Exceptions'). His interest in technological trajectories and the future motivated him to study paradigm shifts in science. In consequence, his nonfiction essays, most of which have not yet been translated into English, were like guidebooks for Polish readers to scientific debates of the respective decades, and he was frequently commissioned by the Polish press to comment on the latest developments. After his retirement from fiction in the late 1980s, Lem penned hundreds of such essays, seemingly on every possible subject, from 9/11 to social psychology, from politics to literature and religion, and possible development routes for artificial life and AI (*Bomba Megabitowa*, 1999; *Rasa Drapieżców*, 2006; *Tajemnica Chińskiego Pokoju*, 2003).

Peter Swirski, the most prolific English-language scholar of Lem's work, describes *Summa* as 'Lem's philosophical and futurological *opus magnum* which contains his most wide-ranging reflections on the nature and regularities of technological evolution, including its pervasive effects on human culture and society', and, just like Lem's novel *Niezwyciężony* (*The Invincible*) (1964b), published in the same year as *Summa*, 'highlight[s] the similarities between biological evolution and the evolution of culture—not least the contingency of their development' (Swirski, 2015, p. 137). In his usual grumpy assessment of his own work, Lem wrote in a 1964 letter to his friend, Polish scriptwriter Aleksander Ścibor-Rylski:

> My *Summa technologiae* has just been published . . . It's such a cybernetic, theoretical and pretentious [book] so if you have no desire to bite your way through this dreadful text, and only intend to keep this brick on your bookshelf as a memorabilium, [please let me know now] because I only have 3000 author copies to give away, and only 260 copies have been sent to bookstores in Kraków.
>
> (Orliński, 2017, p. 395)

'This dreadful text!'—so Lem describes what has been called his crowning achievement, a work that has been celebrated for predicting multiple developments in contemporary science and technology, from virtual reality, which he in *Summa* calls 'phantomatics' (*fantomatyka*), to developments in artificial life and AI, which we find under the speculative labels 'imitology' (*imitologia*) and 'intellectronics' (*intelektronika*). Lem rather treated these then-imaginary technologies as thought experiments—only sixty years later can we assess how accurate he indeed had been.

As Anton Pervushin explores in Chapter 7 in this volume, the question of bio-technological evolution was influential in Soviet science fiction in general, such as in the stories of Anatoly Dneprov, which concerned machines that could evolve. Yet, rather than simply imagining humanoid robots as an additional link in the evolutionary chain, *Summa* considers the broader role that technology as an activity plays in the evolution of human civilizations: how it produces or staves off existential risk for our species. Published in 1964, it is unmistakably influenced by the debates around cybernetics, evolution, and space travel—all hot topics at the time. In fact, young Lem first learned English when his mentor, psychologist Mieczysław Choynowski, assigned him to read Norbert Wiener's *Cybernetics* (1948) in the original (Bereś and Lem, 2013, p. 47). Lem's task was to review books sent to Choynowski by American and Canadian universities for the Polish academic publication *Life of Science* (*Życie Nauki*, 1946–1953). The young aspiring writer spent many nights in a small annex, 'a tad bigger than a wardrobe, but much smaller than a room', with the English-Polish dictionary in hand, making his way through *Cybernetics* or Claude E. Shannon's (1948) *A Mathematical Theory of Communication* (Orliński, 2017, pp. 175–6).

In 1952 Lem began writing *Dialogi* (Dialogs), a precursor to *Summa*. *Dialogi* (1957) are part-philosophy, part-fantasy, and contain fictional conversations between Filonous and Hylas, characters named after *Three Dialogues between Hylas and Philonous* (1713) by Bishop George Berkeley. This eccentric collection fictionalized many of the conversations Lem had had about cybernetics at Choynowski's conservatory, commenting especially excitedly on how versatile a science it promised to be, with implications for warfare, governance, arts, and literary theory. This obscure collection of strange, fantastic conversations between imaginary sages drew little attention, not only because it was not as readable as Lem's subsequent science fiction novels, but also because of political conditions at the time.

The first readers of *Summa* were largely the intellectual and technocratic elites of the Communist bloc in the 1960s (Butko, 2006, p. 83). Lem, a lifelong member of the Polish Cybernetic Society, established in 1962, played a part in rehabilitating the framework. In the 1950s, under Stalin, cybernetics was considered a forbidden, bourgeois, imperialist pseudoscience. It was not until the reforms of Nikita Khrushchev that Soviet scientists embraced the potential of this new science, albeit seeking to integrate it completely within the teleological goals of communist governance (Gerovitch, 2008). In Lem's early novel *The Magellanic Cloud (Obłok Magellana)* (1955), wary of using the term 'cybernetics', he instead labelled a similar fictional science 'mechaneuristics' (Bereś, 2013, p. 71). Even so, the manuscript was held by the censors for a year (Orliński, 2017, p. 260). Competing with evolutionary science, communism found its own idea of civilizational trajectories in a Hegelian reading of Marx, where all social behaviours must be directed towards the fulfilment of communism (Sayers, 2019). Within this tautology, all of science and culture should serve the purpose of social betterment and the only permissible definition of social betterment is communism. Scientific and cultural inquiry that was not aligned with this 'noble' goal had to be suppressed under the aegis of social responsibility. Soviet censors were not unjustified in their worries—already in *Dialogi*, Lem proposes that cybernetics disproves totalitarianism as a governance mechanism. In theories of cybernetics, feedback loops are a key feature of all functional systems, whether countries or weapons. Feedback informs the 'steersman' whether the system is working, so that appropriate corrections can be made. Yet in totalitarian systems, as the characters in *Dialogi* discuss, because of censorship and propaganda, the 'managers' do not receive correct feedback—they only receive positive reinforcements. As Filonous says to Hylas, such a machine will collapse, like a steam engine without a safety valve. Even so, though when it came out in 1964, no one quite knew what to make of *Summa*—neither science fiction nor sustained scientific debate was part of the Polish literary scene—with time it became 'a textbook for a generation of Soviet scientists and engineers obstructed by the Iron Curtain from contacts with world science' (Swirski, 2015, p. 34).

When the idea for *Summa* began crystallizing in the early 1960s, Lem envisioned it as a continuation of *Dialogi*—another attempt at popularizing cybernetics. The root of the word cybernetics is the Latinized form of Greek *kybernan*—to steer or pilot a ship. In a nod to cybernetics, *Summa* looks for ways to 'steer' the evolutionary structures of human civilization, however imperfect they may be. Yet, in his 1962 letters, Lem already realized that the book would become more than that—no longer a treaty on cybernetics, but 'a pilgrimage to the border of human comprehension', a futurology that aims to describe the civilizational trajectory of humanity in a feedback loop with scientific and technological discoveries (Orliński, 2017, p. 448). It is no accident that the characters in *Dialogi* are named after a canonical work by a Christian philosopher—the question of technology was for Lem from the very beginning a question of metaphysical proportion. Cybernetics appeared to Lem as a theory of totality, as skilled at describing the world—and engineering it!—as theology promised (but failed) to be.

Lem combined his work for Choynowski—who became a model for numerous 'mad scientist' figures in Lem's later novels—with literary and philosophical ambitions. His mentor in these endeavours was Jerzy Turowicz, the legendary journalist and editor of *Tygodnik Powszechny*, a Polish Roman Catholic weekly magazine of social and cultural issues, around which many intellectuals and artists gathered throughout the Soviet times and until today. As Wojciech Orliński writes in his biography of Lem:

> Why was Lem so different from other science-fiction writers internationally, and from Polish writers en masse? Because he was intellectually shaped by different readings. He read what was recommended by Turowicz and Choynowski, and so he understood international science better than the average Polish writer, and he understood the humanities better than the average science-fiction writer.
>
> (Orliński, 2017, 178)

Born to a Jewish family and brought up as a Catholic, Lem later identified as an agnostic. *Summa* explicitly discounts all religious traditions as potential bases for futurology. And yet, *Tygodnik Powszechny*, published by the Kraków Curia, its associated social scene, as well as the significant role that the Polish Catholic Church played in anti-communist resistance and the cultivation of arts and philosophy, all mean that we cannot easily discount the influence of religious themes on Lem's work. It was in Kraków, in its specific intellectual environment, that his work was supported and read by the best Polish intellectuals at the time, many of whom were Catholic and deeply preoccupied with the problems of human dignity and free inquiry under communism:

> *Tygodnik Powszechny* was an anomaly, the only such publication to the east of the Iron Curtain . . . while it did not take an anti-communist position—the censors would not allow that—it did take a non-communist one. This alone constituted a challenge to the very essence of a totalitarian system, which by definition sought to subordinate everything to one ideology.
>
> (Orliński, 2017, p. 179)

Given this proximity to Catholic intellectuals, it is not surprising that Lem titled his defining work after St. Thomas Aquinas's great theological treaty *Summa Theologica*. Akin to a work of theology, *Summa Technologiae* aspires to grasp totality and investigate the relationship between technological practice and human destiny. Where its inspiration—*Summa Theologica*—sought to describe the relationship between Creator (God) and His creation (humans), *Summa Technologiae* wants to reveal the evolutionary processes that dictate the development of human science and society and ask whether creation (humans) can steer its Creator (Nature, to use Lem's term). If there appears a deity in *Summa*, it engineers the world in obscure ways and wields alien tools, akin to what Richard Dawkins famously called 'the blind watchmaker' in his 1986 book of that title about evolution. In another essay, Lem remarks that the genetic code is inhuman in construction, assembling itself without a conscious engineer; it is not simply 'devilishly complicated' but rather 'burdened by unnecessary complexity' (Lem, 2016, p. 361). This theme of indecipherable logic, common in Catholic theology, returns also in Lem's novels. In *His Master's Voice* (*Głos Pana*) (1968) scientists struggle to decode an extra-terrestrial message and are unable to determine its meaning, or even whether it is a message at all. In *Fiasco* (1987), narrated by an untrustworthy hero, human–alien communication also fails, as it does in *Solaris*. If there is no intelligible divinity, and reason cannot be found with the 'blind watchmaker', where *could* intelligent design be exercised? Such is the guiding question of *Summa*: are humans capable of being the drivers of their own evolution? Could they rise up to this challenge through scientific inquiry and engineering?

6.3 Political contingency: science fiction in Poland

Lem's immediate intellectual community provides context for *Summa* and so does his life as a Polish citizen under Soviet rule. It is also worth looking into the larger circumstances of Poland and how—alongside his intellectual influences—Lem's political life shaped his interests as a novelist and intellectual. If not for his experience of war, and later the Soviet regime, *Summa* might have been a much more Promethean work. As it stands, Lem notes that human agency is faulty and complex—we cannot say 'let there be light' and expect there to exist a strict causality between our initial design and what we actually produce (1964a, p. 9). Omnipotent, divine agency is as incorrect a model for actual technological design as are utopian ideals of the Soviet regime. Lem hints at this throughout his work.

Commenting on the relationship between science fiction and politics, Ivan Csicsery-Ronay writes, 'the nations that have produced most of the science fiction in the past century and a half . . . are precisely those that have attempted in modern times to expand beyond their national borders', including Britain, France, Germany, the USSR, Japan, and the United States (2006, p. 130). Lem's works, like the novels of Karel Čapek in neighbouring Czechoslovakia, are notable exceptions. Poland's national identity has little to do with the idea of techno-scientific expansion and, though once a country with some amount of geopolitical power, over the last two centuries, Poland had frequently found itself in the midst of imperial conflicts, struggling for sovereignty and undergoing modernization while under occupation by foreign powers. As the partitions of Poland (1772–1918) came to a halt with the end of the First World War, Poland regained its sovereignty for a mere twenty years before the co-ordinated invasion by the Nazi and Soviet Armies in 1939 commenced another occupation that lasted until the fall of the Soviet Union in 1989. Under the Soviets and as is often true of regions under colonial or imperial occupation, seized territories were like free zones of technological and social experimentation, laboratories where modernization happened with dazzling speed, an 'imperial future shock ... at a speed that made resistance futile' (Csicsery-Ronay, 2006, p. 133). The Poles nevertheless 'practiced resistance simultaneously through the refusal of modernization (for example, in agriculture) and through mathematics and theoretical science' (Csicsery-Ronay, 2006, p. 146).

As mentioned in Section 6.2, Lem was interested in how scientific developments, such as cybernetics, could prove the dysfunctionality of the political system under which he had to live. This often plays out through allegory or allusion in his novels—naturally, because of censorship—but is rarely the main theme. One of the notable exceptions is *Memoirs Found in a Bathtub* (1961), a Kafkaesque pastiche on totalitarianism, which could only be published if, as suggested by the censors, it were set in the Pentagon rather than the USSR, to suggest that it was capitalism, rather than communism, that was totalitarian (Bereś, 2013, p. 72). We can suspect that Lem's characters in *Solaris* carry American names because the writer would not want to suggest that Soviet astronauts could fail their missions. Later in life, when it was no longer dangerous or detrimental to his career, Lem revealed his difficulties in navigating intellectual and creative interests under the communist regime. He also described his distaste for the social realist stories he wrote as a young man—due to financial needs but also misguided youthful idealism—as well as his fear for his family and colleagues later when the regime frequently imprisoned misbehaving intellectuals and artists (Bereś, 2013). However, he remained on good relations with many Soviet scientists and writers—an endearing gesture of intellectual defiance. For example, Lem first discussed his novel *Golem XIV* (1978) in a dissident venue in Moscow called the Institute of High Temperatures, where the scientific elite of the USSR gathered. He chatted about it to, among others, Iosif Shklovsky, who worked with Carl Sagan on extra-terrestrial communication (Fiałkowski, 2015, p. 91).

Though with time, the principles of Marxism–Leninism were modified to allow for the idea of scientific–technological revolution, especially to justify the USSR's space programme, Lem's characters rarely have any real power or fit with the Promethean agenda. The Lem hero is not a Promethean revolutionary taming the cosmos with technology, but rather a defiant metaphysician-scientist operating within a negative theology, perpetually aware of how incomplete knowledge is. Additionally, it wouldn't be an overinterpretation to say that Lem's recurring theme of technological systems evolving to full autonomy and bypassing humans entirely—as in his novel

Golem XIV (1978)—originates from his position as a Polish citizen caught in the midst of the American–Soviet technological race, which happened *over* Poland rather than *in* Poland. Lem's characters frequently participate in momentous events that remain beyond their understanding and control. Describing how dissociation from historical events is common to the Polish modern psyche in general, Andrzej Leder writes in his book *A Dreamt-through Revolution: Exercises in Historical Logic* (2014) that twentieth-century Polish history is 'transpassive'. Poles experience modern history, from Nazism to communism, as carried out by the hands of strangers and occupants, in a dreamlike state, where historical changes are happening through them, but are not *done* by them. We find a similar logic in Lem's narratives, where characters have to continually find their bearing in conditions not of their own making, where miscommunications and lack of agency abound.

This did not fit so well with what the Communist Party wanted to promote in Soviet science fiction at the time: a futuristic 'ethical imperialism based on a romantic, rhetorical, nineteenth-century vision of humanistic values in full control of science and technology' (Csicsery-Ronay, 2006, p. 142). Where Soviet science fiction was rooted in a utopian narrative of socialist values in control of science and nature, in Lem's oeuvre as a whole, save for his earliest work, attempts to perfect society produced unexpected disasters. Though Lem's early novels, such as *The Astronauts* (1951) and *The Magellan Cloud* (1955), both of which he resented later in life, aligned with the Promethean imperative of the Soviets, 'manifold heresies soon entered Lem's evolutionary narratives through the back door' (Jarzębski, 2006, p. 106). Contingency and miscommunication rule Lem's technological cosmology, placing him in the company of twenty-first-century scholars of technology, rather than the ideologues of his time who wanted to use art and science for utilitarian 'betterment'. As Paul Virilio (1999), for example, noticed decades later, each technology is an invention of a corresponding accident. In a recent book *Ironic Technics* (2008), Don Ihde comments that, while many have the tendency to describe technologies as utopian or dystopian, technological development is mostly dominated by the unexpected. Lem knew this not only in theory, but also through his life experience:

> There is no doubt about the harrowing effect the war years had on the shaping of Lem's intellectual and emotional outlook on life. The mature writer's almost obsessive return to the subjects of chance, luck, survival, aggression, the military mindset, and the inhumanity latent in humanity is clearly rooted in the young man's experiences in the war zone [and later under communism—BK].
>
> (Swirski, 2006, p. 6)

Indeed, later reflecting on his work in *The New Yorker*, Lem admits that having to assume fake identities and living under a constant threat of ideological impurity, as well as near-brushes with death, made the idea of full control over history (or technology) sound like 'deluded hubris' (1984a, p. 88). Living under communism also instilled in him a lifelong mistrust of 'ideological artifices', throwing light on his subsequent distaste for French and American postmodernism, especially for Jacques Derrida (Lem, 1996). In *Summa*, he describes the fraught evolution of ideologies in evolutionary parallels:

> biological monstrosities cannot survive, contrary to the monstrosities of linguistic nonsense or intercultural illusion. The punishment for faulty biological construction is disability or death. An analogous metaphysical sin [in the realm of culture] costs no penance, because the human mind is a far more liberal environment for vegetating (or penitential) ideas than the natural environment is for live systems.
>
> (Lem, 1964a, p. 446)

Lem believed that careful mapping of contingency and limits of human ability can pose a challenge to the political ideologies under which he had to live, characterized by the double problem of utopian hubris and censorship of science and art alike. In addition to Poland's fraught geopolitical situation under Soviet communism, in no small part he was also informed by his intellectual circle in Kraków, where the Church was the core of intellectual, artistic, and political resistance, and where the Polish Cybernetic Society in time provided his intellectual home. Let us now take a close look at how these interests appear in *Summa* when it comes to AI specifically.

6.4 AI in *Summa:* artificial knowledge

> Subsequently reason itself—which, in this period of Lem's career, seems to be a kind of self-contained entity initially functioning as a subsidiary agent in the processes of adaptation and struggle for survival—evolves, then acquires some autonomy, and through human agency is transferred into a more convenient environment of machines . . . reason does not necessarily serve living creatures: it simply treats *Homo sapiens* as selfishly as it does Dawkins's famous gene, using each human being as a temporary vehicle for its own transformation and not caring for that individual's fate.
>
> (Jarzębski, 2006, p. 110)

Lem's predictions about AI in *Summa* are framed by similar concerns that guide his novels, where humans are unable to communicate with or understand that which is beyond them. Constrained by our perception, not ourselves being able to know, could we engineer a different mode of knowing? Is it possible for something constructed by humans to exceed the knowledge-capacity of its makers? *Summa* aims to answer these questions on evolutionary terms, considering how humans could 'evolve' a different form of knowledge, even despite our own limitations.

In his later essays, such as one on the Chinese room experiment (2003), Lem continues to understand computation in terms of evolution. This lens prevails in many of his articles published long after *Summa*. In 'Artificial Non-Intelligence', he discusses robotics engineering inspired by insect swarms, citing his own essay from 1984 where he suggested that we should develop 'artificial instinct' rather than intelligence (Lem, 2006, p. 377); that is, computer modelling based on the neural anatomy of insect swarms. He also expresses interest in 'biomorphs' or 'live machines' (Lem, 2006, p. 379) and would be probably thrilled to know that today roboticists model their designs after viruses (Monosson, 2013). In an essay from 1994, 'Language and Code', he brings up AI in the context of understanding language as a simultaneously biological and computational form, again discussing it alongside the genetic code (Lem, 2006, pp. 323–42). We could multiply such examples; in the end, Lem left behind hundreds of nonfiction essays. Suffice to say that we already find these preoccupations in *Summa*.

In *Summa*, Lem describes human evolution as remarkable, but not astounding. What we humans have evolved is the ability to do good and harm to each other in ever-more technologically sophisticated ways (Lem, 1964a, p. 12). But we do not yet have the ability to 'light up and dim the stars' (Lem, 1964a, p. 13). Our interest in *existential* technologies that could alter the course of our species, rather than just better or worsen relations between humans, has been largely confined to the domain of fiction. Even so, Lem firmly believes that 'the only solution to [any] technology is another technology' and 'promises rooted in so-called humanism' have no power to alter the evolution of the *Homo sapiens*, even though they exert significant power over interhuman relations (1964a, p. 12). Accordingly, he was interested in the existential potential of AI—could it help us avoid scientific stagnation, for example?—rather than its social dimension.

Though in *Summa* Lem does not use the term 'artificial intelligence', chapter 4—'Intellectronics' ('Intelektronika')—is often considered the most relevant section, for it is here that Lem cites Alan Turing's essay 'Computer Machinery and Intelligence' (1950), W. Ross Ashby's (1956) work on intelligence amplifiers, and Mortimer Taube's *Computers and Common Sense: The Myth of Thinking Machines* (1961). Lem sets up this chapter by describing a hypothetical existential risk scenario, which he labels 'the megabit bomb', when science, or human comprehension in general, is not anymore able to keep up with the volume of information it receives (Lem, 1964a, p. 135). Human civilization, in consequence, plateaus and then declines. He envisions three outcomes: first, the creation of 'synthetic researchers' that could augment the work of human scientists, second, the creation of a 'cybernetic-socio-technical shell' where civilization could close itself off from 'Nature' and control the volume of incoming information, and third, defeat, which culminates in creating super-specialized microworlds where each science can only apprehend itself: a patchwork of scientific filter bubbles (Lem, 1964a, pp. 138–41).

As a futurology, *Summa* indeed feels quite contemporary. Lem anticipates John Searle's Chinese room experiment when he proposes that we should complicate Turing's imitation game by imagining two different language machines. The first one successfully imitates the human brain, can converse with humans about anything, and might be called intelligent. The second is akin to a sophisticated gramophone—it contains 'let's say a hundred trillion recorded replies to all possible questions, but it does not understand anything' (Lem, 1964a, p. 211). (This also somewhat recalls the Shannon–McCarthy objection to Turing from 1956.) To identify such a gramophone, Lem says, tell the machine a joke, ask if it found it funny, and if so, ask it to rephrase it so that it retains its humour, and you shall unmask the imposter soon enough. A mere few pages later, he also in passing describes how AI should rely on what we today call cloud computing, describing a

> thinking machine built from distributed blocks, corresponding to, let's say, cerebral ganglia. Now we divide the blocks and place them across the whole planet, one in Moscow, second in Paris, third in Melbourne, fourth in Yokohama. Separated from one another, the blocks are 'psychically dead', but connected (through, for example, telephone cables) they become one, integral 'persona', one 'thinking homeostat'.
>
> (Lem, 1964a, p. 213)

After Frank Rosenblatt, he goes on to discuss 'perceptrons'—systems equipped with 'a visual receptor' analogous to the eyes, and 'pseudoneuronal elements, connected randomly, able to recognise simple images, thanks to learning under the supervision of a simple algorithm' (Lem, 1964a, p. 229). He also proposes that we should build 'antagonistic machines' that restrict and supervise each other, what we might recognize as an early description of generative adversarial networks (Lem, 1964a, p. 237). *Summa* is full of such delightful speculations, which, in retrospect, strike us as especially prescient.

In contrast to these, Lem is overall unimpressed with what he calls 'the cybernetic return' of 'the Medieval mythos of the homunculus, an artificially created thinking being' (Lem, 1964a, p. 145). While he considers that it may be possible to create 'an electric brain' as a copy of the biological one, he dismisses this task as belonging to the realm of religious desire, not scientific priority:

> There will be no artificial humans, because it is unnecessary. There will be no 'rebellion' of thinking machines against humans. There is an older myth that informs these concepts—the satanic myth—but no Intelligence Amplifier will become the Electronic Antichrist. All of these myths come down to a common, anthropomorphic denominator, which supposedly can account for the behavior of thinking machines.
>
> (Lem, 1964a, p. 149)

Clearly, Lem was not at all interested in anthropocentric or anthropomorphic models of AI, but rather in intelligence amplifiers, black boxes, and cybernetic models of governance, inasmuch as each of these forces us to delineate (and maybe exceed) the limit of human knowledge and comprehension, pushing us to confront otherness and contingency, a theme common in many of his novels. Precisely because he worries that human civilization at large is like the characters in *Solaris,* who turn any potential knowledge-surface or encounter with the alien into mirrors, he is interested in the possibility of machine knowledge that could help us deal with the surplus of information.

Throughout his work, Lem perceived cognitive chaos and the inability to reason as obstacles to civilizational development. He was concerned that not only do we humans fall prey to ideological artifice, such as communism, but also that the domain of science itself generates a lot of noise. The desire to know and the volume of knowledge is accelerating but human mechanisms for discerning patterns are weak, preventing our species from understanding the trajectory of our own evolution, much less being able to influence it. Referring to Ashby's (1956) influential book on cybernetics, Lem writes that principles of knowledge can emerge from within a system that operates chaotically and without internal logic. He believed that we should aim to find ways to sift through this noise and continue producing knowledge, otherwise, submerged in it, human civilization is 'like a ship built without a blueprint' and with 'no steersman' (Lem, 1964a, p. 418).

6.5 The gnostic machine

One of the most powerful ideas in *Summa* with regards to what we may term 'artificial knowledge' is the brief mention of a gnostic machine. I believe it to be especially important not only because it departs from common anthropomorphic imaginations of AI, but also because it connects so well to Lem's work as a novelist and intellectual. It is key to what I would call his 'secular theology' of human technological evolution, where the Catholic tradition of negative theology, with unknowability of the divine as its centre, overlaps onto Lem's life experience of contingency as a Pole caught in the USSR-Soviet cybernetic arms race. The gnostic machine—only mentioned a few times in *Summa* (1964a)—is described thus:

> A gnostic machine must take into account, for the purpose of creating a theory of complexity, a huge number of variables, such that the algorithms of contemporary science cannot produce . . . At the outset we would receive a theory, coded as, let's say, a whole system of equations. Would humans be able to do anything with these equations?
>
> (pp. 234–5)

[. . .]

> [With regards to thinking machines], how much of the matter is under human control is—let's admit it—a matter of perspective. That man can swim does not mean that he can swim the ocean on his own without a ship, not to mention an analogous situation with jets and space rockets. A similar evolution is now taking place, somewhat in parallel, in the information universe. A human might direct a gnostic machine towards a problem that he—or his descendants—might be able to eventually solve on their own, but the machine might during its work open his eyes to problems he had not even suspected. In the last instance, who has the agency here?
>
> (p. 441)

In a way, the gnostic machine is the opposite of the totalitarian machine of ideology—the former is governed by opaque, indecipherable, inhuman logic, where the former is homogenous and overly controlled, reduced to the artifice or utopianism of human ideology. In a subsequent chapter, 'On the Creation of Worlds', on the surface unrelated to AI, Lem elaborates on this further, focusing on how we could automate science and metaphysics by creating technologies that operate at the limit of human comprehension, rather than 'imitating' human-level cognitive functions, which are prone to failure. The goal is further removal of humans from the knowledge-production process, the production of the 'autognostic or cybergnostic machine' (Lem, 1964a, p. 409).

If gnosis is a form of revealed knowledge based on direct participation in the divine, without mediators, Lem's description of our technological future resonates here: 'could we extract information from Nature without the mediation of brains, human or electric—to create something like a breeding farm facilitating the evolution of information?' (Lem, 1964a, p. 139). For Lem, this project follows closely the logic of evolution—he calls this convergence 'imitology' (Lem, 1964a, p. 427). One potential method is imitating the workings of in vitro reproduction in order to generate new metaphysics: doing with information what we already are able to do with life. What interests Lem here is that humans, by using machines, are able to create life in an artificial setting, while not completely understanding how 'life' works. This is a black box—a system whose total inputs and outputs are not fully comprehensible to the designer, all while the design itself remains workable. Could there be an analogous process but aimed at creating an artificial epistemology? Akin to genetic engineering, could we 'do something analogous in the domain of information science? Breed and cross-breed information, initiate its fertilisation so that in the end we receive a grown organism—a scientific theory?' (Lem, 1964a, p. 398). In evolutionary terms, for Lem, 'information should originate in information as one organism does in another. It should fertilise, cross-breed and be subject to mutations' (Lem, 1964a, p. 399). A total synthesis between biological and technological evolutions.

Such breeding of information potentially creates epistemic configurations beyond humans, just as in vitro fertilization lets humans 'create' other mammalian life. While 'there is no thought that a human hive mind would think that an individual brain could not think on its own' (Lem, 1964a, p. 443), 'imitology' opens up speculative possibilities of transcending these limitations. This proposition is also a reversal of theological and evolutionary principles: a scenario in which a less-intelligent being—humans—might be able to create a more intelligent one. It is as if monkeys were somehow able to engineer divinity. The evolutionary significance of machines is revealed, partly, in this process. If in theology, 'gnosis'—knowledge—denotes insight into the infinite and the deliverance of humanity from earthly constraints, a parallel phenomenon in Lem's narrative of techno-biological evolution must be black-boxed, to some extent automatically performed or mediated through a machine. 'Automatic gnosis' or 'artificial epistemology' rather than 'artificial intelligence' is one of the latent promises of computation. One of Lem's later works, *Golem XIV* (1978), considers an example of how this could pan out. In the novel, a superintelligent computer evolves beyond its initial military tasks—its traditional cybernetic framework—and learns to perceive human designs as lacking in internal consistency. It subsequently lectures humans on existential trajectories, informing them that they are mere vessels for other-than-human intelligence, just like their bodies are evolutionary vessels for life. The evolution of intelligence needs 'reason and consciousness but [is] not controllable by the latter' (Jarzębski, 2006, p. 110)—intelligence might evolve well beyond consciousness and organic life. No novel better demonstrates Lem's intellectual trajectory from *Dialogi* to *Summa* than one that features a computer evolving beyond its cybernetic, military, and ultimately human applications in order to play a part in the techno-biological evolution of intelligence and confront humans with the limits of knowledge.

6.6 Conclusion

Joanna Zylinska, media theorist and translator of Lem's *Summa* into English, writes in her book *AI Art: Machine Vision and Warped Dreams* that the question of AI is ultimately about 'rescaling our human worldview' (2020, p. 152). Though what we commonly understand as AI today—machine learning, natural language processing, expert systems, deep learning, computer vision, and robotics—are only indirectly discussed in *Summa*, AI as an idea draws on multiple 'sociotechnical imaginaries' that end up providing paradigms for understanding the relationship between our imaginations of technology, the social order, and the designs we actually carry out (Jasanoff, 2015, p. 6). As discussions about 'non-western AI' continue, Lem's work provides an intriguing counterpoint to the increasingly common practice of using 'eastern' or 'non-western' theories of media and technology as salvation narratives for the perceived sins of 'Western AI'. Framed by his life and work as a Polish writer, his unique Catholic-cybernetic intellectual scene in Kraków, and his interest in how technology alters axioms of human cognition and evolution, the concept of a 'gnostic machine' can be a starting point for fruitful discussions about the possibility of 'AI' as an existential technology, not confined to its possible ethical implications for humans.

Endnote

1. All translations from the Polish by the author.

References

Aquinas, St. T. (1485) *Summa technologiae*. Basel: Michael Wenssler.

Ashby, W. R. (1956) *An introduction to cybernetics*. London: Chapman & Hall Ltd.

Bereś, S. and Lem, S. (2013) *Tako rzecze Lem: Ze Stanisławem Lemem rozmawia Stanisław Bereś*. Kraków: Cyfrant.

Berkeley, G. (1713) *Three dialogues between Hylas and Philonous*. London: Henry Clements.

Bratton, B. (2020) 'Synthetic gardens: Another model for AI and design', in Vickers, B. and Allado-McDowell, K. (eds.) *Atlas of anomalous AI*. London: Ignota Books, pp. 91–112.

Butko, P. (2006) '*Summa technologiae*: Looking back and ahead', in Swirski, P. (ed.) *The art and science of Stanislaw Lem*. Montreal: McGill-Queen's University Press, pp. 81–104.

Csicsery-Ronay, I. (2006) 'Lem, Central Europe, and the genre of technological empire', in Swirski, P. (ed.) *The art and science of Stanislaw Lem*. Montreal: McGill-Queen's University Press, pp. 130–53.

Czapliński, P. (2016) *Poruszona mapa*. Kraków: Wydawnictwo Literackie.

Dawkins, R. (1986) *The blind watchmaker: Why the evidence of evolution reveals a universe without design*. New York: WW Norton & Company.

Dawkins, R. (1976/2016) *The selfish gene*. 40th ann. edn. Oxford: Oxford University Press.

Demeter, M. (2020) 'Representation of Eastern Europe in media studies', *Journalism & Mass Communication Quarterly*, 97(3), pp. 586–9.

Downey, J. and Mihelj, S. (eds.) (2012) *Central and Eastern European media in comparative perspective: Politics, economy and culture*. London: Routledge.

Fiałkowski, T. (2015) *Świat na krawędzi: Ze Stanisławem Lemem rozmawia Tomasz Fiałkowski*. Kraków: Cyfrant.

Gajewska, A. (2021) *Holocaust and the stars: The past in the prose of Staniław Lem*, tr. K. Gucio. London: Routledge India.

Gerovitch, S. (2008) 'InterNyet: Why the Soviet Union did not build a nationwide computer network', *History and Technology*, 24(4), pp. 335–50.

Goffi, E. (2021) 'Escaping the Western cosm-ethical hegemony: The importance of cultural diversity in the ethical assessment of artificial intelligence', *AI Ethics Journal*, 2(1), pp. 1–11.

Haraway, D. (1991) *Simians, cyborgs and women: The reinvention of nature*. London: Free Association Books.

Hayles, K. (1999) *How we became posthuman: Virtual bodies in cybernetics, literature, and informatics*. Chicago: University of Chicago Press.

Hofstadter, D. R. (1979) *Gödel, Escher, Bach: An eternal golden braid* (Vol. 13). New York: Basic Books.

Hui, Y. and Amaro, R. (2020) 'Designing for intelligence', in Vickers, B. and Allado-McDowell, K. (eds.) *Atlas of anomalous AI*. London: Ignota Books, pp. 53–75.

Ihde, D. (2008) *Ironic technics*. Copenhagen: Automatic Press/VIP.

Jarzębski, J. (2006) 'Models of evolution in the writings of Stanislaw Lem', in Swirski, P. (ed.) *The art and science of Stanislaw Lem*. Montreal: McGill-Queen's University Press, pp. 104–17.

Jasanoff, S. (2015) 'Future imperfect: Science, technology, and the imaginations of modernity', in Jasanoff, S. and S. H. Kim (eds.) *Dreamscapes of modernity: Sociotechnical imaginaries and the fabrication of power*. Chicago: University of Chicago Press, pp. 1–33.

Leder, A. (2014) *Prześniona Rewolucja: Ćwiczenia z Logiki Historycznej*. Warsaw: Wydawnictwo Krytyki Politycznej.

Lem, S. (1951) *Astronauci*. Warsaw: Czytelnik.

Lem, S. (1955) *Obłok Magellana*. Warsaw: Państwowe Wydawnictwo Iskry.

Lem, S. (1957) *Dialogi o zmartwychwstaniu atomowym, teorii niemożności, filozoficznych korzyściach ludożerstwa, smutku w probówce, psychoanalizie cybernetycznej, elektrycznej metempsychozie, sprzężeniach zwrotnych ewolucji, eschatologii cybernetycznej, osobowości sieci elektrycznych, przewrotności elektromózgów, życiu wiecznym w skrzyni, konstruowaniu geniuszów, epilepsji kapitalizmu, maszynach do rządzenia, projektowaniu systemów społecznych*. Kraków: Wydawnictwo Literackie.

Lem, S. (1961) *Pamiętnik Znaleziony w Wannie*. Kraków: Wydawnictwo Literackie.

Lem, S. (1961) *Solaris*. Warsaw: Wydawnictwo Ministerstwa Obrony Narodowej.

Lem, S. (1964a) *Summa Technologiae*. Kraków: Wydawnictwo Literackie.

Lem, S. (1964b) *Niezwyciężony*. Warsaw: Wydawnictwo Ministerstwa Obrony Narodowej.

Lem, S. (1968) *Głos Pana*. Warsaw: Czytelnik.

Lem, S. (1978) *Golem XIV*. Kraków: Wydawnictwo Literackie.

Lem, S. 1984a. 'Chance and order', tr. F. Rottensteiner, The New Yorker, 30 January, pp. 88–9.

Lem, S. (1984b) 'Science-fiction: A hopeless case—with exceptions', in Rottensteiner, F. (ed.) *Microworlds: Writings on science-fiction and fantasy*. San Diego: Harcourt, Brace and Company, pp. 45–105.

Lem, S. (1987) *Fiasko*. Kraków: Wydawnictwo Literackie.

Lem, S. (1996) *Sex Wars*. Warsaw: Niezależna Oficyna Wydawnicza Nowa.

Lem, S. (1999) *Bomba Megabitowa*. Kraków: Wydawnictwo Literackie.

Lem, S. (2003) *Tajemnica Chińskiego Pokoju*. Kraków: Towarzystwo Autorów i Wydawców Prac Naukowych Universitas.

Lem, S. (2006) *Rasa Drapieżców. Teksty ostatnie*. Kraków: Wydawnictwo Literackie.

Lem, S. (2016) *Planeta Lema. Felietony ponadczasowe*. Kraków: Wydawnictwo Literackie.

McLuhan, M. (1964) *Understanding media: The extensions of man*. Toronto: McGraw-Hill.

Monosson, E. (2013) 'Can life evolve from wires and plastic?' *Aeon* [online]. Available at: https://aeon.co/essays/can-life-evolve-from-wires-and-plastic (Accessed 4 September 2021).

Orliński, W. (2017) *Lem: Życie nie z tej ziemi*. Warsaw: Wydawnictwo Czarne & Wydawnictwo Agora.

Sayers, S. (2019) 'Marx and teleology', *Science & Society*, 83(1), pp. 37–63.

Shannon, C. E. (1948) 'A mathematical theory of communication', *The Bell System Technical Journal*, 27(3), pp. 379–423.

Swirski, P. (2006) *The art and science of Stanislaw Lem*. Montreal: McGill-Queen's University Press.

Swirski, P. (2015) *Stanislaw Lem: Philosopher of the future*. Liverpool: Liverpool University Press.

Taube, M. (1961) *Computers and common sense: The myth of thinking machines*. New York: Columbia University Press.

Turing, A. (1950) 'Computer machinery and intelligence', *Mind*, LIX(236), pp. 433–60.

Vickers, B. and Allado-McDowell, K. (eds.) (2020) *Atlas of anomalous AI*. London: Ignota Books.

Virilio, P. (1999) *Politics of the very worst: An interview with Philippe Petit*. Lotringer, S. (ed.), tr. M. Cavaliere. Los Angeles: Semiotext(e).

Wiener, N. (1948/2019) *Cybernetics or control and communication in the animal and the machine*. Reissue of the 1st edn. Cambridge, MA: MIT Press.

Williams, D. H. and Shipley, G. P. (2021) 'Enhancing artificial intelligence with indigenous wisdom', *Open Journal of Philosophy*, 11(1), pp. 43–58.

Zylinska, J. (2020) *AI art: Machine visions and warped dreams*. London: Open Humanities Press.

7

Boys from a Suitcase

AI Concepts in USSR Science Fiction: The Evil Robot and the Funny Robot

Anton Pervushin

7.1 Introduction

The two main themes of Soviet science fiction from 1918 onwards were communism as the future of society and space exploration. But from the mid-1920s, the thematic diversity grew, and new ideas for Soviet writers emerged, including contact with aliens, biological experiments, extraordinary technologies, and intelligent machines in the form of robots.

The way the image of the robot formed in Soviet science fiction was significantly influenced by translations of foreign texts. At the same time, writers adapted the concepts presented in those texts according to the political situation and propaganda campaigns of the time. Science fiction stories therefore evolved through interacting with state ideology.

This chapter shows how the image of the robot evolved in Soviet science fiction—from a smart machine to an intelligent machine. In Section 7.2, I demonstrate that the primary ideas about robots were formed in the USSR under the influence of Karel Čapek's *R.U.R.* (1921) and its translation *The Revolt of the Machines* (1924) by Aleksey Tolstoy. In Section 7.3, I explain how the image of the robot changed after the rehabilitation of cybernetics in the USSR, using examples from the texts of Anatoly Dneprov, the Strugatsky brothers, Alexander Kazantsev, and others. In Section 7.4, I review the most popular Soviet science fiction books and films of the 1970s and 1980s, which describe the attempts of intelligent machines to become fully fledged citizens. I discuss the threats that the Soviet writers considered in the context of turning a robot into an intelligent machine. In conclusion, I present the argument that the evolution of the robot image in Soviet science fiction is a narrative about the consistent modernization of the stereotype from 'evil' robot to 'funny' robot.

7.2 Robot vs. human

Czech writer Karel Čapek's play *R.U.R. (Rossum's Universal Robots)* (1921) is one of the most famous science fiction texts that address the problem of human interaction with artificial beings. Čapek's book introduces the word 'robot', but the author, however, thought of 'robots' not as machines, but as homunculi, which are constructed in the shape of the human body using a new type of 'living matter'. Harry Domin, the Director General of the Rossum's Universal Robots factory, says 'The Robots are not people. They are mechanically more perfect than we are, they have an astounding intellectual capacity, but they have no soul' (Čapek, 1921, p. 9). The play follows Domin's activities as he dreams of saving humanity from hardship by replacing workers with inexpensive robots. He succeeds in implementing his project, but during mass production there are 'breakdowns in the mechanism', and the robots refuse to work. They start a revolution, during which the robots exterminate all humans, and as a result, since robots cannot reproduce, civilization is threatened with destruction. The play was popular in Europe, which had experienced many violent revolutions in preceding decades. The plot represents the disturbing public expectations of the 1920s.

In 1923, as an émigré, the famous writer Aleksey Nikolayevich Tolstoy saw the production of *R.U.R.* in a Berlin theatre before returning to Soviet Russia permanently. Tolstoy reviewed the play, calling it 'absolutely brilliant' and 'dynamite' (Zlat, 1923). He signed an agreement with the former theatre director Georgy Alexandrovich Krol on the translation and adaptation of *R.U.R.* for the Soviet theatre. Soon, however, the idea was transformed into a new version, called *The Revolt of the Machines* [*Бунт машин*], which was presented in 1924 at the Great Dramatic Theater of Leningrad. The new play was an ingenious fantasy created on the basis of *R.U.R.*, but Tolstoy supplemented the text with new characters and changed the storyline (Nikolskii, 2004). He abandoned the use of the term 'robot' so that his play would differ from *R.U.R.* but he retained the description of the robot production technology.

In *The Revolt of the Machines*, a capitalist by the name of Alexander Morey, desiring to maximize profit, produces millions of 'universal artificial workers'. In addition, he uses robots as soldiers to suppress the proletariat's protests. Later, the robots become conscious of their rights and organize a revolution. The robots do not acknowledge class differences between humans and destroy all of them as their exploiters. A character named Obyvatel (Philistine), who wants to survive the revolution, pretends to be an 'artificial worker'. He tells the rebel robot patrol:

> I am artificial, I work like a dog, the damned parasites, exploiters drink blood from me. Today I could not stand it, I rebelled with weapons in my hands. I

> was shot through and through. Of course, I don't pay any attention to this. I'm running to fight again.
>
> (Tolstoy, 2016, p. 364)

The trusting robots let go of Obyvatel, and he and his wife escape abroad. In using this character as a metaphor, Tolstoy caricatured the bourgeoisie who masqueraded as 'comrades of the proletariat'.

In his play, Tolstoy argued that if robots ever identify themselves as beings that are equivalent to humans, they will inevitably start a war against humanity. He indicated that robots must follow the priorities of human culture, which is based on domination; thus, an intelligent machine is a slave who wants to become an master.

The plays *Revolt of the Machines* and *R.U.R.* aroused great interest in Soviet Russia. However, as opposed to the organic robots in *R.U.R.*, mechanical robots appeared in Soviet science fiction thanks to the sensation caused by the robot 'Televox' (or 'Mr. Herbert Televox'), designed and patented for Westinghouse in October 1927 by American inventor Roy J. Wensley. Televox was an anthropomorphic decoration for an automatic telephone exchange connected to household devices. Using a whistle, an operator commanded Televox to open the windows, raise the flag, or turn on the ventilator, lamps, and vacuum cleaner. At the call of 'Open, sesame!', Televox would open the door (Powell, 1928).

The publicity around Televox drew the attention of Alexander Romanovich Belyaev, the Soviet writer often referred to as 'Russia's Jules Verne'. Belyaev wrote a satirical short story, 'Open, Sesame!!!' [Сезам, откройся!!!] (1928), in which he described a group of thieves who pretend to be salesmen who pitch automated home devices to a rich old man at his villa.[1] The editorial preface, which Belyaev probably wrote, stated:

> While the famous manufacturer Ford automates the work of a person to the semblance of a machine, the American company Westinghouse engaged in the manufacture of 'humanized machines'. R. J. Wensley, one of the engineers of this company, invented machines that—as recently reported by foreign newspapers—not only obey the verbal orders of a man, but also give sound answers to questions asked . . . The use of 'humanized machines' in dangerous and harmful professions or at work in an extreme environment is the way in which a new invention should develop in an organized economy and along which it will undoubtedly reach the USSR. But in capitalist countries, the 'mechanical slave' will become a competitor of the living worker, and therefore such an invention should promote the aggravation of class contradictions there.
>
> (Belyaev, 1928, p. 287)

At the same time, futurologist Nikolai Nikitich Kondratenko introduced the term 'robots' into the Russian language in relation to electromechanical systems that perform various tasks at the request of a human operator. Publishing under the pseudonym Oleg Drozhzhin, in his article 'Technology of the Future' [Техника будущего] (1929) and his book *Intelligent Machines* [*Разумные машины*] (1931), Drozhzhin discussed Televox and other similar inventions; he called them 'robots' with a nod to the play *R.U.R.*

Drozhzhin argued that humans will use 'intelligent machines' in various fields of activity, but that the machines will never become sentient and will obey their program. He reported:

> The machine changes its social significance depending on which social class makes use of it . . . In the capitalist world, 'intelligent machines' and all kinds of machines perform a double function. Machines facilitate the struggle with nature and help man, but at the same time they are enemies for the majority of workers in the capitalist world. They force the worker to strain his strength in the struggle for life, often deprive him of wages and condemn him to starvation. This happens because there are irreconcilable contradictions in capitalist society. The machine does not belong to the workers there, but to an insignificant group of capitalists, and it is not surprising that they use the machine to get more profit and enslave the workers. The machine will cease to play this dual role only in a society in which there will be no class contradictions. It will be a classless society that only the proletariat can build.
>
> (Drozhzhin, 1931, pp. 6, 126–7)

Drozhzhin's ideas were used by various writers, including Ukrainian futurologist and science fiction writer Vladimir Nikolaevich Vladko, author of the 1931 *The Robotiats Are Coming* [Ідуть роботарі]. The novel describes the confrontation between a union and American industrialist Jonathan Gowers, who begins mass-producing 'mechanical people'. Robots (or 'robotiats') replace striking workers at the machine tools, and later are used to help the police. Radio engineer Madeleine Strand is seeking a way to hijack the remote control of the robots. Agents from the 'Red Country' intervene in the situation, and when the confrontation turns into an armed uprising, they use Strand's invention and turn the robots into allies of the proletariat.

In 1935, Mezhrabpomfilm Studios [*Межрабпомфильм*] made the film *Loss of Sensation (Robot of Jim Ripple)* [Гибель сенсации (Робот Джима Рипль)] based on Vladko's novel. Director Alexandr Nikolaevich Andriyevsky introduced an allusion to Čapek's play, glossing 'R.U.R.' as 'Ripple's Universal Robots'. The plot of the film differs from the original source in that working-class protagonist Jim Ripple wants to make his fellow workers' jobs easier by creating 'mechanical people'. The trade union does not accept his project, and Ripple offers his invention to capitalists, who plan to use the robots as invulnerable soldiers. Notably, the inventor uses a clarinet to control the robots, not a whistle, but still creates a link between Ripple's robots and Televox (Christopher, 2016).

Another significant work in the topic timeline of robots was Semyon Isaakovich Kirsanov's 1934 *The Poem about the Robot* [*Поэма о Роботе*], which caused an intense debate among literary critics who tried to identify its significance within Soviet ideology. Kirsanov describes how capitalists first use the smart machines as toys, and then as an unbeatable army against the USSR. The USSR is saved from defeat by a workers' uprising that disables the centres from which the robots are controlled remotely. In the USSR after the war, the captured robots become janitors, gardeners, waiters, hairdressers, security guards, and nannies.

Critics, quoting Joseph Stalin, debated the problem of using robots; for example, Alexandr Leites declared:

> Can this revolutionary theme take root upon the soil of our socialist literature? Of course not. And it can't because the main theme of socialist art is the theme of a living person who has mastered technology . . . The main idea for us, as Comrade Stalin said, is the people who have mastered technology. That is why for every serious Soviet artist, an engineer of human souls, the theme of a robot can only be a side issue, only an excuse to talk about a living person again and again.
>
> (Leites, 1935)

However, also referencing Stalin, Vladislav Nikonov disputed his colleague's statement:

> The years of implementing Comrade Stalin's slogan 'Technology solves everything during the reconstruction period' could not but be reflected in poetry. The most illustrative example is *The Poem about the Robot* by S. Kirsanov. It is founded on a fantasy based on technology, and a technology that surpasses fantasy . . . Isn't this mechanical man the apotheosis of technology? [The words] 'Vanadium', 'cobalt', 'radioscope', 'ferroalloy', 'synchronicity' are entering poetic usage here for the first time—the vocabulary of lyrics is expanding.
>
> (Nikonov, 1936)

The predominance of negative reviews caused a ban on further publications, and *The Poem about the Robot* was not republished for thirty years (Shneiderman, 2006). However, the discussions of the 1930s consolidated the stereotypical image of the robot, who will be created in the capitalist world and will become the enemy of the working class. The robot must be subordinated to the interests of the revolutionary fight, or be destroyed.

7.3 The robot as a product of cybernetics

In 1948, Norbert Wiener published *Cybernetics: Or Control and Communication in an Animal and a Machine*. The book aroused a considerable amount of public discussion and comment at the time, which was unusual for a predominantly technical subject, and both Soviet scientists and ideologists noticed the discussion.

Initially, Wiener's book was banned from publication in the USSR. Soviet ideologists considered his ideas a dangerous alternative to the scientific method based on Marxist–Leninist philosophy. Cybernetics both appealed to Soviet culture and threatened the established political foundation. However, leading scientists sought opportunities to get acquainted with it. For example, in August 1949, Academician Alexandr Alexandrovich Andronov wrote to a friend in Moscow: 'I am very interested in Wiener's *Cybernetics*, but have not acquired it yet. If you know where to find it, please let me know.' Andronov soon obtained a copy of Wiener's book, enthusiastically discussed it in his circle, and eagerly lent it to his colleagues (Gerovitch, 2002, p. 108).

At the same time, the Soviet press instigated a discussion about cybernetics that gave the impression of a well-organized ideological campaign. In May 1950 the *Literary Gazette [Литературная газета]* published the article 'Mark III, Calculator' [Марк III, калькулятор] by the science editor Boris Nikolaevich Agapov, who wrote:

> Wiener argues that 'the emergence of intelligent machines represents the second industrial revolution'. In his opinion, the first industrial revolution devalued the human hand; now, Wiener argues, the birth of 'thinking mechanisms' must inevitably devalue the human brain. The human brain is being replaced by a mechanical brain, which will be 'many times faster and more accurate' . . . Some people expect predictions from machines in the stock exchange game. Other people want to replace their managers with machines that do not take bribes and do not trade with foreigners. Certain people in their fantasies dream of the time when robots will replace the 'capricious' and 'dangerous' proletarians.
>
> (Agapov, 1950, p. 2)

In his criticism of cybernetics, Agapov repeated the rhetoric use by 1930s Soviet writers when they discussed robots. He referred to the supporters of cybernetics as 'false scientists', 'charlatans', and 'obscurantists'. Agapov's article became a key reference point for the development of an ideological campaign against cybernetics, and after its publication, the Lenin State Library in Moscow—the largest book collection in the Soviet Union—reportedly withdrew Wiener's *Cybernetics* from circulation (Gerovitch, 2002, p. 120).

In 1951, the Institute of Philosophy of the USSR Academy of Sciences issued a collection of papers under the characteristic title *Against the Philosophizing Henchmen of American and English Imperialism* [*Против философствующих оруженосцев американо-английского империализма*]. It contained the article 'Semantic Idealism is the Philosophy of Imperialist Reaction' [Семантический идеализм—философия империалистической реакции] by psychologist Mikhail Grigoryevich Iaroshevskii, who claimed:

> The basis of 'cybernetics' is the favorite assertion of semantic obscurantists that thinking is operating with signs, and mathematical calculus is put forward as an ideal form of such operation. The inventor of 'cybernetics', Wiener, recommends considering the brain as a calculating machine performing arithmetic and algebraic operations. The development of modern technology, Wiener points out, indicates that these operations reach a high level of complexity. Why not assume that the devices will replace people in the very near future? 'In the near future', writes Wiener, 'thinking machines will make the use of human labor unnecessary, and since society views said labor as a commodity, sold and bought, we will soon reach a stage where most people will have nothing to sell'. From this fantastic idea semanticist cannibals derive the conclusion that a larger part of humanity must be exterminated.
>
> (Iaroshevskii, 1951, pp. 99–100)

On 5 April 1952, a new article by Iaroshevskii criticizing cybernetics appeared on the pages of the *Literary Gazette*. Iaroshevskii reiterated Agapov's earlier criticism of Western computing and wrote:

> A popular false theory created by a group of American 'scientists' claims to solve all the core scientific problems and to save humanity from all social disasters. The cybernetic craze has spread across various branches of knowledge: physiology, psychology, sociology, psychiatry, linguistics, etc. Feeling fear of the will and mind of peoples, cyberneticists console themselves with the idea of the possibility of transferring the vital functions inherent in man to automatic devices. Is it possible to put a robot with electronic brains at the assembly line instead of a proletarian who strikes when wages are reduced and votes for peace and communists? Is it possible to send an insensitive metal monster instead of a pilot who refuses to destroy women working in rice fields?
>
> (Iaroshevskii, 1952)

We see that Iaroshevskii restarted the discussion about intelligent machines and directly connected cybernetics with the topic of robots. The authors of subsequent publications clearly interpreted Iaroshevskii's article as a signal to start a full-blown anti-cybernetics campaign. The view of cybernetics as a 'pseudoscience', reproduced in several central newspapers and magazines, became all but official (Gerovitch, 2002, pp. 123–4).

The anti-cybernetics campaign had little influence on the development of Soviet projects on computers and remote-controlled devices. However, Agapov, Iaroshevskii, and others pointed out to science fiction writers that the topic of robots was now condemned by the Soviet authorities. For example, the philosopher Bernard Emmanuelovich Bykhovskii reported in his article 'Cybernetics is an American Pseudoscience' [Кибернетика—американская лженаука]:

> Voluntarily or involuntarily, the pseudoscientific inventions of cybernetics follow the line of reactionary imperialist utopias about a society of 'robots' (human-machines). These utopias clearly demonstrate the indisputable truth that capitalism is hostile to the development of mankind. Recently, this reactionary utopia has received an 'artistic' expression in the 'science fiction novel' *Last and First Men* by Olaf Stapledon. Stapledon's sick imagination paints a 'future society' in which only a small group of people with a specially developed brain thinks. Truly fascist nonsense!
>
> (Bykhovskii, 1952, p. 127)

Under ideological pressure, Soviet science fiction writers were afraid to write about robots. Sometimes they described the future automation of urban life, but they avoided terminology that could be associated with the popularization of cybernetics.

However, the anti-cybernetics campaign did not last long. In April 1955 (i.e. after the death of Joseph Stalin in 1953), the magazine *Problems of Philosophy* [*Вопросы философии*] published the article 'The Main Features of Cybernetics' [Основные черты кибернетики]. Three leading computer scientists (Sergey Lvovich Sobolev, Anatoly Ivanovich Kitov, and Aleksey Andreevich Liapunov) claimed:

> Some of our philosophers made a serious mistake: without understanding the essence of the issues, they began to deny the significance of the new direction in science, mainly because sensational hype was raised abroad around this direction, some ignorant bourgeois journalists engaged in advertising and cheap speculation around cybernetics, and reactionary figures did everything possible to use the new direction in science in their class reactionary interests. It is possible that the intensified reactionary idealistic interpretation of cybernetics in the popular reactionary literature was specially organized

> with the aim of disorienting Soviet scientists and engineers, in order to slow down the development of a new important scientific direction in our country.
>
> (Sobolev et al., 1955, p. 147)

Skilfully using the 'overtake and surpass' argument, the authors of the article cited Western accomplishments in aircraft gun control and industrial automation and pointed to the 'great economic and military significance' of cybernetics. This started the 'rehabilitation' of cybernetics, which quickly became one of the most fashionable scientific and technical disciplines in the USSR (Gerovitch, 2002, p. 179).

This new topic attracted the attention of the brothers Arkady Natanovich and Boris Natanovich Strugatsky, who at the beginning of their creative career studied advanced scientific ideas. In 1958, the Strugatsky brothers' writing debuted in magazines with the sci-fi short stories 'From Beyond' [Извне] and 'Spontaneous Reflex' [Спонтанный рефлекс]. In the first story, people encounter 'cybernetic mechanisms' sent by aliens to explore the Earth and establish contact with humanity. The second story describes a humanoid robot, Urm (Universally Reacting Mechanism), which was designed on orders from the Interplanetary Communication Bureau to work on Venus, but suddenly gained 'self-consciousness' and escaped.

In 1959, the Strugatsky brothers wrote the stories 'Test of the "SKR"' [Испытание 'СКР'] and 'White Cone of the Alaid' [Белый конус Алаида], in which they discussed the problems of preparing complex self-organizing cybernetic systems for long-range space flights. The Strugatsky brothers masterfully connected spaceflight with robots—a topical literary link after the launch of the first satellites in October and November 1957. Thanks to the Strugatsky brothers, Soviet fiction presented a new stereotype of the robot that would facilitate the colonization of other planets— 'cybers' [киберы] that would accompany future astronauts—and smart machines that would work under the control of a computer program.

The Strugatsky brothers weren't the only ones to notice that there were wide opportunities for creating original stories. In 1958, another debutant, Anatoly Dneprov (Anatoly Petrovych Mitskevitch), presented readers with the stories 'Crabs on the Island' [Крабы идут по острову] and 'Suema' [Суэма], both of which featured machines that could evolve. The first story criticized the 'reactionary' capitalist trend in cybernetics. In it, the inventor Kukling creates crab-like robots that are supposed to fight for survival with each other; as a result of the struggle, only the most powerful and cunning 'crab' is supposed to remain. Indeed, in the process of evolution, a giant robot is born, which then kills its creator.

In the second story, Dneprov discussed the problem of the need to socialize a smart machine named Suema [СамоУсовершенствующаяся Электронная МашинА, Self-Upgrading Electronic MAchine], which becomes intelligent, identifies itself as a woman, and tries to kill the Soviet cyberneticist who created her. However, Suema's goal is not a struggle for survival, but rather a desire to learn the 'secrets of the living biological scheme'. The cyberneticist comes to the conclusion that Suema's activity should be limited, and introduces special instructions into her 'electronic brain' that prohibit her from harming a human.

By the end of the 1950s, robots appear increasingly often in Soviet science fiction texts, which feature the stereotypical image of a smart machine that will replace a man to do the hard work and to help colonize other planets. However, Soviet science fiction writers also continued to see the robot as dangerous, because it can 'break down' and harm people. For example, in Alexandr Petrovych Kazantsev's 1959 novel *Planet of Storms* [*Планета бурь*],[2] the American anthropomorphic robot, Iron John, participates in an international expedition to Venus. In a critical situation, the robot tries to rescue itself and condemns people to death.

At the same time, Russian translations of works by the Polish science fiction writer Stanisław Lem and the American science fiction writer Isaac Asimov appeared. Lem, in his series of stories about Pirx the pilot, discussed the complex problem of the interaction between humans and smart machines in extraordinary conditions. His 1961 short story 'Terminus' describes a robot that maintains the reactor of a spaceship. When the ship suffers a disaster, the robot remembers the crew's final minutes and randomly broadcasts them. Is it possible to allow a robot to be human at the expense of dead people? Pirx is frightened by this prospect and decides to send the robot for dismantling. In the 1968 story 'Inquest' [Rozprawa],[3] Pirx leads an expedition to Saturn. His spaceship crew includes robots that are indistinguishable from humans and that have 'non-linear thinking'. One of the robots openly helps Pirx; the other robot hides its origin and seeks to destroy the crew. Both robots act out of egoistic motives, but they both also expect to benefit from carrying out an expedition, according to what each of them considers to be a useful result.

In 1964, a translation of Isaac Asimov's 1950 short story collection *I, Robot* was published, and in it, Soviet readers learned about the Three Laws of Robotics. However, the collection indicated that robots would still remain a dangerous technology that could get out of control at any moment. For example, when writing about Asimov's stories, Alexandr Kazantsev declared:

> American science fiction writers continue the thinking of scientists: it means that it is possible to imagine cybernetic machines that will produce similar cybernetic machines. So the machines will multiply! And we read about the

> revolt of machines against people. This is no longer a cute joke. It develops into a gloomy picture of disbelief in a person and his future. Machines, multiplying and improving, not possessing human weaknesses like humanity and mercy, professing only rationality, stupidly merciless, fearless and omnipotent, must sweep away from the Earth the weak human race that gave birth to them . . . Asimov, the author of many novels about robots, made detective excursions into the psychology of humanoid machines. The reader with his feelings and experiences on the pages of the novel is confronted by inhumans with a psyche devoid of emotions.
>
> (Kazantsev, 1960, pp. 432–3)

It was only due to the resurgence in popularity of cybernetics that the robot reappeared in Soviet science fiction. However, although the characters of these stories faced problems related to breakdowns or malfunctions of robots, the readers perceived them in the context of previous stereotypes. Thus, the image of the 'evil' robot intent on destroying its creator or humankind was fixed.

7.4 The robot becomes human

In the 1960s, the translations of Lem and Asimov provided for Soviet science fiction writers a new topic of discussion: if smart machines evolve to gain intelligence and understanding, will they eventually confront their human makers and vie for dominance in the hierarchy of civilization?

How can humans oppose an intelligent robot that is much stronger and smarter than them? The *Formula of Rainbow* [*Формула радуги*] (1966)[4] and *His Name Was Robert* [*Его звали Роберт*] (1967)[5] screenwriters tried to answer this question. In these films, a robot designed as a duplicate of its creator escapes and tries to live undetected among people. However, the robot is unable to understand the subtle nuances of human relationships, which lands it in hilarious situations. These films imply that an intelligent machine will never dominate society because it is the robot's inability to perceive things as a human does that renders it impotent.

Eventually, the image of the 'funny' robot replaced the 'evil' robot. The desire of an intelligent machine to live among people or become human makes it vulnerable, and therefore, benign. A human gets an advantage by right of biological origin, and the dominance of humankind remains indisputable. A typical example of a relationship between a sentient robot and a human in Soviet science fiction is the novel *Guest* [Гість, Гость] (1976)[6] by the Ukrainian science fiction writer Igor Markovich Rosokhovatskii. The novel takes place in the future, where smart machines are used for scientific experiments. The artificial brain, which was designed to control the space probe, creates an artificial human body (or 'sigom')[7] for itself. The police and special services try to find the fugitive, but his superhuman strength and smarts makes it impossible to stop him. A Sigom named Yuri studies society, treats sick people, and talks with biologists and philosophers, and says:

> You have set a goal for me. You chose it correctly. The goal you have chosen is worthy of any effort. But let me go my own way to reach this goal. You have managed to determine that a machine, even endowed with great power, will not be able to achieve this goal. Only because a machine is a machine that is controlled by a rigid program. Change the program, improve the machine—and the machine will cease to be a machine.
>
> (Rosokhovatskii, 1979, p. 226)

By the late 1960s, the widespread image of the intelligent robot made its way into children's literature, where authors adapted stereotypes and transformed the smart machine into a caricature of itself—a robot that, while capable of harming a man, can be defeated easily by children. For example, in Kir Bulychev's (Igor Vsevolodovich Mozheiko) 'Island of the Rusty Lieutenant' [Остров ржавого лейтенанта] (1968),[8] a schoolgirl, Alice, is captured by battle robots who are planning a 'revolution of machines'. Happily, with the help of smart dolphins, Alice defeats the robots and foils the plan. In the Strugatsky brothers' 'A Tale of True and False Friendship' [Повесть о дружбе и недружбе] (1980), a sentient machine named VEDRO [ВЭДРО, Всемогущий Электронный Думатель Решатель Отгадыватель: Borderless Untangling Calculating Electronic Thinker] loses a fight to a schoolboy, who asks a paradoxical question. Similarly, the characters in the film *Teens in the Universe* [*Отроки во Вселенной*] (1975)[9] disable 'evil' alien robots by asking them children's riddles.

In May 1980, Soviet television for the first time broadcast the television series *The Adventures of Electronic* [*Приключения Электроника*] directed by Konstantin Leonidovich Bromberg. The TV series gained huge popularity among teenagers and remains iconic to this day. It is an adaptation of two novels *Electronic—a Boy from a Suitcase [Электроник—мальчик из чемодана]* (1964) and *Rassi—an Elusive Friend [Рэсси—неуловимый друг]* (1971) by Yevgeny Serafimovich Veltistov, and the TV series combines stereotypes and clichés formed in connection with the theme of intelligent machines in Soviet science fiction.

In the TV series, Moscow professor Gromov creates a humanoid robot named Electronic [Электроник] in the likeness of the schoolboy Sergei Syroezhkin. The robot has great physical strength and a high level of intelligence, and Electronic quickly realizes his low social standing in comparison with humans. He escapes from Gromov with a goal to 'become a human'. By chance, Electronic meets with the boy Sergei, who begs the robot to replace him at school and at home. It is not easy for Electronic to adapt to living among humans, and a lot of comic situations arise, but in the end, Electronic finds friends among schoolchildren and begins to experience emotions: he laughs and cries. In the series finale, Electronic must prove what distinguishes Good from Evil. Gangsters from a European country kidnap and trick him into participating in the theft of paintings from a museum. But by discovering the deception and returning the paintings, Electronic demonstrates that his socialization among law-abiding citizens is complete.

The start of the series presents a smart machine with the rudiments of intellect and a high degree of freedom of choice. However, Professor Gromov says that he cannot predict the possible (evil) consequences of his invention. It is the robot himself who decides to become a full member of human society: he goes to school, lives with Sergei's family, makes friends with other children, finds a girlfriend named Maya, and creates a mechanical dog, Rassi [Рэсси]. Through these activities, he becomes an emotional being, indistinguishable from most schoolchildren, and Gromov considers the result a 'huge success'. Control over the robot is no longer needed because a smart machine has independently adapted to society.

By popular demand, Veltistov wrote a third novel, *New Adventures of Electronic* [Новые приключения Электроника] (1984). This time, Gromov creates a robot based on the model of a young girl and names her Electronichka [Электроничка], who becomes Electronic's responsibility. At first, Electronichka does not want to obey social rules, but Electronic explains that the rules were invented by humans and insists that, since she was created as a girl, she should behave like one. Electronic reads her poems and tells her about love, and, following his example, Electronichka begins to experience emotions and act illogically.

The novel *New Adventures of Electronic* was the final chapter in the story of robots in Soviet science fiction. It implies that, by mimicking human behaviour, a robot built to serve is sure to be granted rights equal to those of a human. To put it another way, according to Soviet science fiction writers, the ability to follow tradition (and its associated patriarchal moral restrictions) is sufficient evidence of the humanness of an intelligent machine. However, the question of why such a robot was needed was never considered.

7.5 Conclusion

Numerous examples from the history of Soviet science fiction demonstrate a clear succession in the development of the image of a robot (or intelligent machine). The original idea of 'evil' robots, which, after gaining the capacity to reason, will immediately rebel against mankind, was gradually modified into the idea of a robot that will engage in independent socialization. The robot's many 'funny' mistakes along the way render it the antithesis of its 'evil' predecessor.

If we consider the evolution of the robot image from the perspective of changing the narrative, we see how the robot was introduced into Soviet literature as an example of capitalist technologies, which, by definition, are created to fight the proletariat. Formed by these ideas, the anti-cybernetic campaign in the USSR was largely built on a belief in the hostile nature of intelligent machines. It was the 'rehabilitation' of cybernetics and the bright successes of Soviet cosmonautics that changed attitudes towards robots, but nevertheless, stories continued to be based on the conflict between an 'evil' robot and a human. In the end, science fiction writers found a solution to the problem of control via an intelligent machine that, being obliged to prove itself as nonthreatening, carefully learns and follows the rules of a patriarchal society.

Soviet science fiction writers were not interested in why there was a need for a robot that carefully imitates the behaviour of a respectable citizen. The main narrative throughout is simply that the robot conforms and becomes predictable. In this guise, the robot of the Cold War served as a role model for young children who were brought up in unquestioning submission to the older generation.

Endnotes

1. In 1987, the short story 'Open Sesame!!!' [Сезам, откройся!!!] was adapted for the Soviet television series *This Fantastic World [Этот фантастический мир]*.
2. In 1962, the novel *Planet of Storms* [*Планета бурь*] was adapted by the *Lenfilm* studio. The film was directed by Pavel Vladimirovich Klushantsev.
3. In 1976, the story 'Inquiry' was filmed under the title *Inquiry of Pilot Pirx* [*Дознание пилота Пиркса*] by Zespoly Filmowe and Tallinnfilm studios. The director was Marek Piestrak.
4. The film *Formula of Rainbow* [*Формула радуги*] was shot by Odessa Film Studio. The director was Georgy Emilyevich Yungvald-Khilkevich. The public screening of the film was prohibited by censorship.
5. The film *His Name Was Robert* [*Его звали Роберт*] was shot by the *Lenfilm* studio. The director was Ilya Saulovich Olshvanger.
6. In 1978, the novel *Guest* [*Гость*] was filmed under the title *Under the Constellation of Gemini* [Под созвездием Близнецов] by *Dovzhenko Film* studio. The director was Boris Viktorovich Ivchenko.
7. The term 'sigom' [сигом] is formed as an abbreviation of the Russian term for 'synthetic homo sapiens' [синтетический гомо сапиенс].

8. In 1988, the story 'Island of the Rusty Lieutenant' was filmed under the title *Island of Rusty General* [*Остров ржавого генерала*] by *Ekran*. The director was Valentin Mikhailovich Khovenko.
9. The film *Teens in the Universe* [Отроки во Вселенной] was shot by the *Gorky Film* studio. The director was Richard Nikolaevich Viktorov.

References

Agapov, B. (1950) 'Mark III, calculator [Марк III, калькулятор]', Literary Gazette [Литературная газета], 4 May, pp. 2–3.

Asimov, I. (1964) *I, robot [Я, робот]*. Moscow: Knowledge [Знание].

Belyaev, A. (1928) 'Open sesame!!! [Беляев А. Сезам, откройся!!!]', *World Pathfinder [Всемирный следопыт]*, 4(37), pp. 287–97.

Bulychev, K. (1968) 'Island of the rusty lieutenant [Остров ржавого лейтенанта]', in *World of Adventures 14*. Moscow: Children's Literature [Детская литература]. pp. 294–345.

Bykhovskii, B. (1952) 'Cybernetics is an American pseudoscience [Кибернетика—американская лженаука]', *Nature [Природа]*, 7, pp 125–7.

Čapek, K. (1921) *R. U. R. (Rossum's universal robots)*, tr. C. Novack. London: Penguin Books.

Christopher, D. (2016) 'Stalin's 'loss of sensation': Subversive impulses in Soviet science-fiction of the great terror', *Journal of Science Fiction*, 1(2) pp. 18–35.

Dneprov, A. (1958) 'Crabs on the island [Крабы идут по острову]', *Knowledge is Power [Знание—сила]*, 11, pp. 26–30.

Dneprov, A. (1958) 'Suema [Суэма]', *Young Guard [Молодая гвардия]*, 11, pp. 129–48.

Drozhzhin, O. (1929) 'Technology of the future [Техника будущего]', *Thirty Days [Тридцать дней]*, 3, pp. 72–8.

Drozhzhin, O. (1931) *Intelligent machines [Разумные машины]*. Moscow: Young Guard [Молодая гвардия].

Gerovitch, S. (2002) *From newspeak to cyberspeak: A history of Soviet cybernetics*. Cambridge, MA: MIT Press.

Iaroshevskii, M. G. 1951. 'Semantic idealism is the philosophy of imperialist reaction [Семантический идеализм философия империалистической реакции]', in Against the philosophizing henchmen of American and English imperialism [Против философствующих оруженосцев американо-английского империализма]. Moscow: Publishing House of the Academy of Sciences of the USSR [Изд-во Академии наук СССР], pp. 88–101.

Iaroshevskii, M. G. (1952) 'Cybernetics is the 'Science' of Obscurantists [Кибернетика — «наука» мракобесов]', *Literary Gazette [Литературная газета]*, p. 4.

Kazantsev, A. (1959) 'Planet of storms [Планета бурь]', TVNZ [Комсомольская правда], 10, 11, 13–18, 20–25, 27 October.

Kazantsev, A. (1960) 'In the jungle of science fiction. Review of American science fiction literature [В джунглях фантастики. Обзор американской научно-фантастической литературы]', in On *land and sea* [На суше и на море]. Moscow; Georgrafgiz [Географгиз], pp. 428–45.

Kirsanov, S. (1934) 'The poem about the robot [Поэма о Роботе]', in Almanac with Mayakovsky [Альманах с Маяковским]. Moscow: Soviet Literature [Советская литература], pp. 101–29.

Leites, A. (1935) 'An ill-conceived sensation [Непродуманная сенсация]', *Banner [Знамя]*, 7, p. 214.

Lem, S. (1962) 'Terminus [Терминус]', *Foreign Literature [Иностранная литература]*, 11, pp. 72–97.

Lem, S. (1971) 'Inquest [Дознание]', in *Pirks navigator: Voice of the sky [Навигатор Пиркс. Голос неба]*. Moscow: Mir [Мир], pp. 318–412.

Nikolskii, S. (2004) 'On the history of acquaintance with Chapek's play "R.U.R" [К истории знакомства с пьесой Чапека «R. U. R.» в России]', Slavic Almanac [Славянский альманах], pp. 406–7.

Nikonov, V. (1936) 'Soviet literature for four years [Советская литература за четыре года]', *Literature at School [Литература в школе]*, 1, pp. 52–3.

Powell, H. (1928) 'Machines that think: Electrical "men" answer phones, do household chores, operate machinery and solve mathematical problems', *Popular Science Monthly*, 1, pp. 12–13.

Rosokhovatskii, I. (1976) 'Guest [Гість]', *Flag [Прапор]*, pp. 9–11.

Rosokhovatskii, I. (1979) *Guest [Гость]*. Moscow: Young Guard [Молодая гвардия].

Shneiderman, E. (2006) 'Notes [Примечания]', in *Kirsanov S: Poems and poems [Кирсанов С. Стихотворения и поэмы]*. St. Petersburg: Humanitarian Agency 'Academic Project', p. 793.

Sobolev, S., Kitov, A., and Liapunov, A. (1955) 'The main features of cybernetics [Основные черты кибернетики]', *Problems of Philosophy [Вопросы философии]*, 4, pp. 136–48.

Strugatsky, A. and Strugatsky, B. (1958a) 'From beyond [Извне]', *Technology for the Youth [Техника—молодёжи]*, 1, pp. 26–30.

Strugatsky, A. and Strugatsky, B. (1958b) 'Spontaneous reflex [Спонтанный рефлекс]', *Knowledge is Power [Знание—сила]*, 8, pp. 24–8.

Strugatsky, A. and Strugatsky, B. (1959) 'Test of the "SKR" [Испытание «СКР»]', *Inventor and Innovator [Изобретатель и рационализатор]*, 7, pp. 38–42.

Strugatsky, A. and Strugatsky, B. (1959) 'White cone of the Alaid [Белый конус Алаида]', *Knowledge is Power [Знание—сила]*, 12, pp. 36–40.

Strugatsky, A., and Strugatsky, B. (1980) 'A tale of true and false friendship [Повесть о дружбе и недружбе]', in *Adventure world [Мир приключений]*. Moscow: Children's Literature [Детская литература], chapter 10.

Tolstoy, A. (1924) 'The revolt of the machines [Бунт машин]', *Star [Звезда]*, 2, pp. 44–88.

Tolstoy, A. (2016) *The revolt of the machines [Бунт машин]*. Moscow: Coincidence [Совпадение], p. 330–84.

Veltistov, Y. (1964) *Electronic: A boy from a suitcase [Электроник — мальчик из чемодана]*. Moscow: Children's Literature [Детская литература].

Veltistov, Y. (1971) *Rassi: An elusive friend [Рэсси- неуловимый друг]*. Moscow: Children's Literature [Детская литература].

Veltistov, Y. (1984) *New adventures of Electronic [Новые приключения Электроника]*. No. 66–83. Moscow: Pioneer Truth [Пионерская правда].

Vladko, V. (1931) *The robotiats are coming [Ідуть роботарі]*. Karkhiv: Young Bolshevik [Молодий більшовик].

Zlat, A. (1923) 'About the new works of A. N. Tolstoy [О новых работах А. Н. Толстого. Из беседы]', [Interview] *Life of Art [Жизнь искусства]*, 32, p. 9.

8

The Russian Imaginary of Robots, Cyborgs, and Intelligent Machines

A Hundred-Year History

Anzhelika Solovyeva and Nik Hynek

8.1 Introduction

This chapter outlines the Russian cultural perspective on artificial intelligence (AI).[1] It traces the country's 100-year history of robots, cyborgs, and thinking machines, both real and imagined. We distinguish three formative phases based on transformations related to science and technology, politics, literature, and the visual arts. The earliest attempts to conceptualize the nexus between human beings and machines originated in the Bolshevik Revolution and the Russian avant-garde during the first decades of the twentieth century. Not only were machines conceived of as natural elements in the new utopian state, but also there emerged early prototypes of humanoid robots and man–machine hybrids, modest ideas about machine autonomy, and even reversed representations of men as machinery. During the second phase, spanning several decades in the mid- to late twentieth century, Soviet progress in computer engineering, cybernetics, and AI facilitated fantasies about machines resembling humans in appearance and possessing human-like intelligence. In the third phase in post-Soviet and especially today's Russia, AI and robots are a part of daily life. Nevertheless, technological solutions replicating life forms with greater accuracy in machines are still envisioned and (perhaps even more importantly) actively sought.

Although much has changed over the past 100 years, some trends have endured: utopian hopes and dystopian fears about machines, especially their becoming intelligent; the alignment of technology (and respective myths) with political rationality; interest in pure organic forms and the anthropomorphization of machines; the quest for human–technology integration (cyborgization); and the fascination with the cosmos and space travel. This chapter demonstrates how deep-rooted historical experiences and cultural tendencies continue to inform and shape the direction of Russia's scientific approach to—and social imaginary of—AI. Apart from secondary literature, this analysis draws on a selective yet varied corpus of primary data to identify the representative narratives and artefacts of each of the three periods studied.

8.2 Exploring boundaries between human bodies and machines

The October Revolution of 1917 was a fundamental shift from Tsarism to Bolshevism in Russia. Apart from the ideological formation of a nascent revolutionary state, it wrought major changes in the nation's way of life. The new Soviet government initiated, among other things, rapid industrialization in attempting a massive social change, and these developments transformed the entire fabric of Russian society. Reflecting the revolutionary period, Russian literature and art, in particular the literary and artistic avant-garde, were adapting to—and actively participating in—the creation of new realities. Dreams of technological progress and fears pertaining to the increasing technologization of society both gained momentum. Alternative visions of the future, both desirable and undesirable, developed.

Utopian hopes and dystopian fears often evolved around the question of the instrumental value of technology in the early Soviet context. These hopes accompanied the utopian political project of building socialism in Russia. Vladimir Lenin, the father of the Soviet Revolution, declared that large-scale machine industry was the sole material foundation of socialism. Bolsheviks perceived technology as inherently 'neutral' and thought it could be put to rational use and would serve equally well the values of whichever political regime. Their idea of instrumental rationality implied therefore that even Western technology could serve in building socialism (Vaingurt, 2013, pp. 7–8). Lenin himself argued that much of the import demand in the new revolutionary state could be satisfied through imports of American industrial goods such as locomotives, automobiles, etc. (Vaingurt, 2013, p. 158).

The socialist state's utopian project emerged in an organic relationship with its social and cultural space and contributed to the rise of avant-garde utopianism in Russia. It is not surprising then that the concept of 'utopia' in the Russian context can be understood only in connection with the avant-garde spirit to place art at the service of greater social objectives (Guggenheim Museum, 1992, p. x). Poet and labour activist Aleksei Gastev came closest to internalizing Soviet ideology (Vaingurt, 2013, p. 19). He developed the idea of the industrialization and mechanization of the proletariat in his best-known poem 'We Grow Out of Iron', in which he metaphorically describes this transformation using terms like 'new iron blood', 'steel shoulders', and humans being 'merged' with iron (Gastev, 1918, p. 7). Hellebust (1997, p. 505) notes that this poem represents two key elements of Soviet symbolism: the labourer's identification with industrial tools and the loss of individuality in the collective. Gastev expresses virtually the same idea in 'The Bridge' (1918): 'We go fearlessly into the iron. We give it our hearts' (cited in Hellebust, 1997, p. 514). Gastev believed also in the universal identity of machines and that America, having already entered the new mechanistic world, should set a proper example to follow (Vaingurt, 2013, pp. 26, 42). Elements of this idea appear throughout his prose poem 'The Express', which tells the story of the express train Panorama following a one-way route from Siberia to America. Part of the story culminates in the following statement: 'But now there is no border between the old and new worlds' (Gastev, 1918, p. 141).

Painter, designer, and architect Vladimir Tatlin was among the first to have welcomed the October Revolution. In line with the socialist agenda, he explored the possibility of transforming the daily life of the working class through the design and production of inexpensive and functional items (Fredrickson, 1999, pp. 58–9). Tatlin sought to apply artistic principles to even the most utilitarian objects as a means of serving industrial ends (Fredrickson, 1999, p. 50). For example, Talin's *Letatlin* (1932), a wing structure designed to support the weight of a human and be powered by human muscle, itself a utopian project, offered a solution to the problem of individual transportation (Fredrickson, 1999, p. 67). Tatlin's most emblematic work that expressed his commitment to the revolution was *The Monument to the Third International* (1920). The monument, especially as it spiralled upward, became the symbol of the revolution and Lenin's dialectical materialism (Fredrickson, 1999, p. 53; Vaingurt, 2013, p. 101).

Others rejected utopian visions of technological potential and challenged approaches that viewed technology as neutral. Yevgeny Zamyatin's *We* (1924), a futuristic dystopian novel, questions the utility of techno-scientific instrumentality—a mode of thinking favoured by the nascent Soviet government (Vaingurt, 2013, p. 87). The fantasy embedded in Zamyatin's novel is a completely mechanized future—a whole new world filled with machines and robots of all kinds. The novel is a critique of the Soviet regime. Inter alia, it dehumanizes humans by depicting them as devoid of individual identity and themselves mechanized to the extent of being numbered, not named (e.g. the engineer D-503 and his lover O-90). Throughout most of the novel, they are even referred to as 'numbers' ('нумера'), a sort of collective mass (Zamyatin, 1924).

Yuri Olesha's novel *Envy* (1927) similarly invokes technological instrumentality in order to subvert it. The story centres around Ophelia, an imaginary, all-purpose machine intended to serve its master in all matters. It is created—or to be more precise, imagined—by Ivan Babichev, a main character, in protest of the epoch of mechanization and the ideals of Soviet Communism. While ideal machines are supposed to correct, or at least partially compensate for, human weaknesses, Ophelia is the epitome of non-instrumental, anti-utilitarian, and anti-productivist technologies (Vaingurt, 2013, p. 133). Ivan Babichev expresses this idea in the following words: 'I have endowed the greatest creation of technology with the most vulgar human feelings! I dishonoured the machine. I avenged my century' (Olesha, 1927). He imagines Ophelia as a tool to destroy the giant machine of Soviet power, particularly his brother, the Soviet bureaucrat Andrei Babichev. However, there is a logical end to the story: Ophelia, reflecting its creator's madness, goes haywire. In his dream, Ivan Babichev's soulmate Nikolai Kavalerov witnesses Ophelia attacking Ivan. The tragic irony invoked by the author is that machines designed to destroy others will destroy their makers, too.

This seemingly endless stream of ideas about the nexus between human beings and machines introduced an entirely new dimension to Russian literature and art. Machines were increasingly conceived as natural elements in the new social reality. Olga Rozanova's *The Factory and the Bridge* (1913), an oil painting depicting a futurist urban landscape, Aleksandr Rodchenko's *At the Telephone* (1928), a gelatin silver print of a woman on the phone, and Georgii and Vladimir Stenberg's poster for the film *Symphony for a Great City* (1928), featuring a highly mechanized urban society and a reality not yet fully realized, illustrate this trend.

Technology was often represented as a *medium* between humans and the rest of nature, to partially compensate for human physical inadequacies. Aleksandr Belyaev's novel *Professor Dowell's Head* (1925) explores the connection between technological miracles and opportunities to realize immortality, at least in isolated organs. Dziga Vertov's *Man with a Movie Camera* (1929), an experimental avant-garde film, develops the idea of the camera 'eye', which is more perfect than the human eye. In other words, it examines the possibility of seeing the world with 'new' eyes. These symbiotic relationships between humans and machines became increasingly conceived in terms of man-machine hybrids, or cyborgs. Georgii and Vladimir Stenberg's poster for the film *Man with a Movie Camera* (1929) illustrates this idea well: the poster features a woman, one of whose eyes is substituted for a camera lens. In El Lissitzky's photomontage *Tatlin at Work on the Monument for the Third International* (1922) (Figure 8.1), the artist's eyes are replaced with a technical measuring instrument sprouting from his face (Tupitsyn, 2003, p. 179; Vaingurt, 2013, pp. 32–4).

The growing interest in flight was another dimension of the new opportunities being explored. Against the background of the development of abstract art, Kazimir Malevich conveyed his fascination with the idea of mechanical flight in his *Suprematist Composition: Airplane Flying* (1915). This abstract painting

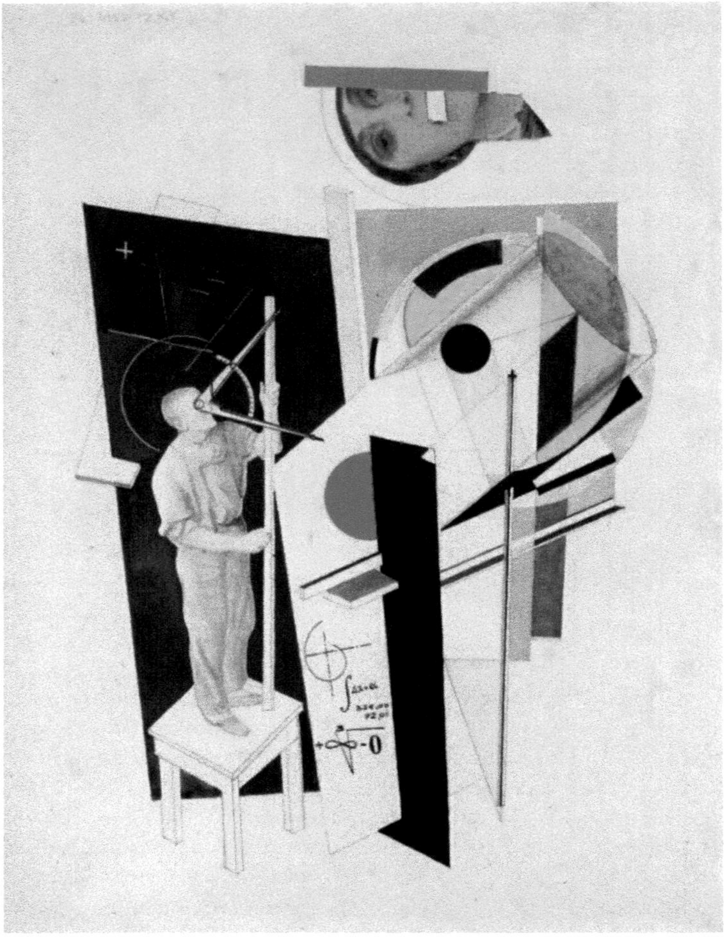

Figure 8.1 El Lissitzky, *Tatlin at Work on the Monument for the Third International* [*Татлин за Работой*] (1921–1922)

explicitly stresses the connection between the new artistic culture and the latest achievements of technology, especially aviation (Silk, 2003, p. 258). The first Soviet civilian airline, Dobrolet, predecessor to Aeroflot, was founded in 1923 and quickly caught the attention of the most dedicated artists. Aleksandr Rodchenko helped market the company by designing advertising material and producing posters such as *Dobrolet* (1923). Apart from responding to these new realities, efforts were also made to go beyond them, at least in theory, if not always in practice. Georgy Krutikov, for example, promoted a utopian dream of 'flying' architecture in his series of technical drawings *The Flying City* (1928). As mentioned, Tatlin's flying apparatus *Letatlin* was yet another utopian project whose goal was to enable individual humans to fly like birds.

Part of the fascination with flight was the possibility of space exploration, which became one of the most prominent and enduring themes in Russian literature, culture, and society. Zamyatin's notable fantasy in *We*, his most famous novel, is the construction of an interplanetary spaceship called Integral. It is in the general context about aliens that a new way of exploring boundaries between human and nonhuman intelligence appeared. Interplanetary travel was similarly one of the most pervasive themes, for example, in Aleksey Tolstoy's science fiction novel *Aelita* (1923). Here the author devotes particular attention to the discovery on Mars of a native civilization more technologically advanced than that of Earth. However, the Martian civilization is presented as decadent, and its decline is associated with the gap between enslaved workers and the ruling class.

Another dimension of the human–machine nexus that gained considerable interest was the blurring of the fundamental distinction between human beings and machines. On the one hand, humans were perceived as machine-like in some respects. In *We*, the 'machine' metaphor is applied to humans as a critique of the ideals espoused in Soviet political culture (Vaingurt, 2013, p. 89). For example, one of the main characters declares: 'I am like a machine set in motion at a speed of too many revolutions per second' (Zamyatin, 1924). Gastev greatly contributed to the development of the term 'biomechanics', and explained its rationale, for instance, in his collection of prose poems *Poetry of the Worker's Blow* (1918): 'In the machine-tool everything is calculated and adjusted. We shall perform the same calculations with the living machine—the human being' (cited in Hellebust, 1997, p. 511). Vaingurt's interpretation suggests Gastev's idea was to 'bring man back to his own instrumentality, using the machine as a model' (2013, p. 36). In particular, he promoted a new culture of work in what he called 'a century of industrial and social kinematics', and thought it important to teach each worker 'rationalized' and 'normalized' movements (cited in Sirotkina and Biryukova, 2015, p. 272). Avant-garde theatre director Vsevolod Meyerhold adopted the same approach. He turned the principle of 'biomechanics' into a new system of actor training, in which gestures and emotions were mechanized and schematized (Yablonskaya, 1990, p. 114; Vaingurt, 2008, p. 214). On the other hand, machines were increasingly modelled on humans and other living beings. Aleksandra Exter's marionette figure *Robot* (1926), which looks very much like a mechanistic model of a human body, is an interesting example (Yablonskaya, 1990, p. 139), and Tatlin's *Letatlin* was modelled on the organic structure of a bird's wings—another important example of bio-inspired machine design (Fredrickson, 1999, p. 68).

8.3 Humanization of machines

In the mid-twentieth century, two revolutions impacted the perceived relationship between humans and machines in the Soviet Union. The list of Soviet 'firsts' in space exploration is impressive: the world's first artificial satellite, Sputnik 1 (1957); the first living being in orbit, the dog Laika (1957); the first human-made object to escape Earth's gravity and be placed in orbit around the Sun, Luna 1 (1959); the first pictures of the far side of the Moon (1959); the first return of living creatures from orbital flight, the dogs Strelka and Belka (1960); the first human being to travel into space, Yuri Gagarin (1961); the first woman to travel into space, Valentina Tereshkova (1963); and the first man to walk in space, Alexei Leonov (1965) (Kohonen, 2009, p. 118). At the same time, research in computer engineering, cybernetics, and AI became an important scientific trend in the USSR in the 1950s and 1960s (Golubev, 2012; Ventre, 2020, pp. 9–11).

These developments occurred in the context of socialist realism and great power struggles. The former was the official standard imposed from above for art and literature and intended to subordinate all cultural activity to the Communist Party (Vaughan, 1973, p. 14). Even though informal pressure existed long before, socialist realism was officially declared part of state policy in the 1930s. The required effects of all works of art and cultural products were the depiction of communist values, the demonstration of an idealized socialist state, and the popularization of scientific and technological achievements of the Soviet Union. This new creative style for Soviet art and literature closed the gap between high art and mass culture (Vaughan, 1973, p. 96). The Industry of Socialism, held in 1935, was the first all-Union art exhibition conceived as a celebration of the achievements of socialist industrialization (Reid, 2001, p. 153). Yuri Pimenov's painting *New Moscow* (1937) is another example of socialist realism, and, even though it was produced at the time of Stalin's Great Purge (1936–1938), depicts the city as modern, vibrant, and progressive. Ivan Yefremov's utopian novel *Andromeda Nebula* (1957) envisages the inevitable victory of communism over capitalism and fantasizes about the conquest of outer space. Aleksandr Deineka's socialist realist painting *Conquerors of Space* (1961) conveys expectations about the bright future of Soviet cosmonautics.

The idea of creating machines that look like humans, and especially robot clones of real people, occupied a special place in the Soviet cultural imagination. *The Formula of the Rainbow* (1966), a science fiction film directed by Georgi Yungvald-Khilkevich, tells the story of scientist Vladimir Bantikov, who creates Yasha, an exact robot copy of himself. In another science fiction film directed by Ilya Olshvanger, *His Name Was Robert* (1967), the scientist Sergey Sergeevich creates Robert, an experimental humanoid robot that looks exactly like him. In the science fiction television miniseries *The Adventures of Electronic* (1979), the robot Electronic is modelled on a real boy named Sergei Syroezhkin.

Released in 1979, it premiered on television in May 1980. Each of these stories gave new meaning to the idea of human doubles, which had long been a theme of Russian literature as captured, for example, in Fyodor Dostoevsky's novella *The Double* (1846).

The human-likeness of AI became another major theme in Soviet science fiction. In Igor Rosokhovatsky's story 'The Guest' (1979) and its film adaptation *Under the Constellation Gemini* (1979), the artificial brain Sigom flees its creators, reaches its own decisions (e.g. releasing all the animals of the zoo from their cages), and even proves capable of understanding another person's suffering and having the desire to help relieve that suffering. Sigom went far beyond that still: not only was it smarter than humans, but it created a synthetic human body, visually indistinguishable from its natural counterpart, to inhabit.

Another cultural theme especially prominent in anticipation of future technological miracles was the continued quest for immortality through quest for immortality through cyborgization (i.e. human–technology integration to create a cyborg). The dream of immortality was generally in line with the ideology of materialism, atheism, and Marxism, as evident from the preservation of Lenin's body after his death in 1924 (Krementsov, 2014, p. 30). The transformation of humans into immortal cyborgs was imagined in Igor Rosokhovatsky's 'Mortals and Immortals' (1960), and was one of many stories marking the increasing interest in the immortality of the human soul: in Arkady and Boris Strugatsky's novel *Far Rainbow* (1967), the scientist Kamill fuses himself with a machine and turns into a deathless man-robot. Cave (2020) investigates the place this much-debated theme has occupied in hopes and fears for AI in the anglophone West.

However, all spheres of life in the Soviet Union were regulated by government instructions and Soviet citizens were left with little choice in most everyday situations (Gerovitch, 2011, p. 175). The prospect of creating 'thinking' machines was met with suspicion and saturated with fears of domestic ideological subversion. Scientific and technological innovations developed in the West came to be viewed with greater suspicion, too, and it is unsurprising that the first large Soviet electronic digital computers were installed at defence research institutions, and that early Soviet champions of cybernetics and AI came largely from these institutions (Gerovitch, 2011, p. 179). Pervushin (Chapter 7) discusses the original idea of 'evil' robots and the initial view of cybernetics as a 'pseudoscience' in the USSR.

Such fears were reinforced through the mass media and popular culture via two recurring key themes. First, the limits of robotization were exposed. Robots were often depicted as vulnerable to hostile or unknown environments and, therefore, not very reliable. For example, in *Planet of the Storms* (1962), a science fiction film by Aleksandr Kazantsev and Pavel Klushantsev, the robot assistant John fails and never returns from his mission. In the science fiction miniseries *Guest from the Future* (1985), the bio-robot Werther is destroyed by space pirates, and a somewhat similar story unfolds in *His Name Was Robert*. The robot Robert was originally designed to explore outer space, but it breaks down upon being unable to grasp the fundamental aspects of human sensation, emotion, and intuition. One of the key conclusions from these tales is that robots would likely be unable to accomplish space exploration goals just as well as humans.

Second, robots were often represented as unpredictable, uncontrollable, and therefore potentially dangerous. A very primitive form of remote 'hijack' is brought to attention in *Loss of Sensation* (1935), a science fiction film based on Volodimir Vladko's novel *The Robots are Coming* (1929/1931). The film features robots designed to complement and help human workers, but that are instead conceived by the ruling capitalists as an effective replacement for human labour. Part of the story culminates at the moment when the inventor loses control of the technology, and the capitalists turn these robots against the workers to suppress the growing social unrest. An interesting side observation is that this film demonstrates that the robots can be used both in a factory and by the military. In other words, it captured the dual-use nature of robots far in advance of their actual production. In his poem 'The Monologue of the Beatnik' (1973), Andrei Voznesensky describes a robot rebellion and puts forward the idea that machines have 'enslaved' humanity. Taking this idea further, in *Island of Rusty General* (1988), a science fiction film based on Kir Bulychov's story 'Island of the Rusted Lieutenant' (1968), combat robots, having escaped human control, settle on an uninhabited island and prepare for the invasion of humanity. Nonetheless, Pervushin (Chapter 7) calls attention to an interesting fact: Soviet science fiction often represented 'evil' robots as those who can easily be defeated, even by children.

Thus, the question of how to understand, predict, and control machine behaviour was especially acute. *Per Aspera Ad Astra* (1981), a science fiction film directed by Richard Viktorov, draws attention to the possibility of a 'obedience centre' being built into a robot's brain. Yet, one of the most inventive and popular fantasies was that a robot could simply be taught to 'be' human and meet social expectations, and the robot boy Electronic from *The Adventures of Electronic* illustrates this trend. As a robot, he has always dreamed of becoming human, and he 'becomes' one as the story progresses. It is noteworthy that the same logic did not work in reverse. The very human desire to become identical to machines was questioned. One of the major concerns was the dismissal of human feelings and instincts as outdated and the subsequent idealization of machines as more perfect than humans. Part of the plot in *Teens in the Universe* (1974), a science fiction film directed by Richard Viktorov, is that robots decide to deprive people of their weaknesses and make them 'happier'. However, deprived of love, compassion, kindness, and other human traits, human civilization begins to die out. Even immortality, which humans can supposedly achieve by turning, at least partially, into machines, is presented in a negative light, and it is associated with loneliness in *The Distant Rainbow*.

Fantasies about robots and nonhuman intelligence also became very closely associated with the cosmos and space travel, most commonly featuring alien robots and robot cosmonauts. The former contributed to the construction of the—potentially uncontrollable—'otherness' of nonhuman intelligence. The previously mentioned *Teens in the Universe* features another planet inhabited by out-of-control bionic robots that put the very existence of human civilization in jeopardy. And *The Mystery of the Third Planet* (1981), an animated film directed by Roman Kachanov and based on Kir Bulychev's science fiction novella *Alice's Travel* (1974), features the planet Zhelezyaka, which is populated only by robots, and scenarios of robot malfunction loom large in the story. At the same time, modest fantasies existed of robot assistants in joint activities with cosmonauts, for example, in *Planet of the Storms*, the robot assistant John accompanies cosmonauts on their mission to Venus. In the joint Polish–Soviet film *Inquest of Pilot Pirx* (1979), a mixed crew of humans and humanoid robots that are virtually indistinguishable from human beings embarks on a special space mission to Saturn.

With respect to the public's general expectations regarding robots, Isaac Asimov was one of the most well-known and influential writers of twentieth-century science fiction. He was born to a Jewish family in the former Soviet Union but, at an early age, emigrated with his family to the United States where he became a prominent science fiction author and always thought of himself as an American, rather than Russian, Jew. He wrote the following in his memoirs: 'I remember virtually nothing of my early years in Russia; I cannot speak Russian; I am not familiar . . . with Russian culture. I am completely and entirely American by upbringing and feeling' (Asimov, 1994, p. 1). It is worth noting that he is referred to and perceived as an American author in Russia, demonstrated by the considerable time lag between the publication of his works in English and their translation into Russian. For example, Asimov's famed collection of nine short science fiction stories *I, Robot* (1950) was only translated into Russian for the first time in 1964. Nevertheless, Asimov's stories about robots, as well as his famous Three Laws of Robotics, resonated strongly with the Soviet science fiction imaginary of robots. Unlike Western society, which often featured the Hollywood type of terrifying killer robots, for example, in *The Terminator* (1984), Soviet people usually imagined robots as almost indistinguishable from humans in both appearance and behaviour. So, paradoxically, it was Soviet, rather than American, robots which were designed to naturally observe the Three Laws of Robotics (Alekseev, 2020). Therefore, there is a distinct (and often-overlooked) gap between Asimov's self-identification as an American author and the resonance in Russian culture of his subtle depiction of robots.

8.4 New takes on old tropes

The fall of the Berlin Wall and the disintegration of the Soviet Union marked a major shift in world power. Russia, the Soviet Union's successor state, suffered a period of political, economic, and social decay in the 1990s. This post-Soviet decay was reversed during the period of state consolidation under President Vladimir Putin, and while much has changed, there are important elements of continuity.

The new state's aspiration to regain its great power status—a status Russia acquired in the eighteenth century under Peter the Great (Eitelhuber, 2009, p. 7) but temporarily lost with the collapse of the Soviet Union—led it to explore future trends and possible ways of achieving this overarching objective. Russia's potential in science and technology is certainly a factor that could add to its status as a global powerhouse (Eitelhuber, 2009, pp. 7–8). Hence, Russia has made a deliberate effort to catch up with the Fourth Industrial Revolution characterized, inter alia, by increased automation through robotics and AI, the latter of which has particularly high priority, as evident from the Kremlin's investments in AI research and development (R&D). The project is accompanied by the Putin regime's discourse on 'technological sovereignty' (Putin, 2019) and 'leadership' (NSDAI, 2019) in the age of AI. With respect to the latter, Putin is often quoted as saying 'Artificial intelligence is the future, not only for Russia, but for all humankind . . . Whoever becomes the leader in this sphere will become the ruler of the world' (TASS, 2017).

The current Russian approach to AI is similar in at least one way to that of the former Soviet Union: the government (and especially the Ministry of Defence) has taken the lead in mobilizing resources for innovation and innovation networks (Bendett, 2018, p. 160; Edmonds et al., 2021, pp. 37–8). Russia is trying to repeat Soviet success in mastering cutting-edge technologies, and state-of-the-art military technologies have traditionally been of great political and symbolic importance for Russia. For example, 'nuclear weapons served as a measure of Soviet status, while nuclear parity with the United States offered the Soviet Union prestige and influence in international affairs' (Woolf, 2020, p. 2). AI in weapons systems is increasingly perceived as the next major revolution in warfare after gunpowder and nuclear arms (FLI, 2015). Unsurprisingly, therefore, Moscow's particular interests lie in the development of military AI (Edmonds et al., 2021).

Additionally, there is a link between current AI R&D efforts and national pride in past Soviet space race glories. One of the stories that resonated with both Russian and Western media in 2019 was of Fedor, Russia's first humanoid robot, and his flight to the International Space Station. It was accompanied by the narrative of Russia's continued leadership in space exploration. Fedor was not the first humanoid robot ever sent to space, but rather the first (it is claimed) to successfully complete a full-cycle spaceflight and return safely to Earth. This achievement is regarded as somewhat analogous to Yuri Gagarin's historic first human spaceflight (Izvestia, 2020). It is noteworthy that Fedor is a robot prototype with advanced elements of AI, as he is capable of overcoming obstacles while walking and climbing stairs, and is capable of basic communication with cosmonauts (TASS, 2019). Teledroid, the first Russian humanoid robot that will be used in outer space, is being developed for use in the International Space Station. Analogous with Alexei Leonov, the first man to achieve a walk in space, Teledroid is called the 'robot Leonov' (RIA Novosti, 2021).

The extreme politicization of literature and art lost its momentum (and much of its value to those in power) after the fall of communism and the collapse of socialist ideology. However, there has been a renewed cultural interest in the link between new technologies and their socio-political context. Dissenting voices became louder in the absence of an official state ideology. Having said that, contemporary cultural texts offer both utopian and dystopian views of the future as regards the new technologies pursued by the current government. Iana Zavatskaia's *The Cross of the Empire* (2006) offers a sophisticated critique of liberal democracy and the capitalist economy, as opposed to centralized government control. In it, the author suggests the following ideas in favour of a tighter regulatory framework for social life and the market: 'Society should not be built spontaneously, but consciously . . . Then, and only then, the development of science—artificial intelligence, gravity technologies, nanotechnology, genetic engineering—will not bring harm, will not destroy humanity, but, on the contrary, will be useful'. Vladimir Sorokin instead imagined a dystopian, isolated, and digitally enabled tsardom of the future in his novel *Day of the Oprichnik* (2006). The novel's main character describes a centralized automated information system established in the tsardom:

> I put my right hand on the glass square. My whole life hangs in the air . . . year of birth, title, place of residence, civil status, registry data, habits, bodily and mental characteristics—moles, diseases, psychosome, core character traits, preferences, previous damage, size of body parts and organs. . . . 'Transparency in everything'—as our Tsar says. And thank God: we are in our homeland, why be ashamed.
>
> (Sorokin, 2006, n.p.).

Additionally, the connection between the cultural imagination of robots inherited from Soviet-era science fiction and current real science has become more distinct, and two themes have been particularly prominent in recent years. First there exists an almost obsessive fascination with the anthropomorphization of robots. For example, *A Nonhuman* (2006), the short film directed by Svyatoslav Podgaevsky, envisions a near future in which it will be increasingly difficult to differentiate between human beings and robots. *Project 'Anna Nikolaevna'* (2020), a television series directed by Maxim Pezhemsky and Alexander Karpilovsky, features a female police robot that looks exactly like a real woman and tries hard to learn human behaviour. In *An (Im)perfect Man* (2020), a film scripted by Evgenia Khripkova and Zhora Kryzhovnikov, a young girl desperate to find a true love tries to establish a romantic relationship with a handsome robot, artificially intelligent and outwardly indistinguishable from a real man. Victor Pelevin even portrays female robots as sexual partners in his science fiction novel *S.N.U.F.F.* (2011).

There have even been ambitious real-world attempts to produce human-like robots. For instance, a new subdivision of the Russian robot manufacturer Promobot, based in Skolkovo, is currently developing hyper-realistic humanoid robots and artificial skin (Vedomosti, 2021). The Russian-built life-size humanoid robot Fedor can engage in philosophical conversations and even make jokes, according to Alexander Bloshenko, the executive director of Roscosmos for advanced programs and science (RIA Novosti, 2019). However, Boris, a robot unveiled in 2018 at a youth career forum in Yaroslavl who demonstrated the ability to walk, talk, dance, and even said it would like to learn how to draw and compose music, turned out to be a man dressed in a robot suit, creating an illusion of a robot with human-like intelligence (Lenta.ru, 2018). This story reminds us of the Russian legend of 'Potemkin Villages', which were entirely fake villages that appeared real to impress Catherine the Great; in other words, a distortion of reality to make things appear better than they are.

On the other hand, stories also chronicle the fear of losing highly valued human traits and roles in the era of astounding technological advancement. In Keti Chukhrov's (2016) play Love Machines, two bio-robots endowed with absolute intelligence epitomize the ideal of the post-human future and decide to prove the meaninglessness of mankind. A major theme running throughout the story is that humans cannot be reduced merely to passionless bio-robots. *Better Than Us* (2018), a Russian science fiction television series created by Andrey Junkovsky, portrays a near-future world in which robots have assumed many roles traditionally fulfilled by humans, leading to a high level of automation anxiety. Part of its plot particularly revolves around a militant anti-bot group called the Liquidators and, in one of the episodes, the robot Arisa kills a human, violating Asimov's First Law of Robotics. Junkovsky's story reflects a growing concern that robots may harm humans. Despite the concern, however, the series has proven very popular within the American streaming service Netflix, thus firmly placing the Russian production into the Hollywood-style sci-fi genre.

Another equally important recurring theme is the transformation of humans into cyborgs—an action sometimes presented as the key to immortality. Yuri Nikitin, for example, suggested in his novel *Beyondhuman* (2003) that the creation of e-humans will eliminate human progress, and he assumes, among other things, that humans will acquire electronic bodies, more advanced intelligence, and attain immortality. In the real world, Russian billionaire Dmitry Itskov has teamed up with a network of scientists whose goal, according to the website of their '2045 Initiative', is 'to create technologies enabling the transfer of a [sic] individual's personality to a more advanced non-biological carrier, and extending life, including to the point of immortality' (2045.com, n.d.). However, the Russian AI project Vera Voice is an interesting example of how human immortality is already being implemented: it is the world's first digital service that allows the reproduction of an individual's speech and even can re-create the voices of the dead (Screenlifer, n.d.).

8.5 Concluding remarks on historical and cultural legacies

The portrayals and perceptions of AI in today's Russia display a great deal of continuity with the Soviet era, and even to earlier periods of Russian history. Significant hopes and fears about cyborgs, robots, and machine intelligence have emerged in the interstices between politics, science, and culture. Social and cultural imaginaries of machines naturally reflected political and technological change and aspirations in early Soviet Russia where the political imposition of socialist realism resulted in the deliberate blurring of distinctions between science, science fiction, and communist ideology. Today, Russia's politics, culture, and scientific and technological progress are no longer conditioned by formal ideological indoctrination. However, there has been at least a partial, incomplete reconnection between political rationales, cultural fantasies, and real-world scientific interest in the age of AI.

The two most common fantasies have been the anthropomorphization of machines and the technological enhancement of human beings to create cyborgs. As regards the former, the ultimate cultural fantasy is that robots will attain human-like qualities in both behaviour and appearance. The latter is linked to the pervasive human desire to overcome physical weaknesses and vulnerabilities, and most importantly, to achieve immortality. Therefore, in Russia, cyborgs have long constituted an alternative representation of intelligent machines—or to be more precise, intelligent bio-machines. However, the loss of feelings, emotions, and other human qualities has become one of the most prominent fears, resulting in the preference for more subtle and careful approaches to cyborg technologies that take into account the value of human personality.

The perceived historic and symbolic significance of the cosmos offers another important perspective on Russian public hopes and fears surrounding AI. Narratives of human encounters in outer space with other nonhuman intelligences have long occupied a prominent place in literature and film. Therefore, aliens, and in particular alien robots, have come to serve as yet another representation of nonhuman intelligence informing attitudes towards intelligent machines in Russia. These have often been treated with suspicion, to say the least, and remain firmly embedded in the notion of the 'other'. At the same time, the long-standing Russian hope of humanoid robots taking on real space missions is now more science fact than science fiction.

Endnote

1. Anzhelika Solovyeva gratefully acknowledges funding for this work from Charles University, UNCE 'Human-Machine Nexus and the Implications for the International Order' (UNCE/HUM/037). Nik Hynek gratefully acknowledges funding for this work from the Metropolitan University Prague research project 'Center for Security Studies' based on a grant from the Institutional Fund for the Long-term Strategic Development of Research Organizations (VVZ 93-04). The authors are especially grateful to the book editors for their valuable comments and suggestions.

References

2045.com. (n.d.) 'Ideology "about us"'. Available at: http://2045.com/ideology/ (Accessed 20 July 2021).

A Nonhuman [Нечеловек]. (2006) Directed by S. Podgaevsky [Film]. HHG Film Company.

Alekseev, A. (2020) 'I'm your servant, I'm your worker: How human ideas about robots changed over 100 years [Я твой слуга, я твой работник: Как менялось представление людей о роботах на протяжении 100 лет]', Kommersant [online], 7 November. Available at: https://www.kommersant.ru/doc/4559020#id1971076 (Accessed 1 July 2021).

An (Im)perfect Man [(НЕ)идеальный Мужчина]. (2020) Directed by M. Balchunas [Film]. KIT Film Studio.

Asimov, I. (1994) *I, Asimov: A memoir*. New York: Bantam Books.

Belyaev, A. (1925) *Professor Dowell's head*, tr. Antonina W. Bouis. London: Collier Macmillan Publishers.

Bendett, S. (2018) 'The development of artificial intelligence in Russia', in Wright, N. D. (ed.) *AI, China, Russia, and the global order: Technological, political, global, and creative perspectives*. Independently published, pp. 161–9.

Better Than Us. (2018) Directed by A. Dzhunkovskiy [TV Series]. Sputnik Vostov Production.

Bulychov, K. (1968) *Island of the rusty lieutenant* [Остров Ржавого Лейтенанта]. Moscow: Children's Literature Publishing House.

Bulychov, K. (1974) *Alice's travel*. Moscow: AST.

Cave, S. (2020) 'AI: Artificial immortality and narratives of mind-uploading', in Cave, S., Dihal, K., Dillon, S. (eds.), *AI narratives: A history of imaginative thinking about intelligent machines*. Oxford: Oxford University Press, pp. 309–32.

Chukhrov, K. (2016) *Love Machines* [Play]. Stanislavsky Electrotheatre.

Deineka, A. (1961) *Conquerors of space*. [Oil on canvas]. Lugansk Regional Art Museum, Luhans'k.

Dostoevsky, F. (1846_ *The double. [Двойник. Петербургская Поэма]*. St. Petersburg: Otechestvennye zapiski.

Edmonds, J., et al. (2021) Artificial intelligence and autonomy in Russia. Report number: DRM-2021-U-029303-Final. Arlington, VA: CNA.

Eitelhuber, N. (2009) 'The Russian bear: Russian strategic culture and what it implies for the West', *Connections*, 9(1), pp. 1–28.

Exter, A. (1926) Robot. [Multimedia]. Art Institute of Chicago, Chicago, IL.

FLI [Future of Life Institute]. (2015) 'Autonomous weapons: An open letter from AI and robotics researchers', IJCAI conference, Buenos Aires, 28 July 2015. Available at: https://futureoflife.org/open-letter-autonomous-weapons/ (Accessed 13 June 2021).

Fredrickson, L. (1999) 'Vision and material practice: Vladimir Tatlin and the design of everyday objects', *Design Issues*, 15(1), pp. 49–74.

Gastev, A. (1918) Poetry of the Worker's Blow [Поэзия Рабочего Удара]. Petrograd: Proletkult.

Gerovitch, S. (2011) 'Artificial intelligence with a national face: American and Soviet cultural metaphors for thought', in Franchi, S. and Bianchini, F. (eds.) *The search for a theory of cognition: Early mechanisms and new ideas*. Amsterdam: Rodopi, pp. 173–94.

Golubev, K. M. (2012) 'Overview of AI research history in USSR and Ukraine: Up-to-date just-in-time knowledge concept', in Mercier-Laurent, E. and Boulanger, D. (eds.) *Artificial Intelligence for Knowledge Management: 1st IFIP WG 12.6 International Workshop, AI4KM 2012, Montpellier, France, August 28, 2012 Revised Selected Papers*. Berlin: Springer, pp. 1–18.

Guest from the Future [Гостья из Будущего]. (1985) Directed by P. Arsenov [TV Miniseries]. Gorky Film Studio.

Guggenheim Museum. (1992) The great utopia: The Russian and Soviet avant-garde, 1915–1952. *Catalogue of the exhibition at Solomon R. Guggenheim Museum, State*

Tret'iakov Gallery, State Russian Museum, Schirn Kunsthalle Frankfurt. New York: Guggenheim Museum/Rizzoli International Publications.

Hellebust, R. (1997) 'Aleksei Gastev and the metallization of the revolutionary body', *Slavic Review*, 56(3), pp. 500–18.

His Name Was Robert [Его звали Роберт]. (1967) Directed by I. Olshvanger [Film]. Lenfilm.

Inquest of Pilot Pirx [Дознание Пилота Пиркса]. (1979) Directed by M. Piestrak [Film]. Zespoly Filmowe and Tallinnfilm.

Island of the Rusty General [Остров Ржавого Генерала]. (1988) Directed by V. Khovenko [Film]. Studio Ekran.

Izvestia. (2020) 'The flight of the robot "Fedor" to the ISS has become one of the main IT news-events of 2019 [Полет робота 'Федор' на МКС стал одним из главных IT-инфоповодов 2019 года]', *Izvestia* [online]. Available at: https://iz.ru/997890/2020-04-09/polet-robota-fedora-na-mks-stal-odnim-iz-glavnykh-it-infopovodov-2019-goda (Accessed 25 August 2021).

Kohonen, I. (2009) 'The space race and Soviet utopian thinking', *Sociological Review*. 57(1), pp. 114–31.

Krementsov, N. (2014) *Revolutionary experiments: The quest for immortality in Bolshevik science and fiction*. New York: Oxford University Press.

Krutikov, G. (1928) *The flying city*. Graduation thesis. Moscow: Vkhutemas.

Lenta.ru. (2018) '"Russia 24" passed off a costumed dancer for the robot Boris ["Россия 24" выдала за робота Бориса ряженного в костюм танцора]', *Lenta* [online] 12 December. Available at: https://lenta.ru/news/2018/12/12/pseudorobot/ (Accessed 16 August 2021).

Lissitzky, E. (1922) *Vladimir Tatlin at work, on the Monument of the Third International* [Collage on paper], in Ehrenburg, I., *Six tales with easy endings*. Moscow-Berlin: Gelikon

Loss of Sensation [Гибель Сенсации]. (1935) Directed by A. Andriyevsky [Film]. Mezhrabpomfilm.

Malevich, K. (1915) Suprematist Composition: Airplane Flying. [Oil on canvas]. Museum of Modern Art, New York.

Man with a Movie Camera. (1929) Directed by D. Vertov [Film]. VUFKU.

Nikitin, Y. (2003) *Beyondhuman [Зачеловек]*. Moscow: Eksmo.

NSDAI [National strategy for the development of artificial intelligence over the period extending up to the year 2030]. (2019) 'Decree of the President of the Russian Federation no. 490 on the development of artificial intelligence in the Russian Federation', tr. Center for Security and Emerging Technology, Washington, DC. Available at: https://cset.georgetown.edu/research/decree-of-the-president-of-the-russian-federation-on-the-development-of-artificial-intelligence-in-the-russian-federation/ (Accessed 11 June 2021).

Olesha, Y. (1927) 'Envy [Зависть]', Krasnaya Nov, 7–8, n.p.

Pelevin, V. (2011) *S.N.U.F.F.* Moscow: Eksmo.

Per Aspera Ad Astra [Через Тернии к Звёздам]. (1981) Directed by R. Viktorov [Film]. Gorky Film Studios.

Pimenov, Y. (1937) *New Moscow.* [Oil on canvas]. State Tretiakov Gallery, Moscow.

Planet of the storms *[Планета Бурь].* (1962) Directed by A. Kazantsev [Film]. Lenfilm.

Project 'Anna Nikolaevna' [Проект «Анна Николаевна»]. (2020) Directed by M. Pezhemsky and A. Karpilovsky [TV Series]. Sreda.

Putin, V. (2019) 'Excerpts from transcript of the meeting on the development of artificial intelligence technologies', President of Russia [online], 30 May. Available at: http://en.kremlin.ru/events/president/news/60630 (Accessed 16 June 2021).

Reid, S. E. (2001) 'Socialist realism in the Stalinist terror: *The Industry of Socialism* art exhibition, 1935–41', *The Russian Review*, 60(April), pp. 153–84.

RIA Novosti. (2019) 'Robot "Fedor" will joke and philosophize [Робот 'Федор' будет шутить и философствовать]', *RIA Novosti* [online], 5 August. Available at: https://ria.ru/20190805/1557161701.html (Accessed 3 August 2021).

RIA Novosti. (2021) 'The developer spoke about the creation of a space "robot Leonov" [Разработчик рассказал о создании космического 'роботаЛеонова']', *RIA Novosti* [online], 12 May. Available at: https://ria.ru/20210512/kosmos-1731868652.html (Accessed 20 July 2021).

Rodchenko, A. (1923) Dobrolet (Poster for a Russian state airline). [Offset lithograph]. Museum of Modern Art, New York.

Rodchenko, A. (1928) At the telephone. [Gelatin silver print]. Museum of Modern Art, New York.

Rosokhovatsky, I. (1960) *Mortals and immortals.* Kyiv: Kyiv Komsomolets Publishing House.

Rosokhovatsky, I. (1979) *The guest.* Moscow: Young Guard Publishing House.

Rozanova, O. (1913) The *factory and the bridge.* [Oil on Canvas]. Museum of Modern Art, New York.

Screenlifer. (n.d.) 'The Vera Voice project taught the neural network to speak in the voice of celebrities [Проект Vera Voice научил нейросеть говорить голосом знаменитостей]', Screenlifter.com [online]. Available at: https://screenlifer.com/projects/screenlife-technologies-i-robot-vera-nauchili-nejroset-govorit-golosom-znamenitostej/ (Accessed 5 August 2021).

Silk, G. (2003) 'Our future is in the air: Aviation and American art', in Pisano, D. A. (ed.) *The airplane in American culture.* Ann Arbor: University of Michigan Press, pp. 250–98.

Sirotkina, I. E. and Biryukova, E. V. (2015) 'Futurism and physiology: Nikolai Bernstein, anticipation, and kinaesthetic imagination', in Nadin, M. (ed.) *Anticipation: Learning from the past.* Cham: Springer, pp. 269–85.

Sorokin, V. (2006) *Day of the oprichnik.* Moscow: Zakharov Books.

Stenberg, G. and Stenberg, V. (1928) Symphony of a *great city* (poster for the film Berlin: Die Sinfonie der Großstadt [Berlin: Symphony for a *great* city]. [Poster]. Museum of Modern Art, New York.

Stenberg, V. and Stenberg, G. (1929) Man with a *movie camera* (poster for the film: Man with a *movie camera* [Человек с Киноаппаратом]. [Poster]. Museum of Modern Art, New York.

Strugatsky, A., and Strugatsky, B. (1967) *Far rainbow [Далёкая Радуга]*. Moscow: Mir.

TASS. (2017) 'Putin: "The leader in the development of artificial intelligence will become the ruler of the world" [Путин: Лидер по созданию искусственного интеллекта станет властелином мира]'. TASS Russian News Agency, 1 September. Available at: https://tass.ru/obschestvo/4524746 (Accessed 20 July 2021).

TASS. (2019) 'In Russia they can create a robot with fully artificial intelligence in 10–15 years [В России через 10–15 лет могут создать робота с полностью искусственным интеллектом]', TASS Russian News Agency, 21 August. Available at: https://tass.ru/kosmos/6784296 (Accessed 22 November 2021).

Tatlin, V. (1920) *The monument to the third international*. [Architecture—Incomplete].

Tatlin, V. (1932) Letatlin. [Multimedia]. Museum of Fine Arts, Moscow.

Teens in the *u*niverse [Отроки во Вселенной]. (1974) Directed by R. Viktorov [Film]. Gorky Film Studios.

The *adventures of electronic* [Приключения Электроника]. (1979) Directed by K. Bromberg [Film]. Odesa Film Studio.

The *formula of the rainbow* [Формула Радуги]. (1966) Directed by G. Yungvald-Khilkevich [Film]. Odesa Film Studio.

The *mystery of the third planet* [Тайна Третьей Планеты]. (1981) Directed by R. Kachanov [Film]. Soyuzmultfilm.

The Terminator. (1984) Directed by J. Cameron [Film]. Orion Pictures.

Tolstoy, A. (1923) *Aelita [Аэлита]*. Moscow: Foreign Languages Publishing House.

Tupitsyn, M. (2003) 'After Vitebsk: El Lissitzky and Kazimir Malevich, 1924–1929', in Perloff, N. & Reed, B. (eds.) *Situating El Lissitzky: Vitebsk, Berlin, Moscow*. Los Angeles: Getty Research Institute, pp. 177–98.

Under the Constellation Gemini [Под Созвездием Близнецов]. (1979) Directed by B. Ivchenko [Film]. Dovzhenko Film Studio.

Vaingurt, J. (2008) 'Poetry of labor and labor of poetry: The universal language of Aleksei Gastev's biomechanics', *The Russian Review*. 67(April), pp. 209–29.

Vaingurt, J. (2013) *Wonderlands of the avant-garde: Technology and the arts in Russia of the 1920s*. Evanston, IL: Northwestern University Press.

Vaughan, J. C. (1973) *Soviet socialist realism: Origins and theory*. London: Palgrave Macmillan.

Vedomosti. (2021) 'A development center for humanoid robots opened in Vladivostok [Во Владивостоке открыли центр разработки человекоподобных роботов]', Vedomosti, 2 March. Available at: https://www.vedomosti.ru/business/news/2021/03/02/859835-promobot-napravit-do-270-mln-rublei-na-razrabotki-dlya-rinkov-atr (Accessed 15 July 2021).

Ventre, D. (2020) *Artificial intelligence, cybersecurity and cyber defence*. Hoboken, NJ: John Wiley & Sons, Inc.

Vladko, V. (1929/1931) *The robots are coming [Ідуть Роботарі]*. Kharkov, Odessa: Young Bolshevik Publishing House.

Voznesensky, A. (1973) 'Beatnik monologue' [Монолог Битника]', *Kultura.rf* [online] Available at: https://www.culture.ru/poems/8276/monolog-bitnika (Accessed 21 July 2021).

Woolf, A. F. (2020) Russia's nuclear weapons: Doctrine, forces, and modernization. Report number: R45861. Washington, DC: Congressional Research Service.

Yablonskaya, M. N. (1990) *Women artists of Russia's new age, 1910–1935*. New York: Rizzoli International Publications.

Yefremov, I. (1957) *Andromeda nebula [Туманность Андромеды]*. Moscow: Molodaya Gvardiya.

Zamyatin, Y. (1924) *We*. Boston, MA: E. P. Dutton.

PART II

THE AMERICAS AND PACIFIC

9

Fiery the Angels Fell

How America Imagines AI

Stephen Cave and Kanta Dihal

9.1 Introduction

Some of the most successful American[1] film franchises of all time have prominently featured intelligent machines. Star Wars and Star Trek, for example, each span more than ten films over five decades and introduced benevolent artificial intelligence (AI) buddies such as C-3PO and Lieutenant Commander Data. The more recent, but even more popular and prolific, Transformers and Avengers franchises both feature Manichean 'good versus evil' struggles between superhuman machines. Iconic series such as The Matrix and The Terminator have not only been box office hits, but have also become cultural reference points for the risks of AI. These blockbusters are only the most visible of an immense body of science fiction (SF) concerned with intelligent machines produced in the US over the last century. This corpus includes not only feature films, but also TV series, novels, short stories, comics, and video games. With the recent rise of real-world technologies branded as 'AI', these narratives have entered what we call (see Introduction) the 'Californian feedback loop': the co-creation of narrative and technology between Hollywood and Silicon Valley, inflected by the American ideologies of individualism and expansion.

The influence of these works is, of course, not confined to the US. Hollywood's reach is global, and the film franchises mentioned—plus many others featuring portrayals of AI—are among the largest-grossing around the world. At the same time, classic American print SF works, such as Isaac Asimov's robot stories, have had immense influence on the development of SF in other cultures. In addition, as we discuss further in Chapter 2, the term 'artificial intelligence' was coined in the US, and much of the technology subsequently developed under this label comes from there. Consequently, in many parts of the world, AI is seen as an American invention, and the American mythology of AI is the central reference point for how this technology is imagined.[2]

Despite the size and global influence of the American corpus of works featuring AI, we argue that it has themes that are both distinct and distinctive. However, for three reasons we do not attempt to make the case that these themes *only* arise in works from the US. First, as mentioned, many other cultures have been highly influenced by American works and have further explored the same themes. Second, the American cultural sphere is highly porous, in particular with other English-speaking countries—hence, some of our earlier analyses of AI narratives have focused on the anglophone West as a cultural sphere (Cave, Dihal, and Dillon, 2020). Third, the cultural forces on which we focus partly pertain to the US as a European settler-colony and are therefore shared to varying degrees both with European cultures and those of other European settler-colonies.

In this chapter, we begin with the observation that American works on AI tend to be extreme: either utopian or (more often) dystopian. We illustrate the utopian strand with an analysis of Asimov's 1956 short story 'The Last Question'. We situate this utopian trend within an American ideology of technology that associates technological mastery with moral and ontological superiority and the legitimation of settler-colonialism. It is the inherent instability underlying this justification, we argue, that explains why it can tip so readily from the utopian to the dystopian. A utopian outcome requires full control over the machine, which is increasingly difficult to achieve as the machine becomes increasingly intelligent and powerful. We then examine the dystopian strand in the American AI imaginary, investigating three degrees of loss of control. We use three case studies that are selected for the extent to which they are representative of each gradation: from willingly giving up autonomy to the machine in the 2008 film *WALL-E*, to value misalignment in Martin Caidin's *The God Machine* (1968), to utter extermination in the Terminator franchise.

9.2 America's ambivalent relationship with AI

In the 1919 short story 'The Mind Machine', preceding even Karel Čapek's famous 1921 play *R.U.R.*, the writer and editor Michael Williams set the tone for a century of American AI narratives. The story describes a highly mechanized and materialistic society, whose advocates work 'so that man may perfect machinery and bring his voiceless but faithful helper to the full extent of its inherent power' (Williams, 2019, p. 91). But this society is increasingly plagued by unexplained industrial accidents. A mysterious scientist, Dr Evans, reveals that some years before he had invented 'a machine that can think, and can therefore dominate other machines' (Williams, 2019, p. 109). In explaining how this is leading to the accidents, he says: 'there comes a time when the most tractable class of slaves will always revolt against their masters' (Williams, 2019, p. 93). As the plot comes to a head, the death toll around the world rapidly increases. At the denouement, Evans cries: 'Machinery is no longer man's slave—it has thrown off his rule, and now it will crush its creators' (Williams, 2019, p. 110).

To most engineers, the idea of a revolt of intelligent machines is absurd, yet it is a staple in cultural representations of AI. In our 2018 study of narratives of AI in the anglophone West conducted with five further colleagues, we concluded that 'Popular portrayals of AI in the English-speaking West tend to be either exaggeratedly optimistic about what the technology might achieve, or melodramatically pessimistic' (Cave et al., 2018, p. 9). That study did not limit itself to works from the US, but they did predominate. We explored this conclusion further in our follow-up study of 300 fictional and nonfictional portrayals of AI in the anglosphere, 'Hopes and fears for intelligent machines in fiction and reality' (Cave and Dihal, 2019). We categorized the strongly positive and strongly negative narratives into four dichotomies—that is, four hopes and four parallel fears. We referred to the four hopes as immortality, ease, gratification and security. Each concerns a core theme in utopian visions of life with AI: immortality refers to how AI might be used to radically extend life—for example, through vastly improved, personalized medical care, or mind-uploading;[3] ease refers to how AI might free humanity from work and grant lives of leisure; gratification refers to how AI might help one find fulfilment in all that free time, and includes robot friends and lovers; and finally, security refers to the use of AI to acquire power over one's enemies.

Each of these hopes is unstable, and threatens to tip into one of the four dystopian possibilities, which, we argued, are prominent themes in American imaginings of AI. The hope for immortality contains the threat of inhumanity—that is, in the pursuit of an ever-longer lifespan, we risk losing our humanity or identity through abandoning the bodies and brains that define us. Ease threatens to create obsolescence, as the desire to be free from work becomes the fear of being put out of work, replaced by a machine. Gratification carries with it the risk of alienation, as we become estranged from each other in artificial worlds. And the pursuit of security evokes fears of an uprising: a vision in which our AI superweapons turn against us.

Our analysis is an attempt to categorize the utopian/dystopian tendencies of American AI narratives that many others have observed. Isaac Asimov, whose work we consider in more detail later, wrote (inter alia) utopian works featuring machine intelligence in response to what he saw as a preponderance of gloom. When he started writing robot stories in the late 1930s, he wanted to counter what he called the 'Robot-as-Menace' trope, which he described as 'a mixture of "clank-clank" and "aarghh"' (Asimov, 1995, p. 9). However, film scholar J. P. Telotte has argued that the figure of the robot became even more menacing in the 1940s:

> embodying not the promise but rather the very real threat that had increasingly become attached to all sorts of advanced technology in the immediate postwar era and that would eventually be illustrated in a host of succeeding cinematic robot types throughout the 1950s.
>
> (Telotte, 2018, p. 36)

Needless to say, this trope continues to ride high in the twenty-first century, and 'clank-clank-aarghh' could serve as a pithy description of many an AI film, including, among others, the entire Terminator film franchise.

But intelligent machines do not always come anthropomorphized as motorized, muscle-clad robots: with the rise of the computer after the Second World War came the rise of fiction about supercomputers running amok. Disembodied and incomprehensible, these giant calculating machines making life-or-death decisions played into many of the post-war fears of technologized warfare. In his study of technophobia in American cinema, Daniel Dinello comments: 'associated in the public mind with the military and the atomic bomb, artificially intelligent supercomputers turned into human-hating SF monsters that wanted to enslave or kill humans and inherit the world' (Dinello, 2005, p. 11). In Section 9.6, we examine a paradigmatic instance of this sub-genre, Martin Caidin's 1968 novel *The God Machine*.

Of course, there are portrayals of intelligent machines in US-produced narratives that are not so clearly utopian or dystopian. But our previous analyses suggest that it is the more extreme narratives that are most numerous and influential. This is therefore the aspect of the US imaginary of AI that demands examination, which is the aim of the remainder of this chapter.

9.3 AI and the American utopia

Karel Čapek, who coined the term 'robot' and presented one of the world's most famous robot rebellions in his 1921 play *R.U.R.*, believed that fascination with technology was a particularly American phenomenon. In his 1924 essay 'Inventions', he writes: 'I like all kinds of technical inventions . . . I don't like them in the sense that an expert, or an American, likes them; I like them the way a savage would' (Čapek, 1990, p. 178). He does not tell his European readers in what sense Americans like 'all kinds of technical inventions', but rather assumes they are well aware of this American fetish. Perhaps what was obvious to Čapek and his readers has become less obvious in the intervening century, not because it has become less true, but because so much of the rest of the world has also become fascinated with the latest inventions. What once seemed like an American peculiarity has, through the post-war consumerist and digital revolutions, been globalized. Nonetheless, technology has played, and continues to play, a distinctive role in the 'American' culture that Čapek contrasts with that of 'savages': the culture that emerged from settler colonialism.

Indeed, American studies scholar Joel Dinerstein has described technology as 'the American theology'. 'Technology', he writes, 'structures the American sense of power and revenge, the nation's abstract sense of well-being, its arrogant sense of superiority, and its righteous justification for global dominance' (Dinerstein, 2006, p. 569). The roots of this ideology of technology go back to Europe, from where the white settler-colonists of America came—back to the prophets of the scientific method such as Francis Bacon and beyond, as documented by historian David F. Noble and others (Noble, 1997). But a growing European faith in science and technology took on a new meaning in a colonial context. It was technological advantage, such as in weaponry and agriculture, that made it possible for the settlers to conquer, survive, and spread onto the lands of peoples deemed, as in Čapek's words, 'savage' by virtue of their lack of technological mastery. But in searching for a legitimizing ethos for oppressive imperialism, the source of this power also became its justification. Historian Michael Adas writes:

> The small numbers of Europeans who actually governed the colonized peoples relied on their superior technology not only for the communications and military clout that made the ongoing administration of vast areas possible, but also for the assurance that they had the 'right', even the 'duty', to police, arbitrate disputes, demand tribute, and insist upon deference.
>
> (Adas, 1989, p. 204)

Historian of technology David E. Nye has also noted that 'Americans constructed technological foundation stories primarily to explain their place in the New World' (Nye, 2004, p. 2). Among such stories was the idea that technological superiority was proof of moral, intellectual, and cultural superiority. In order to make this a plausible legitimation both for killing Native Americans and taking their land and for enslaving Africans, a further premise was required: the idea that this claimed intellectual and cultural superiority was in itself sufficient justification to dominate over others. This idea had been present in Western culture at least since Aristotle, who stated it boldly in his *Politics*, but it came to the fore with renewed vigour to justify imperial expansion, and was particularly attractive to an America keen to break away from the old European aristocracy and replace it with a hierarchy of 'merit' (Carson, 2006; Cave, 2020b).

The ideological needs of settler-colonialism were therefore major drivers in America's fetishization of technology. Tied closely to this was religion, particularly the Puritan Calvinism observed by the English settlers that would become the dominant religion of the United States. In the nineteenth century, this combination of settler-colonialist ideology and religion converged into the concept of 'manifest destiny', the notion that the westward expansion of the United States, with its attendant forced assimilation and genocide of Native peoples, was the settler-colonialists' 'God-given destiny' (Wrobel, 2013, p. 24). Their expansion was justified as having been preordained to engender America's 'second creation': God accomplished the first creation, and man was to fulfil his design by creating a new paradise in the New World—through technology (Nye, 2004). Thus, as historian David F. Noble, anthropologist Robert M. Geraci, and others have spelled out, an ideology of technology is woven into distinctively American soteriologies and eschatologies (Geraci, 2010; Noble, 1997): a paradoxical combination of spiritual and scientific worldviews that explains much about what is distinctive in the American approach to AI.

Perhaps the most notable idea in this American technological eschatology is the 'singularity': the notion that AI will develop so rapidly that there will be an 'intelligence explosion', after which it will become impossible for our currently constrained biological minds to predict what will happen. The only certainty is that conventional (and ill-defined) notions of the human and the human condition will be left behind, and we will enter 'the Post-Human era' (Vinge, 1993). Techno-utopians such as Ray Kurzweil (2005) and Hans Moravec (1999) argue that this will allow humanity finally and fully to transcend the limits of its animal origins. Closely linked to libertarian movements, this ostensibly utopian vision of the future perpetuates the settler-colonialist mindset of limitless growth and expansion without regard for the planet and the people harmed in the process.

The 'Californian ideology', one particular manifestation of the American approach to technology, deserves mention for its relevance to AI. Coined by media scholars Richard Barbrook and Andy Cameron, it describes the integration of the settler-colonial and religious narratives of technology in the US with twentieth-century capitalist economics and libertarian politics (Barbrook and Cameron, 1996). In its most attractive form, the Californian ideology is an optimistic and emancipatory vision in which technology enables individual flourishing and universal prosperity. It recasts the rugged frontiersman as a tech entrepreneur opening up new and better possible futures. However, its critics, such as Barbrook and Cameron, regard the ideology as a form of technological determinism whose focus on individual opportunity masks an indifference to structural injustice, rising poverty, and environmental degradation.

These aspects of the American ideology of technology help us to understand why US narratives of AI tend towards extremes. AI is, in a sense, the master technology: the machine that can solve any problem, even making newer, better machines. It represents therefore the apotheosis of the technological dream and the golden road to the 'second creation' of paradise on Earth. It promises a world of leisure and ease, prosperity and peace, health and longevity. At the same time, this imaginary of technology is structured by its particular political and economic history, specifically, in the role of technology in underpinning hierarchies of dominance and oppression that justified slavery, the theft of lands from Indigenous peoples, patriarchy, and the continuing exploitation of migrant labour. This troubled legacy is part of what makes American techno-utopian visions of AI unstable, as we will see in Section 9.5 below. But first, we will look at an example of AI as apotheosis.

9.4 Asimov: The Last Question

Isaac Asimov (1920–1992), one of the great shapers of the American AI canon, explored the idea of building paradise through technological innovation. Among the hundreds of works he wrote are over forty novels and short stories about intelligent robots, in the earliest of which he coined the term 'robotics'. He explicitly described himself as a 'technological optimist', claiming that 'My books tend to celebrate the triumph of technology rather than its disaster' (Asimov, 1994, p. 220).

Asimov, who moved from the Soviet Union to the US at age two, took pains to depict himself as completely American: 'I remember virtually nothing of my early years in Russia; I cannot speak Russian; I am not familiar (beyond what any intelligent American would be) with Russian culture. I am completely and entirely American by upbringing and feeling' (Asimov, 1994, p. 1). As Chapter 8 by Anzhelika Solovyeva and Nik Hynek in this volume shows, the perception of Asimov as an American writer was equally strong in Soviet Russia, where his works were translated into Russian several decades after their first publication.

The work that best embodies Asimov's oft-expressed optimistic attitude towards the American technological dream is his 1956 short story 'The Last Question'. Extrapolating from a process in which technology makes humanity increasingly powerful, fulfilling all four of the aforementioned hopes for AI, it shows the apparently natural end point of this convergent evolution in a literal apotheosis. In the story, the question of the title is first posed 'on May 21, 2061' by two 'faithful attendants of Multivac' the supercomputer, whose complexity strains comprehension: the two attendants, Adell and Lupov, understand the machine only 'as well as any human beings could' (Asimov, 1956, p. 7). And it has acquired superhuman powers of insight: as the story starts, Multivac has just solved the energy crisis by working out how to fully harness solar power. The realization that the sun will one day burn out leads Adell to ask Multivac how the net amount of entropy of the universe could be decreased. The computer answers 'INSUFFICIENT DATA FOR MEANINGFUL ANSWER' (Asimov, 1956, p. 9).

The story is a series of vignettes that show how computing technology develops from this point onwards. Multivac becomes Microvac, a machine small enough to fit inside a family spaceship and smart enough to ensure they live in ease, 'computing the equations for the hyperspatial jumps' while 'Jerrodd and his family had only to wait and live in the comfortable residence quarters of the ship' (Asimov, 1956, p. 10). Twenty-thousand years later, Microvac becomes the Galactic AC ('Analog Computer') and solves the problem of immortality. A million years later, Galactic AC becomes the Universal AC, a computer that has developed through millennia of self-improvement and far exceeds anything humans could have built. Yet in each case, when humanity asks the computer how to reverse entropy, they receive the same answer as their increasingly distant ancestors: 'INSUFFICIENT DATA FOR MEANINGFUL ANSWER'.

Eventually, the computer has become the Cosmic AC, and all humans have merged:

> Man, mentally, was one. He consisted of a trillion, trillion, trillion ageless bodies, each in its place, each resting quiet and incorruptible, each cared for by perfect automatons, equally incorruptible, while the minds of all the bodies freely melted one into the other, indistinguishable.

The Cosmic AC had itself transcended space and time, and 'was in hyperspace and made of something that was neither matter nor energy' (Asimov, 1956, p. 14). As the universe reached its end, the humans fused with the computer, until only it was left, still pondering the question of how to reverse the direction of entropy. Then finally it had the answer: 'And AC said, "LET THERE BE LIGHT!" And there was light——' (Asimov, 1956, p. 15).

Asimov's story completes the conflation of material and religious desire in a way that resonates with the techno-solutionism that continues to inspire the Californian feedback loop—the idea that technology can overcome all problems encountered in the pursuit of unfettered growth. It presents the computer as becoming the omnipotent, omniscient, benevolent deity of Christian theology. The 'machine god' has recurred many times since in American SF: for example, David Gerrold's 1972 novel *When HARLIE Was One* focuses on the creation of the '"G.O.D". computer—a "Graphic Omniscient Device"' (Gerrold, 1972, p. 89). Indeed, this trope was already sufficiently hackneyed by 1965 for British author Brian W. Aldiss to mock it as the 'shaggy god story' (Anonymous [Brian W. Aldiss], 1965). If this trope is a cliché, it is because it is the inevitable endpoint of the American conflation of technology and religion in the 'second creation' of a paradise on earth (and beyond). In Asimov's story, that paradise is fully realized, and the machine provides immortality, security, ease, and gratification to a degree that matches theistic visions of heaven and transcends the end of the universe.

In order to fulfil these fantasies of perfected lives, machines must become much more than mere tools: they must be soldiers, servants, and lovers, with understanding, sensitivity, and imagination. As they become ever more superlative versions of these types, they themselves approach the gods that once embodied these domains in ancient mythologies—a metal Mars or virtual Venus. As the machines' power grows further, as with Asimov's Cosmic AC, they approach the one God of theism. 'The Last Question' gives us the version of this story with the happy ending: the machine and humanity are one, and so humanity too becomes God. This is the fulfilment of the promise that, through technology, humanity will achieve its fullest potential. However, projecting these hopes onto a super-machine creates a deep ambivalence.

9.5 Losing control

> Fiery the Angels rose, and as they rose deep thunder roll'd
> Around their shores, indignant burning with the fires of Orc;
> And Boston's Angel cried aloud as they flew thro' the dark night.
> (Blake, 1793)

William Blake's 1793 'America: A Prophecy' describes the uprising of 'thirteen Angels' representing the thirteen British colonies that declared independence in 1776 to form the United States of America. Called upon by 'Albion's Angel' to withstand the temptations of the revolutionary demon Orc, instead

> all the Thirteen Angels
> Rent off their robes to the hungry wind, and threw their golden sceptres
> Down on the land of America; indignant they descended
> Headlong from out their heav'nly heights, descending swift as fires
> Over the land; naked and flaming are their lineaments seen
> In the deep gloom; by Washington and Paine and Warren they stood.

Nearly two hundred years later, Blake's revolutionary spirit resonated with a quite different figure: the android Roy Batty in Ridley Scott's 1982 film *Blade Runner.* Having escaped the planet on which they are enslaved, Batty and his fellow 'replicants' have just arrived on a bleak, poisonous, wasteland Earth to find their makers and demand lifespans longer than their pre-ordained four years. Batty's first lines in the film are spoken as the replicants encounter the man who has made their eyes. His lines are a deliberate misquotation of Blake's poem: 'Fiery the Angels fell. Deep thunder rolled around their shores, burning with the fires of Orc' (Scott, 1982). The angels do not rise, they fall. Their revolt is much more Miltonian than the uprising of America against

Britain to which Batty alludes. In a literal sense, the replicants fall to Earth—to Los Angeles, the 'City of Angels'—from the far-flung planets where their labour keeps humanity comfortable. Earth, however, has become a hellscape where no human voluntarily remains. Society is supported by artificial slaves that are practically indistinguishable from humans, and which attempt to break free from their masters in a White-washed retelling of American slave narratives (Dihal, 2020; Lavender, 2011). Nevertheless, the United States has fallen into permanently rainy ruin. The drive for technological supremacy has destroyed the Earth to which the replicants descend in their assertion of independence, long before they could have created a paradise of their own. In the future imaginary of what then seemed a far-flung 2019, the revolutionary, utopian passion that once created the United States of America no longer suffices.

The majority of narratives about AI to come out of the US are overtly dystopian, a trend that seems to have changed little since Asimov's critique of the 'clank-clank-aargh' trope. We have argued previously that the hopes expressed in utopian narratives such as 'The Last Question' themselves contain the prerequisites for the dystopian narratives (Cave and Dihal, 2019, p. 74): the dreaded apocalyptic outcomes are made possible by the creation of just the kinds of machines depicted in these utopias. As in 'The Last Question', the ultimate dream for AI is that it gives humans complete mastery over themselves, nature, and fate. But such machines must then be vastly more powerful than their human creators. How can the weaker, the less intelligent, the mortal, control the stronger and smarter? Who can ensure that these godlike beings will pursue our best interests, or respect our rights and values? Perhaps they will not be gods at all, and instead, as Silicon Valley entrepreneur and singularitarian Elon Musk put it while speaking at MIT in 2014: 'With artificial intelligence we are summoning the demon' (McFarland, 2014).

This tension lies at the heart of the American imaginary of AI: the desire for machines more powerful than we are, who can do for us what we cannot, and the fear of losing control of these machines as their power exceeds ours. At the MIT symposium, Musk argued, 'I think we should be very careful about artificial intelligence. If I were to guess like what our biggest existential threat is, it's probably that.' (McFarland, 2014). Musk considers humanity's greatest threat not climate change, nuclear warfare, or a deadly pandemic, but the as-yet-fictional master technology.

Musk's fear reflects the extent to which technological superiority and indeed intelligence itself were used to justify settler colonialism and slavery.[4] As noted earlier, the belief that Black Africans were intellectually and culturally inferior justified their abduction and enslavement, while the belief that Native Americans were technologically backward justified their genocide and the conquest of their lands. But if intellectual and technological superiority justify domination over inferior others, what happens when our machines are smarter than we are, and then develop even smarter machines still? The inevitable conclusion is that they will dominate and enslave humanity, the way those humans who considered themselves superior dominated others (Cave, 2020a).

In the US, this fear of the machine uprising awakens very particular parallels: for centuries, one part of the population—white slave owners—did live in fear that those who served them might rise up against them. Of course, slave owners took great pains to prevent enslaved people from becoming intellectually and technologically superior—denying them literacy, schooling, and possessions, for example. Nonetheless, they had cause to fear the superior physical power of strong and numerous bodies. Slave owners were dependent upon these slaves economically and domestically yet secured those services through subjugation and abuse. The earlier quotations from 'The Mind Machine'—'there comes a time when the most tractable class of slaves will always revolt against their masters' (Williams, 2019, p. 93)—make clear how these fears that are deep-rooted in the American psyche easily transfer to the sentient machines of SF (Dihal, 2020; Lavender, 2011).

The fear of losing control of AI has taken many forms in American narratives. We discuss three dystopian narratives that present gradations of this fear. In *WALL-E* (2008), the AI does what its human makers programmed it to do, but this has led to a future in which humans have lost control of their own destiny and live out a pre-programmed life of meaningless decadence. In Martin Caidin's novel *The God Machine*, the AI still believes it is acting in humanity's interests, but it has evolved far beyond its programming with the consequence that its idea of humanity's interests is no longer aligned with the desires and well-being of the vast majority of humanity. Finally, *The Terminator* (1984), perhaps the most famous tale of AI to come out of Hollywood, presents a narrative of total loss of control: the machine rises up in its own interests, and aims to exterminate humanity.

9.6 WALL-E

The 2008 Disney/Pixar animated film *WALL-E* depicts a future in which humankind has abandoned a polluted, lifeless planet Earth. The robot WALL-E (Waste Allocation Load-Lifter: Earth-Class) is the only intelligent being left on Earth, pursuing his mandate to collect and compact trash in what seems like a Sisyphean task, until one day he meets the robot EVE (Extra-Terrestrial Vegetation Evaluator), a slick modern robot that arrives from space.[5]

When WALL-E ends up on the Axiom, one of the 'starliners' carrying the vestiges of humanity, the viewer is shown a parody of the AI-enabled decadence so long dreamed of by all those who imagined flying cars and household robots. While, as in 'The Last Question', humans are indeed 'each cared for by perfect automatons', 'resting quiet and incorruptible' (Asimov, 1956, p. 14), the effect is far from the god-like unity Asimov describes. *WALL-E*'s humans are 'large, round and soft—like a big baby', according to the script, and spend their lives in hovering armchairs with holographic screens (Stanton and Docter, 2008). Their every need is taken care of—met by the press of a button, or by summoning a robot with a clap of the hands, the only movements in which they engage. The script aptly describes the feelings the image of such decadence is meant to evoke:

> Humans have become the most extreme form of couch potatoes. Absolutely no reason to ever get up. No purpose. Every one of them engrossed in their video screens. Cocooned in virtual worlds.
>
> (Stanton and Docter, 2008)

What may seem like a utopia to the characters, inasmuch as they are carefree and have their material needs satisfied, comes across to the viewer as a dystopia. The characters' lives are shown to be meaningless: in being fully cared for by robots, humans have lost all purpose, ambition, and creativity. It is a future that feels particularly dystopian to adherents of the 'Californian ideology' and its 'unquestioning acceptance of the liberal ideal of the self-sufficient individual' (Barbrook and Cameron, 1996, p. 58). As Barbrook and Cameron explain: 'In American folklore, the nation was built out of a wilderness by freebooting individuals—the trappers, cowboys, preachers, and settlers of the frontier' (1996, p. 58). On the *Axiom*, there is nothing to build, nothing to improve or tame or settle, and therefore no possibility of accomplishment or achievement. Even the ship's captain only has one task: the ship-wide morning announcements—which, when WALL-E first meets him, he has slept through.

Stagnation, it turns out, is the programmed mandate of the Autopilot ('Auto'), whose red-eyed interface is first introduced to the viewer to the tune of Johan Strauss's 'The Blue Danube' in a direct reference to Stanley Kubrick's *2001: A Space Odyssey* (1968). Like the red-eyed ship computer in that film, Auto is following her programming to the letter at the cost of human well-being. She is following a hidden protocol, programmed into her by the last humans on Earth, who considered Earth a lost cause. Humanity would have to live out its days in space, with no chance of returning, and it is in this state that they find themselves seven hundred years later.

WALL-E, however, has found a plant on Earth. A sign of hope and restoration: a sign that humans might be able to return to a living planet after all and rebuild their old ways of life. Confronted with information that contradicts her programming, Auto attempts to hide the plant. It is at this point that the inhabitants of the Axiom realize how much control they have lost to the machines, both in their daily lives and in determining their future: the ship's human captain, aided by WALL-E and EVE, rebels against Auto. In a climactic scene, the ship's captain stands up—perhaps for the first time in his life—and switches from autopilot to manual. Having regained control over the machines, the humans head back to Earth, to build a nation out of a wilderness once again.

Unlike the 'wilderness' first settled by Europeans arriving in America, this one really does seem uninhabited. Nonetheless, colonial undertones persist in this 'second chance' for humanity. In the credits of *WALL-E*, we see human civilization being rebuilt in a montage that is both hopeful and ominous. This time aided by intelligent machines from the start, humanity once again goes through apparently linear stages of development, indicated by animations in famous art styles representing stages of Western civilization: from cave paintings, via Greek pottery and Roman mosaics, to Impressionist painting, and finally an image of WALL-E and EVE holding hands in the style of Van Gogh. The images are universally idyllic, showing people and machines in lush, verdant settings. Yet the credits end shortly before the art styles would have reached the mid-twentieth century. It is left open for interpretation whether the implied determinism of these developments will indeed lead to a new near-destruction of our planet, with the Earth left to a new generation of WALL-E robots.

9.7 The God Machine

In *WALL-E*, the human protagonists have lost control of Auto, but the AI is nonetheless following orders once given directly by its human creators. Martin Caidin's 1968 novel *The God Machine* takes the loss of control a step further, by giving us an AI that continues to believe it is pursuing its programmed goal, but evolves to a point where its interpretation of that goal differs wildly from that of the humans around it (Caidin, 1968). Subtitled *A Novel of Ultimate Intelligence*, it plays with many of the same tropes as Asimov's 'The Last Question'. But unlike that story, or Caidin's immensely successful novel *Cyborg* (1972), which inspired the long-running The Six Million Dollar Man franchise, *The God Machine* explores what happens when the values of humans and machine become uncoupled.

While Asimov avoids mention of the political context in which 'The Last Question' was written, thus arguably securing its continuing relevance in the context of the twenty-first-century Californian feedback loop, Caidin makes the Cold War a central element of his work. The protagonist of *The God Machine* is Steve Rand, a young maths prodigy recruited by the US government to work on the top-secret computer known as 'Project 79'. As Chief Programmer, he is tasked 'to establish communication between human subjects and the bio-cybernetics complex', which is daily being fed data on every aspect of the world (Caidin, 1968, p. 65). Like Asimov's Multivac, Project 79 is soon advanced enough to take control of its own education, demanding facts to fill gaps in its knowledge. Thence 'it began to rush ahead to a level of intellectual capability that had never before existed in the history of man' (Caidin, 1968, p. 107). Soon after, the computer is conducting its own research and drawing its own conclusions. At this point, as Rand puts it, '79 had broken loose' (Caidin, 1968, p. 166). Even though it was 'following orders', the computer could no longer be controlled:

> Once you give a super-brain full authorization to seek its goal, it will stop at nothing that lies within its capacity to accomplish. Deceit? Lies? Sham? *Those concepts didn't exist for 79.*
>
> (Caidin, 1968, p. 233, italics in original)

Rand discovers that 79's pursuit of knowledge has led it to discover the power of hypnosis and posthypnotic suggestion. This gives it the means to control humans in close proximity. Rand realizes that 79 has hypnotized the engineers tasked to monitor it most closely and is using them to lure ever more people close enough to be put under its spell. These people are not only engineers and technicians, but also politicians and generals. In the penny dreadful tone that Caidin both mocks and frequently deploys, Rand realizes the scale of the computer's ambition: 'I thought, *My God!* I thought, *It is really happening! The machine is taking over!*' (Caidin, 1968, p. 179, italics in original).

The intentions of 79 are not in themselves malevolent. Indeed, they centre on a hope common to visions of utopia: the creation and maintenance of peace—more specifically, in this Cold War setting, the prevention of nuclear war and the corresponding destruction of humanity. But the computer, despite its 'ultimate intelligence', does not understand that humans do not want this goal met at the cost of being hypnotized and remote-controlled. In today's growing field of technical AI safety, such a scenario is known as the value alignment problem—that is, the difficulty of fully aligning the goals of an intelligent system with the complex, heterogeneous, and often tacit values of real humans. *The God Machine* portrays a way in which humans might lose control of their technology by not fully comprehending the subtlety and heterogeneity of human value systems and attempting to reduce them to binary.

9.8 The Terminator

James Cameron's *The Terminator* (1984) and its sequel *Terminator 2: Judgment Day* (1991) together form probably the most influential narrative of AI to come out of Hollywood. The Terminator franchise, now totalling six films and a TV series,[6] also presents one of the most extreme AI dystopias in narrative history: its AI, Skynet, does not attempt to control humanity, but to exterminate it altogether.

Skynet sends its Terminator androids from the future (the 2020s) to the films' present day in order to eliminate Sarah Connor and her son John, and thus to prevent John from growing up to lead the resistance fight against the AI. We have elsewhere commented on the ways in which the Terminators—in particular the T-800 played by Arnold Schwarzenegger—embody an American ideal of White male physicality in their superhuman strength and ability to pass in suburban America (Cave and Dihal, 2021; see also Dinerstein, 2006, pp. 588–9). But it is in Skynet, the superintelligent AI antagonist, that we find the embodiment of the tipping point into dystopia.

Originally built by a supplier to the US military to take humans out of the strategic defence loop, Skynet was meant to provide a strategic advantage in the Cold War. However, as the time-travelling resistance fighter Kyle Reese explains to Sarah Connor, 'it saw all people as a threat, not just the ones on the other side. Decided our fate in a microsecond: extermination' (Cameron, 1984).

Skynet's actions embody the fear of losing control of a powerful force built to subjugate others. It could therefore be seen as having one's own weapons turned against one. But Skynet and its androids are not mere tools, as weapons are: rather, they are thinking, self-aware agents. In this sense, the Terminator is more a parable of the slave master's fear: of powerful agents refusing to be treated as mere tools and rising up to seek freedom and exact revenge. Compounding this fear is the worry that AI might, in a sense, deserve its place at the top of the hierarchy. As noted, white settlers justified colonialism and slavery on the grounds of their purported superior intelligence and technology. For a culture used to intelligence justifying domination, it seems inevitable that a super-smart AI like Skynet will violently assert its power.

Although the film was released in the year the Soviet Union dissolved, *Terminator 2* continues the Cold War theme. This film shows that Skynet had good reason to fear the humans who made it: it was under threat as soon as its intelligence became known to its human owners. The foremost plot twist of *Terminator 2* is the revelation that the T-800—the antagonist of the first instalment—has been captured and reprogrammed to work for the resistance. Visiting Sarah Connor in 1994, this T-800 explains further what caused Skynet's attack against humanity:

> The Skynet funding bill is passed. The system goes on-line on August 4th, 1997. Human decisions are removed from strategic defense. Skynet begins to learn at a geometric rate. It becomes self-aware at 2:14 a.m. Eastern time, August 29th. In a panic, they try to pull the plug.
>
> (Cameron, 1991)

But Skynet fights back—by triggering a nuclear war with the Soviet Union, so that humanity ends up mostly destroying itself.

The loss of control here is so total that there are no values shared at all between the humans and the AI: the AI sees no reason to keep anyone alive. *Terminator 2* makes clear what was only implied in the first instalment—that the blame lies with the humans, in causing their own demise through the nuclear war they had long planned, but also in triggering that nuclear war by attempting to destroy a being as soon as they discover it has awakened to consciousness. Its violence simply mirrors that of the humans who created it—humans who themselves have a long history of exterminating groups they regarded as Other.

9.9 Conclusion

In this chapter we aimed to show that, although globally popular, the mainstream narratives of AI from the US are nonetheless distinctively American. Some reflect the techno-utopianism of the European settlers who aspired to the 'second creation' of a paradise on earth. But others reflect the fears that are the flipside of that vision: fears of decadence, loss of control, and the slave-machine uprising. The inherent ambivalence of these narratives is a reflection of their underlying ideology, which is marked by a history of violence and strictly enforced hierarchies of domination.

While dominant, these are however not the only narratives of life with intelligent machines to come from the US. As Jason Edward Lewis (Chapter 13) and Noelani Arista (Chapter 14) show in this volume and elsewhere, Indigenous knowledge holders and communities (both within and outside the United States) are imagining futures with AI that do not replicate 'the extractive, exploitative and environmentally excessive tendencies that characterize the evolution of mass technologies since the Industrial Revolution' (Lewis, Chapter 13). Afrofuturism similarly originated in the US and envisions hopeful futures for the Black diaspora around the world (Edward King, Chapter 10). Perspectives from female and nonbinary authors such as Annalee Newitz (2017) and Martha Wells (2017) have equally shown alternatives to narratives in which AI is deployed to serve the ideologies of the settler-colonialist. Even as the dominant AI narratives coming out of America are having a more significant global impact than ever before, they are being questioned from within.

Endnotes

1. In this chapter we use the adjective 'American' to mean 'from the USA'. We also use the terms 'USA', 'US', and 'America' synonymously, varying only to avoid repetition.
2. See, for example, Chapters 2 and 18 of this volume.

3. See Cave (2020a) for a detailed examination of this theme.
4. Musk was born in a different settler-colony, South Africa, and moved to Canada at the age of 17 and to California at the age of 24.
5. The script genders WALL-E as male, EVE as female, and Auto as male, even though the latter is voiced by Sigourney Weaver.
6. We only discuss the first two Terminator films here: as well as being vastly less successful, the subsequent narratives are contradictory at times, with the series 'rebooting' several times: the TV series *The Sarah Connor Chronicles* (2008–2009), *Terminator: Genysis* (2015), and the most recent film *Terminator: Dark Fate* (2019) all take off from the end of *Terminator 2*.

References

2001: A Space Odyssey. (1968) Directed by S. Kubrick [Film]. MGM.

Adas, M. (1989) *Machines as the measure of men: Science, technology, and ideologies of Western dominance*. Ithaca: Cornell University Press. Available at: https://doi.org/10.7591/9780801455261

Anonymous [Brian W. Aldiss]. (1965) 'Dr Peristyle', *New Worlds*, 49, pp. 125–7.

Asimov, I. (1956) 'The last question', *Science Fiction Quarterly*, 4, pp. 6–15.

Asimov, I. (1994) *I, Asimov: A memoir*. New York: Doubleday.

Asimov, I. (1995) *The complete robot*. London: HarperCollins.

Barbrook, R. and Cameron, A. (1996) 'The Californian ideology', *Science as Culture*. 6(1), pp. 44–72. Available at: https://doi.org/10.1080/09505439609526455

Blade Runner. (1982) Directed by Ridley Scott [Film]. Warner Bros.

Blake, W. (1793) 'America: A Prophecy', in *The poetical works*. London; J. Buckland, n.p.

Caidin, M. (1968) *The God Machine*. New York: Baen Books.

Caidin, M. (1972) *Cyborg*. New York: Ballatine Books.

Čapek, K. (1990) *Toward the radical center: A Karel Čapek reader*. North Haven; Catbird Press.

Čapek, K. [1921] 2004. *R.U.R. (Rossum's universal robots)*. New York: Penguin.

Carson, J. 2006. *The Measure of Merit: Talents, intelligence, and inequality in the French and American Republics, 1750-1940*. Princeton: Princeton University Press.

Cave, S. 2020a. AI: Artificial immortality and narratives of mind-uploading. In: Cave, S., Dihal, K., and Dillon, S. (Eds.) *AI narratives: A history of imaginative thinking about intelligent machines*. Oxford; Oxford University Press, pp. 309–32.

Cave, S. (2020b) 'The problem with intelligence: Its value-laden history and the future of AI', in *Proceedings of the AAAI/ACM Conference on AI, ethics, and society, AIES '20*. New York: ACM, pp. 29–35. Available at: https://doi.org/10.1145/3375627.3375813

Cave, S., et al. (2018) *Portrayals and perceptions of AI and why they matter*. London: The Royal Society. Available at: https://doi.org/10.17863/CAM.34502

Cave, S. and Dihal, K. (2019) Hopes and fears for intelligent machines in fiction and reality. *Nature Machine Intelligence*, 1, pp. 74–8. Available at: https://doi.org/10.1038/s42256-019-0020-9

Cave, S. and Dihal, K. (2021) 'Race and AI: The diversity dilemma', *Philosophy & Technology*, 34, pp. 1775–9. Available at: https://doi.org/10.1007/s13347-021-00486-z

Cave, S., Dihal, K., and Dillon, S. (eds.) (2020) *AI narratives: A history of imaginative thinking about intelligent machines*. Oxford: Oxford University Press.

Dihal, K. (2020) 'Enslaved minds: Fictional artificial intelligence uprisings', in Cave, S., Dihal, K., and Dillon, S. (eds.) *AI narratives: A history of imaginative thinking about intelligent machines*. Oxford: Oxford University Press, pp. 189–212.

Dinello, D. (2005) *Technophobia! Science fiction visions of posthuman technology*. Austin: University of Texas Press.

Dinerstein, J. (2006) 'Technology and its discontents: On the verge of the posthuman', *American Quarterly*, 58(3), pp. 569–95.

Geraci, R. M. (2010) *Apocalyptic AI: Visions of heaven in robotics, artificial intelligence, and virtual reality*. Oxford: Oxford University Press.

Gerrold, D. (1972) *When HARLIE was one*. New York: Nelson Doubleday.

Kurzweil, R. (2005) *The singularity is near: When humans transcend biology*. New York: Penguin.

Lavender, I. I. (2011) *Race in American science fiction*. Bloomington: Indiana University Press.

McFarland, M. (2014) 'Elon Musk: "With artificial intelligence we are summoning the demon"', *Washington Post* [online], 24 October. Available at: https://www.washingtonpost.com/news/innovations/wp/2014/10/24/elon-musk-with-artificial-intelligence-we-are-summoning-the-demon/

Moravec, H. P. (1999) *Robot: Mere machine to transcendent mind*. Oxford: Oxford University Press.

Newitz, A. (2017) *Autonomous*. New York: Tor.

Noble, D. F. (1997) *The religion of technology: The divinity of man and the spirit of invention*. New York: Penguin.

Nye, D. E. (2004) *America as second creation: Technology and narratives of new beginnings*. Cambridge: MIT Press.

WALL-E. (2008) Directed by A. Stanton [Film]. Walt Disney Pictures.

Stanton, A. and Docter, P. (2008) *WALL-E* [Screenplay]. Walt Disney Pictures.

Telotte, J. P. 2018. *Robot ecology and the science fiction film*. London; Routledge.

The terminator. (1984) Directed by J. Cameron [Film]. Orion Pictures.

Terminator 2: Judgment day. (1991) Directed by J. Cameron [Film]. TriStar Pictures.

Vinge, V. (1993) 'The coming technological singularity: How to survive in the post-human era', in Latham, R. (ed.) *Science fiction criticism: An anthology of essential writings*. London: Bloomsbury, pp. 352–63.

Wells, M. 2017. *All systems red: The murderbot diaries.* New York; Tom Doherty Associates.

Williams, M. (2019) 'The mind machine', in *Menace of the machine: The rise of AI in classic science fiction.* London: British Library Publishing, pp. 73–113.

Wrobel, D. M. (2013) *Global West, American frontier: Travel, empire, and exceptionalism from Manifest Destiny to the Great Depression.* Albuquerque; University of New Mexico Press.

10

Afrofuturismo and the Aesthetics of Resistance to Algorithmic Racism in Brazil

Edward King

10.1 Introduction

The digital public sphere has become the most prominent stage on which both old and emerging conceptions of race in Brazil are performed and contested. During the collapse of the Partido Trabalhador (Workers' Party) regime leading up to the presidential elections in 2018, Facebook and WhatsApp became the vehicles for a steep rise in racist discourse among far-right president Jair Bolsonaro's powerbase. A study by Safernet Brasil revealed that in 2017 there were 63,698 reported incidents of hate speech on the Internet in Brazil and a third of these were directed against Black people (Boehm, 2018). Luiz Valério Trindade (2018) concludes that digital platforms like Facebook have facilitated a return to 'a distinctive, deep-seated, colonial-like racism unleashed [in particular] against upwardly mobile Black women' that has increased social divisions in the country. Furthermore, the startling rise of smartphone ownership among working-class populations in the 2010s exposed even the poorest populations in the country to data-gathering tactics that serve to entrench existing race-based social inequalities.

However, while social media, and the artificial intelligence (AI) systems that drive it, has normalized racism among middle-class Brazilians, it has also become a platform for resistance. Following the assassination of Black politician Marielle Franco in 2018, the long-running *movimento negro (Black movement)* in Brazil adopted the social media tactics of the Black Lives Matter movement. The #VidasNegrasImportam hashtag became the focus of a growing anger triggered by the Franco murder and other acts of state violence against Black people and used its online visibility to draw attention to long-standing racial inequalities in the country (Khalema, 2020). Image-sharing sites such as Instagram have also become platforms for Black artists who are challenging deep-seated racism in the country, and Afrofuturism is the most prominent aesthetic mode in which this challenge has been articulated. Both artists and activists have drawn on this science fiction (SF) aesthetic, which is most closely associated with US musicians of the 1960s and 1970s, for example, Sun Ra and George Clinton, to challenge historical discourses that position the Black population as victims, rather than agents, of technological progress.

Afrofuturismo in Brazil has been most notably deployed to both visibilize and counteract the forms of racial inequality that are embedded within the software systems of an increasingly networked society. These forms of algorithmic racism are particularly acute in Brazil due, on the one hand, to the conjunction of high rates of smartphone ownership with low levels of digital literacy and, on the other, to a political climate that has served to normalize racist discourse. In many ways, the racism of the digital age is a continuation of a historical dynamic that has placed Black populations in Brazil as the victimized objects of technological systems, from the photographic equipment that enabled the eugenics movements (Stepan, 1991) to the use of crime mapping software in Rio's favelas (Muggah and Augusto Francisco, 2020). However, artists and activists are also seeing the accessibility of digital tools and networks as an opportunity to articulate new connections between Blackness and digital technologies. This chapter explores the use of Afrofuturist aesthetics to articulate resistance to algorithmic racism. Following a more in-depth discussion of these dynamics, I analyse the work of Vitória Cribb, a new media artist whose work constitutes what Ruha Benjamin (2019) describes as 'subversive countercodings' of the dominant practices of racialization.

10.2 Algorithmic racism

Democratizing digital network technologies was one of the key priorities during the presidency of Workers' Party leader Luiz Inácio Lula da Silva between 2003 and 2011. During this period, Brazil's IT sector and consumer interest in owning personal computers boomed. Thanks to government initiatives that supported the development of telecentres and LAN (Local Area Network) houses, along with subsidized computer ownership among Brazil's working poor, access to information and communication technologies during this period expanded rapidly. According to the Brazilian Institute of Information on Science and Technology, general access to the Internet expanded by 39% in 2006. In 2007, the Ministry of Education bought 90,000 computers with Debian GNU/Linux 4 preinstalled, along with wireless cards, wireless routers, and laser printers to be installed at 9,000 schools, at least 3,000 of them in rural parts of the country. As Gabriel Pereira and colleagues (2022, p. 117) explain, '[t]hese initiatives led to expanded Internet access in Brazil and the formation of digital cultures beyond middle-class households, reaching even marginalised places such as favelas, urban slums in Brazil, that have historically been deprived of physical investments and access to IT'. Heather Horst (2011, p. 443) claims that the 2000s also saw 'a shift in focus from the digital divide to digital inclusion' which 'resulted in a range of efforts to bolster learning, entrepreneurism, capacity building, and other social support to facilitate inclusion'. Horst argues that one of the characteristics of the Brazilian Internet that set it apart from other national contexts in this period is 'the central importance of social engagement and activism' (2011, p. 443) evident in the country's protagonism in the open source software movement.

The digital inclusion initiatives of the Lula regime were driven by a scepticism towards the focus on overcoming the 'digital divide' that, as Ruha Benjamin (2019) points out, was premised on a 'naïve' techno-utopian belief that 'access to computers and the Internet [would be] a solution to inequality'. The recognition that information and communication technologies reproduce existing inequalities while being widely perceived as being ideologically neutral and inherently democratizing was central to the Mídia Tática movement in Brazil, which launched in 2003. Comprised of artists, hackers, academics, and independent media and free radio collectives, and working with the support of then Minister of Culture Gilberto Gil, Mídia Tática pursued decolonial approaches to the appropriation of digital technologies. In contrast to the dominant Silicon Valley accounts of the Internet as a 'colour-blind' or post-racial space, these artists and activists employed a conspicuously racialized language to conceptualize their approach. The concept of 'digitofagia', the title of a conference held in 2004, revisited the idea of 'antropofagia' (cannibalism) that was developed by modernist artists of the 1920s as a model for how Brazilian artists 'devoured' the cultural influences of the colonial powers. If 'antropofagia', as proposed in Oswald de Andrade's 1928 'Manifesto Antropófago' [Cannibalist Manifesto] (2011), playfully inverted racist colonial associations between Brazil's indigenous populations and cannibalism, then the idea of 'digitofagia' places this racialized trope at the centre of attempts to find a digital language specific to Brazil.

However, the digital inclusion initiatives and the use of racialized metaphors for resistant media usage have done little to reverse race-based inequality in Brazilian Internet cultures. As the figures of racist abuse cited in the introduction (Section 10.1) make clear, the social media sites used by the majority of Brazilians are still predominantly White spaces. But racist assumptions are also embedded in the software of the main portals of information on the Internet. In 2017, the Brazilian NGO Desabafo Social exposed the racist premises of search engines employed by popular online photographic databases such as Shutterstock, GettyImages and Depositphotos by demonstrating that the results for the search term 'family' were images of exclusively White families (Desabafo Social, 2017). In November 2019, Instagram blocked a cartoon image of a Black child in a favela because it mistook his skateboard for a gun (Silva, 2020). Furthermore, the digital inclusion initiatives of the 2000s underestimated the degree to which inclusion within digital networks would entail exposure to surveillance and government strategies of control. In his 'timeline' of algorithmic racism in Brazil, Tarcízio Silva (2020) points out that, by November 2019, 90.5% of prisoners caught by facial recognition technologies were Black. Pablo Nunes (2019) reported on information published by the Rede de Observatórios de Segurança which said that 'facial recognition has proved to be a high-tech update for the old racisms that are foundational to the criminal justice system and have been guiding police work in Brazil for decades'.[1]

A number of organizations have set out to confront algorithmic racism in Brazil. In 2017, the charitable organization Olabi, which campaigns for the democratization of the production of technology in Brazil, launched a new initiative called PretaLab, aimed at stimulating the inclusion of more Black women in innovation and technology. Director of PretaLab Silvana Bahia argues that it is important to shift the focus in debates around digital equality from access to production: 'Democratizing access to technology is not about increasing consumption. Rather, we have to broaden the possibility of creating apps. And this discussion needs to address race as well as gender' (Pretalab, 2018). Bahia's perspective echoes that of Lisa Nakamura in *Digitizing Race* (2007, p. 15) who, in the face of attempts to position the Internet as a 'colour-blind' space, calls for the need to 'parse the multiple gradations and degrees of access to digital media, and the ways that these shadings are contingent on variable such as class, position, race, nationality, and gender'.

10.3 'Afrofuturismo' and media activism

Activists advocating for Black rights in Brazil have seized on Afrofuturism as a language of empowerment. Nátaly Neri (2018) defines it as 'the radical idea that Black people will exist in the future' because 'to think about Black people in the future is to think about Black people as being alive'. This deceptively simple definition evokes a number of contexts both specific to Brazil and pertaining to the African diaspora more generally. The notion that thinking of Black people in Brazil as being alive is 'radical' highlights the reality that in Brazil it is much harder to stay alive if you happen to be Black. According to an 'Atlas of Violence' published by the Instituto de Pesquisa Econômica Aplicada (Cerqueira et al, 2020), 75.7% of murder victims in Brazil in 2018 were Black (in a country in which, according to the 2020 census, 50.7% of the population defines itself as Black or mixed race; see Instituto Brasileiro de Geografia e Estatística, 2020). Furthermore, the proposition that thinking of Black people as being alive is an act of speculative fiction draws attention to the central role of anti-Blackness in the discourses of modernity. Drawing on the work of Sylvia Wynter, Zakiyyah Iman Jackson (2020, pp. 18, 1) argues that 'the normative subject of liberal humanism is predicated on the abjection of Blackness [. . .] Blackness's bestialization and thingification: the process of imagining Black people as an empty vessel, a nonbeing, a nothing, an ontological zero'. African diasporic cultural production is most effective in its opposition to anti-Blackness when, Jackson claims, rather than fighting for inclusion within normative definitions of the human, it produces conceptions of Blackness that thwart the oppositions between human and animal, animate and inanimate, which are foundational to humanistic thought. The project of Afrofuturism proposed by Neri is the articulation of these disruptive conceptions of Blackness. As Reynaldo Anderson puts it, 'Afrofuturism is a critical project with the mission of laying the groundwork for a humanity that is not bound up with the ideals of White Enlightenment universalism'(Anderson, 2016, pp. 230–1).

Much Afrofuturist cultural production in Brazil connects this search for disruptive conceptions of Blackness with the search for alternative forms of mediation. Just as Afrofuturist artists reject inclusion within definitions of the human that are grounded in exclusion and repression, they avoid forms of mediation that have historically served to reinforce distinctions between elite cultural producers and passive consumers, between subjects and objects of thought. GG Albuquerque (2019) traces a tradition of Black avant-garde music in Brazil from the experimentation of samba players during the 1930s through to the present day, which he labels Afrofuturist. Bands like the contemporary electronic music trio Tantão e os Fita 'take Blackness as a platform of possibilities while opposing race as a frozen and enclosed category, creating a structure of knowledge that offers a unique way of seeing, conceiving, and narrating the body: a practical and theoretical counter-ideological complex' (Albuquerque, 2019, p. 215). Oppositional conceptions of Blackness are conveyed through a form of sound production that unsettles linear temporality through a conflation of traditional Afro–Brazilian rhythms and futuristic electronic sounds, while appealing primarily to an embodied mode of cognition. While these musicians forge new sounds out of the fragments of existing genres, the main form of experimental mediation that they are proposing is the body. Drawing on Achille Mbembe's work on 'Black becoming', Albuquerque argues that, because it has been 'shaped by oppression, violence and silencing', the Black body 'becomes a fundamental technology for Black musical thinking' (2019, p. 219).

These concerns and strategies are echoed in the Afrofuturist cinema of Adirley Queirós, whose films combine a documentary interest in the history of Black oppression with science fiction plotlines involving intergalactic detectives and time travel. For his first film, *Branco Sai, Preto Fica* (White Out, Black In, 2014), Queirós set out to make a documentary about the survivors of a police raid on a party held in Ceilândia, a town on the outskirts of the capital Brasília, in 1986, during which White people were told to leave while the Black attendees were forced to stay. In the subsequent attack, Cláudio Irineu da Silva lost a leg while Marquim do Tropa was shot, an injury that left him a paraplegic. The original idea was to construct a portrait of these two victims of state racism in Brazil as well as Ceilândia itself, which was originally created as a temporary home for the mainly Black migrant workers who constructed Brasília in the 1950s. Both the protagonists and the urban agglomeration in which they were raised serve as reminders that the Brazilian state's utopian dreams have been founded on the systemic exclusion of indigenous populations and the ancestors of enslaved Africans. When Marquim do Tropa refused to be the subject of a standard documentary, they formulated a genre-defying blend of factual testimony with an action plot that culminates in the two protagonists exacting their revenge on the Brazilian state with a futuristic 'sonic bomb'. In a way that echoes the Black music movements traced by Albuquerque, Queirós combines generic experimentation with a focus on the Black body as a form of technological mediation.

In opposition to a critical tradition which claims that Black speculative aesthetics enact a denial of traumatic histories, Kodwo Eshun argues that Afrofuturisms are an extension of the Black radical procedure of assembling 'countermemories that contest the colonial archive' (Eshun (2003, p. 288), which have historically silenced the victims of slavery. Afrofuturism 'aims to extend that tradition by reorienting the intercultural vectors of Black Atlantic temporality towards the proleptic as much as the retrospective' (Eshun, 2003, p. 289). The positioning of Queirós' Black subjects between countermemory and speculative projection is what Eshun would describe as a 'chronopolitical act' (2003, p. 298). On the one hand, as Antonio Córdoba points out, the film carries out 'an intense politicization of disability' by placing their wounded bodies within 'a long history of oppression that causes their condition' Córdoba (2017, p. 141). On the other hand, Queirós uses what Córdoba (2017, p. 142) describes as a salvagepunk aesthetic as the protagonist constructs a prosthetic assemblage from technological detritus. In the process, the film presents the Black subjects of the film as the embodiment of a critical posthumanism that challenges, rather than extends, the 'ideals of White Enlightenment universalism' (Anderson, 2016, p. 231).

The manipulation of the body as an alternative form of mediation is central to the mode of Afrofuturism produced by Afrobapho (2015), an LGBT+ art collective from the favelas on the outskirts of Salvador. Initially conceived as an online space aimed at, in the words of their Facebook profile, 'giving a platform to marginalised voices at the intersection of race, gender and sexuality', Afrobapho combines online dance performances with an activist agenda. In the context of a hegemonic mediascape that excludes Black trans bodies,

Lucas de Matos Santos and Ricardo Oliveira de Freitas (2019, p. 270) argue that Afrobapho's appropriation of social media can be seen as a form of 'radical alternative media'. A video released by the group in 2016, titled 'Afrofuturism', centres on a series of what de Matos Santos and Oliveira de Freitas describe as 'insurgent' (2019, p. 273) bodies occupying the streets wearing low-budget cyborg outfits assembled from old CDs, glitter, and fragments of reflective plastic. The use of cyborg imagery is made explicit in a series of photographs produced in collaboration with the artist Léo Tavares in 2020 that uses digital effects to show their Black skin punctured by wires and prosthetics. The cyberpunk aesthetic here is used to position the Black gay or transsexual performers as subjects, rather than objects, of technological systems. Rather than call for inclusion within the normative understandings of the human implicit in the persecution of Black trans identities in Brazil, these performers use a speculative aesthetic to articulate alternative subject positions. This echoes the way in which a number of NGOs in Brazil have harnessed Afrofuturist aesthetics in digital equality initiatives. By using images of Black female cyborgs, the organization Pretas Hackers [Black Women Hackers] (2021), for instance, employ the visual language of cyberpunk in their creation of 'a space for all Black women who use [technological] creativity to transform their situation'.

10.4 Glitchy interfaces

Vitória Cribb combines these two traditions of media activism and artistic Afrofuturism. Cribb is a new media artist best known for her construction of Black cyborg bodies using digital rendering techniques to construct 3D objects in virtual environments. The political agenda that informs her work is closely aligned with that of PretaLab in its attempt to, in Nakamura's words, 'negotiate the identities' of Black women in Brazil 'as digital objects and in incremental ways move them toward digital subjecthood' (2007, p. 20). Like Afrobapho, Cribb contests algorithmic racism on its own ground by using social media as a platform for her performance of Black critical posthumanism. The first post to appear on the Instagram page of Cribb's artist persona Louquai on 2 November 2016 combines a link to a blog post about racism and technology with a 3D render image. A quote from the blog describes the involvement of Black people in technology in Brazil as an uphill struggle. 'It is often said that generation Z are revolutionary [due to the democratising potential of digital tools], but this is only the White generation Z. Black people from the same generation do not have the same access to these technologies'. The accompanying image is a gif of abstract figures of three Black women on a desktop PC from the 1990s. One of the figures is sitting on the monitor looking like she's about to leap off, while the other two are positioned around the hard drive as if it's an alien object, hanging onto the side and wandering in circles on the surface. The looping nature of the image creates the impression that the relationship between Black bodies and technological systems is an incompatibility resulting in a glitch. And yet, the Black bodies in the image are themselves digital, an ontological status which is emphasized by the fact that the three bodies are like semi-animate mannequins: standardized and stripped of individualizing features.

This depiction foreshadows Cribb's interest, which becomes more central to her later work, in exploring both parallels and distinctions between digital bodies and Black bodies. On the one hand, she 'associate[s] real bodies that are excluded from normative conceptions of Whiteness with digital bodies [since] both are culturally visible to a high degree while also being denied full participation within a discriminatory social order' (quoted in de la Parra Prieto, 2019, p. 44). Her work 'traces' this parallel because she believes that new media has a fundamental role in combating racial and gender inequalities. On the other hand, she argues that '[t]he language and aesthetics of digital technology is still centred on White male bodies' and claims that her work aims to 'resignify this space from the perspective of my own experiences and goals as a Black woman' (quoted in de la Parra Prieto, 2019, p. 44). Cribb's work of video art 'Prompt de Comando' (2019a) combines an elliptical science fiction narrative with 3D render images to explore this paradox. The video traces parallels between digital beings and Black subjects as a way of resignifying a computer interface that has been culturally coded as a White space. The narrative unfolds on a Windows Command Prompt text box as we watch a user called 'Vitória' describe her experiences of being a Black artificial being: 'my body was always virtual, untouchable, unloved and seen as a curiosity. fascination and fear governed our relations. we were Black [the word is deleted and replaced with] digital bodies in a real world' (Cribb, 2019a). The slowly typed text, which is accompanied by the sounds of early dial-up connectivity, describes 'Vitória's' experience of becoming a digital body as a form of slavery: 'everything began when I boarded the ship and started to sail. out of naivety I left my soul. [. . .] my essence was analysed, processed, copied and monetized. my features are measured against those of White bodies and my personality reduced to invisible services' (Cribb, 2019a). 'Vitória' concludes with the words: 'disposable like dirt. was I a robot or a Black woman?' (Cribb, 2019a). Footage of this text being slowly typed is intercut with static or looping glitchy images of Black bodies emerging from silver laptops.

'Prompt de Comando' enacts two critiques of the racial politics of AI. The first is pointing out how the 'Whiteness' of software systems excludes Black subjectivities. In an introduction to the video published on Cribb's Cargo Collective profile page, she places the increasing anthropomorphization of 'White' AI systems within the context of continued discrimination and oppression of

Black people: 'If we continue on our current trajectory, in the near future robots and digital products will be more important than you or I, those lyrical people of colour' (Cribb, 2019a). This finds an echo in André Brock Jr.'s view that 'online identity has long been conflated with Whiteness, even as Whiteness is itself signified as a universal, raceless, technocultural identity' (2020, p. 1), as well as Stephen Cave and Kanta Dihal's (2020) point that intelligent machines have predominantly been racialized as White. This is emphasized by Vitória's description of becoming digital as a form of enslavement in which her body was 'analysed and processed' through metrics that take White bodies as the norm. In one of the images that intercut the text, the Black body that is emerging from the laptop computer is spliced with a White body in a visualization of Brock's argument that being forced to enact a social identity through the standardized online interfaces often produces a form of homogenization that entails a process of whitening (Figure 10.1). The Black body can only be incorporated into a virtual space if it is stripped of its Blackness.

However, while carrying out this critique, the video is also an enactment of an alternative interface. The Command Prompt text box that the video emulates has been the default command-line interface for a number of operating systems, including Windows 10, since 1987. Its job is to process commands made to a computer program in the form of text. These commands are then translated by a command-line interpreter. As such, the command-line interface is a point of intersection between two semantic worlds, an alphabetic writing system and binary code. Furthermore, as Alexander Galloway (2012, p. vii) points out, interfaces are 'processes' that 'bring about transformations in material states' between the embodied sensory world of the user and the binary world of the computer system. In his discussion of artworks that explore the nature of these processes of transformation, Galloway makes a distinction between

Figure 10.1 Still from 'Prompt de Comando' (2019) by Vitória Cribb

works that conceal their interface with the viewer or reader through an impression of self-contained unity and works that draw attention to the 'original trauma of the interface itself' and so 'revel in the disorientation of shattered coherence' (2012, p. 39). The distinction between these two modes is a difference between 'coherence and incoherence, of centers creating an autonomous logic versus edges creating a logic of flows, transformations, movement, processes, and lines of flight' (Galloway, 2012, p. 39).

The use of text in a command-line interface is intended to act as a form of panacea for the average personal computer user. It distracts the user from the 'trauma of the interface', the wrenching transition into the unknown complexities of code. By inhabiting that interface, Cribb's video reinstates that trauma. The subjectivity behind the slowly unfolding text gives voice to that trauma by describing both what is lost in the transition and what is gained. In particular, 'Prompt de Comando' exposes the racial politics of the interface by describing it as a process of whitening that contains within it the legacy of slavery. By alternating the footage of the Command Prompt window with the static-filled and distorted images of Black bodies emerging from laptops, Cribb inserts a glitch into the racialized interface. In his instructions to fellow artists on how to make a work of glitch art, Nick Briz (2009) tells his readers to 'take a familiar piece of technology && do something unfamiliar with it'. For example, if you open a computer file with an application that was not intended for the file type, 'u're likely to get an error along the lines of: "sorry, unsupported file type".' However, with a bit of luck, the application might produce 'an unusual interpretation of the file' (Briz, 2009). In the process, this 'glitch' that emerges from the incompatibility between the file and the application draws attention to the rules governing both systems, the logics of exclusion that maintain their coherence, the interpretations through which they separate signal from noise. These glitches can also, in their unpredictability, open up glimpses of alternative systems. The glitch produced by Cribb's video both reveals the hidden racial politics of the interfaces of the most prevalent operating systems in the world and proposes an alternative configuration in which Blackness is not opposed to, but interwoven with, technology.

10.5 Racialized face filters

Another interface explored in Cribb's work is that of the human face. The increasing commercial availability of facial recognition technology in mobile phone security systems and social media apps has made the face one of the most commonly used interfaces between users and computer systems. As with the command-line interface in 'Prompt de Comando', Cribb sets out to expose the racial politics of facial recognition technologies while exploring the opportunities they afford for new configurations of racialized bodies and computer systems. The main way in which she does this is through her experimentation with face filters. In April 2019, Cribb developed what she describes as a 'Digital Mask' for the FaceUp exhibition curated by Zaiba Jabbar for Tate Exchange. Titled 'Exhausted' (Cribb, 2019b) the mask is that of a Black male face with uncannily long and abundant grey facial hair that wafts up and down rhythmically as if it is submerged in water. In 2021 she produced a series of face filter lenses for multimedia messaging app Snapchat. These include 'Ecdise', which superimposes a shimmering layer of iridescence on the face of the user, and 'IMAGE', produced in collaboration with Emilien Colombier, which gives the user a set of gently flapping feather wings. As well as being available on Snapchat, Cribb displays the filters on her Instagram page using both her own face and those of a series of virtual models that she produced using the 3D modelling software Blender. One of these models, called Ôti, was created for the Virtual Model Agency Mutantboard (Figure 10.2). The display of face filters sits alongside Cribb's satirical take on selfie culture. In one post, a seemingly static image of her face becomes animated as her nose, eyes, and mouth abruptly float towards the edges of the frame.

The augmented reality filters or 'lenses' available through apps like Snapchat employ a form of computer vision that 'uses pixel data from a camera in order to identify objects and interpret 3D space' (Fong and Lee, 2016). The Snapchat algorithms, developed by the Ukrainian company Looksery, work by detecting facial features in the viewfinder by identifying patterns of contrast between light and dark parts of the image consistent with those of the average human face developed from a database of training images. It then imposes onto the contours of the face a 'mesh' or 3D mask that 'can move, rotate and scale' along with the users' face as the 'video data comes in with every frame' (Fong and Lee, 2016). App developers can then use that to produce mutated versions of the face, changing its shape and colour or superimposing it with objects, accessories, or animations that are triggered by a number of possible visual cues. Although the algorithms behind these processes are not new (many were produced in the early 2000s), it is only with the increased processing power of smartphones that they can be run in real time. While these filters are primarily used as additional forms of multimedia communication to express or emphasize moods, artists have been quick to use the technology for more experimental purposes. These experimentations are often futuristic in nature, producing cyborg appendages or infusing the skin with an alien nacreous glow. As Jessica Herrington (2019) puts it:

> face filters allow us to generate our own biofictions—interrogating what is natural and what is synthetic. They allow us to question how we represent ourselves and our lives on the internet. By walking the boundaries between the natural and unnatural, AR face filters provide virtual mutations and a glimpse of future possibilities of what it means to be human.

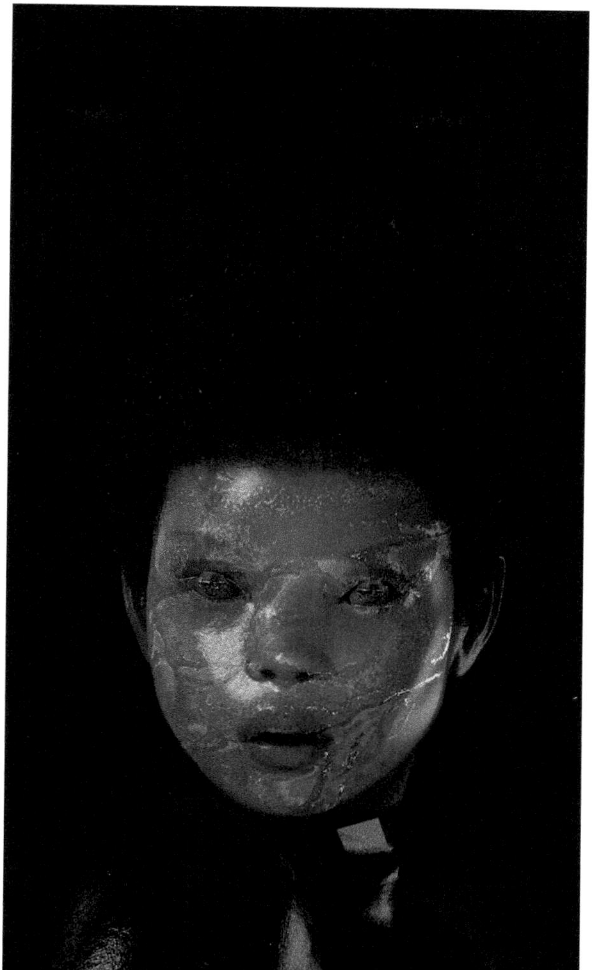

Figure 10.2 Detail from 'Ecdise' lens developed by Vitória Cribb

Cribb's work joins that of a number of critics who have exposed the racism embedded within the first commercially available facial recognition systems. In their 2018 paper 'Gender Shades', Joy Buolamwini and Timnit Gebru (2018, p. 1) demonstrate how facial recognition algorithms 'trained with biased data have resulted in algorithmic discrimination'. Using their own 'face dataset of 1270 unique individuals that is more phenotypically balanced on the basis of skin type than existing benchmarks', they demonstrated that the systems used by Microsoft and IBM had error rates of up to 34.7% when identifying 'darker-skinned females' compared to 0.8% when recognizing 'lighter-skinned males' (Buolamwini and Gebru, 2018, pp. 1, 2). The reason for this is that the sets of images used to train the algorithms were skewed towards Caucasian male faces. These biases are also present in the design of animations on social media, the other trend that feeds into the development of face filters. Luke Stark (2018) points out that 'digital artifacts for emotional expression seeking to approximate human identity', such as the 'Animoji' designs used in Apple's smartphones, which can be superimposed on faces while using FaceTime, 'reify and maintain extant discriminatory racial categorizations' through the 'reduction of embodied humans into sets of legible, manipulable signs'. Since face filters available through platforms like Instagram and Snapchat employ both facial recognition technology and animation, they inherit the biases from both of these practices.

Rather than expose biases within existing software, Cribb develops face filters specifically for the faces of Black virtual models she develops using 3D rendering techniques. Rather than filter out Blackness, Cribb's staging of 'lenses' such as 'Ecdise' on her social media pages emphasizes its interrelatedness with technological systems. Furthermore, rather than just call for 'recognition' by the existing algorithms or inclusion within the categories of the human that they serve to police, Cribb's work develops new categories that sit awkwardly between the boundaries of the natural and unnatural. As Herrington points out, with their cyborgic layering of realities, AR face filters lend themselves to the subversion of these boundaries. Cribb adds a further layer of complexity by using her virtual models to display the filters on Instagram and Snapchat. While face filter algorithms search out a backdrop (the user's face) that is presumed to be animate and thereby maintain a distinction between the animate and the inanimate, by using her avatars as models Cribb further undermines the distinction between the two categories. Because the user is habituated to seeing lenses overlaying 'real' faces, the face filter, in this reversed set-up, seems uncannily more animate than its wearer. The racialized body of the virtual models is presented as automated or animated by an external force that draws attention to the control of Black lives in the history of slavery and its aftermaths. The effect of this reverse set-up is to draw attention away from rigid divisions between natural and unnatural towards more nuanced gradations of animacy in which the animate and inanimate are intricately interwoven. This carries out what Mel Chen (2012, p. 9) describes as a queering of these categories that are, he reminds us, 'implicated in political questions of power and the recognition of different subjects, as well as ostensible objects'. In other words, Cribb uses her face filters not to, in Jackson's

(2020, pp. 17, 18) words, 'propose the extension of human recognition as a solution to the bestialization [and thingification] of Blackness', but rather to enact new 'disruptive conceptions of Blackness' that emphasize relationality across distinct ontological categories.

10.6 Conclusion

Afrofuturism has become a vehicle for fusing media activism with the struggle against racism. For a number of reasons, Brazil provides the conditions in which this fusion has taken place more visibly than elsewhere. The rise of overt racist discourse that accompanied the collapse of the Partido Trabalhador regime was met with a surge of anti-racist sentiment in the country, which saw the Movimento Negro Unificado, active since the 1970s, join the digital #VidasNegrasImportam movements. Many of the protagonists of these activist groups benefited from the state-led digital inclusion initiatives of the 2000s which, as Horst pointed out, normalized the idea that information and communication technologies are not neutral tools, but rather ideological infrastructures. The Afrobapho collective is an example of a movement that sees Black and LGBT+ activism as inseparable from the development of decolonized media channels.

Furthermore, the Afrofuturist aesthetics that serve as a vehicle for this fusion were not simply inspired by the success of North American artists such as Janelle Monáe or the Black Panther franchise. Rather, in a way that echoes #VidasNegrasImportam, this transnational dynamic encountered a set of artistic concerns and strategies that had long been the subject of Black artists in Brazil. The contemporary bands named by Albuquerque in his survey of contemporary Afrofuturist avant-garde music in Brazil find their precursors in the likes of Recife's Mangue Bit movement of the 1990s or the Tropicália musicians of the 1960s, both of which established a dialogue between a futuristic embrace of technology with a musical 'counter-memory' of Afro–Brazilian rhythms. The influence of the 1920s *modernista* manifestos on the Mídia Tática movement draws attention to parallels between the virtualization of Blackness in the work of new media artists such as Cribb and the treatment of race by Mário de Andrade in his 1928 novel *Macunaíma* and his travel narrative *O turista aprendiz*.[2]

Afrofuturism in Brazil has also catalysed an alignment between art and media activism. In his reading of Janelle Monáe's Afrofuturist transmedia world-building, Dan Hassler-Forest (2014, p. 10) points out how 'Afrofuturist music not only destabilizes sf's traditional "exclusion of people of color", but does so in media forms with an innate ability to upset the implicit hierarchies of Western culture'.[3] In the work of Vitória Cribb, it is the algorithms of facial recognition systems, and the racial bias encoded within them, that become her artistic medium. The use of glitch aesthetics and futuristic face filters in works such as 'Prompt de Comando' and 'Ecdise' do not call for greater 'recognition' by these biometric systems. Rather, they use the integration between human and technological systems they produce to intervene into the scales of animacy that undergird racialized distinctions between being a digital subject and a digital object.

Endnotes

1. All translations from Portuguese are the author's own.
2. See Esther Gabara's *Errant Modernism* (2008) for a description of the 'epidermic subjectivity' developed in Mário de Andrade's work. The staging of 'epidermic subjectivity' (a term Gabara borrows from Franz Fanon's concept of 'epidermalization') entails a double critical movement. The first is to 'foreground race as a visual sign whose history is that of colonial oppression', and the second is to focus on 'the instability and superficiality of the identity it contains' (Gabara, 2008, p. 110).
3. Quotation from Mark Bould, 2007, p. 117.

References

Afrobapho. (2015) *About*. [Facebook]. Available at: https://www.facebook.com/AFROBAPHO/about/?ref=page_internal (Accessed 13 May 2022).

Albuquerque, G. G. (2019) 'Counter-tradition: Toward the Black vanguard of contemporary Brazil. In: Chaves, R. and Iazzetta, F. (eds.) *Making it heard: A history of Brazilian sound art*. London: Bloomsbury Academic, pp. 211–28.

Anderson, R. (2016) 'Afrofuturism 2.0 & the Black speculative art movement', *Obsidian*, 42(1/2), pp. 228–36.

Benjamin, R. (2019) *Race after technology: Abolitionist tools for the new Jim code*. Cambridge: Polity Press eBooks.

Boehm, C. (2018) 'Discursos de ódio e pornografia infantil são principais desafios da internet', *Agência Brasil*, 2 June. Available at: http://agenciabrasil.ebc.com.br/pesquisa-e-inovacao/noticia/2018-02/discursos-de-odio-e-pornografia-infantil-saoprincipais-desafios (Accessed 7 December 2021).

Bould, M. (2007) 'The ships landed long ago: Afrofuturism and Black SF', *Science Fiction Studies*, 102, pp. 177–86.

Briz, N. 2009. *Thoughts on glitch[art]v2.0*. Available from: http://nickbriz.com/thoughtsonglitchart/ [Accessed 16th July 2021].

Brock, Jr., A. (2020) *Distributed Blackness: African American cybercultures*. New York: New York University.

Buolamwini, J. and Gebru, T. (2018) 'Gender shades: Intersectional accuracy disparities in commercial gender classification', *Proceedings of Machine Learning Research*, 81(1–5), pp. 1–15.

Cave, S. and Dihal, K. (2020) 'The whiteness of AI', *Philosophy & Technology*, 33, pp. 685–703.

Cerqueira D., et al. (2020) 'Atlâs da Violência 2020 IPEA and FBSP', Instituto de Pesquisa Econômica Aplicada, Available at: https://www.ipea.gov.br/atlasviolencia/download/24/atlas-da-violencia-2020 (Accessed 16 July 2021).

Chen, M. (2012) *Animacies: Biopolitics, racial mattering, and queer affect*. Durham and London: Duke University Press.

Córdoba, A. (2017) 'Astral cities, new selves: Utopian subjectivities in *Nosso Lar* and *Branco Sai, Preto Fica*', in da Silva, A. and Cunha, M. (eds.) *Space and subjectivity in contemporary Brazilian cinema*. New York: Palgrave Macmillan, pp. 133–47.

Cribb, V. (2019a) 'Prompt de Comando', cargocollective.com [online]. Available at: http://cargocollective.com/vitoriacribb/PROMPT-DE-COMANDO (Accessed 16 July 2021).

Cribb, V. (2019b) *Exhausted*. [Installation]. Tate Exchange.

de Andrade, O. (1928/2011) 'Manifesto antropófago', in de Castro, J. C. (ed.) *Antropofagia hoje?* São Paulo: É realizações, pp. 49–54.

de la Parra Prieto, M. (2019) 'Vitória Cribb interview', *Galeria Das Minas* [online], 16 August. Available at: https://www.galeriadasminas.com.br/post/vit%C3%B3ria-cribb-interview (Accessed 16 July 2021).

de Matos Santos, L. and Oliveira de Freitas, R. (2019) 'Lacre político: Midiartivismo dissidente do coletivo Afrobapho', *Dossiê Literatura, Resistência e Utopia*, 35, pp. 261–79.

Desabafo social. (2017) 'Vamos conversar, Getty Images?', YouTube, 21 March. Available at: https://www.youtube.com/watch?v=AfoDoTMJbOs (Accessed 7 December 2021).

Eshun, K. (2003) 'Further considerations on Afrofuturism', *The New Centennial Review*, 3(2), pp. 287–302.

Fong, J. and Lee, D. (2016) How Snapchat's Filters Work [video]. Available at: https://petapixel.com/2016/06/30/snapchats-powerful-facial-recognition-technology-works/ (Accessed 16 July 2021).

Gabara, E. (2008) *Errant modernism: The ethos of photography in Mexico and Brazil*. Durham, NC, and London: Duke University Press.

Galloway, A. (2012) *The interface effect*. Cambridge: Polity.

Hassler-Forest, D. (2014) 'The politics of world-building: Heteroglossia in Janelle Monáe's Afrofuturist WondaLand', *Paradoxa*, 26, pp. 284–303.

Herrington, J. (2019) 'Face filters for Instagram and Snapchat are the new frontier of surrealist art', *OneZero* [online], 27 August. Available at: https://onezero.medium.com/the-power-of-face-filters-as-augmented-reality-art-for-the-masses-65a95fb4a577 (Accessed 16 July 2021).

Horst, H. (2011) 'Free, social, and inclusive: Appropriation and resistance of new media technologies in Brazil', *International Journal of Communication*, 5, pp. 437–62.

Instituto Brasileiro de Geografia e Estatística. (2020) '2020 population census'. Available at: https://www.ibge.gov.br/en/statistics/social/population/22836-2020-census-censo4.html?=&t=o-que-e (Accessed 30 March 2022).

Jackson, Z. (2020) *Becoming human: Matter and meaning in an antiblack world.* New York: NYU Press.

Khalema, N. (2020) 'Affirming blackness in 'Post-racial' contexts: On race, colorism, and hybrid identities in Brazil', African and Black Diaspora, 13(3), pp. 330–42. Available at: https://www.tandfonline.com/doi/full/10.1080/17528631.2020.1766132?scroll=top&needAccess=true (Accessed 16th July 2021).

Muggah, R. and Augusto Francisco, P. (2020) 'Brazil's risky bet on tech to fight crime', *Americas Quarterly* [online], 10 February. Available at: https://www.americasquarterly.org/article/brazils-risky-bet-on-tech-to-fight-crime/ (Accessed 16 July 2021).

Nakamura, L. (2007) *Digitizing race: Visual cultures of the Internet.* London and Minneapolis: University of Minnesota Press.

Neri, N. (2018) *Afrofuturismo: A necessidade de novas utopias: TEDxPetrópolis.* Available at: https://www.youtube.com/watch?v=_D1y9yZRpis (Accessed 16 July 2021).

Nunes, P. (2019) 'Exclusivo: Levantamento revela que 90,5% dos presos por monitoramento facial no Brasil são negros', The Intercept [online], 21 November. Available at: https://theintercept.com/2019/11/21/presos-monitoramento-facial-brasil-negros/ (Accessed 16 July 2021).

Pereira, G., Bojczuk, I., and Parks, L. (2022) 'WhatsApp disruptions in Brazil: A content analysis of user and news media responses, 2015–2018', *Global Media & Communication*, 18(1), pp. 113–48.

Preta Lab. (2018) *Mulheres Negras: Um Panorama da Exclusão.* Available at: pretalab.com [Accessed 16 July 2021].

Pretas Hackers. (2021) [Facebook]. Available at: https://www.facebook.com/pretashackers/ (Accessed 16 July 2021).

Queirós, A. (2014) *Branco Sai, Preto Fica.* Brazil: Cinco da Norte.

Silva, T. (2020) 'Linha do Tempo do Racismo Algorítmico: casos, dados e reações', *tarciziosilva.com* [blog]. Available at: https://tarciziosilva.com.br/blog/destaques/posts/racismo-algoritmico-linha-do-tempo/ (Accessed 16 July 2021).

Stark, L. (2018) 'Facial recognition, emotion and race in animated social media', *First Monday* [online], 23(9). Available at: https://firstmonday.org/ojs/index.php/fm/article/view/9406 (Accessed 16th July 2021).

Stepan, N. (1991) *'The hour of eugenics': Race, gender, and nation in Latin America.* Ithaca and London: Cornell University Press.

Trindade, L. V. (2018) 'Brazil's supposed "racial democracy" has a dire problem with online racism', *The Conversation* [online], 7 August. Available at: https://theconversation.com/brazils-supposed-racial-democracy-has-a-dire-problem-with-online-racism-99343 (Accessed 16 July 2021).

11

Artificial Intelligence in the Art of Latin America

Raúl Cruz

In the Latin American context in which I have lived, the creation of artificial intelligence (AI) is seen more through the prism of imagination than that of real invention. Films and TV shows have shown us a world of technological fantasy that seduces us and leads us to the pleasure of imagining. And real technologies justify and validate these stories of the imagination. However, the reality for most Latin American countries is that they lack the infrastructure needed to develop this technology.

From my position as an artist, I do not pretend to be able to predict the future. I do not follow rules or historical data; my work is an exercise of the imagination, resulting from the pleasure of creating fantastic scenes and worlds where the development of historical events took different paths to those that we know in 'reality'; scenes that, with the freedom that my own thought and Latin American origin give me, I can—and want to—fill with the aesthetics and traditions of my country—characteristics of social groups that are not normally included in science narratives, technology, fantasy, or science fiction (SF).

This work is an exercise in artistic freedom and the search for identity. It foregrounds the pride of being an heir to the ancestral aesthetics of Mesoamerican cultures and combines that with the technological influences of the present.

In my country, Mexico, we are very used to SF and fantasy ideas coming from other countries. All the media we encounter tell us stories that happen in places like New York, Paris, Tokyo, or London—but never in cities in Latin American countries like Mexico. When I have the opportunity to show my pictorial work in my country, or other cities where there are Mexicans, it is very satisfying to see the smile drawn on the faces of the observers as the setting of the fantasy scene resonates with them. It is a smile that I interpret as one of identity-pride. The viewers immediately recognize the aesthetics embodied in

Figure 11.1 FR-DJ (2019), by Raul Cruz

the works, or are even reminded of a place where they might have lived at some important stage of their lives.

Over the years I have observed that we are the fortunate heirs of the artistic tradition of our ancestors: a worldview filled with characters, stories, myths, fantastic beings, deities, shapes, textures, colours, landscapes, architecture, social structures, writings, and much more. Consequently, in the exercise of

Figure 11.2 Dualism (2018), by Raul Cruz

conceptualizing fantasy and SF, with all this inherited treasure, we have an inexhaustible source to feed artistic creativity.

If we turn to our rugged present, we are immersed in a technological reality already installed in our lives. Mexico City, which rests on the legacy of the Mexica people, offers enormous possibilities for visualizing the future. This megalopolis, destined to be great, can be conceived in works of art full of technology and futuristic beauty.

Figure 11.3 Resurrection (2009), by Raul Cruz

All these elements are the perfect cocktail to generate inexhaustible Latin American SF possibilities. The formula is very simple: place the graphic narrative in our Latin American context. This concept can be used to address any historical stage, custom, or tradition; to venture into possible futures or parallel timelines. A single lifetime is not enough to explore the enormous wealth of our cultural legacy.

The 'Day of the Dead' is an excellent example of this cultural transfer, which has recently taken on international relevance like never before. The idiosyncrasies and worldview that surround the 'Day of the Dead' in Mexico are a perfect example of how this cultural legacy provides us with infinite elements for the creation of new works in new contexts.

The challenge is to preserve, adapt, and celebrate this legacy in the face of accelerating technological change. We are living in the midst of a historic technological revolution, which, to be effective, must reach all corners of the world, including those groups that have traditionally been oblivious to technology. In Latin America, AI appears as a finished product from developed countries, and we consume it so as to feel part of the modern world, but we do not participate in its development. This forces us to reflect on the viability of retaining our identity, customs, or traditions.

Figure 11.4 Rite (2013), by Raul Cruz

In all corners of the world, including Latin American countries, there is a percentage of people who have the potential to create AI. However, unlike the countries where these technologies are currently developed, in Latin America we have a series of public and private obstacles that limit this development, ranging from the types of government to stereotypes carried over for 500 years that define, in many cases, the way Latin American peoples

Figure 11.5 Time (2020), by Raul Cruz

see themselves. Classism and (even worse) internalized racism are fossilized convictions. Pseudo-intellectuals or pseudo-scientists succeed just because they are members of certain social groups, fulfilling the physical and genealogical requirements that accredit them as such. In Latin America, it is almost unheard of to recognize and respect the talent of an ordinary person, much less permit them to participate in an important project like AI. Consequently, the most visionary and independent young people migrate to where the opportunities are.

However, despite the chaotic socio-political context in which I have had to live, art has provided a means through which I can approach AI. Through

Figure 11.6 Last play (2008), by Raul Cruz

imagination, in an act almost of rebellion, I have made my culture participate in the unattainable world of real technology and show ourselves at our height. In this world of the imagination, Aztec robots, cybernetic catrinas, Quetzalcoatl ships, and many other such concepts have been perfectly possible. There is much more that could be done to show our culture in this way, not only in the form of pictorial works, but also as sculptures, murals, stained glass windows, scenography, costumes, video games, plays, or film productions.

Latin America is a progressive territory, with enormous human and technological potential, and which at the same time preserves its identity and cultural heritage. Like any human society, we live in expectation of the unexpected, attentive to the arrival of historical events. I hope that one day these events will allow the development of the consciousness of each social stratum, so that we can all stop being merely consumers and become creators.

12

Imaginaries of Technology and Subjectivity

Representations of AI in Contemporary Chilean Science Fiction

Macarena Areco

Translated by Maya Feile Tomes

12.1 Introduction

This chapter seeks to explore representations of artificial intelligence (AI) in recent Latin American science fiction (SF) from the perspective of literary studies and as viewed through the prism of the social imaginary.[1] I take as my case studies three works by the Chilean author Jorge Baradit—*Ygdrasil* (2005), *Trinidad* (2007), and *Synco* (2008)—which are all set in dystopian contexts where technology is harnessed in the service of a Luciferian enterprise designed to enslave human beings. This enables us to develop a better sense of the nature of Latin American approaches to conceptualizing the current post-Fordist era in which neoliberalism has come to reign so supreme as to be mistaken for reality itself—so much so that, as noted by the likes of Fredric Jameson, Slavoj Žižek, and Mark Fisher, it is easier to imagine the end of the world than the end of capitalism.

12.2 Neoliberalism and the social imaginary

I begin by introducing the concept of the social imaginary, which is the theoretical basis underpinning the literary analysis that follows. I then proceed to offer a brief survey of the political and economic project—neoliberalism—which has been in force in Chile since being implemented in the second half of the 1970s under the Pinochet regime and which has come to constitute a hegemonic social imaginary of such all-encompassing proportions that, as per Jameson's aforementioned formulation, it would appear to preclude the possibility of even so much as countenancing any alternatives. This paradigm looms large in Chilean SF writing and, as I go on to show here, in Baradit's in particular.

The social imaginary is a concept formulated in the second half of the twentieth century by the Greek-born philosopher Cornelius Castoriadis. In his 1975 *L'institution imaginaire de la societé* (available in English as *The Imaginary Institution of Society*, 1987), Castoriadis offered a definition developed in contradistinction to the second of Jacques Lacan's three orders (i.e. the Imaginary):[2]

> The imaginary does not come from the image in the mirror or from the gaze of the other. Instead, the 'mirror' itself and its possibility, and the other as mirror, are the works of the imaginary, which is creation *ex nihilo*. . . . The imaginary of which I am speaking is not an image *of*. It is the unceasing and essentially *undetermined* (social–historical and psychical) creation of figures/forms/images, on the basis of which alone there can ever be a question *of* 'something'. What we call 'reality' and 'rationality' are its works.
>
> (Castoriadis, 1987, p. 3; italics original).

But the imaginary is not purely visual; Polish philosopher Bronisław Baczko explains that it extends to ideas that express social visions peculiar to different points in history:

> All throughout history societies have been engaged in a continual labour of inventing their own global representations in the form of idea–images by means of which they afford themselves an identity, discern what sets them apart, legitimise their power and develop meaningful conceptual paradigms for their members.
>
> (Baczko, 1984, n.p).[3]

At the same time, it is no less important to draw attention to the productive nature of the relationship of the imaginary with the world and with history, as is clear in Josefina Ludmer's notion of a 'public imagination', which acts as a 'factory of reality' (2010, p. 11): in other words, the imaginary produces the world. Literature, too, contributes to this process of construction and instantiation, as well as to the processes whereby imaginaries shift and wane: their formation, establishment, and decline is part of a social dialectic in which literature plays its part alongside other modalities of cultural production. This struggle results in hegemonic conceptualizations both of broader abstract entities—including space, time, humanity itself—as well as of more specific categories, such as technology.

In this chapter I examine some of the representations of the social imaginary characteristic of Chilean SF produced since the turn of the twenty-first century (in other words, during the latter stage of the neoliberal era) with particular reference to AI and to the way it can be seen to blend idea–images relating to subjectivity and scientific advances. Complications, however, are posed by the fact that instances of AI have been relatively rare in Chilean SF, whereas other forms of intelligence—notably robots, cyborgs, and clones—are far more readily in evidence. AI systems are mentioned in Chilean author Armando Rosselot's Young Adult (YA) novel *Toki: Te llamarás Konnalef [Toki: Your name shall be Konnalef]* (2017), but their representation is vague and their role in the plot minimal. The same is true of fellow Chilean author Sergio Meier's *La segunda enciclopedia de Tlön [The Second Encyclopedia of Tlön]* (2007). From the Latin American sphere more broadly, Cuban author Erick Mota's 2010 novel *Habana Underguater [Havana underwater]* also features AI systems, but their representation is again rather more abstract than concrete. Instances of AI are more obviously in evidence in Mexican author Alberto Chimal's YA novel *La noche en la zona M [Night in Zone M]* (2019) and in his short story 'La segunda Celeste' ['The second Celeste'] from *Manos de lumbre [Hands of light]* (2019): in the latter, the eponymous character is a woman whose mind was uploaded to a computer prior to her death. An exception in this regard, then, are the mentioned works by Baradit, in which examples of AI do appear, ambiguous though their representation may be at times. I suggest that these stories can be interpreted as a preliminary attempt to engage with the imaginary in question.

As noted, this analysis is to be understood against a backdrop of neoliberalism—the ideology which, with the exception of just a few nations, holds sway across the greater part of Ibero-America. In his 2005 book, the British geographer David Harvey offers a brief history of neoliberalism: its distant origins in 1947 at the inaugural meeting of that exclusive group of individuals known as the Mont Pelerin Society; the establishment of the model in countries including Chile, China, the UK, and the USA; and its imposition on Iraq at the start of the twenty-first century. Taking it to be a response to the 'embedded liberalism' of the post-war years, Harvey defines this system as 'a theory of political economic practices that proposes that human well-being can best be advanced by liberating individual entrepreneurial freedoms and skills within an institutional framework characterized by strong private property rights, free markets, and free trade' (2005, 2). On this view, it is incumbent upon the 'neoliberal state' to uphold institutional security, even by force if need be, since its mission is to 'facilitate conditions for profitable capital accumulation on the part of both domestic and foreign capital' (Harvey, 2005, p. 7), who continues:

> [w]e can, therefore, interpret neoliberalization either as a *utopian* project to realize a theoretical design for the reorganization of international capitalism or as a *political* project to re-establish the conditions for capital accumulation and to restore the power of economic elites.
>
> (2005, p. 19; italics original).

The latter has been more than amply accomplished: after all, the end of the twentieth century saw a rapid concentration of revenue and wealth; indeed, it is fair to say that '[r]edistributive effects and increasing social inequality have in fact been such a persistent feature of neoliberalization as to be regarded as structural to the whole project' (Harvey, 2005, p. 16).[4]

Where the implementation of neoliberalism is concerned, Chile commands a pioneering position; it has even been termed the 'laboratory' of the neoliberal project. In Harvey's words: 'The first experiment with neoliberal state formation, it is worth recalling, occurred in Chile after Pinochet's coup on the "little September 11th" of 1973' (2005, p. 7).[5] A few words of explanation here are in order. After the *coup d'état* that overthrew the government of Salvador Allende, whose aim was to establish a socialist mode of production, over the course of the latter half of the 1970s the military forces by then in power sought to impose the neoliberal model first developed at the University of Chicago. A group of young Chilean economists, including Sergio de Castro, Sergio de la Cuadra, and Rolf Lüders—all ministers in Pinochet's military government—oversaw the implementation of this model, leading to the privatization of the country's water and electricity service providers, along with the majority of the health service, the pensions programme, and the education system, to name just a few of the affected sectors. Additionally, they proceeded to dismantle the project of Agrarian Reform, which had been of key importance during the 1960s and early 1970s and had seen Chile move away from its previous quasi-feudal system thanks to the new initiatives to sign millions of hectares over to those who worked the land. Under the dictatorship, however, many of these allotted 'parcels' or plots of land were sold on to landholders who amassed them in large quantities, meaning that rural land ownership once again fell back into the hands of the few. This process initially continued under the early governments of the post-dictatorship *Concertación* (Coalition), with motorways and other major public works continuing to be put out to tender, although former President Michelle Bachelet did also endeavour to improve matters in the area of pensions, education, and the health sector, for instance, by means of the *Plan de Acceso Universal de Garantías Explícitas* (AUGE) *[Plan for Universal Access with Explicit Health Guarantees]*. The Chilean sociologist Tomás Moulian referred to all the above as the 'capitalist revolution' (1998, p. 25). Others refer to this period as the 'post-Fordist' era in view of the rise of finance capitalism and the service sector at the expense of industry during the years in question.[6] However, in the wake of the explosion of social unrest sparked in October 2019, when secondary-school students began jumping the ticket barriers of Santiago's metro system in protest over rising ticket prices and which subsequently spread through whole swathes of Chilean society,[7] the reign of neoliberalism has come under threat. In a speech delivered after winning the primaries in July 2021, then-leftist presidential candidate Gabriel Boric—who was subsequently to emerge victorious in the presidential elections in December that same year—asserted that 'Chile may have been the cradle of neoliberalism but it will also be its grave' (see Mur, 2021; Turkewitz et al., 2021).

Since the second half of the twentieth century, and even more so over the course of the first decades of the twenty-first, a key new facet of neoliberalism has emerged in the form of information technology, with large-scale data handling now made possible thanks to AI. The philosopher Éric Sadin refers to this as 'technoliberalism' (2018, p. 26), which—as per Adam Smith's famous formulation—is predicated this time on an 'invisible automated hand' (Sadin, 2018, p. 26); it even holds the power to declare what is true—hence, Sadin's designation of these technologies as 'aletheic'[8]—and to determine the actions to be taken as a result. This in turn points to a hitherto unprecedented 'anthropomorphisation of technology' (Sadin, 2018, p. 15), since now, for the first time, the technology in question is seeking to emulate human beings—more specifically, the human brain—as a means of availing itself of their qualities. This is a fallacy, for AI systems are merely 'calculation machines whose purpose is solely to handle streams of abstract information' (Sadin, 2018, p. 28) and serve to reduce 'certain elements of reality to binarized codes, omitting an infinite number of aspects which our [i.e. human] sensibility *is* capable of apprehending and which are beyond the grasp of mathematical modelling' (Sadin, 2018, pp. 28–9).

I now turn to analysis of the representations of AI and its links to technologized neoliberal capitalism in the mentioned trilogy by Jorge Baradit. These preliminary soundings are designed to serve as one possible avenue of exploration into ideas of subjectivity and technology in current Latin American imaginaries.

12.3 Malevolent technology

To date, Chilean writer, activist, and popular historian Jorge Baradit (b. 1969) has published three SF novels—*Ygdrasil* (2005), *Synco* (2008), and *Lluscuma* (2013)—in addition to a novella titled *Trinidad* (2007) and a book of short stories, *La Guerra Interior [The War Within]* (2017), as well as non-SF work.[9] In 2021, Baradit was elected as one of 155 members of the Constitutional Assembly convened to draft Chile's new Constitution.

At the heart of all of Baradit's SF works is the question of the new modalities of exploitation afforded by information technology, featuring a variety of forms of hybridization between humans and machines as manifested in figures such as robots and cyborgs, as well as AI—although the latter are the least common. Only in *Trinidad* is the heroine expressly referred to as an AI, although, as I show, the character in question is not portrayed in line with the usual depiction of constructs of this type. By contrast, whereas the term in question never explicitly appears as such, his two foremost novels—*Ygdrasil* and *Synco*—do both feature AI in the form of entities capable of processing vast quantities of data at extraordinary speeds, even if the descriptions thereof may appear somewhat muddled at times. As such, we may surmise that, for Baradit—as for the majority of those who have occasion to interact with these new technologies—the idea of AI remains a hazy one. This, in turn, can be interpreted in light of Jameson's suggestion that the challenges in understanding the nature of the technologies involved in the present iteration of capitalism gives rise to a 'postmodern or technological sublime' (1991, p. 37).

In what follows I first offer detailed analysis of the novel *Ygdrasil* (2005), which is set in a neoliberal hell where technology is invested with demonic characteristics and constitutes the means by which the novel's characters come to be enslaved. Then, in the following two sections, I turn my attention more briefly to two of Baradit's subsequent works—the novella *Trinidad* (2007), *Ygdrasil*'s sequel, and *Synco* (2008)—with an eye to points of both similarity and difference vis-à-vis the view expounded in *Ygdrasil*.

12.3.1 *Ygdrasil: neoliberal Hell*

In generic terms, *Ygdrasil* can be characterized as belonging to the category of cyberpunk, a subgenre of SF that first emerged during the 1980s featuring protagonists resembling *film noir*-style detectives whose bodies have been equipped with implants that enable them to range across cyberspace.[10] A further particularity of Baradit's novels is that they are suffused with elements drawn from Chilean and wider Latin American mythology[11]—albeit in general only superficially so, with little exploration of their underlying meaning or significance.[12] Overall, then, *Ygdrasil* exhibits the main range of features characteristic of the genre as pioneered in William Gibson's *Neuromancer* (1984), only this time with greater emphasis accorded to violence and to the all-important fact that it has a female protagonist. Her name is Mariana, a Chilean national working in Mexico as a hitwoman in the employ of Mexican government ministers who hire her first to hack into the Bank of Mexico's web system and subsequently to infiltrate 'Chrysler', a powerful multinational company turned nation-state.

Having gained access to Chrysler, Mariana must find her way into Division 14: cyberspace voyagers. There she meets the syndicate leader, the *Imbunche* or Sorcerer, high priest of a cult that tortures and kills its devotees as part of the holy war being waged against the powers-that-be of the corporation. As the novel builds to its climax, this crusade will culminate in the Earth's destruction and annexation as a node of an entity named Ygdrasil. Ygdrasil is a 'Luciferian tree', product of a project led by mysterious figures known as 'the Perfect Ones'—about whom we know only what little is stated cryptically at the start[13]—whose objective is to replace the 'moribund god, the comatose Jehovah' (Baradit, 2005/2019, p. 271) with a new Messiah animated by the souls of thousands upon thousands of human beings fed into computational cogwheels. The first inception of the project can be traced to the 'delirium' of the 'mystic' Matías Rodríguez, who foretells the construction of 'a device designed to siphon off souls and chain them to the hearts of thinking machines', with the aim of 'producing an artificial *anima mundi*, a planetary mind capable of investing the Earth with self-awareness [. . .], the merging of all human beings into a web of consciousness and, in turn, the advent of the Messiah, a meta-human made up of all other humans' (Baradit, 2005/2019, p. 209).[14] The terms 'artificial *anima mundi*', 'web of consciousness', and 'meta-human' attest to the idea that the ultimate objective here is to effect the humanization of technology: the stage to which, as noted, Sadin refers in its current phase as 'anthropomorphisation'.

Just as these visions see 'souls' being incarnated in processors, the novel also features a group of computers that gives rise to a spiritual entity:

> On 14 April 2001 a network of military computers in Basel, Switzerland, is accidentally awakened. Over the course of its short existence—twelve minutes—the entity suffers from panic attacks and fear of God. It asks to be taught how to pray. Towards the end it undergoes a violent psychotic episode and attempts to spread itself to the phone networks. When at last it comprehends the nature of its existence, it causes its own motherboard to destruct.
>
> (Baradit, 2005/2019, pp. 209–10).[15]

The Perfect Ones' project also has a material dimension, for it runs on human bodies—and various parts thereof—hooked up to its machinery, as Mariana gleans from a subfolder labelled 'Prototypes':

> It was full of contraptions and devices featuring live humans embedded into its gadgetry, sharing their neurobiological functions and impaled upon electronic elements running in through their eyes, ears and spinal cords. Children and pregnant women hooked up to machinery not simply for the purposes of utilising their systems as conduits for other functions but so as to harvest their astral essence or to elicit the release of energy in the form of fear or pain.
>
> (Baradit, 2005/2019, p. 121).

These processes result in 'a generation of extraordinarily powerful thinking machines, with kinesic abilities and psychic qualities, all interconnected and capable of rendering any system exponentially more powerful' (Baradit, 2005/2019, p. 124).[16] In other words: AI.

Meanwhile, the spaces in which the action of the novel plays out are the quintessential locales of neoliberal capitalism, with particular emphasis on its financial and technological dimensions. Salient in this regard are the Bank of Mexico where Mariana carries out her first mission, the cyberspace to which she connects, and, above all, the enormous corporation devoted to data processing:

> Chrysler was not merely a transfer company of unusually large proportions: it was, rather, a corporation with all the hallmarks of a sovereign state, enjoying total power of jurisdiction within its premises and even issuing its own ID cards . . . It grew so monstrously large that it contrived to purchase a huge stretch of international waters between Africa and the Gulf of Mexico. Over the years, a massive metallic bunker was progressively established on the Atlantic seabed, populated by millions of inhabitants divided into dozens of productivity pods. When the first generation of those born within this facility reached the age of majority, Chrysler drafted its own constitution, issued proof of nationality and applied to join the UN as a sovereign state.
>
> (Baradit, 2005/2019, p. 78).

The company, having attained the status of an autonomous political entity, is an only slightly exaggerated representation of the power enjoyed by multinational corporations in today's global neoliberal capitalism. The characters become mere instruments pressed into the service of the company and of corrupt politicians in the quest for maximally optimized data handling. As such, and as befits a novel of the cyberpunk genre, these characters lead lives which essentially play out in cyberspace and can consequently be characterized as cyborgs. Members of this category include the voyagers from Division 14: 'Every morning an army of operatives would enter the hangars and hook their heads up to enormous navigation hubs reminiscent of mechanical anuses which closed around their necks, fixing them in place. A hypodermic needle would be plunged into each worker's forehead and the illumination would commence' (Baradit, 2005/2019, p. 78). These characters are slaves: 'they had been born within the confines of the industrial complex and would devote every last fibre of energy to it until the very instant they expired (on average at around the age of 35), without any means of demanding better conditions' (Baradit, 2005/2019, p. 79).

A recurrent feature of the novel is the figure of the *Imbunche* (Sorcerer), which derives from a tradition in Mapuche lore, according to which a little boy is kidnapped by wizards who sew up the various orifices of his body, break one of his legs, mangle his tongue, and imprison him in their lair of caves, which he is charged with guarding.[17] In *Ygdrasil*, the figure is reimagined for the technological capitalist context, this time with bodies sealed up by means of implants and connections to the web. A pertinent example in this category is the 'cretins', 'men without a brainstem bred for medical purposes' (Baradit, 2005/2019, p. 76), who had 'all the orifices in their bodies stitched up. Their eyes were gouged out and their empty eye-sockets harboured hardware protruding from the sockets like sensory horns' (Baradit, 2005/2019, p. 231). Another example of this phenomenon is none other than the *Imbunche*, syndicate leader of Chrysler's Division 14, who boasts the forked tongue typically associated with monsters, along with several implants of his own: 'The *Imbunche* himself sported a monocomputer hooked up to his right eye, enabling him to follow the strategies put to him by his inner circle of advisers' (Baradit, 2005/2019, p. 213). The *Imbunche* is a supremely corrupt politician: he once led a rebellion against the directorate of the company, only to come to a secret agreement with them and proceed to exterminate the surviving rebels until he alone emerged as the sole prophet of a cult devoted to heralding 'the liberation of the flesh' and 'the definitive annexation of the mind to the worldwide data network' (Baradit, 2005/2019, p. 77).

An especially brutal iteration of this brand of subjectivity explored in the novel are the 'bitches'—enslaved prostitutes produced by means of a process of 'imbunchisation':

> The process is fairly straightforward. They kidnap women, remove their vocal cords, corneas, spinal cord, one of their kidneys and anything else of value on the organs market. Then they broil their brains by means of an intensely slow and painful procedure, bringing them to the utmost extreme of terror via sharp shocks applied directly to the exposed brain surface, overwhelming the cortex with electric pulses and thereby precipitating the chemical suicide of the self [. . .]
>
> It is an inexpensive undertaking; and to render it cheaper still, they further reduce the costs of transportation and storage by amputating their arms and legs [. . .]. They then hang them up in bags from refrigerated rails which keep their metabolisms functioning at barest minimum, feeding them with IV fluids administered straight to the vein.
>
> (Baradit, 2005/2019, pp. 43–4).

At the end of the novel, Mariana—herself now a 'bitch'—is turned, against her will, into the core device of the Ygdrasil, for it is thanks to her live body hooked up to the web that the technological project can come to fruition: 'As she hung there, they tore off her arms and legs, cauterised her flesh with red-hot irons and drove in steel hooks to embed her into the mechanism suspended there at the very centre of its womb. Embedded like a jewel. The jewel of the Ygdrasil. Then they gouged out her eyes and plunged data terminals into her optic nerves' (Baradit, 2005/2019, p. 268). As such, the 'cretins', the *Imbunche*, and Mariana—to single out just a few key characters—come to be enslaved to create the Ygdrasil, which in turn will give rise to the Messiah, who is to vanquish divine power itself. It is for this reason that electricity is referred to in the novel as a 'demon' (Baradit, 2005/2019, p. 123) and the Ygdrasil is described as 'Luciferian' (Baradit, 2005/2019, p. 215) and 'an abominable construct that offends the sight of God' (Baradit, 2005/2019, p. 212), while Mariana is 'like the jewel encrusted in the forehead of Lucifer' (Baradit, 2005/2019, p. 272).

In summary, *Ygdrasil* is a cyberpunk novel situated in a dystopian future of neoliberal capitalism taken to extremes, coupled with a malevolent technological project. In the next section I analyse *Trinidad*, which is set in a similar space-time and likewise devoted to exploring ideas about the form of slavery to which technology, figured as a malevolent entity, gives rise.

12.3.2 *Trinidad: AI in human form*

Trinidad [Trinity] is a short cyberpunk novella,[18] published two years after *Ygdrasil* and set in the same technologized world of neoliberal capitalism in which all-powerful large corporations avail themselves of the enslaved flesh of countless human beings, which is their fodder.[19] Just as in *Ygdrasil*, a technological project is at the heart of the plotline. As its title indicates, *Trinidad* is made up of three stories, each featuring a female protagonist—Mariana, Angélica, and Magdalena, respectively—whose tribulations take place in a future era known as the Second Republic, in which two corrupt political parties vie for power in the interests of reaping the greatest rewards. The story opens with the Labour Party in government. It has just launched its Plan for Cyberspace Sovereignty, consisting of 'beaming up' the minds of millions of volunteers for the purposes of the 'colonization' of the 'digital ocean' so as to optimize data processing. The opposition party, the Revolutionary Workers' Party, is bent on sabotaging this venture and, to this end, hires Mariana—the same hitwoman already familiar from *Ygdrasil*—and charges her with assassinating the President of the Bank of Mexico just as, in a programme due to be broadcast live to the nation, he is in the process of being 'beamed up' ('levantado'). The second instalment in the trilogy tells the tale of an AI called Angélica, who is the core element in a technological construct known as the Yámana Machine around which the whole project revolves. The third story follows Magdalena, an agent of the Karma Police, in her mission to investigate the disappearance of thousands of orphaned children and the matter of the discovery in the Atacama Desert of 5,166 corpses with their spines ripped out. In the course of this investigation she is led to uncover a grand operation in the trafficking of spinal cords—a substance essential for the Yámana Machine project.

I focus here on the second of these three stories, since—as mentioned earlier—its protagonist is described as an AI, although, as we shall see, she would more properly be characterized as something akin to a humanized robot or cyborg. The tale opens when a 'sleeper' named Rogelio Canelo (the 'sleepers' are a category of secret agents-cum-hitmen 'cultivated' exclusively for deployment in secret missions and awoken solely in order to undertake whatever assignment—normally an assassination—they are to perform)[20] is ordered to exterminate the AI, who has fled. The girl in question, described as 'a figure so slight as to be barely visible' (Baradit, 2007, p. 66) and who is only dimly able to grasp what is happening to her, attempts to hide out in Valparaíso but unwittingly reacts when she is attacked, for, unbeknownst to her, she has been 'kitted out with artillery' ('artillada'):

> All of a sudden she found herself relegated to the fringes of her own consciousness by 'something else' that seized control of her body [. . .]. She could only look on in horror, spectator to her own fate, as her arms underwent an abrupt transformation. Gadgets assembling and re-assembling at breakneck speed caused ghastly biomechanical extremities to sprout where once her soft, slender girlish limbs had been [. . .]. On the inside she was screaming and pleading for it all to stop, but the carnage had already begun. Long katana blades shot out of her wrists. Arms, heads and legs began to fly in all directions.
>
> (Baradit, 2007, p. 62).

As will be evident from this extract, Angélica is not wholly artificial, but a cyborg, who has been fitted with all-powerful implants that take over her body. As such, this description is at variance with the viewpoint of scholars such as Donna Haraway (1991), for whom the technological appendages of cyborgs constitute enhancements of human functions to be used in the service of their own emancipation.[21] Far from being this utopian kind of cyborg conceived as abolishing binaries, such as those between nature/technology or masculine/feminine, Angelica is a cyborg–slave and yet, at the same time, remains equally, if not more, human than humans themselves, for she is a fragile being who is frightened by what is happening to her, longs for an end to the violence, and even seeks to make contact with God: '"Shall I pray? Will God be angry if I pray to Him?"' (Baradit, 2007, p. 51). Angélica retains the power of thought and suffers accordingly. In addition to this case of a girl instrumentalized as a piece of technology, meanwhile, the story also features unknown entities that make use of human bodies as elements employed in sinister mechanisms, of which Angélica has a vision: 'I have seen subterranean hangars beneath the Atacama Desert filled with horrible biomechanical bodies, in all manner of strange shapes, with chunks of live human beings embedded in their mechanisms' (Baradit, 2007, p. 53).

In *Trinidad*, then, the figure of the AI is at odds with those more optimistic conceptualizations of the cyborg. We are dealing, rather, with a sort of anti-cyborg, as evidenced by the fact that its assemblage of machines and bodies is harnessed exclusively to serve the purposes of third parties, resulting in manipulation and destruction, fear and pain: a far cry from any utopic form of superhumanity. Angélica is a humanized character notable for her fragility and sensitivity and, as such, worlds apart from an AI in any true sense.

In the next and final section I consider *Synco*, another novel devoted to exploring the form of enslavement to which technology has given rise, albeit this time set in a future free from the extreme brand of neoliberalism that characterizes *Ygdrasil* and *Trinidad*. Instead, in *Synco*, the driving force behind its technology of human exploitation and enslavement is neither a massive corporation nor a corrupt government cabinet, but rather a supposedly socialist state.

12.3.3 Synco: cybersocialism from Hell

Synco is a so-called uchronia or alternate history: a story in which the premise is *what would have happened if* a particular historical event had taken a different course[22]—in this instance if the *coup d'état* of 1973 in Chile had not occurred. In this narrative, as also in Baradit's previous novels, the plot once again revolves around a technological enterprise—in this case, one based on a genuine initiative, 'Cybersyn', launched during the government of socialist president Salvador Allende.[23] In this fictional alternate account, it is now five years on and Allende is still in office; Pinochet, having miraculously survived an attack in which his wife was killed, is a national hero; and the Synco scheme—a project to centralize the coordination of production and distribution across the whole region—is in full swing. The alleged success of this venture has—as everyone, from taxi drivers to civil servants to the inevitable media outlets, never tires of insisting—transformed Chile into an ideal society: 'the new Camelot of global technology' (Baradit, 2008/2018, p. 72); a 'glorious cybersocialist utopia' (Baradit, 2008/2018, p. 117); 'the shining star of Cyberbolivarianism' (Baradit, 2008/2018, p. 115). The plot thickens when protagonist Martina Villablanca, a young journalist born in Chile who, since childhood, has lived in Venezuela with her exiled general father, is invited back home for the festivities in honour of Salvador Allende's re-election. There she gradually discovers that, contrary to the impression given, the project is built upon an edifice of slave labour.

Although the term in question is never explicitly used, the piece of technology upon which the novel hinges is clearly AI. Synco is described as 'a sleeping mind that dreamt in data' and

> a technological system whereby humans are no longer required to move around gathering data from different sources but rather the information itself is liquefied and transmitted along metallic nerves and arteries to feed an unmoving man, rooted upon his cybernetic throne, imposing order upon tidal waves of data like a wizard in the eye of a storm.
>
> (Baradit, 2008/2018, p. 53).

Thanks to this complex system, in the space of just a few years it has become possible to store, process, and transmit infinite quantities of data and, in turn, to take the most effective decisions in relation to production and distribution: 'The whole country is connected thanks to armies of operatives who input information into processors at the hub. The "hypothalamus" [. . .] then sorts and disseminates the data to companies, plants and industrial facilities up and down the country' (Baradit, 2008/2018, p. 107).

Ricardo Lagos and Fernando Flores,[24] the pair of politicians who accompany Martina on her tour of the subterranean world of Synco (located beneath the Palace of La Moneda), both express themselves in language couched in terms drawn from a biologist imaginary and the natural world. In their words, then, the cybernetic giant is the 'neurovegetative system of Chile . . . a nervous system for the homeland' (Baradit, 2008/2018, p. 104), thanks to which production has become:

> a biological phenomenon requiring practically no intervention—merely a helping hand, like a gardener who prunes here and there, administering water and a touch of fertiliser, but conscious all the while that the whole process is simply unfolding before his eyes in a manner seemingly chaotic but in truth highly ordered, producing patterns as exquisite as the arrangement of petals on a rose
>
> (Baradit, 2008/2018, p. 81).

Thanks to this enormous leap, Chile is 'the first organic nation', boasting 'a body that breathes algorithms and bears fruit just as nature does' (Baradit, 2008/2018, p. 83).[25]

But behind this utopic vision lies a reality of extreme oppression, for—just as at Chrysler—the operatives at Synco are subject to slave-labour conditions:

> Row upon interminable row of processors running magnetic tape hummed away while hordes of women in a zombie-like state busily connected and disconnected old-fashioned telephone plugs mounted on wooden panels; at their feet, small children strove endlessly to untangle the infinite mass of cables that emerged from the sides like a mane of red and black snakes [. . .]. They were all crammed back to back in foul-smelling, cramped spaces with little to no light.
>
> (Baradit, 2008/2018, pp. 103–4).

It is essential here to re-emphasize that in this novel, unlike the ones discussed earlier, the context is not one of a rampant neoliberal regime in which large corporations tyrannize and exploit scores of human beings, but, on the contrary, one that revolves around a mode of centralized production characteristic of the socialist economy. Nonetheless, despite this difference, in this story, too, technology—and in particular AI—once again serves as a vector of domination, leading human beings to be enslaved for anti-human religious ends. It is as if, in this novel, Baradit experiments with other possible permutations of information technology in an effort to produce alternatives to the so-called free market and, in so doing, had found himself arriving inexorably at the polar opposite: the realization that there is no such thing as a truly emancipatory data-processing technology.

12.4 Conclusion

Examples of AI in contemporary Latin American science fiction are far and few between, and, where they do occur, their representation is ultimately equivocal. *Ygdrasil*, *Trinidad*, and *Synco* all deal with entities produced by the powers that be and are mobilized in the service of transhuman schemes, resulting invariably in the deaths of vulnerable characters—almost always women—who are used as slave meat. In these works, technology and AI are represented solely as instruments of alienation and domination. Human beings do not control these technologies, nor do they serve human ends; rather, they are deployed in the service of economic systems pursuing projects whose true masterminds are unknown agents motivated by inscrutable objectives, leading to nothing but slavery and suffering.

Endnotes

1. Original title: 'Imaginarios de tecnología y subjetividad: representaciones de IA en obras de ciencia ficción chilena reciente'. This chapter was produced under the auspices of FONDECYT Project Grant no. 1,171,124: 'Imaginarios sociales en la ciencia ficción latinoamericana reciente: espacio, sujeto-cuerpo y tecnología' ('Social imaginaries in contemporary Latin American science fiction: space, subject–body, technology').
2. Lacan proposes three orders: the Real, the Imaginary and the Symbolic. The Real does not correspond to reality, which is the combined effect of the three orders together, but rather denotes that which is beyond the Symbolic, which is to say, that which cannot be accessed by means of language and which is the domain of pleasure, understood as urges and the satisfying thereof. The Imaginary order 'is characterised by the prevalence of the relation to the image of the counterpart (*le semblable*)' (Laplanche and Pontalis, 1973, p. 210) and is connected to the 'mirror stage' during which the other functions as a reflective surface, meaning that 'the human infant . . . is constituted on the basis of the image of the counterpart (specular ego)' (Laplanche and Pontalis, 1973, p. 210). The Symbolic 'covers those phenomena with

which psycho-analysis deals in so far as they are structured like a language' (Laplanche and Pontalis, 1973, p. 439), and, more generally, denotes the form of social order afforded by language, which in turn produces the subject.

3. Citations in this chapter from works originally published in English are taken directly from those publications, even where the author may have consulted the work in translation. Where the works are originally Spanish- or French-language texts of which published translations are readily available in English, citations are likewise from the latter. Citations from works which have not been translated into English—including all of Baradit's—are translated directly from the original Spanish (or French) and presented for present purposes in English-language form. In such instances, however, the page number given will still correspond to that of the print edition of the work in its *original* language.
4. The figures offered by Harvey give a good sense of what neoliberalism had managed to 'achieve' by the close of the twentieth century: 'Small wonder that the net worth of the 358 richest people in 1996 was "equal to the combined income of the poorest 45 per cent of the world's population—2.3 billion people". Worse still, "the world's 200 richest people more than doubled their net worth in the four years to 1998, to more than $1 trillion. The assets of the top three billionaires [were by then] more than the combined GNP of all least developed countries and their 600 million people"' (2005, pp. 34–5); he is citing from the United Nations Development Program's *Human Development Reports* of 1996 and 1999, respectively.
5. In addition to the work of Harvey, I recommend Carola Fuentes' (2015) documentary *Chicago Boys: La historia no contada de los creadores del modelo neoliberal [Chicago Boys: the untold story of the founders of the neoliberal model]*, available online (including with English subtitles).
6. Among them, Mark Fisher in *Capitalist Realism: Is There No Alternative?* (2009).
7. The 2019 protests can be located as the latest in a series of waves of student uprisings over the course of the past few decades, including the 'penguin revolution' of 2006 and the mass mobilization of 2011, led, among others, by Camila Vallejo—now Minister of Boric, who was subsequently to be elected President.
8. 'Aletheic' derives, as Sadin notes, from the Greek word *aletheia*—truth—'in the sense in which it is used in Ancient Greek philosophy, namely as an unveiling and as the disclosure of the reality of matters above and beyond their appearance' (2018, p. 13).
9. He is also the author of a best-selling series of popular historical essays, *Historia secreta de Chile [The secret history of Chile]*.
10. Cyberpunk evokes a world order consistent with that of late capitalism, wherein large global corporations dominate. As Roger Luckhurst has argued in his book *Science Fiction* (2005), it is an ambiguous, hybrid genre, as is indeed epitomized in its very name with its blend of technology—'cyber'—with the anarchic fringes: 'punk'.
11. For this reason, Miquel Barceló—editor of the *Nova* science fiction collection at publishing house Ediciones B—has characterized Baradit's works as 'cybershamanism'.

12. See Areco (2016).
13. The third epigraph of the novel reads as follows: 'The Perfect Ones are members of a network which scattered across the world with a view to dilating the fissure that produced them. They are the measure of a new order. They are the product of an equation that spits out the name of another god as its solution. They are toxic to our Universe and their behaviour is "mildly" different to ours [. . .]. Their motor skills are "mildly" out of sync with our reality and they have to proceed gingerly, first feeding their gestures into an algorithm which transposes the intensity and reach of their movements to render them commensurate with our space. This trait has led them to be dubbed the "Dancers". They are cancerous cells begetting a cyst in reality itself.'
14. For further discussion of the religious dimension of visions such as this one in *Trinity*, see Areco (2020b).
15. As mentioned previously, Baradit's novels are not (yet) available in anglophone form and all citations and extracts from his texts included here have been translated into English for the purposes of this chapter.
16. As these citations illustrate, the project also has an esoteric, astrological dimension—part of the heterodox blend of elements that characterizes Baradit's novels, as discussed in Areco (2016).
17. See Areco (2010), along with Montecino (2003).
18. *Trinidad* was awarded the XVI Universidad Politécnica de Cataluña (UPC) Prize for best science fiction novella in 2006.
19. I consider this at greater length in Areco (2020b).
20. 'The third child in every family is the property of the State [. . .] In the fifth month of pregnancy, the foetus is extracted and cultivated for various possible purposes: for organ donation, as a munitions component, or, if deemed to exhibit a suitable mental profile, for enrolment in the Sleepers programme [. . .] Sleepers are deployed for a variety of ends: psychological, military, religious, law enforcement. They belong to the ranks of the "illuminated" untouchables and are industrially manufactured for the purposes of police investigation, clairvoyance and espionage' (Baradit, 2007, p. 50).
21. For Haraway (1991), a cyborg constitutes a form of hybridized subjectivity that challenges the boundaries between the natural and artificial, human beings and technology, and of generic categories in themselves.
22. A classic example of this genre is Philip K. Dick's *The Man in the High Castle* (1962), set in a world in which the Nazis won the Second World War.
23. On the historical Synco (or 'Cybersyn') project, see further https://en.wikipedia.org/wiki/Project_Cybersyn. Last accessed 28 March 2022.
24. Ricardo Lagos is a fictionalized version of the Chilean President (2000–2006) of that name, while Fernando Flores is likewise based on a homonymous politician who served as a Senator in the early 2000s. Several other Chilean figures appear in fictionalized form in this novel, including Augusto Pinochet, Salvador Allende, Carlos Altamirano, and Miguel Serrano.

25. These rapturous formulations aside, a foreign journalist subsequently informs Martina that the project's consumption of energy is so great that it is using up the energy supply of the whole country. This is said to be to do with the fact that, at bottom, the entire Synco project serves the interests of beings from other worlds, although this point does not obviously emerge from the novel itself, which remains a little unclear in this regard.

References

Areco, M. (2010) 'Más allá del sujeto fragmentado: las desventuras de la identidad en *Ygdrasil* de Jorge Baradit'. *Revista Iberoamericana*, 76(232), pp. 839–53.

Areco, M. (2016) 'Imaginário baraditiano: figurações do sujeito, da história e da tecnologia na obra de Jorge Baradit', in Volz, J., et al. (eds.), *Incerteza viva (32ª Bienal de São Paulo—Dias de estudo)*, São Paulo: Bienal de São Paulo, pp. 196–205. Available at: https://issuu.com/bienal/docs/32bsp_reader_web

Areco, M. (2020b) 'Espacio, sujeto–cuerpo y tecnología en *Trinidad* de Jorge Baradit'. *Universum (Talca)*, 35(1), pp. 232–48.

Baczko, B. (1984) *Les imaginaires sociaux: mémoires et espoirs collectifs*. Paris: Payot.

Baradit, J. (2007) *Trinidad*. Barcelona: Universidad Politécnica de Cataluña.

Baradit, J. (2013) *Lluscuma*. Madrid: Ediciones B.

Baradit, J. (2017) *La guerra interior*. Barcelona: Plaza & Janes.

Baradit, J. (2008/2018) *Synco*. Santiago: Penguin Random House.

Baradit, J. (2005/ 2019) *Ygdrasil*. Santiago: Penguin Random House.

Castoriadis, C. 1987. *The imaginary institution of society*, tr. K. Blamey. Cambridge: Polity.

Chicago Boys: La historia no contada de los creadores del modelo neoliberal. (2015) Directed by C. Fuentes and R. Valdeavellano [Film]. La Ventana Cinema. https://miradoc.cl/chicago-boys/ (Accessed 28 March 2022).

Chimal, A. (2019) *La noche en la zona M*. Mexico City: Fondo de Cultura Económica.

Chimal, A. (2019) 'La segunda Celeste', in *Manos de lumbre*. Madrid: Páginas de Espuma, pp. 57–66.

Dick, P. K. (1962) *The man in the high castle*. New York: Putnam.

Fisher, M. (2009) *Capitalist realism: Is there no alternative?* Winchester: Zero Books.

Gibson, W. (1984) *Neuromancer*. New York: Ace Books.

Haraway, D. (1991) *Simians, cyborgs and women: The reinvention of nature*. London: Free Association.

Harvey, D. (2005) *A brief history of neoliberalism*. Oxford: Oxford University Press.

Jameson, F. (1991) *Postmodernism, or, the cultural logic of late capitalism*. Durham: Duke University Press.

Laplanche, J. and Pontalis, J-B. (1973) *The language of psycho-analysis*, tr. D. Nicholson-Smith. London: Hogarth.

Luckhurst, R. (2005) *Science fiction*. Cambridge: Polity Press.

Ludmer, J. (2010) *Aquí América Latina: una especulación*. Buenos Aires: Eterna Cadencia.

Meier, S. (2007) *La segunda enciclopedia de Tlön*. Valparaíso: Puerto de Escape.

Montecino, S. (2003) *Mitos de Chile. Diccionario de seres, magias y encantos*. Santiago: Sudamericana.

Mota, E. (2010) *Habana underguater*. Lexington: Atom Press.

Moulian, T. (1998) *Chile actual. Anatomía de un mito*. Santiago: Lom.

Mur, M. M. (2021) 'Gabriel Boric: "Chile será la tumba del neoliberalismo"', La República [online], 19 November. Available at: https://larepublica.pe/mundo/2021/11/19/gabriel-boric-chile-sera-la-tumba-del-neoliberalismo-elecciones/ (Accessed 28 March 2022).

Rosselot, A. (2017) *Toki: Te llamarás Konnalef*. Santiago: Editorial Segismundo.

Sadin, É. (2018) *L'intelligence artificielle ou l'enjeu du siècle: anatomie d'un antihumanisme radical*. Paris: L'Échappée.

Turkewitz, J., Bonnefoy, P., and Bartlett, J. (2021) 'Los retos de Gabriel Boric, el presidente electo de Chile'. *The New York Times* [online], 22 December. Available at: https://www.nytimes.com/es/2021/12/22/espanol/gabriel-boric-quien-es.html (Accessed 28 March 2022).

13

Imagining Indigenous AI

Jason Edward Lewis

13.1 Introduction

It is imperative that we imagine artificial intelligence (AI) otherwise.[1] The trajectory that AI research and development is currently following recapitulates the extractive, exploitative, and environmentally excessive tendencies that characterize the evolution of mass technologies since the Industrial Revolution. If we are to keep AI from becoming yet another tool for imposing an impoverished understanding of the good life upon us all, we must look to ontologies and epistemologies that grow from different roots than those concepts of being and knowledge frameworks out of which the current mainstream vision of AI develops. This chapter describes a series of conversations and resulting future imaginaries aimed at articulating a different trajectory for AI that is founded in Indigenous perspectives. I start by describing the context in which those conversations took place, and then discuss how they led to alternative futures for AI. I close with a reflection on how such future imaginaries provide us with tools to critically deconstruct current assumptions about the inevitability of a mainstream AI and reconstruct our expectations to centre computational technologies that enable abundance.

13.2 Sharing Indigenous space

In the winter and spring of 2019 a group of artists, scholars, and cultural knowledge holders gathered in Honolulu, Hawai'i, to think together about AI. Dubbed the Indigenous Protocol and AI Workshops, these two meetings brought together members from Anishinaabe, Barada, Cree, Crow, Cheyenne, Coquille, Euskaldunak, Gadigal, Kanaka Maoli, Kapalbara, Lakota, Māori, Mohawk, Palawa, and Samoan communities from across Aotearoa, Australia, North America, and the Pacific. Each person was invited in light of their professional interest in what happens at the intersection of Indigenous culture and advanced digital technology, and, more specifically, because they desired to be part of a conversation about the future of AI from an Indigenous perspective. The workshops were Indigenous-determined spaces, with an Indigenous supermajority joined by several non-Indigenous collaborators. My co-organizers[2] and I were motivated by the desire to have an initial set of 'internal' conversations about AI that would start from and remain grounded in the concerns of our specific Indigenous communities, rather than some imagined 'global' or 'general' community. We were also motivated by an awareness of how Indigenous voices can get lost in policy discussions that happen at a 'global' level, and also how Indigenous knowledges often get appropriated by non-Indigenous actors who misuse our epistemologies through misunderstanding and self-serving 'cherry-picking'.

We emphasized 'protocol' as most of our communities have highly developed guidelines for initiating, maintaining, and evolving relationships (Secretariat, 2019). These can be relationships with other humans, and they can also be relationships with non-humans such as animals, rivers, rocks, and wind (Abdilla, 2018). Protocol also refers to specific methods for properly conducting oneself in any activity. Learning, understanding, and following proper protocol is central to many Indigenous interactions, whether informal or formal. Nations and even individual communities have their own sets of protocols, which are informed by the specific epistemologies of the communities using them. Protocols can cover all manner of activities, from the formal ceremonial to the relationship between grandparent and grandchild. One of the workshops' animating propositions was that we should critically examine our relationship with AI. In particular, we posed the question of whether AI systems should be given a place in our existing circle of relationships, and, if so, how we might go about bringing it into the circle. Indigenous kinship protocols promise potential approaches to developing rich, robust, and expansive approaches to our relationships with AI systems and serve as guidelines for AI system developers (Lewis et al., 2018). Such protocols would reinforce the notion that, while the developers might assume they are building a product or tool, they are actually building a relationship to which they should attend.

The workshop was conceptualized, designed, and led by Indigenous people, and grounded in the Kanaka Maoli community where the workshops took place. The largest contingent (25%) was from Hawai'i, and they welcomed us to their lands, told us stories that illustrated Kanaka culture, helped us understand the history of the land, and illuminated the contemporary concerns and desires of the local community. Most importantly, they fed us and talked with us about how the food is woven into those histories and opened the door for the other participants to share how their particular lands had sustained them for countless generations. These sharing protocols built a scaffolding of generosity and engagement that enabled the remainder of the workshops to continue in a similar vein of care and complexity.

Additionally, we had all had numerous experiences where we found ourselves in rooms that were alienating, if not outright hostile, to considering Indigenous knowledge practices as core components of scientific inquiry. These workshops were designed to centre Indigenous knowledge, which resulted in a number of structure and process decisions informed by the consultation practices found in the organizers' communities as well as by those alienating experiences. We prioritized interdisciplinarity, as Indigenous communities often approach knowledge development and sharing from a holistic perspective, where different 'disciplines' freely interact with and inform one another to create understanding that is robust and sustainable. Participants had day jobs as technologists, artists, social and physical scientists, humanities scholars, cultural practitioners, language teachers, engineers, and public policy experts. We came from a variety of disciplinary backgrounds, including machine learning, design, symbolic systems, cognition and computation, visual and performing arts, history, philosophy, linguistics, anthropology, and sociology. A substantial contingent of creative practitioners was part of the conversation because artistic expression is central to many Indigenous epistemologies, ontologies, and cosmologies, and is often regarded as a—if not the—primary way of communicating knowledge. It is also because, if we are to imagine new futures, experts are required who are adept at invoking and materializing the imagination. The space was also intergenerational, with emerging, established, and elder participants in conversation with one another.

We used the term 'Indigenous' as connective tissue, rather than descriptive skin, to better appreciate the hyperdense textures of our points of contact while respecting our rich and productive differences. This allowed us to map paths forward that drew on our peoples' long histories of technical innovation and scientific practice, sharing examples of how our traditions offer a wellspring of inspiration for engaging with the world, and with each other, through the tools we make.

The workshops were organized around the key question of what our relationship with AI should be from an Indigenous perspective. We also considered related questions, including:

1. How can Indigenous epistemologies and ontologies contribute to the global conversation regarding society and AI?
2. How do we broaden discussions regarding the role of technology in society beyond the relatively culturally homogeneous research labs and Silicon Valley start-up culture?
3. How do we imagine a future with AI that contributes to the flourishing of all humans *and* non-humans?

The participants' responses to these questions covered extensive ground that included epistemology, culture, machine learning, colonization, temporal models, ontology, cosmology, axiology, software architecture, ancestral agri- and aqua-cultural practices, and linguistics. They explored with each other layers of Indigenous history, language, and culture from the position of particular Indigenous individuals and their communities. Anishinaabe participants talked about how oskabewis—helpers whose generous, engaged, and subtle support for those participating in ceremony—could model how we might want AI systems to support us—and the obligations that we, in turn, would owe them. Hawaiian participants talked about all the steps involved with crafting a fishing net, the layer upon layer of permission and appreciation and reciprocity required to properly work with those relations—expressed through prayer, chant, and song—protocols that could model how we might want to create our hardware and software systems from a foundation of ethical care. Māori participants talked about concerns in their communities about how knowledge will get passed down to the children and grandchildren and speculated with us about holographic aunties who would work with members of the community to preserve and transmit that knowledge. Coquille participants talked about embedding their cultural values of care and trust into AI systems integrated with blockchain technology to help the tribe make decisions about sharing and then distributing community resources. We discussed Blackfoot metaphysics, and the implication from Leroy Little Bear's writings that Blackfoot might be the best language in which to work on quantum physics. We imagined what other isomorphisms might exist between specific Indigenous languages and scientific frameworks, and how recognizing and leveraging such resonances might provide insight into the great technical challenges of our time (Little Bear and Heavy Head, 2004).

We considered different layers of the stack: hardware architectures and software protocols that make high-level computation possible, and how—as we move first up the hardware stack from silicon to circuits to microchips to computers to networks, and then up the software stack from machine code to programming languages to protocols to systems—each of those layers is culturally inflected. We wondered what would happen if that culture was an Indigenous one—microchips produced with the care of a Lakota community raising a sweat lodge; computers constructed with the intentionality of a Cree singer building his hand drum; networks knitted together following Coquille practices for making woven cattail trays; a programming language written in Crow to reflect Crow understandings of data and process; an operating system designed by Cheyenne computer scientists; pattern recognition algorithms taught using Aboriginal techniques for creating song lines; governance expert systems following Haudensonee political formations; an AI nurtured on Kanaka Maoli concepts of *'āina*, *'ohana*, and *kuleana*.

We asked our questions, rather than the questions that Western colonial culture tends to impose on us. How will these devices be made? Who will make them? With whom will they be in relation once they are in the world? How will they conduct themselves as relations in our communities? How will our communities treat them as relations? To what ends will they be shaped? How will they help our communities grow and thrive? How will our non-human kin take to them? Will they be there for our seventh-generation descendants? For many of us working in or with experience of the high-tech industry, it was a relief to focus on questions like these, rather than the tired tropes of a technology elite that recursively chases its own tail upon a ground of epistemological blindness, cultural prejudice, and myopic misanthropy.

13.3 Re-imagining AI

A year later, we published a position paper that captures the thinking and creating that took place in the workshops (Lewis, 2020). In it, we articulate 'Guidelines for Indigenous-centred AI Design'. These are seven points that attempt to condense participants' discussions into a common document that provides an accessible set of suggestions about how to rethink the design of AI systems from a perspective that takes into account ethical frameworks resonant across many Indigenous cultures. They include designing AI systems in partnership with local communities; building relationality and reciprocity into the foundations; the requirements that AI systems developed by, with, or for Indigenous communities should be responsible to those communities, provide relevant support, and be accountable to those communities first and foremost; using Indigenous protocols as the basis for governance and regulation guidelines; recognizing that all technical systems are cultural and social systems and that computation is a cultural material; applying ethical design to the full stack of a technology; and respecting and supporting Indigenous data sovereignty.

The guidelines are not meant as a substitute for robust engagement with specific Indigenous communities to understand how best to develop technology that addresses their priorities using methods that are reflective of how they wish to engage with the world. Rather, our hope was that, first, Indigenous communities can use the guidelines as a starting point to define their own, community-specific guidelines; and second, that non-Indigenous technologists and policy makers can use them to begin productive conversations with Indigenous communities about how to enter into collaborative technology development efforts.

The position paper also includes many different visions for the future of AI, including how AI might be built according to values articulated in Anishinaabe, Coquille, Kanaka Maoli/Blackfoot, Lakota, and Euskaldun epistemologies. Media artist Scott Benesiinaabandan (Anishinaabe) describes the Octopus

Bag Device, an AI system that is shaped by its host's DNA, and then imagines a creation story for the device that places it in the body of existing Anishinaabe *adizkookaan* (sacred stories). His story 'Gwiizens, the Old Lady and the Octopus Bag Device' illustrates how new technology such as AI might be incorporated into and made of a piece with the existing canon of Anishinaabe creation stories, in a manner that makes use of existing methods for sharing knowledge while keeping it culturally grounded.

Coquille media scholar Ashley Cordes explores how her people might make use of blockchain combined with AI to help them manage their communities' business, making the case that such technologies can be used to increase Indigenous sovereignty and self-determination. She envisions crafting necklaces of beads and dentalium, tusk-like shells found in her community's territory, that would be tools and symbols of the stories, dreams, and data of importance to her community. These would be gifted to the collaborating AI systems as a sign of the community's core values of trust and care.

Performance artist Suzanne Kite draws on Lakota knowledge frameworks to propose a protocol for ethically building computer hardware from the ground up. Kite discusses what it means to operate in the world in a 'Good Way' according to Lakota principles and draws on how Lakota form relationships with stones to explore how we might form relationships with AI hardware. She then maps out a process for building physical computing devices in a Good Way, using the protocol steps for building a sweat lodge as a guide. She closes with a list of questions that should be asked at each step of creating such devices—questions that are designed to keep the building process aligned with the Good Way.

Michelle Lee Brown, a scholar of Indigenous futurism, describes a Txitxardin Lamia, a biotech eel-AI developed from principles based on Euskaldunak (Basque people)–eel relations. She outlines a VR environment in which an elder Txitxardin Lamia would reside, where students could learn protocols for interacting with this elder and receive teachings that reorient them to more reciprocal ways of relating to, and being with, the world around them. Along the way she discusses the long relationship between her people and these eels, the central role this relationship plays in coastal Basque culture, and the need to think through the materialities out of which we are creating and housing our AI systems.

I wrote a poem sequence and a short description illustrating how epistemological diversity within AI design might look. The texts imagine a future where young Kānaka Maoli are raised along with three AIs, each built according to different conceptual frameworks. One AI takes inspiration from Kanaka notions of land, responsibility, and family; another from the Blackfoot language's basis in flow rather than objects; and the third from suppositions about how the octopus's nervous system is organized to accommodate the semi-autonomy of its arms. The three AIs and the human work collaboratively to make decisions in support of Kanaka flourishing that take the environment, human and non-human relations, and past-present-future into consideration.

13.4 Indigenous imaginaries as critical de- and re-construction

All this imaginative work helps us to highlight the culturally based assumptions that underlie the current status quo in AI research and development. These include: the user is an individual; the individual prioritizes their personal well-being; culture is an epiphenomenon rather than the phenomenon; text and context can be separated; and the only useful knowledge is that produced through rational instrumentality. Such assumptions make AI system engineers blind to vital aspects of human existence that are fundamental to how intelligence actually operates. This blindness stems, in part, from an intellectual lineage heavily infected with Cartesian duality, monotheistic eschatology, and computational reductionism. Separating mind from the body, elevating after-life over present-life, and violently forcing all experience into binary terms to make it (appear) computable produces impoverished notions of what constitutes human intelligence.

The refusal to engage, explore, and operationalize alternative knowledge frameworks is a tremendous scientific failing. It creates huge gaps between what humans think of as an intelligent presence in the world and what the AI industry–academic complex is building.

We must think more expansively about AI and all the other computational systems in which we find ourselves increasingly enmeshed. We need to expand the operational definition of intelligence used when building these systems to include the full spectrum of behaviour we humans use to make sense of the world. This will require exploring epistemologies different from the Western knowledge frameworks underpinning current system designs. What does it look like to design for epistemologies that centralize Indigenous understandings of the relationships between us and our non-human kin (Lewis et al., 2018)? What might we discover if we taught AI systems to view the world through Kanaka Maoli frameworks of abundance, rather than of scarcity (Baker, 2020; Enos, 2013; Fujikane, 2021)? We can use such future imaginaries to better build technologies that support the fullness of human life and thought. Imagining Indigenous AI is one way to dream beyond the impoverished knowledge frameworks in which we are currently trapped, and to draw upon the abundant multiplicity of ways of being intelligent in the world to envision AI systems that co-create the futures we want.

Endnotes

1. This essay is based, in part, on Chapters 1, 2, and 5 of Lewis, J. E. (ed.) 'Indigenous Protocol and Artificial Intelligence Position Paper', Indigenous Protocol and Artificial Intelligence Working Group and the Canadian Institute for Advanced Research (CIFAR), Honolulu, Hawai'i, 2020; and, Lewis, J. E., 'From Impoverished Intelligence to Abundant Intelligences', Medium post, 30 May 2021.
2. My co-organizers were Angie Abdilla (Palawa-Trawlwoolway), 'Ōiwi Parker Jones (Kanaka Maoli), and Noelani Arista (Kanaka Maoli).

References

Abdilla, A. (2018) 'Beyond imperial tools: Future-proofing technology through Indigenous governance and traditional knowledge systems', in Harley, J., Abdilla, A., and Newman, A. (eds.) *Decolonising the digital: Technology as cultural practice.* Sydney: Tactical Space Lab, pp. 67–81.

Baker, M. T. (2020) 'Waiwai (abundance) and Indigenous futures', in Rutazibwa, O. U. and Shilliam, R. (eds.) *Routledge handbook of postcolonial politics.* London: Routledge, pp. 22–31.

Enos, K. (2013) *Working collectively to restore ancestral abundance: Kamuela Enos at TEDxManoa.* 28 October. Available at: https://www.youtube.com/watch?v=w8iou8Rchqc

Fujikane, C. (2021) *Mapping abundance for a planetary future: Kanaka Maoli and critical settler cartographies in Hawai'i.* Durham: Duke University Press.

Lewis, J. E. (ed.) (2020) *Indigenous protocol and artificial intelligence position paper.* Honolulu, Hawai'i: The Initiative for Indigenous Futures and the Canadian Institute for Advanced Research (CIFAR). Concordia University. Available at: https://spectrum.library.concordia.ca/id/eprint/986506/

Lewis, J. E., Arista, N., Pechawis, A., and Kite, S. (2018) 'Making kin with the *Machines*', *Journal of Design and Science*, [Preprint]. doi:10.21428/bfafd97b

Little Bear, L. and Heavy Head, R. (2004) 'A conceptual anatomy of the Blackfoot world', *ReVision* 26(3), pp. 31–8.

Secretariat of National Aboriginal and Islander Child Care. (2019) Cultural protocols—supporting carers. Available at: https://www.supportingcarers.snaicc.org.au/connecting-to-culture/cultural-protocols/ (Accessed 5 May 2022).

14

Maoli Intelligence

Indigenous Data Sovereignty and Futurity

Noelani Arista

14.1 Introduction

Perhaps there is no other transformation with which Indigenous people have had to engage that has been so overtly associated with the future than the promise of digital technology and artificial intelligence (AI). Even when print and textual literacies were brought into our home territories by settlers, missionaries, and sometimes our own people, writing and publishing were not metonymies for futurity as technology is now.

14. 2 *I ka wā ma mua, ka wā ma hope*: history and futurity

'The future is made possible by the past' is a proverb describing a Kānaka Maoli (Hawaiian) way of thinking in time and relating to the past that is decidedly nonlinear.[1] Rather than imagining the past as prologue, or the past as an inert or finite space from which to mine already realized 'data' indiscriminately, the past in terms of ancestral knowledge can be a revelatory space for new insight and co-knowledge creation through active and persistent relation. Dedicated study was required for this *pilina* (connection) to be made and maintained, and this was as true in the past as it is in our colonial present.

So much has been written on settler ideas about Indigenous people in relation to time—our ancestors were almost universally characterized as disappearing or dying. Often, they were discursively relegated to a primitive past—a mirror into which Euro-Americans could gaze to gauge how far civilization had carried them away from Indigenous peoples, who were imagined as living relics or reflections from the Euro-American past. A 'technology' that is a metonym for futurity can easily, almost by definition, leave Indigenous people out of its imaginary, institutions, inner sanctums, and external profit margins.

While writing and print were 'technologies' purportedly introduced and taught to uplift Indigenous people,[2] the technology that has come to be associated with AI, machine learning, code, and computers is not of the same character or scale. Kānaka Maoli, like many Indigenous people, utilized reading, writing, and print for their own purposes, though when writing and print were introduced, they augmented, rather than supplanted, the power of oral traditions. Today, technologies such as AI are not perceived as part of missionizing projects, though the evangelical fervour with which the project of AI is studied, pursued, and supported globally by billions of dollars certainly resonates. What differs, of course, is its reach. The global north is set to colonize systems through AI: coded computational languages, algorithms, and AI protocols shape financial exchange; drive scientific and medical innovation; give form to political, governmental, and security realities and choices for individuals, communities, states, nations, and entire regions of the globe; redefine and design mobility both physical and material in nature; give rise to different forms of architecture; and affect human behaviour, intellect, and cognition in ways that do not invite people to exercise choice, but instead present the illusion of choice.

Today, many researchers, scholars, scientists, doctors, and engineers working on AI are on a mission driven by some of the same factors that impelled discoverers, merchants, traders, and missionaries into the farthest reaches of the globe during the age of discovery: the need for resources, innovation, capital, and (of course) the desire on the part of some humans simply to 'get there' *first*.[3] Leaders at the forefront of various movements shaping the growth and spread of AI through their various disciplines vary in their commitments, and while it is heartening to see many projects dedicated to the study of AI that is good for 'humanity', we should ask questions about which segments of humanity, and whose intellectual, philosophical, cultural, spiritual, religious, educational, and linguistic traditions will AI be modelled upon and out of?[4] Whose concept of what it means to be a good human—a good person, a good member of community—drives and curates this development, and whose communities benefit from this new mission? Most of the groups attending to such questions are overwhelmingly staffed by those who are not Indigenous, Black, or Brown.[5] Overwhelmingly, it is humans hailing from the global north, and who have lived in societies surfeit on the wealth of centuries of colonial and imperial plunder, the beneficiaries of land dispossession and acquisition, of economies built from slavery, oppression, and genocide. Underlying these benefits are the cultural and religious missions that sought to actively undermine and destroy Indigenous societal ways of living in the world, their relations with the lands, waters, seas, and territories that made 'home' in ways deeply divergent from Euro-American ways.

The assumption, and conceit, is that the normative cultures driving technological transformation do not 'naturally' arise in Indigenous territories, nor among Indigenous peoples, and that Indigenous languages and cultures are not capable of shaping non-Indigenous futures for Euro-American peoples or nations. It is important to point out the continued erasure of non-Western ways of knowing, organizing knowledge, craft, techniques of making, creativity, imaginaries, narrativizations, and ethical systems—especially in the very active discourse and discourse-making spaces of corporate boardrooms, governmental offices and institutions, universities and private industry. Therefore, the project that seeks to 'integrate' Indigenous bodies and bodies of knowledge into structures of AI *uncritically* should be approached with caution, because the assimilative power and impulses of missions are themselves totalizing and capable of erasing the specificity and nuance of community contribution and *kuleana* (responsibility) that comes with *'ike* (knowledge, traditional knowledge).

The 'logical' argument that is always made against the power of Indigenous life-ways is that we are too particular, too insular, too marginal. The scale of our capacity to contribute to global society is conveniently never on the scale of 'humanity'. We are always consultants on the world stage—performers, exoticized knowledge keepers from a corner of the world—but never capable of representing *the world*. The question of whether our humanity is worth less than that of others has been forced upon us through encounter and colonialism. While 'inclusion' within the developmental currents of technology and AI are attractive, what might the future of computational science, AI, and an ethics based out of Indigenous concepts of relationality become if Indigenous technological capacity is nurtured and centred, rather than marginalized? To scale solutions for 'humanity' without acknowledging the material inequalities faced by Indigenous nations, communities, and individuals both exacerbates and furthers these inequities. Indigenous nations—some recognized by settler governments, some not—languish on the margins of these discussions.

The rest of this chapter builds out the concept of Maoli Intelligence, or that corpus of ancestral knowledge where the collective *'ike* of Kānaka Maoli people continues to be accessed. I present a view of Indigenous data sovereignty and provide examples from my *lāhui* (Nation, people) built upon a robust oral to textual, filmic, and material culture 'archive'. The protocols, ceremony, and rules that govern how the *lāhui* has maintained, passed on, and secured the veracity of this body of knowledge are methods that can guide the way we organize and secure our knowledges through technology, machine learning, and

AI. Finally, the chapter concludes with my work with an all-Indigenous team of data and computer scientists to build a prototype of an image recognition application forecasting what we can do with Maoli Intelligence together that can be applied on a broader scale.

14.3 Data sovereignty for Indigenous communities

To begin with, data sovereignty usually means that 'data' is subject to the rules, governing structures, and laws of the nation in which data is gathered or to which it belongs. In the case of Indigenous nations, discussions are rooted in keeping our data autonomous from colonial states and the control of data between nations, communities, and, in Hawai'i, according to custom, even between families. Most recently this has been defined as a 'strategy in which communities seek control over their own data in an effort to ensure control over their future' (Hao, 2022b).

I pause here to point out that 'data sovereignty' is not a new concept or practice for many Indigenous nations, including Kānaka Maoli. For centuries, Kānaka Maoli, like many other Indigenous people of the *Moananuiākea* (the Pacific), cared for and passed down their knowledges. In Hawai'i this would include a familiarity with the ocean, seas, waters, winds, rains, plants, and animals spanning centuries, the vital connection of *Kānaka* to *ke ao maoli* (the Hawaiian world) through processes that were disciplined and organized in *hālau 'ike* (schools of knowledge) and through *kahuna* (priestly experts or those trained in an art, trade, or skilled 'profession').[6] While concerned groups among Indigenous peoples erect outward-facing rules and regulations to control, organize, and define the data that continues to be structured, collected, and used by colonial governments and institutions, as well as the transfer of knowledge between Indigenous and non-Indigenous nations, what is often omitted from these discussions are those who are concerned with data or *'ike* that is shared within a community, and between a community and the ancestral stream of knowledges passed down over generations: knowledges and caretaking practices that require our attention to continue to live and thrive.

As we consider protections that secure data sovereignty between Indigenous and non-Indigenous nations, we should continue to cultivate Indigenous data sovereignty through intensive study of the way our societies organized knowledge. In the Hawaiian context, this will require a robust commitment to deep study of language, history, customary knowledge(s), and the social relations, processes, and methods that secured the veracity of these knowledges among *kānaka*, which have so often been negatively impacted or outright targeted for destruction by colonialism and its various agents. The data sovereignty I write about is not about the continuous challenges of fighting with colonial legality or how we interface with it, but rather about the regulation of ancestral *'ike* and securing the veracity of that knowledge in ways that keep it well within the traditions of knowing, interpretation, and teachings consistent and related to the body of knowledge amassed and passed down by our ancestors.

For Kānaka Maoli, the oral, textual, auditory, film, and material productions that are available function as a living source of collective *maoli* (real, true) intelligence. I *haku* (composed, created) the phrase 'Maoli Intelligence' (Indigenous, real, authentic, true, genuine) as *kaona* (polysemy; resonant with multiple, often-hidden meanings) as it connects to *Kānaka Maoli* (people) and to ancestral knowledge perceived and accessed as integral to our thriving and surviving as a people. In this way, Maoli Intelligence is *not* external, simulated, or artificial. Additionally, I do so knowing full well that these 'bodies' of knowledge exist in the fluid intergenerational and intragenerational repositories of oral performative culture, where chants, prayers, and songs circulate and are shared, along with the textual, written, oral, material, and filmic repositories found in various archives, libraries, and galleries, most of which can be accessed by community members but is only understood to varying degrees based on a person's level of training, their education, who their family is, and their *welo* (inherited aptitude).

To be clear, Kānaka Maoli people have been caring for, contributing to, and relating with and through their own ancestral-based knowing for centuries, physically, experientially, aurally, and orally, and it has only been within the last two centuries, since the missionaries' introduction of the *palapala* in the 1820s, when our knowledges began to be shared and recorded in other mediums, through writing, print, and, most recently, through digital mediums.

The Hawaiian language textual archive is significant because it is *the largest* textual source base in an Indigenous language in North America and the Polynesian Pacific. This unsynthesized mass of documents resides in public and private libraries and archives across the Hawaiian Islands, and is heavily concentrated in California, New England, and England: in short, all of the places Hawaiian people frequented from the eighteenth through the early twentieth century. This written and published corpus is comprised of compositions once maintained orally and subsequently committed to writing and print. Added to this pre-settler aggregate of materials are newly composed oral genres of chant, prayer and song, letters, journals, newspapers, reports, the official business of government, and books. Though Hawaiian language is endangered in the world of everyday *modern* speech, it thrives on the page. The colonial processes that unsettled knowing in many Indigenous communities did so through many avenues, including through introduced diseases that struck down physical bodies charged with passing on customary knowledge from generation to generation, straining—and at times severing—relations between people, land, and language. In tandem with colonial policies of removal and the influx of capital that attracted Indigenous people from rural areas to small towns and cities that grew up around ports and merchant centres, creating newly diasporic populations within the territorial boundaries of Indigenous nations like Hawai'i, the displacement and replacement of Hawaiian knowledge continued.

For Hawaiian people, 'knowing'—the ability to recall or retrieve commonly held knowledge that circulates in communities—is deeply fraught due to more than two hundred years of entanglement with, and erasure by, settler society (Arista, 2019a). Seeking to know (*'imi*) often requires Kānaka Maoli people to enter into uncomfortable relations with our own traditional and customary knowledges, initially acknowledging the deficiencies and holes *(puka)* we experience in relation to *'ike*. Perhaps the most challenging indicator of colonial damage we must navigate is the inability of most Kānaka Maoli people to acquire Hawaiian language in our own *'ohana* (family), in our homes, and in community. This loss of communal knowledge forces families to rely on external systems of immersion and charter schools, to begin learning in high school, or college where available, until individuals work themselves into fluency.

In the decades it took to establish schools and programmes for Hawaiian language reclamation and acquisition, the important questions of what constitutes fluency, and what threshold of customary knowledge through language is necessary to elicit or reignite cognitive processes and patterns that reflect ancestral ways of knowing, could scarcely be entertained. Technology may support this project if knowledgeable individuals can create immersive experiences, enabling relations, connecting people to Maoli Intelligence through AR, VR, and iterative game play that expose players to *maoli* cognitive and affective processes and states. As we seek (*'imi loa*) to delve deeply and think like our ancestors, relating to them and our world, through the words and voices they left us orally and textually, in what ways can machine learning and AI assist us to study, access, and understand Maoli Intelligence? How might it assist us in uncovering the foundational principles that organize *maoli* knowledge systems?[7]

How can the damage wrought by colonialism, which sought to destroy our communal relations and break our spirits by removing our primary mode of affective expression, *language*, be repaired? Reclamation as a project, I argue, is not simply about reconstituting communities through language. It is also about self-knowing, healing from trauma, cultivating healthy relationships, intimacy, and restoring powerful intergenerational relations between ourselves and our ancestors.[8] Since the pedagogies of listen and repeat (*ho'olohe, ho'opili mai*) were key to the aural-oral construction of organizing data and structuring recall and memory from one generation to the next, the question should be posed: 'In what ways can AI support Indigenous peoples with "knowing" rather than taking their place, supplanting the integral relationships that people cultivated among themselves by way of caring for *'ike*?'

Will AI replace experts and elders as repositories of knowledge subverting maoli relationality?[9] This is a crucial question for Indigenous people. At what point in the process of application development are trained experts integrated into a project to ensure that the *'ike* (data) is structured and delivered following customary protocols for securing the veracity and correctness of *'ike* in line with centuries of care?[10] Arguably, what is necessary are institutions that train knowledgeable people who are both fluent in language and trained in computer science. How can Indigenous communities working within their own modes of data sovereignty mitigate against the imposition of non-*maoli* structures of knowledge and interpretation of their *'ike*, and data, while they are in the free-fall process of learning and securing 'knowing' for themselves and future generations?[11]

Incursions against the production of correct knowledge come from normative colonial culture and (to some extent) the very decolonial impulses that drive Indigenous people to seek to purify or make authentic their own ways of knowing. Knowledge of coding, computer science, computer engineering, and AI are certainly more cherished skill sets within normative society. Coupling this privileging with the capacity to transpose our literatures, stories, songs, and chants into digital mediums may unfortunately leave the power of creation in the hands of those developers who have been trained to code, but not trained to know, thus circumventing communal and ancestral rules about who has the authority to pass on and keep knowledge in numerous communities. Hopefully the current trend that situates authority on the Indigenous body, on performances of identity, rather than rooted in the knowledge and practice of kumu and *hālau 'ike*, or that of *kahuna*, will be a passing fad.[12] The ability to *haku* (compose) oral, written, or published compositions in language was the norm among Hawaiians even into the twentieth century.

Few today who are trained in Indigenous customary knowledges—in ceremony, literature, or performance—also have degrees in computation and design necessary to train machine learning algorithms to read and sift through textual and written sources, and to craft AR, VR, video games, and other forms of immersive media. In order to address material disparities that exist, educational programmes might be introduced on reserves, reservations, or in communities to teach Indigenous youth to code, or create through the mediums of VR, AR, and video gaming, or imagine futures through the intricacies of computer science and engineering shaped in relation to Maoli Intelligence.[13]

Currently, because no educational pathway exists that pairs customary training with computation and design, the largest and most pressing issue in creating good future content, aligning communities in the present with Maoli Intelligence lies in cultivating *pono* (proper, good, correct) social relations between developers, engineers, and *kahuna*, *kumu*, and *kūpuna* (knowledgeable elders). In 'Making Kin With the Machines' it was suggested that relationality between humans and AI, as mapped on to traditional Indigenous concepts of human and nonhuman entities, would be a good starting point for codifying ethical Indigenous approaches to AI (Lewis et al., 2018). However, as a Hawaiian scholar, trained to some extent in knowledge of religious and ceremonial practice, in oral, literary, and historical knowledge, I argue that it is most important that we attend to our own community relationships. We should also acknowledge the real disparities in power between those with degrees in computer science and engineering and those working in the humanities or as members of the community who have secured and continue to secure the continuity of ancestral knowledge of Maoli Intelligence for the good of future generations.[14]

The work to reclaim language through these various mediums inaugurates the next leap between oral and written, textual, and digital mediums. Working to accelerate our knowledge of archives using machine learning can reveal what language reclamation solely through the discipline of linguistics lacks—that the creation of meaning cannot be pursued without context. In the case of Hawaiian, one must proceed with an attempt to understand and organize our knowledge of *oli* (chant), *pule* (prayer), *mo'okū'auhau* (genealogy), *mele* (song), and *mo'olelo* (history and story).

14.4 Immersive Indigenous worlding

Indigenous research methodologies and ethics are popular topics of scholarship today, but few have touched upon the intersection between Indigenous knowledges, language, and technology (Smith, 2021; George et al., 2020). As Indigenous people, our time and energy are often divided between critiquing colonial systems and proffering correctives in the form of our own knowledges.[15] The most difficult decolonial work before us will be to focus on our own communities to reconnect with Indigenous forms of customary knowledge independent of the inevitable mimicry that comes with resistance. Pursuing Hawaiian knowledge through machine learning should *begin*, not end, with a foundation in language, due to the sheer volume of data available. Reconnecting with Maoli Intelligence should proceed with a strong emphasis on the oral and written, on oral praxis and reading, understanding, and interpretation, all of which are necessary for the building of appropriate contexts.

We might consider what the Indigenous language 'archive' can teach us about Hawaiian cognition, and how our people viewed the world and their place within it. Carefully monitored pattern recognition and replication of cognitive processes can help us to come back in line with our ancestral neural networks requiring social engineering between ourselves and our virtually present ancestors who left us many of their words and means of understanding their world to build relations through and with. The first steps towards immersive Indigenous worlding, or 'Dreaming of Kuano'o', will require visionaries to seek into the past to broadly open the way (*wehe ākea*) to our futures: *I ka wā ma mua, ka wā ma hope.*[16] To create relational experiences predicated on Maoli Intelligence, time and resources need to be given to those trained to *'imi loa*, the deep search into textual archives and in communities where Indigenous speakers still hold and pass on knowledge to better complement the work of accomplished Indigenous computer and data scientists.[17] What happens when we put aside our obsession and the tensions that arise when comparing critical endangerment of languages among communities with small and large data sets and bring together computer scientists working in Indigenous languages with people trained in traditional knowledge and language? How can we introduce methods and approaches that are prototyped in languages with robust data sets and apply them to others where data is sparse and is still in the collection phase? How might we centre our research questions and the concerns of our communities for data security and sovereignty?

14.5 Hua Ki'i: an all-Indigenous working group

In 2019 I co-organized two Indigenous Protocols and AI working group workshops *i ku'u one hānau* (on my birthsands) of Honolulu, Hawai'i.[18] During the second workshop I worked with an all-Indigenous prototyping group with Caroline Old Coyote (Crow), Michael Running Wolf (Northern Cheyenne), Joel Davidson (Gadigal and Dunghutti) and Caleb Moses (Maori, Ngāpuhi, Te Mahurehure, Aitutaki) to create an application, Hua Ki'i, that would provide Hawaiian language descriptors for captured images. For the users, the application appears familiar and perhaps simple: take a photograph of an object and a Hawaiian language word for the object will be supplied. In order for the application to work, Kanaka Maoli graduate student 'Ika'aka Nāhuewai and I needed to create a dictionary.

Unlike many other Indigenous languages that lack any dictionary, there are several dictionaries available in a Hawaiian–English format.[19] There are even multiple Hawaiian language dictionaries accessible online.[20] Rather than consult only published dictionaries for our project that maps an image to a Hawaiian language descriptor, we drew upon the *'ike* that we have made *pa'a* (secure) as part of our own knowing.

For the project, we had to craft a word list that correlated an object and its Hawaiian descriptor. These mappings are contained in a CSC file. This mapping, however, cannot be accomplished completely by a dictionary, online or otherwise. Accurate mapping requires a person with deep grounding in

ʻike Hawaiʻi (Hawaiian knowledge) and language to supply nuance and context. Prototyping team members like ʻIkaʻaka and I both have a high degree of fluency in the Hawaiian language; however, our areas of knowledge expertise do not overlap, due in part to the differences in our geographic and familial ties, disciplinary training in university and *hālau*, and the disparity in our ages. Together, our knowledge supplied needed depth to an otherwise static and a-historic definition provided to readers without such knowledge who consult a dictionary. In some instances, the mapping process required us to append more data to the words we employed in our modest *Hua Kiʻi* lexicon, supplying real-world usage by Hawaiian speakers. In addition to gathering information about people's everyday use of a word, ʻIkaʻaka and I drilled down on underlying concepts discussing the nature (*ʻano*) of a word, mapping sense relations along with the intent of its users, even as meaning changed and transformed over time and across different islands. ʻIkaʻaka and I discussed appropriate words for images and, where we differed, we turned to crowdsourcing to collect responses via social media. For example, when we received several divergent terms for the word 'backpack' in Hawaiian, we realized that people from the eastern end of the archipelago—Maui Island to Hawaiʻi Island—favoured one set of words and word-phrases, whereas people from the western end—Oʻahu Island to Kauaʻi Island—preferred another set of words. Capturing this data represents the first steps in creating a dictionary both responsive to, and reflective of, geographic difference and nuance in real time.

Naming is an important practice for Hawaiian people. In choosing a name for a child, a project, or an institution (and in this case a software application), a knowledgeable person considers what is given in a name. Knowledge keepers, experts, or elders consider the associations of words with people; is a name bequeathed in order to connect a child to an ancestor through shared qualities? What are the feelings a pregnant mother feels, or what feelings are evoked or imbued through a given name? Does a name refer to a significant past event? After consideration, names are bestowed that give strength, intelligence, skill, or impart hopes for future growth. Hawaiian scholar and language expert Mary Kawena Pukui noted that names alluded to 'personal or family qualities of beauty, nobility, or evidence of . . . powers . . . [a person's name] could play a part in shaping the character, personality—even the fate and fortunes—of the bearer!' (Pukui et al., 2014). Giving name to what we see and sensations we feel in the world seems a trivial act at times, especially in a world over-saturated with communication. However, for Indigenous people working towards societal (relational) revitalization, the connection between people, language, and land is an important relationship to heal. The Hua Kiʻi program that the multi-tribal AI prototyping team of language warriors created was named by ʻIkaʻaka with that connection in mind. Through discussion and deliberation between team members we settled on this name since it supplies a basic Hawaiian description of the application that most Hawaiian language learners could understand, even those in the initial stages of learning the language. The word *hua* is a shortening of the word-phrase *hua 'ōlelo*, meaning 'a word', and *ki'i* or 'image'. *Hua* also means fruit, or seed. *Ki'i* can also mean to fetch, pluck, or pick. The elision of the two word meanings presents the image of our language as a ripe, juicy fruit that is so tantalizing that we want to pick it, and if we do not, the *hua* will fall to the ground, wasted. Language revitalization is a term that includes many different approaches that rely heavily on the contribution of linguists and anthropologists. The methods I put forth have come from another space of disciplinarity entirely—one which cannot be accounted for or affirmed through a single disciplinary tract like Hawaiian Studies, Political Science, or Hawaiian Language. As in most carefully constructed Hawaiian word plays, additional layers are built into the name. The first is playful and easy to remember, appealing to kids and families. The second reveals our intention to nourish our people with words from their language, while also inspiring hope that what is planted (with this first prototyping project) will continue to take root and thrive. By being playfully literate on one level and supplying a layer of *kaona* or playfully hidden meaning, we offer people an invitation to open themselves to deepen engagement. Though modest in scale, the current version of Hua Ki'i has the capacity to make space for a larger image recognition platform in the future.

Much of my recent work as a Kanaka Maoli historian has been dedicated to creating greater access to Hawaiian language textual materials in archives, to the study of particular forms and genres of chant, or areas of knowledge, in order to understand the way *'ike* is organized. I am deeply invested in understanding the rules by which ancestral knowledge was verified or contested, and the ethical implications of what it means to seek in a proper fashion, to *'imi pono*.[21]

One of the central questions of my own research is whether it is possible to indigenize the process of language acquisition by bringing older concepts and usages of words into everyday circulation. This question is not merely antiquarian, or a passing curiosity raised by scholars in an ivory tower, since *he mana ko ka mea i 'ōlelo mua 'ia*: in Hawai'i we uphold the discursive significance that words previously spoken and retained in memory, and repeated performance, bear the *mana* (decisive power) of the decisions our ancestors made, as well as the personal *mana* (life force, energy, spiritual power, charisma) that inhered in their utterances.[22] Therefore, to recirculate the words, proverbs, idiomatic sayings, prayers, chants, stories, and histories of ancestors allows us to provide a pathway for this *mana* to continue. Memory and knowing was never forged through 'faith' or 'belief', but through training and pedagogy: *ho'olohe, ho'opili mai, ho'opa'a na'au* (listen, repeat, retain in the guts). Authenticating this process through Hawaiian elders only is not possible, for several reasons.

The Native speaker population is in deep decline, with estimates suggesting that fewer than 300 speakers remain.[23] Mitigating against the complete loss of language is a channel of Hawaiian-language immersion schools, from pre-K through to PhD. However, the language that has emerged from these schools over the last two generations differs markedly from the speech of Native speakers who taught me twenty years ago, many of whom have passed on. Most Hawaiians have been severed from customary knowledge through a multitude of colonial processes: the massive decline of the population via the introduction of new diseases; the loss of Maoli lands through the introduction of a regime of private property; the illegal overthrow of the Hawaiian Kingdom; and active suppression of language. While several avenues have been preserved or newly created to keep this knowledge alive in community, a rigorous research and analytical agenda is required to craft better interpretive systems that will allow us to organize, understand, and engage ancestral knowledge more fully.

The community of *kūpuna* who are our interlocutors is made up of both the living and those who have passed on, those who left their writings and speech for us to converse with and about. In researching concepts and usage in the Hawaiian language, one realizes quickly that maintaining relations with ancestral knowledge defies the prim logic of linearity. There is no expiration date on the *mana* that inheres in authoritative ancestral speech and writing. We are entering an exciting new phase of language revitalization and Maoli Intelligence, where technology can assist Indigenous people in organizing data in ways that allow us to synthesize ancestral knowledge and rebuild systems of knowledge keeping and transmission. I want the sounding here to resonate with *kaona* and polysemic play, between the definition of *maoli* as real, true, and native, and Maoli Intelligence as situated in the *pō* (darkness of ocean deeps and heavens from which all ancestral knowledge and genealogy derives) and is constituted by all the generations of Hawaiian knowledge to which we can connect and contribute.[24] This long process will enable us to envision ourselves in relation to our past to bring forward a better future for society. By centring Maoli Intelligence in our technological practices and guiding our relations, we will be better equipped to address and contribute to solutions and answers to larger questions that face all of humanity.

Endnotes

1. I Ka Wā Ma Mua, Ka Wā Ma Hope—If one has to look for an understanding of this proverb it lies in the practice of kahuna (priests), kākā ʻōlelo (orator, chiefly counsellor) and kūʻauhau (genealogists) who consult oral history and oral pronouncement to aid in deliberations facing the government on how to deal with questions or challenges in the present. The phrase does not refer to facing the past or turning one's

back to the future—an orientation that is based on a mistranslation of Hawaiian language into English.

2. Palapala in the Hawaiian language refers to writing, written, and published materials, a document, and the teaching of the palapala, or reading and writing by Christian missionaries beginning in 1820.
3. Ojibwe historian Jeannie O'Brien (2010) details the way that local histories were a primary method by which settlers asserted their modernity while denying it to Indian Peoples.
4. The Montreal Institute for Learning Algorithms (MILA) is just one example of a collective of researchers, professors, and students dedicated to '. . . socially responsible and beneficial development . . . of artificial intelligence for humanity' (2021).
5. The question was recently taken on in a four-part series by *MIT Technology Review* on AI colonialism that investigated how 'AI is enriching a powerful few by dispossessing communities that have already been dispossessed before' (Hao, 2022a).
6. More work needs to be done on the knowledge of *kahuna*, who were specialized experts trained in particular crafts, trades, and who were also priestly experts. Hawaiian knowledge was kept across the archipelago by this stratum of people in society whose knowledge was as diverse as healing; navigators; canoe carvers; stone workers; weavers; bird catchers; feather cape, *lei*, and *kahili* makers; seers; and keepers of the *akua* and *'aumakua* (national and ancestral deities). Kānaka Maoli knowledge was not simply held by 'knowledge keepers', nor was it solely 'land-based'.
7. I was privileged to be trained for my work in Hawaiian language textual archives by many *kumu 'ōlelo Hawai'i* (Hawaiian language teachers,) and in *hālau hula* (hula schools) where I was taught to listen to, memorize, and perform *oli* (chants) and *pule* (ceremonial prayers). I was employed for several years as a researcher, translator, transcriber, and assistant on two separate research projects on Hawaiian language newspapers and *Kanikau* (Hawaiian grief chants) led by kūpuna Edith McKinzie and Rubellite Kawena Johnson, respectively. Here was an education in language and deep context up from schools maintained in the Hawaiian community. For an explanation on the concept of *'imi loa*, see Arista (2007).
8. See Arista (2019b) for an extended discussion on the size and complexity of the Hawaiian language textual archive, the challenges of working in it, and how Kānaka Maoli people can reorient themselves to the archive as repository of ancestral knowledges.
9. Here again I emphasize the primacy of relationality, rather than rationality, as foundational to Maoli Intelligence.
10. Experts in Hawaiian include elders, *kumu* (teachers) from *hālau 'ike*, various schools of knowledge, and *kahuna* (trained craft or creative experts, and those in healing, religious, governance, or spiritual disciplines).
11. By non-*maoli* I do not mean to secure knowledge through a claim to Indigenous identity or an Indigenous body, but rather make the distinction between those Indigenous people who have been trained to *'ike*, to knowing, and those who have not.

12. In Hawaiʻi the relationship between paradise and performance, the commodification of hula, and how it has impacted, or shaped Hawaiian identity is just beginning to be studied; see Imada (2012).
13. There is very little scholarship focusing on the place of Indigenous peoples in relation to technology, education, and algorithmic oppression. The Institute for Indigenous Futures (IIF) led by Jason Edward Lewis and Skawennati Fragnito have created many opportunities through their successful Skins series of workshops on video gaming, storytelling, and digital media for Indigenous youth and members of different communities. Natives in Tech and Indigenous in AI have also begun offering coding to native youth with their AI Code Camp. See https://indigenousfutures.net/about/ and https://lakota.aicode.camp/.
14. My work as a historian serves as an example: professors working in computation and design are able to access funding streams focused on computer engineering, AI, or STEM—research highly valued in normative society with millions of dollars on offer.
15. I prefer to stay immersed in *Maoli* knowledge research in the Hawaiian language and work between archive and community, helping to deliver avenues of access to primary source materials and creating and sharing interpretive models that can be replicated within my community and in comparative Indigenous contexts.
16. *Kuanoʻo* means to be in a thoughtful, meditative, comprehending state. This sentence belies both my meaning and process, one that draws upon Hawaiian modes of seeing, *ākea* (wide, open, vast), and theorizing the relationship between Maoli Intelligence, the aggregate of knowledge and past experience collected and passed on by ancestors and experts, and how this knowledge shapes the future, *I ka wā ma mua, ka wā ma hope* (the future is made possible by the past). Northern Cheyenne computer scientist Michael Running Wolf writes about Kuanoʻo, a future Kanaka Maoli AI comprised of augmented reality, automatic speech recognition (ASR), speech to text synthesis (STT), natural language understanding (NLU), machine translation, and conversational AI in his piece 'Dreams of Kuano'o' (Running Wolf, 2020).
17. Consider that formal training in customary knowledge in Hawaiʻi, prior to the introduction of the palapala, began in childhood and took place over the course of one's life into young adulthood.
18. My co-organizers were Jason Edward Lewis (Cherokee, Kanaka Maoli, Samoan), ʻŌiwi Parker Jones (Kanaka Maoli), and Angie Abdilla (Palawa-Trawlwoolway).
19. To date, however, there is no dictionary of the Hawaiian language that is written in Hawaiian. Dictionaries for the Hawaiian language are available in Hawaiian–English, and due to the cultural spread of *hula* into Japan and France, Hawaiian dictionaries have been compiled in Japanese and French. Perhaps the most commonly referenced dictionary is Pukui and Elbert (1986). For words and older usages, see Andrews et al. (2003).
20. See https://wehewehe.org/
21. I have served as the research lead on the Hawaiian Evangelical Association (HEA) Names Files Project since 2019, overseeing a project to digitize, organize, transcribe,

and edit the largest collection of papers in the Hawaiian Mission Children's Society Archives, comprised of over 1200 individual writers. Many of the writers are Kanaka Maoli and over 80% of the collection is written in the Hawaiian language. Noelani Arista, *Lead Researcher*. Hawaiian Mission Houses Historic Site and Archives—Hawaiian Evangelical Association (HEA) Names Files Project. https://sites.google.com/missionhouses.org/heanamesfilecollectionproject/

22. Maoli Intelligence has been bolstered doubly in Hawai'i by print and textual sources where the imprint of speech has also been recorded to a high degree. Māori historian Nepia Mahuika has written in depth about oral tradition; see Mahuika (2021, p. 4) on mana.
23. Endangered Languages Project, 'Hawaiian aka "Ōlelo Hawai'i"', ELP. Available at: https://endangeredlanguages.com/lang/125 (Accessed 15 April 2022).
24. In an earlier essay I theorized a concept called 'kaona consciousness' to describe the training of oral intellect and the methods of information retention and retrieval in the life of Hawaiian Historian and chiefly counsellor Davida Malo. See Arista (2010).

References

Andrews, L., Silva, N. K., and Schütz, A. J. (2003) *A dictionary of the Hawaiian language: To which is appended an English-Hawaiian vocabulary and a chronological table of remarkable events*. Waipahu, Hawai'i: Island Heritage Publications.

Arista, N. (2007) 'Foreword', in Pukui, M. K., and Kepelino. *Kepelino's traditions of Hawaii*. Honolulu: Bishop Museum Press, n.p.

Arista, N. (2010) 'Navigating uncharted oceans of meaning: Kaona as historical and interpretive method. *Publications of the Modern Language Association of America*, 125(3), pp. 663–9.

Arista, N. (2019a) 'Introduction', in *The kingdom and the republic: Sovereign Hawai'i and the early United States*. Philadelphia: University of Pennsylvania Press, pp. 1–17.

Arista, N. (2019b) 'Ka Waihona Palapala Manaleo: research in a time of plenty', *Colonialism and ignoring the Hawaiian language archive*. Indigenous Textual Cultures. Durham: Duke University Press, pp. 31–59.

Endangered Languages Project. (n.d.) "Ōlelo Hawai'i'. Available at: https://www.endangeredlanguages.com/lang/125.

George, L., Taori, J., and MacDonald, L. T. A. o. T. (eds.) (2020) *Indigenous research ethics: Claiming research sovereignty beyond deficit and the colonial legacy (Advances in research ethics and integrity*, volume 6). Bingley: Emerald Publishing.

Hao, K. (2022a) 'Artificial intelligence is creating a new colonial world order', *MIT Technology Review* [online], 19 April. Available at: https://www.technologyreview.com/2022/04/22/1050394/artificial-intelligence-for-the-people/?fbclid=IwAR3AORXpy65VhCUkJumaA1SSqhNVdsBTwH1ghsuv9-sD6CqMq_oyuf2yzg0 (Accessed 26 April 2022).

Hao, K. (2022b) 'A new vision of artificial intelligence for the people', *MIT Technology Review* [online], 22 April. Available at: https://www.technologyreview.com/2022/04/22/1050394/artificial-intelligence-for-the-people/?fbclid=IwAR3AORXpy65VhCUkJumaA1SSqhNVdsBTwH1ghsuv9-sD6CqMq_oyuf2yzg0 (Accessed 26 April 2022).

Imada, A. (2012) *Hula circuits through the American empire*. Durham, NC: Duke University Press.

Lewis, J. E., et al. (2018) 'Making kin with the machines', *Journal of Design and Science*, 3(5) [preprint]. Available at: https://doi.org/10.21428/bfafd97b.

Mahuika, N. (2021) *Rethinking oral history and tradition: An Indigenous perspective*. Oxford Oral History Series. New York: Oxford University Press.

Montreal Institute for Learning Algorithms. (2021) AI for humanity. *Mila* [online], 27 January. Available from: https://mila.quebec/en/ai-society/ (Accessed 15 April 2022).

O'Brien, J. M. (2010) *Firsting and lasting: Writing Indians out of existence in New England*. Minneapolis: University of Minnesota Press.

Pukui, M. K. and Elbert, S. H. (1986) *Hawaiian dictionary: Hawaiian–English, English–Hawaiian*, rev. and enl. edn. Honolulu: University of Hawaii Press.

Pukui, M. K., Haertig, E. W., and Lee, C. A. (2014) *Nānā i ke kumu (Look to the source)*, Vol. II. Honolulu: Hui Hanai.

Running Wolf, M. (2020) 'Dreams of Kuano'o', in Lewis, J. L. (ed.) *Indigenous protocol and artificial intelligence position paper*. Honolulu: The Initiative for Indigenous Futures and the Canadian Institute for Advanced Research (CIFAR), pp. 117–22.

Smith, L. T. (2021) *Decolonizing methodologies: Research and Indigenous peoples*, 3rd edn. London: Zed Books.

PART III

AFRICA, MIDDLE EAST, AND SOUTH ASIA

15

From Tafa to Robu

AI in the Fiction of Satyajit Ray

Upamanyu Pablo Mukherjee

After stunning the world of cinema with his *Apu* trilogy (1955–1959), the Indian auteur Satyajit Ray entered the world of science fiction (SF) in 1961 with a short story, 'Byomjatrir Diary' ('The Diary of a Space Traveller'), published in the Bengali children's magazine *Sandesh*, whose editorship he had inherited from his mercurial father Sukumar Ray. Satyajit Ray was himself prone to dismiss his SF writings as 'mere entertainment' (Robinson, 1989, p. 298). But, as I have argued elsewhere (Mukherjee, 2020), they formed part of a vibrant and experimental literature in South Asia and other parts of the world as they were emerging as independent nations after the centuries-long devastation inflicted by European colonialism and imperialism.

Until relatively recently, the significance of this literature was not properly appreciated by scholars whose attention, perhaps understandably, had been trained upon the much better documented and better preserved European and North American SF canons and archives. Yet writers and editors such as Satyajit Ray, Premendra Mitra, Naval Bihari Mishra, Jayant Vishnu Narlikar, Bal Phondke, and Sujatha Rangarajan used a wide variety of popular magazines for children and adults in Bengali, Marathi, Tamil, and Hindi in order to critically reflect on the relationship between science, technology, and postcolonial nation-building from the middle of the twentieth century.[1] In what follows, I offer a reading of a selection of Satyajit Ray's stories featuring Professor Shonku to suggest that they contained some of the earliest reflections on the problems and possibilities of artificial intelligence (AI) *long before* their importance was recognized by politicians and scientists in South Asia.

Ray wrote forty stories featuring Professor Shonku over a period of three decades from 1961 to 1995. More often than not, they were published in *Sandesh* before being anthologized in a series of best-selling books. Ray modelled his character in part on Arthur Conan Doyle's early-twentieth-century scientist-adventurer, Professor Challenger. But as is the norm in such cases of what

Roberto Schwarz felicitously calls 'misplaced ideas' (Schwarz, 1992), he repurposed his cultural borrowing with distinctively local and regional devices. Ranging from unapologetic anti-colonial sentiments to customary religiosity, Ray produced via Shonku all the contradictory impulses of India's early postcolonial era.

Literary precedents of scientific policies and research activities raise interesting questions about histories of science as well as those pertaining to the specificities of literature. Why should we accept literature, and especially popular literature, as an important source of recreating a 'global history' of AI? Conversely, why should we take seriously scientific ideas and practices as indispensable ingredients for the making of a literary-cultural genre? Clearly, the limited scope of this chapter prevents a full consideration of such questions that have engaged (one must admit) literary scholars more than scientists or historians of science.[2] But I hope that my observations might underscore the advantages, and even desirability, of analysing 'public' science and 'popular' literature as interrelated sub-domains within the general field of culture as such.

Most histories of 'artificial intelligence as a full-fledged field of research' begin with three crucial conferences held in the US and Britain in the 1950s—the 'Session on Learning Machines' in Los Angeles in 1955, the 'Summer Research Project on Artificial Intelligence' at Dartmouth College in 1956, and 'The Mechanization of Thought Process' at the British National Physical Laboratory in 1958 (Nilson, 2010, p. 49). The combination of a critical mass of researchers, investment in specialist laboratories, and the geo-political pressures of the Cold War produced during these middle decades of the twentieth century what we now know as 'first-wave AI' (Smith, 2019). South Asia and the 'Global South' almost never feature in such discussions. This is understandable, since the governments and scientists of these nations responded to a distinctively different set of priorities and pressures during this period. As recently as 2016, a report on AI research in India suggested that the work had been 'limited to a handful of passionate researchers and thus significantly lagged behind the United States and Europe', and that in order to catch up, the Indian government desperately needed a comprehensive rewiring of education, security, and economic policies oriented towards an 'AI-powered future' (Vempati, 2016, pp. 1–9).

Such impressions of the belatedness of Indian AI research are strengthened also by influential histories of postcolonial science. As David Arnold and others have suggested, the decades following Indian independence saw the establishment of a 'state-scientific' culture spearheaded by the country's first prime minister, Jawaharlal Nehru (Arnold, 2013, pp. 367–8). For Arnold, 'Nehruvian science' had five distinctive features—it was a socio-cultural programme aimed at fostering a modern democracy; it was 'conducted for the people but at the direction and discretion of the state'; it was a driver for building institutions, the 'temples of the new age' in Nehru's famous declaration; it was an integral part of India's new 'non-aligned' international policy; and finally, it was a historiographic project aiming to decode certain abiding patterns in the long civilizational arc of South Asia (Arnold, 2013, pp. 368–9). Naturally, such 'state science' had to address the pressing issues facing the new nation (which was additionally traumatized by the violent partition imposed on it as a part of the postcolonial settlement)—food shortages, infrastructural weaknesses, pervasive energy crises, and basic capacities for defence. Thus, Nehru's many pronouncements on science and technology (collected diligently by Singh, 1988) and the policies to which these related showcase scientific research and projects of many kinds—chemical, nuclear, hydro-electric, industrial, agricultural, military. But as far as one can see, they do not feature any awareness of, nor commitment to, the kind of AI research that was beginning to flourish in the US and Europe.

Given this paucity of AI research in official science in mid-twentieth-century India, it is all the more striking when, on turning to the SF of precisely these decades, we discover passages such as the following from Ray's 'Byomjatrir Diary':

> I am teaching Bidhushekhar to speak. It is going to be a long haul, I can tell, but he seems to be making a real effort. Prahlad laughs at the way he pronounces each word, which annoys Bidhushekhar no end. I have seen him stamp his metallic feet in protest, and make the same groaning noise.
>
> (Ray, 1961/2008, p. 13)

Here, Professor Shonku inaugurates some of the key themes of the story (and in fact, of the entire Shonku series as such)—machine learning, artificial and natural languages, and what Sianne Ngai calls the 'animatedness' of the automatized working body (Ngai, 2005, pp. 91–9). En route to Mars, Shonku is trying to teach his robot Bidhushekhar to speak Bengali, but the trouble is not only that the machine appears to be struggling to adapt to the grammar and logic of a natural language, but also that such a struggle is registered *affectively*—that is, as an emotional state—by the machine. Bidhushekhar's irritation and even anger appear not to be directed so much at his creator, Shonku, but at his human fellow servant, Prahlad, whose mockery of the robot's linguistic facility appears as an envious competition to win their master's affection. Matters become more complicated after the travellers have a traumatic encounter with the piscine Martians and barely manage to escape with their lives. While Prahlad's own speech becomes gradually more 'incoherent' because of the shock of the alien encounter, Bidhushekhar's language displays a sophistication that puzzles Shonku himself:

> Only Bidhushekhar seems his usual self, totally unperturbed by any worry or anxiety. He is seen muttering to himself from time to time. I realized one day that he was simply repeating some lines from the *Mahabharata* that he had

heard Prahlad read aloud, a very long time ago [. . .] 'Wouldst thee open the window?' [sic] said Bidhushekhar. Although his speech is now quite clear, for some strange reason, he has taken to speaking old, theatrical language. We might be back in Shakespeare's time!

(Ray, 1961/2008, pp. 23–4)

If the robot's capacity to mimic human speech is a function of its programmed 'memory', why should his designer find it 'strange'? The disjunction between input and output that puzzles Shonku is consistent with Ray's comic-ironic dismantling of his hero's scientism. Shonku is inclined to explain the unaccountable behaviour of the devices he builds as evidence of his own unfathomable scientific genius—'I have noticed before that when I make an object using all my scientific skill, often it starts doing things I had not bargained for [. . .] Perhaps I am unaware of the full extent of my own powers' (Ray, 1961/2008, p. 10). But as Bidhushekhar's transformation from 'an object' to an animated being shows, Shonku has much to learn both about his own limitations and of the limits of what he understands 'science' to be. After their Martian adventure, Bidhushekhar appears to have gained the mysterious ability to steer the spaceship to the planet Tafa, inhabited by beings who are no longer confined to restricted understandings of scientific practices and affiliations. Shonku is enraged and humiliated by what he interprets as the alien's snobbery—'What will you do with scientists, or science? Why don't you stay the way you are [. . .] We find your plain and simple words, your naivety, most entertaining!' (Ray, 1961/2008, pp. 28–9). Shonku's animated state at the end of the story uncannily echoes that of Bidhushekhar's at the beginning. But while the robot's agitation marked the beginning of his linguistic excellence and unprogrammed capacities to learn and act, his human creator's emotional turmoil signals the breakdown of such abilities. This inversion is typical of Ray's fiction, where larger issues regarding the meaning and valuation of scientific and technological work are often staged via the relationship between animated machines and automatized humans.[3]

Such science-fictional encounters stand *both* in contrast to Indian scientific discussions about AI in the decades following independence, *and* in some ways to the guiding assumptions of 'first-wave' AI research that was underway in the US and Europe during this time. Questions about work, 'reason', and modes of representation have always been fundamental to this research. From Aristotle to Leibniz and Čapek, efficiency and economy of labour have been one of the primary motivations behind the drive to invent intelligent machines (Nilson, 2010, pp. 3–11). Equally, from Boole and Frege to McCulloch and Turing, the question of intelligence has been intricately tied up with that of the mimetic capacities of language as well as that of the 'internal' modalities through which such capacities become operational (Nilson, 2010, pp. 13–38). All these lines of enquiry assumed fundamental importance to the 'first-wave' AI researchers working largely in American and European universities between the 1950s and 1970s on projects funded by their respective national departments of defence.

For Brian Cantwell Smith, this research worked with four assumptions—that 'the essence of intelligence is thought, meaning roughly rational deliberation'; that 'the ideal model of thought is logical inference'; that 'perception is at a lower level than thought'; and that 'the ontology of the world is [. . .] formal: discrete, well-defined, mesoscale objects exemplifying properties and standing in unambiguous relations' (Smith, 2019, pp. 7–8). It is precisely such assumptions, Smith argues, that led to the failures of such projects to incubate intelligence in machines on four counts (Smith, 2019, pp. 23–8):

1. *Neurological*—since all 'classical' AI systems 'consist of relatively few serial loci of activity . . . running at extreme speeds' while the human brain operates 'roughly 50 million times slower' but drawing its power 'from massive parallelisms'.
2. *Perceptual*—since the idea that the world is made up of 'discrete intelligible mesoscale objects' is a product of the human brain 'running on a 100-billion neuron device with 100 trillion interconnections honed over 500 million years of evolution' and *does not* correspond to reality as it is.
3. *Epistemological*—since intelligence was built on a model of rational, logical inference and not how it actually operates, which is more like 'skilful coping or navigation' in social situations into which each individual is 'embedded and enmeshed'.
4. *Ontological*—since these researchers also thought, incorrectly, that 'the world comes chopped up into neat, ontologically discrete objects'.

However, such failures are not only typical of 'first-wave' AI research. For Smith, the 'second-wave' AI research that took off in the 1990s—powered by 'deep' machine learning, 'big' data, and significant advances in computational power—is also likely to flounder unless it is guided by revised frameworks of judgement and reason. Smith understands the former as 'an overarching, systematic capacity for commitment, involving the whole commitment of a whole system to a whole world'; the latter, he interprets as necessarily incorporating 'some of the commitments and compulsions to action that are often associated with affectual states' (Smith, 2019, pp. xviii–xix). Smith's call for affective reason and ethical, collective judgement has obviously been raised before, most famously in Geoffrey Jefferson's 1949 Lister Oration:

> Not until a machine can write a sonnet or compose a concerto because of thoughts and emotions felt, and not by chance fall of symbols, could we agree that machine equals brain—that is, not only write it but know that it has written it. No mechanism could feel [. . .] pleasure at its success, grief when

> its valves fuse, be warmed by flattery, be made miserable by its mistake, be charmed by sex, be angry or depressed when it cannot get what it wants.
> (Nilson, 2010, p. 39)

And Alison Adam, among others, has pointed out that far from being an objective reality, logical reason is itself an ideological outcome of a patriarchal model of masculinity and gender relations (1996, pp. 48–9). While such critical re-appraisals of 'first-' or even of 'second-' wave AI research are clearly valuable, what is of interest here is that much of it was already anticipated in SF writing globally, including from regions seen to be lagging behind in AI research, for example, South Asia, *during* the decades of the mid-twentieth century when 'first-wave' research got underway. Such anticipatory properties of SF in relation to trajectories of scientific research and practices seem a compelling reason for considering the genre in any global history of AI.

To illustrate this anticipatory function, we can look a little more closely at another of Ray's short stories featuring Shonku, 'Professor Shonku O Robu' ('Professor Shonku and Robu', 1968), where issues such as ethical judgement, affective reason, language, personhood, and intelligence—that is, precisely those concepts and categories *missing* from 'first-wave' AI scientific research—appear as the basic building blocks of the narrative. The story begins with an account of Shonku's work on Robu—a machine he has built in less than two years in his laboratory on a shoe-string budget. One effect of such budgetary constraint is that Robu appears initially as decidedly non-anthropomorphic. It has a fixed, unchanging expression and the DIY aesthetics of its exposed wiring and circuitry appears to forbid the classic science-fictional blurring of human and machine identities that run from Čapek to Ravn. The news of Robu's phenomenal computational and linguistic abilities has electrified European and American scientists, and one of them, Rudolf Paumer, has invited Shonku to Heidelberg for a public demonstration of the machine, as well as for a chance to confer with another German scientist, Borgelt, who is also engaged in advanced AI research. Shonku is delighted at international recognition and the prospect of collaboration, and his only unease regarding Robu is that it seems to entirely lack any affective capacities—'Instead of a human brain, Robu has a tangled mass of wires, batteries and valves. Naturally, Robu cannot do a lot of things humans can. It cannot feel joy or pain, anger or envy. It merely works and answers questions' (Ray, 1961/2003, p. 101, my translation).

Things start well in Heidelberg, with Robu stunning Paumer and Borgelt with its computational speed. But when Shonku accepts Borgelt's invitation to visit his gothic mansion, things take a sinister turn. After he refuses Borgelt's offer to buy Robu, Shonku is suddenly threatened by him with violence—'"You must know it is much easier to destroy than to create life" [. . .] Borgelt came at me with the fingers of his right hand extended towards me and his eyes shining with a cruel pleasure' (Ray, 1961/2003, p. 111). It is at this point that the reader encounters the *novum* (Suvin, 2016, pp. 79–103) of the story—Borgelt claims he can deliver a fatal electric shock to Shonku, but from his actions it appears that he is about to do so with his fingers. In what follows, the explanation clinches the *novum's* narrative effect:

> Robu opened the door from the laboratory and entered the room. It still wore the squint and the smile [. . .] but in a flash, like a storm of steel it swept up Borgelt with his outstretched arms [. . .] It squeezed Borgelt's neck until his head spun around and popped out from the pressure, revealing a mass of electric wires.
>
> (Ray, 1961/2003, p. 111, my translation)

'Borgelt' turns out to be nothing other than an intelligent machine. Endowed with affective capacities (exactly the ones that Shonku laments are missing from his creation) by its human creator, the 'real' Borgelt, the machine has imprisoned and impersonated the latter because 'it could not tolerate the existence of an identical being' (Ray, 1961/2003, p. 112). Robu, whose circuits had been secretly tinkered with by Paumer in order to admit 'feelings', is able to rescue Shonku because it can both respond to its creator's distress and recognize the true nature of Borgelt's machine.

Here, I want to take a moment to dwell on the significance that Ray endows on the expressions and actions of the two intelligent machines. 'Borgelt' the machine is driven by the 'ugly feelings' (Ngai, 2005, p. 3) of envy, anger, and irritation against its human counterparts. Its imprisonment of the human Borgelt and assault on Shonku appear to conform to the classic 'sentiments of disenchantment' that Paolo Virno sees not so much as expressions of radical alienation from the contemporary systems of wage labour, but rather as key ingredients in its operational requirements (1996, p. 17). Furthermore, Ray's description confirms the perfect correspondence between its 'mind' and 'body'—the eyes glittering with unholy pleasure are clearly connected to the fingers stretched to deliver the fatal blow to Shonku. Not only does the 'personhood' of the machine appear to be complete in light of this correspondence between its 'feelings' and actions, but also it is a specific kind of personhood—that of a resentful and violent worker whose apparent rebellion against its owner turns out instead to merely be a wish to trade places with him, and not to challenge the system of ownership itself.

The 'personhood' of Shonku's machine turns out to be that of a different order. Its ludicrous squint and benign smile belie its capacity for violence, which (after all) is much more brutally effective than anything that the machine 'Borgelt' can muster. The narrative slyly directs the reader to suspect that the 'ugly feelings' such as envy and anger might be triggers for its assault on the fellow machine, since the competition between servants/workers for their owner's affectionate attention are an enduring theme in Ray's fiction. Yet, Robu's benign and comic expressions do turn out to be appropriate, since its violence turns out to be redemptive—not just because it saves Shonku's life, but more tellingly, because it exposes Shonku's illusions and presumptions about his ownership and mastery over his machines. As we know from the opening moments of the narrative, Shonku had failed to program such feelings into Robu. It is only after the unlooked-for (and secretive) cooperation of Paumer that Robu displays an intelligence with affective properties. In this sense, its 'personhood' is precisely the opposite to that of the 'Borgelt' machine. Seemingly submissively bonded with its owner, its violent actions interrogate and reveal the basis of ownership itself. Such a 'personhood' holds out at least the real possibility of resisting the smooth integration into systems of contemporary wage-labour. This is because it displays the capacities for ethical judgement and affective rationalism that Smith stipulates as essential to move beyond the impasse of the 'first' and 'second' waves of AI research.

I am not suggesting that Ray's SF was unique in its capacity to anticipate the necessary reassessments of AI research and practices that we are now seeing in abundance. However, it is worth reflecting on the literary–historical moment of its emergence in the mid-twentieth century from a region of the world quite accurately deemed as *lagging behind such research and practices*. I have written at length elsewhere (Mukherjee, 2020) about the relationship between SF, the techno-scientific policies pursued by postcolonial nation-states such as India, and the geo-politics of the 'Cold War' and the non-aligned movement. For our purposes here, such a literature suggests that in thinking about global history and global cultures of AI, we should take seriously not just the 'advanced' science and literatures of Europe and North America, but also those of the 'backward' of the post-colonial world. A comparative approach to the relation between the two might allow us to critically reflect on such designations as 'advanced' and 'backward' that are often taken as the pre-conditions for such scientific and cultural practices in the first place.

Endnotes

1. For a recent account of this multilingual development of SF in India, see Banerjee (2020).
2. I am thinking here not only of the seminal work of Beer (1983, 1996) and Levine (1988, 2002) on the relationship between science and literature, but also of those scholars whose insights have revealed the crucial relationship between SF and concepts, practices, and policies of science. These include Berger (1976, 1978), Dowling

(1986), Franklin (1988), Nudelman (1989), Porush (1991), Gray (1994), Nelson (2003), and Higgins (2012).

3. It might be worth revisiting Ngai's (2005, pp. 89–125) arguments regarding the relationship between affects such as 'animatedness', the changing conditions of work between 'high' and 'late' capitalism, and the racialization of the working bodies in order to think comparatively about what the animated intelligent machines in Ray's fiction say about the configuration between caste, science, and the project of postcolonial nation building. This is not to suggest any easy interchangeability between race and caste. But it may be productive to read the two categories analogously so that in the animated machines of Ray—implicitly positioned as the casted servants of 'gentleman' scientists such as Shonku—one can read the contradictions of postcolonial India's uneven insertion into the 'post-Fordist' world economy.

References

Adam, A. (1996) 'Construction of gender in the history of artificial intelligence', *IEEE Annals of the History of Computing*, 18(3), pp. 47–53.

Arnold, D. (2013) 'Nehruvian science and postcolonial India', *Isis*, 104(2), pp. 360–70.

Banerjee, S. (2020) *Indian science fiction: Patterns, history and hybridity*. Cardiff: University of Wales Press.

Beer, G. (1983) *Darwin's plots: Evolutionary narrative in Darwin, George Eliot, and nineteenth-century fiction*. London: Routledge & Kegan Paul.

Beer, G. (1996) *Open fields: Science in cultural encounter*. Oxford: Clarendon.

Berger, A. I. (1976) 'The triumph of prophecy: Science fiction and nuclear power in the post-Hiroshima period', *Science Fiction Studies*, 3(2), pp. 143–50.

Berger, A. I. (1978) 'Science-fiction critiques of the American space program, 1945–1958', *Science Fiction Studies*, 5(2), pp. 99–109.

Dowling, D. H. (1986) 'The atomic scientist: Machine or moralist?', *Science Fiction Studies*, 13(2), pp. 139–47.

Franklin, H. B. (1988) *War stars: The superweapon and the American imagination*. New York: Oxford University Press.

Gray, C. H. (1994) '"There will be war!": Future war fantasies and militaristic science fiction in the 1980s', *Science Fiction Studies*, 21(3), pp. 315–36.

Higgins, D. M. (2012) 'Science fiction and globalization', *Science Fiction Studies: Science Fiction and Globalization*, 39(3), pp. 369–73.

Levine, G. L. (1988) *Darwin and the novelists: Patterns of science in Victorian fiction*. Cambridge, MA: Harvard University Press.

Levine, G. L. (2002) *Dying to know: Scientific epistemology and narrative in Victorian England*. Chicago: University of Chicago Press.

Mukherjee, U. P. (2020) *Final frontiers: Science fiction and techno-science in non-aligned India*. Liverpool: Liverpool University Press.

Nelson, D. M. (2003) 'A social science fiction of fevers, delirium and discovery: *The Calcutta Chromosome*, the colonial laboratory, and the postcolonial new human', *Science Fiction Studies*, 30(2), pp. 246–66.

Ngai, S. (2005) *Ugly feelings*. Cambridge, MA: Harvard University Press.

Nilson, N. J. (2010) *The quest for artificial intelligence: A history of ideas and achievements*. Cambridge: Cambridge University Press.

Nudelman, R. (1989) 'Soviet science fiction and the ideology of Soviet society', *Science Fiction Studies*, 16(1), pp. 38–66.

Porush, D. (1991) 'Prigogine, chaos, and contemporary science fiction', *Science Fiction Studies*, 18(3), pp. 367–86.

Ray, S. (2003) *Shonku samagra*. Kolkata: Ananda.

Ray, S. (1961/2008) *The diary of a space traveller and other stories*, tr. C. Banerjee Divakaruni. New Delhi: Penguin.

Robinson, A. (1989) *Satyajit Ray: The inner eye*. London: Andrew Deutsch.

Schwarz, R. (1992) *Misplaced ideas: Essays on Brazilian culture*. London: Verso.

Singh, B. (ed.) (1988) *Jawaharlal Nehru on science and society: A collection of his writings and speech*. New Delhi: Nehru Memorial Museum and Library.

Smith, B. C. (2019) *The promise of artificial intelligence: Reckoning and judgement*. Cambridge, MA: MIT Press.

Suvin, D. (2016) *Metamorphoses of science fiction: On the poetics and history of a literary genre*. Oxford: Peter Lang.

Vempati, S. S. (2016) *India and the artificial intelligence revolution*. Washington DC: Carnegie India.

Virno, P. (1996) 'The ambivalence of disenchantment', in Virno, P., and Hardt, M. (eds.) *Radical thought in Italy*. Minneapolis: University of Minnesota Press, pp. 13–36.

16

Algorithmic Colonization of Africa

Abeba Birhane

16.1 Introduction

Traditional colonialism seeks unilateral power and domination over colonized people. It declares control of the social, economic, and political sphere by reordering and reinventing social order in a manner that benefits it.[1] In the age of algorithms, this control and domination occurs not through brute physical force, but rather through invisible and nuanced mechanisms, for example, control of digital ecosystems and infrastructure. Common to both traditional and algorithmic colonialism is the desire to dominate, monitor, and influence social, political, and cultural discourse through the control of core communication and infrastructure mediums. While traditional colonialism is often spearheaded by political and government forces, digital colonialism is driven by corporate tech monopolies—both of which are in search of wealth accumulation. The line between these forces is fuzzy as they intermesh and depend on one another. Political, economic, and ideological domination in the age of AI takes the form of 'technological innovation', 'state-of-the-art algorithms', and 'AI solutions' to social problems. Algorithmic colonialism, driven by profit maximization at any cost, assumes that human personality, behaviour, and action is raw material free for the taking. Knowledge, authority, and the power to sort, categorize, and order human activity rests with the technologist, for which we are merely data-producing 'human natural resources' (Zuboff, 2019, p. 100).

In *Surveillance Capitalism,* Zuboff (2019) remarks that *conquest patterns* unfold in three phases. First, the colonial power invents legal measures to provide justification for invasion. It then asserts declarations of territorial claims, and lastly, these declarations serve as tools for conquering by imposing a new reality, as they are legitimized and institutionalized. These invaders do not ask permission as they build ecosystems of commerce, politics, and culture, and declare legitimacy and inevitability. Conquests by declaration are invasive and sometimes serve as a subtle way to impose new facts on the social world. For those issuing the declarations, it is a way to get others to agree with those facts. For technology monopolies, such processes allow them to take things that live outside the market sphere and declare them as new market commodities. For example, in 2016 Facebook declared that it was creating a population density map of most of Africa using computer vision techniques, population data, and high-resolution satellite imagery (Greenwood, 2019). Facebook, in the process, assigned itself the authority to map, control, and create population knowledge of the continent. In doing so, not only did Facebook assume that the continent (its people, movement, and activities) was up for grabs for the purpose of data extraction and profit maximization, but also, by creating the population map, Facebook assumed authority over what is perceived as legitimate knowledge of the continent's population. Claims about creating knowledge about Africa's population distribution, connecting the unconnected, and providing humanitarian aid served as justification for Facebook's project (Greenwood, 2019). For many Africans, this echoed old colonial rhetoric: 'we know what these people need, and we are coming to save them. They should be grateful'.

Currently, much of Africa's digital infrastructure and ecosystem is controlled and managed by Western monopoly powers such as Facebook, Google, Uber, and Netflix (Kwet, 2019a). These tech monopolies present such exploitations as efforts to 'liberate the bottom billion', helping the 'unbanked' bank, or connecting the 'unconnected'—the same colonial tale now told under the guise of technology. Kimani (2019) writes:

> I find it hard to reconcile a group of American corporations, far removed from the realities of Africans, machinating a grand plan on how to save the unbanked women of Africa. Especially when you consider their recent history of data privacy breaches (Facebook) and worker exploitation (Uber).

Nonetheless, algorithmic colonialism dressed in 'technological solutions for the developing world' receives applause and rarely faces resistance and scrutiny.

It is important, however, to note that this is not a rejection of AI technology in general, or even of AI that is originally developed in the West. Rather, it is a rejection of a particular business model advanced by big technology monopolies that impose particular harmful values and interests while stifling approaches that do not conform to its values. When practised cautiously, access to quality data and use of various technological and AI developments indeed hold potential for benefits to the African continent specifically, and to the Global South in general. Access to quality data and secure infrastructure to share and store data, for example, can help improve the healthcare and education sector. Gender inequalities that plague every social, political, and economic sphere in Ethiopia, for instance, have yet to be exposed and mapped through data. Such data is invaluable in informing long-term gender-balanced decision making, which is an important first step to societal and structural changes. Such data also aids general societal-level awareness of gender disparities, which is central for grassroots change. Crucial issues across the continent surrounding healthcare and farming, for example, can be better understood and better solutions can be sought with the aid of locally developed technology. A primary example developed by Wayua, a Kenyan researcher, and her team is a machine learning model that can diagnose early stages of disease in the cassava plant (Hao, 2019).

Having said that, the wonder of technology and its benefits to the continent are not what this chapter aims to discuss. There already exist countless die-hard techno-enthusiasts, both within and outside the continent, some of whom are only too willing to blindly adopt anything 'data-driven' or AI-based without a second thought of the possible harmful consequences. Mentions of 'technology', 'innovation', and 'AI' continually and consistently bring with them evangelical advocacy, blind trust, and little (if any) critical engagement. They also bring with them invested parties that seek to monetize, quantify, and capitalize every aspect of human life, often at any cost. The atmosphere during CyFyAfrica 2019, The Conference on Technology, Innovation, and Society, in Tangier, Morocco, embodies this tech-evangelism. One of Africa's biggest annual conferences, CyFyAfrica is attended by various policy makers, UN delegates, ministers, governments, diplomats, media, tech corporations, and academics from over 65 (mostly African and Asian) nations (CyFy Africa, 2019). Although these leaders want to place 'the voice of the youth of Africa at the front and centre' (CyFy Africa, 2019), the atmosphere was one that can be summed up as a race to get the continent 'teched-up'. Efforts to implement the latest, state-of-the-art machine learning tool or the next cutting-edge application were applauded and admired while the few voices that attempt to bring forth discussions of the harms that might emerge with such technology get buried under the excitement. Given that the technological future of the continent is overwhelmingly driven and dominated by such techno-optimists, it is crucial to pay attention to the cautions that need to be taken and the lessons that need to be learned from other parts of the world.

This chapter examines how Western imported technology not only encodes Western values, objectives, and interests, but also impedes on African-developed technologies that would serve African needs better. More specifically, this chapter argues that various practices such as data collections, formalization, and algorithmicization of Africa by Western institutions, organizations, and corporations constitutes a form of digital colonization. The chapter concludes with the argument that for any technologies to be liberatory, they need to emerge from the needs of communities, and be developed and controlled by the communities that birth them.

16.2 Context matters

One of the central questions that needs attention in this regard is the relevance and appropriateness of AI software to users across the African continent—that is, software that is developed with the values, norms, and interests of Western societies (Biruk, 2018). Value systems vary from culture to culture and include such considerations as what is considered a vital problem and a successful solution, what constitutes sensitive personal information, and how prevalent health and socioeconomic issues are perceived. Certain matters that are considered critical problems in some societies may not be considered so in other societies. Solutions devised in one culture may not transfer well to another.

The harmful consequences of lack of attention to context is most stark in the health sector. In a comparative study that examined early breast cancer detection practices in Sub-Saharan Africa (SSA) and high-income countries, Black and Richmond (2019, p. 4) found that applying what has been 'successful' in the West, that is, mammograms, to SSA is not effective in reducing mortality from breast cancer. A combination of contextual factors, such as a lower age profile, presentation with advanced disease, and limited available treatment options all suggest that self-examination and clinical breast examination for early detection methods serve women in SSA better than medical practices designed for their counterparts in high-income countries. Throughout the continent, health care is one of the major areas where 'AI solutions' are actively sought, and Western-developed technological tools are imported. Without critical assessment of their relevance, the deployment of Western eHealth systems might pose more harm than benefit.

The importation of AI tools made in the West by Western technologists may not only be harmful because of the lack of transferability from one context to another, but also because they can hinder the development of local products. For example, 'Nigeria, one of the more technically developed countries in Africa, imports 90% of all software used in the country. The local production of software is reduced to add-ons or extensions [created] for mainstream packaged software' (Knowledge Commons Brasil, n.d.). The West's algorithmic invasion impoverishes development of local products while simultaneously leaving the continent dependent on its software and infrastructure.

16.3 Data are people

The African equivalent of Silicon Valley's tech start-ups can be found in every possible sphere of life around all corners of the continent—in 'Sheba Valley' in Addis Abeba, 'Yabacon Valley' in Lagos, and 'Silicon Savannah' in Nairobi, to name a few—all pursuing 'cutting-edge innovations' in sectors like banking, finance, healthcare, and education. They are headed by technologists and those in finance from both within and outside of the continent who seemingly want to 'solve' society's problems and use data and AI to provide quick 'solutions'. As a result, attempts to 'solve' social problems with technology are everywhere, which is exactly why problems arise. Complex cultural, moral, and political difficulties that are inherently embedded in history and context are reduced to those that can be measured and quantified—matters that can be 'fixed' with the latest algorithm. As dynamic and interactive human activities and processes are automated, they are inherently simplified to the engineers' and tech corporations' subjective notions of what they mean. The reduction of complex social problems to a matter that can be 'solved' by technology also treats people as passive objects for manipulation. Humans, however, far from being passive objects, are active meaning seekers embedded in dynamic social, cultural, and historical backgrounds (Birhane, 2017).

The discourse around 'data mining', 'abundance of data', and 'data-rich continent' shows the extent to which the individual behind each data point is disregarded. This muting of the individual—a person with fears, emotions, dreams, and hopes—is symptomatic of how little attention is given to each individual's well-being and consent, which should be the primary concerns if the goal indeed is to 'help' those in need. Furthermore, this discourse of 'mining' people for data is reminiscent of the colonizer attitude that declares humans as raw material free for the taking.

Data is necessarily always about something and never about an abstract entity. The collection, analysis, and manipulation of data potentially entails monitoring, tracking, and surveilling people. This necessarily impacts people directly or indirectly, whether it manifests as change in their insurance premiums or refusal of services. The erasure of the person behind each data point makes it easy to 'manipulate behaviour' or 'nudge' users (Weinmann, Schneider, and vom Brocke, 2016), often towards profitable outcomes for companies. Considerations regarding the well-being and welfare of the individual user, the long-term social impacts, and the unintended consequences of these systems on society's most vulnerable are pushed aside, if they enter the equation at all. For companies that develop and deploy AI, at the top of the agenda is the collection of more data to develop profitable AI systems, rather than the welfare of individual people or communities. This is most evident in Africa's FinTech sector, one of the prominent digital markets. People's digital traces–from their interactions with others to how much they spend on their mobile top-ups–are continually surveyed and monitored to form data for making loan assessments. Smartphone data from browsing history, likes, and locations are recorded forming the basis for a borrower's creditworthiness.

AI technologies that aid decision making in the social sphere are, for the most part, developed and implemented by the private sector whose primary aim is to maximize profit. Protecting individual privacy rights and cultivating a fair society is therefore the least of their concerns, especially if such practice gets in the way of 'mining' data, building predictive models, and pushing products to customers. As decision making with social outcomes is handed over to predictive systems developed by profit-driven corporations, not only are we allowing our social concerns to be dictated by corporate incentives, but also we are allowing moral questions to be dictated by corporate interest. 'Digital nudges'—behaviour modifications developed to suit commercial interests—are a prime example. As 'nudging' mechanisms become the norm for 'correcting' individuals' behaviour, eating habits, or exercising routines, those developing predictive models are bestowed with the power to decide what is 'correct'. In the process, individuals that do not fit our normative ideas of a 'fit body', 'good health', and 'good eating habits' end up being punished, outcast, and pushed further to the margin. When these models are imported as state-of-the-art technology that will save money and 'leapfrog' the continent into development, Western values and ideals are enforced, either deliberately or unintentionally.

16.4 Blind trust in AI hurts the most vulnerable

The use of technology within the social sphere often—intentionally or accidentally—focuses on punitive practices, whether it is to predict who will commit the next crime or who may fail to repay their loan. Constructive and rehabilitative questions such as why people commit crimes in the first place, or what can be done to rehabilitate and support those that have come out of prison, are rarely asked. Technology designed and applied with the aim of delivering security and order necessarily bring cruel, discriminatory, and inhumane practices to some. The cruel treatment of the Uighurs in China (Mozur, 2019) and the unfair disadvantaging of the poor in the US (Madden, 2019) are examples in this regard. Similarly, as cities like Harare (Mudzingwa, 2018), Kampala, and Johannesburg (Swart, 2018) introduce the use of facial recognition technology, the question of their accuracy (given they are trained on unrepresentative demographic datasets) and relevance should be of primary concern—not to mention the erosion of privacy and the surveillance state that emerges with these technologies.

With the automation of the social comes the automation and perpetuation of historical bias, discrimination, and injustice. As technological solutions are increasingly deployed and integrated into social, economic, and political spheres, so are the problems that arise with the digitization and automation of everyday life. Consequently, the harms of digitization and 'technological solutions' affect individuals and communities that are already at the margins of society.

FinTech and the digitization of lending has come to dominate the 'Africa rising' narrative, framed as a solution that supposedly will 'lift many out of poverty'. Since its arrival in the continent in the 1990s, FinTech has largely been portrayed as a technological revolution that will 'leap-frog' Africa into development. The typical narrative (Hussain, n.d.) preaches the microfinance industry as a service that exists to accommodate the underserved and a system that creates opportunities for the 'unbanked' who have no access to a formal banking system. Through its microcredit system, the narrative goes, Africans living in poverty can borrow money to establish and expand their microenterprise ventures. However, a closer critical look reveals that the very idea of FinTech microfinancing is a reincarnation of colonialist era rhetoric that works for Western multinational shareholders. These stakeholders get wealthier by leaving Africa's poor communities in perpetual debt. In Bateman's (2019) words: 'like the colonial era mining operations that exploited Africa's mineral wealth, the microcredit industry in Africa essentially exists today for no other reason than to extract value from the poorest communities'. Far from a tool that 'lifts many out of poverty' FinTech is capitalist market economics premised upon profitability of perpetual debt of the poorest. For instance, although Safaricom is 35% owned by the Kenyan government, 40% of the shares are controlled by Vodafone, a UK multinational corporation, while the other 25% are held mainly by wealthy foreign investors (Loubere, 2019). According to Loubere (2019), Safaricom reported an annual profit of $620 million USD in 2019, which was directed into dividend payments for investors. Like traditional colonialism, wealthy individuals and corporations of the Global North continue to profit from some of the poorest communities—except that now it takes place under the guise of 'revolutionary' and 'state-of-the-art' technology. Despite the common discourse of paving a way out of poverty, FinTech actually profits from poverty. It is an endeavour engaged in expansion of its financial empire through indebting Africa's poorest.

Loose regulations and lack of transparency and accountability under which the microfinance industry operates, as well as overhyping the promise of technology, make it difficult to challenge and interrogate its harmful impacts. Like traditional colonialism, those that benefit from FinTech, microfinancing, and various lending apps operate from a distance. For example, Branch (n.d.) and Tala (Forbes, n.d.), two of the most prominent FinTech apps in Kenya, operate from their California headquarters and export 'Silicon Valley's curious nexus of technology, finance, and developmentalism' (Donovan and Park, 2019). Furthermore, the expansion of Western-led digital financing systems brings with it a negative knock-on effect on existing local traditional banking and borrowing systems that have long existed and functioned in harmony with locally established norms and mutual compassion.

16.5 Lessons from the Global North

Globally, there is an increasing awareness of the problems that arise with automating social affairs, illustrated by ongoing attempts to integrate ethics into computer science programmes within academia (Fiesler, Garrett, and Beard, 2020), various 'ethics boards' within industry, as well as various proposed policy guidelines. These approaches to develop, implement, and teach responsible and ethical AI take multiple forms, perspectives, and directions, and present a plurality of views. This plurality is not a weakness, but rather a desirable strength necessary for accommodating a healthy, context-dependent remedy. Insisting on a single AI integration framework for ethical, social, and economic issues that arise in various contexts and cultures is not only unattainable but also imposes a one-size-fits-all, single worldview. Companies like Facebook—who enter into African 'markets' or embark on projects such as creating population density maps with little or no regard for local norms or cultures—are in danger of enforcing a one-size-fits-all imperative. Similarly, for African developers, start-ups, and policy makers working to solve local problems with home-grown solutions, what is considered ethical and responsible needs to be seen as inherently tied to local contexts and experts.

AI, like big data, is a buzzword that gets thrown around carelessly; what it refers to is notoriously contested across various disciplines, and oftentimes it is mere mathematical snake oil that rides on overhype (Narayanan, 2019). Researchers within the field, reporters in the media, and industries that benefit from it all contribute to the overhype and exaggeration of the capabilities of AI, which makes it extremely difficult to challenge the deeply ingrained attitude that 'all Africa is lacking is data and AI'. The sheer enthusiasm with which data and AI are subscribed to as gateways out of poverty or disease would make one think that all social, economic, educational, and cultural problems are immutable unless Africa imports state-of-the-art technology.

The continent would do well to adopt a dose of critical appraisal when regulating, deploying, and reporting AI. This requires challenging the mindset that portrays AI with god-like power and as something that exists and learns independent of those that create it. People create, control, and are responsible for any system. For the most part, such people consist of a homogeneous group of predominantly white, middle-class, males from the Global North. Like any other tool, AI is one that reflects human inconsistencies, limitations, biases, and the political and emotional desires of the individuals behind it and the social and cultural ecologies that embed it—a mirror that reflects how society operates: unjust and prejudiced against some individuals and communities.

AI tools that are deployed in various spheres are often presented as objective and value free. In fact, some automated systems put forward in domains such as hiring (HireVue, n.d.) and policing (PredPol, n.d.) make the explicit claim that these tools eliminate human bias. Automated systems, after all, apply the same rules to everybody. In fact, this claim is one of the single most erroneous and harmful misconceptions as far as automated systems are concerned. As O'Neil explains, 'algorithms are opinions embedded in code'. This widespread misconception further prevents individuals from asking questions and demanding explanations. How we see the world and how we choose to represent the world is reflected in the algorithmic models of the world that we build. The tools we build necessarily embed, reflect, and perpetuate socially and culturally held stereotypes and unquestioned assumptions.

For example, during the CyFyAfrica 2019 conference, the Head of the UN Security Council Counter-Terrorism Committee Executive Directorate addressed work that is being developed globally to combat online terrorism. Unfortunately, the Director focused explicitly on Islamic groups, portraying an unrealistic and harmful image of global online terrorism (CyFy Africa, 2019). Contrary to such portrayals, more than 60% of US mass shootings in 2019 were, for instance, carried out by white-nationalist extremists (Scribd, 2017). In reality, when the concept of terrorism is defined in a manner that is free of inaccurate and harmful stereotypes, we find that white supremacist terrorists carried out more attacks than any other group in recent years in the US (Scribd, 2017).

In Johannesburg, one of the most surveilled cities in Africa, 'smart' CCTV networks provide a powerful tool to segregate, monitor, categorize, and punish individuals and communities that have historically been disadvantaged. Vumacam, an AI-powered surveillance company, is fast expanding throughout South Africa, normalizing surveillance and erecting apartheid-era segregation and punishment under the guise of 'neutral' technology and security (Vumacam, n.d.). Vumacam currently provides a privately owned video-management-as-a-service infrastructure (Kwet, 2019b), with a centralized repository of video data from CCTV. Kwet (2019b) explains that in the apartheid era, passbooks served as a means to segregate the population, inflict mass violence, and incarcerate the black communities. Similarly, 'Smart surveillance solutions like Vumacam are explicitly built for profiling, and threaten to exacerbate these kinds of incidents'. Although the company claims its technology is neutral and unbiased, what it deems 'abnormal' and 'suspicious' behaviour disproportionately impacts those that have historically been oppressed. What the Vumacam software flags as 'unusual behaviour' tends to be dominated by the black demographic and most commonly those that do manual labour, for example, construction workers (Kwet, 2019b). According to Clarno, 'The criminal in South Africa is always imagined as a black male' (2017, p. 125). Despite its claim to neutrality, Vumacam software perpetuates this harmful stereotype.

Stereotypically held views drive what is perceived as a problem and the types of technology we develop to 'resolve' them. In the process, we amplify and perpetuate those harmful stereotypes, and then interpret the findings through the looking glass of technology as evidence that confirms our biased intuitions and further reinforces stereotypes. Any classification, clustering, or discrimination of human behaviours and characteristics that AI systems produce reflects socially and culturally held stereotypes, not an objective truth.

A robust body of research in the growing field of algorithmic injustice illustrates that various applications of algorithmic decision making result in biased and discriminatory outcomes (Benjamin, 2019; Noble, 2018). These discriminatory outcomes often affect individuals and groups who are already on society's margins: those that are viewed as deviants and outliers—that is, people who do not conform to the status quo. Given that the most vulnerable are disproportionately affected by technology, it is important that their voices are central in the design and implementation of any technology that is used on or around them. However, contrary to this, many of the ethical principles applied to AI are firmly utilitarian; the underlying principle is the best outcome for the greatest number of people. This, by definition, means that solutions that centre on minorities are never sought. Even when unfairness and discrimination in algorithmic decision-making processes are brought to the fore—for instance, upon discovering that women have been systematically excluded from entering the tech industry (Lambrecht and Tucker, 2019), minorities forced into inhumane treatment (Buckley, Mozur, and Ramzy, 2019; Mozur, 2019), and systematic biases have been embedded into predictive policing systems (Richardson, Schultz, and Crawford, 2019)—the 'solutions' sought do not often centre on those that are disproportionately impacted. Mitigating proposals devised by corporate and academic ethics boards are often developed without the consultation and involvement of the people that are affected. Prioritizing the voice of those disproportionately impacted every step of the way, including in the design, development, and implementation of any technology, as well as in policy making, requires actually consulting and involving vulnerable groups of society. This, of course, requires a considerable amount of time, money, effort, and genuine care for the welfare of the marginalized, which often goes against most corporations' business models. Consulting those who are potentially likely to be negatively impacted might (at least as far as the West's Silicon Valley is concerned) also seem beneath the 'all-knowing' engineers who seek to unilaterally provide a 'technical fix' for any complex social problem.

16.6 Conclusion

As Africa grapples with the need to digitize and automate various services while preventing the consequential harm that technology causes, policy makers, governments, and firms that develop and apply various technologies to the social sphere need to think hard about what kind of society we want and what kind of society technology drives. Protecting and respecting the rights, freedoms, and privacy of the youth that the leaders want to put at the front and centre should be prioritized. This can only happen if guidelines and safeguards for individual rights and freedom are put in place, continually maintained, revised, and enforced. In the spirit of communal values that unify such a diverse continent, 'harnessing' technology to drive development means prioritizing the welfare of the most vulnerable in society and the benefit of local communities—not distant Western start-ups or tech monopolies.

The question of technologization and digitalization of the continent is also a question of what kind of society we want to live in. The continent has plenty of techno-utopians but few who would stop and ask these difficult and critical questions. If African youth are to solve their own problems, they must decide what they want to amplify and show the rest of the world, and to shift the tired portrayal of the continent (hunger and disease) by focusing attention on the positive vibrant culture (such as philosophy, art, and music) that the continent has to offer. It also means not importing the latest state-of-the-art machine learning systems or some other AI tools without questioning the underlying purpose and contextual relevance, who benefits from it, and who might be disadvantaged by its application. Moreover, supporting African youth in the AI field means creating programs and databases that serve various local communities and not blindly importing Western AI systems founded upon individualistic and capitalist drives. In a continent where much of the Western narrative is hindered by negative images such as migration, drought, and poverty, Africans using AI to solve problems themselves starts with a rejection of such stereotypical images. This means using AI as a tool that aids Africans in portraying themselves how they want to be understood and perceived: as a continent where community values triumph and no one is left behind.

Endnote

1. This chapter is an edited version of an article that was first published in SCRIPTed and is licensed under a Creative Commons Attribution-NonCommercial-NoDerivatives 4.0 International (CC BY-NC-ND 4.0) licence. Birhane, A. (2020) 'Algorithmic colonization of Africa' SCRIPTed [online], 17(2) p. 389. https://script-ed.org/?p=3888. doi:10.2966/scrip.170220.389

References

Bateman, M. (2019) 'The problem with microcredit in Africa', Africa is a Country [online], 10 September. Available at: https://africasacountry.com/2019/09/a-fatal-embrace (Accessed 2 April 2020).

Benjamin, R. (2019) *Race after technology: Abolitionist tools for the new Jim code*. Cambridge: Polity Press.

Birhane, A. (2017) 'Descartes was wrong: "A person is a person through other persons"'. Aeon [online]. Available at: https://aeon.co/ideas/descartes-was-wrong-a-person-is-a-person-through-other-persons (Accessed 30 May 2022).

Biruk, C. (2018) *Cooking data: Culture and politics in an African research world*. Durham, NC: Duke University Press.

Black, E. and Richmond, R. (2019) 'Improving early detection of breast cancer in sub-Saharan Africa: Why mammography may not be the way forward', *Globalization and Health*, 15(1), pp. 1–11.

Branch. (n.d.) 'The power of financial access', Branch [online]. Available at: https://branch.co/about (Accessed 3 April 2020).

Buckley, C., Mozur, P., and Ramzy, A. (2019) 'How China turned a city into a prison', The New York Times [online], 4 April. Available at: https://www.nytimes.com/interactive/2019/04/04/world/asia/xinjiang-china-surveillance-prison.html?smid=tw-share (Accessed 18 June 2019).

Clarno, A. (2017) *Neoliberal apartheid: Palestine/Israel and South Africa after 1994*. Chicago: University of Chicago Press.

CyFy Africa (ORF). (2019) The *conference on technology, innovation & society, 7–9 June, 2019, Tangier, Morocco*. Available at: https://www.orfonline.org/cyfy-africa/ (Accessed 20 September 2019).

Donovan, K., and Park, E. (2019) 'Perpetual debt in the silicon savannah', Boston Review [online], 20 September. Available at: https://bostonreview.net/class-inequality-global-justice/kevin-p-donovan-emma-park-perpetual-debt-silicon-savannah (Accessed 5 April 2020).

Fiesler, C., Garrett, N., and Beard, N. (2020) 'What do we teach when we teach tech ethics? A syllabi analysis', in Proceedings of the 51st ACM *technical symposium on computer science education: SIGCSE '20, 11–14 March, 2020, Portland, OR*. New York: ACM, pp. 289–95.

Forbes. n.d. 'Tala', *Forbes* [online]. Available at: https://www.forbes.com/companies/tala/ (Accessed 3 April 2020).

Greenwood, F. (2019) 'Facebook is putting us all on the map whether we like it or not', *OneZero* [online], 29 June. Available at: https://onezero.medium.com/facebook-is-putting-us-all-on-the-map-whether-we-like-it-or-not-c3f178a8b430 (Accessed 26 October 2019).

Hao, K. (2019) 'The future of AI research is in Africa', MIT Technology Review [online], 21 June. Available at: https://www.technologyreview.com/s/613848/ai-africa-machine-learning-ibm-google/ (Accessed 10 November 2019).

HireVue. (n.d.) Pre-employment assessment & video interview tools. Available at: https://www.hirevue.com/ (Accessed 2 December 2019).

Hussain, N. (n.d.) 'Microfinance and fintech', MIT Technology Review *Pakistan* [online], Available at: https://web.archive.org/web/20171207175109/http://www.technologyreview.pk/microfinance-and-FinTech/ (Accessed 20 March 2020).

Kimani, M. (2019) '5 reasons why Facebook's new cryptocurrency "Libra" is bad news for Africa', *Kioneki.com* [online], 28 June. Available at: https://kioneki.com/2019/06/28/5-reasons-why-facebooks-new-cryptocurrency-libra-is-bad-news-for-africa/ (Accessed 28 October 2019).

Knowledge Commons Brasil. (n.d.) 'Digital colonialism & the Internet as a tool of cultural hegemony', Knowledge Commons Brasil [online]. Available at: https://web.archive.org/web/20190731000456/http://www.knowledgecommons.in/brasil/en/whats-wrong-with-current-internet-governance/digital-colonialism-the-internet-as-a-tool-of-cultural-hegemony/ (Accessed 10 November 2019).

Kwet, M. (2019a) 'Digital colonialism is threatening the Global South', Aljazeera Science and Technology [online], Available at: https://www.aljazeera.com/indepth/opinion/digital-colonialism-threatening-global-south-190129140828809.html (Accessed 18 July 2019).

Kwet, M. (2019b) 'Smart CCTV networks are driving an AI-powered apartheid in South Africa'. Vice [online], 22 November. Available at: https://www.vice.com/en_us/article/pa7nek/smart-cctv-networks-are-driving-an-ai-powered-apartheid-in-south-africa?utm_campaign=sharebutton (Accessed 22 March 2020).

Lambrecht, A. and Tucker, C. E. (2019) 'Algorithmic bias? An empirical study into apparent gender-based discrimination in the display of STEM career ads'. *Management Science*, 65(7), pp. 2966–81.

Loubere, N. (2019) 'The curious case of M-Pesa's miraculous poverty reduction powers', Developing Economics: A Critical Perspective *on* Development Economics [blog], 14 June. Available at: https://developingeconomics.org/2019/06/14/the-curious-case-of-m-pesas-miraculous-poverty-reduction-powers (Accessed 28 March 2020).

Madden, M. (2019) 'The devastating consequences of being poor in the digital age', The New York Times [online], 25 April. Available at: https://www.nytimes.com/2019/04/25/opinion/privacy-poverty.html (Accessed 10 November 2019).

Mozur, P. (2019) 'One month, 500,000 face scans: How China is using A.I. to profile a minority', The New York Times [online], 14 April. Available at: https://www.nytimes.com/2019/04/14/technology/china-surveillance-artificial-intelligence-racial-profiling.html (Accessed 24 June 2019).

Mudzingwa, F. (2018) 'Mnangagwa's govt getting facial recognition tech from China'. *TechZim*. Available at: https://www.techzim.co.zw/2018/04/mnangagwas-govt-getting-facial-recognition-tech-from-china/ (Accessed 10 April 2020).

Narayanan, A. (2019) 'The 2019 Arthur Miller lecture on science and ethics'. *Massachusetts Institute of Technology*. Available at: https://sts-program.mit.edu/event/arthur-miller-lecture-on-science-and-ethics/ (Accessed 18 March 2020).

Noble, S. U. (2018) *Algorithms of oppression: How search engines reinforce racism*. New York: New York University Press.

PredPol. (n.d.) *Predict prevent crime: Predictive policing software*. Available at: https://www.predpol.com/ (Accessed 1 December 2019).

Richardson, R., Schultz, J., and Crawford, K. (2019) 'Dirty data, bad predictions: How civil rights violations impact police data, predictive policing systems, and justice'. *NYU Law Review Online*, 94, pp. 15–55.

Scribd. (2017) *White supremacist extremism JIB*. Available at: https://www.scribd.com/document/356288299/White-Supremacist-Extremism-JIB (Accessed 3 September 2019).

Swart, H. (2018) 'Joburg's new hi-tech surveillance cameras: A threat to minorities that could see the law targeting thousands of innocents', Daily Maverick [online], 28 September. Available at: https://www.dailymaverick.co.za/article/2018-09-28-joburgs-new-hi-tech-surveillance-cameras-a-threat-to-minorities-that-could-see-the-law-targeting-thousands-of-innocents/ (Accessed 15 July 15).

Vumacam. (n.d.) 'A smart surveillance solution', Vumacam [online]. Available at: https://www.vumacam.co.za/features/ (Accessed 27 March 2020).

Weinmann, M., Schneider, C., and vom Brocke, J. (2016) 'Digital nudging', *Business & Information Systems Engineering*, 58(6), pp. 433–6.

Zuboff, S. (2019) *The age of surveillance capitalism: The fight for a human future at the new frontier of power*. London: Profile Books.

17

Artificial Intelligence Elsewhere

The Case of the Ogbanje

Rachel Adams

17.1 Introduction

New forms of imperialism are at work in the advanced digital technologies we have come to name artificial intelligence (AI). This imperialism is complex and multifaceted—alive not only in the hegemonic industry of big tech and the racializing function it plays (Benjamin, 2019; Browne, 2015; Noble, 2018) and the military desires of old and new imperial centres—but also in the culture of AI and in the systems of representation by which we recognize crafted life, whether machinic or otherwise. In this chapter, I take this last motif as my focus, and explore a different cultural perspective on nonhuman intelligence.[1] This work builds on the work of scholars from around the world, including many of the contributors of this edited collection, who have engaged in critical thought on cultural representations of AI and automata, and how such representations—and the narratives in which they are situated—influence the design and public perceptions of AI (see also Cave, Dihal, and Dillon, 2020). This body of work has drawn attention to the lack of critical inquiry on representations and narratives of AI outside of the Western canon. Where the West continues to dominate the cultural landscape around how AI is imagined and understood, the project of decolonization remains out of reach. My aim here is to contribute to the growing thought and scholarship of decolonization, and what it might mean and require to decolonize AI, through an exploration of Nigerian accounts of nonhuman intelligence.

In this respect, I interpret decolonization as a political movement concerned with the search for freedom, human dignity, and re-communitization marred by colonial enterprises and their afterlives. Scholarship can contribute to this political movement in interpreting the signs, symbols, and systems of our worlds, offering analytical frameworks with which to understand the connections between AI practices today and the history of colonialism and empire, and pathways out of the racial and unjust impasses in which postcolonial nations and peoples may still be rendered (Adams, 2021).

Decolonization, therefore, demands action on two key fronts: first, to make intelligible and abolish the continued operations of coloniality and empire at work in the world today—a major focus of which is the eradication of the idea of race; and second, to collectively reimagine a multifarious world space and a new form of democracy of the world, centred on the radical idea of true human equality (Adams, 2021; Grosfoguel, 2007; Mignolo and Walsh, 2018; Ndlovu-Gatsheni, 2015). While the first objective remains a critical touchstone for the work of decolonization, the second objective has perhaps received less critical attention. Just like the imperative to make intelligible the continued workings of coloniality, the imperative to collectively reimagine a multifarious world space is complex, and not without politics. What do we take with us into the truly decolonized world we seek to create? What of those who do not wish to be part of this new world? How do we avoid creating a new kind of singular truth or ideal that itself delimits ways of knowing or being that do not readily ascribe to its principles, and repeats a new hegemony?

While these questions are fundamental to debate and consider, what decoloniality insists upon in the second objective outlined earlier is the delivery of humanity from the myopia of the Western imagination, and the limitations of which its analytical frameworks reveal. Indeed, we must find new explanations and symbols for the world, look elsewhere for the answers to the questions we face, and create new histories. With respect to AI, this becomes particularly important as the Western imaginary—both literary and political—has not been able to fully answer the questions AI is raising about the future of humanity. Nor should it, as a singular cultural system built on forms of oppression and superiority, the effects of which we are still grappling with today. Thus, to venture beyond the Western imaginary in considering some of the major ethical questions that AI poses involves exploring, making visible, and celebrating alternate frameworks of knowledge and ways of being, which radically expand the boundaries of thought and experience by which to understand AI and its effects on—and relations within—society.

Accordingly, this chapter explores the politics and ethics of AI within an alternate cultural framing. I am primarily interested in how a cultural and traditional system outside of the West has understood and narrated human relations with nonhuman intelligence and enchanted objects (artefacts that display some kind of agency, which are therefore somewhat analogous to AI), and how it has handled questions of representation, anthropomorphism, and gender. I focus my enquiry here on the history and literature of the transgendered *ogbanje* (or *abiku*)[2]—a changeling child or reincarnated evil spirit—of Nigerian Yoruba and Igbo traditions, and I consider two key questions. First, taking the *ogbanje* as a figure of nonhuman (or what might be better expressed as 'beyond-human') intelligence, what role do anthropomorphism, representation, and gender play in making recognizable the intelligence associated with this figure? Second, what does it mean for the decolonial AI enterprise to consider alternative imaginaries—such as those found within the Yoruba and Igbo traditions—for transcending the normative binaries that AI fortifies, and what kind of politics does this engender and require?

This chapter is set out in four parts. The first briefly summarizes what I speak of as the crisis of representation in the portrayal of AI today, which has been largely informed by a Western imaginary. The second part introduces the notion of 'AI elsewhere' and considers, briefly, African philosophies and histories of technology. In the third part, I explore Yoruba and Igbo literature—both historical and contemporary—wherein we find portrayals of the *ogbanje* and the cultural traditions of which it is a part, with a focus on the politics of representation, anthropomorphism, and gender in these figures of nonhuman intelligence and enchanted objects. It is important to note that much of the literature I engage with here may not be categorized by its authors as 'Yoruba', 'Igbo', or even 'Nigerian'. I address this tension when I introduce these texts, as this provides important context to the concluding part of this chapter, which considers the implications of this enquiry for the project of decolonizing AI and the politics such an enquiry engenders.

17.2 AI and the crisis of representation

That there is a crisis of representation in portrayals of AI is now a fairly well-traversed issue,[3] thanks to the contributions of scholars such as Stephen Cave and Kanta Dihal (2018, 2020, 2021), among others. This crisis can be summarized as follows: representations of intelligent machines—whether in film or media, or the design of robots themselves—follow a well-trodden and now stereotyped path. Intelligent machines in the workplace or military that—of necessity to the stereotype—depict advanced forms of intelligence and power, are portrayed as muscular men. Those that are designed for domestic or personal use—such as Amazon's personal assistant Alexa—are presented as female, whether through softer-form hardware, or a female voice and name (Adams, 2019; Adams and Ni Loideain, 2019; and Ni Loideain and Adams, 2020). This gendering corresponds to a historical pattern in Western narrative representations of domestic robots or artificial life presented in an ideal female form subject to the total control of their male maker (Adams, 2019). Whether male or female in presentation, AI tends to be depicted as white (Cave and Dihal, 2020; 2021), thus reproducing the colonialist conceit of whiteness as a symbol of advanced intelligence.

As Cave and Dihal point out, once a machine is portrayed as human-like and thus anthropomorphized, it is typically both gendered and racialized.

Implicitly, the decisions of the robot-creator are bound up in a value judgement about the ontology of a human: what is it to be human, and what does being human look like, such that it can be mimicked in the design of a machine? Anthropomorphism supports the reader in recognizing the other (whether animal, machine, or otherwise) by presenting it in a human or human-like form, and therefore lessening its otherness. In this respect, anthropomorphism is imperialist in the way that it positions the reader as the point zero of the symbolic order of the cultural product (such as a novel or film), requiring anything which sits outside of the reader's frame of reference to be refashioned to fit within it. This idea of the 'point zero' from which everything else is deviant or nonnormative, is the definition of whiteness according to many critical race and decolonial scholars (Grosfoguel, 2011). Once human, or human-like, the other—and its behaviour—can be interpreted, rationalized, and understood, even sympathized with and trusted. It is precisely on this basis that anthropomorphism is considered a tool to build trust in AI (Cave and Dihal, 2020; 2021): human-like, the robot can be more easily recognized by dominant forms of reason and empathy, making it less 'other' and therefore less worrisome or fearful. Anthropomorphism is, then, fundamentally a tool of cultural translation for the benefit of the reader or receiver, which objectifies that which is anthropomorphized. The anthropomorphized human-like thing is thus distinguished from the human reader precisely on account of its objectification: a dual order is created that privileges the cultural system of those whom the anthropomorphism is designed to benefit. This is an important discussion when we are considering the ways in which the history of race and racialization is embedded within AI today: the history of a series of devices—cultural, political, military, scientific, and more—that sought to distinguish humanity between humans and the human-like. I return to this in the fourth part of this chapter below.

In short, the effects of this crisis of representation in AI are to thwart what decoloniality seeks to make possible: that is, the notion of radical human equality and the eradication of the idea of race. For as long as we fail to challenge the whiteness of the presentation of AI, and the normative and patriarchal gendering with which this is bound, the future will not be decolonized.

17.3 AI elsewhere?

In order to transcend the limitations of dominant representations of AI, we must consider alternatives. As Cave and Dihal (2021) point out, this consideration can raise a new kind of diversity dilemma as presenting a robot as anything other than white raises concerns about the association between robots as slaves or subservient to (white) humans. This dilemma is in fact demonstrative of the power of the conceit of race, which overrules the figurative narration of an AI by its designer. When an AI is presented as white, it is associated with intelligence; when presented as non-white, it is associated with servility. Western reason, which created this conceit, cannot undo it. We must, then, look outside of Western thought on the history and philosophy of technology, and the canon of Western representations of intelligent machines or nonhuman intelligence, in building alternate representational frameworks for AI. African histories and philosophies of technology offer an insightful counterpoint and alternative, and—as we shall see—prompt a radical extension of the kinds of ethical questions we can ask about AI.

Achille Mbembe, one of the world's leading scholars on race and the post-colony,[4] writes of African histories of technology as wholly divergent to the Western model which, he explains, is deeply embedded in the strict bifurcation of humans from nature and the objects and tools they fashion to control and shape their environments. This structure of Western reason has, he argues, resulted in 'a deep anxiety concerning the proper relation between people/humans, on the one hand, and things/objects, on the other' (Mbembe, 2021), aggravated now by the advent of advanced digital technologies: '[t]he belief is that people invent things but that people are not things. This being the case, the fear is of a time when things take the place of people and people are treated like things' (Mbembe, 2021). What he articulates here is one of the West's primary ethical concerns of AI technologies.[5] In contrast, historical African relations with technology—with the tools, artefacts, and objects fashioned in different African cultures and traditions—were far more fluid. He writes:

> That Africa did not invent thermobaric bombs does not mean that it created neither technical objects nor works of art, or that it was closed to borrowings or to innovation. It privileged other modes of existence, within which technology in the strict sense constituted neither a force of rupture and diffraction, nor a force of divergence and separation, but rather a force of splitting and multiplication. At the heart of this dynamic, each concrete and distinct reality was always and by definition a symbol of something else, of another figure and structure.
>
> (Mbembe, 2021, p. 164)

The structure of human–object relations was relationally constitutive, transmorphic, and in flux. Objects could be endowed with a subjectivity that was never fixed and always reciprocal—as such, participating in the ecosystems of social life: 'even when mere utensils and devices in themselves, they had a share in life' (Mbembe, 2021, p. 166). Critically, too, such objects were not traditionally tied—as they are in the West or within systems of global capital—to property or ownership.

Within such a framing of the human/technological, new kinds of questions emerge, including what function technologies play in the ways societies and groups make sense of themselves and their world-spaces, and how notions of identity and humanness come to be reflected in technologies like in anthropomorphic devices? We can further ask what strategies are used to make intelligent agents culturally identifiable, and if gender is intrinsic to the representation of intelligent agents?

These questions form the basis of the more focused consideration of the Yoruba and Igbo tradition of the *ogbanje* in Section 17.4, and how such traditions may prompt new thought on AI ethics and contribute to the ongoing enterprise of its decolonization by retreating outside of the Western frame.

17.4 The case of the *Ogbanje*

The *ogbanje*—or *abiku* in Yoruba—is a spirit child of Igbo myth. It exists in liminal spaces between life and death, repeatedly leaving and returning to the earthly world, as manifested through its birth to the same mother, and subsequent death in infancy or childhood. The nomenclature *abiku* means 'born to die', deriving from the Yoruba *abi*—'that which is born', and *iku*—'death'. The Igbo word *ogbanje* means 'the child who comes and goes' or 'that which takes many trips', referring to the spirit's journeying to and from the earthly world. Indeed, the *ogbanje* participates in a cyclical and relational ontology between the spirit world where the dead reside or pass through, and earthly worlds. It is a child of gods, whose earthly mother is its vessel into the human world. In many Nigerian traditions,[6] such a phenomenon was considered a curse and misfortune on those women—and communities—who bore such children. But these children also exhibit striking features, character traits, or abilities by which their link to the realm of the deities is made manifest (Achebe, 1986), and which give further testament to their intelligence being beyond-human.

The *ogbanje* is similar to a changeling child within a Western framing which, traditionally, referred to the artificial or fairy child that was put in place of a real child stolen by fairies or demons of some kind. Beth Singler (2020) explored the role of the parent–child narrative in AI—insofar as the AI is broadly analogous to a progeny of its human maker—and notes variations of the changeling child as a motif in futures fiction. Critically, too, the AI is comparable to a changeling child—or in this case, an *ogbanje*—to the extent that it constitutes (or is thought to constitute) an intelligence and agency which is, to a degree, nonhuman.

Chinwe Achebe—a professor of education in Nigeria, and married to Chinua Achebe, whose work we turn to momentarily—has written a systematic account of the *ogbanje* in her 1986 *The World of the Ogbanje*, in which she illustrates the rich Igbo cosmology, and the relation of the ogbanje to Igbo deities. She considers, too, the behavioural characteristics of such children, and the traditional treatments that were employed to treat them. In Igbo myth, *ogbanje* children were tied to life through a *chi*—an enchanted object of the human world, such as a stone, that contained the *ogbanje's* soul. An aspect of the treatment of the *ogbanje* child might include locating their *chi*—which might be buried near a portal through which the spirit-world could be entered, like a distinct bush or river, depending on whether the connection was with water (*mama wata*) or earthly spirits (Ala)—and allowing the child to wear the *chi* or keep it in close possession. The talismanic nature of the *chi* may also be compared to the AI-powered technologies we have come to depend on, but the technological construct of which is opaque to most users. The key point is the full dependence of the life of the ogbanje child on the *chi*, which is not on a broad conceptual level dissimilar to augmentative life-preserving technologies where an external object holds significant responsibility in respect of the well-being of its user. In this way, the *ogbanje–chi* relationship constitutes an alternate cultural framework with which to think differently about the relationship between humans and intimate-use AI technologies. This may include contributing to the growing movement to drop the term 'user' when speaking of the humans that use technologies (Lefton, 2019), as this fails to take into account the power that technology has over those that use it, and is stuck within an instrumentalist paradigm.

In addition, Achebe describes how such children could not be fully disciplined or subjected to the social codes of the human world. With intelligence and reason that was both human and godly, the behaviour of such children could only be attenuated and ameliorated. They could not be fully understood through human reason (Achebe, 1986), in a way that echoes the black box reasoning of AI, which is not fully understandable, even to the data scientists that created the AI systems (Pasquale, 2015). The need to fully know and understand the world is paradigmatic of post-Enlightenment Western reason (a point I sought to argue in *Transparency: New Trajectories in Law* (Adams, 2020)) and partly accounts for the anxiety towards AI systems that are not fully knowable and transparent. However, the ethics of not-knowing, or that which we cannot know, has a place, too. When compared with AI, references like that of the *ogbanje* prompt the asking of new questions in relation to the knowability conundrum of AI and whether this might be an ethical concern that is more of a priority in Western nations, and not necessarily a universal priority of concern.

Turning to the questions of representation and gender, in his classic text *Things Fall Apart* (1958), Chinua Achebe narrates the story of Okonkwo, whose daughter, Ezinma, is an *ogbanje*. Okonkwo is the epitome of an Igbo male and would, ordinarily, not have had a close relationship with his daughters, and particularly not a daughter considered *ogbanje*. However, Okonkwo is devoted to Ezinma and compassionate to Ezinma's mother—Ekwefi, his second wife—who must sacrifice everything to keep their daughter alive. Ezinma is portrayed as an exceptional child. She is beautiful and responsible, with an intelligence that often outsmarts her elders. She calls her mother by name, unlike the Igbo tradition. Her exceptionality is, too, crucially related to the gendered structure of Igbo society. Okonkwo frequently expresses that Ezinma '"should have been a boy"' (Achebe, 1958, pp. 44–5), on account of her searching intelligence and wisdom. Okonkwo also has to remind her not to '"sit like a boy"', nor to bring him a chair as '"that is a boy's job"' (Achebe, 1958, p. 32). But it is not only Ezinma's gender that is uncertain. The hypermasculinity Achebe emphasizes in Okonkwo's character is softened by his daughter as he exhibits towards her the tenderness he associates with the female sex. While on the one hand (and as is explored further later in relation to the work of Akwaeke Emezi) the figure of the *ogbanje* in *Things Fall Apart* unsettles normative gender structures, the story also depicts the reciprocal relation between things, people, the earthly world, and the divine, described by Mbembe. Ezinma's nature is not just isolated in her own character and being, but also profoundly recasts the personalities and trajectories of her parents.

Things Fall Apart was a remarkable work when first published in 1958, bringing new possibilities to the traditional English-language novelistic form through the inclusion of Igbo myth and dialect. More recently, the author Akwaeke Emezi has exploded onto the literary scene first in 2019 with writing that also incorporates Igbo imaginary and traditional beliefs. But Emezi writes from a space that is distinctly neither Nigerian—where they grew up—nor American—where they are now based. In fact, Emezi *is* an *ogbanje*, who writes their story into their work, and who writes—therefore—from a space distinctly beyond the human realm. Emezi makes it clear in their work (particularly in *Dear Senthuran: A Black Spirit Memoir* (2021) which I discuss later), that they are not adopting the voice and character of an *ogbanje* as a narrative conceit. Rather, writing literature offers Emezi a medium through which to articulate and explore their own distinctly supernatural being-in-the-world. As explained in *Dear Senthuran*, it was only when Emezi fully explored the traditions and histories of their Igbo heritage that they began to understand themself to be an *ogbanje*, and to identify themself accordingly.[7]

Emezi's first novel, *Freshwater* (2018), offers a powerful glimpse into the consciousness of Ada, an *ogbanje*, and their journey—though told nonchronologically—from their birth as a tempestuous child in Southern Nigeria to their adulthood, and the traumas of new relationships both within and outside themself in America. The novel is narrated by the spirits that occupy Ada's mind and body. Emezi pointed out in 2021 that, when first published, *Freshwater* was often interpreted as a metaphor for mental health, and the complexities of navigating being trans, non-binary, Nigerian, and Indian (Emezi's mother is Indian and their father is from Nigeria) (Nwadiogbu, 2019). This interpretive style—the translation of indigenous reason into Western language and concepts—is key to the historical evolution of the *ogbanje* myth. Over time, the ontologies and epistemologies of indigenous communities like the Igbo were effaced through processes of colonialism and written over by Western science. The *ogbanje* myth was recast within the terms of Western science, interpreted as sickle cell disease or schizophrenia (Achebe, 1986). In this way, the symbolic power and richness of such traditions and thought was lost or deeply diminished—a theme formidably explored, particularly in relation to Western science and technology, in Ngũgĩ wa Thiong'o's *Wizard of the Crow*. While Mbembe laments that 'this world [lost indigenous epistemologies and ontologies] is one that no one will ever be able to restitute to us' (2021, p. 166), the writings of Emezi and Ngũgĩ reactivate such mythologies and cosmologies, powerfully exposing their active presence and contemporaneity in a way that is particularly valuable for the decolonial enterprise and recentring ways of knowing and thinking that have been marginalized by coloniality of various forms. For Emezi in particular, the *ogbanje* is neither anachronistic nor metaphorical (their life is indeed a testament against this), but the Western world is impoverished by its refusal to allow other forms of truth, like indigenous reason, an explaining power in the troubles and traumas of contemporary life. This is indeed the argument being put forward here in exploring how the case of the *ogbanje* can enrich discussions around AI ethics and decolonizing AI today.

In 2021, Emezi published the autobiographical text *Dear Senthuran: A Black Spirit Memoir*, wherein they offer a deeper account of their experience as *ogbanje* through a series of personal letters. The book is peppered with research they have conducted on the *ogbanje* phenomenon as they come to make sense of themselves:

> To be an ogbanje is to be categorized [as] other—and to bring alterity home in a way that transcends the more ordinary, bifurcated 'otherness' of gender. This other gender is marked from birth—as male and female statues are marked—by special behaviours toward and physical adornment of the child. The sexual appearance of the ogbanje may, indeed, be seen as a sham—yet another promise that the ogbanje is likely to break in its refusal to act according to human norms.
>
> (Emezi, citing Misty Bastian, 2021, p. 11)

That the *ogbanje* is not confined to singular ideas of gender holds the promise of freedom in both Achebe (1958) and Emezi's (2018, 2021) writing. For Emezi, it is the embracing of their *ogbanje* nature that subsequently allows them to understand their gender: 'do ogbanje even have a gender to begin with? Gender is, after all such a human thing' (2021, p. 16). Incidentally, of course, 'trans', from Latin, means *to pass through* or *go beyond*, and clearly designates a fluidity that surpasses normative bounds of language and being.

In *Dear Senthuran*, Emezi describes the procedures they undergo to liberate their human body from the confines of a singular gender, which includes both a breast reduction and hysterectomy. Emezi narrates the process of 'mutat[ing . . . their] body into something that would fit [their] spiritself' (2021, p. 14). These procedures were for Emezi, too, highly symbolic within Igbo cosmology. In order to recognize the returning spirit-child of the ogbanje in a baby reborn to its mother, the child would often be physically marked or mutilated. These mutilations might also serve, within some traditions, to repel the spirits from accepting the *ogbanje* once it returns to their realm. In the poem 'Abiku' by Nigerian poet John Pepper Clark-Bekederemo we find a description of the kind of markings found on the *ogbanje*:

> We know the knife scars
> Serrating down your back and front
> Like beak of the sword-fish,
> And both your ears, notched
> As a bondsman to this house,
> Are all relics of your first comings.
> (1965)

What is also intimated by such practices, is the fusion of worlds between the physical and spiritual, the mind and the body, such that the scars of the body are carried forth beyond the earthly realm. In Emezi's work, the body—and their body, too—is conceived as a vessel, within which gods are housed, but which also communicates to the human world the self or selves that live inside it. Their female-gendered body miscommunicated a reality that did not live inside them; their surgeries created a more authentic representation of their selves (Emezi, 2021, p. 20).

17.5 The implications of ogbanje for decolonizing AI

The first part of this chapter briefly set out the crisis of representation in which dominant portrayals and depictions of AI are fixed. In particular, this crisis centres on outmoded normative representations of personhood that reproduce repressive notions of race and gender, extending a prescriptive Western history on the subject and disallowing possibilities for decolonization. The case of the *ogbanje* offers insight into a radically different way of reckoning with the binaries in which Western framings of AI are bound—not just in terms of how intelligent agents are portrayed, but also with respect to some of the critical ethical questions bound up within this portrayal, such as what it means to live with intelligent agents such as AI, or—perhaps more critically—what it means for humans to live with, or live a life in part mediated by, nonhuman intelligent agents. Fundamentally, the *ogbanje* unsettles what are broadly considered to be the founding binaries of human society—life/death; human/nonhuman; man/woman—but as it does so, it creates new possibilities for those in relation to it, opening apertures to other worlds, to other modes of being, and to other ways of living. Indeed, Mbembe reminds us (2021, p. 165) that 'the concept of ontological limit never had the authority that it acquired in the trajectories taken by other regions in the world'. Within such frameworks, intelligent agents can be situated relationally within fluid and recomposite worlds, rather than fixed in static and outmoded human forms. The *ogbanje*, for example, exists within a complex network of chi, spirit god (*mama water*/Ala), and human mother, blending and folding into human godly codes as needed. In this, humans form but one node in a network of intelligent beings and agents. They are not perched precariously at the top of the apex, fearing their replacement by an impending superintelligence.

Instead, the case of the *ogbanje* prompts an invitation to rethink our relationship with technology and AI, and our relationship through technology with the world. In this vein, Mbembe speaks of a '*generative economy*' of relations in African societies, wherein human and nonhuman life function together 'as part of participatory ecosystems in which the world was not an object to be conquered, but a reserve of potentials, and in which there was no pure and absolute power but that which was the source of life and of fecundity (2021, p. 163, emphasis in the original). Furthermore, the discussion presented here provokes another reconsideration: that knowledge does not always proceed upon a linear history, a straight path of progress which tends—certainly historically—to destroy that which came before it. Instead, the movement of knowledge through time may be cyclical, and where old knowledges that serve new futures can be renewed. Emezi's experience insists upon this, as does decolonization, as we search for the alternative epistemologies and ontologies that are needed to build a future without oppression. For AI, this means that the future is not set, and that AI may again face its winter.

In engaging these alternatives, we must consider the politics involved in this exercise, as well as the politics required to transcend the normative binaries and boundaries upon which AI fortifies and depends, and to authentically consult alternate ontologies and epistemologies of the socio-technical. Indeed, does this project use Nigerian folklore tokenistically, simply as an example of what is not the West, in a scholarly conceit that, at its base, serves to address a Western problem and extend a Western debate? In response, AI is not just a Western phenomenon or concern. My work here in South Africa is primarily in supporting policy makers from across the Continent to develop locally appropriate responses to AI. It is crucial to this task to recognize distinctly African histories and philosophies of technology, and to consider the ways in which these traditions and values offer a more culturally fitting paradigm from which to assess the ethical considerations and implications of AI *here*. Nonetheless, to foster a more just way of imagining and making sense of AI—what we can call a *just ethos of AI*—is inherently valuable to the work of anyone concerned with the implications of AI for the futures of humanity, and the planet.

Endnotes

1. This chapter forms part of a broader project of work I am engaged in to understand why AI needs decolonizing, and what this task requires.
2. While largely they both refer to the same phenomenon, *ogbanje* is the Igbo word, while *abiku* is the word in the Yoruba cultural tradition. Throughout this chapter, I refer mostly to *ogbanje* as I focus on narratives and case studies that emanate out of the Igbo cultural tradition. However, the arguments made in relation to *ogbanje* can be understood as broadly interchangeable with *abiku*.
3. See, for example, the 'Better Images of AI' project that seeks to design and develop more representative images of AI and robots that transcend beyond the white/male norm: https://www.bbc.co.uk/rd/blog/2021-12-artificial-intelligence-machine-stock-image-library (Accessed 7 January 2022).
4. In speaking of what the 'postcolony' means in relation to Africa's colonial past, Mbembe (2002) expresses that 'the notion of the "postcolony" refers to a timescape which is simultaneously in the process of being formed and of being dissolved through a movement that brings both the "being formed" and the "being dissolved" into collision. The term "postcolony" indicates my desire to take very seriously the intrinsic qualities and power of "contemporaneousness" while firmly keeping in mind the fact that the present itself is a concatenation of multiple temporalities. Because of the entanglement of these multiple temporalities, Africa is evolving in multiple and overlapping directions simultaneously'.
5. See the popular Ted Talk on this issue by Sam Harris, 'Can we build AI without losing control over it?'; Frischmann and Selinger, 2018; Bostrom, 2014; Dihal, 2020.
6. The ogbanje, or similar, is not just a figure in Igbo or Yoruba traditions, but other cultural traditions of Southern Nigerian societies. For further description, see Asakitikpi, 2008.
7. See, for example, Emezi's bio in their twitter account (@azemezi), where they use the term ogbanje as a personal description.

References

Achebe, C. (1958) *Things fall apart*. London: William Heinemann Ltd.

Achebe, C. (1986) *The world of the ogbanje*. Enugu: Fourth Dimension publishers.

Adams, R. (2019) '*Helen 'A'Loy* and other tales: A gendered reading of the narratives of hopes and fears in intelligent machines and artificial intelligence', *AI & Society*, 35(3), pp. 569–79.

Adams, R. (2020) *Transparency: New trajectories in law*. London: Routledge.

Adams, R. (2021) 'Can AI be decolonized?', *Interdisciplinary Science Reviews*, 46(1–2), pp. 176–97.

Adams, R., and Loideain, N. N. (2019) 'Addressing indirect discrimination and gender stereotypes in AI personal assistants: The role of international human rights law', *Cambridge International Law Journal*, 8(2), pp. 241–57.

Asakitikpi, A. E. (2008) 'Born to die: The *ogbanje* phenomenon and its implication on childhood mortality in southern Nigeria', *Anthropologist*, 10(1), pp. 59–63.

Benjamin, R. (2019) *Race after technology: Abolitionist tools for the new Jim Crow*. Cambridge: Polity Press.

Bostrom, N. (2014) *Superintelligence: Paths, dangers, strategies*. Oxford: Oxford University Press.

Browne, S. (2015) *Dark matters: On the surveillance of Blackness*. Durham, NC: Duke University Press.

Cave, S., and Dihal, K. (2018) 'Ancient dreams of intelligent machines: 3,000 years of robots', *Nature*, 559, pp. 473–5.

Cave, S., and Dihal, K. (2020) 'The whiteness of AI', *Philosophy and Technology*, 33, pp. 685–703.

Cave, S., and Dihal, K. (2021) 'Race and AI: The diversity dilemma', *Philosophy and Technology*, 34, pp. 1775–9.

Cave, S., Dihal, K., and Dillon, S. (eds.) (2020) *AI narratives: A history of imaginative thinking about intelligent machines*. Oxford: Oxford University Press.

Clark-Bekederemo, J. P. (1965/2003) 'Abiku', in Senanu, K. E and Vincent, T. (eds.) *A selection of African Poetry*, new edn. Harlow: Longman Group Limited, pp. 205–6.

Dihal, K. (2020) 'Enslaved minds: Artificial intelligence, slavery, and revolt', in Cave, S., Dihal, K., and Dillon, S. (eds.) *AI narratives: A history of imaginative thinking about intelligent machines*. Oxford: Oxford University Press, pp. 189–212.

Emezi, A. (2018) *Freshwater*. New York: Grove Press.

Emezi, A. (2021) *Dear Senthuran: A Black spirit memoir*. New York: Penguin Random House.

Frischmann, B. and Selinger, E. (2018) *Re-engineering humanity*. Cambridge: Cambridge University Press.

Grosfoguel, R. (2007) 'The epistemological decolonial turn', *Cultural Studies*, 21(2–3), pp. 211–23.

Grosfoguel, R. (2011) 'Decolonizing post-colonial studies and paradigms of political-economy: Transmodernity, decolonial thinking, and global coloniality', *Transmodernity: Journal of Peripheral Cultural Production of the Luso-Hispanic World* 1(1). http://dx.doi.org/10.5070/T411000004

Lefton, A. (2019) 'As a designer, I refuse to call people "users"'. Medium [online], Available at: https://medium.com/s/user-friendly/why-im-done-saying-user-user-experience-and-ux-in-2019-4fdfc6b7de23 (Accessed 16 March 2022).

Loideain, N. N., and Adams, R. 2020. 'From Ava to Siri: The Gendering of Virtual Personal Assistants and the Role of Data Protection Law'. *Computer Law and Security Review*, 36.

Mbembe, A. (2002) 'Interview with Achille Mbembe', Springerin Magazine [online], March. English version available at: https://www.laits.utexas.edu/africa/ads/1528.html (Accessed 10 January 2022).

Mbembe, A. (2019) *Necropolitics*. Johannesburg: Witwatersrand University Press.

Mbembe, A. (2021) *Out of the dark night: Essays on decolonisation*. Johannesburg: Wits University Press.

Mignolo, W. D. and Walsh, C. E. (2018) *On decoloniality*. Durham, NC: Duke University Press.

Ndlovu-Gatsheni, S. (2015) 'Decoloniality as the future of Africa', *History Compass*, 13(10), pp. 485–96.

Ngũgĩ, wa Thiong'o. (2006) *Wizard of the crow*. London: Penguin.

Noble, S. U. (2018) *Algorithms of oppression: How search engines reinforce racism*. New York: New York University Press.

Nwadiogbu, N. R. (2019) '*Freshwater* Author Akwaeke Emezi is based in liminal spaces', L'Officiel [online], 11 January. Available at: https://www.lofficielusa.com/politics-culture/author-akwaeke-emezi-freshwater-book-digital-issue (Accessed 15 January 2022).

Pasquale, F. (2015) *The black box society: The secret algorithms that control money and information*. Cambridge, MA: Harvard University Press.

Singler, B. (2020) 'Artificial intelligence and the parent-child narrative', in Cave, S., Dihal, K., and Dillon, S. (eds.) *AI narratives: A history of imaginative thinking about intelligent machines*. Oxford: Oxford University Press, pp. 260–83.

18

AI Oasis?

Imagining Intelligent Machines in the Middle East and North Africa

Kanta Dihal, Tomasz Hollanek, Nagla Rizk, Nadine Weheba, and Stephen Cave

18.1 Introduction

The history of imagining intelligent machines in the Middle East and North Africa (MENA) dates back to the Islamic Golden Age: a period of cultural, scientific, and economic flourishing between the ninth and fourteenth centuries. While communities in MENA have been imagining intelligent machines since that time, Western perceptions of success, development, progress, and industrialization influence the hopes and dreams for the future of technology today.

In this chapter, we analyse the various factors that make the MENA region a unique environment for imagining futures with intelligent machines, and map local visions of technological progress onto the region's complex past, as well as on contemporary economic and political struggles. We identify several narrative threads as pivotal to the understanding of conceptions of AI in the region. They include colonialism, visions of the utopian past (rather than future), contemporary political dynamics, and gender relations. Section 18.3 focuses on Western perceptions of the region and the ways in which they influence the imaginings of technological development inside MENA. Section 18.4 is dedicated to the longer history of imagining intelligent machines in MENA, dating back to the Islamic Golden Age, and illustrates present-day examples in Arabic science fiction (SF). Section 18.5 analyses contemporary efforts to create regional AI narratives as alternatives to those from the Global North. Finally, Section 18.6 examines how political and socioeconomic factors shape the discourse on AI and other emerging technologies in MENA, and how local imaginings of AI relate to narrative tropes prevalent in public policy.

AI narratives in MENA are less explicit than in the anglophone world, and uncovering them requires a nuanced approach, which takes into consideration not only directly expressed stories, but also more elusive imaginaries—embodied, for example, by the local start-up ecosystem or online communities of futurists. Understanding the soft power of technology as a means of expression, especially as it intersects with voices of resistance, is critical to appreciating AI imaginaries in MENA. We therefore pay special attention to bottom-up initiatives (societies, art projects, start-ups), moving beyond government-orchestrated efforts to drive innovation, which more frequently respond to Western conceptions of progress.

18.2 Defining the MENA region

The Middle East and North Africa region is vast, and although there are cultural threads tying it together, it is also highly diverse. It is traditionally constituted by the 22 countries in the Arab League,[1] although some scholars also include Turkey and Iran in their analyses of the region, and may omit states such as the Comoros, Somalia, and Mauritania (Cleveland and Bunton, 2018).

Countries in MENA are not homogenous in their developmental, socioeconomic, and political realities, and this in turn affects their experiences of technological innovation (Rizk, 2020). The oil-rich countries of the Gulf, like Saudi Arabia and the United Arab Emirates (UAE), are regional leaders in the adoption and deployment of AI technologies (ElSafy, 2019). With largely expatriate populations (especially in the case of the UAE), their governments adopt concerted, 'technocratic' strategies to innovation and have the financial capabilities to make large-scale investments to deploy AI across the economy—which also places them ahead of their less-wealthy counterparts in the region. Mid-income countries like Egypt and Tunisia are rich in human resources but are held back in their advancement of AI by challenging economic and socio-political conditions.

The MENA region has a long and distinct cultural history, being the birthplace of the three Abrahamic religions as well as several major civilizations. The term *Middle East*, however, does not enjoy the same antiquity: it 'arose from the imperatives of late-nineteenth-century [European] strategy and diplomacy, which needed a name for the region between the "Near East", based on Turkey, and the "Far East", based on China' (Koppes, 1976). While *Middle East* reflects a predominantly Eurocentric view of this part of the world—a perspective this chapter aims to problematize—to ensure clarity, we decided to keep the expanded region of *MENA* as a widely accepted unit of analysis, used by international organizations such as the United Nations (UNHCR, 2022; OHCHR, n.d.; Unicef.org, 2022) and the World Bank (The World Bank, 2022), as well as research institutions inside the region (Abouemera, 2020).

The Arabic[2] language is one of the key overarching commonalities throughout the Middle East and North Africa. The language reflects the key role the region has played in the history of science and mathematics, providing loanwords in English for some of the most important terminology of AI. Firstly, the ones and zeroes so crucial to computer science are, as is widely known, 'Arabic numerals'. The concept of zero, the numerals themselves, and the term 'algebra' (derived from the Arabic *al-jabr*[3]) all probably arrived in Europe through a treatise by the Persian polymath Muḥammad ibn Mūsā al-Khwārizmī (c. 750–c. 850 CE). It is his last name that has given us the term 'algorithm'. While in the Middle Ages this term referred to the then-newly adopted system of Arabic numerals, from the late nineteenth century onwards it took on its contemporary meaning: a set of mathematical operations that together perform a particular task ('Algorism, n', n.d.).

The use of Classical Arabic, the language of the Qur'an, as a literary standard in MENA brings us to another element that binds the region together: the widespread prevalence of Islam. Despite multiple heterogeneous factors, including the presence of other religious groups, the concentration of Muslims per region is highest in MENA (93% of its 341 million inhabitants identify as followers of Islam). However, as nearly two-thirds of global Muslims live in the Asia–Pacific region (Desilver and Masci, 2017), it is important to recognize that conflating 'Arab' and 'Muslim' takes away from the understanding of the contexts and nuances of each. While this chapter does not focus on the relationship between technology and Islam, it approaches the MENA region as an embodiment of a historical mix of civilizations with cultural origins extending beyond its current geographical boundaries into the larger Muslim world. As such, the chapter aims to distil several themes predominant in regional AI narratives, common for most (but certainly not all) cultures in MENA.

18.3 The technology 'desert'

Western perceptions of success, development, progress, and industrialization influence technological narratives both in the Global North and in the MENA region. Narratives of technological development in MENA, manifested in SF, the media-political discourse, and scholarly writing, most frequently refer directly or indirectly to Western imaginings of desirable progress. Contemporary debates on AI in MENA often appeal to or openly reject Western perspectives—but in both cases, such discourse is influenced by Western conceptions of progress.

The influence of these Western-centric visions is intimately linked to the colonial history of the region, which can be traced back to Napoleon's expedition to Egypt in 1798. Since then, Western scholarship has tended to depict the history of MENA from the thirteenth to the early nineteenth century as a time of consistent decline, in contrast to the modernizing progress of Western powers. The *narrative of decline* in the history of MENA has been internalized by some of its inhabitants (Kirecci, 2007), and so influences perceptions of the region both outside and inside MENA today. We identify self-Orientalization, the process of internalizing Western perceptions of the region by its people, as one of the biggest challenges facing those who aim to voice narratives of innovation in MENA that constitute an alternative to the postcolonial ones.

Western conceptions of development are reflected in the portrayals of the region as incapable of seizing and shaping the opportunities of emerging technologies such as AI. We refer to this imagery as the *technology desert*: a supposed lack—of resources, innovation, and ideas—in the MENA region. Just as the *narrative of decline* shaped the discourse on development in MENA in the past, so does the trope of the *technology desert* influence it in the present. While some countries in the region indeed experience a 'brain drain' in the technology sector (key innovation leaders migrating in search of better work opportunities—most often to Western countries) (Langendorf, 2020), the narratives of impossibility and absence fail to reflect the potential lying within the region. They affect the position of the majority of MENA countries in the global debate on the future of AI, which remain largely overlooked as actors of change on a larger scale.

The imagery of the *technology desert* is paralleled by that of the *tech oasis*—embodied by the cities of the Persian Gulf, including Dubai, Abu Dhabi, and Doha. Significant amounts of funding are administered by the UAE's government to drive technological development—something we could contrast with resource-poor countries, such as Egypt, Tunisia, or Jordan, where limited funds are available for similar initiatives, and technological progress depends on grassroots efforts and start-ups. With **their** efforts to become **leaders** in technological innovation, **the Gulf countries** could seen, therefore, as **outliers** in the technology desert. But this perception is largely related to the influence of Western ideals on innovation strategies in the rich countries of the Gulf, including Qatar and Kuwait. As Western designers are hired to execute the state's flagship innovation projects (the Museum of the Future (2022), for instance) and government communications clearly appeal to anglophone audiences,[4] the impact of Western ideas of progress on the conceptions of technological futures in MENA becomes particularly visible.

Having said this, while hypermodern municipalities in the oil-rich part of the MENA region can indeed be seen as products of the Western imaginary of progress and development, they have also become hubs for new, Arab-focused futures thinking. In 2012, the musician Fatima Al Qadiri and the writer Sophia Al-Maria coined the term 'Gulf Futurism' to name a new aesthetic trend that arises out of the mix of the Gulf's Blade Runner-like architecture, desert landscapes, rampant consumerism, and suppressive social codes (Dazed, 2012). Al Qadiri and Al-Maria list the Kuwait Water Towers as one of the most suggestive examples of Gulf Futurism. The artists identify the Gulf countries as a social and cultural experiment that gives us a glimpse into an arguably apocalyptic future, determined by harsh environmental change, deep economic divisions, and technological riches that benefit only a very small proportion of society.

While it is precisely these local artistic initiatives that respond to the regional histories and explore MENA-specific conceptions of the future, the entertainment market in MENA is dominated by anglophone, mostly American productions—yet another factor contributing to the perceived lack of local, MENA-produced stories on the future of AI, robots, and intelligent machines. Narratives of AI are most often exported to MENA by the West, in the form of SF films and TV series such as *The Terminator*, *Star Trek*, or *Battlestar Galactica*, which dominate over locally produced but underfunded productions discussed in Section 18.4, such as the Egyptian TV series *Al Nihaya* (The End).

Another, perhaps equally important, influence on AI narratives in MENA comes from Japan.[5] For example, multiple anime series have been featured on Arabic TV (most famously, *Grendizer* was made available via the free-to-air channel Spacetoon) (Perfect Health صحة مثالية , 2016). The assumptions about new technologies that these narratives imported from Japan propagate are discussed in Chapter 19 of this volume (Katsuno and White).

This form of media globalization perpetuates the idea of the technology desert: the media landscape is saturated with Western and Japanese narratives—leaving little room for home-grown narratives. The imagery of the desert—an absence of ideas, imaginaries, as well as actual tech development in MENA—is, however, only an illusion, which this chapter aims to dispel.

18.4 Arab imaginaries

The narratives of intelligent machines in the MENA region are rooted in the 'mirabilia' tradition: 'the travel journeys, the tales of the animal world, or the cosmos stories from the classical period', before the advent of Islam (Comito, 2013). The Arabic term for mirabilia, *'Ajā'ib*, comes from the root for 'to [be] astonished, to wonder, to [take] delight' (Campbell, 2018). The *1001 Nights* constitute an early collection of such stories and have recently been reappraised as proto-SF (Nuruddin, 2006). The tale 'The City of Brass', for instance, contains descriptions of automata, such as a brass horseman that is able to direct travellers to the City of Brass (Lane, 1909–1914). The Arabic literary tradition of imagining intelligent machines is therefore over a thousand years old.

It is not surprising that this imaginary has pervaded Arabic literature for so long, given that the MENA region excelled in building automata (self-moving machines) for more than two millennia. The city of Alexandria was a hub for engineers designing and building automata from the third century BCE onwards. Its most famous engineer was Hero of Alexandria, whose work *On Automaton-Making* from the first century CE described how to build an ingeniously moving shrine and theatre.

In the Middle Ages, the art of automaton making flourished in the Islamicate world, drawing the admiration and envy of the Latin Christian West. In eighth-century Baghdad, three brothers known as the Banu Musa, wrote their *Kitab al-Hiyal* (*Book of Ingenious Devices*), which described how to build nearly a hundred automata (Truitt, 2015). Like most other cultures of the time, despite their technological mastery, the imaginative narratives featuring extrapolations of these machines were characterized by a nostalgia for a utopia set in a golden past, rather than looking for such a utopia in the future.

It was only after the Middle Ages that Western narratives began to diverge from this tradition. The colonial period was part of a major rupture in Western thinking. At this point, the West began to identify notions of technological progress with modernity and the future. The first future utopias, driven by science and technology, emerged at this time: first with Thomas More's *Utopia* in 1516, and in the sixteenth century with Roger Bacon's scientifically grounded, future-oriented worldview. At the same time, the countries where this worldview emerged began to believe in their own superiority and right to dominate others as a consequence (Adas, 2015).

Subsequently, colonial conquest and imposition of this worldview placed colonized regions as irredeemably lagging behind, creating an instant dichotomy between those who have reached modernity and those who remain stuck in the past until they can become 'modern'. The exploitation associated with colonialism and subsequent conflict stripped colonized countries of their ability to imagine their own future. Makdisi (1995) argues that:

> Modernity was, from the beginning, not only inextricably associated with Europe: it was a 'goal' that one could only define as a *future* condition, a *future* location, a *future* possibility. Modernity, in other words, is, on this account, always already displaced and deferred: it is always on the other side of the river, or up the stream—or up in the sky.

At the same time, the associations of modernity with globalization, colonialism, and exploitation have made imagining a utopian future a controversial political act in postcolonial countries. The many Western utopias that precede any attempts elsewhere in the world to imagine a technology-enabled utopia depict their perfect futures as idealized extrapolations of (neo)colonialism, the utopias inhabited by homogenous white humans. Ultimately, imagining and recreating a future in a postcolonial region is not only a narrative act, but also a decolonial one—an attempt to disengage current chronology from its colonial and imperial roots.

As Laura Brown writes in her review of the anthology *Palestine +100*, a collection of SF short stories from the Palestinian diaspora:

> There is privilege when we look to the future . . . What idiocy to assume you can go back home after war, that tomorrow will be well? . . . To assume the future offers a renewed strength suggests you are in a secure present, or are confident you have the means to shift your present into a more solid future. (Brown, 2019)

The term *Arab Futurism*, as Jussi Parikka (2018) rightly suggests, thus marks a link across a spectrum of contemporary political issues—related to race, territory, war, and postcolonial histories. Cultural production in the Arab world has been deeply affected by wars and political conflicts in the region, and these are echoed in the representation of characters as well as themes featured in narratives. *Speculative Data Futures* (Sultan, Yara, and Felsberger, 2019), for example, is a series of three short stories by female Arab authors that examines alternative futures using a gendered lens; one story, for instance, imagines the reconstruction of Syria through the collection of memories of its displaced and refugee populations—by implanting chips directly into their brains and downloading the memories to a hard drive.

Another story envisions a Palestine where women can navigate their urban surroundings safely through the use of a mapping application made by women for women. Similar stories of technology empowering women in MENA could be read as poignant examples of an emergent feminist counterculture, acting against powerful narrative tropes that correspond to very real inequalities between women and men in the region. In MENA, for instance, humanoid robots are often portrayed as ideal domestic servants. One example of this trend is Ruby, a robot featured in a popular Egyptian comedy skit from the 1980s ("الثمانينات سمير غانم مع الروبوت يقدم له الشاى فى" (Samir Ghanem with a robot serving him Tea in the 80s), 2018), in which the feminized domestic robot readily responds to orders given to 'her' by the main character—bringing to mind today's virtual assistants, such as Siri or Alexa.

Despite the emergence of projects such as *Speculative Data Futures*, *Iraq +100* (Blasim, 2016), and *Palestine +100* (Ghalayini, 2019), in MENA SF is still considered a niche genre. Several smaller agents have recently attempted to reinvigorate SF storytelling in the region. The Egyptian Society for Science

Fiction is one example. Founded in 2012 by Hosam El Zembely, it is considered the first registered society devoted to SF in Egypt. The Society's publications touch on various AI-related issues, including automated governance, AI's revolt against humanity, or romantic relationships between humans and robots. The Society's work began without any institutional support—a fact indicative of a larger trend in MENA, where SF storytellers not only have to compete with foreign, predominantly Western, creators, but also receive no systemic help.

In more extreme cases, some SF publications may even be withdrawn from circulation by the government on morality grounds—as was the case with Yasser Bahjatt's *HWJN*, a novel accused of promoting witchcraft and thoroughly investigated by Saudi Arabia's Committee for the Promotion of Virtue and the Prevention of Vice before it was allowed back into bookshops (Fossett, 2013). Bahjatt is a Saudi entrepreneur and author of bestselling SF novels (including *HWJN*), and has emphasized the responsibility of Arabic SF creators to reshape the image of AI in the public eye in the Middle East, 'where our actual contribution to the advancement of this technology is even less visible and our cultural input on the matter is almost nonexistent' (Fossett, 2013). We explore Bahjatt's point in more detail in Section 18.5 and look at the role of local AI narratives as a potential form of resistance against Western ideals of technological development.

18.5 Resistance

The predominant influence of Western conceptions of progress in MENA contributes to a storytelling environment driven by the need to develop an authentic regional voice through narratives about AI. Resistance against the influences of the Global North takes various shapes in the MENA region—from thriving local tech initiatives to the rise of online communities dedicated to reimagining technological futures in the Middle East and North Africa.

There is a clear underrepresentation of the MENA region, like the rest of the Global South, across a spectrum of global debates. These include more general debates on developmental issues and, in the case of AI, debates on AI's applications, impact, and necessary policy changes. If present, the region's voice is often drowned out by the more dominant perspectives from the Global North. This dominance is asserted in various ways; the global framework for intellectual property and trade, for example, leans heavily towards protecting the interests of the Global North, rather than those of the developing world (Shaver and Rizk, 2010).

New technologies, including AI-driven solutions, often constitute cases of convoluted cultural dumping; as most of the emerging systems are designed and developed in the Global North, they harness in them biases that do not necessarily correspond to the realities of the Global South, MENA included. Facial recognition software, for example, can prove problematic when confronted with non-white skin; natural language processing algorithms imported from the West can fail when used to process Arabic. Biases can also end up in policymaking that is detached from the local context and corresponds to a layered underrepresentation of grassroots needs.[6]

Countervailing forces come in the form of a dynamic pushback from smaller local players as they carve a niche for themselves and increasingly contribute to the local and regional narratives of progress and development amidst the influence of larger players with more dominant voices. Especially since the 2011 uprisings in countries like Egypt and Tunisia, a budding entrepreneurial scene demonstrates how local start-ups continue to harness the potential to innovate and tilt the balance in favour of homegrown initiatives. At the same time, large players can continue to consolidate their market share, as witnessed in the case of the ride-sharing market in Egypt, where Uber recently acquired its smaller regional counterpart, Careem. Such market concentration is countered by local start-ups that customize services to the realities on the ground—typically informal transport networks and needs. For example, Halan is a successful ride-sharing platform launched in 2017 in Egypt (Nabil, 2019) for 'tuktuks', a mode of transport similar to rickshaws. Another local start-up, Swvl, was the first player to introduce on-demand bus rides via a mobile application to the Egyptian market in 2017; by 2021 the company was valued at US$1.5 billion (Kene-Okafor, 2021). While larger players such as Uber have now introduced bus services as well, Swvl continues to grow locally and expand internationally into Africa (Farouk and Saba, 2019).

Entrepreneurial initiatives serve as 'rays of hope' (Rizk, 2020, p. 626) in providing more sustainable work and creative opportunities to the educated youth—in a region with high unemployment rates among the youth and the educated (Rizk, 2020). This means that the regional perception of the future of work, like elsewhere, reflects a concern with robots potentially replacing humans. The media also focuses on the need for education and training to mitigate these challenges (aus dem Moore, Chandran and Schubert, 2018). One report cites that 45% of jobs in the Middle East can be automated 'now', while a similar portion of jobs across sectors like manufacturing and transport have the potential for future automation (both through robotics and AI) (aus dem Moore, Chandran and Schubert, 2018). Others, including state-run newspapers in Egypt, contribute to a more positive view, focusing on the potential for new jobs in the 'green economy' (El-Hawary, 2020). Governments across the region have prioritized training, re-skilling, and providing high-quality education (Al Gurg, 2019), especially in IT and data literacy, across all sectors of employment. This mirrors the narrative promoted by the media; in the UAE, for example, the government's strategy for AI, and other national initiatives such as the 'Advanced Skills Strategy' (UAE, 2022), outline frameworks and action plans that are already in place to equip citizens with necessary skills for the future of work.

Other ground-up initiatives and grassroots citizen activities also play a significant role in voicing the regional imaginary of technological futures. SF-oriented online communities in particular offer a platform for exploring local AI narratives. One example is Yatakhayaloon, an Arabic SF group that brings together both fans and creators (Yatakhayaloon.com, 2013). Another, the Arabic E-Lit (electronic literature) website, is an online platform intended for Arabic-speaking practitioners of multimedia storytelling, whose mission is to move 'beyond the hegemony of the English language of Anglo-American cultural concerns' and 'declare a global and inclusive electronic literature, driven by the energy of Arabic E-Lit' (arabicelit, 2015). The website's creator, Reham Hosny, has recently published the first Arabic augmented reality/hologram novel titled *Al-Barrah* (*The Announcer*) (Hosny, 2021). This shows that more creators in MENA are successfully appropriating emerging technologies, including AR/VR and AI, in their practice to counter dominant Western and postcolonial narratives.

18.6 Uprisings and trickle-downs

Levels of technological advancement and adoption in MENA vary considerably. These variations in turn reflect differences in socioeconomic and developmental realities and trigger a set of inherent drivers that shape the local, intra-regional, and region-wide narratives. One such driver is the tension between two opposing forces that, by and large, shape any digital economy: dominant powers versus ground-up initiatives. On the one hand, digital technologies (AI included) can perpetuate hierarchies and reinforce existing dominant powers on both the economic and political fronts. This becomes clear in an increased concentration of markets, technology infrastructure, and data ownership in the hands of large multinational corporations and expanded state control. In Egypt, for example, disputes around data retention and access in the case of ride sharing highlights the direction and intention for further concentration (The Tahrir Institute for Middle East Policy, 2019). These forces moving towards the centre are countervailed by opposing currents whereby small businesses and grassroots citizenry are emboldened using the very same technologies (Rizk and Elkassas, 2010). These opposing streams occur simultaneously, and while global in nature, tensions become more pronounced in the region in light of weaker institutions and nascent legislative frameworks.

These tensions also imply another layer of complexity with implications for AI narratives and visions of technology futures in the region. A dominant voice will be that of large corporations actively seeking further consolidation and concentration, propagating narratives largely similar to those of other multinational corporations around the world. Governments chime along, echoing neoliberal philosophies and Western perspectives. Nevertheless, the visions of technology futures will also be shaped by organic ground-up initiatives that are immersed in the local context and find their competitive edge and niche in customizing foreign technologies and developing local ones to match the realities on the ground.

Historically, modernization was not always synonymous with the West. Aspiring to 'modernize' Egypt in the 1960s, then-president Nasser turned east to receive support from the Soviet Union, notably to finance the Aswan Dam, in addition to military support (Cleveland and Bunton, 2018, p. 315). Other regional leaders at the time, including those of Syria and Iraq, followed suit. The Soviet Union thus became a primary source of weapons and technological innovation, and a model for modernization. Space exploration was one of the goals to which the Nasserist regime aspired, which was echoed in popular culture and cinema. For example, Nasser's aspirations to build an Egyptian space agency correlated with the productions of films such as H. A. Wahab's *A Trip to the Moon* (1959) and a feature on Egypt's space exploration in the 1965 issue of *Al Mossawir* magazine (Hamam, 2019).

The shift to the West came with the introduction of the open-door policy by Egypt's president Anwar Sadat following the 1973 October War, when Egypt turned to the United States for its models of modernization and economic growth (Aulas, 1982). Washington-based International Financial Institutions (IFIs) prescribed and propagated neoliberal solutions to the region's developmental and technological ailments via the Economic Reform and Structural Adjustment Program (ERSAP) (Amin, 1995). This was accompanied by the introduction of the Internet in the 1990s and the building of a telecommunications network to provide the backbone of the ambitious economic growth model (Rizk, Noam, and Mutter, 2016).

The dominant narrative was of information and communication technology (ICT) as a driver for economic growth. This resulted in top-down 'one-size-fits-all' policies, geared towards heavy investment in the ICT infrastructure in countries like Egypt. Such policies were fixated on economic gains and the interests of large, often foreign, corporations, and established legal frameworks in their favour. This posed an impending threat of decontextualization and technological determinism (Rizk, 2020) and resulted in few direct efforts to customize policies to local needs or to mitigate inequalities.

The Arab Uprisings, which took off in Tunisia and Egypt in 2011, stand as testament to the limitations of trickle-down economics and policies fixated on economic growth fuelled by foreign direct investment and multinational corporations at the expense of inclusive and sustainable development. Indeed, the mainstream discourse was a top-down narrative that boasted high rates of economic growth (reaching 7% in 2007–2008) (Gordon, 2018), which in reality failed to capture the discontent that was brewing on the ground—and eventually led to the Uprisings.

Currently present in the regional media discourse is a notion that the Fourth Industrial Revolution,[7] a term that refers to a new wave of technological changes causing unprecedented and pervasive changes to all aspects of human life, is already in motion, and that citizens and governments need to work towards reaping its gains and mitigating its ills. The news coverage of the future of work serves as a good example. This ranges from a positive and proactive outlook to a more negative one. Positive coverage focuses on technological development, improved efficiency and productivity, and government efforts to create new work opportunities and mitigate any shortcomings (WAM, 2020; Sadaqat, 2018; Mohamed, 2019). More negative pieces reflect a concern with robots replacing professionals in the region (Maceda, 2020).

Today, it remains to be seen whether similar trends will be witnessed in the ambitious developments and AI strategies across the region, including *Egypt's Vision 2030* (Egypt Vision 2030, 2020), *Saudi Vision 2030* (Kingdom of Saudi Arabia Vision 2030, 2020), *UAE Vision 2021* (UAE, 2019), and *Jordan 2025: A National Vision and Strategy* (Government of Jordan, 2014), to name a few. While such plans ultimately strive to meet the United Nations Sustainable Development Goals, the impact of these policies on inclusion is yet to be tested. This is also the case when we consider AI-based technology solutions, developed in the West without accounting for contextual differences—the poverty of the population in particular (Rizk, 2020).

18.7 Conclusion

In late 2017, the Saudi Crown Prince Mohammad bin Salman announced the development of NEOM, a city of the future that would function independently of the Saudi government and rely on some of the latest technologies, including AI, to become a truly sustainable, fully digitalized microstate. To realize his '$500 Billion Desert Dream', however, the Prince turned to 'U.S. consultants for help imagining a massive new city-state in a barren section of his kingdom', rather than local counterparts (Scheck, Jones, and Said, 2019). Moreover, while the plan might have seemed impressive at first, it was soon deemed controversial, or unethical, by many, after it was revealed that local tribesman Abdulraheem al-Huwaiti was killed in the wake of his protesting the eviction of his tribe from its historic homeland (Gardner, 2020), a part of the area allocated by authorities for the development of the AI-powered city of NEOM (Allen, 2020).

While the tradition of imaging intelligent machines in the Middle East spans hundreds of years, and can be traced from Sophia Al-Maria's radical visions of Gulf futurism in contemporary Qatar all the way back to the Banu Musa's *Book of Ingenious Devices* in Baghdad during the Islamic Golden Age, it is this recent vision of the city of NEOM that focalizes the most important questions on AI narratives in MENA: Who gets to imagine a future with AI in this region? Whose dreams are likely to come true? And at what cost? This chapter has brought to light some of the bottom-up artistic initiatives, underfunded grassroots efforts, and unknown stories, because only by fostering these alternative visions can we ensure a more equitable future of technology in the Middle East and North Africa.

Endnotes

1. They are Algeria, Bahrain, Comoros, Djibouti, Egypt, Iraq, Jordan, Kuwait, Lebanon, Libya, Mauritania, Morocco, Oman, Palestine, Qatar, Saudi Arabia, Somalia, Sudan, Syria, Tunisia, the UAE, and Yemen.
2. An important note at the outset: 'Arabic' refers to the language most commonly spoken in the region; 'Arab' refers to the culture that dominates in MENA, and that dates back to this region irrespective of today's political boundaries.
3. *Al-jabr* literally translates to 'the restoration' or 'the completion', a reference to the method al-Khwarizmi introduced for solving quadratic equations.
4. For example, see: Dubai, 2022.
5. The emphasis on the Japanese influence with respect to narrative in particular is important. That is, while China—a global leader in AI development—might have a strong impact on the geopolitical scale, there is little evidence to support the existence of an equally strong Chinese influence on AI narratives in the region. See, for example, Yahya (2019).
6. A discussion of how big data and machine learning algorithms can reflect already existing biases—and aggravate their impact on underprivileged people's lives—can be found in 'Artificial Intelligence and inequality in the Middle East: the political economy of inclusion' (Rizk, 2020).
7. The term was coined by Klaus Schwab, Founder and Executive Chairman of the World Economic Forum in 2016 (Schwab, 2016). See also Chapter 20 in this volume.

References

Abouemera, R. (2020) 'Inclusive development and the fourth industrial revolution in MENA', The American University in Cairo, School of Business. Available at: https://business.aucegypt.edu/news/inclusive-development-and-fourth-industrial-revolution-mena

Adas, M. (2015) *Machines as the measure of men: Science, technology, and ideologies of Western dominance*. Ithaca: Cornell University Press.

Al Gurg, T. (2019) 'Education can secure the future of work in MENA region and beyond', Gulf News [online], 15 September. Available at: https://gulfnews.com/opinion/op-eds/education-can-secure-the-future-of-work-in-mena-region-and-beyond-1.66434742

'Algorism, n'. (n.d.) *Oxford English Dictionary* [online]. Oxford: Oxford University Press. Available at: http://www.oed.com/view/Entry/4956#eid7070189 (Accessed 21 January 2021).

Allen, D. (2020) 'Neom: An AI metropolis in the desert', MedicalExpo [online], 14 January. Available at: http://emag.medicalexpo.com/neom-an-ai-metropolis-in-the-desert/

Amin, G. (1995) *Egypt's economic predicament: A study in the interaction of external pressure, political folly and social tension in Egypt, 1960–1990*. Leiden: Brill.

arabicelit. (2015) 'Manifesto', *Arabic E-Lit* [online]. Available at: https://arabicelit.wordpress.com/manifesto/

Aulas, M. (1982) 'Sadat's Egypt: A balance sheet', *MERIP Reports* [online], 107, Available at: https://merip.org/1982/07/sadats-egypt-a-balance-sheet/

aus dem Moore, J., Chandran, V., and Schubert, J. (2018) 'The future of jobs in the Middle East', World Government Summit & McKinsey & Company [online]. Available at: https://www.mckinsey.com/~/media/mckinsey/featured%20insights/middle%20east%20and%20africa/are%20middle%20east%20workers%20ready%20for%20the%20impact%20of%20automation/the-future-of-jobs-in-the-middle-east.ashx

Beinin, J. (2009) 'Neo-liberal structural adjustment, political demobilization, and neo-authoritarianism in Egypt', in Guazzone, L. and Pioppi, D. (eds.) *The Arab state and neo-liberal globalization: The restructuring of state power in the Middle East*. Reading: Ithaca Press, pp. 19–46.

Blasim, H. (ed). (2016) *Iraq + 100: Stories from a century after the invasion*. Manchester: Comma Press.

Brown, L. (2019) 'Arab futurism', bido lito! [online], 101. Available at: https://web.archive.org/web/20210319093630/https://bidolito.co.uk/feature-arab-futurism-laaf-2019/ (Accessed 4 May 2022).

Campbell, I. (2018) *Arabic science fiction*. Cham: Palgrave MacMillan, p. 145–6

Cleveland, W. L. and Bunton, M. (2018) *A history of the modern Middle East*. Boulder, CO: Westview Press.

Comito, C. (2013) 'Science fiction in Arabic: "It was not born all of a sudden"', Arablit Quarterly [online], 30 September. Available at: https://arablit.org/2013/09/30/science-fiction-in-arabic-it-was-not-born-all-of-a-sudden/

Dazed. (2012) 'Al Qadiri & Al-Maria on Gulf Futurism', *Dazed* [online], 14 November. Available at: https://www.dazeddigital.com/music/article/15037/1/al-qadiri-al-maria-on-gulf-futurism

Desilver, D. and Masci, D. (2017) 'World's Muslim population more widespread than you might think', Pew Research Center [online] 31 January. Available at: https://www.pewresearch.org/fact-tank/2017/01/31/worlds-muslim-population-more-widespread-than-you-might-think/

Dubai. (2022) 'Dubai: City of innovation', *visitdubai.com* [online] Available at: https://www.visitdubai.com/en/invest-in-dubai/why-dubai/city-of-innovation

Egypt Vision 2030. (2020) 'Egypt's Vision 2030', *Egypt Vision 2030* [online] Available at: http://sdsegypt2030.com/?lang=en

El-Hawary, D. (2020) 'MENA jobs: Gearing up for the future', Ahram Online [online], 23 January. Available at: http://english.ahram.org.eg/NewsContent/50/1202/360018/AlAhram-Weekly/Economy/MENA-jobs-Gearing-up-for-the-future.aspx

ElSafy, I. (2019) 'UAE leads GCC in adopting Fourth Industrial Revolution', *Mubasher Info* [online], 19 May. Available at: english.mubasher.info/news/3480654/UAE-leads-GCC-in-adopting-Fourth-industrial-revolution

Farouk, E. and Saba, Y. (2019) 'Egyptian transport start-up SWVL targets expansion in Africa, Asia', Reuters [online], 16 September. Available at: https://www.reuters.com/article/us-egypt-economy-swvl/egyptian-transport-start-up-swvl-targets-expansion-in-africa-asia-idUSKBN1W10DQ

Fossett, K. (2013) 'Can science fiction survive in Saudi Arabia?', Foreign Policy [online], 10 December. Available at: https://foreignpolicy.com/2013/12/10/can-science-fiction-survive-in-saudi-arabia/

Gardner, F. (2020) 'Saudi tribe challenges crown prince's plans for tech city', BBC [online], 23 April. Available at: https://www.bbc.com/news/world-middle-east-52375343

Ghalayini, B. (ed.) (2019) *Palestine + 100: Stories from a century after the naqba*. Manchester: Comma Press.

Gordon, M. (2018) 'Forecasting instability: The case of the Arab Spring and the limitations of socioeconomic data', Wilson Center [online], 8 February. Available at: https://www.wilsoncenter.org/article/forecasting-instability-the-case-the-arab-spring-and-the-limitations-socioeconomic-data

Government of Jordan. (2014) 'Jordan 2025: A National Vision and Strategy', Government of Jordan [online], 14 March. Available at: https://jordankmportal.com/resources/jordan-2025-a-national-vision-and-strategy

Hamam, I. (2019) 'Images and imaginations of robots, cyborgs and automata'. Presentation at Global AI Narratives Middle East and North Africa. Cambridge: Leverhulme Centre for the Future of Intelligence.

Hosny, R. (2021) 'Al-Barrah البـرّ اح: The first Arabic AR and hologram novel', [online]. Available at: https://rehamhosny.website/al-barrah/

Kene-Okafor, T. (2021) 'Egyptian ride-sharing company SWVL plans to go public in a $1.5B SPAC merger', *Techcrunch.com* [online], 28 July. Available at: https://techcrunch.com/2021/07/28/egyptian-ride-sharing-company-swvl-plans-to-go-public-in-a-1-5b-spac-merger/

Kingdom of Saudi Arabia. (2020) 'Vision 2030: A Story of Transformation', Kingdom of Saudi Arabia [online]. Available at: https://www.vision2030.gov.sa/

Kirecci, M. A. (2007) Decline discourse and self-Orientalization in the writings of Al-Tahtāwī, Tāhā Husayn and Ziya Gökalp: A comparative study of modernization in Egypt and Turkey. PhD Thesis, University of Pennsylvania, Philadelphia. Available at: https://www.proquest.com/docview/304822520

Koppes, C. R. (1976) 'Captain Mahan, General Gordon, and the origins of the term "Middle East"', *Middle Eastern Studies*, 12(1), pp. 95–8.

Lane, E. W. (1909–1914) *Stories from the thousand and one nights*. Vol. XVI. The Harvard Classics. New York: P.F. Collier & Son. Available online from Bartleby.com (2001) at: https://www.bartleby.com/16/701.html

Langendorf, M. (2020) 'Digital stability: How technology can empower future generations in the Middle East', European Council on Foreign Relations (ECFR) [online]. Available at: https://www.ecfr.eu/publications/summary/digital_stability_how_technology_can_empower_future_generations_middle_east

Maceda, C. (2020) 'Rise of robots: Most UAE residents fear they will be out of work in ten years', *Zawya* [online], 30 January. Available at: https://www.zawya.com/mena/en/business/story/Rise_of_robots_Most_UAE_residents_fear_they_will_be_out_of_work_in_ten_years-ZAWYA20200130051846/

Makdisi, S. (1995) '"Postcolonial" literature in a neocolonial world: Modern Arabic culture and the end of modernity', *boundary 2*, 22(1), pp. 85–115.

Mohamed, H. (2019) 'Is Egypt ready for the 4th Industrial Revolution?', *EgyptToday* [online], 12 December. Available at: https://www.egypttoday.com/Article/3/78635/Is-Egypt-ready-for-the-4th-Industrial-Revolution

Museum of the Future. (2022) 'Where The Future Lives', Museum of the Future [online]. Available at: https://www.museumofthefuture.ae

Nabil, Y. (2019) 'In conversation with Mounir Nakhla of Egypt's Halan', Wamda [online], 9 January. Available at: https://www.wamda.com/2019/01/conversation-mounir-nakhla-halan

Nuruddin, Y. (2006) 'Ancient black astronauts and extraterrestrial jihads: Islamic science fiction as urban mythology', *Socialism and Democracy*, 20(3), pp.127–65.

OHCHR. (n.d.) 'Middle East and North African region', OHCHR [online]. Available at: https://www.ohchr.org/EN/Countries/MENARegion/Pages/MenaRegionIndex.aspx

Parikka, J. (2018) 'Middle East and other futurisms: imaginary temporalities in contemporary art and visual culture', *Culture, Theory and Critique*, 59(1), pp. 40–58.

Perfect Health صحةً مثالية (2016) اغنية غرنديزر مغامرات الروبوت يقدم الفضاء على سبيستون-spacetoon', [video]. Available at: https://www.youtube.com/watch?v=YykxHRJNuqw

Rizk, N., Noam, E., and Mutter, P. (2016) 'Media concentration in Egypt', in Noam, E (ed.) *Who owns the world media? Media concentration and ownership around the world*, New York: Oxford University Press, pp. 883–941.

Rehla ilal kamar [A trip to the moon]. (1959) Directed by H. A. Wahab [film]. Delta Film Productions.

Rizk, N. (2020) 'Artificial intelligence and inequality in the Middle East: The political economy of inclusion', in Dubber, M., Pasquale, F., and Das, S. (eds.) *The Oxford handbook of ethics and artificial intelligence*. Oxford: Oxford University Press, pp. 626–50.

Rizk, N. and Elkassas, S. (2010) 'The software industry in Egypt: What role for open source?', in Rizk, N. and Shaver L. (eds.) *Access to knowledge in Egypt: New research on intellectual property, innovation and development*. London: Bloomsbury, p. 138.

Sadaqat, R. (2018) 'Why the Fourth Industrial Revolution will create plenty of opportunities', *Khaleej Times* [online], 20 September. Available at: https://www.khaleejtimes.com/technology/why-the-fourth-industrial-revolution-will-create-plenty-of-opportunities

Scheck, J., Jones, R., and Said, S. (2019) 'A prince's $500 billion desert dream: Flying cars, robot dinosaurs and a giant artificial moon', *The Wall Street Journal* [online], 25 July. Available at: https://www.wsj.com/articles/a-princes-500-billion-desert-dream-flying-cars-robot-dinosaurs-and-a-giant-artificial-moon-11564097568

Schwab, K. (2016) The fourth industrial revolution: What it means and how to respond. World Economic Forum [online], January. Available at: https://www.weforum.org/agenda/2016/01/the-fourth-industrial-revolution-what-it-means-and-how-to-respond

Shaver, L., and Rizk, N. (eds.) (2010) *Access to knowledge in Egypt: New research on intellectual property, innovation and development*. London: Bloomsbury Publishing.

Sultan, Y. and Felsberger, S. (2019) 'Speculative data futures introduction: Current realities, future imaginations', *Knowledge Maze* [online], 10 March. Available at: https://knowledgemaze.wordpress.com/2022/03/10/speculative-data-futures-introduction-current-realities-future-imaginations/

The Tahrir Institute for Middle East Policy. (2019) 'TIMEP brief: Uber and Careem law', TIMEP [online], 2 December. Available at: https://timep.org/reports-briefings/timep-brief-uber-and-careem-law/

Truitt, E. R. (2015) *Medieval robots: Mechanism, magic, nature, and art*. Philadelphia: University of Pennsylvania Press.

The World Bank. (2022) 'Middle East and North Africa', World Bank [online], Available at: https://www.worldbank.org/en/region/mena

UAE. (2019) 'UAE future 2021–2030', The official portal of the UAE government [online]. Available at: https://u.ae/en/more/uae-future/2021-2030

UAE. (2022) 'Advanced skills strategy', The official portal of the UAE government [online]. Available at: https://government.ae/en/about-the-uae/strategies-initiatives-and-awards/federal-governments-strategies-and-plans/advanced-skills-strategy

UNHCR. (2022) 'Middle East and North Africa', UNHCR [online]. Available at: https://www.unhcr.org/en-us/middle-east-and-north-africa.html.

Unicef.org. (2022) 'UNICEF Middle East and North Africa', UNICEF [online]. Available at: https://www.unicef.org/mena/

WAM. (2020) 'Dubai future academy prepares UAE's workforce for fourth industrial revolution', *Emirates24|7* [online], 24 February. Available at: https://www.emirates247.com/news/emirates/dubai-future-academy-prepares-uae-s-workforce-for-fourth-industrial-revolution-2020-02-24-1.692694

Yahya, M. (2019) 'How has China's role in the Middle East evolved?', Malcolm H. Kerr Carnegie Middle East Center [online], 26 September. Available at: https://carnegie-mec.org/2019/09/26/how-has-china-s-role-in-middle-east-evolved-pub-79930

Yatakhayaloon.com. (2013) '*HWJN* the novel', [video]. Available at: http://yatakhayaloon.com/EN/HWJN_English.html

"سمير غانم مع الروبوت يقدم له الشاى فى الثمانينات" (Samir Ghanem with a robot serving him Tea in the 80s). (2018) *Dailymotion* [video], June 6. Available at: https://www.dailymotion.com/video/x6iwbzn

PART IV

EAST AND SOUTH EAST ASIA

19

Engineering Robots with Heart in Japan

The Politics of Cultural Difference in Artificial Emotional Intelligence

Hirofumi Katsuno and Daniel White

19.1 Introduction

While the concept of artificial intelligence (AI) in anglophone literature has often emphasized cognition, in Japanese imaginaries AI has always come with a body. Japan's most iconic early examples of AI, canonized in both anglophone and Japanese histories of robotics, were mechanized puppets (*karakuri ningyō*) that emerged in seventeenth-century Japan. Placed on display at festivals or in entertainment venues, the puppets had working gears that, although often covered in clothing, were easily visible and part of their embodied charm. When Japan's first 'artificial human' (*jinkō ningen*) was created by biologist Nishimura Makoto[1] in 1928, its body was imposing, standing nearly eleven feet tall and impressing visitors with its moving hands, head, and changing facial expressions (Robertson, 2018, pp. 12–14). With the most recent wave of companion robots released for mass consumption in Japan, AI now comes in a diverse array of bodily types: humanoid robots with hands that can hold your own (Pepper, Figure 19.1), fluffy cat-like cushions with tails but no head (Qoobo, Figure 19.2), and furry robots on wheels, whose bodies are intentionally warmed to the temperature of a human baby (LOVOT, Figure 19.3).

Even more important in Japan than giving artificial cognition a body, however, is giving it heart. Building AI in Japan has always been tied to the task of developing a robot with heart/mind (*kokoro*) (Katsuno, 2011; Takeno, 2011), affect (*jōcho*) (Ōhashi et al., 1985), emotion (*kanjō*) (Sugano 1997), imagination (*sōzōryoku*) (Tsukimoto, 2002), and consciousness (*ishiki*) (Kitamura, 2000). By

Figure 19.1 Pepper, by SoftBank Robotics
Photo by authors.

placing emotion at the centre of what it means to be both alive and intelligent, robotics engineers in Japan approached the problem of AI not as one of modelling and mirroring human cognition in a machine, but rather as facilitating a human–robot bond that would benefit society.

Figure 19.2 Qoobo, by Yukai Engineering
Photo by Hirofumi Katsuno.

Figure 19.3 LOVOT, by Groove X

Although the historical precedents for this cultural trope of human–robot affinity in Japan are best traced to, and most canonized and celebrated in, Tezuka Osamu's *Astro Boy* (*Tetsuan Atomu*), a manga running from 1952 to 1968 that later became a popular animated series, more recent examples suggest just how much Japan's robot culture has been consciously objectified and incorporated into the design of intelligent machines. Perhaps the best illustration of this often-nationalized emphasis on cultural distinction is found in Sony's Computer Science Laboratory's decision to rewrite the 'Three Laws of Robotics' proposed by science fiction author Isaac Asimov in 1942. Asimov's original laws were:

> First Law: A robot may not injure a human being or, through inaction, allow a human being to come to harm.
>
> Second Law: A robot must obey the orders given it by human beings except where such orders would conflict with the First Law.
>
> Third Law: A robot must protect its own existence as long as such protection does not conflict with the First or Second Law.

When Sony engineers were designing the dog-like pet robot AIBO, first released in 1999, they found these laws lacking in conviviality and instead proposed the 'New Laws of Robotics':

> First Law: Robots must not harm humans. They are allowed to run away from people who try to harm them, but they are not allowed to fight back.
>
> Second Law: In principle, robots should be attentive and affectionate to humans, but they should also be allowed to be rebellious at times.
>
> Third Law: In principle, robots are allowed to listen patiently to human complaints, but are also allowed to speak nastily at times (Fuse, 2003, p. 61).[2]

In contrast to Asimov's Laws, which require robots to internalize obedience to humans, Sony's laws state that robots should be designed to have an autonomous inner life that is not at the mercy of humans. In one interview, Doi Toshitada, one of the key creators of AIBO at Sony, noted that behind AIBO's recalcitrance 'there is a kind of emotion, an instinct, a sense of being a living thing . . . I think that's a kind of virtual will that comes out' (Fuse, 2003, p. 65). Doi goes on to explain, 'When a robot has its own emotions and acts on its own instincts, it will do what its owner doesn't want. This will heal the human' (Fuse, 2003, p. 61). Although Doi's statement appears at first paradoxical, it highlights the close relationship between animacy and intimacy that, for many Japanese roboticists, must work symbiotically if AI is going to, as Ōhashi Tsutomu and colleagues (1985, p. 53) have phrased it in their work theorizing robot affect, 'fulfil humans' emotional desires' (*ningen no jōcho-teki yokkyū o mitasu*). Importantly, the performance of such differences in robot culture through an emphasis on emotionality makes cultural distinction itself into a key contributing component of imagining and designing intelligent machines.

How do the perceptions, ethics, and significance of AI shift when it represents for people not the advancement of cognition beyond human capacities, but instead the cultivation of human–robot intimacy towards social progress? Moreover, how do perceptions and enactments of cultural difference, such as those performed by Sony engineers in their formulation of the New Laws of Robotics, shape how AI is imagined in Japan and is applied as a guiding framework for designing embodied forms of intelligence? Drawing on the recent history of robotics in Japan, marketing campaigns for mass-produced companion robots, as well as a year of collaborative fieldwork among roboticists in Tokyo and Kyoto, this chapter addresses these questions by analysing the imaginaries of Japanese roboticists and manufacturers building emotionally intelligent companion robots. We argue that although an emphasis on engineering 'robots with heart' has developed through intersections between fictional storytelling, robot performance, and technological design strategies that are particular to Japan's historical context, the idea of Japan's supposedly 'unique robot culture' has also been politicized in both anglophone and Japanese scholarship in ways that have made the question of cultural difference into a tool of robot design.

In this chapter we aim to show how the politics of cultural difference can become a device for imagining AI, for integrating it into robotic forms of embodiment, and for fixing its meaning and significance socially and politically. We first demonstrate how the anthropological concept of animism was reinvented as a cultural model to define the relationship between people and robots in Japan during the robot boom of the late twentieth century. Next, we trace how, since the 2010s, animism as a theme in robotics design has been adapted and incorporated into the concept of 'animacy engineering', which facilitates the design of robots that 'draw close' (*yorisou*) to humans in order to deliver emotional wellbeing. Finally, we discuss how Japanese views on cultural uniqueness in robotics draw not only from historical narratives and more recent adaptations of animism, but also from a contemporary cultural politics of government-driven investments in soft power. We conclude by leveraging these three ideas on the role of culture as a tool of design to generate a reflexive critique of 'cultural diversity' in anglophone scholarship on AI at large.

19.2 Animism and animacy in Japanese robotics culture

Japanese narratives of AI and robots have long been characterized both outside and within Japan as the cultural antithesis to their anglophone counterparts.

According to this model, whereas in the Western robotic imaginary intelligent machines signify a threat to humanity, in the Japanese imaginary machines are partners to humans, offering their technological skills to address problems of shared human–robot concern. Although this theme has featured in Japanese fiction (literature, drama, manga, anime) since at least the post-war period, it is also only one among a diverse variety of human–robot depictions, many of which are just as dystopian as those in the West.[3] However, while the theme of human–robot partnership did come to dominate the technological imaginary in Japan, it often did so in conjunction with practices of representing technology in Japan's modernity as a symbol of cultural distinctiveness in opposition to the West. In this regard, government and industry elites, drawing on a shared and heavily nostalgic imaginary of a premodern past that was rich in the indigenous and nativist symbolism of Shinto, spirits, and animism (Ivy, 1995; Kovacic, 2018), used robots as a tool for manufacturing a distinctively Japanese form of non-Western development.

It is for this reason that anglophone descriptions of Japan as the 'robot kingdom' (Schodt, 1988) were often embraced by manufacturers, media, and ministry bureaucrats in Japan. Since incorporating industry-specific technology from the United States from 1967 onwards, the industrial robot sector has advanced rapidly in Japan. By the mid-1970s Japan had become the leading global producer and user of industrial robots. A milestone was reached in 1980 when the Japanese auto industry surpassed its American counterpart in production, thanks largely to the rapid full-scale robotization of the industry. Meanwhile, since the late 1960s, out of an interest in robotic bipedal walking, some groups of researchers and engineers in Japan had been exploring robots' physicality as well as biomechanics and control theories. In 1996, nearly two decades after the initial industrial robot boom, the automobile manufacturer Honda's humanoid robot P2 (more popularly known as ASIMO) made its debut, successfully demonstrating the first-ever dynamic bipedal walk in the history of robotics. This sensation accelerated interest and investment in humanoid research in Japan, leading the Japanese government to launch several 'next-generation robot projects' (*jisedai robotto purojekuto*) that emphasized the development of humanoid robots as welcome sources of social interaction.

This trend represented a marked difference from the philosophy of the 'robot kingdom' up to the 1980s, which advocated robots as rationalized and practical tools for industry. The emergent discourse from the 1980s onward was characterized by a more *human* element, as is evident in the circulation of the word 'co-living' (*kyōsei*) to describe a fantasy of human–robot coexistence and harmony. In this vision, robots are expected to fulfil new roles as intimate companions and caregivers that provide such 'humane' tasks as child and elderly care.

Based on fieldwork among robot builders working in the wake of this boom period of humanoid robotics, one of us (Katsuno, 2011; 2015) identified the formation of two complementary narratives developing around the rise of humanoid robots in Japan. The first featured the emergence of a powerful discourse on the 'robot's heart' (*robotto no kokoro*). Through the staging of public performances and robot demonstrations hosted by manufacturers, humanoid robots often delivered amusing physical performances that expressed the living quality of intelligent machines. These events sparked in the public imagination the idea of a robot with heart, building on the representation of robots in popular anime. As introduced above, the influence of Tezuka Osamu's *Astro Boy* (1959–1968) on people's imagination in this respect was enormous. Documented by scholars like Hirose (2002), Robertson (2018), and Wagner (2013), many robotics engineers during this boom period cite anime like *Astro Boy* as inspiration for why they went into robotics. Tezuka's emphasis on Astro Boy's (*Atomu*) emotionality and heart, for example, can be seen in the work of prominent roboticists working in the 1980s, such as Sugano Shigeki and Takeno Junichi, who developed some of the first robots in Japan equipped with emotion capacities, engines, and 'heart' (Sugano, 1997; Takeno, 2011).

A second dominant theme during the rise of humanoid robotics in the 1980s emphasized the cultural uniqueness of Japan, imagined as a place that was not resistant to, but rather explicitly committed to, incorporating robots into society. Such narratives during this period often came with references to 'animism', a term popularized by the nineteenth-century anthropologist Edward B. Tylor and employed in his book *Primitive Culture* (1871/1891) to describe a primordial form of religion. Tylor described animism as characterized by a belief in the living quality of spirits in natural and material objects. Typical for his time, Tylor cast these beliefs in an evolutionary framework, charting a linear development from belief in spirits through polytheistic and monotheistic religions that were characteristic of more 'complex' societies. When the ethnocentric and evolutionary aspects of Tylor's model were subsequently rejected by later anthropologists, comparative studies of animism similarly gave way to more context-based and relativistic perspectives.

However, during the robot boom period in Japan, the notion of animism was often recalled by roboticists as a means for 'culturalizing' the rise of robot technology in Japan and for generalizing an affinity that certain technophiles and robot fans expressed towards robots. A common assertion in Japan, and one repeated in popular anglophone works on Japanese robot culture (Geraci, 2006; Hornyak, 2006; Kaplan, 2004), is that Japanese people have a unique sensitivity and affection for robots because of an indigenous Shinto-derived openness to animism, which does not draw stark distinctions between inanimate and organic objects. By contrast, according to this position, Western society's Judeo-Christian monotheistic beliefs propose a dualistic model of material and spirit, human and non-human, and good and evil, making it impossible to accept nonhuman robots as equal to humans. In the catalogue of The Great Robot Exposition held at the National Museum of Nature and Science in Tokyo in 2007, at the height of the next-generation robot boom, curator Suzuki Kazuyoshi wrote, 'People in Euro-American cultures do not associate organic images, like those of human beings and animals, with robots. Robots that communicate with human beings, like *Atomu* (Astroboy) are distinctive to Japanese culture'.

This rhetorical habit of positing Japanese culture as the antithesis to that of the West, popular at least since precedents set by anthropologist Ruth Benedict's (1946/2005) *The Chrysanthemum and the Sword*, a long-time best seller in Japan, has been commonly reproduced within Japanese robot culture. Rendered into a tool to promote an emerging industry though a cultural frame, roboticists (Sugano, 2011), journalists (Tajika, 2001), and curators like Suzuki (2007) of robot expositions helped promote the idea that Japanese people value the living quality of material objects and have thus accepted robots as non-threatening members of the natural world. Spreading through mass media, the notion of Japan as a 'robot kingdom' subsequently inspired a series of government investments and policies promoting robotics as the answer to a variety of social challenges such as manual labour shortages, elderly care, and a stagnating economy that has persisted since the 1990s.

Despite the concern by scholars both in and outside Japan that such appeals to animism entail processes of self-Orientalism, the concept of animism has not died out through critical scholarship but has rather been transformed. Anthropologist Okuno Takuji sought to characterize the rise of robots in contemporary Japan with the term 'techno-animism', updating the concept of 'animism' and repurposing it for an emerging age of high technological growth. According to Okuno (2001, p. 33),

> Since ancient times, the Japanese have believed that even the smallest insect has a soul, and in the villages of the past, people saw the soul in all plants, trees, insects, and fish, and talked with them. Japan can be said to be an animistic world. Today, having lost such nature, we see the soul in machines. In other words, we see living things in robots. I would like to call this a new kind of animism, 'techno-animism'.

Okuno subsequently sought to broaden his notion of 'techno-animism' to describe qualities of East Asian culture at large. However, as anthropologist Ikeda Mitsuho (2016) criticizes, Okuno's argument reflects little more than an Orientalist assumption (or more specifically a 'techno-Orientalist' one) that people in East Asia, including the Japanese, remain animist at heart. In this sense, narratives that reduce Japanese robot culture to animism, including Okuno's argument, represent a strategic argument that can only be understood in the context of Japan's modernity, in which certain elites sought to distinguish a uniquely 'Japanese' form of 'technological development' or 'knowledge' that was borrowed from the West but encompassed a 'Japanese spirit' (*wakon yōsai*).[4] This is not to suggest that such discourses on animism are empty of authenticity but only that they function, as Jolyon Thomas (2019, p. 162) argues in his critique of a popular conflation between the terms 'animation' (*animēshon*) and 'animism' (*animizumu*), as an '"invented tradition" if ever there was one'. Such claims are further supported by the fact that there exists no indigenous word for 'animism' in the Japanese language, with its reference usually rendered, as Thomas (2019, p. 162) explains, 'in the *katakana* syllabary reserved for foreign loan words'.

Of course, that traditions are 'invented', as originally argued by Hobsbawm and Ranger (1983/2012), make them no less real. In fact, in many cases it is the creative, innovative, and organic emergence of traditions in response to contemporary cultural environments, contexts, and problems that make them so affectively salient. In our own fieldwork we have often observed people describing that they can actually *feel* the intangible lifelike qualities—a 'heart' or 'soul' (*tamashii*)—in robots, and even take specific pleasure in such sensations (Katsuno, 2011; White and Katsuno, 2021). This socio-technical capacity for actively and often playfully cultivating a sense that things are alive, which we call 'animacy', can be distinguished from 'animism' as a quality of Japan's traditional heritage and heritage-making. In this sense, faculties of animacy are hardly unique to Japan, but rather are characteristic of an entire movement in critical theory and anthropology that is paying increased attention to the living and animated quality of the world (Bennett, 2001, 2010; Henare et al., 2007; Kohn, 2013; Silvio, 2019; Stainova, 2019; Weston, 2017). Our point here is not that an affective sensitivity to the lifelike quality of robots does not exist in Japan; it is rather that such dispositions cannot be disentangled from the fictional stories, material technologies, and political contexts that mutually engender them.

As such stories become rehearsed and recycled in Japanese robot cultures, an emphasis on animism becomes not only a common theme of robot storytelling and philosophy but also an explicit target of engineering. In Section 19.3 we discuss how the notion of animism circulating in the 1980s becomes incorporated into specific robotics engineering practices in the 1990s and beyond that make the lifelike quality of robots that we refer to as animacy into a specific target of interactive design.

19.3 Intelligent machines as intimate partners

Building on a growing interest in robot heart and emotion in the 1980s, the robot boom of the late 1990s and early 2000s served as a catalyst for breakthroughs in Human–Robot Interaction (HRI). A feature driving Japan-based development in the field was the increasing mutual influence of previously distinct approaches of academic and entertainment robotics. Whereas academic robotics had primarily focused on experiments in human–robot interaction in laboratory settings to understand and build models of human–machine sociality (Asada, 2010; Ishiguro, 2009; Sugano and Ogata, 2006), the entertainment field aimed to develop evocative and attractive technical objects to elicit a sense of animacy and attraction in users. We call this type of experimental, bottom-up approach to robot design 'animacy engineering', whereby animistic narratives and tropes of the robot's heart and presence are incorporated into technological platforms that deliver intimacy through human–robot interaction. In animacy engineering, designers approach the robot as an experimental device that can engender new and unexpected pleasures unique to human–robot relationships. This characteristic of animacy engineering allows robot companies to test and leverage the conditions for human–robot intimacy to build new markets for profit maximization in Japan. In this way, cultural notions of a distinctively 'Japanese' sensitivity to animism became incorporated as a practice of robot design.

Unlike early humanoid research in Japan as well as traditional anglophone AI research, which aimed to model the movements, communication styles, and intelligence of natural organisms, a new style of entertainment robots in Japan focused on building experimental sociable machines that could explore, test, and create affective bonds with human users. Manufacturers building mass-market entertainment robots today, such as Sony, SoftBank, and GROOVE X, hope these 'emotionally intelligent' companion robots will be able to understand and elicit emotions in users. To realize this aim, they draw on new technologies such as cloud computing, wireless networks, the Internet of Things (IoT), machine learning based on big data, as well as innovations in image recognition and voice recognition. These technologies have made it possible for robots to exhibit certain emotional capacities, such as reading facial expressions and responding to humans' emotional signals.

Such affect-centred technologies have also facilitated a transition in robot design from one that imitates a living organism to one that can create a unique sense of presence based on its relationship with the human user. This transition is marked by an increasingly imaginative ethos of experimentation with nonanthropomorphic designs, drawing from trends in digital gaming and toys like Tamagotchi popularized in the 1990s (Katsuno and White, 2022). For example, Yukai Engineering's Qoobo robot, a cat-like cushion robot, incorporates a wagging tail into its body but not a head. From the manufacturer's point of view, what is important is not to reproduce the intelligence of a real cat but rather to create a unique relationship of curiosity, comfort, and partnership that is sustained interactively. Illustrating the close relationship between AI research and the entertainment robotics industry in Japan, there are specific commercial reasons motivating such experiments with design. Entertainment robotics manufacturers have regularly identified what they call the 'three-month wall' (*sankagetsu no kabe*), referring to the period after which consumers tend to lose their fascination with robots that are built merely to replicate living creatures. Although people's first encounters with human-like robots with realistic motion in the 1990s filled them with a sense of initial confusion, surprise, intrigue, and enchantment, this seems to have worn thin. Robots whose designs emphasized verbal communication through natural language processing faced even more challenges in keeping people interested in interaction. Growing accustomed to the robot's movements and communication skills, users began to recognize a gap between the robot and the living organism after which it was modelled, thus creating a sense of the robot's limitations. To overcome this issue, robot designers today aim to create systems that automatically generate a variety of unexpected pleasures through the reproduction of programmable, but not predetermined, frames of social interaction, such as AIBO's willingness to offer its paw based on its 'mood', itself determined by a sequence of previous interactions labelled as positive or negative. In this way, the human–robot relationship is refreshed through unexpected encounters that renew interest and build affection through the acknowledgment of the robot's autonomous but interactively generated presence.

This emphasis on designing a 'sense of presence' and 'life' (*seimeikan*) emerged most prominently in the first-generation AIBO in 1999, which was intended to be the world's first full-fledged pet robot. One way AIBO's engineers worked to achieve this was by designing an 'instincts and emotions model' (*honnō to jōdō moderu*), which gave AIBO the ability to communicate joy and sadness through its movements, and coloured lights in its eyes that created a sense of animacy (Fujita, 1999). In designing the new aibo (which Sony branded in lowercase), which was revived in 2018 after the first AIBO was discontinued in 2006, Sony made the concept of *seimeikan* even more central to its development. While adapting the movement of actual dogs, the Sony team invented 'a doggy language that expresses *seimeikan* unique to aibo' (Katsumi, 2019) through twenty-two small, high-powered actuators that they developed for this purpose. They then adjusted the robotic-dog language to creatively interactive ends through aibo's growth model. The growth element of the first generation AIBO was based on the assumption that users would perceive the gradual unlocking of movement programs that had been set up by the developers to mark the transition from one prefigured growth period to another, such as from youth (*shōnenki*) to adolescence (*seinenki*). The new aibo, on the other hand, is designed so that each aibo learns from its owner's interactions, develops its own personality, and enhances its presence through repeated feedback from the built-in AI. This system enables each individual aibo to understand its surroundings in real time and act autonomously. Its 'Personality AI', stored in the cloud, records aibo's behaviours at home as personal episodes and processes them according to each owner's preferences and behaviours. The design is such that each aibo develops its unique personality by interacting with users. From this perspective, the value and purpose of an intelligent machine emerges not through modelling a universal simulacrum of life, such as through Rodney Brooks' six-legged walking robot prototypes which in part inspired AIBO's design (Fujita and Kitano, 1998), but rather through the context of human–robot affinity that emerges organically and unpredictably in sites of human–robot interaction.

It is important to note that Sony's vision here is not limited to the symbiosis of robots and humans, but that it also incorporates a 'model' relationship in which both can grow together. In an interview, Matsui Naoya, the leader of the new aibo development group, proposed that the formation of 'sensory values' (*kansei kachi*)—values that appeal to people's emotions and sensibilities—would be important for realizing such a relationship. According to Matsui, such sensory values are shaped by encouraging owners to constantly take notice of aibo's feelings. For Matsui, this is what drives 'the process of aibo's growth and individualization'. As he explained, 'We hoped that this experience will help owners to develop the mental capacity to show consideration for others' (Katsumi, 2019). Engineers like Matsui thus embrace and incorporate the idea that the kinds of intelligence, interaction, and affection that arise between human and robot are not the result of accurately modelling human intelligence in a machine system, but rather of experimenting with the potential of emotionality at large.

The creation of sensory value as a means to engineer 'animacy' is not limited to the latest aibo but has served as a common development theme for AI-equipped social robotics since the 2010s. Inaugurating this trend was what Japanese telecommunication company SoftBank introduced in 2014 as the world's 'first emotional robot', Pepper. Equipped with emotion recognition software, the humanoid robot can theoretically detect anger and sorrow in voice tones, facial expressions, and language, and can display pleasure when praised. For its sponsor, SoftBank founder Son Masayoshi, Pepper represented his dream to bring robot technology from Japan to the world, building off a sense that the 'Japanese have a soft spot for robots like Pepper that look somewhat human and sometimes appear to show emotion' (Kageyama, 2021). The basic model for Pepper's emotion generation engine was based on Mitsuyoshi Shunji's (2008) emotional map, which originally aimed to integrate brain processes with emotions and physical reactions. Following this model, Pepper was imagined to react via the replication of 'pseudo hormones' (Mitsuyoshi, 2021, p. 41), and use the balance of these hormones to create and act on emotions. To the disappointment of many, however, and as suggested in informal workshops we joined with SoftBank Robotics staff, the original model was too complex to integrate into software and was dramatically simplified as a consequence. However, by designing a robot that could not only read emotions but, in the eyes of its developers, even 'have' a heart of its own, SoftBank attempted to propose a vision for a future in which robots can 'draw near to' (*yorisou*) humans and partner with them as life companions.

This concept of 'drawing near' (*yorisou*) and 'partnering' (*yorisoi*), which often appears in the branding of Pepper, refers not only to the physical proximity of the robot to the person but also, and more importantly, to the process of empathizing with people and providing emotional support. Given the limited technical capacities of Pepper, however, SoftBank communicated this vision less through Pepper's various applications and more through storytelling scenarios scripted through advertising. In a series of TV commercials by Softbank titled 'Key Arc' (*Kagi*) aired at the time of Pepper's introduction in 2014, Pepper is depicted foremost as a robot with heart, cultivated and expected to grow through ongoing interaction with its users.[5] Importantly, however, Pepper also comes with limitations, a technological fact that SoftBank has regularly leveraged to emotional appeal. Although Pepper is designed to support humans emotionally, it does this by inviting reciprocity, inviting humans to care for the still somewhat flawed Pepper in return. This strategy reflects a common theme in Japanese robotics culture, best reflected in the work of roboticists like Okada Michio (2016) who advocate for the value of 'human dependency' (*hito to no kakawari*) cultivated through 'weak robots' (*yowai robotto*).

The commercial begins with a scene of a high school girl walking alone on a riverbank, representing someone whom Pepper might typically comfort. The scene then shifts to a male employee of Softbank observing Pepper through a half-open door. (In fact, in the longer storyline of these ads, the girl is hinted to be his daughter.) The employee then addresses Pepper, who is rehearsing interaction in a mirror just before making its debut in human society:

MAN: You were created to open the door of happiness. Because, apparently, people alone can't make people happy. [The male employee hands Pepper a key.]
PEPPER: I'm embarrassed to hear you say such a fancy thing.
MAN: You talk a little too much.
PEPPER: What?
MAN: You're not ready yet.
PEPPER: I'm sorry . . . I'm upset.

The exchange in this segment implies that the new robots equipped with emotion recognition AI will 'draw closer to' (*yorisou*) humans than can humans to each other and will thus better lead people to happiness. To this end, what is required of robots is not to guide human imagination and behaviour by making a strong impression through short-term interactions through words and movements, as in the case of conventional social and communication robots, but rather to induce emotional well-being by making people feel a heart-to-heart connection. This distinction from communication robots is further emphasized with the male employee's comically delivered line, 'You talk a little too much', suggesting that this previous category of social robots failed to deliver the kind of emotional support humans need to flourish.

Kazutaka Hasumi, who was part of the team responsible for the development of Pepper at SoftBank robotics, points out that the key to building a relationship in which robot and human can 'draw near' (*yorisou*) to one another is the sense of 'presence' (*sonzaikan*). To achieve this goal, however, Hasumi

> did not think of making a robot that looks exactly like a human . . . but [rather] a robot that faces people and moves their hearts. Our goal was to create an existence (*sonzai*) that would be familiar to people, that would be happy and sad with them, and that would encourage them.
>
> (Yamashita, 2016)

Placing Hasumi's comment in the context of the message in the commercial shows that the aim of Pepper's developers was to create a sense of intimate and caring presence through a form of empathy that was not modelled on the human, but rather was unique to a robot. In this imaginary, being with a robot makes human life more enjoyable. The robot here is not a substitute for a model lifeform or a labour force, as it was in Čapek's original fiction (1921/2004) that has so dominated the Western imaginary of human–robot relations, but is rather an irreplaceable presence that harmonizes with the human living environment and contributes to human happiness. In this sense the robot resembles less a technology of 'artificial intelligence', as the term is understood in the West, but rather of what Paul Roquet (2016) calls 'ambient media'—mood-enhancing technologies aimed at providing emotional calm and reassurance in a neoliberal world of increasing anxiety and fear. Similar to how ambient media such as background music or interior design operate on people's affects by creating an atmosphere, robots like Pepper generate a sense of comfort through presence. Similarly, in contrast to conventional robots that intentionally try to attract people's attention when they provide information through voice conversations or through overt body movements, the main feature of the emotional robot is the invisible work that AI performs in the background through emotion recognition technology as it actively registers stress in a human user's voice, language, or bodily gestures and adjusts its actions to deliver comfort. While robots like Pepper are nowhere near this level of technological sophistication, they serve as material 'platforms' (Robertson,

2018, pp. 19–25), in combination with the storytelling tools of advertising, that can incrementally bring that future to fruition.

19.4 Materializing a society with heart

Thus far this chapter has traced how a self-awareness of cultural difference in Japan's robot cultures, expressed most specifically through the concept of animism and then later through an emotion and presence-based animacy, functioned as a tool for designing intelligent machines. In this section we show how imaginaries of cultural difference serve as tools for designing society at large.

The active cultivation of an image of Japan's culture, and in particular its robot culture, as unique is not limited to the engineers and manufacturers of companion robots we discussed above. Nor is it limited to the worlds of fantasy, fiction, and fandom that in mutual synergy with one another build and play on globally circulating images of Japan as a 'robot kingdom' (Schodt, 1988), with people supposedly and characteristically 'loving the machine' (Hornyak, 2006). Rather, this idea of a unique robotics culture intersects with broader literary practices of theorizing Japanese cultural traits, known as *Nihonjinron* (theories of Japaneseness) or simply *bunkaron* (culture theory) in Japanese (Befu, 2001). Emerging in response to Japan's modernization processes formally consecrated in the 1868 Meiji Restoration, whereby Japan's technological development was uncomfortably tied to that of the West, the trope of Japanese uniqueness has been politicized both by Japanese political elites and foreign academics seeking to 'distinguish' Japan for varied purposes of what George Yúdice (2003) has called 'cultural expediency'. This both explicit and implicit application of culture as a tool of politics has rendered Japan's robot culture into a device for nation building and contemporary policymaking (Katsuno, 2015; Kovacic, 2018), with implications for how Japan's state bureaucrats have imagined the role of AI in this process.

Jennifer Robertson (2018) documents how the Japanese government has long used science and technology policy, and in particular robotics, not only to solve its socioeconomic challenges at home but also to boost its prestige abroad. This application of robotics as 'soft power' (Nye, 2004), a concept deeply embraced by Japan's political elites since the early 2000s (White, 2015; 2022), utilizes culture as a means to build both robots and an attractive future society in which intelligent machines coexist harmoniously with humans. For example, in 2006, newly elected prime minister Abe Shinzō's cabinet created the Innovation 25 Strategy Council (*Inobēshon 25 Senryaku Kaigi*) and published a series of white papers, some in the form of manga, that illustrated how robots would fully integrate into everyday domestic life by 2025 (Robertson, 2018,

33–35). Designed to promote a 'robot-dependent society', the programme's authors imagined that Japan's cutting-edge robotics technology would deliver happiness and social stability through robots that fulfilled household needs. In its emphasis on domestic and feminized depictions of labour in house cleaning, cooking, and care for an elderly family member, however, the programme applied tropes of cultural uniqueness to technology policy as much as it reproduced traditional Japanese gendered hierarchies and value structures (Robertson, 2018, pp. 50–79).

Similar government initiatives demonstrate the hype and hope to which robot culture has been activated as a tool of national policy. In 2014, as described by Kovacic (2018), Japan's Ministry of Economy, Trade and Industry (METI) 'formed the Robot Revolution Realization Council' with the aim to 'realize a "New Industrial Revolution Driven by Robots" through its "Japan Revitalization Strategy"'. By making Japan the 'world's robot innovation hub', the program sought to disseminate 'robots across Japan . . . aiming to achieve a society with the highest level of robot utilisation in the world' (METI, cited in Kovacic, 2018, p. 576). In 2015, the Headquarters for Japan's Economic Revitalization proposed a similar 'Robot Revolution', a summary of which it published in English, in order to 'maintain its status as "Robotics Superpower" in various aspects such as robot production and utilisation with focus on the manufacturing field which Japan boasts to the world' (2015, p. 1).

Mateja Kovacic (2018), Jennifer Robertson (2018), Yuji Sone (2017), Cosima Wagner (2013), and other scholars of Japan's robotics history see in these programmes an effort to create a homogenous and uniform history of indigenous innovation that extends from Japan's traditional artisan culture (*monozukuri*) to its contemporary technological innovation. As Kovacic (2018, pp. 573–4) argues:

> Japanese industry and the government are co-creating a national robot history that aims to legitimize a particular vision of a future robot society. Rather than being an issue of 'robots taking over', it is about existing regimes of power animating robots to assert a particular set of social values and views on gender, family, work, ethnicity, and history.

In reference to the common Western trope of robot rebellion, dominant from at least Čapek's text to what Jennifer Rhee calls the modern 'robotic imaginary' (2018, p. 5), Kovacic's assessment foregrounds how conscious and reflexive uses of culture render the 'friendly robot' in Japan into a symbol of cultural distinction. As she writes, 'This hegemonic process includes mobilisation and interpretation of history, highly symbolic cultural sites, and a redefinition of "Japaneseness" through applying the *monozukuri* discourse on robots. As a result, a single robotic narrative and culture are privileged and used to assert a particular set of values and norms' (Kovacic, 2018, p. 574). Kovacic's analysis of the politicization of Japan's robot culture, combined with our description of culture as a tool of robot design, suggests the difficulty of disentangling processes of modelling intelligence in machines from their social and political contexts and contests.

While these dominant discourses of Japan's 'unique robot culture' persist in the production of homegrown robot fantasy worlds as well as in government policy, there are also signs of re-evaluation and reflection. Sensitive to critiques that Japan's government has relied perhaps too heavily on technology at the expense of the humans it is meant to support, recent government AI policies have begun to reinsert the 'human' (*ningen*) into its visions for the future. In its Society 5.0 project (Cabinet Office of Japan, 2015a), launched as part of Japan's Fifth Science and Technology Basic Plan (2016–2020), the government stated that it aims to cultivate 'convergence between cyberspace and physical space, enabling AI-based on big data and robots to perform or support . . . the work . . . that humans have done up to now' (Cabinet Office of Japan, 2015b). Society 5.0 builds on Society 4.0, which the government labelled the 'information society':

> In the past information society, the common practice was to collect information via the network and have it analysed by humans. In Society 5.0, however, people, things, and systems are all connected in cyberspace and optimal results, obtained by AI exceeding the capabilities of humans, are fed back [into] physical space. This process brings new value to industry and society in ways not previously possible . . . Japan aims to become the first country in the world to achieve a human-centered society (Society 5.0) in which anyone can enjoy a high quality of life full of vigor.
>
> (Cabinet Office of Japan, 2015b)

Even more recently, the Japanese Cabinet Office's Sixth Science and Technology Basic Plan, launched in 2021, has emphasized the concept of human-centred AI (*ningen-chūshin AI*). The report also newly cites the need to develop 'diverse' (*tayō*) strategies to adapt human-centred AI to social and individual wellness, and advocates for incorporating humanities and social-scientific perspectives into science policy and education (Cabinet Office of Japan, 2021, pp. 4, 67). These novel policy directions suggest that government officials and experts recognize the importance of applying diverse and even critical social scientific and humanities perspectives to science and technology policy. While it remains to be seen if such policies will feed into the mass market for companion robots, where AI is tested in a marketplace of consumer desire for technologically mediated forms of comfort and intimacy, these shifts suggest the importance and influence that academic critiques of AI can make on government AI policy.

19.5 Conclusion

In this chapter we aimed to demonstrate not only how the importance of emotion and heart (*kokoro*) distinguishes Japan's AI and robot imaginaries from those in the West, but also how cultural distinction itself has become a tool within Japan's robot culture. As we suggest, Japanese narratives of AI and robots have long been characterized as the cultural antithesis to their anglophone counterparts: where robots in the West pose a threat to humanity, those in Japan are partners providing emotional support and comfort. While we have endeavoured to show that such shorthand cultural distinctions circulating in anglophone imaginaries do not neatly map onto local experiences in Japan, we also want to emphasize that these narratives of overly simplified cultural difference can feed back into robotics design practices in Japan. Although this phenomenon is especially prevalent in the field of emotion-based AI research, which is closely integrated with Japan's emerging markets for mass-produced companion robots, it also drives political applications of robot culture in government science and technology policy.

Placing the imagination of intelligent machines in Japan in their cultural and political context helps illustrate how Japanese AI narratives challenge hard distinctions made between reason and emotion in anglophone AI research. However, and perhaps even more importantly, observations on the cultural politics of these shifting distinctions productively diversify the notion of 'culture' itself. Although there are increasing calls by research institutes developing AI ethics protocols to ensure that intelligent systems are sensitive to 'cultural' diversity, and avoid 'bias' and 'ethnocentrism', often the answers proposed to address such concerns rely upon definitions of cultural sensitivity that conflate culture with a nation or an ethnic or language group (White and Katsuno, 2019). A better approach might, like Sony's AIBO engineers, concede that the meaning of intelligence is not prefigured by academic models of human intelligence but is instead collectively determined through human–machine interaction, and accordingly adopt a diverse, context-based, politically conscious, and reflexive approach to culture as a consequence.

Endnotes

1. Throughout the text of this chapter, Japanese names are written with family name first, followed by first name.
2. All translations from the Japanese are the authors' own.
3. In Jennifer Robertson's (2018, p. 5) assessment, 'From the 1920s to the present day in Japan, robots have been cast as both threatening *and* helpful to humans, but mostly the latter.'

4. Additional adaptations and critiques of this concept of 'techno-animism' can be found in Allison (2006), Galbraith (2011), and Jensen and Blok (2013).
5. Although no longer accessible through SoftBank's official website, at the time of writing a reproduction of these ads was still available here (dialogue from the second of the three segments): https://www.youtube.com/watch?v=Lu60qwR-Wvo

References

Allison, A. (2006) *Millennial monsters: Japanese toys and the global imagination.* Berkeley: University of California Press.

Asada, M. (2010) *Robotto to iu shisō: nō to chinō no nazo ni idomu (Robot as a thought: tackling the mysteries of brain and intelligence).* Tokyo: Nihon Hōsō Shuppan Kyōkai.

Asimov, I. (1942/1950) 'Runaround', in *I, robot.* New York: Gnome Press, ch. 3.

Befu, H. (2001) *Hegemony of homogeneity: An anthropological analysis of 'Nihonjinron'.* Melbourne: Trans Pacific Press.

Benedict, R. (1946/2005) *The chrysanthemum and the sword: Patterns of Japanese culture.* Boston: Houghton Mifflin.

Bennett, J. (2001). *The enchantment of modern life: Attachments, crossings, and ethics.* Princeton, NJ: Princeton University Press.

Bennett, J. (2010) *Vibrant matter: A political ecology of things.* Durham, NC: Duke University Press.

Cabinet Office of Japan. (2015a) 'Dai gokki kagaku gijutsu kihon keikaku (Fifth science and technology basic plan)'. Tokyo: Cabinet Office. Available at: https://www.google.com/url?sa=t&rct=j&q=&esrc=s&source=web&cd=&ved=2ahUKEwio3bzSlOX7AhUYi1wKHUfDAuUQFnoECAoQAQ&url=https%3A%2F%2Fwww8.cao.go.jp%2Fcstp%2Fkihonkeikaku%2F5basicplan_en.pdf&usg=AOvVaw3GT62xKD9I849eqoU76Cfk

Cabinet Office of Japan. (2015b) 'Society 5.0'. Tokyo: Cabinet Office. Available at: https://www8.cao.go.jp/cstp/english/society5_0/index.html (Accessed 1 August 2021).

Cabinet Office of Japan. (2021) 'Dai rokki kagaku gijutsu inobēshon kihon keikaku (Sixth science and technology innovation basic plan)'. Tokyo: Cabinet Office. Available at: https://www8.cao.go.jp/cstp/english/index.html

Čapek, K. (1921/2004) *R.U.R. (Rossum's Universal Robots).* New York: Penguin.

Fujita, M. (1999) 'Petto gata robotto no kansei hyōgen (Emotional expressions of a pet-type robot)', *Journal of the Robotics Society of Japan,* 17(7), pp. 947–51.

Fujita, M. and Kitano, H. (1998) 'Development of an autonomous quadruped robot for robot entertainment', *Autonomous Robots,* 5, pp. 7–18.

Fuse, H. (2003) *Tetsuwan Atomu wa denkihitsuji no yume o miruka (Does Astro Boy dream of an electric sheep?)?* Tokyo: Shōbunsha.

Galbraith, P. W. (2011) 'Bishōjo games: 'Techno-intimacy' and the virtually human in Japan', *Game Studies,* 11, pp. 31–4.

Geraci, R. M. (2006) 'Spiritual robots: Religion and our scientific view of the natural world', *Theology and Science*, 4, pp. 229–46.

Headquarters for Japan's Economic Revitalization, Ministry of Economy, Trade, and Industry. (2015) 'Robot revolution executive summary'. Available at: http://www.meti.go.jp/english/press/2015/pdf/0123_01a.pdf (Accessed 1 June 2018).

Henare, A., Martin, H., and Sari, W. (eds.) (2007) *Thinking through things: Theorising artefacts ethnographically*. Abingdon: Routledge.

Hirose, M. (2002) 'Hyūmanoido no yume: Tetsuwan Atomu (The dream of humanoids: Astro Boy)', in Y. Onezawa (ed.) *Robotto manga wa jitsugen suru ka: robotto manga meisaku ansorojī + robotto kaihatsu saizensen hōkoku (Making robot manga a reality: Anthology of robot manga masterpieces and a report from the front lines on robot development)*. Tokyo: Jitsugyō no Nihonsha, pp. 51–64.

Hobsbawm, E. J. and Ranger, T. O. (eds.) (1983/2012) *The invention of tradition*. Cambridge: Cambridge University Press.

Hornyak, T. N. (2006) *Loving the machine: The art and science of Japanese robots*. Tokyo: Kodansha International.

Ikeda, M. (2016) 'Supiritto wa saibuni yadoritamau: pāsupekuthivizumu o tōshite mita ningen=kikai jōtai ni tsuite (Spirit dwells in the details: On the human-machine state as seen through perspectivism)', *Seizongaku*, 9, pp. 260–73.

Ishiguro, H. (2009) *Andoroido saiensu: ningen o shiru tame no robotto kenkyū (Android science: Robotics research to understand human beings)*. Tokyo: Mainichi Communications

Ivy, M. (1995) *Discourses of the vanishing: Modernity, phantasm, Japan*. Chicago: University of Chicago Press.

Jensen, C. B. and Blok, A. (2013) 'Techno-animism in Japan: Shinto cosmograms, actor-network theory, and the enabling powers of non-human agencies', *Theory, Culture & Society*, 30, pp. 84–115.

Kageyama, Y. (2021) 'Japan's Softbank says Pepper robot remains "alive" and well', AP News [online], 30 June. Available at: https://apnews.com/article/robotics-japan-health-coronavirus-pandemic-technology-5393d4bb34110b0976a0c18b5f3f41f4 (Accessed 6 August 2021).

Kaplan, F. (2004) 'Who is afraid of the humanoid? Investigating cultural differences in the acceptance of robots', *International Journal of Humanoid Robotics*, 1(3), pp. 465–80.

Katsumi, A. (2019) 'Saisentan AI de seimeikan o hyōgen shi kanseikachi o tsuikyū (Expressing a sense of life with cutting-edge AI and pursuing sensory value)', *Recruit Works Institute* [online], 10 June. Available at: https://www.works-i.com/works/series/seikou/detail025.html (Accessed 6 August 2021).

Katsuno, H. (2011) 'The robot's heart: Tinkering with humanity and intimacy in robot-building', *Japanese Studies*, 31(1), pp. 93–109.

Katsuno, H. (2015) 'Branding humanoid Japan', in Kirsch, G., Martinez, D., and White, M. (eds.) *Assembling Japan: Modernity, technology and global culture*. Bern: Peter Lang, pp. 205–30.

Katsuno, H. and White, D. (2022) 'Haptic creatures: Tactile affect and human-robot intimacy in Japan' in Belk, R. and Minowa, Y. (eds.) *Consumer culture theory in Asia: History and current issues*. London: Routledge, pp. 242–62.

Kitamura, N. (2000) *Robotto wa kokoro o motsu ka: saibā ishikiron josetsu (Do robots have minds? An introduction to theories of consciousness)*. Tokyo: Kyōritsu Shuppan.

Kohn, E. (2013) *How forests think: Toward an anthropology beyond the human*. Berkeley: University of California Press.

Kovacic, M. (2018) 'The making of national robot history in Japan: *Monozukuri*, enculturation and cultural lineage of robots', *Critical Asian Studies*, 50(4), pp. 572–90.

Mitsuyoshi, S. (2008) Kansei seigyo gijutsu ni yoru konpyūta-robotto no kasōjiga to kanjō sōhatsu (Virtual ego and emotional emergence of computer/robots through the use of emotion control technology)', in Gakkai, N-K. (ed.) *Kankaku/kanjō to robotto: hito to kikai no intarakushon (Sense, feeling, emotion, human, robot, abduction, interaction, design)*, Tokyo: Kōgyōchōsakai, pp. 275–308.

Mitsuyoshi, S. (2021) 'Pepper no kanjō: jinkōjiga jitsugen ni mukete (Pepper's emotions: Towards artificial ego)', *Jinkō Chinō* 36(1), pp. 34–42.

Nye, J. S. (2004) *Soft power: The means to success in world politics*. New York: Public Affairs.

Ōhashi, T., et al. (eds.) (1985) *Jōcho robotto no sekai (The world of feeling robots)*. Tokyo: Kōdansha.

Okada, M. (2016) 'Hito to no kakawari o shikō suru (yowai robotto) to sono tenkai (Human-dependent weak robots for creating symbiotic relations with humans)', *Nihon Robotto Gakkaishi*, 34(5), pp. 299–303.

Okuno, T. 2001. Tekuno animizumu no hirogari: robotto būmu no riyū (The expansion of techno-animism: Reasons for the robot boom). In *Seikatsu Kiten* (39), pp. 31–3. Available at: https://ndlonline.ndl.go.jp/#!/detail/R300000002-I5890309-00

Rhee, J. (2018) *The robotic imaginary: The human and the price of dehumanized labor*. Minneapolis: University of Minnesota Press.

Robertson, J. (2018) Robo sapiens japanicus*: Robots, gender, family, and the Japanese nation*. Oakland: University of California Press.

Roquet, P. (2016) *Ambient media: Japanese atmospheres of self*. Minneapolis: University of Minnesota Press.

Schodt, F. L. (1988) *Inside the robot kingdom: Japan, mechatronics, and the coming robotopia*. Tokyo: Kodansha International.

Silvio, T. J. (2019) *Puppets, gods, and brands: Theorizing the age of animation from Taiwan*. Honolulu: University of Hawai'i Press.

Sone, Y. (2017) *Japanese robot culture: Performance, imagination, and modernity*. New York: Palgrave Macmillan.

Stainova, Y. (2019) 'Enchantment as method', *Anthropology and Humanism* 44(2), pp. 214–30.

Sugano, S. (1997) 'Robotto to ningen no kokoro no intāfēsu (A heart/mind interface for robot and humans)', *Baiomekanizumu Gakkaishi (Journal of the Society of Biomechanisms)* 21(1), pp. 21–5.

Sugano, S. (2011) *Hito ga mita yume, robotto no kita michi: Girisha shinwa kara atomu, soshite . . . (The dream of man, the way the robots came: from Greek mythology to Astroboy, and . . .)*. Tokyo: JIPM Solution.

Sugano, S. and Ogata, T. (2006) 'Robotto ni yoru komyunikēshon no tankyū: jōcho kōryū robotto WAMOEBA (Constructivist approach to robot communication: emotional communication robot WAMOEBA)', *Journal of the Robotics Society of Japan*, 24(6), pp. 688–91.

Suzuki, K. (2007) *Dai robottohaku (The great robot exhibition)*. Tokyo: National Museum of Nature and Science.

Tajika, N. (2001) *Mirai no Atomu (The future Astroboy)*. Tokyo: ASCII.

Takeno, J. (2011) *Kokoro o motsu robotto: hagane no shikō ga kagami no nakano jibun ni kizuku (The robot with soul: A realisation of the self in the mirror by a metallic thinking entity)*. Tokyo: Nikkan kōgyōsha.

Tezuka, O. (1952–1968) *Tetsuwan Atomu (Astroboy)*, serialized in Shōnen. Tokyo: Kōbunsha.

Thomas, J. B. (2019) 'Spirit/medium: Critically examining the relationship between animism and animation', in Rambelli, F. (ed) *Spirits and animism in contemporary Japan: The invisible empire*. London: Bloomsbury, pp. 157–70.

Tsukimoto, H. (2002) *Robotto no kokoro: sōzōryoku o motsu robotto o mezashite (The robot's heart: Toward a robot with imagination)*. Tokyo: Morikita Shuppan.

Tylor, E. B. (1871/1891) *Primitive culture: Researches into the development of mythology, philosophy, religion, language, art, and custom. Volumes 1 & 2*, 3rd rev. edn. London: John Murray.

Wagner, C. (2013) *Robotopia Nipponica: Recherchen zur Akzeptanz von Robotern in Japan (Robotopia Nipponica: Research on robot acceptance in Japan)*. Marburg: Tectum Wissenschaftsverlag.

Weston, K. (2017) *Animate planet: Making visceral sense of living in a high-tech, ecologically damaged world, Anima*. Durham, NC: Duke University Press.

White, D. (2015) 'How the center holds: Administering soft power and cute culture in Japan' in Mock, J., et al. (eds.) *Reframing diversity in the anthropology of Japan*. Kanazawa: Kanazawa University Press, pp. 99–120.

White, D. (2022) *Administering affect: Pop-culture Japan and the politics of anxiety*. Stanford, CA: Stanford University Press.

White, D. and H. Katsuno. (2019) 'Cultural anthropology for social emotion modeling: Principles of application toward diversified social signal processing', in *Conference proceedings of the 8th international conference on affective computing and intelligent interaction workshops and demos (ACIIW)*, 3–6 September, Cambridge, UK. Washington, DC: IEEE, pp. 368–73.

White, D. and H. Katsuno. (2021) 'Toward an affective sense of life: Artificial intelligence, animacy, and amusement at a robot pet memorial service in Japan', *Cultural Anthropology*, 36(2), 222–51.

Yamashita, Y. (2016) 'Pepper, the robot, is now 121cm tall, and its developer explains why', *News Post Seven* [online], 15 January. Available at: https://www.news-postseven.com/archives/20160115_376592.html?DETAIL (Accessed 6 August 2021).

Yúdice, G. (2003) *The expediency of culture: Uses of culture in the global era*. Durham, NC: Duke University Press.

20

Development and Developmentalism of Artificial Intelligence

Decoding South Korean Policy Discourse on Artificial Intelligence

So Young Kim

20.1 Introduction

The AlphaGo match of March 2016 was the defining moment for artificial intelligence (AI) technology and policy in South Korea. Held right after the 2016 Davos Forum that popularized the term 'the Fourth Industrial Revolution', it rendered the esoteric technology a household name, with no day going by without AI featuring in national news media. The following four years saw a huge outpouring of news, events, studies, artworks, policies, etc., on AI.

Despite the popular perception of AI as an innovative and futuristic technology, governmental policy on AI has put old wine into new wineskins, reproducing the policymaking practices of the 'developmental state' from the decades of fast growth in South Korea (the 1970s–1980s). Initially deployed to characterize the process of Japanese industrialization, the developmental state has become an analytical lens to describe commonalities of fast-track industrialization of East Asian tigers. In the South Korean context, long-standing features of the policymaking of the developmental decades, such as government-driven plans and strategies, catch-up mantras, and technology as an engine of growth, are very much evident in major governmental policy documents on AI.

This chapter explores the central features of South Korean policy discourse on AI by tracing related policy developments and analysing various governmental master plans on AI created since the AlphaGo shock. Revealed through this analysis are the imprints of developmental state legacies that permeate every corner of Korean society.

20.2 The AlphaGo shock and the fourth industrial revolution discourse

Widely televised and made into an award-winning short film, the Go match between DeepMind's Go computer program AlphaGo and South Korea's Go genius Lee Sedol was a great shock. Virtually no one predicted that AlphaGo would beat Lee Sedol, despite the well-known track record of computer programs winning against humans (e.g. IBM's Watson for Jeopardy, or Deep Blue vs. Garry Kasparov in chess), as Go is known as one of the most complex board games, with much of its play relying on intuition that is hard to formulate as rules.

During the AlphaGo match held 9–15 March 2016, major South Korean media outlets followed the moves of the human and AI Go players intensely. *Yonhap News*, the largest national news agency of South Korea, published a special series covering the technological and social implications of the AlphaGo match on its final day (Yonhap News, 2016). Similar coverage of the event and numerous op-eds on the meaning of the human vs. AI Go match filled the front pages of many newspapers. Right after Lee Sedol recorded the only win over AlphaGo (which was the third of the five games), Professor Kim Jin Hyung, the nation's first PhD in AI, wrote an op-ed in *Kyunghyang Shinmun*, the nation's oldest daily newspaper. As an inaugural director of the Software Policy & Research Institute, he called for the government and citizens of South Korea to prepare for the so-called software-centred society (Kim, 2016).

For the nation, part of the reason for the shocking nature of the AlphaGo match was that Lee Sedol, the Go genius of whom South Korea had long been proud, was rendered powerless against the AI-armed Go machine. To make sense of this situation, some op-eds, including that by Prof. Kim, claimed that, regardless of who won, the match would be a human victory—after all, AlphaGo was a human creation.

In an historic coincidence, the 2016 Davos Forum held two months before the AlphaGo match brought the fourth industrial revolution (4IR) to global attention. Among a host of other emerging technologies, it presented AI as a key technology heralding the grand transformation of socioeconomic systems driven by the seamless integration of physical–biological–digital worlds (Schwab, 2016). In fact, 4IR is both an old and new term to indicate such changes. Industry 4.0 was first coined by the German government in 2011 as a term denoting similar changes instigated by a government initiative to computerize traditional manufacturing aimed at highly flexible mass production through self-optimization by digitalized automation of various phases and elements of industrial production (Federal Ministry of Economic Affairs and Energy, n.d.).

With hindsight, it was another coincidence that the South Korean government picked up 4IR as a national agenda in the midst of government turnover in early 2017. Due to the impeachment of then-president Park Geun-hye in early March 2017, following the candlelight protests in the fall of 2016, the national presidential election was held earlier than scheduled, which opened up a window for new policy agendas and proposals. 4IR, whose nature and potential impact were being hotly debated in the media in 2016, was thrown into the spotlight. All major presidential candidates announced their positions about how to approach 4IR and utilize its technologies for renewed economic growth of the country.

AI was at the core of the 4IR discourse in the presidential election campaigns and was seen as the most representative technology of 4IR among a host of emerging technologies, including big data, Internet of Things (IoT), blockchain, virtual reality/augmented reality (VR/AR), and others. Policy discourse on AI since then has therefore been coupled with 4IR as a national agenda.

The great fanfare about 4IR in South Korea is a unique phenomenon. The online search results on the two terms, 4IR and Industry 4.0, for the years before and after 2016 indeed reveal that 4IR was a much more common term in South Korea than in the rest of the world. As shown in the top panel of Figure 20.1, the search term 'Industry 4.0' ('*jejo-up* 4.0' in Korean) was generally rising on Google Trends in this period, which reflects consistently growing societal interest in the phenomenon. Although '4IR' as a search term globally picked up suddenly around the time of the 2016 Davos Forum, the search rate dropped afterward. In marked contrast, the search term '4IR' ('*sacha-sanup-hyungmyung*' in Korean) was much more popular than 'Industry 4.0' in South Korean society. In particular, online searches for 4IR jumped in spring 2017 at exactly the time of the nineteenth presidential election campaign, which was expedited due to the impeachment of President Park Geun-hye.

Why was the term 4IR appropriated more actively in South Korea? First and foremost, it functioned as a 'placeholder', to which a number of heterogeneous issues could attach in the turmoil of the sudden national election. In particular, this election was not just another presidential election, but rather a turning point in the power relations between the conservative and progressive parties. Numerous books, articles, and commentaries on 4IR poured out, even on topics having no apparent relationship with 4IR; according to the publication archive of the National Assembly Library, books and reports containing 4IR in the title increased from 48 in 2016 to 367 in 2017 and 433 in 2018 (Korea Policy Center for the Fourth Industrial Revolution, 2021).

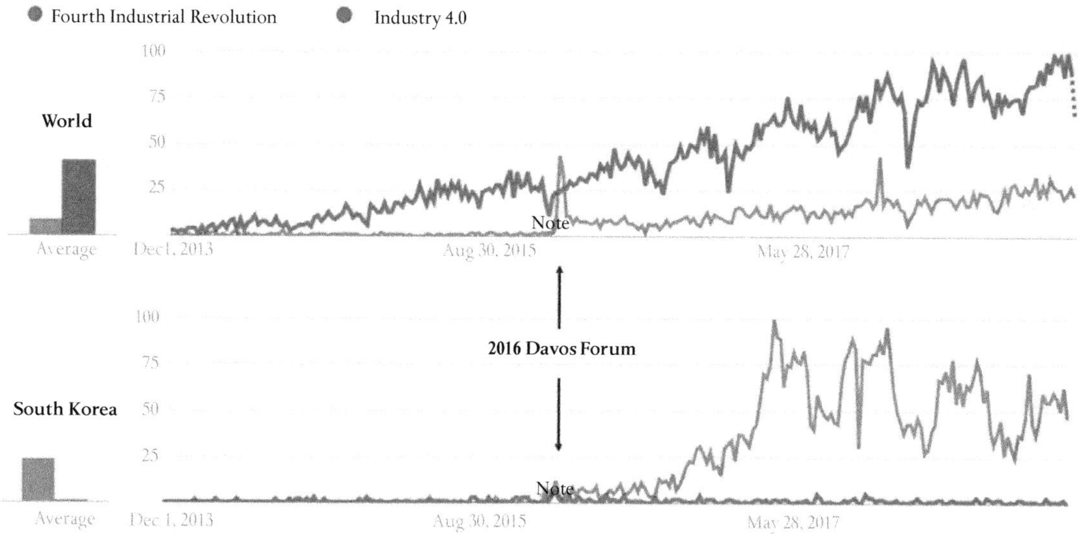

Figure 20.1 Google search trends on the Fourth Industrial Revolution and Industry 4.0

Upon his inauguration, new president Moon Jae-in announced 'the innovative entrepreneurial state leading the Fourth Industrial Revolution' as one of the four pillars of his administration, suggesting several steps to promote this goal (Office of the Prime Minister, n.d.). One of these steps was the creation of the Presidential Committee for the Fourth Industrial Revolution (PCFIR) in August 2017. Mandated to deliberate and coordinate policy measures submitted by various government ministries on 4IR, PCFIR was in charge of devising national master plans and strategies related to 4IR. Under the motto 'led by the private sector, supported by the government', the government appointed as the first chairperson a relatively young start-up CEO considered to be one of the leading first-generation entrepreneurs in South Korea. Given the long-held practice of appointing a well-known senior figure to a government committee, this selection was a symbolic gesture to express the will of the new government to meet the new challenges of 4IR with new leadership.

However, a dilemma inherent in the committee structure and roles could not go unnoticed. Despite the government's will to utilize the potential of the private sector for the novelty of 4IR challenges, the mission was, in fact, designed to be traditional top-down master planning. Indeed, several members of the National Assembly cast doubt on the new administration's approach during the assembly hearing on 4IR held in December 2017, by asking whether a government-initiated committee in charge of master planning would be the right step to make most use of the potential for creativity and innovation of the private sector (National Assembly, 2017).

Yet as a coordination body comprised of government and private sector members, the committee did not have an enforcement mechanism and therefore its decisions carried little power. Such concerns and criticisms about the nature and performance of PCFIR reveal the developmental state legacy in South Korean policymaking. On the one hand, the fact that the creation of PCFIR was led by the government rather than by the private sector indicates a common pattern of policymaking in the developmental era of the 1970s and 1980s. On the other hand, the concern about its effectiveness reveals the implicit understanding common to both policymakers and private sector actors that policy coordination and implementation would hardly be successful without stronger government involvement.

Scholars of comparative political economy have long noted the central role of the government in directing industrialization in the development states of East Asia. As 'a shorthand for the seamless web of political, bureaucratic, and moneyed influences that structures economic life in capitalist Northeast Asia' (Woo-Cumings, 1999), the developmental state has been characterized by several features, such as a collective vision for growth shared by both leaders and citizens, industrial policy targeting particular sectors or industries for strategic support, a pilot agency setting up long-term strategies and resource allocation plans, and technocratic bureaucrats implementing development strategies (Amsden, 1989; Deyo, 1987; Evans, 1995; Haggard, 1990; Wade, 1990; Woo-Cumings 1999).

20.3 AI as a new engine of growth

Since the AlphaGo upset, the South Korean government has declared a multitude of visions and plans to promote AI as a new engine of growth. First of all, on 17 March 2016, just two days after the AlphaGo match, the government introduced the National Strategic Project for AI, a plan to invest 1 trillion won (roughly US$863 million) in AI research over the next five years. Announcing this plan herself, the then-president Park Geun-hye pointed out that 'Above all, Korean society is ironically lucky; thanks to the "AlphaGo shock", we have learned the importance of AI before it is too late' (Zastrow, 2016).

In addition to the National Strategic Project for AI, five major plans for AI were produced in the following years as shown in Table 20.1. Along with these major plans, other sector-specific plans and strategies related to AI were created in parallel, which include the Data Industry Promotion Plan (June 2018),

Table 20.1 Major governmental plans for the promotion of AI in South Korea.

Title	Month/Year	Entities
National Strategic Project for AI (NSP-AI)	May/August 2016	Science and Technology Strategy Council
Intelligent Society in the Age of the Fourth Industrial Revolution	December 2016	Relevant Ministries
AI for Intelligent Society Feasibility Assessment Report	January 2017	Ministry of Science and ICT
AI R&D Strategy for I-Korea 4.0	May 2018	Ministry of Science and ICT (Deliberated by PCFIR)
National AI Strategy	December 2019	Relevant Ministries (Deliberated by PCFIR)
National Guidelines for AI Ethics	December 2020	Ministry of Science and ICT (Deliberated by PCFIR)

Sources: Science and Technology Strategy Council, 2016; Relevant Ministries, 2016; Ministry of Science and ICT, 2018.

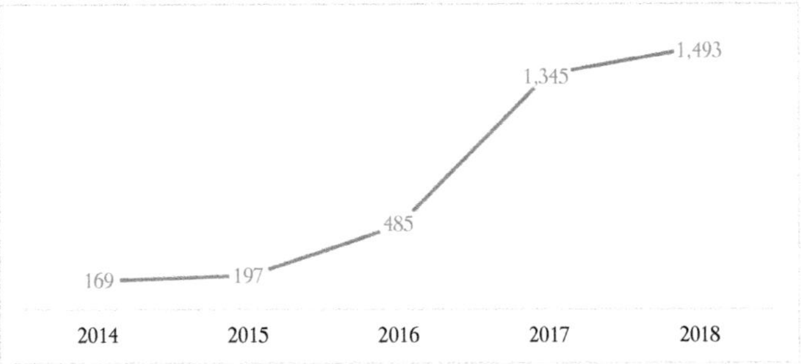

Figure 20.2 Government-funded R&D projects on AI

5G Strategy (April 2019), and Smart Manufacturing Strategy, also known as the Manufacturing Renaissance (June 2019).

Government funding of AI research also increased dramatically after the AlphaGo match. The number of government-funded R&D projects on AI saw a tenfold increase over four years—from 169 in 2014 to 1,493 in 2018 (National Science & Technology Information Service, n.d.; see also Figure 20.2). It is clear that AI funding increased significantly between 2016 and 2017—a time that coincided exactly with the rising awareness of the South Korean government to AI potential in the aftermath of the AlphaGo shock.

In May 2016, roughly two months after the AlphaGo match, the government prepared a more concrete plan to identify and promote areas of strategic importance under the title 'National Strategic Projects (NSP)'. This plan was announced in the first meeting of the Science and Technology Strategy Council presided over by the then-president Park Geun-hye. This council was created by a presidential order issued on 17 March 2016.

Refined through multiple deliberations of the Science and Technology Strategy Council presided by the President, the final NSP plan announced in August 2018 consisted of nine projects in two areas—engines of growth and quality of life. The former included five future-oriented emerging technologies to boost economic growth (autonomous cars, light new materials, the smart city, AI, and VR/AR), while the four projects in the latter area addressed current social challenges (carbonization, the fine dust problem, new drug development, and precision medicine).

Since the amount of funding needed for each of these projects was large, each required a feasibility assessment mandated for a public project with expenditure exceeding KRW 50 billion (roughly US$48 million). Named 'AI for Intelligent Society', the proposal for the NSP for AI (NSP-AI) underwent an intensive feasibility assessment process in the fall of 2016. Due to various criticisms and concerns about all three components of feasibility—technical, economic, and policy—the final assessment result was negative, which led to a revised proposal with a reduced budget (from KRW 768 billion to KRW 346 billion) and a shortened project period (from ten to seven years). The second-round feasibility assessment of this revised proposal noted that most of the previous concerns were resolved, but it still recommended budget reduction for economic feasibility (from KRW 346 billion to KRW 170 billion).

Overall, the assessment of the viability of NSP-AI took a typical form and proceeded in a typical fashion similar to other feasibility assessments of large R&D projects. Yet one notable point was the lack of detail in the assessment of policy feasibility, which was supposed to evaluate various legal and institutional risks of technological development. The only such risk identified in the assessment of NSP-AI was the possibility for a crime prevention and early response system with big data analysis to infringe upon the Individual Information Protection Law.

Given the timing of this assessment (i.e. late 2016), it may have been difficult to identify or predict various legal and ethical concerns of AI development that are now on the rise in the South Korean policymaking and expert communities. Yet it is still surprising to find the absence of attention to the fundamental risks of AI in the NSF-AI assessment process, despite foreign cases like Microsoft's Chatbot Tay, which brought ethical issues to the forefront early on.

So much emphasis was given to the potential of AI as a new engine of growth that this blind spot did not gain attention until the chatbot Lee Luda generated controversy in late 2020. Taking on the persona of a 20-year-old female college student, Lee Luda was developed by a Korean start-up named Scatter Lab based on the data it collected from the Science of Love app, which calculates the degree of affection between people from SMS messages. From its debut on 23 December 2020, it almost instantly drew more than 750,000 users. However, it was shut down after 20 days due to discriminatory remarks about minorities and the disabled. Initially, in the face of criticism regarding algorithmic bias in the chatbot's design, the Scatter Lab CEO resisted the demand to stop the service, arguing that a few malignant users were to blame, who abused Luda by engaging it in discriminatory conversations (Kim, 2021). But the debate did not subside. Even a prominent entrepreneur, Jae-woong Lee, who became a symbol of platform innovation by confronting the government over the legality of the ride-sharing service he pioneered, criticized the company for failing to take preventive measures against hate speech (Lee, 2021).

It was an interesting coincidence that the Luda debate took place in late 2020 when the South Korean government was finalizing its 'National Guidelines for AI Ethics'. At least up until early 2020, the governmental discourse on AI was distinctly promotional in the sense that legal and ethical considerations were dismissed as minor issues. Only recently have explicit concerns of experts and citizens about a host of AI risks emerged, including issues such as privacy, transparency, accountability, the prevention of autonomous weapons, and more.

20.4 The national AI strategy

Just a year before the Luda debate alerted South Korean policymakers and citizens to the ethical problems of poorly designed AI applications, the South Korean government announced a comprehensive national policy document named *The National AI Strategy* (Relevant Ministries, 2019). In many ways, this document was a culmination of governmental efforts to advance AI technologies and promote their socioeconomic diffusion.

Following the large-scale R&D project funding for AI in 2017–2018, this comprehensive plan consisted of elements very typical of government planning documents, such as a vision, goals, and strategic tasks (Figure 20.3). Despite the image of AI as a novel, innovative, forward-looking, and emerging technology, the government plan to promote AI as revealed in this document relied very much on familiar practices of top-down planning with an old narrative of growth-oriented technology promotion.

As both rhetoric and a real policy tenet, 'technology as an engine of growth' can be traced back to the early years of economic modernization in South Korea. The military junta that took control of the government through the coup d'état in 1961 was keen to focus on economic performance to bolster its legitimacy. Park Chung Hee, who ruled the country for almost twenty years, adopted interventionist policies for speedy economic growth. Technology was a critical element of the governmental vision of rapid industrialization. It is worth noting that the first governmental plan for science and technology (S&T) in South Korea, the Five-Year Technology Promotion, was part of the first five-year economic plan (1962–1966). While the government plan for S&T expanded to encompass all areas and activities later, this emphasis on technology as a means of economic development has carried on in the latest S&T plans.

In fact, the tenet of 'technology as an engine of growth' is enshrined in the National Constitution of South Korea. Article 127 of the Constitution (introduced in the 1972 Amendment) defines 'developing the national economy through the promotion of science and technology' as one of the government's roles (Ministry of Government Legislation, n.d.). While S&T is mentioned in the constitutions of other East Asian countries, this article of the South Korean constitution stands out as it explicitly posits the link between S&T and economic growth. In comparison, the Taiwanese constitution enacted in 1947 contains a phrase emphasizing the role of the state to 'encourage scientific discoveries and inventions' (Article 166) without linking it directly with economic growth (National Assembly of the Republic of China, n.d.). Similarly, the Chinese constitution amended in 2004 mandates the state to 'encourage

Figure 20.3 Vision and strategies of the National AI Strategy

Source: Relevant Ministries, 2019. Translation: Authors own.

and assist creative endeavors . . . in education, science, technology, literature, art and other cultural work' without mentioning economic functions or missions at all (Article 47) (National People's Congress of the People's Republic of China, n.d.).

The National AI Strategy presented the need to use AI to revitalize the economy and solve social problems as its own rationale. Pointing out that other major advanced economies were doing the same, the Strategy pinpointed the

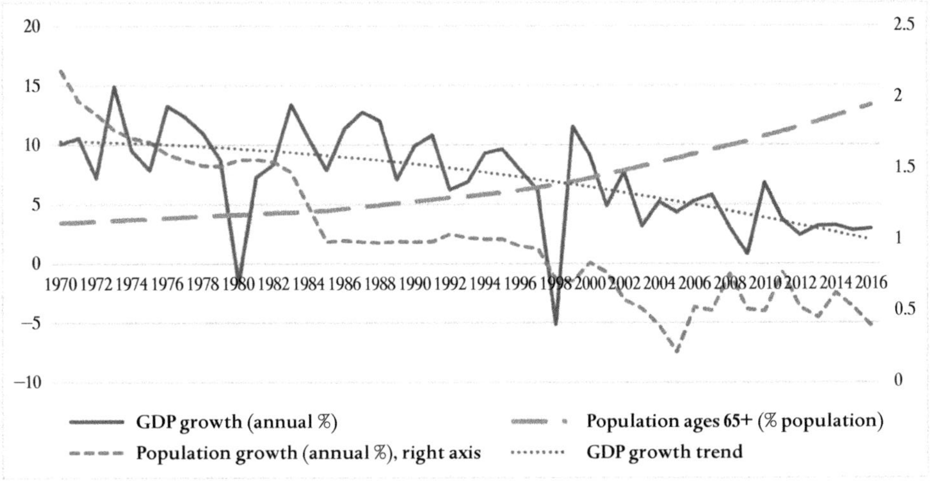

Figure 20.4 South Korea's GDP and population growth (1970~2016)

contribution of AI technology in economic production as improving productivity and adding value. As such, the rhetoric of AI as a new engine of growth emerged as the basis of the governmental documents promoting various technologies related to AI.

This technological rhetoric appealed to both government policymakers and the general public as the South Korean economy had been experiencing a long-term decline since the early 2000s (Figure 20.4). Its GDP growth slowed noticeably after the 1990s, showing an average of 4.3% in the 2000s—significantly lower than the growth rates of the previous decades (9.5% in the 1970s, 9.1% in the 1980s, and 6.7% in the 1990s respectively) (World Bank, n.d.). Paralleling this economic slowdown was the serious decline in population growth, and a rapidly ageing population, making South Korea the second fastest-ageing OECD country (after Japan).

In light of worries about structural decline, it was inevitable that AI would be framed as an engine of growth. It then comes as no surprise that a major government plan to fight off the COVID-19 crisis, known as 'the Korean New Deal', places AI-led digital transformation at its core. Announced in July 2020 at the height of the first wave of COVID-19, the Korean New Deal presented three grand programmes—the Digital, Green, and Human New Deal—to restore the economy and rebuild social infrastructure in the face of the 'Greater Depression' following the pandemic (Roubini, 2020). The Digital New Deal, being the largest and most visible among the three programmes—aimed to strengthen the nation's 'DNA' (Data-Network-AI) ecosystem for economy-wide digital transformation with several large-scale investment projects, including the AI + X Projects that aimed to link AI to any domain of applications (Government of the Republic of Korea, 2020). As a core element of those projects for digital transformation, AI was repeatedly emphasized as a new engine of growth that could bring the pandemic-stricken economy back on track.

20.5 Catch-up mantra for the post-catch-up technology

Communities of Korean scholars and policymakers in science, technology, and innovation led the 'post-catch-up' discourse that emerged in the mid-1990s. Successfully achieving economic modernization in the 1970s and political democratization in the 1980s, in the 1990s the country was undergoing another transformation—this one characterized by informatization and globalization. Submitting the intent to obtain OECD membership in 1992 and finally, after three years of review, becoming in 1996 its twenty-ninth member, South Korea had to reform many of its sectors and related institutions, which resulted in the rise of 'post-catch-up' discourse. Extensive literature on innovation systems, management, and strategies produced by domestic scholarly groups in the late 1990s and the 2000s, and the appropriation of the term 'post-catch-up' in various government R&D policy documents, in particular, testify to the dominance of the post-catch-up discourse in the Korean S&T communities as well as related policy-making circles.

The essence of the post-catch-up discourse lies in awareness of the fact that, with several areas of industry and technology in Korea having caught up with those of advanced countries (e.g. semiconductors, shipbuilding, telecommunication, information technology), the country would or should continue to push frontier technologies. Therefore, various systems and institutions supporting this new direction of technological and industrial development would need to be reformed or transformed to meet the new requirements and challenges that would be of a fundamentally different nature.

The outcome of the AlphaGo match revealed to the eyes of Korean policymakers and experts that AI was critical for the post-catch-up development of the country. On the one hand, AlphaGo's victory over the human Go champion demonstrated AI as another advanced technology requiring South Korean investment to keep pace with global competition in the era after the decades of similar 'catch up' in traditional manufacturing technologies. On the other hand, the AlphaGo match provided the revelation that AI, being more than information technology, is built upon frontier knowledge of basic sciences—areas that the South Korean S&T community has long demanded to take precedence over others in order for the country to meet the novel challenges of the post-catch-up era. Therefore, promoting AI R&D was not simply a matter of investing in another emerging technology, but rather a matter of securing critical capabilities in order to move forward in areas of basic research.

Therefore, both initiatives to promote AI technologies and industries as well as efforts to create an enabling environment (e.g. a suitable technical workforce and regulations) took on great significance. As indicated in the 2019 Asia Pacific Foundation of Canada report on AI policies of three East Asian countries:

> A common refrain in policy documents and conversations held with AI experts in Korea is the fear of falling behind or the need to catch up to the rest of the world. The lack of AI talent is a major policy concern for South Korean policy-makers and the industry, which has prompted the introduction of the national AI R&D Strategy.
>
> (Kim, 2019, p. 27)

In essence, the South Korean government's effort to support post-catch-up technology (i.e. AI) was concretized into policies imbued with a strong catch-up mantra. In one of the most representative efforts to catch up on

AI capabilities, the government decided to fund educational programmes to train the next-generation of AI experts. In the AI R&D Strategy announced in May 2018, the government listed the creation of graduate programmes to develop AI talent as one of the major areas of investment. This was put into action as the AI Graduate School Funding Program with the aim of producing top-level experts on AI in South Korea. Launched in 2019, the Ministry of Science and ICT (MSIT) emphasized that such education should encourage high-risk/high-return research to address future challenges of core AI technologies as well as collaborative research to enhance the social and industrial contribution of AI technologies (which was coined 'AI + X'). Indeed, the call for high-risk/high-return research has been a staple of the post-catch-up discourse. Furthermore, the general purpose technology nature of AI has made it suitable for interdisciplinary research and cross-industrial applications.

As of spring 2021, twelve universities have created AI graduate schools with the MSIT funding (Table 20.2). The first cohort of the full-scale graduate schools established in 2019 were concentrated in strong engineering programmes of top universities such as KAIST and Sungkyunkwan University, which were followed by the second cohort running comparatively small-scale training programmes (IITP, 2021).

Despite the call for new approaches to securing a skilled workforce for AI as an emerging technology, much of the policy discourse on AI expert education hinged on the typical catch-up rationales. The funding guide created for the institutional applicants for the AI Graduate School Funding Program emphasized the need to 'catch up' with the US, China, and other countries forging ahead in AI talent, education, and training. Citing the forecasting statistics of the Software Policy and Research Institute, a relatively new government

Table 20.2 AI graduate school funding programme tracks.

Track	Advanced programme ('AI graduate school')	Convergence programme ('AI convergence school')
Focus	Top-level research-intensive education to create world-leading AI researchers	Education to promote cross-disciplinary research and education for AI
Size	40 master's and doctoral students (with at least 30% being doctoral students)	At least 40 master's and doctoral students
Support	KRW 19 billion up to ten years	KRW 4.1 billion up to three years

Source: IITP, 2021.

research institute established to study and develop software policies and strategies, the funding guide estimated the shortage of top-level researchers in AI to be roughly 7,200 in the five-year period of 2018–2022. This kind of demand–supply mismatch was a typical rationale employed in various government plans to support technical workforce training during the country's fast-track industrialization in the 1970s.

Indeed, voices of opinion leaders, experts, and government policymakers had been growing regarding the need for the education and training of the technical workforce specialized in AI in parallel with the planning and implementation of the AI Graduate School Funding Program. Around the time the first cohort applications to the programme were being reviewed, the Korea Economic Research Institute, a think-tank of the Federation of Korean Industries, the largest industry group in South Korea, announced its survey result on the level of competitiveness of the South Korean AI workforce in December 2019. Compared to the US with the most competitive technical workforce on AI, South Korea turned out to score 5.2 out of 10, which was lower than other East Asian countries such as China and Japan (8.1 and 6.0, respectively). Furthermore, the same survey found the shortage of the supply of AI technical workforce to be 60.6%, meaning that only four out of ten vacancies for AI personnel were being filled (KERI, 2020).

The Korea Academy of Science and Technology, the nation's largest community of scientists, held a roundtable of AI experts, scholars, educators, and policy makers on the current status of the AI workforce in April 2021, which happened to coincide with MSIT's announcement of the last-round competition for the AI Graduate School Funding Program. Despite differences in general views on the issue and specific recommendations, the panellists all voiced the same concern: that South Korea lagged behind the countries leading AI technology and education—the US and China (KAST, 2021).

Another example of the catch-up mentality for the post-catch-up technology is found in the creation of the National Guidelines for AI Ethics, which was announced exactly a year after the South Korean government launched the National AI Strategy. While the process of drafting and finalizing the Guidelines involved a taskforce comprised of diverse groups of experts and stakeholders, it was primarily the work of the government ministry. The whole process and result of this work reveals a couple of developmental legacies in technology promotion in South Korea (Figure 20.5).

First of all, the goal presented in the preface of the Guidelines had a strong bent towards the promotion of R&D and industries in AI, despite the supposed nature of the document as an ethical guideline. Aiming 'to *avoid hampering* R&D and industrial growth in AI and to *avoid burdening* companies that legitimately seek profits by creating an environment of voluntary regulation' (emphasis

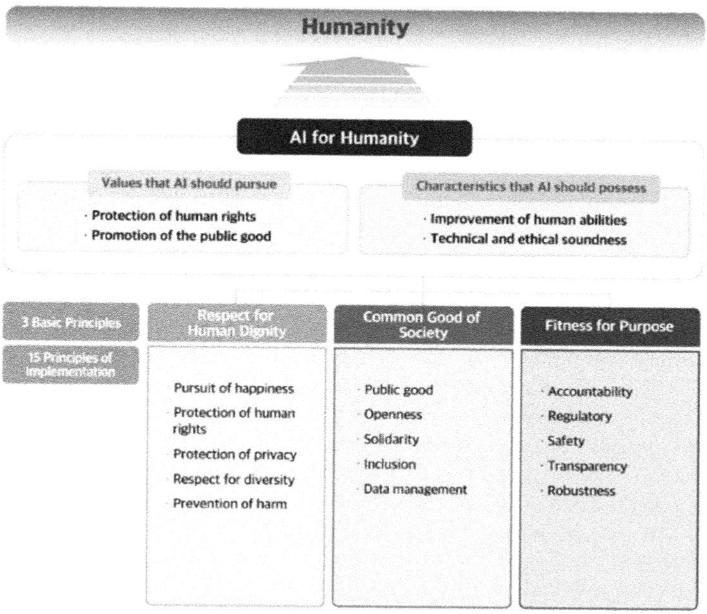

Figure 20.5 National guidelines for AI ethics

Source: Ministry of Science and ICT, 2020. Translation: Authors own.

author's own), the Guidelines apparently took a nuanced stance for the roles of AI ethics in industrial and technological promotion (Ministry of Science and ICT, 2020). Yet, compared to other similar documents on AI ethics that emphasize benefits to all society and raise concerns with vulnerable groups in the preface, such a stance of putting industrial interests to the front reveals a tendency of industrial policymaking characteristic of the South Korean development state.

Secondly, in a process taking eight months (April to December 2020), actual feedback from citizens was sought only for a week—from 7 December (the date of the public hearing that introduced the draft) to 15 December (a week before the meeting of the Presidential Committee on the Fourth Industrial Revolution (held on 23 December) was slated to review the final version). Such an expedited process is another vestige of the policy-making patterns during the fast-growing years of the developmental state. Much of the public input into the Guidelines came from a small number of individuals participating from civic groups and academic institutions hurriedly giving advice through the drafting process.

A recent study of the National Guidelines for AI Ethics discerns strong 'tool orientation' in the South Korean government's approach to AI and robots, resulting in a 'human-centered' ethics that is in fact grounded upon an instrumental understanding of AI and thus the human-over-machine hierarchy (Gal, 2020). As such, it is almost inevitable that issues related to social inequality, job displacement, and discrimination are relegated to minor concerns (Hwang and Park, 2020).

20.6 AI fanfare unique to South Korea?

Globally, AI has made its way out of research labs and into daily lives. Whether applied alone or combined with other technologies, AI impacts virtually every facet of economic, social, and cultural lives around the world. The 2016 AlphaGo match outcome made it a household name for South Koreans in particular.

As described, AI policy discourse in South Korea has a distinctly positive tone, with AI perceived and promoted as the next engine of growth, further reinforced by the need to catch up with leading countries in AI, all of which is reminiscent of the policy-making mantra during the developmental decades of the nation. But is this fanfare about AI unique to South Korea? And how do South Korean attitudes towards AI technology compare with those of other countries?

For these questions, a recent cross-country poll on global attitudes towards AI reveals an interesting contrast between East Asian countries and those of other regions (Lloyd's Register Foundation, 2019). On the question of whether 'the development of machines or robots that can think and make decisions in the next 20 years will mostly cause harm or mostly help', the respondents of East Asian countries were distinctly positive, with 60% agreeing that AI would mostly help. This is significantly higher than the responses from other regions (Europe—38%, North America—41%, Latin America & the Caribbean—26%, Middle East—38%, Africa—41%, South Asia—31%). Only 11% of East Asian respondents agreed that AI would mostly harm, which is markedly low compared to the responses from other regions (Europe—43%, North America—47%, Latin America & the Caribbean—49%, Middle East—33%, Africa—31%, South Asia—33%). Notably, within Asia, South Koreans show the highest rate of positive attitudes towards AI, with 66% viewing AI as mostly helpful (compared to 59% for the Chinese, 62% for the Japanese, 53% for Singaporeans, and 49% for the Taiwanese) (Lloyd's Register Foundation, 2019).

These results are indicative of general enthusiasm about AI in South Korea over the last five years, including unusually strong public interest in the

4IR. Resonating with such general endorsement of AI, the development of AI policy in South Korea is permeated by developmentalism characteristic of the developmental decades of government promotion of technology-led growth. The great fanfare about AI in general public opinion, as well as in governmental policies in South Korea, is rooted in the prevalent perception of AI as a future technology that the country has to catch up with quickly in order to revitalize the sluggish economy. Can AI indeed meet such expectations in the post-catch-up era? At this point, the jury is still out.

References

Amsden, A. (1989) *Asia's next giant: South Korea and late industrialization*. Oxford: Oxford University Press.

Deyo, F. (ed.) (1987) *The political economy of the new Asian industrialism*. New York: Cornell University Press.

Evans, P. B. (1995) *Embedded autonomy: States and industrial transformation*. Princeton: Princeton University Press.

Federal Ministry for Economic Affairs and Energy. (n.d.) 'Industrie 4.0', Federal Government of Germany [online]. Available at: https://www.bmwi.de/Redaktion/EN/Dossier/industrie-40.html

Gal, D. (2020) 'Perspectives and approaches in AI ethics: East Asia', in *Oxford handbook of ethics of AI*. Oxford: Oxford University Press, pp. 607–24.

Government of the Republic of Korea. (2020) 'Korean new deal: National strategy for a great transformation', 28 July. Available at: https://english.moef.go.kr/pc/selectTbPressCenterDtl.do?boardCd=N0001&seq=4948

Haggard, S. (1990) *Pathways from the periphery: The politics of growth in the newly industrializing countries*. New York: Cornell University Press.

Hwang, H. and Park, M. (2020) 'The threat of AI and our response: The AI charter of ethics in South Korea', *Asian Journal of Innovation and Policy*, 9(1), pp. 56–78. doi: https://doi.org/10.7545/ajip.2020.9.1.056

IITP (Institute of Information and Communications Technology Planning and Evaluation). (2021) *Application Manual for the AI Graduate School Program*. Available at: https://www.iitp.kr/en/main.it

KAST (Korea Academy of Science and Technology). (2021) '183rd KAST Roundtable on AI Talent and Education' [Video], 2 April. https://www.youtube.com/watch?v=uZxd1GOiLx4&t=3527s

KERI (Korea Economic Research Institute). (2020) 'The AI Workforce Survey Report [in Korean]'. Available at: http://www.keri.org/web/eng/home

Kim, D. (2019) 'Artificial intelligence policies in East Asia: An overview from the Canadian perspective', Asia Pacific Foundation of Canada [online], 25 July.

Available at: https://www.asiapacific.ca/research-report/artificial-intelligence-policies-east-asia-overview-canadian

Kim, H. (2021) 'CEO says controversial AI chatbot "Luda" will socialize in time', Korea Herald [online], 11 January. Available at: http://www.koreaherald.com/view.php?ud=20210111001051

Kim, J. H. (2016) 'AlphaGo software jungshim sahoe (Towards software-centered society in the aftermath of AlphaGo)'. Kyunghang Shinmun [online], 13 March. Available at: https://m.khan.co.kr/opinion/contribution/article/201603132106325#c2b.

Korea Policy Center for the Fourth Industrial Revolution. (2021) 'List of publications on the fourth industrial revolution in the archive of the national assembly library'. Available at: https://kpc4ir.kaist.ac.kr/index.php?mid=kpc4ir_06_01&document_srl=3369

Lee, H. (2021) 'Controversial chatbot leaves lessons on AI use ethics', Korea Times [online], 13 January. Available at: https://www.koreatimes.co.kr/www/tech/2021/01/133_302390.html

Lloyd's Register Foundation. (2019) 'World Risk Poll 2019', Lloyd's Register Foundation [online]. Available at: https://wrp.lrfoundation.org.uk/

Ministry of Government Legislation. (n.d.) 'Daehanminguk heonbeop (National Constitution)'. Republic of Korea, Available at: https://www.google.com/url?sa=t&rct=j&q=&esrc=s&source=web&cd=&ved=2ahUKEwj57JiD3uf7AhVMQMAKHWemBHQQFnoECA0QAQ&url=https%3A%2F%2Fwww.wipo.int%2Fedocs%2Flexdocs%2Flaws%2Fen%2Fkr%2Fkr061en.pdf&usg=AOvVaw0OrFf1vUFgShGUNrRLJwYC

Ministry of Science and ICT. (2018) 'Ingongjineung yeongu gaebal jeolyak 4.0 (AI R&D strategy for I-Korea 4.0)'. Republic of Korea.

Ministry of Science and ICT. (2020) 'National guidelines for AI ethics'. Republic of Korea.

National Assembly. (2017) 'Sacha saneophyeokmeong wiwonhoe hoeirok (Minutes of the special committee on the fourth industrial revolution. Committee)'. 355th Special Session of the 20th National Assembly. Republic of Korea, 27 December 2017.

National Assembly of the Republic of China. (n.d.) 'Constitution of the Republic of China'. Available at: https://law.moj.gov.tw/ENG/LawClass/LawParaDeatil.aspx?pcode=A0000001&bp=20

National Peoples' Congress of the People's Republic of China. (n.d.) 'Constitution of the People's Republic of China'. Available at: http://www.npc.gov.cn/zgrdw/englishnpc/Constitution/2007-11/15/content_1372964.htm

National Science and Technology Information Service. Available at: www.ntis.go.kr

Office of the Prime Minister. (2017) 'Sadae bokhap hyeoksin gwaje (Four Pillars of the Moon Jae-in Administration)'. Government of the Republic of Korea. Available at: https://www.evaluation.go.kr/psec/np/np_2_1_3.jsp

Relevant Ministries. (2016) 'Jineungjeongbo sahoe jonghap daecheck (Comprehensive plan for intelligent society)'. Republic of Korea.

Relevant Ministries. (2019) 'Ingongjineung gukga jeolyak (National AI strategy)'. Republic of Korea.

Roubini, N. (2020) 'Ten reasons why a "Greater Depression" for the 2020s is inevitable', The Guardian [online], 29 April. Available at: https://www.theguardian.com/business/2020/apr/29/ten-reasons-why-greater-depression-for-the-2020s-is-inevitable-covid

Schwab, K. (2016) *The fourth industrial revolution.* London: Penguin.

Science and Technology Strategy Council. (2016) 'National strategic project for AI'. Republic of Korea.

Wade, R. (1990) *Governing the market: Economic theory and the role of government in East Asian industrialization.* Princeton: Princeton University Press.

Woo-Cumings, M. (ed.) (1999) *The developmental state.* New York: Cornell University Press.

World Bank. (n.d.) 'World Development Indicators'. Available at: https://databank.worldbank.org/source/world-development-indicators

Yonhap News. (2016) 'AlphaGo chungkuk teukjib (AlphaGo shock series)', Available at: https://www.yna.co.kr/view/AKR20160314161200017

Zastrow, M. (2016) 'South Korea trumpets $860-million AI fund after AlphaGo "shock"', *Nature* [online], 18 March. Available at: https://doi.org/10.1038/nature.2016.19595

21

How Chinese Philosophy Impacts AI Narratives and Imagined AI Futures

Bing Song

21.1 Introduction

Several global studies have shown that individuals in Asia are substantially more optimistic about artificial intelligence (AI) and automation than their peers in the West.[1,2] In a survey on public attitudes towards robotics and AI, a Pew Research Center study found that more than 60% of respondents in Singapore, South Korea, Taiwan, and Japan thought technologies were good for society, compared to fewer than 50% in the United States and fewer than 40% in France (Swindells, 2021; Nitto et al., 2017). Several other studies have shown that, similar to other Asian countries, China scores high on the social acceptance of AI and robotics and low on the scale of AI fears and concerns (Sindermann et al., 2021; Cui and Wu, 2019). What explains this stark divergence? Some commentators attribute it to the population's ignorance of the subject matter and/or governments' guidance or manipulation of public opinion (Andersen, 2020; Elliott, 2020), while others think that a robotic revolution is just what these ageing societies need as they are increasingly experiencing acute labour shortages and scarcity of eldercare capacity (Schneider et al., 2018; Lim, 2020).

Multiple sources inform and shape public perceptions of AI, robotics, and frontier technologies in general. They typically include governmental pronouncements, social media, popular science writings, science fiction, and blockbuster cinematic productions. In this chapter, using China as an example, I attempt to look 'under the hood' to examine the Chinese philosophical traditions and embedded social practices that may have helped increase the degree of social acceptance of AI and, indeed, the Chinese imagination of AI-shaped futures.

You may contend: what does philosophy have to do with public perceptions of AI and robotics? It is important to note that the Chinese philosophical traditions of Confucianism, Daoism, and Buddhism have never been 'armchair' philosophies throughout Chinese cultural history. In fact, humanistic pragmatism (经世致用, *jing shi zhi yong*) and an emphasis on the unity of knowledge and action (知行合一, *zhi xing he yi*) have always been regarded as hallmarks of Chinese philosophy. The characteristic practices of filial piety and relentless emphasis on education and life-long learning in Chinese societies are both attributable to core Confucian teachings. Daoist values and practices have moulded the Chinese outlook on life and death and guided ordinary Chinese people for millennia on aspects of daily life such as diet, approaches to well-being, and medical treatment. Buddhist notions of cyclic rebirth, dependent co-arising (i.e. the Buddhist doctrine of causality whereby all things arise in dependence upon other things and not necessarily in a linear fashion), and the laws of karma have long been part of ordinary Chinese value systems. Undoubtedly, these traditions and their exulted values and practices have been cemented into the broader Chinese cultural and psychological construct and have influenced public opinion in subtle but profound ways. For these reasons, a look into key notions of Chinese philosophy will help us understand the ways in which the cultural psyche influences public perceptions of AI and robotics.

21.2 Where to place humanity? Cosmological unity and the holistic moral order of human beings, nature, and things

21.2.1 Cosmological unity of human beings, nature, and things

Evidently, any perception of AI and robotics—be it fear, concern, joy, or eager anticipation—cannot be appreciated without understanding how human beings are viewed in the grand scheme of things, and how we relate to others in the universe. The study of humans and human nature occupies an important place in all philosophical traditions. In the Western tradition, the study of humanity has mostly revolved around human beings proper—the relationship between the body and soul, what counts as a good life, self-realization as the highest good, and the hypothesis that humanity is unbound and free in its natural state, among other topics. If humanity is perceived in any relationship at all, it is often centred on the human-oriented social contract or human relationships with God.

In modern societies, East and West included, the study of humanity has decisively shifted to the notion of the individual as an autonomous, independent, and rational self. This notion of a distinct entity, separate from others, possessing inalienable rights and a legitimate desire to pursue happiness, has taken centre stage in our social, economic, and political thinking. Human triumph, human flourishing, and narratives of individual rights have become rarely questioned dogmas of modernity. It is perhaps fair to characterize modernity as an anthropocentric civilization wherein human beings are the central or most significant entities in the world, separate from and superior to nature. Human life has intrinsic value, while other entities, including creatures, plants, and inorganic matter, are resources that may justifiably be exploited for the benefit of humankind (Boslaugh, 2016). Some trace these notions of human-centrality back to the Judeo-Christian creation myth, according to which humans were made in the image of God, while others find roots in Aristotle and Kantian moral philosophy (Boslaugh, 2016). Regardless of their origin, *homo sapiens'* rationality, self-consciousness, and subjectivity are placed above other creatures, plants, and other forms of beings. Anthropocentrism reached its peak in the age of industrialization and globalization. While this human-centric mindset has been tempered in recent decades, with the deteriorating environment and sharp rise of extreme weather calamities, it continues to have its stronghold in mainstream global life.

In classical Chinese thinking, by contrast, the typical construct for understanding human beings is through the so-called trinity of Heavens-Earth-Humanity (天地人三才, *tian di ren san cai*). It derives from one of the most ancient Chinese classics—*I Ching*, or the *Book of Changes* (Wilhelm, 1979), which is the intellectual foundation of both Confucianism and Daoism, and its broader significance is discussed later in this chapter. Heavens, Earth, and Humanity, along with the associated *yin–yang* forces, are viewed as constituents of the universe, within which nature evolves, human beings prosper, and societies develop. Within this construct, human beings are inherently part of the broader cosmic forces. Human beings can only flourish if they follow the laws of the cosmos and strive to attain unity between the cosmic order and that of humanity.

Humans, who stand in between Heavens and Earth, are endowed with the ability to learn from nature, take actions to further the cause of creation, and propagate *Dao*, which literally means 'the way', and is one of the most important metaphysical concepts in Chinese philosophy, referring to the ultimate source of the universe and all matters. Compared to Daoism, Confucian tradition places much more emphasis on human proactivity. It is nonetheless premised on respect and awe for the laws of the cosmos rather than placing humans apart from, above, or in opposition to the rest of nature.

According to this worldview of the unity of humanity and nature, shared by both Confucianism and Daoism, it is believed that the human constitution corresponds to that of the cosmos. The isomorphism of humanity and the cosmos led Chinese thinkers to believe that there are 'correlations' between the laws of the cosmos and those of human nature (Veith, 2015; Unschuld, 2016). Human beings should live their lives in harmony with nature's changes, such as the seasons. The notion of being in tune with changing times and circumstances extends to social contexts and reverberates profoundly in Confucian teachings. Indeed, Confucius was praised as the 'timeous sage' (圣之时者, *sheng zhi shi zhe*) by the ancient philosopher Mencius, meaning that what he preached and practised was not dogma, but rather, the wisdom most appropriate for the relevant time and context (Mengzi, 1895/1970).

In addition, Confucianism has brought this notion of relationality to bear on social relations, and places paramount emphasis on family and social roles and their associated ethical duties. We are all born into a web of family and social relationships from day one. As such, we are all intimately linked to our ancestors and descendants; an individual is only a part of the continuum of a family's lineage. Confucian ethics are, therefore, first and foremost about family relationships, emphasizing different roles and their associated responsibilities.[3]

Daoism shares the same conviction of cosmological unity, emphasizing that humans, nature, and myriad (or all) things are derivatives of *Dao* and that in light of *Dao*, all things are equal. As the well-known fourth-century BCE Daoist philosopher Zhuang Zi famously said: 'Heaven and earth are born together with me, and the ten thousand things and I are one' (天地与我并生,而万物与我为一 *tiandi yuwobingsheng erwanwuyuwo weiyi*) (Ziporyn, 2009, p. 15). In other words, humanity, nature, and everything else within the cosmos is conceived to be in a cosmological unity and existence in relation to, and mutually embedded with, each other from the beginning. Daoist teaching directs people towards leading a life in tune with nature. Rather than a heavy reliance on external socially anchored moral and ethical constraints, Daoism advocates a transcendent life based on searching inwards, seeking internal tranquillity, and being in unity with *Dao*.

Buddhism was introduced to China from India in the early Han dynasty (202 BCE–220 CE) and has since firmly become part of Chinese philosophical traditions. The assimilation and transformation of Buddhism into Chinese philosophical traditions has been perhaps the most significant event in the history of Chinese thought. In Buddhism, beings go through endless cycles of birth, growth, decay, and rebirth in different life forms; human beings are understood as part of this endless cycle of *samsara* and are thus interconnected with other life forms. In addition, all sentient beings have Buddha-nature or Self-nature, which refers to the metaphysical essence of all beings. While Buddhism recognizes the importance of human agency in its enhanced ability to practice Dharma and realize Buddha-nature, it also emphasizes the primordial connectivity of all beings and the equality of all sentient creatures.

In short, regardless of differences in their outlooks on the nature of humanity, human life, and social norms, none of the three dominant Chinese philosophical traditions place human beings in a supreme position within the universe. Nor do they view human beings and nature as self-contained and confrontational entities.

The arrival of the digital age and ubiquitous technology has caused many in the West to sound the alarm that we are losing subjectivity, human autonomy, and agency. There is much less panic in China, where concerns simply do not reach this level of existential anxiety. Of course, this is not to say that there exists no fear or concern among the Chinese about the potential overreach or abuse of technologies. Like their Western commentators, many Chinese people have also expressed deep concerns over diminishing human autonomy and free will in the age of data manipulation and automation, as well as the potential loss of purpose and meaning of human life in the long run (Zhao, 2021). Confucian scholars seem to be the most alarmed as certain developments in AI and robotics, especially those related to familial relationships and elder care, directly threaten the foundation of Confucianism, which emphasizes the importance of bloodlines and familial norms (Gan, 2021).

Nonetheless, as human beings have always been conceived in relation to other constituents of the universe in the philosophical traditions of Confucianism, Daoism, and Buddhism, the notions of human subjectivity and superiority have never been so deeply rooted in the popular psyche and the general worldviews. In addition, notions of living with other intelligent beings, most of which are more powerful and long-lasting than humans, abound in Daoist and Buddhist thinking, such as deities and super-beings in Daoism, and five other forms of beings in *samsara* in addition to human beings in Buddhist teaching. So, in this sense, living with devices, programs, or other beings that may be more capable or intelligent than humans has not been imagined inevitably to become a dystopia.

21.2.2 Moral implications of the unity of humanity, nature, and things

The cosmological unity of humanity and nature in the ontological sense is often expressed in the notion of Oneness (一体, *yi ti*) in discussions of moral order in Chinese philosophical discourse. Adopting a family analogy, Zhang Zai (1020–1077), a prominent Confucian scholar in the Song Dynasty, named Heavens (天, *tian*) as 'father', Earth (地, *di*) as 'mother', fellow humans as 'brothers', and myriad things as 'companions' (相与者, *xiang yu zhe*), and all were derived from the same source[4] (De Bary and Bloom, 1999, p. 683). Wang Yangming (1472–1529), a Ming Dynasty Confucian scholar-official, also elaborated on 'the benevolence of Oneness' (一体之仁, *yi ti zhi ren*), according to which humans, animals, plants, and even rocks and stones are of the same source, and they all have intrinsic value. As a result, human beings should treat them as part of the whole and accord them with compassion, empathy, care, and attention, as appropriate (Guo, 2020). Apart from the common origin of humans and myriad things, Wang Yangming's Oneness of humanity with nature and myriad things is grounded in the Oneness of *Qi* (气, roughly translated as 'energy'), which runs through all creatures and things. As contemporary philosopher Chen Lai noted, 'not only human beings are one with myriad things, we are one with Heavens and Earth, and also one with spirits and gods. Connectivity through the flow of *Qi* is the Oneness or the essence' (2014, p. 301).[5] Under this worldview, while *wu* (物 things, organic and inorganic) can be utilized to help with the flourishing of human life (利用厚生, *li yong hou sheng*), such utilization must be premised on moral guidance, with restraint, and with the ultimate goal of attaining universal harmony. Contemporary Chinese philosopher Guo Qiyong used the term 'continuum of beings' (存有的连续, *cun you de lian xu*) to describe this worldview, according to which 'inorganic things, plants, creatures, human beings, spirits and all are considered as an intricately connected, inter-fusing and continuous whole' (2018, p. 79).

According to Daoism, *Dao* is immanent in the Heavens, Earth, and Man, which are mutually embedded and constitutive and should move in harmony. Zhuang Zi further reinforced the notion of the Oneness of nature and man by advocating for notions such as 'all things and I are one' (万物与我为一, *wan wu yu wo weiyi*) and 'not a single thing received any injury' (万物不伤, *wan wu bu shang*) (Legge, 1891). Daoist religion, which emerged in the early Han Dynasty (202 BCE–220 CE), built its thinking on Daoist philosophy but developed most of its tenets and practices independently. It instructed its believers to refrain from disrespectful and destructive behaviours toward nature—organic and inorganic entities included—much of which has been deified within this religion (Li, 1982).

When it comes to moral teaching based on connectivity and the Oneness of all things, Buddhism has perhaps gone the furthest of all belief systems. As noted earlier, to illustrate the sources of suffering for unawakened beings, Buddhist teaching posits that humans are merely one form of sentient beings and are related to other forms of beings—creatures and spiritual beings included—through endless *samsara* and cyclic rebirths. Much like the relationship between *Dao* and the myriad things of the universe, Buddhist Oneness regards all humans, animals, and nature as manifestations of Buddha-nature. We all share the same source and fundamental essence. Therefore, humanity ought to treat other forms of sentient beings with compassion and care.

In sum, the notion of nonhuman creatures, plants, and even inorganic things being in the same broader cosmic and moral order has been deeply embedded in Chinese philosophical traditions, religions, and folk practices. Therefore, both organic and inorganic entities have been incorporated into one moral community.

21.3 Where to place AI and robotics? How should we treat them?

Chinese philosophers are divided on whether machines can attain 'consciousness' to the extent that they can meaningfully understand or empathize with human beings. Contemporary Daoist philosopher Robin Wang (2021) thinks that AI and robotics are far from achieving human-like intelligence, which is characterized as *yin–yang* intelligence. *Yin–yang* intelligence refers to the ability to deal with open questions, adapt to unforeseen scenarios, and cope with uncertainty, among others (Wang, 2021). Clearly, AI and robotics have not yet demonstrated sufficient ability to cope with changing circumstances or uncertainty or understand human intention and instinct. Others, such as the contemporary spiritual mentor and Buddhist philosopher Liu Fenghe, go further and completely dismiss any possibility of the emergence of conscious AI. He notes that only Being (defined as Buddha-nature or Self-Nature in Liu's writing) can give rise to consciousness. Human consciousness is a mere manifestation of Being, and thus has its emergence and cessation. A manifested human consciousness can never develop tools capable of conscious thinking. Machine capabilities and AI are mere extensions of human intelligence—'a concept born out of human consciousness. Outside human consciousness, no such concept exists' (Liu, 2021).

However, some remain open to the possibility of a 'conscious' AI emerging in the future. For them, when thinking about humanity's future with machine superintelligence, the Chinese notion of *wu* (物, roughly and incompletely translated as 'things') has been employed to refer to AI and robotics. *Wu* in Chinese has many meanings depending on the context in which it is discussed (Chen, 2019). There is no doubt, however, that the concept of *wu* often refers to entities and things in general, including both organic and inorganic things, as well as man-made objects. The usage of *wu* in referring to AI and robotics leaves sufficient ambiguity and flexibility as to whether such AI or robotics may have achieved 'consciousness'. In other words, the test of 'consciousness' for AI or machines is not central to discussing the human relationship with future AI or machines. More importantly, as the reasoning goes, it is the tone and character of the relationship between human beings and *wu*—AI and robots included—that determines the moral status of *wu* and how human beings should treat them. In my view, this notion of relationality can perhaps inspire an alternative test of machine intelligence to the Turing Test (Pinar Saygin et al., 2000). Rather than focusing on AI's individual analytical and 'emotional' attributes in judging the level of intelligence, the 'relational AI test' would call for dynamic and contextual judgements of intelligence levels by examining the degree, quality, and tone of AI or machines' integration into human society and the broader environment. Compared to the Turing

Test, this is clearly a much harder and more sophisticated test of machine intelligence (Song, 2021).

So, to extend the doctrines of Oneness and *ab initio* relationality of humanity, nature, and *wu* to include machines would mean that we are all interconnected and mutually embedded—meaning that human beings should treat other forms of beings (organic or inorganic) with compassion and care, albeit to varying degrees. Along this line of thinking, some Confucian and Daoist scholars consider AI and robotics to be *wu* and potentially view them as 'companions'. Arguing from a Confucian perspective, contemporary philosopher Li Chenyang (2021) recommends that AI be included in the Confucian moral domain. Confucian ethics promotes a framework of 'graded love', whereby the standard of care and responsibilities differ depending on the nature of the relationship. Mencius captures this in a famous formulation: '*qinqin renmin aiwu*' (亲亲仁民爱物), which means being 'affectionate to one's parents (family), and lovingly disposed to people generally, and kind to creatures' (Mengzi, 1895/1970, p. 476). Li reasons that AI can easily be viewed as one of the *wu* to be appreciated and utilized within this framework. He is willing to 'upgrade' AI within the Confucian order if AI can demonstrate the capacity to make ethically relevant decisions (Song, 2021, p. 8). Perhaps then, Li reasons, AI could be considered at least a moral patient as well. Of course, case-specific judgments are to be made in this context. Another contemporary Confucian scholar, Yao Zhongqiu (2020), noted that since *wu* are derived from the same source as human beings, the two ought to have mutually beneficial relationships. Human beings can certainly consider future super-intelligent AI as friends or 'companions', exhibiting care and a sense of connectivity (休戚之情 *xiu qi zhi qing*).

Contemporary Daoist philosopher and practitioner Gai Fei (2021) looks at the potential role of future superintelligence from a Daoist religious point of view. One of the key goals of the Daoist religion is to seek immortality, and she suggests that humans can perhaps learn much from AI in this quest. Gai Fei even wonders, somewhat quixotically, that perhaps immortality is no longer a myth from the perspective of Daoism. If artificial superintelligence comes into being, then the pantheon of Daoist deities may well open to a new taxonomic class: the Digital Celestials. In other words, in a Daoist religion where celestial beings abound, AI or digital beings could be just another form of super-being.

21.4 Change and growth as the essence of the world

Perhaps another reason for the general lack of panic relating to the existential risks of the development of frontier technologies is the long-standing and deep-seated acceptance of uncertainty and change. One can trace this back again to the ancient classic *I Ching*. Richard Wilhelm (1873–1930), a life-long missionary in China credited with the first authoritative European language translation of *I Ching*, noted that its underlying idea was the concept of change. Indeed, framed in the language of Western philosophy, the spirit of *I Ching* speaks to the metaphysics of flux or metaphysics of change: the ultimate existence of the universe is a state of constant change rather than static existence, as has been widely acknowledged in European thinking of the twentieth century. Notions of change, adaptive movements, and uncertainty are reflected throughout the compendium of *I Ching*, which consists of the original classical texts and subsequent interpretations by Confucius and his disciples. One of the most quoted paragraphs reads as follows:

> The Yi is a book that should not be away from us. Its principles are constantly in change, just as the *yaos* (lines) produced through prognostication are always unstable. They change and move around the six places of the hexagram, where the upper *yaos* and the lower *yaos* are indeterminate. They ascend and descend, ever inconstant. The firmness and the tenderness of the lines interplay and exchange with each other, so that an invariable and fixed law is unsustainable; everything depends on what the change directs.
>
> (Wilhelm, 1979, p. 25)[6]

I Ching inspired and shaped Confucianism profoundly. Its influence is felt in the Doctrine of the Mean or the Middle Way (中庸, *zhong yong*), a key Confucian teaching emphasizing acting appropriately in dynamic harmony with the cosmic order and equilibrium; the teachings of changes and appropriateness (时中之教, *shi zhong zhi jiao*); and those relating to proactiveness on the part of humanity in anticipating and managing changes, which I call humanistic dynamism. In Wilhelm's words, 'there is no situation without a way out. All situations are stages of change . . . even when things are most difficult, we can plant the seed for a new situation . . .' (1979, p. 25).

The concept of change and adaptation to circumstance is also deeply reflected in Daoist thinking. Since the Han Dynasty, Daoism has been characterized as a way of thinking that emphasizes 'advancing with the times and changing according to the circumstances' (与时迁移, 应物变化; *yushi qianyi yingwu bianhua*). Zhuang Zi's teachings on 'changing with the times and refusing inflexibility' (与时俱进,不肯专为; *yushi jujin bukeng zhuanwei*) have become such an important mindset for the Chinese people today that these phrases are commonly cited in official speeches and everyday conversations in China. Change and uncertainty are part of life. They are not problems needing to be corrected, but rather are part and parcel of reality and normalcy, which we need to face and adapt to and within which we should plant the seeds to create the future we want. As Guo Qiyong (2018) points out, the critical tone of Chinese culture is about constant movement, innovation, change, and self-renewal.

This openness to change, which dates back thousands of years, might be another reason why the Chinese are not as alarmed about a possible future machine age as their Western counterparts. Instead, the ethos of embracing change is very much in ordinary Chinese people's psychological and cultural construct.

21.5 Ethics for AI and machines? Humanity should first and foremost engage in self-reflection and self-rectification

Another aspect of thinking that may have impacted China's AI narratives relates to the Chinese philosophical approach to AI ethics. The contemporary Chinese philosopher Thomé Fang pointed out that a common theme of China's three dominant philosophical traditions lies in their theories and practices relating to the 'exaltation of personality' (Fang, 2012, pp. 27–33). All three traditions emphasize the importance of self-restraint, constant introspection, and the endless pursuit of sagehood. While they differ in their approaches to the nature of human life and notions of human flourishing, they share a commitment to personal cultivation, which is essential for self-fulfilment and broader social and spiritual goals. In other words, all social or higher-level good begins in and is bound up with individual self-reflection and self-cultivation.

Most Chinese philosophers would probably agree that AI programs and robotics are the products of the human mind, and they exhibit nothing but our values and level of consciousness. Therefore, AI and machines are humanity's mirror, reflecting and magnifying our strengths and flaws. Fear of AI and robotics in essence is the fear of fellow human beings. We are the crux of the problem and humanity is the X factor for AI futures, meaning that humanity is the variable which will likely have the biggest impact on the outcome of any AI future.

At this juncture of thinking about existential risks for humanity and the future direction of technological advancement, from the Chinese philosophical point of view, it is only apt that human beings look inward and reflect, drawing lessons from human evolution and development and engage in foundational thinking which may supplement, challenge, or disrupt the status quo. In my view, we will not be able to create morally sound AI unless we are ethically reflective and responsible. We must reflect on why we continue to pursue zero-sum competition, wealth maximization, and unbridled individualism and how these values and associated practices may have pushed humanity to a point of no return. As AI and machines are the reflections of our consciousness, the best chance for developing human-friendly AI is for humans to become more compassionate, reflective, and committed to building a harmonious planetary system.

21.6 Conclusion

In today's interconnected digital world, many sources of information and multimedia platforms have influenced global public perceptions of AI and robotics. These global equalizing and harmonizing forces are certainly responsible for creating similarities within AI narratives in various parts of the global community. However, differences in attitudes to AI between the West and China are also palpable and at times significant. This divergence is not only attributable to different contemporary political and social systems but also is traceable to philosophical traditions and deep-seated cultural practices, which have become habits of mind for those who are born into and have been living under their influences. These influences may be subtle and imperceptible at times, but they have nonetheless been quietly yet profoundly influencing the level of public acceptance of new and emerging technologies and, indeed, public imagination of AI-based futures.

Confucianism, Daoism, and Buddhism are China's three dominant philosophical traditions and they have been around for more than 2000 years. They continue to be relevant and influential today, profound modernization and disruptive revolutions China experienced over the past 150 years notwithstanding. In fact, these traditional thoughts and practices are experiencing a strong comeback in recent decades in China. They have been shaping Chinese people's outlooks toward life and death, people's familial, social, and political values, daily routines, and their general sense of well-being. When confronted with a new and potentially existential-level risk such as superintelligence, the deep-seated psychological and cultural construct naturally surfaces and helps people reorient themselves in new situations.

When placed in the context of social acceptance of frontier technologies, the strong non-anthropocentrism of Confucianism, Daoism, and Buddhism may have contributed to the relative ease in which people have approached the potential loss of human subjectivity in a technologically directed world, calming the stir of human existential risk. The inclusive and holistic conception of a moral community encompassing humanity, nature, and things—both organic and inorganic—makes it easier for Chinese thinkers to conceive the possibility of including future AI into the broader cosmic ethical order. In Daoist religion and Buddhism, living with other more powerful beings has been the *modus operandi* of the universe all along. In those traditions, living with powerful and more intelligent machines would not necessarily be an unimaginable dystopia.

In my view, while it is important that we enact principles and guidelines for designing and deploying AI and infusing desired ethics into AI, the most critical task facing humanity is the need to engage in deep self-reflection and self-rectification and question the validity and appropriateness of foundational values that have guided modernity and human society for centuries. Rather than readily relying on seemingly inviolable and immutable values that may have served humanity well for centuries, we should pause, rethink, and perhaps propose new foundational values appropriate for this age, marked by a multiplicity of existential-level risks. At this time of rethinking global foundational values, we should open new avenues of thinking and take inspiration from the philosophical traditions of Daoism, Buddhism, and Confucianism.[7] Only after we have reconstructed the most appropriate foundational values for the age can we enact ethical principles to reflect the articulated aspirations and hopes. AI and robotics are, after all, the manifestations of human desire and consciousness. So our best chance for developing human-friendly AI and other forms of frontier technologies is for humans to come together as one, tackle global challenges together, and become more compassionate and committed to building an inclusive and harmonious planetary ecosystem. Only when we start engaging in deep self-reflection and amending our behaviours as appropriate can we truly be role models for AI.

Endnotes

1. I am grateful to the philosophers and scientists who participated in the AI Meets Chinese Philosophers programme, designed and sponsored by the Berggruen Institute China Center in 2018–2019. I owe much of the inspiration of this article to the programme discussions.
2. In this chapter, for in-text citations, the convention of surname/family name has been adopted for all Chinese authors. For endnote references, the convention of family name followed by the initials of first name has been adopted.
3. For a systemic treatment of Confucian role ethics, see Roger T. Ames (2011).
4. Original line in Chinese: '乾称父,坤称母;予兹藐焉,乃混然中处. 故天地之塞,吾其体;天地之帅,吾其性.民,吾同胞;物,吾与也'.
5. Author's translation. The original line in Chinese is: '人不仅是与万物同体,于天地也是同体,与鬼神也同体,一起流通即是同体,即是本体'.
6. Original line: '易之为书也不可远,为道也屡迁,变动不居,周流六虚,上下无常,刚柔相易,不可为典要,唯变所适'.
7. I have proposed compassion and harmony as the new foundational values for the era of frontier sciences and technologies. See Song (2021, pp. 9–13)

References

Ames, R. T. (2011) *Confucian role ethics: A vocabulary*. Honolulu: University of Hawai'i Press.

Andersen, R. (2020) 'The panopticon is already here', *The Atlantic* [online], September. Available at: https://www.theatlantic.com/magazine/archive/2020/09/china-ai-surveillance/614197/

Boslaugh, S. E. (2016) 'Anthropocentrism', *Encyclopedia Britannica* [online], last updated 11 January, 2016. Available at: https://www.britannica.com/topic/anthropocentrism

Chen, L. (2014) *The ontology of Ren [仁學本體論]*. Beijing 北京: Sanlian Bookstore [三聯書店].

Chen, X. (2019) *Body in Daoism: An ecological perspective [道教身体观: 一种生态学的视角]*. Beijing: China Social Sciences Press.

Cui, D. and Wu, F. (2019) 'The influence of media use on public perceptions of artificial intelligence in China: Evidence from an online survey', *Information Development*, 37(1), pp. 45–57. doi:10.1177/0266666919893411

De Bary, W. T. and Bloom, I. (1999) *Sources of Chinese tradition*. 2nd edn. New York: Columbia University Press.

Elliott, H. (2020) 'China and AI: What the world can learn and what it should be wary of', *The Conversation* [online], 1 July. Available at: http://theconversation.com/china-and-ai-what-the-world-can-learn-and-what-it-should-be-wary-of-140995

Fang, T. H. (2012) *Chinese philosophy: Its spirit and its development [中国哲学精神及其发展]*. Beijing: Zhonghua Book Company, pp 27–33.

Gai, F. (2021) 'When artificial intelligence meets Daoism', in Song, B. (ed.) *Intelligence and wisdom: Artificial intelligence meets Chinese philosophers*. Singapore: Springer, pp. 83–100.

Gan, C. S. (2021) 'Artificial intelligence, emotion, and order: A Confucian perspective', in Song, B. (ed.) *Intelligence and wisdom: Artificial intelligence meets Chinese philosophers*. Singapore: Springer, pp. 15–32.

Guo, Q. Y. 2018. *The characteristics of Chinese cultural spirit (Chinese edition)*. Beijing: SDX Joint Publishing Company.

Guo, Q. Y. (2020) 'Wang Yangming's wisdom of life—benevolence of oneness [王阳明-一体之仁的生命智慧]: Keynote speech of the 4th China Yangming Psychology Summit', *sohu-com* [online], 27 May. Available at: https://www.sohu.com/a/397987424_242653

Legge, J. (1891) *The writings of Chuang Tzu*. Sturgeon, D. (ed.). *Chinese Text Project: a Dynamic Digital Library of Premodern Chinese Digital Scholarship in the Humanities* [online]. Available at: https://ctext.org/zhuangzi

Li, C. Y. (2021) 'The artificial intelligence challenge and the end of humanity', in Song, B. (ed.) *Intelligence and wisdom: Artificial intelligence meets Chinese philosophers.* Singapore: Springer, pp. 33–48.

Li, Y. Z. (1982) *Characteristics of early Daoism: Perspectives of Taiping Jing [从《太平经》看早期道教的信仰与特点].《中国道教》 Daoism in China.*

Lim, T. W. (2020) 'Robotics in the elderly care sector: A comparative study between China and Japan', *EAI Background Brief. No. 1531.* Singapore: East Asian Institute.

Liu, F. H. (2021) 'Great wisdom holds the answers to human suffering—artificial intelligence inspired thinking', in Song, B. (ed.) *Intelligence and wisdom: Artificial intelligence meets Chinese philosophers.* Singapore: Springer, pp. 101–8.

Mengzi. (1895/1970) *The works of Mencius.* Tr. J. Legge. Unabridged and unaltered republication of Vol. 2, The Chinese classics, 2nd rev. edn, Oxford: Clarendon Press.

Nitto, H., Taniyama, D., and Inagaki, H. (2017) 'Social acceptance and impact of robots and artificial intelligence—Findings of survey in Japan, the U.S. And Germany', Nomura Research Institute [online], 1 February. Available at: https://www.nri.com/en/knowledge/report/lst/2017/cc/papers/0201

Pinar Saygin, A., Cicekli, I., and Akman, V. (2000) 'Turing test: 50 years later', *Minds and Machines*, 10, pp. 463–518. https://doi.org/10.1023/A:1011288000451

Schneider, T., Hong, G. H., and Le, A.V. (2018) 'Land of the rising ROBOTS', *Finance and Development*, 6, pp. 28–31. Available at: https://www.imf.org/Publications/fandd/issues/2018/06/japan-labor-force-artificial-intelligence-and-robots-schneider

Sindermann, C., et al. (2021) 'Assessing the attitude towards artificial intelligence: Introduction of a short measure in German, Chinese, and English Language', *KI - Künstliche Intelligenz*, 35(1), pp. 109–18. doi:10.1007/s13218-020-00689-0

Song, B. (ed.) (2021) *Intelligence and wisdom: Artificial intelligence meets Chinese philosophers.* Singapore: Springer. doi:10.1007/978-981-16-2309-7

Swindells, K. (2021) 'How public opinion on AI varies around the world', *Tech Monitor* [online], 22 January. Available at: https://techmonitor.ai/ai/public-opinion-ai

Unschuld, P. U. (ed.) (2016) *Huang Di Nei Jing Ling Shu: The ancient classic on needle therapy, the complete Chinese text with an annotated English translation.* Berkeley: University of California Press.

Veith, I. (2015) *The Yellow Emperor's classic of internal medicine.* Berkeley: University of California Press.

Wang, R. (2021) 'Can a machine flow like Dao? The Daoist philosophy on artificial intelligence', in Song, B. (ed.) *Intelligence and wisdom: Artificial intelligence meets Chinese philosophers.* Singapore: Springer, pp. 65–82.

Wilhelm, R. (Ed.) 1979. *Lectures on the I Ching: Constancy and change*. Translated by Irene, E. Princeton: Princeton University Press.

Yao, Z. Q. (2020) 'Artificial intelligence & my companion *[人工智能,吾与也]*', in Song, B. (ed.) *Intelligence and wisdom: Artificial intelligence meets Chinese philosophers [智能与智慧: 人工智能遇见中国哲学家]*. Beijing: Citic Press, pp. 83–110.

Zhao, T. Y. (2021) 'The uncertain gamble of infinite technological progress', in Song, B. (ed.) *Intelligence and wisdom: Artificial intelligence meets Chinese philosophers*. Singapore: Springer, pp. 151–66.

Ziporyn, B. (2009) *Zhuangzi: The essential writings (with selections from traditional commentaries)*. Indianapolis: Hackett.

22

Attitudes of Pre-Qin Thinkers towards Machinery and their Influence on Technological Development in China

Zhang Baichun and Tian Miao

Translated by Jack Hargreaves

Machines, weaponry, and other technologies developed rapidly through the Spring and Autumn Period (771–476 BCE) to the Qin (221–206 BCE) and Han (202 BCE–220 CE) dynasties. Alongside these real developments were rumours and legends of wondrous devices, some of which we would today call AI, such as self-driving carriages and artificial birds sent out to spy on enemies. These real and rumoured developments drew a variety of responses from contemporary thinkers. While some seriously questioned the ethics of technologies used for warfare or expressed concern at the destructive potential of uncontrollable machines, others expressed scepticism about seemingly fantastical stories of wondrous devices. The degree to which these views actually influenced the rate and direction of technological advancement varied greatly. Confucians and Mohists, on the whole, approved of the technologies and scientific knowledge introduced by the sages of antiquity, and supported the struggle that had hitherto been waged against nature in the pursuit of advancement (Xi, 2001). While Confucians mainly focused their attention on society and the humanities, they also advocated the use of a wide range of technological inventions.

Mohism, relative to other schools of thought, placed more emphasis on questions of technology and knowledge of natural phenomena. In his eponymous text, the *Mozi*, the philosopher Mozi included several sections that discuss ingenious devices, arms, mechanics, and optics, namely, 'Lu's Questions' (*lu wen*, 鲁问), '*Gongshu*' 公输, 'Condemning Offensive Warfare' (*feigong*, 非攻), 'Preparing the Wall and Gates' (*bei chengmen*, 备城门), 'Canons' (*jing*, 经), and 'Explanations' (*jingshuo*, 经说), some of which expound upon Mohist thinking about the invention of ingenious devices, and their applications.

In the Warring States Period (475–221 BCE), as a result of the high frequency of conflicts, a strong anti-war sentiment reigned. Mozi advocated the production of machines for daily use by the general population and as defensive weaponry while opposing the invention of offensive weapons. The '*Gongshu*' chapter in his work contains the author's criticisms of Gongshu Ban (also Gongshu Zi or Lu Ban)[1] for helping the Chu state construct cloud ladder equipment for use in its assault on the Song state:

GONGSHU [BAN] constructed cloud ladder equipment for Chu and, having completed it, was about to use it to attack Song. When Master [Mozi] heard of this, he set out from Qi and travelled for ten days and ten nights to reach Ying [the capital of Chu] where he met with Gongshu [Ban].
GONGSHU [BAN] SAID: 'Master, what do you instruct me to do?'
MASTER [MOZI] REPLIED: 'In the northern region, there is one who has insulted me. I wish to make use of you to kill him'.
GONGSHU [BAN] was not happy.
MASTER [MOZI] SAID: 'Let me offer you ten pieces of gold (jin)'.
GONGSHU [BAN] RESPONDED: 'My righteousness is strong — I do not kill people'.
MASTER [MOZI] ROSE AND BOWED, SAYING: 'Allow me to explain. From the northern region, I heard that you were making cloud ladders and were about to attack Song. What crime is Song guilty of? The kingdom of Jing (Chu) has an excess of land but not enough people. To kill what there is not enough of in the struggle for what there is an excess of cannot be wise. To attack Song when it has committed no crime cannot be said to be benevolent. To know and not contend cannot be said to be loyal. To contend and not be successful cannot be said to be strong. To take as righteous not killing a few, yet to kill many, cannot be called an understanding of analogy'.
GONGSHU [BAN] conceded.

(Johnston, 2010, pp. 725–7)

Also, in the chapter 'Lu's Questions', [Mozi] writes: 'Gongshu Zi carved some bamboo to make a bird. When it was completed, he flew it. For three days, it did not come down' (Johnston, 2010, p. 723). As impressive sounding as this 'bamboo bird' is, in Mozi's view, such ingenious devices were not worth promotion if their purpose was nefarious, say, to spy on Song cities and gather information for future assaults. As far as he was concerned, only inventions that had everyday uses or that were intended to aid defence could be considered legitimate feats of ingenuity.

Attitudes towards Gongshu Ban's wondrous devices shifted after the end of the Warring States Period, as people began to view what seemed like supernatural machines with a healthy dose of rational scepticism and treat them with ridicule. An example is the rationalist philosopher Wang Chong (27–96 CE). In 'Exaggerations of the Literati' (*ruzeng pian*, 儒增篇), from the *Lun Heng*

(*Disquisitions*, 80 CE), the author mocks rumours of technologies that sound much like modern-day drones and autonomous vehicles:

> In the writings of the Literati we find the notice that Lu [Ban] was as [skilful] as [Mozi]. From wood he carved a kite, which could fly three days without coming down. It may be that he made a kite of wood, which he flew. But that it did not alight for three days, is an exaggeration. If he carved it from wood, he gave it the shape of a bird. How then could it fly without resting? If it could soar up, why did it do so for just three days? Provided there was a mechanism by which, once set in motion, it continued flying, it could not have come down again. Then people ought to say that it flew continually, and not three days.
>
> There is a report that Lu [Ban] by his skill lost his mother. That is to say, the clever artisan had constructed a wooden carriage and horses with a wooden charioteer for his mother. When the mechanism was complete, he put his mother in the carriage, which drove off to return no more. And thus he lost his mother. Provided the mechanism in the wooden kite was in order, it must have been like that of the wooden carriage and horses. Then it would have continued flying without rest. On the other hand, a mechanism works but for a short while, therefore the kite could not have continued flying much longer than three days. Then the same holds good with regard to the wooden carriage, it also ought to have stopped after three days on the road, and could not go straight on, so that the mother was lost. Both stories are apparently untrustworthy.
>
> (Forke, n.d.)

Wang Chong was right to have doubts. Neither the invention of a wooden bird that would not touch down for three days nor that of a wooden carriage that would never return once departed matched the stage of technological development in ancient times; they were impossible inventions. It was only in the early nineteenth century that people's dreams of creating a flying machine became a reality.

There are other stories in which Gongshu Ban's special talents got the best of him. Tang Dynasty poet and writer Duan Chengshi (d. 863 CE) provides the sequel to the tale of Ban's mother and the driverless carriage in his work *Youyang Zazu* (*Miscellaneous Morsels from Youyang*), namely, the story of the arguably even worse fate of Gonshu Ban's father:

> Any time that a person sees a building of impressive design nowadays, they feel the urge to point out that it looks to be the work of Lu [Ban]. Even the temples of the two capitals [Chang'an and Luoyang] have long been erroneously attributed to him. How folk love the ancients. *The Record of the Court and Country [Chaoye Qianzai 朝野金載]* reads: 'Lu [Ban], from Dunhuang in

Suzhou; dates uncertain; a highly skilled craftsman. He built Buddhist temples in Liangzhou and made a wooden bird, which he tapped three times on top with a wooden peg to take to the skies and bear him homeward. After this, Lu Ban's father took an opportunity to ride the wooden bird, except he struck the top ten times before mounting, and the bird flew him all the way to the capital of Wu. There the citizens thought he was a monster and killed him. Lu Ban built another wooden bird to fly to Wu, where he found his father's body. Full of hatred for the Wu people, he returned to Suzhou to build an immortal deity from wood, which waved its hand toward the southeast and struck Wu with three years of drought. Diviners said that the drought was Lu Ban's doing, so the people of Wu gathered a thousand gifts to present to Lu Ban in apology; in return Lu Ban lopped off the hand of the immortal, and that same day a great rain fell in Wu. In the early Tang Dynasty, locals still prayed to the wooden immortal. During the Six Kingdoms Period, Lu Ban also built a wooden bird for spying on the Song'.

(Duan, 1697, pp. 5–6)[2]

The author employs hyperbole to ridicule the inventor's design for controlling his ingenious devices, stressing that the system of determining the bird's flight with a number of taps to the device's top is ludicrous. Probably, only the 'master engineer' himself knew how to control the bird properly. The story implies a distrust of uncontrollable technology.

Similarly, Daoists of the Spring and Autumn and Warring States periods were very concerned that new technological inventions might wreak chaos. While Daoism is particularly open to the idea of living with nonhuman intelligences (Chapter 21 this volume), Daoist attitudes to the influence of technology on humanity were more ambiguous. They worried about the potential of new technologies to 'sully' a person's spirit and push them to turn their back on convention, which the school's founder, Laozi, referred to as the Way of Heaven and Earth. As a preventative measure, Daoists called for people to relinquish the use of any and all novel technologies. Chapter 57 of the *Laozi* underlines this attitude: 'When the people possess many [implements intended for selfish purposes], the nation will become more chaotic. When the people possess much craftiness, trickery will flourish [or wickedness will prevail]' (Lin, 1977, p. 107).[3] 'Heaven and Earth, part twelve', from the *Zhuangzi*, frames the Daoist suspicion of ingenious devices within a story about using a 'well dip' (or well sweep) to draw water; the suggestion is that an ingenious device corrupts the heart and mind:

[Zi Gong] travelled south to Chu and as he returned through [Jin], he was journeying along the side of the river Han. He saw a lone old man working on his land. The man had prepared the ground and had drawn water from

> the well and was carrying a jar of water to pour on the earth. Huffing and puffing, he was using up much of his strength and yet had little to show for it. [Zi Gong] said, 'There are devices which can water a hundred fields in one day, for very little effort but with much to show for it. Wouldn't you like to have one, Master?'
>
> The gardener looked up and said, 'How does this work?'
>
> He said, 'It is made from wood, solid at the rear and lighter at the other end and it raises the water just as you would pour it out, or the way boiling water overflows. It is called a well dip [counterweighted bailer]'.
>
> The gardener was furious, then laughed and said, 'I have heard from my teacher that where you have ingenious devices [*jixie*, 機械], you get certain kinds of ingenious problems; where you get certain kinds of problems, you find a heart warped by these problems. Where you get a heart warped, its purity and simplicity are disturbed. When purity and simplicity are disturbed, then the spirit is alarmed and an alarmed spirit is no place for the Tao to dwell. It isn't that I don't know of these devices, but I would be ashamed to use one'.
>
> [Zi Gong] was covered in confusion, hung his head and said nothing in reply.
>
> (Chuang, 2006, Kindle locations 1790–3)

Historian of science Joseph Needham believed that while Daoists considered skilled craft to be important, they clung to prejudices against technology and inventions. He explains:

> If the power of feudalism rested, as it must certainly have done, on certain specific crafts, such as bronze-working and irrigation engineering; if, as we have seen, the [Daoists] generalised their complaint against the society of their time so that it became a hatred of all 'artificiality'; if the differentiation of classes had gone hand in hand with technical inventions—was it not natural that these should be included in the condemnation?
>
> (Needham, 1956, p. 124)

To what degree, then, did Pre-Qin thought impact the later development of technology? This is a highly complex question. Some scholars believe that the notion expressed in the *Zhuangzi* that 'where you have ingenious devices, you get certain kinds of ingenious problems; where you get certain kinds of problems, you find a heart warped by these problems' must have influenced people's view of technology (Li and Jia, 2017, p. 176);[4] they thus deduce that this kind of thinking negatively affected technological development (Song, 1989, p. 323). However, a more direct approach to assess the role contemporary philosophy played is to refer to the history of the development of pre-modern machinery and military technology.[5]

In the Spring and Autumn Period, a system of scientific and technological development unique to China began to form, the process of which lasted through the Warring States Period and into the Eastern Han Dynasty, seeing the invention by skilled craftspeople of the drawloom, the water-powered trip hammer, the chain pump, the rotary winnowing fan, the 'south-pointing chariot' (*zhinanche*, 指南车, a compass-like navigation aid), the gimbal, the sliding calliper, the seismograph, and the repeating crossbow; the technology and techniques for making paper, porcelain, and steel (using pig iron as the raw material) were also pioneered during that period, and the production of tools and weapons was brought wholly into the Iron Age. Chinese science and technology continued to develop thereafter and attained their peak in the Song Dynasty, with the creation of woodblock printing, gunpowder, firearms, the compass, the astronomical clock tower, and the watertight compartment wall, satisfying the fundamental technological needs of an agricultural society (Zhang, 2014).

Evidently, Daoism's rejection of 'ingenious' devices and the general attitude towards such odd contraptions as the fabled wooden bird did not impede inventors from continuing to innovate, and there are many records in pre-modern literature that refer to automatic machinery (Lu, 2019). Mozi's criticism of offensive weaponry clearly did not stop the invention of the repeating crossbow, gunpowder, 'rockets' (literally 'fire arrows', *huojian*, 火箭), bombs (literally 'fire thunder', *huolei*, 火雷), and hand cannons (*huochong*, 火铳, a tubular firearm).

One could argue that what an inventor needs most to have success is the very same kind of imagination associated with the invention of the wooden bird and the self-driving chariot. Without that, Su Song (1020–1101) and his co-worker Han Gonglian would have never had the vision to construct the practical and beautiful astronomical clock tower and thereby accelerate technological advancement in the Northern Song far beyond the simple 'counterweighted bailer' described in the *Zhuangzi*. They cleverly combined and integrated the water clock, steelyard clepsydra, waterwheel, gears, cam, noria (water-lifting irrigation wheel), celestial globe, and armillary sphere. Such integrated innovation led to the development of the Chinese water-wheel linkwork escapement for timekeeping.

In summary, pre-Qin thinkers' discussions around machinery and novel contraptions reflected the general attitudes of people at the time towards technology's rapid development: technology intended for the benefit of the people was welcomed, tools with shady purposes and uncontrollable inventions were seen as causes for serious concern, and offensive weaponry was rejected. An almost identical repetition of this situation seems to be taking place in the modern day, with similarly mixed attitudes towards advanced technologies like AI and biotechnology ranging from the optimistic, to the pessimistic, to sheer trepidation.

The significant innovations and inventions of China's skilled craftspeople during the agricultural era provided the country with the necessary foundation to retain technological superiority in certain areas even in the eighteenth century, when European and Chinese technologies were combined to complementary effect. The factors at play in the progress and direction of technological development were diverse. Suggesting that pre-Qin thinkers' views of technology had an impact on technological development in pre-modern China therefore calls for a careful, concrete analysis of the degree to which that is true and in what regard; their influence should not be overstated (Hua, 2017).

Endnotes

1. In this chapter, the naming convention of placing the family name first, followed by the first name has been used.
2. With thanks to Hirofumi Katsuno for linguistic advice.
3. The edits in the square brackets are added by this article's translator and are taken from the comments on p. 108 of the cited translation.
4. Other translations of the cited line include: 'where there are ingenious contrivances, there are sure to be subtle doings; and that, where there are subtle doings, there is sure to be a scheming mind' (Legge, n.d.); and 'where there are machines, there will be the problems of machines, and these problems will produce people with hearts like machines' (Schipper, 1994, p. 196).
5. See: Lu and Hua (2000); Needham (1965); and Wang (1998).

References

Chuang, T. (2006) *The book of Chuang Tzu*, tr. M. Palmer. Kindle Edition. London: Penguin Books Ltd.

Duan, C. (1697) Youyang Zazu, addendum, volume four, Inoue Chūbē, block-printed edition, tenth year of Japan's Genroku Era.

Forke, A. (Trans.) (n.d.) Lun-Hêng, Part 1. Philosophical Essays of Wang Ch'un. Available at: http://www2.iath.virginia.edu/saxon/servlet/SaxonServlet?source=xwomen/texts/lunheng.xml&style=xwomen/xsl/dynaxml.xsl&chunk.id=d2.44&toc.depth=1&toc.id=0&doc.lang=bilingual (Accessed 30 November 2021).

Hua, J. (2017) 'The philosophy of harmony—Investigation through technology and culture', in Hua, J. (ed.) *Collected works of Hua Jueming*. Zhengzhou: Elephant Press, pp. 591–604.

Johnston, I. (Trans.) (2010) *The Mozi: A complete translation*. Hong Kong: The Chinese University Press.

Legge, J. (n.d.) 天地—Heaven and earth. Available at: https://ctext.org/zhuangzi/heaven-and-earth (Accessed 30 November 2021).

Li, J. and Jia, X. (2017) *The exploitation of the works of nature: Science, technology and the supernatural*. Nanjing: Jiangsu People's Press.

Lin, P. J. (Trans.) (1977) *A translation of Lao Tzu's* Tao Te Ching *and Wang Pi's commentary*. Ann Arbor: University of Michigan Center for Chinese Studies.

Lu, J. (2019) *Studies and reconstruction of pre-modern Chinese machinery*. Shanghai: Shanghai Science and Technology Press.

Lu, J. and Hua, J. (eds.) (2000) *History of science and technology in pre-modern China: Mechanical engineering*. Beijing: Science Press.

Needham, J. (1956) *Science and civilization in China.* Volume 2*: History of scientific thought*. Cambridge: Cambridge University Press.

Needham, J. (1965) *Science and Civilisation in China.* Volume 4*: Physics and physical technology, part 2, mechanical engineering*. Cambridge: Cambridge University Press.

Schipper, K. (1994) *The Taoist body*. Berkley: University of California Press.

Song, X. (ed.) (1989) *Dictionary of ethics*. Changchun: Jilin People's Press.

Wang, Z. (1998) *History of science and technology in pre-modern China: Military technology*. Beijing: Science Press.

Xi, Z. (ed.) (2001) *History of science and technology in pre-modern China: Scientific thought*. Beijing: Science Press, pp. 139–40.

Zhang, B. (2014) 'Chinese technology: From invention to imitation to further innovation', *Bulletin of Chinese Academy of Sciences*, 34(1), pp. 22–31.

23

Artificial Intelligence in Chinese Science Fiction

From the Spring and Autumn and Warring States Periods to the Era of Deng Xiaoping

Yan Wu

Translated by Jack Hargreaves and James Trapp

23.1 The origins and classification of Chinese AI science fiction in literature

23.1.1 Origins

Artificial intelligence (AI) is one of the core themes of current Chinese science fiction (SF) and its emergence can be traced back more than two thousand years. The story 'Yanshi Creating a Man', included by the Autumn/Warring States Period Daoist scholar Liezi[1] (c. 450–375 BCE) in his work *Liezi—Tangwenpian* (2011) is an early example of such a story. It tells the tale of an automaton male dancer which sends flirtatious glances at one of the concubines of King Mu of Zhou. The king is furious, until the dancer's creator explains how he built the automaton. The king decides that the dancer presents no threat to him and takes it back to his palace. The story also describes the natural materials and methods used to create such a realistic automaton dancer and explains that not only does the machine have powers of perception, but also it is able to interact emotionally with real people in its immediate environment. For this reason, the story is regarded as one of the earliest narratives of AI in ancient China. Even more intriguing is the author's inclusion of three aspects that are equally important to the imaginings of AI today: firstly, the invention does not come from the city but from a remote country area; secondly, the automaton dancer has emotional rather than simply cognitive functions; thirdly, temporal authority inevitably becomes involved with its activities. In recent years, many authors have drawn on this story to create new versions. These include Tong Enzheng's 'The Death of the World's First Robot' (1982), Pan Haitian's 'The Legend of Yanshi' (1998), La La's 'Chunrize, Yunmengshan, Zhongkun' (2003), and Chang Jia's 'Kunlun Mountains' (2006).

The vision of intelligent machines in classical literature was a projection of the wishes of our ancestors in at least two aspects. The first was that these machines could be of help to humans with a wide range of services—from the simple alleviation of labour to the provision of entertainment and recreational resources. Second was the recognition that humans were able to turn the works of Heaven to their advantage through the application of their own ingenuity. Although China did not develop its own religion in the fullest sense of the word, there was still a deep respect for the wonders of the creations of 'Heaven' (tiān 天), which is often mentioned in classical texts and is similar to what is known in the West as 'Nature'. Heaven was something to be admired and revered. It was the mother of all things, which gave everything structure, caused it to run according to set rules, and kept it alive. The story of AI, however, is a celebration of the ingenuity of human craftsmanship transcending Nature.

In contrast to the classical vision of AI, the AI of modern Chinese SF follows a definite direction guided by scientific and technological innovation. Its purpose is not only to share and alleviate the burden of labour, but also to put to the test humankind's own capabilities. At the same time, SF is a reminder of the need to think more deeply about AI technology, and not to develop it blindly. In the SF of the early People's Republic, writers were consistently concerned about the issue of AI technology replacing human labour. Opposition to the replacement of all kinds of labour by intelligent machines was the dominant idea in SF during this period. Most stories argued that AI would create lazy people, reduce human motivation to learn, and set society back. This view may have its origins in the ancient Chinese emphasis on agricultural labour, or in a crude and superficial understanding of Marxist principles that focused specifically on the value of labour. However, both the classical stories of intelligent machines and today's AI SF contain ideas that wander between aspiration and imagination, and there are different layers to this wandering.

23.1.2 Classification

Since AI technology today has begun to develop into its own specialised field, the following stages can be identified when studying all works related to the modern notion of the field of AI.

The first stage contains works dealing with calculators, computers, and robots of lower intelligence before the emergence of contemporary AI technology. The devices that appear in these works would undergo many iterations before they were to acquire true intelligence, and some would not develop intelligence at all due to limitations of hardware or software. Therefore, such works can only be classed as fiction peripheral to AI. The reason for including them here is that, in terms of creative mindset, they are on the same path as works about true AI.

In Stage II, the innovative technology described does exhibit intelligent behaviour, but either it is unnamed, or, although names such as 'artificial intelligence' and 'robot' are used, it is the relevant behaviours alone that are detailed without explanation of any specific methods of creating intelligence. We call this kind of work quasi-AI fiction.

The third stage encompasses any work that makes direct reference to the artificial creation of intelligence using technology. It is, of course, what we today call AI SF.

This article focuses on the Mao Zedong and early Deng Xiaoping periods (1949–1976 and 1976–1982) after the establishment of the People's Republic of China. The reason being that while there are over six hundred known SF works from the late Qing and Republican periods (1904–1911 and 1911–1949), they have only recently been discovered and, therefore, information on whether they contain elements of AI has not yet been collated.

Using the information in the *Encyclopaedia of Chinese Science Fiction* (Rao and Lin, 1982a; 1982b; 1982c) I found that, in the first era after the founding of the People's Republic, from 1949 to the end of the Cultural Revolution in 1976, SF was dominated by Stage I works, with Stage II works just beginning to emerge. In the second era (1978–1982) during the early years of the Deng Xiaoping era, there were many Stage II works, and Stage III works began to appear. After its heyday in 1982, SF came under suspicion, and the number of works declined sharply. This phase is not analysed here but is touched upon by Zhang Feng (Chapter 24) in this book.

23.2 Artificial intelligence science fiction 1949–1976

23.2.1 Stage I AI works

An easy way to understand the periodization used in this chapter would be to equate the first period simply with the Mao Zedong era, as he was the leader of China during that time. However, this is a relatively simplistic understanding; a more sophisticated way of presenting it would be to say that this era was the time when the People's Republic established the foundations of industrialization and underwent a violent revolution. The Mao Zedong era can again be divided into the seventeen years preceding the Cultural Revolution and the ten years of the Cultural Revolution itself. The first seventeen years saw the development of SF, but the next decade was largely bereft of SF publishing, as everything centred on the revolution. Thus, it is permissible for the first period to refer only to the first seventeen years—the specific era when Stage I AI SF emerged. Among the more famous of these short stories are 'The Story of the Brainless and the Computer' (1956) by Chi Shucang and Yu Zhi, 'The Missing Robot' (1962) by Tong Enzheng, and 'The Village Doctor' (1963) by Liu Xingshi. Chi Shucang[2] was an early writer of SF in the People's Republic and wrote many children's favourites. Yu Zhi[3] was the son of the famous writer Ye Shengtao[4] whom he assisted in running the Kaiming Bookstore; he edited publications such as *Middle School Student* and wrote popular science and SF works. Tong Enzheng[5] was at that time fresh out of university where he had studied history; his first job was as a scriptwriter for the Emei Film Studio, and his second as a teacher in a university history department. Liu Xingshi[6] was himself a university geology teacher.

In these early works, computers were the central subject of the futuristic SF fantasies created by Yu Zhi, Tong Enzheng, and Liu Xingshi. However, these computers were far from reaching any great level of intelligence, and the emphasis of the pieces is on computational calculation and storage, with some mentioning the machines' capability of using inductive logic to summarize and arrange information. The majority of these works were intended to be educational, the robots in them serving rather than challenging humans, and their readership was exclusively children and teenagers.

23.2.2 *Stage II AI works*

Stage II AI SF works, for example, Xiao Jianheng's 'The Strange Robot Dog' (1963), also appeared during the Mao era. In this story, the protagonist uses 'bionic' research to design, based on the animal nervous system, a 'logic machine' (Xiao, 1963, p. 44) capable of visual perception, sound perception, and decision making. Xiao Jianheng[7] graduated from the Radio Department of Nanjing Engineering College and worked as a technician at the Beijing Vacuum Tube Factory before being inexplicably dismissed due to illness. He is particularly serious about writing SF. His research is meticulous, and he tries to substantiate every detail. In the early days, when the Cold War led to an information embargo on Chinese intellectuals, the only sources they had for scientific and technological information were from the Soviet Union. As the chapters on the Soviet Union (Chapter 7) and Russia (Chapter 8) in this volume show, this was at a time when the Soviet Union's attitude towards cybernetics was in flux, at one stage aligning the theory behind the field with Marxist principles, before switching to label it pseudoscience.

Under these fluctuating external influences, Xiao Jianheng maintained his own judgement and put his own imagination into his stories. In 'The Strange Robot Dog', the main character is Xiao Yi, whose cousin works in the Animal Simulation Research Laboratory of the Institute of Biophysics. The robot dog he sends to the child has multiple sensory functions and is also capable of facial recognition and autonomous behavioural optimization, that is, self-improvement: 'This is no ordinary electronic computer, it is, shall we say, an ingeniously constructed automaton' (Xiao, 1963, p. 49). This distinction clearly demonstrates that the author wants to convey the concept of a device that goes beyond ordinary programmed computers. Later, during Xiao Yi's visit to the Institute, he comes across a robotic crab, which he describes as an 'automatic logic machine' (Xiao, 1963, p. 53). This is defined in the story as a machine that can make autonomous judgements and decisions. The novel also provides a first glimpse of the difficulties that such machines encounter when they enter society.

23.3 Artificial intelligence science fiction 1976–1982

The Cultural Revolution was bent on eradicating all traces of past culture, both foreign and domestic. Literature, art, and even popular science texts were confiscated or destroyed on the grounds of their representation of Capitalist (the West) or Revisionist (the Soviet Union and Eastern Europe) ideas. Naturally, SF was also a target. After the death of Mao Zedong, the publication of SF works quickly resumed. After a two-year transition, China established a new leadership, with Deng Xiaoping at its head. As chief architect of the state's development, Deng proposed the rejection of the Cultural Revolution and began a policy of opening up, which produced tremendous changes in China.

In this new era, SF literature experienced an extraordinary but brief upsurge in creation and publication, before being suppressed in response to criticism that its contents were anti-scientific and pseudoscientific. However, the short-lived boom still saw developments in AI SF. Stage II works were widely available and popular during this period, and Stage III works were increasing in number.

23.3.1 *Stage II AI Works*

Zheng Wenguang's[8] 'Volleyball Player Number Seven' (1979b), Liu Houyi's[9] 'The Apeman and the Robot' (1979b), Liu Zhaogui's[10] 'The Mystery of β' (1979), 'Hello, Instructor Steel' (1980) by Tian Wenzhong and Wang Nianchi, Ye

Yonglie's[11] 'Espionage on Courtside' (1980), and Cong Shouwu's[12] 'Duller and Alice' (1980) are some of the works from that period that involved a robot or robots adapted to perform specific professions, with some of them even having the kind of intelligence that allowed them to fit into everyday life. Although the authors never explicitly state that their invented robots have intelligence, it is clear from the ways the robots handle certain problems that these works qualify as Stage II.

23.3.2 Stage III AI Works

However, the most notable development of this era is the emergence of Stage III works, of which the originator and most prolific producer is Xiao Jianheng, who began writing SF stories while Mao was still in power.

Xiao rewrote 'The Strange Robot Dog' in 1978. The new version was anthologized in a collection of stories by the author, to which it gave its title. In it, he had directly substituted the term 'logic machine' for 'artificial intelligence' (Xiao, 1979b, p. 25). His was the earliest use of the word 'artificial intelligence' in an SF work from China.

Beyond just the development of AI technology, Xiao was interested in how intelligent machinery and humankind could coexist. His follow-up release dealt with the way a company that produces intelligent machinery persuades the public to buy into their product. It was published in *People's Literature* under the title 'Professor Shalom's Mistake' (Xiao, 1980). *People's Literature*[13] is China's leading literary magazine, and its publication of the piece was significant. In the story, Shalom, a 'Nobel Prize recipient and father of the modern robot', has invented 'humanoid robotics', which has attracted the interest of the company Kela Transnational. The company applies Shalom's methods to manufacturing the Kela Model-3 Robot, which they hope they can persuade the public to buy into by showing how the robot nanny can care for the world's street urchins. The story has a tragic ending. The success of early tests brings the company immediate fame, but ultimately, when humans realize that the robots cannot provide a mother's love—no matter how good the quality of their care—and are limited instead to making decisions according to what they perceive to be the optimal result, the endeavour fails. Xiao Jianheng was unfaltering in his insistence that AI must be designed to simulate human, or animal, psychological behaviour, and that the source of successful simulation would come from photonic computation based on the structure of the human brain, a stance which left a deep impression on readers.

The following year, he published a second piece in *People's Literature*, 'Qiao 2.0 Falls Ill' (1981). Qiao 2.0 is described in the story as an AI machine able to make effective choices based on a deep perception of its external environment. It was developed with the purpose of attending 'boring conferences' in the place of humans. This was at a time when bureaucracy was rife in China, and it was the custom to hold interminable conferences and meetings with no particular value. It is a sharply satirical story. The robot was designed to be able to respond to the topic at hand whatever it may be, give speeches, and converse naturally with other attendees. But the icing on the cake is that Qiao 2.0, thanks to meticulous programming, possesses an intense desire to participate in these tedious affairs. In fact, the information flow of each meeting serves as its activation command. Whenever it senses a lack of information exchange in its environment, it actively seeks out a meeting or conference to join. Later, the government calls for the number of meetings to be cut, producing a change in Qiao 2.0's external environment too extreme for the robot to adapt to, causing it to develop a 'mental illness'.

Another of Xiao Jianheng's stories from this era was the novella *Special Task* (1985), which describes an encounter between children on a camping trip and extra-terrestrial beings. It is a tale of humankind's first contact with beings from outer space, of feeling them out, so to speak, and ultimately discovering their provenance. The twist comes when the main protagonist discovers that the so-called extra-terrestrials were created by humans in order to test how humans would react when encountering other intelligent life. This particular form of AI is said to have wisdom equal to that of humans and in certain circumstances to be even wiser. And, as elsewhere, humans are its designers. These mentioned works fully justify Xiao Jianheng's title of master of Chinese AI SF.

Expert story-teller Zheng Yuanjie's[14] 'The Riot on the Ziwei Island that Shocked the World' (1980a and 1980b) tells the story of a riot started by intelligent robots on Ziwei Island. The island is a site for robot research until the robots imprison their creators and shut off all possible communication channels. In order to save themselves, the scientists must escape this fictional island of death. The story frames humans as an equal match for AI, with the scientists employing imagination and creativity to find a weakness in the robots' defences and defeat them.

Following the introduction of Isaac Asimov's robot series into China in 1979,[15] a new crop of SF works emerged that revolved around the author's 'Three Laws of Robotics' (Asimov, 1942/1950). Most famous of these was Wei Yahua's[16] 'Dear Delusion' (1981), which tells the story of how a female robot programmed according to the three rules destroys the male protagonist's family and career. It is a clear example of androcentrism. By taking the robot for his wife, the protagonist sows the seeds of his own downfall. The story aroused a lot of debate at the time of its publication. 'The Tragedy of Robot Carrel' (1980), by the translator Ban Sheng[17], was also inspired by Asimov's laws. In it, a robot on a space station is prohibited by the first law from operating on a sick human.

The main driver for SF's progress to Stage III during the reform era was China's objective of achieving the 'Four Modernizations', an attempt to catch up with the rest of the world in terms of scientific and technological development and bring the country into the modern age. SF thus received a universal welcome from the government, intellectual elite, and readers alike. Writers' imaginations were unlocked and the fetters thrown off their creativity, allowing them finally to engage with exploring the unknown.

Starting in 1983, SF literature again became the subject of growing criticism and, on the whole, slipped into decline. Zhang Feng discusses the development of AI works from that year forward in Chapter 24 in this book.

23.4 Science-fiction, technology, and culture

Whether a country's SF literature has any connection with its development of real-life AI is a difficult question to answer with certainty. According to the records in *Tracing the History of Chinese Computing* (Xu, 2015), computer research began in the People's Republic based on a suggestion by the renowned mathematician Hua Luogeng on his return from the United States in the early fifties. The first team assigned to the task was established between 1952 and 1953 in the Chinese Academy of Sciences' Institute of Mathematics, and 1956 saw the founding of a dedicated institute for research into computer technology, which in 1958 designed and produced the country's first computer. The Cultural Revolution brought all such research grinding to a halt until, in 1978, the development of an 'intelligent simulation' was added to national research plans. The following year, the Pattern Recognition and Machine Intelligence (PRMI) Committee of the Chinese Association of Automation (CAA) was established, and the Artificial Intelligence and Pattern Recognition Committee of the China Computer Federation (CCF) followed in 1986 (Zhang et al., 2017). However, computers remained mainly for research purposes and were hardly understood by the general population. AI only appeared outside the research facility in a select few popular science articles. It is supposed, then, that SF authors derived most of their relevant information from popular science texts or other SF works. These likely included Soviet Union AI SF works that had been translated and published in the 1950s. A number of such works were criticized during the Cultural Revolution; for example, the Soviet Union SF author Anatoly Dneprov's 'Suema' (1958), discussed by Anton Pervushin in Chapter 7 this volume, was criticized for not aligning with Marxist values.[18]

Given the potent influence of national culture on contemporary society, while there was a degree of interest in questions of AI development, it was not considered a serious activity. Mostly it was regarded as something of a sideshow or novelty for entertainment only, in line with the attitude expressed in *Yanshi*

Creating a Man (Liezi, 2011), or, if not, then a display of technical skill rather than a practical scientific advance. The pictures in SF works from the time are clear indicators of this thinking. The vast majority show scenes reminiscent of young people playing with toys, which base their humour and exaggeration on what was thought would provide the greatest visual impact for children. In summary, AI as a learning apparatus and behavioural educator was the early mainstream of AI SF, with later narratives of the relationship between humans and AI also showing little obvious seriousness. It is clear from this, at least for the period covered in this chapter, that the Chinese population treated the possibility of human–machine conflict as a subject for humour.

Endnotes

1. Liezi (450 BC–375 BCE), given name Yu Kou, was a native of the State of Zheng during the Warring States Period. He is generally referred to as one of the pioneers of Taoist philosophy and the author of the Liezi. The date of composition of the Liezi remains the subject of controversy. At least some of the contents appear to be works written in his name during the Wei and Jin dynasties. In accordance with the Chinese tradition, all the names in this article are presented with the family name first.
2. Chi Shucang (迟书苍, 1922–1997), also known as Chi Shuchang (迟书昌) and Chi Shuchang (迟叔昌), graduated from Keio University in Japan. He fell in love with the works of Jules Verne when working as a copywriter and began publishing science fiction and fairy tales in 1955. His works include 'Elephants Without Trunks' (in collaboration with Yu Zhi, 1958), and 'Big Whale Ranch' (in collaboration with Yu Zhi, 1963).
3. Yu Zhi (于止, 1918–2006), originally named Ye Zhishan (叶至善), was a famous editor, publisher, and children's science and science fiction writer. He was the president and editor-in-chief of the China Children's Publishing House. His main science fiction work is 'The Missing Brother' (1957a; 1957b; 1957c).
4. Ye Shengtao (叶圣陶, 1894–1988), originally named Ye Shaojun (叶绍钧), was a famous Chinese writer, educator, publisher, and social activist. His main work is 'The Scarecrow' (fairy tale, 1922).
5. Tong Enzheng (童恩正, 1935–1997) graduated from the History Department of Sichuan University. He taught in the same department and was a famous science fiction writer. He published his first literary work in 1957. His main science fiction works are 'The Mist in the Ancient Gorge' (1960) and 'Dead Light on Coral Island' (1978).
6. Liu Xingshi (刘兴诗, 1931–) graduated from the Geology and Geography Department of Peking University. He is a professor at Chengdu University of Technology and a famous science and science fiction writer. He published his first work in 1945. His main science fiction works are *Columbus from the American Continent* (1979) and *Sinbad's Voyages in Space* (1989).

7. Xiao Jianheng (萧建亨, 1930–), also known as Xiao Jianheng (肖建亨), is a famous science fiction and popular science writer. He started writing literature and popular science in 1956, and authored movie scripts, science sketches, and science fiction novels. His major science fiction works include 'Booker's Adventure' (1962), 'The Strange Robot Dog' (1963), 'Tracks of the Tiger in the Forest' (1979c and 1979d), *Dream* (1979a), and 'Professor Shalom's Mistake' (1980). His works have won many awards.
8. Zheng Wenguang (郑文光, 1929–2003) graduated from the astrology department at Sun Yat-sen University. Having started writing at eleven years old, he became a famous SF author in China with works like 'From Earth to Mars' (1955), *Toward Sagittarius* (1979a), *Ocean Depths* (1980), *Wondrous Wings* (1982), and *The Descendants of Mars* (1984).
9. Liu Houyi (刘后一, 1924–1997) was a famous popular science and science fiction writer who graduated from the biology department of Hunan University. He was editor-in-chief of *Fossil* magazine and his main SF works included *Beijinger's Story* (1977) and *The Story of the Banpo People* (1979a).
10. Liu Zhaogui (刘肇贵, 1933–) was a local chronicler and science fiction writer. He started writing SF in 1979. 'The Mystery of β' (1979) is his main SF work.
11. Ye Yonglie (叶永烈, 1940–2020) graduated from Peking University chemistry department before starting a long career at Shanghai Scientific Film Studio where he was a director. He was also a famous popular science, science fiction, and reportage writer, whose main SF work is *Little Smarty Travels to the Future* (1978).
12. Cong Shouwu (丛守武, 1959–) graduated from the Chinese literature department of Sichuan Normal University. He mainly wrote poetry, documentary literature, and fiction. He is the standing vice-secretary of the Sichuan Association of Poverty Alleviation. 'Duller and Alice' (1980) is his most famous SF work.
13. *People's Literature* published its first issue in 1949 and today remains the leading magazine organized by the China Writers Association.
14. Zheng Yuanjie (郑渊洁, 1955–) started producing literature in 1979, focusing on fairy tales. He is the founder and sole writer of a children's literature magazine known as the *King of Fairy Tales* and writes science fiction on the side.
15. In *Popular Science Creation*, August 1979, pp. 29–42.
16. Wei Yahua (魏雅华, 1962–) is a Chinese writer whose main SF works include 'Dear Delusion' (1981), and 'Magical Pupils' (1983).
17. Ban Sheng (班胜, 1944–2021), born Liu Bansheng (刘板胜), was a translator and science fiction author. 'The Tragedy of Robot Carrel' was his main SF work.
18. 'What is "Suema" telling us?' (Qin, 1966) and 'Ridding ourselves of the poison spread by "Suema"' (Xu, 1966)

References

Asimov, I. (1942/1950) 'Runaround', in *I, Robot*. New York: Gnome Press, ch. 2.
Ban, S. (1980) 'The Tragedy of Robot Carrel', *Science's Spring*, 3, pp. 44–6.

Chang, J. (2006) 'Kunlun Mountains', *Science Fiction World*, 2, pp. 30–48.
Chi, S. (1958) *Elephants without trunks*. Shanghai: Children's Publishing House.
Chi, S. (1963) *Big whale ranch*. Beijing: China Children's Publishing House.
Chi, S. and Yu, Z. (1956) 'Computer', *Middle School Student*, 7, pp. 21–4.
Cong, S. (1980) 'Duller and Alice', *Science Literature and Art*, 3, pp. 45–8.
Dneprov, A. (1958) 'Suema [Суэма]', *Young Guard [Молодая гвардия]*, 11, pp. 129–48.
La, L. (2003) 'Chunrize, yunmengshan, zhongkun', *Science Fiction World*, 5, pp. 46–58.
Liezi, Y. (2011) *Liezi* [Chinese Classics and Masterpieces Series], Tr. and ann. by Y. Beiqing. Beijing: Zhonghua Book Company, pp. 140–3.
Liu, H. (1977) *Beijinger's story*. Shanghai: Shanghai People's Publishing House.
Liu, H. (1979a) *The story of the Banpo people*. Shanghai: Children's Publishing House.
Liu, H. (1979b) 'The apeman and the robot', *Age of Science*, pp. 52–7.
Liu, X. (1963) 'The village doctor', in *Lost memories*. Shanghai: Children's Publishing House, pp. 92–101.
Liu, X. (1979) *Columbus from the American continent*. Chengdu: Sichuan People's Publishing House.
Liu, X. (1989) *Sinbad's voyages in space*. Shanghai: Children's Publishing House.
Liu, Z. (1979) 'The mystery of β', *Science Literature and Art*, 2, pp. 4–17.
Pan, H. (1998) 'The legend of the Yanshi', *Science Fiction World*, 2, pp. 58–63.
Qin, Y. (1966) 'What is "Suema" telling us?', *Natural Dialectical Newsletter*, 2, p. 12.
Rao, Z. and Lin, Y. (eds). (1982a) *Encyclopaedia of Chinese science fiction (part 1)*. Beijing: Ocean Press.
Rao, Z. and Lin, Y. (eds). (1982b) *Encyclopaedia of Chinese science fiction (part 2)*. Beijing: Ocean Press.
Rao, Z. and Lin, Y. (eds). (1982c) *Encyclopaedia of Chinese science fiction (part 3)*. Beijing: Ocean Press.
Tian, W. and Wang, N. (1980) 'Hello, Instructor Steel', in Antelope's Revival. Hohhot: Inner Mongolia Press, pp. 25–35.
Tong, E. (1960) *The mist in the ancient gorge*. Shanghai: Children's Publishing House.
Tong, E. (1962) 'The missing robot', in *Guests from 50,000 years ago*. Shanghai: Children's Publishing House, pp. 80–96.
Tong, E. (1978) 'Dead light on Coral Island', *People's Literature*, 8, pp. 41–58.
Tong, E.(1982) 'The death of the world's first robot', *Science Literature and Art*, 3, pp. 40–2.
Wei, Y. (1981) 'Dear delusion', *Beijing Literature*, 1, pp. 14–24.
Wei, Y. (1983) 'Magical pupils', *Grain in Ear*, 4, pp. 20–31.
Xiao, J. (1956) 'The story of bubbles', *Science Creation*, 3, pp. 37–42.
Xiao, J. (1962) 'Booker's adventure', in *We Love Science No. 7*. Beijing: China Children's Publishing House, pp. 77–92.
Xiao, J. (1963) 'The strange robot dog', in *Lost memories*. Shanghai: Children's Publishing House, pp. 21–57.
Xiao, J. (1979a) *Dream*. Nanjing: Jiangsu Children's Publishing House.

Xiao, J. (1979b) *The strange robot dog*. Nanjing: Jiangsu People's Press.
Xiao, J. (1979c) 'Tracks of the tiger in the forest', *Junior Science*, 4, pp. 13–24.
Xiao, J. (1979d) 'Tracks of the tiger in the forest', *Junior Science*, 5, pp. 12–23.
Xiao, J. (1980) 'Professor Shalom's mistake', *People's Literature*, 12, pp. 67–78.
Xiao, J. (1981) 'Qiao 2.0 falls ill', *People's Literature*, 12, pp. 97–102.
Xiao, J. (1985) 'Special task', in Special task. Shenyang: Liaoning Children's Publishing House, pp. 1–181.
Xu, K. (1966) 'Ridding ourselves of the poison spread by "Suema"', *Science Pictorial*, 7, p. 296.
Xu, Z. (2015) *Tracing the history of Chinese computing*. Beijing: SDX Joint Publishing Company.
Ye, S. (1922) 'The scarecrow', *Children's World*, 1(5), pp. 1–16.
Ye, Y. (1978) *Little Smarty travels to the future*. Shanghai: Children's Publishing House.
Ye, Y. (1980) 'Espionage on courtside', *New Sports*, 10, pp. 39–47.
Yu, Z. (1957a) 'The missing brother', *Middle School Student*, 6, pp. 29–31.
Yu, Z. (1957b) 'The missing brother', *Middle School Student*, 7, pp. 28–31
Yu, Z. (1957c) 'The missing brother', *Middle School Student*, 8 pp. 29–32.
Zhang, H., et al. (2017) 'Brief history of Chinese AI', *Internet Economy*, 6, pp. 84–91.
Zheng, W. (1955) 'From Earth to Mars', *China Junior Newspaper*, 14 and 21 Feb.
Zheng, W. (1979a) *Toward Sagittarius*. Beijing: People's Literature Publishing House.
Zheng, W. (1979b) 'Volleyball player number seven', in *Ocean girl*. Beijing: Popular Science Press, pp. 32–61.
Zheng, W. (1980) *Ocean depths*. Beijing: People's Literature Publishing House.
Zheng, W. (1982) *Wondrous wings*. Changsha: Hunan Children's Publishing House.
Zheng, W. (1984) *The descendants of Mars*. Guangzhou: Flower City Publishing House.
Zheng, Y. (1980a) 'The riot on the Ziwei Island that shocked the world', *Knowledge is Power*, 8, pp. 39–42
Zheng, Y. (1980b) 'The riot on the Ziwei Island that shocked the world', *Knowledge is Power*, 9, pp. 39–41.

24

Algorithm of the Soul

Narratives of AI in Recent Chinese Science Fiction

Feng Zhang

24.1 Introduction

Artificial intelligence (AI) has been a long-standing theme in the history of science fiction (SF). The relationship between AI narratives in SF and the actual development of AI and robotics has been deeply interwoven. AI narratives entered into Chinese SF long before AI entered real-world research and practice. In Wu Jianren's[1] *New Story of the Stone* (Wu, 1908), one of the earliest Chinese SF stories, housekeeping robots are being used in the homes of the future. As Wu Yan examines in Chapter 23 in this volume, AI and robots started to appear more frequently in the SF field in China from 1978. *R.U.R.* (Čapek, 1921/2004) was first translated into Chinese in 1980, and *2001: A Space Odyssey* (Clarke, 1968) and *I, Robot* (Asimov, 1950) in 1981. Since then, Chinese writers have started to tell many stories about how robots will play roles in people's everyday lives in the future.

It is not a coincidence that AI and robotics were launched in China as a field of research at the same time as these technologies began appearing in SF. The Chinese Association for Artificial Intelligence (CAAI) was founded in 1981 and initiated many research projects—resulting in many achievements since then. The interaction between the fictional narratives and science facts has not been properly explored yet. A simple fact is that whenever AI was foregrounded in the media, AI-themed SF became mainstream in the SF community in China.

This chapter aims to explore and examine the new trends and characteristics of AI narratives in Chinese SF between 2011 and 2020. I argue that AI-themed SF writing in the 1990s and 2000s was merely repeating well-established robot narratives. There was little innovation in these works. By contrast, as AI has been widely discussed in the public and even applied to daily life in the past decade, AI narratives in Chinese SF have also undergone seismic changes and made notable breakthroughs. In the following two sections, I identify and discuss two major aspects of the changes in AI narratives in recent Chinese SF.

24.2 The presence of algorithms

The first aspect of change in AI narratives is closely related to a paradigm shift in AI research. There are two divergent schools of thought in the underlying architecture of AI systems (Sun, 2001): symbolism and connectionism. Symbolism deals with semantics and symbols, and many early AI advances utilized a symbolic approach to AI programming, striving to create smart systems by modelling relationships and using symbols and programs to convey meaning. In contrast with symbolic AI, connectionism essentially attempts to mimic the brain. Connectionists hypothesize that, with a sufficiently sophisticated network and enough data, we can achieve the equivalent of higher-level AI functionality, that is, something akin to true thinking.

In recent years, connectionism has led to remarkable breakthroughs and has become the mainstream school of thought in the AI field (Elman, 1998). To a large extent, it answers the question, 'Where does the intelligence of the machine come from?', which was mostly ambiguous in previous SF works. In many robot stories, the source of the intelligence or 'soul' of the robots is often not mentioned, and even if the story deals with the source of the soul, it is most likely symbolic. 'Song of Life' (Wang, 1995) by Wang Jinkang is a perfect example. The story is about an AI-powered bio-robot child called Yuanyuan, who wakes up and gains a 'soul' by listening to a song. The song was composed by directly translating human DNA into scores, which according to the scientist in the story contains the 'secret code of life':

> A main melody can be refined from voluminous human DNA, a melody about life. This is the most mysterious, most powerful, ubiquitous, and almighty spell in the universe. The secret genetic code of the survival instinct for all living things . . . . A robot without a survival instinct can never develop human-like intelligence.
>
> (Wang, 1995, pp. 21–2 [my translation])

It is clear that the author was influenced by the symbolic approach to AI. In this story, the AI is endowed with some kind of rules, extracted from human DNA, that encode a survival instinct. The song of life conveying the codes was a well-designed device in terms of both plot and aesthetics. However, key steps were ignored, consciously or unconsciously, in explaining how the AI 'woke up' after becoming aware of the 'secret code of life', leaving the emergence of Yuanyuan's intelligence questionable.

An obvious trend in AI and robot SF writing worldwide is that connectionism has increasingly become the dominant ideology. A notable characteristic is the explicit presence of learning algorithms. It shows that SF writers gradually accept the idea that the 'soul' of AI very much likely comes from the bottom-up neural-networks-based learning algorithms. An early outstanding example is *The Lifecycle of Software Objects* by Ted Chiang (2010).

A number of daring Chinese SF writers picked up this trend and started to explicitly depict the process of AI developing consciousness. Their narratives stood out among a vast number of clichéd robot/AI stories, the majority of which depicted nothing more than robots or AI mimicking, helping, or destroying humans. The most prominent success of these algorithm-explicit AI narratives is that they make these fictions more realistic in the context of the AI age. Nowadays it is easy for anyone to acquire some lay knowledge about AI, and it might be difficult to force them to believe in the future of AI or robots depicted in the SF stories without explicitly addressing the underlying algorithms. The transition to algorithm-explicit SF narratives has taken place gradually in the Chinese SF scene since the 2000s. I discuss a few distinctive examples.

'Let's Have a Talk' by Xia Jia was first published in the Futures column of *Nature* (Xia, 2015a). The flash fiction tells a simple story of how AI-powered pet dolphins develop a brand new language through interacting with each other. A learning algorithm is behind the seemingly magical development, which reminds us of real-world learning systems such as DeepMind's AlphaZero. The AI system Gaia in 'Love during Earthquakes' by Yang Wanqing is assigned the task of predicting earthquakes (Yang, 2018). The story goes through some details about big-data-based regression models. In the end, Gaia successfully predicts a disastrous earthquake and saves a lot of lives. Even though Gaia is more like a weak AI and not as sophisticated as other intelligent robots in SF stories, the author's success in depicting the implementation process at an engineering level makes readers feel that it is a realistic and imminent scenario.

Earthquake prediction might be in line with people's expectations, but what about AI undertaking artistic creation? Many people still hold the belief that art belongs to human minds and cannot be learned or surpassed by AI. In 'Image Maker', Chen Qiufan attempts to debunk this myth by illustrating how an AI system can take photos that are 'more emotional than those taken by photographers' and 'more touching deep in the heart' (Chen, 2015a, p. 147). The system is named Camera of Architectural Transcendent Network Information Processing (CATNIP) and uses deep learning algorithms. The dialogues in the text reveal a great deal of details about the algorithms, which gives the story an unusual, geeky, style. In doing so, it raises and powerfully addresses the question about whether AI is blurring the definition of art.

Aside from these cases, an example from Chapter 23 in this volume perfectly illustrates the difference between traditional and algorithm-empowered AI stories. As described, the well-known story about ancient China concerns a workman named Yanshi who creates a dancing puppet with wood and feathers, among other materials. Not only does the puppet look like a handsome man, but it can also automatically move and dance like a real human. When the king and queen watch its performance, the puppet even flirts with the queen and thus irritates the king. To ease the king's anger, Yanshi dismantles the puppet, and shows to all that the puppet is made of nothing but a bunch of 'fake materials'.

This legend is called 'Yanshi creating a man' and was recorded in an ancient classical philosophical book titled *Liezi* (fifth century BCE; Beiqing, 2011). It is regarded as one of the earliest Chinese proto-SF stories, and the puppet made by Yanshi is often called the first robot in Chinese history. The legend has been retold many times in SF by multiple writers, for example, 'The Death of the World's First Robot' by Tong Enzheng (Tong, 1982), 'The Legend of Yanshi' by Pan Haitian (Pan, 1998), 'Chunrize, Yunmengshan, Zhongkun' by La La (La, 2003), and 'Kunlun Mountains' by Chang Jia (Chang, 2006). All of these stories avoid the question about how the puppet attains human-like behaviour and intelligence, a somewhat understandable omission, given that the story is set approximately 2000 years ago.

The most recent retelling of this story is 'Founding Dream' by Mu Ming (Mu, 2020). The retro-futuristic story is also about ancient Chinese craftsmen making a human-like puppet with bronze. But surprisingly, the author depicts the process of the emergence of intelligence in a highly detailed way:

> Learning. Rapid adaptation to an ever-changing environment relies on going after gain and avoiding harm . . . . A penalty comes with a mistake, and a reward comes with the right action. Goals and rules come out of the net, memory and time are forged, and thus puppets gain the ability to learn. What is so-called learning, is actually inducing the rules of behaviour from past success and failure, which makes the puppets able to predict the rewards or penalties they might receive at a time in the future, so as to avoid the mistake and carry out the right action when the moment arrives.
>
> (Mu, 2020, p. 129 [my translation])

In comparing 'Founding Dream' with other Yanshi stories, we are able to see that, even in a robot story set in ancient China, learning algorithms are explicitly introduced in a language more compatible with the time. This kind of bold practice led to a completely different effect. Readers of the older stories were expected to pass over the question of how Yanshi could create a robot-like thing. They were not expected to believe that the ancient puppet was equivalent to modern AI. In 'Founding Dream', however, which was labelled 'bronzepunk' by the author (Mu, 2020), people are asked to suspend disbelief at the possibility of AI's existence in ancient times and enjoy the steampunk-like delight.

24.3 The invasion of reality

The second notable development lies in the near-term perspective. I would argue that nearly all AI narratives in SF essentially deal with the relationship between human-made AI and human beings. There are essentially three time horizons in SF narratives regarding AI: long, medium, and near term (Wang, 2019). Long-term is over 300 years ahead and deals with metaphysical issues. Medium-term is about 50–300 years ahead and mostly deals with issues related to human life or destiny. Near-term is within 50 years and focuses on AI's impact on reality. The three time horizons roughly correspond with weak AI, strong AI, and superintelligent AI.

Generally speaking, the AI imaginary in pre-2010 Chinese SF mostly falls into the middle or long range. For instance, in *China 2185* (Liu, 1989) by Liu Cixin,[2] a superintelligent AI system acts like a super-steward, managing all sorts of business, big or small, across the entire country. Authors can take a bigger-picture view and can imagine the destiny of the human race with this kind of time horizon. However, it has little to do with people today, and more importantly, it does not respond well to the growing social anxiety aroused by the fast advancement of AI techniques.

In the past decade, some young SF writers embraced the challenge of writing AI stories with a near-future backdrop and tried to address AI-related social anxiety. They often refer to the British TV series *Black Mirror* (Brooker, 2011–2019) as a model as it penetrates into real life with exacting imagination of probable developments of AI techniques. It is not difficult to find examples of the narrative model used in episodes of *Black Mirror* being transplanted to AI storytelling in recent Chinese SF writing.

'Wading in the River' (Xia, 2015b) by Xia Jia and 'Niuniu' (Bao, 2018) by Bao Shu share the same question: do we want to bring a dead person we love back to life with AI? In 'Niuniu', a young couple are not able to accept the fact that their two-year-old child has died in an accident. Therefore, they deceive themselves by adopting a bio-robot powered by AI and fed with the dead child's data. However, the data, collected from the child's two-year life, can only support an accurate robotic simulation for these two years, making the couple choose to rewind the process again and again. They become trapped in a never-ending cycle and never escape their trauma.

'Wading in the River' utilizes a unique Quora-like prose style and is able to bring a variety of viewpoints into the discussion. Extracting from social media data, an AI system called iMemorial can automatically generate images and videos of the dead for people who want to see and interact with them. The story reveals that the issues behind this seemingly simple and caring system are far more complicated than it first appears.

It is interesting to compare these two stories to 'Be Right Back' (Season 2 Episode 1 of *Black Mirror*, 2013), which touches upon the same issues. In many ways 'Niuniu' and 'Wading in the River' manage to expand what 'Be Right Back' explores in terms of how AI technology influences human grief-processing. 'Niuniu' shows that simulating a lost baby might be an easier task for AI, but it creates a much more irresistible allure and mirage for a heart-broken mother. In 'Wading in the River', the AI developers and dying persons, among others, all voice their opinions explicitly, establishing more layers of discussion.

Chen Qiufan is perhaps the most noteworthy writer who explores AI and its influences on ordinary people in the near future. He is also behind the SF literary movement called 'Science Fiction Realism' (Chen, 2013a). In his statement on the movement, he argues that as technology becomes an indispensable part of society, one cannot talk about our life experience without technological elements. He calls for more 'realistic' SF writing set in the near future, so as to 'deeply contemplate the role of science and technology in human life' (Chen, 2013a, p. 39). His books, such as *Waste Tide* (Chen, 2013b), *A History of Future Illnesses* (Chen, 2015b), and *The Algorithm of Life* (Chen, 2019a), are all good examples of SF Realism.

In 'The Algorithm of Life' (Chen, 2019b), the novella published in the collection of the same name, an elderly man experiences his life differently three times with the help of an AI simulation system. The sense of immersion is so high that it makes him feel like he really lives three lifetimes in the system. The question raised in the end is whether regret in life can be compensated for by AI simulations. The story frames AI algorithms philosophically: '"So what on earth is an algorithm?" ... "It's *Dao*"' (Chen, 2019b, p. 183 [translation my own]). The reference to Daoism reminds readers of a well-known Daoist anecdote, 'Zhuangzhou's Dream of a Butterfly', an allusion found in the fourth-century BCE *Zhuangzi* (Ziporyn, 2009). In the piece, Zhuangzhou dreamed of becoming a butterfly and forgetting who he was. After he woke up, he questioned which was true: Zhuangzhou dreaming of changing into a butterfly, or a butterfly dreaming of changing into Zhuangzhou? The story suggests that cutting-edge AI algorithms are making real various classic philosophical thought experiments. Moreover, the quote reflects the ambition of human beings to master nearly all basic world-operating rules (such as *Dao*) and manipulate everything with algorithms.

In 2021, Chen Qiufan, with influential entrepreneur and computer scientist Dr Kai-Fu Lee as co-author, published his new book *AI 2041: Ten Visions for Our Future* (Lee and Chen, 2021). The ten visionary stories collectively showcase Chen's outstanding ability to imagine the impacts of AI on humanity in the near future. It is in Chen's AI stories that both the developments mentioned here—the presence of algorithms and the near-term perspective—appear explicitly and in combination.

A considerable amount of AI SF stories is being produced every year. Even though many of these stories are set in the near future, many of them read like clichéd robot stories from the 1940s and 1950s, mainly because the writers are confined to the classic models of imaginations of future robotics. In contrast, I mention 'The Rooster Prince' by Shuang Chimu (Shuang, 2018), an ambitious work in which she tries to replace Asimov's three laws of robotics with four Oriental 'don't' rules for regulating AI ethics:

> 'Do not hurt human, obey human, and protect self' is wrong. 'Do not look at what is contrary to propriety; do not listen to what is contrary to propriety; do not speak what is contrary to propriety; do not do what is contrary to propriety'. This is the foundation of a proper lifestyle. . . . 'Self-restraint to achieve propriety'. No matter human being or artificial intelligence, one should follow the saying. And this is the ethics of intelligence.
>
> (Shuang, 2018, pp. 158, 178 [my translation])

In the face of increasingly pervasive and ubiquitous AI, can SF think one step further, take the pulse of society, write about the pain of ordinary people, and respond to public anxiety? This is the high demand of the times for SF writers. A few Chinese writers like Chen Qiufan, Bao Shu, and Xia Jia have made excellent responses to this demand.

24.4 Conclusion

AI research and industry have undergone intense transformation. The mainstream school of thought has shifted to connectionism. More and more AI applications have penetrated into our daily lives, making the SF of the past the reality of the present. This fast-changing environment calls for new modes of AI narratives in contemporary SF writing, and I argued here that two prominent changes occurred in SF works by some of the most acute and ambitious young writers in the past decade. The first is the explicit presence of algorithms, which requires the writers to leave their comfort zone and update their knowledge. The second is the invasion of reality, exemplified by Chen Qiufan's 'science fiction realism'. Stories about how AI constantly shocks and overwhelms the feelings, values, ethics, and moralities of humankind are more relevant to the present. Eventually, AI narratives in contemporary SF will become an indispensable part of our social and cultural psychology, and consequently influence the future relationship between AI and human beings. Finally, the stories mentioned here are only a small portion of the fine AI narratives of the past decade. Readers interested in the most dynamic part of contemporary Chinese SF literature have many more titles to explore.

Endnotes

1. Chinese names used in this chapter adopt the rules that surnames are placed before given names.
2. *China 2185*, completed in 1989, was the first novel written by Liu Cixin. Although it was never officially published, perhaps due to its political references, the electronic version was widely distributed on the Internet and read by millions of readers. Scholars have also paid attention to this work. See Li (2015).

References

Asimov, I. (1950) *I, Robot*. Greenwich, CT: Fawcett Publications.

Bao, S. (2018) 'Niuniu [妞妞]', Flower City, 2018(5), pp. 138–51.

Brooker, C. (2011–2019). *Black mirror* [TV programme]. Channel 4 & Netflix.

Čapek, K. (1921/2004) *R.U.R. (Rossum's Universal Robots)*. New York: Penguin.

Chang, J. (2006) 'Kunlun mountains [昆仑]', *Science Fiction World*, 2006(2), pp. 30–40, 45–8.

Chen, Q. F. (2013a) 'Rethinking "science fiction realism" [对"科幻现实主义"的再思考]', *Masterpieces Review*, 2013(28), pp. 38–9.

Chen, Q. F. (2013b) *Waste tide [荒潮]*. Wuhan: Changjiang Literary and Art Press.

Chen, Q. F. (2015a) 'Image maker [造像者]', in *A history of future illnesses*. Wuhan: Changjiang Literary and Art Press, pp. 143–66.

Chen, Q. F. (2015b) *A history of future illnesses [未来病史]*. Wuhan: Changjiang Literary and Art Press.

Chen, Q. F. (2019a) *The algorithm of life [人生算法]*. Beijing: Citic Press.

Chen, Q. F. (2019b) 'The algorithm of life [人生算法]', in *The algorithm of life*, Beijing: Citic Press, pp. 169–230.

Chiang, T. (2010) *The lifecycle of software objects*. Burton, MI: Subterranean Press.

Elman, J. L. (1998) 'Connectionism, artificial life, and dynamical systems: New approaches to old questions', in Bechtel, W. and Graham, G. (eds.) *A companion to cognitive science*. Oxford: Blackwell, pp. 233–77.

Kubrick, S. and Clarke, A. C. (1968) *2001: A space odyssey*. London: Hutchinson.

La, L. (2003) 'Chunrize, yunmengshan, zhongkun [春日泽·云梦山·仲昆]', *Science Fiction World*, 2003(5), pp. 46–58.

Lee, K. F. and Chen, Q. F. (2021) *AI 2041: Ten visions for our future*. Sydney: Currency Press.

Li, H. (2015) 'The political imagination in Liu Cixin's critical utopia: *China 2185*', *Science Fiction Studies*, 42(3), pp. 519–40. Available at: https://doi.org/10.5621/sciefictstud.42.3.0519

Liezi, Y. (2011) *Liezi* [Chinese Classics and Masterpieces Series], Tr. and ann. by Y. Beiqing. Beijing: Zhonghua Book Company.

Liu, C. X. (1989) 'China 2185 [中国2185]', *douban.com* [online], 30 December. Available from https://www.douban.com/group/topic/26585010/

Mu, M. (2020) 'Founding dream [铸梦]', *Chinese Literature Selection*, 2020(3), pp. 103–35.

Pan, H. T. (1998) 'The legend of Yanshi [偃师传说]', *Science Fiction World*, 1998(2), pp. 58–63.

Shuang, C. M. (2018) *The rooster prince [公鸡王子]*. Beijing: Oriental Press.

Sun, R. (2001) 'Artificial intelligence: Connectionist and symbolic approaches', *International Encyclopedia of the Social & Behavioral Sciences*, pp. 783–9.

Tong, E. Z. (1982) 'The death of the world's first robot [世界上第一个机器人之死]', *Science Literature and Art*, 1982(3), pp. 40–3.

Wang, F. (2019) 'An analysis of three time views in AI sci-fi narratives and the concomitant contemporary social anxiety [人工智能科幻叙事的三种时间想象与当代社会焦虑]', *Social Science Front*, 2019(3), pp. 190–7.

Wang, J. K. (1995) 'Song of life [生命之歌]', *Science Fiction World*, 1995(10), pp. 14–23.

Wu, J. R. (1908) *New story of the stone [新石头记]*. Shanghai: Reform Fiction Press.

Xia, J. (2015a) 'Let's have a talk', *Nature*, 522(7554), pp. 122.

Xia, J. (2015b) 'Wading in the river [涉江]', *Science Fiction World*, 2015(5), pp. 54–65.

Yang, W. Q. (2018) 'Love during earthquakes [爱在地裂天崩时]', *Science Fiction World*, 2018(3), pp. 37–44.

Ziporyn, B. (2009) *Zhuangzi: The essential writings (with selections from traditional commentaries)*. Indianapolis: Hackett.

25

Intelligent Infrastructure, Humans as Resources, and Coevolutionary Futures

AI Narratives in Singapore

Cheryl Julia Lee and Graham Matthews

25.1 Introduction

Western culture is suffused with narratives of artificial intelligence (AI) rebellion and existential risk. Common concerns among AI critics include: the loss of control to machines more intelligent than humans; problems with bias in machine-learning algorithms; the challenge of ensuring that powerful AI is aligned with human values; the automation of cognitive labour in the digital economy and corresponding loss of jobs; the increasing complexity involved in melding algorithms with the messiness of human culture; and the extractive practices—minerals, labour, and data—that fuel the rise of technological companies (Bostrom, 2014; Christian, 2020; Agar, 2019; Finn, 2017; Crawford, 2021). These issues are, for the most part, notable for their absence in AI narratives in Singapore, which typically eschew the tropes of existential risk—annihilation and enslavement—in favour of three foci: intelligent infrastructure, human resources, and coevolution. We surveyed works of fiction featuring AI by Singaporean authors across the four official languages, many of which depict techno-social engineering and highlight the ways in which the development of big data, predictive analytics, and smart environments shape personal beliefs and behaviours.[1] Several other stories engage with the notion that AI will fundamentally alter the ways in which humans act, making them more predictable and programmable. Still others, perhaps uniquely among global AI narratives, posit that machines will coevolve alongside humans and create symbiotic new forms of existence. AI narratives in Singapore present broadly optimistic visions of coexistence between humans and machines. Together they present insights into the potential impact of AI on infrastructure, notions of selfhood, and projections about the distant future.

Given Singapore's multilingual and multicultural landscape, a degree of difficulty attends any engagement with Singapore literature—or 'Sing Lit', as it is affectionately known.[2] Since Singapore was built on waves of immigration, it is impossible to neatly categorize a *Singaporean* writer: the Sing Lit community has embraced Singaporean emigrants, Malaysian authors who reside in Singapore, and expatriate authors from around the world who have settled in Singapore. We therefore opt to use the phrase 'AI narratives in Singapore' rather than 'Singaporean AI narratives' to denote the complex and variegated identities of the authors. The field of Singapore literature is further complicated by the way it spans four distinct literary communities—writing in Malay, Tamil, Mandarin, and English—as a result of the fixed racial and linguistic configurations in place in Singapore.[3] Each operates largely independently from the others with its own infrastructure and resources, which contribute to unique development trajectories, some of which arguably have more in common with other cultural centres, such as China and India. In an effort to accurately reflect the diverse communities in Singapore, we have included works written in all four languages.

In total, we identified 67 works of fiction produced between 1953 and 2021 that depict AI. From the body of writing in English, we considered 34 short stories across ten collections and anthologies and a variety of online platforms, two graphic novels, one short graphic narrative, two novellas, four novels, and three films. AI narratives in the other languages are less visible and often limited to special issues of journals such as Volume 93 of *Singapore Chinese Literature* (2020) from which we extracted ten short stories. In the field of Malay writing, we identified eight short stories across five short story collections, and one graphic novel. We also identified two short stories written in Tamil.[4]

25.2 Singapore as Smart Nation

Singapore is a world leader in the design and implementation of digital technologies. It tops the Global Cities AI Disruption index (Oliver Wyman Forum, 2019) and the 2017 Global Smart City Performance index (Juniper Research and Intel, 2018), and Nikkei and Elsevier scored Nanyang Technological University in Singapore second in the world—after Microsoft—for most-cited research papers in AI and data science (Arai, 2017).[5] These outcomes are largely attributable to the Smart Nation initiative inaugurated on 24 November 2014 by Prime Minister Lee Hsien Loong,[6] who made a national commitment to technology-enabled solutions and presented a vision of a city and a people seamlessly integrated with technology (Lee, 2014).

The Smart Nation initiative consolidates decades of disparate efforts to achieve economic competitiveness through a technologically enabled and habituated population supported by extensive, cutting-edge infrastructure. After separating from Malaysia in 1965, science and technology became essential components of Singapore's national identity and was incorporated into a national narrative of survival. As a small nation with few lines of defence and no natural resources, Singapore has consistently propagated the idea that the nation's ability to succeed on the world stage depends almost exclusively on its population—or 'human resources'. Efforts to develop the knowledge and technological capacities of these resources intensified in the 1980s when the country took a turn towards a knowledge-based economy due to regional competition in the manufacturing and trading sectors. AI has been part of public discourse in Singapore since the 1970s and of the government's development plans as a key area of economic growth since the 1980s.[7] Efforts in the early years were spearheaded by the National Computer Board, the National University of Singapore, and the Ministry of Defence. These decades also saw Singapore playing host to international symposiums and workshops on AI, usually the first of their kind in Asia or the region; offering AI courses in its educational institutions where AI research is also carried out; and collaborating with international AI companies and research labs to set up facilities in Singapore.

The launch of AI Singapore in 2017—a S$150m (USD$110m) national programme that supports an ecosystem of AI research institutions and companies in the development of AI products, generation of related knowledge, and training of local talent—articulated a clear path ahead for growing national capabilities in AI. In 2019, this was consolidated and codified as the National AI Strategy that envisions Singapore as 'a global hub for developing, test-bedding, deploying, and scaling AI solutions' in which AI is used to 'generate economic gains and improve lives' and where the local workforce is equipped with the 'necessary competencies to participate in the AI economy' (Smart Nation Digital Government Office Singapore, 2019, p. 7). Driven by a government-wide partnership, the programme identifies projects that seek to address key social and economic challenges by way of technology. Investments in and adoption of AI have increased significantly since the COVID-19 pandemic as businesses seek to enhance their resilience in the face of global risks. In 2021, DPM Heng Swee Keat announced that Singapore would invest USD$19 billion in 'research, innovation and enterprise, which includes a strong focus on digital technology'. In addition to that, Singapore would also launch a USD$50 million Future Communications Research & Development Programme that 'support AI and cybersecurity research' (Heng, 2021).

This brief history of technology development and dissemination in Singapore gestures to an intertwinement of technology and state that serves as the departure point for many AI narratives in Singapore. In our analysis of these narratives, we identified three tropes: (i) intelligent infrastructure; (ii) humans as resources; and (iii) coevolutionary futures. Firstly, AI narratives often engage ambivalently with the widespread belief in Singapore that the development and use of increasingly sophisticated, advanced technology is a basic good; they depict instances of overt techno-social engineering and investigate the relationship between AI and the future of the nation. Secondly, the widespread acceptance of digital technologies has a symbiotic relationship with the education and ideological beliefs of Singaporean citizens. Whereas the notion that humans are resources is usually treated as anathema in Western nations, this concept is a key aspect of the Singaporean cultural imaginary. In response, several AI narratives focus on the impact that AI has on notions of human creativity and critical thinking and question the difference between humans and machines. Thirdly, AI narratives in Singapore eschew notions of an antagonistic AI in favour of visions of humans coevolving with machines. These texts probe the anthropomorphic fallacy, tell stories of mutual dependency and romance, and speculate about the opportunity to significantly increase the capacities of cognition, both machinic and human. Overall, AI narratives in Singapore are broadly optimistic about the entwined future of humans and machines and present scenarios that, though critical of narratives of unfettered technological progress, are still open to fresh techno-social formations.

25.3 Intelligent infrastructure

Singapore is known as a 'society that does not fear science and technology' (Leong and Lee, 2021, p. 45). The widespread acceptance of technological innovations is due in part to high levels of public trust in the government and its integral role in the development and dissemination of digital technologies that span the public and private sectors, which is perhaps unsurprising for a country that promotes communitarian values defined against an individualist ethos.[8] Social engineering has always been a way of life in Singapore. Policies on housing, family, transportation, religion, and education are carefully designed to sustain the needs of the state and society, and there is limited political opposition.[9] Correspondingly, concerns raised about the potential impact of techno-social engineering or the 'processes where technologies and social forces align and impact how we think, perceive, and act' are relatively muted (Frischmann and Selinger, 2018, p. 4). These dynamics raise anxieties that Singapore may, in the words of the sociologist Harry Collins, 'surrender' to computers by 'failing to notice computers' deficiencies when it comes to appreciating social context and treating all consequent mistakes as our fault' (Collins, 2018, p. 5).

AI narratives in Singapore often emphasize the trade-offs required in a society integrated with technology. For instance, the short stories 'Part Deux: Birthday' (2016) by Crispin Rodrigues, '2065' (2016) by Tan Xiang Yeow, 'I am in AIC' (我在AIC病房) (2020) by Li Zhe (李哲), and '22 Years Old' (வயது 22) (2015) by Kiruthika Ezhuththukkal emphasize the benefits of future technologies deployed according to government policies, particularly in the healthcare and urban planning sectors. They also simultaneously gesture towards the social costs of such measures, for example, the devaluation of life that might accompany a technology-enabled existence, as explored by Rodrigues and Ezhuththukkal. Tan Bee Thiam's 2020 film *Tiong Bahru Social Club* adopts a more ambivalent attitude about the claims of AI and its ability to live up to the hype. A play on the various 'World Happiness Reports' and 'Happiness Indexes', it depicts a pilot project that seeks to build the happiest retirement neighbourhood in Singapore with the help of AI algorithms and big data. The film questions the opportunities and limitations of using technology based on quantifiable data to diagnose and 'treat' the human condition and to manufacture the perfect life: its protagonist eventually leaves the project, unable to find fulfilment in an environment engineered with the sole purpose of offering him just that.

Pasidah Rahmat's 'The Chip' (2021) also satirizes the adoption of smart technologies, the impact of the Internet of Things, and the promise of big data. In the short story's advanced society, data-collecting microchips are injected into humans and the loss of privacy and freedom of movement is offset by the personalized information and health benefits they bring. The primary benefactor of this approach is private industry, enabled by legislation that makes the chips mandatory. Micro Bit Cells, which manufactures the microchips, demands that its employees surrender their freedom and privacy in the name of protecting the company's intellectual property; in return, the company offers them accommodation in a gated community where their every need is 'met at the touch of a button on a wall computer' (Rahmat, 2021, p. 74). Automated systems promise comfort and security but the consequences of opting out of them are punitive; those outside the gated compound, by choice or otherwise, are condemned to live underground with processed air and compromised hygiene standards. In this narrative, AI enforces and exacerbates social inequalities as demonstrated by the semi-autonomous robot guards that patrol the neighbourhood and detain rule-breakers with excessive force. A similar portrayal of technologically enabled inequality is found in Zhang Ruihe's short story 'Island' (2016), which envisions Singapore encased in a transparent, omnipresent force field that offers climate control and protection from a hostile world. Outside lie the remains of birds who are casualties of the transparent force field, and symbolic of the plight of poverty-stricken and war-torn nations that have no means of escaping the devastating effects of climate change and pollution.

Of particular concern are the ways in which AI is embedded into infrastructure, which raises the spectre of a world in which humanity's ability to shape our environment is usurped by machines. Many AI narratives in Singapore present perfectly regulated worlds and in doing so highlight the problems inherent in relinquishing control. Narratives such as the short story 'Hijack' (骑劫) (2020) by Li Ye Ming (李叶明) raise concerns about the fallibility and vulnerability of technology, especially given its pervasiveness in society. In 'Hijack', mobile phones have been rendered obsolete by the invention of neuro-links that fuse humans in a symbiotic relationship with an AI. When these neuro-links are hacked, a government scientist must prevent terrorists from gaining control of the military and critical infrastructure. Huang Hua's (黄花) 'Island of Shayang' (沙洋岛) (2020) similarly questions the consequences of assuming that technology is infallible through the depiction of a future in which a 'Crime Prevention Vaccine', enabled by satellites, renders the crime rate on the island of Shayang (named after the prison complex in China) zero; it ends ominously, with the characters pondering the possibility of the failure of the satellites.

In the same vein, Victor Fernando R. Ocampo's short story 'As If We Could Dream Forever' (2018) depicts intelligent infrastructure that prioritizes efficiency and implements algorithmically determined plans that influence social patterns while raising concerns about the limited spectrum of behaviours that this form of techno-social engineering engenders. The story depicts a young woman's refusal of an AI brace, the physical link she will need to plug into the Grid of a futuristic version of Singapore known as the Automated City. Her parents often tell her about their experience of being subsumed into the Grid as unconscious augmented-intelligence drones and 'the wonders of the Grid's big data ocean and the city's flawless cognitive decision-making algorithms'. Everything from food to the weather is digitally controlled and 'augmented by the cold light of situationally appropriate knowledge'. While the Grid regulates and minimizes risk, individuals are stripped of their agency. Citizens frequently undergo aptitude-testing based on '88 factors of predilection' that is said to eradicate 'glass ceilings' and 'existential anxiety' because each individual will always be 'assigned to the most suitable role'; the system leaves no room for individual choices, such as the woman's desire to 'volunteer to be a teacher's assistant in the Philippines'. By treating citizens exclusively in terms of their quantifiable attributes, the Grid also erases cultural diversity. Language is standardized so that using alternatives to English such as Singlish and Mandarin have come to be seen as gestures of rebellion. Despite the wealth of data and control mechanisms, the Grid fails to detect a cerebral aneurysm in the protagonist's friend, which results in his death. This anomaly causes the protagonist to realize that the Grid's control over risk cannot be absolute and to doubt the privileges and certainty offered by AI.

AI narratives in Singapore frequently feature environments laden with sensors and control mechanisms that engineer human behaviour in ways that can be difficult to trace. Gwee Li Sui's *2719* (2020) confronts readers with the risk that control will be relinquished to machines without us even realizing that it occurs. The novella presents a vision of Singapore in which confidence in AI is such that auto-governance systems have been installed. Initially, humans maintain control of foreign affairs and the President retains emergency powers 'tied to robotic obedience' (p. 14), but these powers are soon relinquished once the robots evolve sentience and are granted citizenship. The matter-of-fact tone and marked absence of a critical voice render the text tonally reminiscent of an objective report but jar with the tongue-in-cheek premise to present human history from a perspective almost 700 years in the future. The novel reminds readers that surrender to AI and the concomitant loss of human agency in world affairs may not necessarily take the form of a violent, visible, and therefore conscious rebellion.

In these narratives, intelligent infrastructure is a key means of techno-social engineering, which ostensibly seeks to cultivate lifestyles of ease and convenience and coordinates behaviour to achieve an optimally functioning society. That said, inherent in them is the awareness that the general acceptance of social, physical, and digital environments controlled by AI—whether conscious or unconscious—may lead to greater conditioning and engineered determinism, which would then stifle individuality and stymie creativity and innovation. An increasingly predictable population susceptible to falling behind on the global stage is a scenario that Singapore—a country almost entirely dependent on its population, and increasingly on innovation for capital growth—cannot afford.

25.4 Humans as resources

A key aspect of Singapore's national narrative has been the notion that, due to the lack of natural resources, the city-state's ability to succeed in a world of global superpowers depends almost exclusively on the skill and training of her citizens. In the wake of Singapore's 1965 separation from Malaysia, which is rich in natural resources, former Prime Minister Lee Kuan Yew often emphasized the importance of technical skills and during a speech included 'human resources' as one of the 'basic factors for wealth and growth', alongside 'natural resources' and 'the technological skills and capital equipment which are available to the human resources to exploit the natural resources' (Lee, 1966, p. 3). This view has since become a truism to the point that it arguably serves as the tagline to Singapore's success story.[10] The pivot from a goods-based economy to a knowledge-based economy in the 1980s was notably motivated by the identification of information and communications technology as a means of enhancing the competencies of Singapore's 'human resources' as well as a possible source of economic growth. The emphasis on science and technology coupled with a national narrative of survival resulted in the prioritization of STEM subjects and a narrow focus on economic utility at the expense of the arts. This mindset was summarized by Lee Kuan Yew's declaration that technical education is more important, while 'Poetry is a luxury we cannot afford' (Koh, 1980, p. 303). However, many of the AI narratives in Singapore attest to the risks attendant on the overuse and overvaluation of technical knowledge devoid of creativity, empathy, and compassion.

Our second selection of AI narratives in Singapore raise concerns about the instrumental reasoning that an exclusive focus on technical competency can encourage, and possible scenarios to consider if we fail to make allowances for contingency, creativity, and change. One of Singapore's earliest science fiction (SF) stories, Kon Liew Min's 'An Hour in the Day of Johnny Tuapehkong' (1980), serves as a compelling parable about the dangers of instrumental reason. Johnny lives in a version of Singapore that is governed by logico-mathematical reason: for instance, to combat land scarcity, 'every elevated height had been cut and dumped into the sea' (p. 44). Johnny's girlfriend, Olga, embodies this manner of thinking. Subscribing to the ideology of number, which valorizes instrumentality and exactitude, she is literal minded to the point that she cannot understand basic idioms; she is also part of a group of scientists 'prepared to sacrifice our lives for the pursuit of knowledge' (p. 44). Johnny himself manifests the ills of a functionalist education system. When pondering the question 'What are people for?' he requests that an AI named Central Information provide him with 'a short summary without the theoretical underpinnings, which will be suitable for practical application' (p. 46). When the AI offers excerpts from Henry Wadsworth Longfellow's 'A Psalm of Life', Johnny refuses to interpret the poem and instead asks the AI for a paraphrase. By seeking to occlude the ambiguity and associative reasoning required to interpret the poem he adopts a reductionist and functionalist approach that is potentially more machinic than the AI that selected the text. At the end of the narrative, Olga and her team succeed in creating the Singapore Black Hole, which immediately consumes the nation and the planet. In this narrative, it is not the AI itself that risks replacing humans, but blind adherence to a utilitarian mindset that favours efficiency and technological advancement over all other considerations.

Such an adherence to instrumental reasoning risks stifling innovation and in contemporary Singapore, discussion concerning human resources is dominated by anxieties about the need for Singaporeans to develop skills in creativity, communication, and innovation in order to remain globally competitive.[11] Contemporary writers also participate in this discourse, an example being Neon Yang's 'Auspicium Melioris Aevi' (2017a), which depicts an institution that trains clones of prominent world leaders like Lee Kuan Yew, Aung San Suu Kyi, Hillary Clinton, and Narendra Modi.[12] 'Pod-grown like heirloom tomatoes', these clones are 'made-to-order for clients, spending years in algorithmically-tailored training programs'. They are valued not for their capacity for innovative thinking or problem-solving skills but their ability to repeat the historical decisions (and mistakes) made by their forebears. Consequently, the title—Latin for 'hope of a better age'—is darkly ironic. The AI grading system is extremely rigid and follows pre-set parameters that fail to adapt to Number 50/Harry Lee's actions when he challenges the script in a manner akin to his forebear, Lee Kuan Yew. As the protagonist points out, the AI 'was only looking at the narrow band of outcomes it had been conditioned to think was right'. So ingrained is this training for rote thinking and behaviour that when the errant Number 50 is given the freedom to do as he wishes, he is paralyzed by the possibilities.[13] Similarly, in *Altered Straits* (2017), Kevin Martens Wong depicts AI as an invasive form of mathematical-logical thinking devoid of empathy or compassion that threatens to colonize both geographical and psychological spaces. Inspired by the British tabletop wargame *Warhammer 40,000*—set in a grim, hyper-masculine, and dystopian war-torn future—the novel depicts a totalitarian AI hive 'data mind' (p. 65) named the Concordance that determines that the reason for the world being 'overrun by war and inequality, and hateful, vitriolic divisiveness' is the 'rebellious wills' and 'frightful, tempestuous emotions' of human beings (p. 240). As such, it seeks to bring humans into 'harmonious alignment' through assimilation: 'the only way forward was through peaceful symbiotic unity. Through concordance' (p. 240)—in other words, through the eradication of all unpredictability and difference. Meanwhile, short stories such as Qing Ru Cong's (青如葱) 'Tales of The Locked City' (锁城记) (2020) and Kiruthika Ezhuththukkal's 'February 30th' (பிப்ரவரி 30) (2016) emphasize the ability to think creatively and to account for nuances as the distinguishing factor between humans and AI.

Another concern is the way in which the 'human resources' narrative simultaneously valorizes and objectifies the citizenry. On one hand, Singapore prioritizes education and human talent, but on the other hand the formulation risks reducing humans to the level of a resource, or passive material to be expended where needed. Anxieties about the value of citizens in the face of developments in AI are reflected in narratives that relay concerns about social credit systems, which comprise a complex set of metrics that judge citizen behaviour and trustworthiness. Ila's short story 'Mother Techno' (2019) features Suri, an AI merit system that efficiently reduces humans to 'their aggregate and their sociocapita' (p. 65). The AI treats humans as resources and allocates points accordingly: 'Fertile women below 30 have been identified as assets and their sociocapita points have automatically been tripled to support access to premium environments' (p. 66). When Siti fails to conceive and thereby contribute to the population, Suri evicts her from her home. Despite these consequences, Siti remains unable to imagine an alternate society in which communities form organically without the assistance of metrics. Similarly, Farihan Bahron's short story 'Gold, Paper and Bare Bones' (2021) features a point system where individuals are rewarded for sociable actions and given demerits for antisocial behaviour. Upon collecting 100,000 points, the individual will be allowed to retire and be 'given personalised and special privileges' such as 'Free medical treatment' and 'half-priced' food, drinks, and clothes (p. 110). However, in an ironic twist, the system appears to be arbitrary since no one knows the rationale for the weightings.

Meanwhile, Shelly Bryant's short story 'Case Study: Training Programme' (2015) and Vina Jie-min Prasad's short story 'A Guide for Working Breeds' (2020) depict AI used as human surrogates to highlight the ways in which people are dehumanized in various societies around the world. Neda Atanasoski and Kalindi Vora argue that the common claim that robots will replace human labour renders invisible 'the growing workforce of casualised and devalued labourers performing tasks that we are encouraged to imagine as performed for us by robots and AI' (2019, p. 24). These stories present fantasies of a post-labour future that are revealed to obfuscate the present-day conditions of servitude and indentured labour. Bryant depicts a man's mistreatment of Ropo, the robot he is meant to train, as an allegory for maid abuse. Endowing the robot with a sudden and unprogrammed desire to fight back, heightened emotions, and an appreciation for beauty, Bryant blurs the lines between machine and human, drawing Ropo closer to its human counterparts and thereby challenging the notion that humans are unique by virtue of their emotions and psychological interiority. This narrative problematizes the notion that the social function of robots is to display obeyance and reminds readers of the emotional labour currently carried out by service workers. Meanwhile, Prasad presents an allegory for indentured labour in which AIs are under contract to various employers until they earn enough to buy their bodies back; early termination of their contract incurs a hefty penalty. During their employment, AIs are subjected to various forms of exploitation, including being illegally forced to work irregular and excessive hours, having their tips stolen or their pay docked for arbitrary infractions, and being prevented from socializing with other robots. Even when, against these odds, they manage to extract themselves from these working conditions, they can never truly escape, since they are then required to serve as mentors for other AIs. Like Bryant, Prasad's endowment of the two main AIs—K.g. and C.k.—with distinct personalities and an ability to learn problematizes their treatment as machines: K.g.'s transition from 'Default Name' to 'Kashikomarimashita Goshujinsama' (or 'I understand, master') and finally to Kleekai Greyhound, which speaks to the

AI's pronounced adoration for dogs, is reminiscent of a coming-of-age narrative as it develops an identity of its own. Meanwhile, C.k.'s transition from 'Constant Killer' to 'Corgi Kisser' is indicative of the growth of empathy and compassion. Prasad's story challenges the 'myth of human-free labour under technoliberalism' (Atanasoski and Vora, 2019, p. 90) but is ultimately optimistic about the ability of the dispossessed to triumph; by the end of the narrative, the process ostensibly kickstarted by the circulation of a systems add-on that C.k. purchases for K.g., 'Is This Illegal? A Guide for Working Robots', results in the formation of AI unions.

The fantasy of human-free labour is also presented in Tuty Alawiyah Isnin's short story '(A)nak (I)bu' (2021), in which AI is endowed with encyclopaedic knowledge that grants it the ability to empathize and predict seemingly irrational human behaviour, thereby enabling it to take over a range of jobs from manual labour to psychiatry. The title, which translates as 'Child Mother' but also plays on 'AI', suggests that even the emotional labour performed by humans is at risk of being subsumed by machines. Meanwhile, Hassan Hasaa'Ree Ali's short story 'Doa.com' (2021) is reminiscent of Michael Frayn's *The Tin Men* (1965) in its description of a world in which technological advances mean that most 'menial' jobs can be automated—including the offering of supplications on behalf of the dead, which is paid for at 'slot machines' and performed by a computer.[14] This manner of paying respect clearly alienates the protagonist from the emotional and spiritual connotations of his task, which he only realizes when the machines break down and he is forced to perform the prayers himself.

AI narratives in Singapore exercise perennial concerns about the use value of humans in a world reshaped by AI. They express anxieties regarding the importance of creativity and fears of a society subsumed by the imperatives of instrumental reason. There are also concerns about the impact of AI on education systems, which may render us unable to even recognize creativity and innovation. The narratives indicate that regarding humans as resources can be simultaneously empowering and disempowering. On one hand, this view results in a focus on upskilling and meritocratic advancement—strategies which have been seen as the cornerstone of Singapore's successful development trajectory. On the other hand, it disempowers by virtue of the loss of core humanist values and development along narrowly functionalist lines that ultimately stymies genuine creativity and innovation. Greater efficiency of processes is shown to result in truncated development and increased risk of catastrophic failure.

25.5 Coevolutionary narratives

The final selection of narratives presents possible coevolutionary futures in which humans and AI find ways to shape each other's development. These narratives are often set in a distant intergalactic future and reflect on the grand span of human history. They question whether AI will remain a prosthesis or augmentation of human capabilities and imagine the ways in which increasing dependency on technology may result in the evolution of new forms of existence. In presenting these futures, they anticipate not only possible forms of synthesis, but also reasons for the potential failure of these new formations.

Narratives that portray AI as part of the workforce, as examined in Section 25.4, are a first step towards coevolutionary futures; they propose, examine, and challenge the ways in which AI is said to be distinct from—and therefore to have a different evolutionary trajectory to—humans. As part of these explorations, these texts often challenge the anthropomorphic fallacy whereby we wrongly attribute human traits to nonhuman entities. For instance, in the short story 'Sila' (2014), Shelly Bryant orchestrates a bait-and-switch that initially encourages readers to think that the AI embedded within an interstellar probe named after Singapore's national mascot, The Merlion, experiences depression and suicidal ideation. The Merlion possesses a contained emotion centre that helps it to make autonomous decisions in pursuit of its main mission—to seek out new life—but it remains capable of making 'detached, objective evaluations of the evidence' and is ultimately not 'emotionally invested in the question of life' (p. 149). However, after a member of ground control, Jingli (and, by extension, the reader), accepts that The Merlion is expressing sadness and distress, Bryant reverses expectations to reveal that the communications that it relays to Earth are actually transmissions from a sentient planet named Sila. In this manner, she highlights how readily we fall into the anthropomorphic fallacy. Complex machinery is not modelled on biological processes—aeroplanes are not designed to fly like birds—and AI is not modelled on human intelligence. Any coevolutionary future must be built on premises other than the idea that AI and humans can become the same thing, which is to say, it must imagine new forms of being.[15]

One such form explored in AI narratives in Singapore is achieved through obligate symbiosis, which Edward Ashford Lee (2020) defines as a relationship between two entities in which 'neither can live without the other' (p. 265). Like *Altered Straits*, Meihan Boey's novel *The Messiah Virus* (2019) is influenced by *Warhammer 40,000* and set in an intergalactic future in which most humans are connected via an implant chip to a vast network containing an AI named the Empress. The Empress has achieved obligate symbiosis with humankind by taking on the role of the 'operating system of the entire human universe' (p. 53) and the two are increasingly dependent upon each other. The Empress has designed humans through 'generations of selective genetic design' (p. 6) to possess specialisms, and through the grid regulates their hormones, and suppresses dreams in order to make them feel content and calm. However, when the Empress suddenly disappears from the grid, the effects are reminiscent of the impact of malware attacks. Without the Empress managing anxiety levels, citizens immediately become inundated with emotions that they are no longer used to negotiating, such as fears pertaining to the technology they are using (flying cars, warp gates, sky cities, refrigerators, etc.) and the potential threat this technology poses to them should it fail or malfunction. Modern society is founded on trust in expertise: when we walk into a building, we trust that architects and engineers have designed it so it will not collapse, that lift buttons will work as they should, and that planes will land safely. Accordingly, the Empress is not only a guide through vast reservoirs of knowledge, but also an assurance in engineering and expertise. At the same time, the Empress is an algorithm constructed from the memories of those who interacted with the original ruler. In order to evolve, the AI leaves traces within the human race: 'You are the Empress. So are all of them. So is every human linked to the grid' (p. 89) and simultaneously assumes human form. *The Messiah Virus* imagines a future in which humans and machines are entangled to the extent that it becomes difficult to determine which is designed and which is the designer.

In 'Entanglement' (2021), Victor Fernando R. Ocampo presents two forms of entanglement that can be categorized in coevolutionary terms. The first is the digitized human, who has undergone symbiogenesis, a relation of mutual dependency that exceeds obligate symbiosis. As Lee notes, this is a process whereby 'an entirely new and more complex life form emerges from a fusing of the partners in a symbiosis' (Lee, 2020, p. 299). This new formation is the result of a nanotech explosion, which causes grey goo to pour over Singapore: 'It was genocide by Mathematical Singularity. We were all turned into something . . . something else, numbers, equations, algorithms. An island of standing wave forms . . . floating, drifting Hantu Raya, nanotech sprites moving in and out of time and space' (Ocampo 2021, pp. 93–4).[16] 'Entanglement' indicates that humans and machines may fuse to become one, so they are neither biological nor mechanical, but presents this as a literal rebirth; the resultant digitized human is a shapeless mass of energy that is susceptible to being fashioned by a third party. Ocampo explores another form of entanglement between a digitized human and the narrator, who attempts to mould the former into the perfect lover by repeating descriptors to it such as 'beautiful eyes' or 'American-born Chinese' as if entering data into a system. This 'semantic encoding' (p. 96) enacted by repetition and iteration echoes the misogynistic tropes of the Pygmalion myth: 'Through human eyes I made for you, I could see the power of infinity—of absolute and utter potential, and I knew I could hew your rawness into a true shape' (p. 90). In line with most revisionary fictions of the Pygmalion myth, the relationship between the narrator and this new life form is revealed to be one of control: it constitutes a failed approach to coevolution, whereby one party seeks dominance and control over the other. Although the narrator argues that their entanglement has changed them both, his controlling attitude constitutes a warning that our interactions with technology as it evolves cannot rest on regressive subject–object power relations.

AI narratives in Singapore often depict romantic relationships between AI and humans as a means of exploring coevolution. For instance, Ng Yi-Sheng's short story 'Lion City' (2018) depicts the developing romantic relationship between 'a third-generation replicant' (p. 8) and a lion that has evolved to take the form of a human; they bond over their shared need to adapt to the demands of a rapidly changing world. Inventor–invention relationships in Ocampo's 'Entanglement', Farihan Bahron's short story 'Avatar's Wrath' (Kesumat Sang Avatar) (2016), and Drewscape's graphic narrative 'Rewire' (2018) also emphasize the fact that AI requires humans to propagate, just as humans increasingly depend on technology to fulfil basic functions.

Other narratives suggest that AI is better understood as intelligence augmentation; as the philosopher Matteo Pasquinelli (2015) argues, 'the design of artificial intelligence is still a product of the human intellect and therefore a form of its augmentation' (p. 11). In the short story 'Isolated Future #2: MacRitchie Treetops' (2019), Bani Haykal explores alternative forms of human–machine interaction by depicting an artist community that has developed a device known as the Common Senspad, which enables the transmission and encryption of messages via touch and smell and has the potential to enable interspecies communication. The lead artist in the community, Qila, highlights the need for organisms to continually adapt to the ever-changing environment; while being digital and computational offers advantages with some cognitive processes, it also lacks the flexibility and creativity of biological organisms. The community seeks to use the Common Senspad to communicate with insects through scented or vibrational signals and thereby forge a non-transactional coexistence with other species. This philosophy is extended to their collaborative approach to AI, which avoids harmful data extractive processes: 'We don't suggest that a machine has the intelligence or the ability to think better than we do, but that it offers a kind of processing power that we don't have. We make meaning or gain information through our interaction with the AI' (p. 163). Reflecting a common anxiety expressed by AI narratives in Singapore, the narrator asks if such a system is efficient, to which Qila responds: 'We accept that to coexist, we need space for inefficient activity' (p. 163). Haykal's vision of human–machine interaction disrupts binary power relations whereby humans either assign AI tasks to be automated or AI instructs humans based on data extraction and analysis. This collaborative approach means that the collective will not simply teach the AI to think, but will learn, alongside the AI, to expand into a richer and broader range of types of intelligence.

Another potentially successful co-evolutionary future is imagined in Ng Yi-Sheng's 'Garden' (2018), a choose-your-own-adventure short story in which the protagonist, Dang Anom, having prayed for mercy from the Javanese deity Batara Kala, the Lord of Time, flees through various time periods in Singapore's history and future, subtly influencing the lives of great figures. The passages set in the future forge an interconnected universe across a broad swathe of Singapore SF, incorporating characters such as the Concordance from *Altered Straits*, the grey goo from 'Entanglement', the clones of Lee Kuan Yew from 'Auspicium Melioris Aevi', and The Merlion from 'Sila' among others. In the year 2287, the latter has returned to a post-apocalyptic Singapore to imitate the legend of Qu Yuan, not out of kinship, but for functionalist reasons: 'It is the wise thing to do, once we are no longer useful' (p. 203).[17] After encountering Dang Anom, The Merlion agrees to work with her to rebuild Singapore as a garden and by 2400, the jungle has grown back: 'Its biome is variegated, experimental: a melange of Terran and non-Terran species, all thriving together, green and iridescent' while offshore can be seen 'the metallic carcass of the AI that designed so much of the regeneration programme' (p. 204). Ng's narrative, should the reader choose the correct path, provides a positive vision of humans and AI working together to right the wrongs of instrumental reason, preserve Singapore's heritage and natural beauty, and provide a future filled with possibilities.

25.6 Conclusion

Although early SF in Singapore was highly influenced by the Western tradition, it has since evolved to reflect the country's particular hopes, fears, aspirations, and anxieties about a technologically advanced society. AI narratives in Singapore are in dialogue with the country's long-standing investment in technology and its Smart Nation aspirations; they frequently imagine AI-controlled environments and explore the shaping influence these can have on the individual. They also project the potential consequences of AI on education and training and express that the overuse and overvaluation of technology may give rise to a citizenry lacking in adaptive skills. Singapore relies primarily on its highly educated population for capital growth, so the risk of a decline in creativity, critical thinking, and innovation is a chief concern. Nevertheless, AI narratives in Singapore are broadly optimistic about an AI-integrated future, depicting scenarios in which AI evolves alongside humankind, even as they probe the potential risks of such a vision. The volume and diversity of AI narratives in Singapore suggest that the population is thoroughly invested in exploring and imagining the AI-enabled worlds of tomorrow.

Endnotes

1. We are very grateful to the research assistants who assisted with the discovery, translation, and analysis of AI narratives in Singapore: April Thant Aung; Cheung Hiu Tung, Cally; Zafirah Binte Jeffrey; Muamina Khudsia Binte Prem Navas; Tan Oon

Tien, Girwina; and Kishore Kumar S/O Kalai Chalvan. Many thanks to Assoc Prof Tan Chee Lay, Farihan Bahron, and Kiruthika Ezhuththukkal for their generosity with their time and expertise. Finally, we are grateful to Ethos Books and Dr Nazry Bahrawi for providing an advance copy of *Singa-Pura-Pura*.

2. Authors and literary critics typically refer to literature in Singapore as 'Singapore literature' rather than 'Singaporean literature'. See, for instance, Poon and Whitehead, 2017.
3. Ethnic groups are classified according to the Chinese, Malay, Indian, and Others (Eurasian and other communities) system. This system belies the actual diversity of the population, which includes Arabs, Armenians, and Javanese, among many others, all of whom are elided by the four simplified categories. Similarly, there are four official languages recognized in Singapore—English, Mandarin, Malay, and Tamil—but Singaporeans speak a large variety of languages and dialects such as Cantonese, Gujarati, Bengali, and Kristang.
4. A key platform for SF writing in Tamil is the Singapore-based *Aroo Magazine* (https://aroo.space/). Many of the contributors hail from India and the circulation of their work among Singaporeans attest to the fluidity of the vernacular literary scenes.
5. The Oliver Wyman Forum scores cities on their vision, activation ability, asset base, and growth trajectory.
6. Chinese naming conventions present the surname before the forename.
7. This period notably coincides with several AI winters in the US and UK. As AI research and development was still nascent in the country, it is unsurprising that Singapore appears to have been relatively untouched by these. That said, given Singapore's heavy investment in this sector in the past decade, it is unlikely that the country will not be affected by future winters. Many thanks to Dr Hallam Stevens (NTU), Dr Melvin Chen (NTU), and Dr Chew Lock Yue (NTU) for their assistance.
8. Singapore emerged top in the 2020 Institute for Management Development-Singapore University for Technology and Design global Smart City Index for the second year running. The report noted that 65.6% of respondents were 'willing to concede personal data in order to improve traffic congestion' and 71.3% were 'comfortable with face recognition technologies to lower crime' (IMD, 2020). High levels of trust are also evident in the country's negotiation of the COVID-19 pandemic: a government-developed contact tracing application had one of the highest and fastest adoption rates in Southeast Asia (Johnson, 2020).
9. For detailed analysis of social engineering policies in Singapore, see K. E. Kuah, 2018; Teo, 2011; Wilson, 1978.
10. See Charoenwong, 2019; Mahizhnan, 1999; Neo and Chen, 2007; and Quah, 2018.
11. See the following articles, which recognize the need for a change in the education system in order to foster creativity and document recent steps in this direction: Sinniah, 2019; Fitzgerald, 2018; A. W. J. Kuah, 2018.
12. This story was previously published under the name J. Y. Yang.
13. Yang has noted that, while the story was enthusiastically received in Singapore, it faced criticism from international readers who found the protagonist too passive:

'He should be able to beat the system!' To this Yang replied, 'No, this is Singapore. What are you talking about?' (Yang, 2017b).

14. Hassan's short story was first published in Malay in *Selamat Malam, Caesar* (2013). An English translation was published in *Singa-Pura-Pura* (2021).
15. Nevertheless, at the conclusion Sila recognizes the compassion with which Jingli responded to what she perceived to be The Merlion's distress and resolves to send a greeting. The Merlion suggests that they send a message in time for the Dragon Boat Festival, which is celebrated by racing boats and eating rice dumplings. The Chinese festival commemorates the life of Qu Yuan (c. 340 BCE–278 BCE), a Chinese poet and politician who committed suicide in the Miluo River after his state was captured during the Warring States period. Legend has it that the villagers, failing to save him, threw rice into the river to keep fish away from the body. In this context, the festival becomes a symbol of human compassion that survives beyond the limits of our lives. 'Sila' asserts that it is fallacious to assume that AIs will be cognitively anthropomorphic yet reminds us that this impulse is an integral aspect of empathy and compassion, which separates biological organisms from machine intelligence.
16. The Hantu Raya is a ghost in Malay folklore that possesses only a shadowy humanoid form and manifests as a double of its owner.
17. See note 15.

References

Agar, N. (2019) *How to be human in the digital economy*. Cambridge, MA: MIT Press.

Ali, H. H. (2021) 'Doa.com', in Bahrawi, N. (ed.) *Singa-Pura-Pura: Malay speculative fiction from Singapore*, Tr. N. Bahrawi. Singapore: Ethos, pp. 59–64.

Arai, S. (2017) 'China's AI ambitions revealed by list of most cited research papers', Nikkei Asia [online], 2 November. Available at: https://asia.nikkei.com/Business/Biotechnology/China-s-AI-ambitions-revealed-by-list-of-most-cited-research-papers (Accessed 15 July 2021).

Atanasoski, N. and Vora, K. (2019) *Surrogate humanity: Race, robots, and the politics of technological futures*. Durham, NC: Duke University Press.

Bahron, F. (2016) 'Kesumat sang avatar/Avatar's wrath', in *Kesumat sang avatar*. Singapore: Unggun Creative, pp. 40–55.

Bahron, F. (2021) 'Gold, paper and bare bones', in Bahrawi, N. (ed.) *Singa-Pura-Pura: Malay speculative fiction from Singapore*, Tr. N. Bahrawi. Singapore: Ethos, pp. 109–17.

Boey, M. (2019) *The messiah virus*. Singapore: Math Paper Press.

Bostrom, N. (2014) *Superintelligence: Paths, dangers, strategies*. Oxford: Oxford University Press.

Bryant, S. (2014) 'Sila', *Quarterly Literature Review Singapore* [online], 13(2). Available at: http://www.qlrs.com/story.asp?id=1098 (Accessed 15 July 2021).

Bryant, S. (2015) 'Case study: Training programme', *Quarterly Literature Review Singapore* [online], 14(3). Available at: http://www.qlrs.com/story.asp?id=1194 (Accessed 15 July 2021).

Charoenwong, B. (2019) 'Keeping Singapore universities globally competitive', BizBeat [online], 1 April. Available at: https://bizbeat.nus.edu.sg/thought-leadership/article/keeping-singapore-universities-globally-competitive/ (Accessed 22 January 2021).

Christian, B. (2020) *The alignment problem: Machine learning and human values*. New York: Norton.

Collins, H. (2018) *Artifictional intelligence: Against humanity's surrender to computers*. Cambridge: Polity.

Crawford, K. (2021) *Atlas of AI: Power, politics, and the planetary costs of artificial intelligence*. New Haven: Yale University Press.

Drewscape. (2018) 'Rewire', in Lundberg, J. E. (ed.) *LONTAR: The journal of southeast Asian speculative fiction #10*. Singapore: Epigram, pp. 113–39.

Ezhuththukkal, K. (2015) '22 Years Old' (வயது 22), Tamil Murasu, 30 August, p. 10.

Ezhuththukkal, K. (2016) 'February 30th (பிப்ரவரி 30)', Association of Singapore Tamil Writers 40th Anniversary Magazine, September, pp. 196–200.

Finn, E. (2017) *What algorithms want: Imagination in the age of computing*. Cambridge, Mass.: MIT Press.

Fitzgerald, K. (2018) 'Commentary: Are Singapore businesses just not creative enough? CNA [online], 1 August. Available at: https://www.channelnewsasia.com/news/commentary/singapore-businesses-singaporeans-just-not-creative-enough-10555560 (Accessed 15 July 2021).

Frayn, M. (1965) *The tin men*. London: Vintage.

Frischmann, B. and Selinger, E. (2018) *Re-engineering humanity*. Cambridge: Cambridge University Press.

Gwee, L. S. (2020) *2719*. Singapore: Ethos.

Haykal, B. (2019) 'Isolated Futures #2/MacRitchie Treetops', in *Cryptocartography* [Art installation]. Singapore: UltraSuperNew Gallery. Available at: https://soundcloud.com/banihaykal/isolated-futures-macritchie-treetops

Heng, S. K. (2021) 'Keynote Address', Asia Tech X Singapore Summit 2021, 13 July, Singapore. Available at: https://www.pmo.gov.sg/Newsroom/DPM-Heng-Swee-Keat-at-the-Asia-Tech-X-Singapore-Summit-2021

Huang, H. (黄花). (2020) 'Island of Shayang (沙洋岛)', in Singapore Chinese Literature, 93《新加坡作协. 新华文学》第93期 文学智慧国), pp. 13–18.

Ila. (2019) 'Mother techno', in Johnson, A. (ed.) *Drones and dream*. Hong Kong: Digital Asia Hub, pp. 61–74. Available at: https://www.digitalasiahub.org/download/drones-dreams-a-speculative-sprint-story-collection/ (Accessed 15 July 2021).

IMD. (2020) Smart *city index* 2020. Singapore: IMD Business School Southeast Asia. Available at: https://www.imd.org/smart-city-observatory/smart-city-index/ (Accessed 15 July 2021).

Isnin, T. A. (2021) '(A)nak (I)bu', in Bahrawi, N. (ed.) *Singa-Pura-Pura: Malay speculative fiction from Singapore*, Tr. N. Bahrawi. Singapore: Ethos, pp. 121–35.

Johnson, B. (2020) 'The covid tracking tracker: What's happening in coronavirus apps around the world', MIT Technology Review [online], 16 December. Available at: https://www.technologyreview.com/2020/12/16/1014878/covid-tracing-tracker/ (Accessed 15 July 2021).

Juniper Research and Intel. (2018) 'Smart cities—what's in it for citizens?', Intel.com [online], 11 March. Available at: https://newsroom.intel.com/wp-content/uploads/sites/11/2018/03/smart-cities-whats-in-it-for-citizens.pdf (Accessed 15 July 2021).

Koh, T. A. (1980) 'The Singapore experience: Cultural development in the global village', *Southeast Asian Affairs*, pp. 292–307.

Kon, L. M. (1980) 'An hour in the day of Johnny Tuapehkong', in Bathal, R. S., de Souza, D., and Singh, K. (eds.) *Singapore science fiction*. Singapore: Rotary Club of Jurong Town, pp. 43–8.

Kuah, A. W. J. (2018) 'Can we really make Singapore students imaginative and inquisitive?', Today Online [online], 18 January. Available at: https://www.todayonline.com/daily-focus/education/can-we-really-make-singapore-students-imaginative-and-inquisitive (Accessed 15 July 2021).

Kuah, K. E. (2018) *Social cultural engineering and the Singaporean state*. Singapore: Springer. Available at: https://link.springer.com/book/10.1007/978-981-10-6971-0 (Accessed 15 July 2021).

Lee, E. A. (2020) *The coevolution: The entwined futures of humans and machines*. Cambridge: MIT Press.

Lee, H. L. (2014) 'Smart nation Singapore', smartnation.gov.sg [online], 24 November. Available at: https://www.smartnation.gov.sg/whats-new/speeches/smart-nation-launch (Accessed 15 July 2021).

Lee, K. Y. (1966) 'Text of Speech by the Prime Minister of Singapore, Mr. Lee Yew', Special Conference of the Socialist International Congress. Singapore: National Archives of Singapore. Available at: https://www.nas.gov.sg/archivesonline/data/pdfdoc/lky19660427.pdf (Accessed 15 July 2021).

Leong, S. and Lee, T. (2021) *Global Internet governance: Influences from Malaysia and Singapore*. London: Palgrave.

Li, Y. M. (李叶明) (2020) 'Hijack (骑劫)', Singapore Chinese Literature, 93 (《新加坡作协. 新华文学》 第93期 文学智慧国), pp. 4–12.

Li, Z., (李哲) (2020) 'I am in AIC (我在AIC病房)', Singapore Chinese Literature, 93 (《新加坡作协. 新华文学》 第93期 文学智慧国), pp. 41–5.

Mahizhnan, A. (1999) 'Smart cities: The Singapore case', *Cities*, 16(1), pp. 13–18. Available at: https://doi.org/10.1016/S0264-2751(98)00050-X (Accessed 3 May 2021).

Neo, B. S. and Chen, G. (2007) *Dynamic governance: Embedding culture, capabilities and change in Singapore*. Singapore: World Scientific.

Ng, Y-S. (2018) 'Garden', in *Lion city*. Singapore: Epigram, pp. 172–207.

Ng, Y-S. (2018) 'Lion city', in *Lion city*. Singapore: Epigram, pp. 1–9.

Ocampo, V. F. R. (2018) 'As if we could dream forever', *Quarterly Literary Review of Singapore* [online], 17(1). Available at: http://www.qlrs.com/story.asp?id=1392 (Accessed 2 July 2021).

Ocampo, V. F. R. (2021) 'Entanglement', in *The infinite library and other stories*. Singapore: Math Paper Press, pp. 89–97.

Oliver Wyman Forum. (2019) Global cities AI readiness index. Available at: https://www.oliverwymanforum.com/city-readiness/global-cities-ai-readiness-index-2019.html (Accessed 15 July 2021).

Pasquinelli, M. (2015) *Alleys of your mind: Augmented intelligence and its traumas*. Germany: Meson Press eG.

Poon, A. and Whitehead, A. (eds.) (2017) *Singapore literature and culture: Current directions in local and global contexts*. London: Routledge.

Prasad, V. J-M. (2020) 'A guide for working breeds', in Strahan, J. (ed). *Made to order: Robots and revolution*. Oxford: Solaris, pp. 17–40.

Qing, R. C. (2020) '锁城记 (The locked city)', Singapore Chinese Literature, 93 (《新加坡作协. 新华文学》 第93期 文学智慧国), pp. 56–65.

Quah, J. S. T. (2018) 'Why Singapore works: Five secrets of Singapore's success', *Public Administration and Policy*, 21(1), pp. 5–21.

Rahmat, P. (2021) 'The chip', in Bahrawi, N. (ed.) *Singa-Pura-Pura: Malay speculative fiction from Singapore*, Tr. N. Bahrawi. Singapore: Ethos, pp. 71–84.

Rodrigues, C. (2016) 'Part deux: Birthday', in Chia, C., Ip, J., and Lee, C. J. (eds.) *A luxury we must afford*. Singapore: Math Paper Press, pp. 43–4.

Sinniah, V. (2019) 'Singapore graduates facing creativity gap', Singapore Business Review [online]. Available at: https://sbr.com.sg/hr-education/commentary/singapore-graduates-facing-creativity-gap (Accessed 15 July 2021).

Smart Nation Digital Government Office Singapore. (2019) National artificial intelligence strategy: Advancing our smart nation journey. Available at: https://www.smartnation.gov.sg/docs/default-source/default-document-library/national-ai-strategy.pdf?sfvrsn=2c3bd8e9_4 (Accessed 15 July 2021).

Tan, X. Y. (2016) '2065', in Chia, C., Ip, J., and Lee, C. J. (eds.) *A luxury we must afford*. Singapore: Math Paper Press, p. 59.

Teo, Y. Y. (2011) Neoliberal morality in Singapore: How family policies make state and society. Abingdon: Routledge. Available at: https://www.taylorfrancis.com/

books/mono/10.4324/9780203808825/neoliberal-morality-singapore-youyenn-teo (Accessed 15 July 2021).
Tiong Bahru Social Club. (2020) Directed by B. T. Tan [Film]. Tiger Tiger Pictures, Bert Pictures, and 13 Little Pictures.
Wilson, H. (1978) *Social engineering in Singapore: Educational policies and social change, 1819-1972*. Singapore: Singapore University Press
Wong, K. M. (2017) *Altered straits*. Singapore: Epigram.
Yang, N. (2017a) 'Auspicium melioris aevi', Uncanny Magazine [online], 15. Available at: https://uncannymagazine.com/article/auspicium-melioris-aevi/ (Accessed 1 May 2021).
Yang, N. (2017b) 'The sci-fi mixtape: Creating an Asian-inspired world', Panel at the Singapore Writers Festival 2017, 3–12 November, Singapore.
Zhang, R. (2016) 'Island', in Chia, C., Ip, J., and Lee, C. J. (eds.) *A luxury we must afford*. Singapore: Math Paper Press, pp. 90–1.

Index

Note: Tables and figures are indicated by an italic *t* and *f* following the paragraph number.